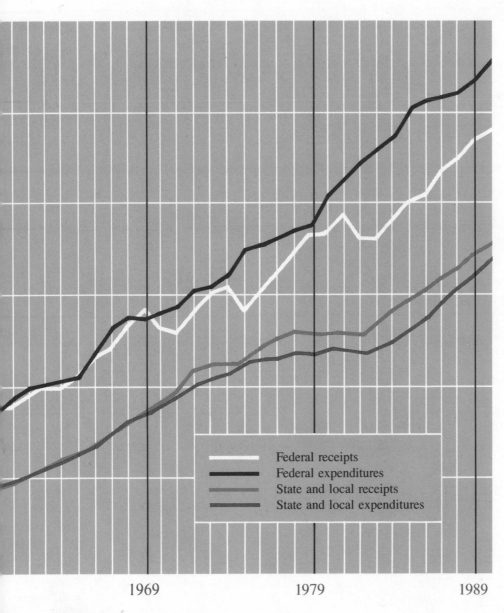

Federal receipts
Federal expenditures
State and local receipts
State and local expenditures

1969   1979   1989

Year

Public Finance

Public Finance

EDITION 3

Harvey S. Rosen

Department of Economics
Princeton University

IRWIN

Homewood, IL 60430
Boston, MA 02116

© RICHARD D. IRWIN, INC., 1985, 1988, and 1992

Sponsoring editor: Gary Nelson
Developmental editor: Patricia McCabe
Project editor: Waivah Clement
Production manager: Irene H. Sotiroff
Cover and interior designer: Mary Sailer
Part and chapter illustrator: Poli Garza
Artist: Mary Jo Szymanski
Compositor: Bi-Comp, Inc.
Typeface: 10/12 Times Roman
Printer: R. R. Donnelley & Sons Company

Library of Congress Cataloging-in-Publication Data

Rosen, Harvey S.
　　Public finance / Harvey S. Rosen. — 3rd ed.
　　　　p.　　cm.　　(The Irwin series in economics)
　　ISBN 0-256-08376-2
　　ISBN 0-256-11393-9 (International student edition)
　　1. Finance, Public—United States. I. Title.

HJ257.2.R67   1991
336.73—dc20　　　　　　　　　　　　　　　　91–19228
　　　　　　　　　　　　　　　　　　　　　　　　CIP

Printed in the United States of America
2 3 4 5 6 7 8 9 0 DOC 8 7 6 5 4 3 2

*To Lynne and Jonathan**

* Order of names was determined by the flip of a fair coin.
The author loves you both the same.

Preface

"It is a foolish thing to make a long prologue." (II Maccabees 2:32)   I shall once again follow this Biblical advice, and be brief in describing the features of this third edition. The field of public finance has been changing rapidly in recent years. On the theoretical side, one of the main achievements has been to integrate the analysis of government spending and taxing more closely with basic economic theory. A prime example is the literature on optimal taxation, which has attempted to *derive* prescriptions for government fiscal behavior using standard economic tools, rather than to annunciate a set of ad hoc "principles" for tax design. On the empirical side, the most exciting development has been the widespread application of the tools of econometrics to understanding how expenditure and tax policies affect individual behavior and how the government itself sets its policies.

The results of modern research have been slow in entering traditional texts. This book takes its readers to many of the frontiers of current research. The approach to the material, while accessible to undergraduates, is the same as the approach shared by most economists who are now active in the field.

The development of public finance has not proceeded free of controversy. In this book, disputes concerning both methodological and substantive issues are discussed at length. One reviewer of an early draft of the manuscript warned against displaying too much of the profession's dirty laundry in public. My feeling, however, is that "full disclosure" should apply not only in the market for securities, but also in the market for ideas.

There is some tendency for economic analysis to lose touch with the reality it is supposed to describe. I have tried to avoid this tendency. The relevant institutional and legal settings are described in ample detail. Moreover, the links between economic analysis and current political issues are constantly emphasized.

Organization

Part One consists of two short chapters that provide a broad perspective on the role of government in the economy. Part Two discusses the methodological tools used in the study of public finance. These include the methods of empirical analysis (Chapter 3) and the fundamentals of theoretical welfare economics (Chapter 4). The remainder of the book follows the conventional tactic of analyzing government expenditure and revenue-raising activities separately. Part Three (Chapters 5 through 12) deals with the expenditure side of the budget; various government programs are described and evaluated. Part Four (Chapters 13 through 15) provides a theoretical framework for discussing taxation. The major revenue-raising instruments are analyzed using this framework in Part Five (Chapters 16 through 20). Finally, Part Six deals with the special issues that arise under a federal system of government.

Some instructors may choose to do the tax side (Parts Four and Five) prior to the expenditure side (Part Three); the book is designed so that this can be easily done. In the same way, the chapters within Parts Three, Four, and Five can generally be taken up in any order desired without serious loss of continuity.

This book is designed for use in undergraduate curricula as well as graduate programs in public administration. It is assumed that readers are familiar with microeconomic theory at the level of the standard introductory course. Because some use is made of indifference curve analysis, a topic that is not covered in all introductory courses, indifference curves are carefully explained in the Appendix to the book. In addition, this Appendix provides a brief review of other topics in basic microeconomics, including the supply and demand model and marginal analysis. This review should be adequate to refresh the memories of readers who have been away from microeconomics for a while. A glossary of key terms appears after the Appendix.

It is hoped that this book will whet readers' appetites to learn more about public finance. To this end, a large number of articles and books are cited within, and at the ends of, the chapters. A typical citation consists of the author's name followed by the date of publication in brackets. The full reference can then be found by consulting the consolidated bibliography that appears at the back of the book. These references vary considerably in technical difficulty; those who wish to pursue specialized topics further have to pick and choose.

What's New in the Third Edition?

"Are you doing anything beside updating the tables?" That's the question many of my colleagues asked when they heard that I was revising *Public Finance*. The answer is, "Quite a bit, actually." The material on Social Security (Chapter 10) has been augmented with a discussion of the surplus that is accumulating in the trust fund. The focus is on how the surplus affects the economy and the implications for proposals to restructure the Social Security system. The chapters dealing with federal taxation have been thoroughly revised in light of the Omnibus Budget Reconciliation Act of 1990. Chapter 21 on public finance in a federal system now includes a section on the economics of public education. The discussion covers traditional topics such as the impact of grants on educational spending as well as more recent research on whether the public education system requires fundamental restructuring.

In addition, several organizational changes have been made in the third edition: First, a glossary has been added to the end of the book. I hope that this will be a helpful pedagogical feature. Second, in response to suggestions from a number of readers, the material on consumption taxes and wealth taxes has been consolidated into a single chapter. Third, and most important, is the elimination of the separate chapter on international tax issues that appeared in earlier editions. The material that was formerly in that chapter has been integrated throughout the other relevant chapters. (For example, the section on the tax treatment of multinational corporations now appears in the chapter on corporate taxation.) This organizational change is a response to the increasing internationalization of the U.S. economy. It simply no longer makes sense to view open-economy issues as segregable from mainstream topics.

Despite these changes, the basic thrust of the book is unchanged. As in the first and second editions, the goal is to interweave institutional, theoretical, and econometric material to provide students with a clear and coherent view of government spending and taxing.

Harvey S. Rosen

Acknowledgments

It is a pleasure to acknowledge all the people who have helped in the preparation of this book. As a graduate student, I was fortunate to be taught by two of the world's outstanding figures in public finance, Martin Feldstein and Richard Musgrave. Feldstein and Musgrave differed considerably in their approaches to the subject, but they shared a fundamental outlook—public finance is not a mere academic exercise; its goal is to help us understand and perhaps improve real-world situations. The intellectual influence of both these men is evident throughout the text.

Nearly 200 academic colleagues who teach public finance responded to a survey that provided useful material on how they focus their courses. Their input afforded an insight on how they teach and on the students who take this course. Instructors who identified places for refinement and reorganization in this edition are

Lawrence P. Brunner
Central Michigan University

Edward Coulson
The Pennsylvania State University

Kevin T. Duffy-Deno
Southeastern Massachusetts University

Amihai Glazer
University of California, Irvine

Bradley S. Loomis
Rochester Institute of Technology

Alfredo M. Pereira
University of California, San Diego

Michael Wasylenko
Syracuse University

Thanks are also due to Douglas Holtz-Eakin (Syracuse University) and Wallace Oates (University of Maryland), who read various chapters and provided useful suggestions.

I am particularly grateful to Eleanor Brown of Pomona College. She made numerous excellent suggestions, and without her help, timely publication of this edition would have been impossible.

Recognition of and an expression of appreciation to the people who reviewed and made useful suggestions for earlier editions of this text is also appropriate.

Roy D. Adams
Iowa State University

James Alm
University of Colorado

Charles L. Ballard
Michigan State University

Douglas Blair
Rutgers University

Rebecca Blank
Northwestern University

David Bradford
Princeton University

Neil Bruce
Queens University

O. Homer Erekson
Miami University

J. Fred Giertz
University of Illinois

Roy T. Gobin
Loyola University of Chicago

Timothy J. Gronberg
Texas A & M University

Jonathan H. Hamilton
University of Florida

Rich Hanson
University of California, Irvine

Roger S. Hewett
Drake University

Robert Inman
University of Pennsylvania

Robert Kelly
Fairfield University

Edward Kienzle
Boston College

Helen Ladd
Duke University

Randall Mariger
University of Washington

Roger P. Mendels
University of Windsor

Robert Moore
Occidental College

Susan Parks
University of Wisconsin—Whitewater

Anthony Pellechio
World Bank

James Porterba
Massachusetts Institute of Technology

B. Michael Pritchett
Brigham Young University

Uwe Reinhardt
Princeton University

Robert Rider
University of Southern California

Efraim Sadka
Tel-Aviv University

Gian S. Sahota
Vanderbilt University

John L. Solo
University of Iowa

Richard Steinberg
Virginia Polytechnic Institute and State University

Thomas F. Stinson
University of Minnesota

George Zodrow
Rice University

Finally, I thank my family lawyer for technical advice and encouragement.

H. S. R.

Contents in Brief

P A 4 R T A Framework for Tax Analysis

P A 5 R T The United States Revenue System

P A R T **Multigovernment Public Finance**

Contents

P **A** 4 **R** T   **A Framework for Tax Analysis**

P A **5** R T **The United States Revenue System**

16 The Personal Income Tax *368*

P A **6** R T **Multigovernment Public Finance**

Public Finance

PART 1 Introduction

People's views on how the government should conduct its financial operations are heavily influenced by their political philosophies. Some people care most about individual freedom, others care more about promoting the well-being of the community as a whole. Philosophical differences can and do lead to disagreements as to the appropriate scope for government economic activity.

However, forming intelligent opinions about governmental activity requires not only a political philosophy but also an understanding of what the government actually does. Where does the legal power to conduct economic policy reside? What does government spend money on, and how does it raise revenue?

Chapter 1 discusses how political views affect attitudes toward public finance, and Chapter 2 outlines the operation of the U.S. system of public finance. Together these two chapters provide a broad perspective that is useful to remember as we discuss various details in the rest of the book.

Public Finance and Attitudes toward Government

Sometimes it is said that man cannot be trusted with the government of himself. Can he, then, be trusted with the government of others? Or have we found angels in the forms of kings to govern him? Let history answer this question.

THOMAS JEFFERSON

The year is 1030 B.C. For decades, the Israelite tribes have been living without a central government. The Bible records that the people have asked the prophet Samuel to "make us a king to judge us like all the nations" [1 Samuel 8:5]. Samuel tries to discourage the Israelites by describing what life will be like under a monarchy:

> This will be the manner of the king that shall reign over you; he will take your sons, and appoint them unto him, for his chariots, and to be his horsemen; and they shall run before his chariots. . . . And he will take your daughters to be perfumers, and to be cooks, and to be bakers. And he will take your fields, and your vineyards, and your oliveyards, even the best of them, and give them to his servants. . . . He will take the tenth of your flocks; and ye shall be his servants. And ye shall cry out in that day because of your king whom ye shall have chosen. [1 Samuel 9:11–18]

The Israelites are not deterred by this depressing scenario: "the people refused to hearken unto the voice of Samuel; and they said: 'Nay; but there shall be a king over us; that we also may be like all the nations; and that our king may judge us, and go out before us, and fight our battles' " [1 Samuel 8:19–20].

This biblical episode illustrates an age-old ambivalence about government. Government is a necessity—"all the nations" have it, after all—but at the same time it has undesirable aspects. These mixed feelings toward government are inextricably bound up with its taxing and spending activities. The king will provide things that the people want (in this case, an army), but only at a cost. The resources for all government expenditures ultimately must come from the private sector. As Samuel so graphically explains, taxes can become burdensome.

Centuries have passed, mixed feelings about government remain, and much of the controversy still centers around its financial behavior. This book is about the taxing and spending activities of government, a subject usually called **public finance**, but sometimes referred to as **public sector economics** or simply **public economics.**

Our focus is on the microeconomic functions of government, the way government affects the allocation of existing resources and the distribution of income. Nowadays, the macroeconomic functions of government—the use of taxing, spending, and monetary policies to affect the overall level of unemployment and the price level—are usually taught in separate courses.

It is not always exactly clear whether certain subjects belong in public finance. Governmental regulatory policies have important effects on resource allocation. Such policies have goals that sometimes can also be achieved by government spending or taxing measures. For example, if a goal of the government is to limit the size of corporations, one possible policy is to impose large taxes on big corporations. Another policy is to issue regulations making firms that exceed a particular size illegal. However, while corporate taxation is a subject of intense study in public finance, antitrust issues are generally treated only tangentially in public finance texts, and are covered instead in courses on industrial organization. Such a practice seems arbitrary, but it is necessary to limit the scope of the field. This book follows tradition by confining most attention to governmental spending and revenue-raising activities.

Alternative Views of Government

Public finance economists analyze not only the effects of actual government taxing and spending activities but also what these activities ought to be. Views of how government should function in the economic sphere are influenced by general attitudes concerning the relationship between the individual and the state. Political philosophers have distinguished two major approaches.

Organic View

Society is conceived of as a natural organism. Each individual is a part of this organism, and the government can be thought of as its heart. Yang Chang-chi, Mao Tse-tung's ethics teacher in Peking, held that "A country is an organic whole, just as the human body is an organic whole. It is not like a machine which can be taken apart and put together again.'' (Quoted in Johnson [1983, p. 197].) The individual has significance only as part of the community, and the good of the individual is defined with respect to the good of the whole. Thus, the community is stressed above the individual. For example, in the *Republic* of Plato, an activity of a citizen is desirable only if it leads to a just society. Perhaps the most infamous instance of an organic conception of government is provided by Nazism: "National Socialism does not recognize a separate individual sphere which, apart from the community, is to be painstakingly protected from any interference by the State. . . . Every activity of daily life has meaning and value only as a service to the whole."[1]

The goals of the society are set by the state, which leads society toward their realization. Of course, there are considerable differences with respect to the choice of goals. Plato conceived of a state whose goal was the achievement of a golden age in which human activities would be guided by perfect rationality. On the other hand, Adolf Hitler [1971/1925, p. 393] viewed the state's purpose to be the achievement of racial purity: "The state is a means to an end. Its end lies in the preservation and advancement of a community of physically and psychically homogeneous creatures." According to Lenin [1968/1917, p. 198] the proletarian state has the purpose of "*leading the whole people* to socialism, . . . of being the teacher, the guide, the leader of all the working and exploited people."

Because societal goals can differ, a crucial question is how they are to be selected. Proponents of the organic view usually rely on some notion that certain goals are *natural* for the societal organism to pursue. Pursuit of sovereignty over some geographical area is an example of such a natural goal. (Think of the Nazi drive for domination over Europe.) However, despite the fact that philosophers have struggled for centuries to explain what natural means, the answer is far from clear.

Mechanistic View

In this view, government is not an organic part of society. Rather, it is a contrivance created by individuals to better achieve their individual goals. As the American statesman Henry Clay suggested in 1829, "Government is a trust, and the officers of the government are trustees; and both the trust and the trustees are created for the benefit of the people." Thus, the individual rather than the group is at center stage.

Accepting that government exists for the good of the people, we are still left with the problem of defining just what *good* is and how the government should act to promote it. There is virtually universal agreement that it is good for individuals when government protects them from

---

[1] Stuckart and Globke [1968, p. 330]. (Wilhelm Stuckart and Hans Globke were ranking members of the Nazi Ministry of the Interior.)

violence. To do so government must have a monopoly on coercive power. Otherwise, anarchy develops, and as the 17th-century philosopher Thomas Hobbes [1963/1651, p. 143] noted, "the life of man 'becomes] solitary, poor, nasty, brutish and short." Recent events in such countries as Lebanon and Northern Ireland, where private armies are common, confirm Hobbes's observation. Similarly, in *The Wealth of Nations,* Adam Smith argues that government should protect "the society from the violence and invasion of other independent societies," and protect "as far as possible every member of the society from the injustice or oppression of every other member of it" [1977/1776, Book V, pp. 182, 198].

The most limited government, then, is one whose sole function is to prevent its members from being subjected to physical coercion. Beyond that, Smith argued that government should have responsibility for "creating and maintaining certain public works and certain public institutions, which it can never be for the interest of any individual, or small number of individuals, to erect and maintain" [1977/1776, Book V, pp. 210–11]. Here one thinks of items such as roads, bridges, and sewers—the infrastructure required for society to function.[2]

At this point, opinions within the mechanistic tradition diverge. Libertarians, who believe in a very limited government, argue that there is no further economic role for the government. In Smith's words, "Every man, as long as he does not violate the laws of justice, is left perfectly free to pursue his own interest his own way" [1977/1776, Book V, p. 180]. In contrast, those whom we might call social democrats believe that a substantial amount of government intervention is required for the good of individuals. These interventions can take such diverse forms as safety regulations for the workplace, laws banning racial and sexual discrimination in housing, or welfare payments to the poor. When social democrats are confronted with the objection that such interventions are likely to impinge on individual freedom, they are apt to respond that freedom refers to more than the absence of physical coercion. An individual with a very low income may be free to spend that income as he or she pleases, but the scope of that freedom is quite limited indeed. Of course, between the libertarian and social democratic positions there is a continuum of views with respect to the amount of government intervention that is appropriate.

Viewpoint of This Book

The notion that the individual rather than the group is paramount is relatively new. Historian Lawrence Stone [1977, pp. 4–5] notes that prior to the modern period,

---

[2] Some argue that even these items should be provided by private entrepreneurs. Problems that might arise in doing so are discussed in Chapter 5 under "Efficient Provision of Public Goods."

It was generally agreed that the interests of the group, whether that of kin, the village, or later the state, took priority over the wishes of the individual and the achievement of his particular ends. "Life, liberty and the pursuit of happiness" were personal ideals which the average, educated 16th-century man would certainly have rejected as the prime goals of a good society.

Since then, however, the mechanistic view of government has come to dominate Anglo-American political thought. This is not to say that its dominance is total. Anyone who claims that something must be done in the "national interest," without reference to the welfare of some individual or group of individuals, is implicitly taking an organic point of view. More generally, even in highly individualistic societies, people sometimes feel it necessary to act on behalf of, or even sacrifice their lives for, the nation. As Kenneth Arrow [1974, p. 15] observes, "the tension between society and the individual is inevitable. Their claims compete within the individual conscience as well as in the arena of social conflict."

Not surprisingly, Anglo-American economic thought has also developed along individualistic lines. The individual and his or her wants are the main focus in mainstream economics, a view reflected in this text. However, as stressed earlier, within the individualistic tradition there is much controversy with respect to how active a role government should take. Thus, adopting a mechanistic point of view does not by itself provide us with an ideology that tells us whether any particular economic intervention should be undertaken.[3]

This point is important because economic policy is not based on economic analysis alone. The desirability of a given course of government action (or inaction) inevitably depends in part on ethical and political judgments. As this country's ongoing public debate over what we have chosen to call public finance illustrates, reasonable people can disagree on these matters. We attempt to reflect different points of view as fairly as possible.

Summary

- Public finance, also known as public sector economics or public economics, focuses on the taxing and spending activities of government and their influence on the allocation of resources and distribution of income.

- Economists dealing with public finance both analyze actual policies and develop guidelines for government activities. In the latter role, economists are influenced by their attitudes toward the role of government in society.

---

[3] Note that this question really makes no sense in the context of an organic view of government, in which the government is above the people, and there is an assumption that it should guide every aspect in life.

- In an organic view of society, individuals are valuable only in their contribution to the realization of social goals. These goals are determined by the government.
- In a mechanistic view of society, government is a contrivance erected to further individual goals. There is considerable disagreement over how the government should promote sometimes conflicting individual goals.

- Individual decision making is the focus of much economics and is consistent with the mechanistic view of society adopted in this book. This does not eliminate much controversy over the appropriate role of the government in our economy.

Discussion Questions

1. In *The End of Liberalism,* Theodore Lowi [1979, p. xii] offers the following article as part of a present-day constitution:

   Article VI: The public interest shall be defined by the satisfaction of the voters in their constituencies. The test of the public interest is reelection.

   What does this imply about the role of government in society? Do you agree or disagree? Why?

2. In *The Closing of the American Mind,* Alan Bloom writes:

   In the tightest communities, at least since the days of Odysseus, there is something in man that wants out and senses that his development is stunted by being just a part of a whole, rather than a whole itself. And in the freest and most independent situations men long for unconditional attachments. The tension between freedom and attachment, and attempts to achieve the impossible union of the two, are the permanent condition of man. But in modern political regimes, where rights precede duties, freedom definitely has primacy over community, family and even nature.

   Does Bloom identify modern society with a dominance of individuals' rights? Does such a correspondence seem appropriate to Western cultures? What about non-Western societies?

   One area of public debate that has highlighted the tension between individual rights and social control is the regulation of handguns. Can you think of other areas of debate that reflect this tension Bloom refers to?

Selected References

Arrow, Kenneth J. *The Limits of Organization.* New York: W. W. Norton, 1974.

Johnson, Paul. *Modern Times.* New York: Harper and Row, 1983.

Lenin. "The Marxist Theory of the State and the Tasks of the Proletariat in the Revolution." In *Lenin on Politics and Revolution,* ed. James E. Connor. Indianapolis: Bobbs-Merrill, 1968, pp. 184–232.

Smith, Adam. *The Wealth of Nations.* London: J. M. Dent and Sons, 1977 (1776). (Book V, Chapter 1.)

APPENDIX A   Doing Research in Public Finance

Throughout the text, we cite many books and articles, both within and following the chapters. These references are useful for those who want to delve into the various subjects in more detail. Students interested in writing term papers or theses on subjects in public finance should also consult the following journals which specialize in the field:

Journal of Public Economics
National Tax Journal
Public Finance
Public Finance Quarterly

The *Journal of Public Economics* is relatively technical compared to the others and is of most use to those who have had a course in microeconomic theory at the intermediate level and have a working knowledge of calculus.

In addition, all the major general-interest economics journals frequently publish articles that deal with public finance issues. These include, but are not limited to:

American Economic Review
Econometrica
Journal of Economic Perspectives
Journal of Political Economy
Quarterly Journal of Economics
Review of Economics and Statistics

Articles on public finance in these and many other journals are indexed in the *Journal of Economic Literature*.

There are vast amounts of data available on government spending and taxing activity. The following useful sources of information are published by the U.S. Government Printing Office:

Statistical Abstract of the United States
Economic Report of the President
Budget of the United States
U.S. Census of Governments

All of the preceding are published annually, except for the *U.S. Census of Governments,* which appears every five years. *Facts and Figures on Government Finance,* published annually by the Tax Foundation, is another compendium of data on government taxing and spending activities. For those who desire a long-run perspective, data going back to the 18th century are available in *Historical Statistics of the United States from Colonial Times to 1970* (U.S. Government Printing Office). Readers with a special interest in state and local public finance will want to read the reports issued by the U.S. Advisory Commission on Intergovernmental Relations.

In addition, students should consult the volumes included in the Brookings Institution's series *Studies of Government Finance.* These books include careful and up-to-date discussions of important public finance issues using relatively nontechnical language. The American Enterprise Institute and the Hoover Institution also provide useful tracts on current policy controversies. The working paper series of the National Bureau of Economic Research, available in many university libraries, is another good source of recent research on public finance. The technical difficulty of these papers is sometimes considerable, however.

Government at a Glance

I don't make jokes—I just watch government and report the facts.

WILL ROGERS

It is useful to have a broad description of the U.S. system of public finance before delving into its details. We begin with a brief discussion of the legal framework within which government conducts its economic activities. Then we consider problems that arise in attempts to quantify the role of government in the economy.

The Legal Framework

The Founding Fathers' concerns about the role of government in the economy are reflected in the Constitution. We first discuss constitutional provisions relating to the spending and taxing activities of the federal government and then turn to the legal status of states.

Federal Government

By virtue of Article 1, Section 8 of the Constitution, Congress is empowered "to pay the Debts and provide for the common Defense and general Welfare of the United States." Over the years, the notion of "general welfare" has been interpreted very broadly by Congress and the courts, and at the present time this clause effectively puts no constraints on government expenditure activity.[1] The Constitution puts no limits on the size of federal expenditure, either absolutely or relative to the size of the

---

[1] Article 1 also mandates that certain specific expenditures be made. For example, Congress has to appropriate funds to maintain both an army and a court system.

economy. Bills to appropriate expenditures (like practically all other laws) can originate in either house of Congress. An appropriations bill becomes law when it receives a majority vote in both houses and is signed by the president. If the president chooses to veto an expenditure, it can still be passed into law if it receives a two-thirds majority in each house.

How is Congress to raise the money to pay for these expenditures? Federal taxing powers are authorized in Article 1, Section 8: "Congress shall have Power to lay and collect Taxes, Duties, Imposts, and Excises." Unlike expenditure bills, "All Bills for raising Revenue shall originate in the House of Representatives" (Article 1, Section 7). In light of the enormous dissatisfaction with British tax policy during the colonial period, it is no surprise that considerable care was taken to constrain governmental taxing power, as described in the following paragraphs:

1. "[A]ll Duties, Imposts and Excises shall be uniform throughout the United States" (Article 1, Section 8). Congress cannot discriminate among states when it sets tax rates. If the federal government levies a tax on gasoline, the *rate* must be the same in every state. This does not, of course, imply that the per capita *amount* collected will be the same in each state. Presumably, states in which individuals drive more than average have higher tax liabilities, other things being the same. Thus, it is still possible (and indeed, likely) that various taxes make some states worse off than others.[2]

2. "No . . . direct Tax shall be laid, unless in Proportion to the Census or Enumeration herein before directed to be taken" (Article 1, Section 9). A direct tax is a tax levied on a *person* as opposed to a *commodity*. Essentially, this provision says that if State A has twice the population of State B, then any direct tax levied by Congress must be such that it yields twice as much revenue from State A as from State B. In general, the only permissible direct tax is a *head tax,* under which every citizen has the same tax obligation.

In the late 19th century, attempts to introduce a federal tax on income were declared unconstitutional by the Supreme Court because income taxation leads to different tax burdens for different citizens. Given this decision, the only way to introduce an income tax was via a constitutional amendment. The 16th Amendment, ratified in 1913, declares that "Congress shall have power to levy and collect taxes on incomes, from whatever source derived, without appointment among the several states, and without regard to census or enumeration." Today, the individual income tax is one of the mainstays of the federal revenue system.

---

[2] No tax law in history has ever been struck down for violating this clause. However, a close call occurred in the early 1980s. Congress passed a tax on oil, which exempted oil from the North Slope of Alaska. A federal district court ruled that the tax was unconstitutional, but this decision was ultimately reversed by the Supreme Court.

3. "No person shall be . . . deprived of life, liberty, or property, without due process of law; nor shall private property be taken for public use, without just compensation" (Fifth Amendment). From the point of view of tax policy, this clause means that distinctions created by the tax law must be reasonable. However, it is not always simple to determine which distinctions are "reasonable" and doing so is an ongoing part of the legislative and judicial processes.

4. "No Tax or Duty shall be laid on Articles exported from any State" (Article 1, Section 9). This provision was included to assure the southern states that their exports of tobacco and other commodities would not be jeopardized by the central government. It has not had much of an impact on the development of the public finance system.

The federal government is not required to finance all of its expenditures by taxation. If expenditures exceed revenues, it is empowered "To borrow Money on the credit of the United States" (Article 1, Section 8). Recently, there has been some political support for a constitutional amendment to require a balanced federal budget, but so far the movement to adopt such an amendment has not succeeded.

State and Local Governments

According to the Tenth Amendment, "The powers not delegated to the United States by the Constitution, nor prohibited by it to the States, are reserved to the States respectively, or to the people." Thus, explicit authorization for states to spend and tax is not required. However, the Constitution does put some limitations on states' economic activities. Article 1, Section 10 states that "No State shall, without the Consent of the Congress, lay any Imposts or Duties on Imports or Exports." Thus, international economic policy is in the hands of the federal government. In addition, various constitutional provisions have been interpreted as requiring that the states not

1. Levy taxes arbitrarily.
2. Discriminate against outside residents.
3. Levy taxes on imports from other states.

For example, in 1986 the Supreme Court declared unconstitutional an Alaska law mandating that 95 percent of workers on public projects be Alaskans.

States can impose spending and taxing restrictions on themselves in their own constitutions. State constitutions differ substantially with respect to the types of economic issues with which they deal. In recent years, one of the most interesting developments in public finance has been the movement of some states to amend their constitutions to limit the size of public sector spending.

From a legal point of view, the power of local governments to tax and spend is granted by the states. As a 19th-century judge put it:

> Municipal corporations owe their origin to, and derive their powers and rights wholly from, the [state] legislature. It breathes into them the breath of life, without which they cannot exist. As it creates, so it may destroy. If it may destroy, it may abridge and control. [*City of Clinton* v. *Cedar Rapids,* 1868]

It would be a mistake, however, to view localities as totally lacking in fiscal autonomy. Many towns and cities have substantial political power and do not respond passively to the wishes of state and federal governments. An interesting development in recent years has been the competition of states and cities for federal funds. The cities often are more successful in their lobbying activities than the states [Perlez, 1983, p. B1]!

The Size of Government

What has been the result of these legal prescriptions for government taxing and spending activities? The first item that belongs in any such description is a measure of their magnitude. Just how big is government? The whole public debate concerning whether government is too big presupposes that there is some way of measuring it.

One measure often used by politicians and journalists is the number of workers in the public sector. However, inferences about the size of government drawn from the number of workers it employs can be misleading. Imagine a country where a few public servants operate an enormous computer that guides all economic decisions. In this country, the number of individuals on the government payroll certainly is an underestimate of the importance of government. Similarly, it would be easy to construct a scenario in which a large number of workers is associated with a relatively weak public sector. Although for many purposes it is useful to know the number of public sector employees, it does not cast light on the central issue—the extent to which society's resources are subject to control of government.

A more sensible (and common) approach is to measure the size of government by the volume of its annual expenditures. These expenditures are basically of three types:

1. Purchases of goods and services. The government buys a wide variety of items, everything from missiles to services provided by forest rangers.
2. Transfers of income to people, businesses, or other governments. Here the government takes income from some individuals or organizations and transfers it to others. Examples are welfare programs such as food stamps and subsidies paid to farmers for production (or nonproduction) of certain commodities.
3. Interest payments. The government often borrows to finance its activities and, like any borrower, must pay interest for the privilege of doing so.

The federal government itemizes its expenditures in a document referred to as the **unified budget.**[3] In 1990, federal expenditures (excluding grants made to state and local governments) were $1,143 billion. When we add state and local government expenditures made that year, we arrive at a total of $1,907 billion [*Economic Report of the President,* 1991, pp. 380, 381].[4] Figures on government expenditures are easily available and widely quoted. Typically when expenditures go up, people conclude that government has grown and vice versa.

Unfortunately, conventional budget expenditures can convey a misleading impression of the extent to which society's resources are under government control. There are at least two reasons for this, the existence of off-budget items and hidden costs of government.

Off-Budget Items

Off-budget federal agencies are federally owned and controlled, but their fiscal activities are excluded by law from budget totals. These include entities such as the Rural Electrification and Revolving Telephone Fund (which makes loans to support the construction and operation of electric and telephone utilities in rural areas), and the better-known Tennessee Valley Authority, a regional supplier of electricity. The most important activities of off-budget agencies are making loans and providing insurance.[5] Our discussion focuses on the difficulties that off-budget credit activity creates for measuring the size of government.

The three main types of federal loans are direct loans, loan guarantees, and loans by government-sponsored enterprises. *Direct loans* are made to individuals, businesses, nonprofit institutions, and local governments. Often the government lends at rates below the market rate of interest. By the end of 1989, there were $207 billion in direct loans outstanding. *Loan guarantees* are promises to repay principal and interest in case a borrower defaults on a loan. Two important examples are student loans and some home mortgages. The values of outstanding guaranteed loans in 1989 stood at $588 billion. Analogously, the federal government insures savers against the insolvency of savings institutions. The federal government's largest insurance commitment is for deposits at banks and savings and loan institutions. Deposit insurance covered $2.9 trillion in deposits by the end of 1989. Further, the federal government insures $963 billion in pension funds against insolvency. *Government-sponsored enterprises* (GSEs) are privately owned institutions generally perceived to be quasi-governmental because they are federally established. GSEs provide

---

[3] The publication of some kind of budget document is constitutionally required: "a regular Statement and Account of the Receipts and Expenditures of all public Money shall be published from time to time" (Article 1, Section 9).

[4] Federal grants to state and local governments were $130 billion in 1990.

[5] On-budget agencies also make loans, but the amount is relatively small. See Congressional Budget Office [1982d, p. 3].

credit to housing, agriculture, and education. Their total loans outstanding in 1989 were $763 billion [Executive Office of the President, 1990, p. 229].

Note that figures on outstanding credit and insurance represent only potential liabilities of the government. Most borrowers do not default, and most savings institutions remain solvent. As the savings and loan crisis has demonstrated dramatically, however, these government commitments can prove to be costly. In 1989 the federal government spent more than $60 billion to cover the losses of over 400 bankrupt savings institutions. In 1990 the White House was projecting that the cost of the crisis would amount to some $500 billion over the next four decades ["No End in Sight," *Time*, August 13, 1990, p. 50].

Clearly, even though they are omitted from the unified budget, government credit and insurance activities are important. If government expenditures fell slightly at the same time that credit and insurance activities rose substantially, one might erroneously conclude that the role of government in the economy was diminishing. In recognition of this fact, in the 1970s Congress mandated the creation of a credit budget that estimates for each fiscal year the volume of new direct loans and loan guarantees made by the federal government. In addition, the federal budget document reports the face value of major federal insurance programs.

However, it is not easy to interpret the economic significance of government credit and insurance programs. For example, if the government taxes away $1 million from the private sector and spends the money on a tank, the cost to the private sector is $1 million.[6] If the government loans $1 million to a small business at a rate of interest below the market rate, as long as the loan is repaid, apparently all that the private sector loses is the difference between the subsidized interest rate and the market rate.

This line of reasoning suggests that government direct loans made at the market rate of interest have no net cost to the private sector. If the money is paid back, what's the difference? However, such reasoning fails to take into account the effect of government loan programs on the allocation of credit.

Assume for simplicity that there is a fixed amount of available credit during a given year. In competitive markets, the funds are allocated to projects on the basis of their expected rates of return. Lenders help to finance projects likely to be successful in the sense of making a lot of money. When the government steps in, funds are allocated to projects that otherwise might not have been able to gain financing. Our assumption that the amount of credit is fixed implies that some projects that otherwise would have been undertaken are crowded out.

---

[6] Actually, the loss in welfare exceeds $1 million if the tax induces a less efficient pattern of economic activity. The notion of efficiency that is relevant here is described in Chapter 14.

Of course, it may be the case that the recipients of government loans are entirely worthy of support, even though they would not have been successful in borrowing on the private market. ("Welfare Economics" in Chapter 4 presents criteria for establishing which projects are worthy.) The point is that the reallocation of credit induced by government loans has a cost in private investment projects that are crowded out. Therefore, an assessment of the economic significance of the credit budget requires knowing which private sector projects were sacrificed and what the returns on those projects would have been. Needless to say, this information is very hard to obtain.

To summarize: The federal government's off-budget credit and insurance activity is large in magnitude and scope. It is not included in the conventional budget, so the latter tends to underestimate the extent to which government is affecting use of resources. However, the savings and loan crisis is likely to create pressure to find ways to integrate credit and insurance obligations into the conventional budget.

Finally, some financial obligations incurred by the federal government appear in neither the unified budget nor the credit budget. Under the Social Security program, for example, government commits itself to pay citizens pensions when they retire. In the private sector, when such obligations are made, it is considered prudent practice to establish a reserve fund sufficient to meet them. Additions to such reserves are considered a current expense. The federal government does not engage in this practice. If it did, the net obligation of the Social Security system for the future would have required setting aside about $133 billion during the fiscal year ending in 1984 [Arthur Andersen and Company, 1986]. We see, then, that measures of the size of the official government budget depend on somewhat arbitrary accounting decisions concerning which items are to be included.

Hidden Costs of Government

Some government activities can have substantial effects on resource allocation even if they involve little in the way of explicit outlays. For example, issuing regulations per se is not very expensive, but compliance with the rules can be very costly. Air bag requirements raise the cost of cars. Various permit and inspection fees increase the price of housing. Some have argued that labor market regulations such as the minimum wage create unemployment, and that regulation of the drug industry slows the pace of scientific development.

It has been suggested that the costs imposed on the economy by government regulations be published in an annual **regulatory budget.** In this way, an explicit accounting for the costs of regulation would be available for public scrutiny. Unfortunately, it is exceedingly difficult to compute the costs of regulation. For example, we can easily imagine even pharmaceutical experts disagreeing on what new cures would have been developed in the absence of drug regulation. Similarly, it is hard to estimate how much government mandated safety procedures in the workplace increase production costs. In view of such problems, it is unlikely that there will ever be an official regulatory budget.[7]

Some Numbers   We reluctantly conclude that there is no feasible way to summarize in a single number the magnitude of government's impact on the economy. Having made this admission, we are still left with the practical problem of finding some reasonable indicator of government's size that can be used to estimate trends in the growth of government. Most economists are willing to accept conventionally defined government expenditure as a rough but useful measure. Like many other imperfect measures, it yields useful insights as long as its limitations are understood.

With all the appropriate caveats in mind, we present in Table 2.1 some data on expenditures made by all levels of U.S. government over time. The first column indicates that annual expenditures have increased by a factor of about 190 since 1929. This figure is a misleading indicator of the growth of government for several reasons:

1. Because of inflation, the dollar has decreased in value over time. In column 2, the expenditure figures are expressed in 1990 dollars. In real terms, government expenditure in 1990 was about 20 times the level in 1929.

2. The population has also been growing over time. We expect that an increasing population by itself creates demands for a larger public sector. (For example, more roads and sewers are required to accommodate more people.) Column 3 shows real government expenditure per capita. Now the increase from 1929 to 1990 is a factor of about 10.

3. For some purposes it is useful to examine government expenditure compared to the size of the economy. If government doubles in size but at the same time the economy triples, then in a relative sense, government has shrunk. Column 4 shows government expenditure as a percentage of gross national product (GNP), the market value of goods and services produced by the economy during the year. In 1929, the figure was 9.9 percent, and in 1990, it was 34.9 percent.

In light of our previous discussion, the figures in Table 2.1 convey a false sense of precision. Still, there is no doubt that in the long run the

---

[7] Regulation is not necessarily a bad thing just because it creates costs. Like any other government activity, it can be evaluated only by assessing the benefits as well as the costs. (Problems in doing cost-benefit analysis are discussed in Chapter 12.)

Table 2.1   **State, local, and federal government expenditures** *(selected years)*

	(1) Total Expenditures *(billions)*	*(2)* 1990 Dollars *(billions)**	*(3)* 1990 Dollars per Capita	*(4)* Percent of GNP
1929	$ 10	$ 93	$ 767	9.9%
1940	19	187	1,418	18.4
1945	93	778	5,598	43.5
1950	61	338	2,223	21.3
1955	99	476	2,886	24.3
1960	137	584	3,228	26.6
1965	190	738	3,802	26.9
1970	317	994	4,848	31.3
1975	545	1,208	5,620	34.1
1980	890	1,365	5,987	32.6
1985	1,403	1,663	6,959	34.9
1990	1,907	1,907	7,598	34.9

* Conversion to 1990 dollars done using the GNP deflator.

SOURCE: Calculations based on *Economic Report of the President 1991* (Washington, D.C.: U.S. Government Printing Office, 1991), pp. 286, 290, 321, 379.

Table 2.2   **Government outlays as a percentage of gross domestic product** *(selected countries, 1987)*

Australia	34.4%	Japan	33.2%
Canada	39.5	Sweden	62.7
France	49.4	United Kingdom	37.9
Germany	44.4		

SOURCE: Computed from *National Accounts of OECD Countries 1975–1987,* volume II (Paris: OECD Department of Economics and Statistics, 1989), various pages.

economic role of government has grown enormously. With more than a third of GNP going through the public sector, government is an enormous economic force.[8]

To put the U.S. data in perspective, it helps to make some international comparisons. Table 2.2 shows figures on government expenditure relative to gross domestic product for a number of developed countries.[9]

---

[8] Interestingly, relative to the size of GNP, the rate of expenditure growth has tapered off in the last decade. But as growth slowed in this area, other dimensions of government activity (such as off-budget lending) have been increasing. It is hard to say what the effect is on balance.

[9] Gross domestic product differs from GNP in its treatment of production by foreign-owned companies. GNP includes U.S. production abroad and excludes the output of foreign-owned companies in the United States. GDP does the opposite, including the output produced domestically (although foreign owned) and excluding production abroad (even though it is U.S. owned).

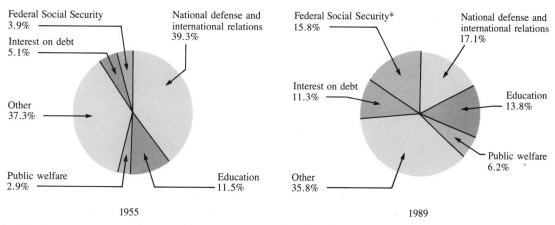

Federal Social Security
3.9%

Interest on debt
5.1%

National defense and
international relations
39.3%

Other
37.3%

Public welfare
2.9%

Education
11.5%

1955

Federal Social Security*
15.8%

National defense and
international relations
17.1%

Interest on debt
11.3%

Education
13.8%

Public welfare
6.2%

Other
35.8%

1989

* Officially known as OASDHI—old-age, survivors, disability, and health insurance.

SOURCE: For 1955 computed from U.S. Bureau of the Census, *Historical Statistics of the United States, Colonial Times to 1970* (Washington, D.C.: U.S. Government Printing Office, 1975), pp. 1120–21. For 1989, U.S. Bureau of the Census, *Governmental Finances in 1988–89* (Washington, D.C.: U.S. Government Printing Office, 1991), p. 1.

Figure 2.1
Expenditures by all levels of government, 1955 and 1989

The data indicate that the United States is not alone in having an important public sector. Indeed, compared to countries such as Sweden and France, the U.S. public sector is relatively small.

Expenditures

We now turn from the overall magnitude of government expenditures to their composition. It is impossible to reflect the enormous scope of government spending activity in a brief table. In the federal budget for fiscal year 1991, the list of programs and their descriptions required over 800 pages! The major categories of government expenditure and their growth over time are illustrated in Figure 2.1. For 1955 and 1989, the figure shows the percentage of total government expenditure spent on each category. The following aspects of the figure are noteworthy:

1. National defense is and always has been an important component of government expenditure.[10] In 1989, the percentage of government expenditure devoted to defense (17.1 percent) was larger than it was at the turn of the century (9.9 percent), but quite a bit smaller than in 1955 (39.3 percent). Of course, this observation by itself tells us little about whether too much or too little is spent on defense.

[10] The bulk of expenditure on "national defense and international relations" is for military services.

2. The Social Security program has grown at an enormous rate. Essentially this program transfers income to individuals who are not working either because they are disabled or retired. Social Security did not even exist 50 years ago; now it absorbs almost as much of the budget as defense. Chapters 10 and 11 include a detailed analysis of the program.

3. Public welfare activities have generally been increasing as a proportion of government spending, but in recent years, the proportion has fallen. Public welfare includes programs such as old-age assistance, Aid to Families with Dependent Children (AFDC), and the Medicaid program (which pays medical bills for the indigent).

4. Payments of interest on debt are increasing in relative importance. This is because both interest rates and the size of the debt have been growing over time.

Note that fast growing areas such as Social Security and interest payments are relatively uncontrollable in the sense that they are determined by decisions made in previous years. Indeed, much of the government budget consists of so-called **entitlement programs**—programs with cost determined not by fixed dollar amounts, but by the number of people who qualify. The laws governing Social Security, many public welfare programs, farm price supports, and so forth include rules that determine who is entitled to benefits and how much recipients receive. Expenditures on entitlement programs are therefore out of the hands of the current government, unless it changes the rules. Similarly, debt payments are determined by interest rates and previous deficits, again mostly out of the control of current decision makers. According to most estimates, about three-quarters of the federal budget is relatively uncontrollable. In Chapter 7, we discuss whether government spending is out of control and if so, what can be done about it.

It is useful to break down total expenditures by the level of government making them. Of the $1.9 trillion of direct expenditures made in 1989, the federal government accounted for about 57.1 percent, the states for 17.4 percent, and localities for 25.6 percent [U.S. Department of Commerce, 1990, p. 2]. State and local governments thus play a very important role in U.S. public finance. They account for the bulk of spending on items such as police and fire protection, education, and transportation. A substantial amount of public welfare expenditures is also made through the states. The complications that arise in coordinating the fiscal activities of different levels of government in a federal system are discussed in Chapter 21.

Revenues

The principal components of the U.S. tax system are noted in Figure 2.2. For 1955 and 1989, the figure shows the percentage of total revenues attributable to each of the major taxes. Currently, personal income taxa-

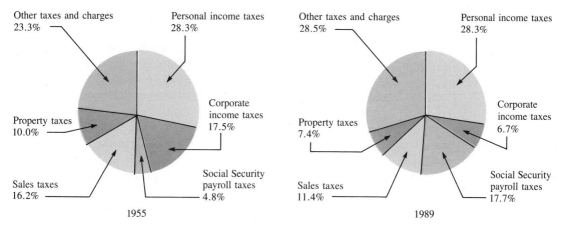

Other taxes and charges
23.3%

Personal income taxes
28.3%

Corporate
income taxes
17.5%

Property taxes
10.0%

Sales taxes
16.2%

Social Security
payroll taxes
4.8%

1955

Other taxes and charges
28.5%

Personal income taxes
28.3%

Corporate
income taxes
6.7%

Property taxes
7.4%

Sales taxes
11.4%

Social Security
payroll taxes
17.7%

1989

SOURCES: For 1955, computed from U.S. Bureau of the Census, *Historical Statistics of the United States, Colonial Times to 1970* (Washington, D.C.: U.S. Government Printing Office, 1975), p. 1119. For 1989, U.S. Bureau of the Census, *Governmental Finances in 1988–89* (Washington, D.C.: U.S. Government Printing Office, 1991), p. 1.

Figure 2.2

Revenue collections
by all levels of
government, 1955
and 1989

tion is the single most important source of revenue, accounting for about 28 percent of taxes raised by all levels of government. Note the importance of the Social Security payroll tax. It yields more revenue than either sales, corporation, or property taxation. At the same time that Social Security expenditures have been increasing (see Figure 2.2), so have the taxes raised to pay for them.

Property and sales taxes used to play a much greater role in the revenue structure than they do now. In 1902, property taxes accounted for 41 percent of all revenues raised, and sales taxes, 30 percent. By 1989, the comparable figures were 7 percent and 11 percent. It is also interesting to observe the relative rise and fall of corporation income taxes during this century. In 1902, taxes on corporate income did not exist. In 1955, they accounted for 17.5 percent of all revenue collected, but by 1989 this figure was down to 6.7 percent.

In 1988, the federal government collected about 56.3 percent of all tax revenues. But the federal government has not always been the biggest tax collector. In 1902, for example, only 37.4 percent of revenues were raised by the federal government; 51.3 percent were raised by localities, and the rest by the states.

Changes in the real value of debt.   In popular discussions, taxes are usually viewed as the only source of government revenue. However, when the government is a debtor and the price level changes, changes in the real value of the debt may be an important source of revenue. To see why, suppose that at the beginning of the year you owe a creditor $1,000, and the sum does not have to be repaid until the end of the year. Suppose further that over the course of the year, prices rise by 10 percent. Then the dollars that you use to repay your creditor are worth 10 percent less than those you borrowed from him. In effect, inflation has reduced the real value of your debt by $100 (10 percent of $1,000). Alternatively, your real income has increased by $100 as a consequence of inflation. Of course, at the same time, your creditor's real income has fallen by $100.[11]

At the end of fiscal year 1990, the federal government's outstanding debt was about $2.40 trillion. During 1990, the rate of inflation was 6.1 percent. Applying the same logic as previously, inflation reduced the real value of the federal debt by $146 billion ($2.40 trillion $\times$ 0.061). In effect, this is as much a receipt for the government as any of the taxes listed in Figure 2.2. However, the government's accounting procedures do not allow the inclusion of gains due to inflationary erosion of the debt on the revenue side of the account. We defer to Chapter 18 further discussion of issues related to the measurement of the debt and its economic significance.

Agenda for Study	This chapter has set forth a collection of basic "facts"—facts on governmental fiscal institutions, on the size and scope of government spending, and on the methods used by government to finance itself. Parts of the rest of this book are devoted to presenting more facts—filling in the rather sketchy picture of how our fiscal system operates. Just as important, we seek to explore the significance of these facts, to ask whether the status quo has led to desirable outcomes, and if not, how it can be improved.

Summary

- Legal constraints on federal and state government economic activity are embodied in the Constitution.

- The federal government may effectively undertake any expenditures it wishes and may use debt and taxes to finance them. The federal government may not discriminate among states when choosing tax rates, and may not place a levy on state exports. The 16th Amendment empowers the federal government to levy a tax on personal income.

- State governments are forbidden to levy tariffs on imports, discriminate against outside residents, or tax other states' products. Many states have adopted self-imposed requirements for a balanced budget.

- All common measures of the size of government—employees, expenditures, revenues, etc.—involve some deficiency. In particular, these items miss the impact of off-budget activities and the costs of regulations. Nonetheless, there is strong evidence that the impact of the government sector on the allocation of national resources has increased over time.

- The level of government expenditures has

---

[11] If the inflation is anticipated by borrowers and lenders, one expects that the interest rate charged will be increased to take inflation into account. This phenomenon is discussed in Chapter 16 under "Taxation and Inflation."

increased in both nominal and real absolute terms, in per capita terms, and as a percentage of gross national product.

■ The share of defense spending in federal expenditure has fallen in the long run, while Social Security, public welfare, and payments on outstanding debt have increased in importance. The combination of entitlement programs and interest payments has resulted in reduced yearly control over the level of expenditures.

■ Personal income and Social Security payroll taxes are currently the largest sources of government revenue. Since the turn of the century, property taxes have declined in importance, while corporate income taxes rose and then recently declined.

Discussion Questions

1. In each of the following circumstances, decide whether the impact of government on the economy has increased or decreased and why. In each case, how does your answer compare to that given by standard measures of the size of government?

    a. Congress replaces federal student loan guarantees with outright, but smaller, direct grants to students.

    b. The ratio of government purchases of goods and services to gross national product falls.

    c. The federal budget is brought into balance by reducing grants-in-aid to state and local governments.

2. The federal government guarantees loans of $100 million to the Theta Beta Phi Sorority Sweatshirt Company. If the market interest rate is currently 10 percent, what is the cost of the program? Suppose that instead, the government makes a direct loan at a rate of 8 percent. What is the cost now?

3. Proponents of student loans argue that "the only objection is the reported default rate" [Drinan, 1983, p. E17]. Similarly, the vice chairman of Chrysler Corporation, which received millions of dollars of federal loan guarantees, stressed "we never really got a dime from the federal government. We only got guarantees" [Chrysler's Stock Plea, 1983, p. D6]. Evaluate these claims.

Selected References

Executive Office of the President. *Budget of the United States Government Fiscal Year 1991* (Section One). Washington, D.C.: U.S. Government Printing Office, 1990.

Facts and Figures on Government Finance. Washington, D.C.: Tax Foundation, 1991.

Tools of
Public Finance

The dual tasks of an economist are to explain how the economy works—**positive economics**—and to determine whether or not it is producing good results—**normative economics.** In principle, positive analysis does not require value judgments, because its purpose is descriptive. Normative analysis, on the other hand, requires an ethical framework, because without one, it is impossible to say what is good. Although it is sometimes difficult to keep the positive and the normative from getting entangled, most economists agree that the distinction is worthwhile. Discussions of how the world *is* should not be colored by a view of how it *ought* to be.

The next two chapters describe the tools used by public finance economists to analyze both normative and positive issues. To a large extent, they are the same as those used in other fields of applied economics. Despite the popularity of these tools, they are far from perfect. It is important to know their deficiencies as well as their strengths. Given their imperfections, why are the tools so widely used? A common response to this query is the story about the compulsive gambler who plays roulette every night at the local casino, despite the fact that the wheel is fixed. When asked by a friend why he continues to play, the gambler replies, "It's the only game in town." Similarly, most modern public finance economists are convinced that flawed as they may be, the standard tools of economics are the best available for studying the relationship between government and the economy.[1]

---

[1] Most, but not all! For example, a lively group of radical economists has rejected the standard tools. See Mermelstein [1973].

CHAPTER 3

Tools of Positive Analysis

Numbers live. Numbers take on vitality.

JESSE JACKSON

A good subtitle for this chapter is "Why Is It So Hard to Tell What's Going On?" We constantly hear economists—and politicians—disagree vehemently about the likely consequences of various government actions. Consider the controversy over the likely effects of reduced income tax rates on the amount of labor that people supply. Conservatives argue that lower tax rates create incentives for people to work harder. Liberals are skeptical, arguing that no major changes can be expected. On each side there are economists to testify that their opinion is correct. Is it surprising that the cynical viewpoint expressed in the following cartoon is so widespread?

An important reason for the lack of definitive answers is that economists are generally unable to perform carefully controlled experiments with the economy. To determine the effects of a fertilizer on cabbage growth, a botanist can treat one plot of ground with the fertilizer and compare the results with an otherwise identical unfertilized cabbage patch. The unfertilized patch serves as the control group. Economists do not have such opportunities. Although the government can change the economic environment, there is no control group with which to make comparisons. Therefore, we never know for certain the extent to which changes in the economy are consequences of policy changes.

In the absence of controlled experiments, economists use other methods to analyze the impact of various government policies on economic behavior. Indeed, one of the most exciting developments in public finance

"That's the gist of
what I want to say.
Now get me some
statistics to base it
on."

Drawing by Joe Mirachi;
© 1977 The New Yorker
Magazine, Inc.

in the last several decades has been the widespread use of modern statistical tools to study public policy issues.

Next, the debate over the effect of taxes on labor supply provides an
understanding of how empirical work is done in public finance. The general principles used are applicable to any number of problems.

The Role of Theory

An assertion often heard in all kinds of arguments is that "The numbers
speak for themselves." What do the numbers say about income tax rates
and labor supply? Table 3.1 gives information on how the proportion of
the last dollar of earnings taken by the tax collector—the **marginal tax
rate**—varied over the period 1955 to 1988. The table also shows how the
average weekly hours per worker have changed over time. The figures
indicate that tax rates have generally increased, and the hours of work
have decreased. The numbers appear to say that taxes have depressed
labor supply.

Is this inference correct? At the same time that tax rates were changing, so were numerous other factors that might influence labor supply. If
unearned income—income from dividends, interest, and so forth—were
rising over the period, people may have worked less because they were
richer. Alternatively, changing attitudes—a decrease in the Protestant
ethic—might have decreased labor supply. Neither of these effects, and
you can certainly think of many more, is taken into account by the numbers given. Clearly, what we need to know is the *independent* effect of
taxes on labor supply. This effect simply cannot be learned solely from

Table 3.1   **Income tax rates and labor supply**

Year	Marginal Federal Tax Rate* (percent)	Average Weekly Hours†
1955	20.00%	39.6
1960	20.00	38.6
1965	17.00	38.8
1970	19.50	37.1
1972	19.00	37.1
1974	20.00	36.6
1976	22.00	36.1
1978	25.00	35.8
1980	30.13	35.3
1982	31.70	34.8
1984	28.70	35.2
1986	29.15	34.8
1988	22.51	34.7

* Lerman, Allen H., "Average and Marginal Income Tax and Social Security (FICA) Tax Rates for Four-Person Families at the Same Relative Positions in the Income Distribution, 1955–1988," Office of Tax Analysis, Department of the Treasury, mimeo, 1988.

† *Economic Report of the President, 1991.* Washington, D.C.: Government Printing Office, 1991.

examining the trends in the two variables over time. Here is a typical situation; when we turn to data for answers, *the numbers never speak for themselves*.

In a sense, this observation opens a Pandora's box; an unlimited number of variables change over time. How do we know which ones have to be considered to find the tax effect? One major purpose of economic theory is to help isolate a small set of variables that are important in influencing behavior. The taxes and labor supply example illustrates how basic economic theory is useful in organizing thoughts.

The dominant theory of labor supply is that the work decision is based on the rational allocation of time.[1] Suppose that Mr. Rogers has only a certain number of hours in the day: How many hours should he devote to work in the market, and how many hours to leisure? Rogers derives satisfaction (utility) from leisure, but to earn income he must work and thereby surrender leisure time. Rogers's problem is to find just the combination of income and leisure that maximizes his utility.

---

[1] The theory of labor supply is presented here verbally. A graphical exposition appears in Chapter 17 under "Labor Supply."

Suppose that Rogers's wage rate is $w per hour. The wage is the cost of Rogers's time. For every hour he spends at leisure, Rogers gives up $w in wages—time is literally money. However, a "rational" individual generally will not work every possible hour, even though leisure is costly. People spend time on leisure to the extent that it generates satisfaction that is valued in excess of its cost.

This model may seem absurdly simple. It does not account for the possibility that an individual's labor supply behavior may depend on the labor supply decisions of other family members. Neither does the model take into account whether the individual can work as many hours as desired. Indeed, the entire notion that people make their decisions by rationally considering costs and benefits may appear unrealistic.

However, the whole point of model building is to simplify as much as possible, so that a problem is reduced to its essentials. The literary critic Lytton Strachey said that "Omission is the beginning of all art" [Lipton, 1977, p. 93]. Omission is also the beginning of all good economic analysis. A model should not be judged on the basis of whether or not it is true, but on whether the model is plausible and informative. Most of the work in modern economics is based on the assumption that maximization of utility is a good working hypothesis [see Becker, 1962]. This point of view is taken throughout the book.

Imagine that Mr. Rogers has found his utility maximizing combination of income and leisure based on his wage rate of $w. Now the government imposes a tax on wage income of t percent. Then Rogers's after-tax or *net wage* is $(1 - t)w$. How will a rational individual react—work more, work less, or not change at all? In public debate, arguments for all three possibilities have been made with great assurance. In fact, however, the impact of an earnings tax on hours of work *cannot* be predicted on theoretical grounds.

To see this, first observe that the wage tax lowers the effective price of leisure. Prior to the tax, consumption of an hour of leisure cost Rogers $w. Under the earnings tax, because Rogers's net wage is lower, an hour of leisure costs him only $(1 - t)w$. Since leisure has become cheaper, there will be a tendency to consume more of it—to work less. This is called the *substitution effect*.

Another effect occurs simultaneously when the tax is imposed. Assume that Rogers will work a certain number of hours regardless of all feasible changes in the net wage. After the tax, Rogers receives only $(1 - t)w$ for each of these hours, while before it was $w. In a real sense, Rogers has suffered a loss of income. To the extent that leisure is a *normal good*—consumption increases when income increases and vice versa—this income loss leads to less consumption of leisure. But less leisure means more work. Because the earnings tax has made Rogers poorer, it has induced him to work more. This is called the *income effect*.

Thus, the tax simultaneously produces two effects: It induces substitution toward the cheaper activity (leisure), and it reduces real income. Since the substitution effect and the income effect work in opposite directions, the impact of an earnings tax cannot be determined by theorizing alone. Consider the following two statements:

1. "With these high taxes, it's really not worth it for me to work as much as I used to."
2. "With these high taxes, I have to work more to maintain my standard of living."

For the person making the first statement the substitution effect is dominating, while in the second statement the income effect is dominating. Both statements can reflect perfectly rational behavior for the individuals involved.

The importance of the uncertainty caused by the conflict of income and substitution effects cannot be overemphasized. Only **empirical work**—analysis based on observation and experience as opposed to theory—can answer the question of how labor force behavior is affected by changes in the tax system. Even intense armchair speculation on this matter must be regarded with considerable skepticism.

Although we have developed the argument with a labor supply example, the lesson is more general; one major purpose of theory is to make us aware of the areas of our ignorance.

Methods of Empirical Analysis

Theory helps to organize thoughts about how people react to changes in their economic environment. But it usually cannot tell what the magnitude of such responses will be. Indeed, in the labor supply case just discussed, theory alone cannot even predict the *direction* of the likely changes. Empirical work becomes necessary. The three types of empirical strategies are personal interviews, experiments, and econometric estimation. With each technique, the connections to theory are vital. Theory influences how the study is organized, which questions are asked, and how the results are interpreted.

Interviews

The most straightforward way to find out whether some government activity influences people's behavior is simply to ask them. In a crude way, this is the kind of empirical "analysis" done by reporters. ("Tell me, are you going to delay your retirement if the government lowers your Social Security benefit?") A number of quite sophisticated interview studies have been done to assess the effect of taxes on labor supply. A group of British lawyers and accountants were carefully questioned as to how they determined their hours of work, whether they were aware of the tax rates they faced, and if these tax rates created any incentives or disincentives to work. The responses suggested that relatively few people were affected by taxes [Break, 1957, p. 549]. A later survey of a group of affluent Americans told much the same story. "Only one-eighth . . . said that they have actually curtailed their work effort because of the progressive income tax. . . . Those facing the highest marginal tax rates reported work disincentives only a little more frequently than did those facing the lower rates" [Barlow, Brazer, & Morgan, 1966, p. 3].

Pitfalls of interviews.   However, interpretation of these survey results must be done cautiously. After all, just because an individual cannot recite his or her tax rate does not mean that the individual is unaware of the discrepancy between before- and after-tax pay.

An old Chinese proverb counsels, "Listen to what a person says and then watch what he does." The fact that people *say* something about their behavior does not make it true. Some people are embarrassed to admit that financial considerations affect their labor supply decisions. ("I work for fulfillment.") Others complain about government just for the sheer fun of it, while in reality they are not influenced by taxes at all. If you want to find out what radio station a family listens to, what makes more sense: to ask them, or to see where the radio dial is set?

Experiments

At the outset, we stressed that the basic problem in doing empirical work in economics is the inability to do controlled experiments with the economy. However, the federal government has funded several major attempts to use experimental methodologies in the study of economic behavior. The idea underlying these social experiments is illustrated in the Income Maintenance Experiment conducted during the late 1960s.

The problem was to find out how the labor supply of the poor would change (if at all) when poor people were allowed to participate in certain income support programs.[2] By random selection, a sample of poor families was sorted into two groups. Families in the first group were allowed to participate in the income support program. The second group served as a control. At the end of several years, the labor supplies of the two groups were compared. Any differences in work effort, it was thought, could be attributed to the experimental treatment.

Pitfalls of social experiments.   Although such an experiment seems to be a promising way to learn about economic behavior, technical problems tend to diminish the usefulness of its results because classical methodology for experiments requires that samples be truly random. That is, the members of the sample must be representative of the population whose behavior is under consideration. In social experiments, it is virtually im-

---

[2] Essentially, the programs provided poor families with a guaranteed annual payment, the amount of which depended on their earnings in the labor market. See Stafford [1985] and Chapter 9 under "Aid to Families with Dependent Children."

possible to maintain a random sample, even if one is available initially. Some people leave the program to take new jobs. Others simply decide that they don't want to participate. Because such people *self*-select out of the sample, the characteristics of the group left are no longer representative of the population.

In addition, unlike plants or laboratory animals, human beings are conscious of the fact that they are participating in an experiment. This consciousness itself affects their behavior. A related point is that people within the group may react differently to a program when only a small number of participants is involved than they would when the program is universal. Or an experiment that lasts only a few months may produce different behavior than a program expected to be permanent.

One thing is certain. Social experiments are costly. An experiment conducted to learn how the housing decisions of the poor would be affected by rent subsidies cost $163.3 million.[3]

Social experiments are more likely to be worth their cost when existing evidence on the value of expensive social programs is inconclusive. In a paper assessing the value of controlled experiments in labor training programs, Gary Burtless and Larry Orr [1986] point out that while the Supported Work experiment for disadvantaged workers took six years and $80 million to complete, federal expenditures on training and placement during that time exceeded $10 billion. If there were any substantial doubt about the programs' effectiveness and this doubt could be resolved only through a carefully controlled experiment, the potential for avoiding misdirected spending could easily outweigh the costs of the experiment.

Laboratory experiments.   Certain kinds of economic behavior can also be studied in laboratory experiments, an approach often used by psychologists. An investigator recruits a group of people (subjects) who perform various tasks. The investigator observes their behavior. To study labor supply, an investigator might begin by noting from the theory of labor supply that a key variable is the net wage rate. A possible experimental strategy would be to offer subjects different rewards for completing various jobs and record how the amount of effort varies with the reward.

Laboratory experiments are subject to some of the pitfalls of social experiments. The main problem is that the environment in which behavior is observed is artificial. Moreover, the characteristics of the subjects, who are often college undergraduates, are unlikely to be representative of the population as a whole. However, laboratory experiments are much cheaper than social experiments and provide more flexibility. Their popularity has been growing in recent years, and as we see in later chapters, they have provided a number of very interesting results.

---

[3] In this Experimental Housing Allowance Program, $55.9 million went for payments to the members of the sample. The remainder was spent on administration and analysis of the data. See Ingram [1985].

Econometric Studies

Econometrics is the statistical analysis of economic data. It does not rely on asking people for their opinions or subjecting them to experiments. Rather, the effects of various policies are inferred from the analysis of observed behavior.[4] While economists are unable to control historical events, econometrics makes it possible to assess the importance of events that *did* occur.

In the simple labor supply model, it was suggested that annual hours of work *(L)* depend on the net wage rate *(w_n)*. [By definition, $w_n = (1 - t)w$.] A bit of thought suggests that variables like nonlabor income *(A)*,[5] age *(X_1)*, and number of children *(X_2)* may also influence the hours of work decision. The econometrician chooses a particular algebraic form to summarize the relationship between hours of work and these explanatory variables. A particularly simple form is:

$$L = \alpha_0 + \alpha_1 w_n + \alpha_2 A + \alpha_3 X_1 + \alpha_4 X_2 + \varepsilon \tag{3.1}$$

The α's are the **parameters** of the equation and ε is a **random error.** The parameters show how a change in a given right-hand side variable affects hours of work. If $\alpha_1 = 0$, the net wage has no impact on hours of work. If α_1 is greater than 0, increases in the net wage induce people to work more. The substitution effect dominates. If α_1 is less than 0, increases in the net wage induce people to work less. The income effect dominates.

The presence of the random error ε reflects the fact that there are influences on labor supply that are unobservable to the investigator. No matter how many variables are included in the study, there is always some behavior that cannot be explained by the model.

Clearly, if we knew the α's, all debate over the effect of taxes on labor supply would be settled. The practical side of econometrics is to estimate the α's by application of various techniques. The most popular method is called **multiple regression analysis.** The heat of the debate over labor supply indicates that this technique does not always lead to conclusive results. To understand why, we consider its application to the labor supply example.

For this purpose, ignore for the moment all variables in Equation (3.1) other than the net wage. Assume that hours of work decision can be written simply as

$$L = \alpha_0 + \alpha_1 w_n + \varepsilon \tag{3.2}$$

Equation (3.2) is characterized as *linear* because if it is graphed with *L* and w_n on the axes, the result is a straight line.

Suppose now that information is obtained on hours of work and on after-tax wages for a sample of people. Plotting those observations gives a

---

[4] Note that econometric methods can also be applied to data generated by surveys and experiments. However, these methods are applied most often to data based on observed behavior.

[5] The sum of dividends, interest, and so forth.

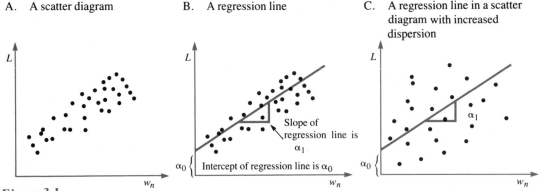

A. A scatter diagram

B. A regression line

C. A regression line in a scatter diagram with increased dispersion

Figure 3.1

Multiple regression analysis

scatter of points like that in Figure 3.1A. Obviously, no single straight line can fit through all these points. The purpose of multiple regression analysis is to find the parameters of that line which fits best.[6] Such a **regression line** is illustrated in Figure 3.1B. The regression line is a geometric representation of Equation (3.2), and its slope is an estimate of α_1. (A parameter estimate is sometimes called a *regression coefficient*.)

After α_1 is estimated, its reliability must be considered. Is it likely to be close to the "true" value of α_1? To see why this is an issue, suppose that our scatter of points looked like that in Figure 3.1C. The regression line is identical to that in Figure 3.1B but the scatter of points is more diffuse. Even though the estimates of the α's are the same as those in Figure 3.1B, there will be less faith in their reliability. Econometricians calculate a measure called the *standard error* which indicates how much an estimated parameter can vary from the true value. When the standard error is small in relation to the size of the estimated parameter, the coefficient is said to be **statistically significant.**

This example assumed that there is only one explanatory variable, the net wage. Suppose that instead there were two variables in the equation: the net wage and nonlabor income. In analogy to fitting a regression *line* in a two-dimensional space, a regression *plane* can be fitted through a scatter of points in a three-dimensional space. For more than two variables, there is no convenient geometrical representation. Nevertheless, similar mathematical principles are applied to produce estimates of the parameters for any number of explanatory variables (provided that there are fewer variables than observations). The actual calculations are done with computers.

With estimates of the α's in hand, inferences can be made about the changes in L induced by changes in the net wage. Suppose that $\alpha_1 = 100$. Then if a tax increase lowered the wage by 50 cents, it can be predicted an individual would work 50 hours ($100 \times \$.50$) less per year.

---

[6] The best line is that which minimizes the sum of the squared vertical distances between the points on the line and the points in the scatter. See Gujarati [1978].

Pitfalls of econometric analysis.   There are difficulties involved in doing econometrics that explain why different investigators may reach contradictory conclusions. For example, implicit in Equation (3.1) is the assumption that the same equation can describe everyone's behavior. However, different types of people may have different hours-of-work equations. Married women may react differently than married men to change in the net wage. Similarly, the young and the old have different behavioral patterns. Grouping together people with different behavior results in misleading parameter estimates. Investigators generally do not know beforehand along what lines their samples should be divided. Somewhat arbitrary decisions are required, and these may lead investigators to different results.

A related problem is that the parameters may change over time. The female labor supply equation using data from 1960 would very likely show different results from an equation using 1992 data. In part, this would be due to the impact of the women's movement on attitudes toward work, and hence, on the values of the α's. More generally, the reality that econometricians seek to understand is constantly changing. Estimates obtained from various data sets may differ even if the techniques used to obtain them are the same.

In addition, for an estimate of α_1 to be reliable, the regression equation must include all the relevant variables. Otherwise, some effects that are actually due to an omitted variable may be attributed to the net wage. Important variables are sometimes left out of an equation because information on them is simply not available. For example, it is very difficult to obtain reliable information on people's sources of nonlabor income. Suppose that:

1. As nonlabor income increases (other things being the same), people tend to work less.
2. There is a tendency for people with high wages also to have high nonlabor income.

If nonlabor income is omitted from the equation, part of its effect on hours of work would be attributed to the wage, and the estimate of α_1 would be lower than its true value. In general, an estimate of α_1 is biased unless all the other variables that affect hours of work and that are also systematically related to the net wage are included.

A more severe version of this problem occurs when a potentially important variable is inherently unmeasurable. Attitudes like aggressiveness may very well influence work decisions, but there are no satisfactory ways for quantifying these attitudes.

Sometimes there are controversies over which variables should be included in a regression equation. Should an individual's educational level be included? Some argue that education affects attitudes toward work and therefore should be included as an explanatory variable. Others believe that education only affects work decisions to the extent that it changes the wage, and therefore should not be included. While economic theory helps give some structure to the search for explanatory variables, it is rarely definitive. Different investigators make different judgments.

Also, to the extent that the variables are mismeasured, it is difficult to obtain reliable estimates of the behavior we seek to understand. Consider problems in measuring hours of work. Superficially, this seems like a straightforward issue—merely find out how much time elapses at the workplace. But a better measure would take into account coffee breaks and "goofing off" time. These are obviously more difficult to measure. Measuring the wage rate also presents substantial problems. Ideally, the computation should include not only what a worker receives in the pay-check at the end of the week, but also the value of fringe benefits—pension rights, insurance programs, access to a company car, and so forth.

Equation (3.1) assumes that all the explanatory variables affect hours of work in a linear fashion. This is a very convenient assumption, but certainly not the only possibility. An investigator might believe that hours of work depend on the net wage and the net wage squared—a quadratic relationship. It is therefore necessary to augment the equation with the variable w_n^2. Human behavior is sufficiently complex that any equation can be only an approximation of the truth. Unfortunately, economic theory gives little guidance with respect to what the correct functional form is, so investigators must choose specifications largely on the basis of intuition or convenience.

Finally, an important assumption is that variables on the right side of the equation affect the choice of the left-hand variable. If the reverse is true, serious problems arise. Suppose that α_1 of Equation (3.1) is found to be positive. One interpretation is that when the net wage increases, people choose to work more. Another plausible interpretation is that employers pay higher wages to people who work longer hours. Indeed, it might be the case that wage rates affect hours worked and simultaneously hours worked affect wages. If this is so, then the estimate of α_1 generated by multiple regression analysis does not measure just the effect of changes in the net wage on people's work decisions.

Several statistical techniques are available for dealing with the simultaneity problem. They tend to be complicated, and different techniques can lead to different answers. This is another source of discrepancies in the results of econometric studies.

Concluding Remarks

A number of tools are available for those who seek to describe economic behavior. Theory plays a crucial role in helping to isolate a set of potentially important variables. Empirical work is then needed to see whether the theory is consistent with real-world phenomena. Currently the most widespread method of empirical work in economics is econometric analysis, because economists tend to be most comfortable with results based on data from real-world environments. However, honest econometricians may come to very different conclusions. The data they use are imperfect, and implementation requires that assumptions be made. Reasonable people can disagree on the proper interpretation of a particular set of "facts":

> Facts are simple
> and facts are straight
> Facts are lazy
> and facts are late
> Facts all come with points of view
> Facts won't do what I want them to.[7]

This does not mean that all hope of learning about the factors that influence economic behavior should be abandoned. The economist researching an empirical question will doubtless come across a number of studies, each making somewhat different assumptions, each emphasizing a somewhat different aspect of the problem, and each therefore arriving at a somewhat different conclusion. In many cases it is possible to reconcile the different studies and construct a coherent picture of the phenomenon under discussion. Martin Feldstein has likened the economist who undertakes such a task to the maharajah in the children's fable about the five blind men who examined an elephant:

> The important lesson in that story is not the fact that each blind man came away with a partial and "incorrect" piece of evidence. The lesson is rather that an intelligent maharajah who studied the findings of these five men could probably piece together a good judgmental picture of an elephant, especially if he had previously seen some other four-footed animal. [1982b, p. 830]

On the numerous occasions throughout this book when we refer to the results of empirical studies, the caveats presented should be kept in mind. In cases where the profession has failed to achieve consensus, the opposing views are discussed. But more generally, it is hoped that this introduction to empirical methodology induces a healthy skepticism concerning claims about economic behavior that occur in public debate and begin with the magic words "studies have proved."

Summary

- Because economists are unable to perform carefully controlled experiments with the economy, the effects of economic policy are often hard to determine.

- Economic theory helps specify the factors that might affect a given kind of behavior. Generally, however, theory alone cannot say how important any particular factor is.

---

[7] From "Cross-Eyed and Painless" © 1980 Bleu Disque Music Co., Inc., Index Music, Inc., and E. G. Music, Ltd. by permission of David Byrne and Brian Eno.

- Empirical research attempts to measure both the direction and size of the effect of government policy changes on behavior. Common types of empirical studies are interview studies, social and laboratory experiments, and econometric analysis.

- Interview studies consist of directly asking people how various policies affect their behavior. However, people may not actually react to policies in the way they say they do.

- Social experiments subject one group of people to some policy and compare their behavior with that of another group that is not subject to the policy. These attempts are not entirely satisfactory because the experiment itself may affect people's behavior, because it is difficult to obtain a random sample, and because social experiments are quite costly.

- Laboratory experiments are used to study some types of economic decisions, but in the artificial atmosphere subjects may not replicate real-world behavior.

- Econometrics is the statistical analysis of economic data. In econometrics, the effects of various policies are inferred from the analysis of observed behavior.

- Techniques such as multiple regression analysis are used to pick the "best" parameters for the model. It is the size and sign (positive or negative) of the estimated parameters that allow prediction of the effects of policy changes.

- Econometrics is not without pitfalls. Misleading results are obtained if data from greatly dissimilar groups are combined; if important variables are omitted; if the wrong mathematical form is adopted; if variables are incorrectly measured; or if the direction of causation is not only from the explanatory variables to the left-hand variable, but in the reverse direction, as well.

Discussion Questions

1. Like economists, astronomers are generally unable to perform controlled experiments. Yet astronomy is considered more of an exact science than economics. Why?

2. In 1991, the Bush administration argued that reducing tax rates on interest paid on savings accounts would increase saving. Opponents said that such a change would have no such effect.

   a. Does the theory of consumer behavior tell you which view is correct?

   b. How would you construct a survey to investigate this issue?

   c. If you were to conduct an experiment to investigate the issue, would it be a social or laboratory experiment? Why? Describe your experiment.

   d. How would you conduct an econometric investigation? Which data would you need? Which algebraic function would you choose?

   e. In any of your studies did you consider variables other than tax rates? If so, why did you choose them?

3. In 1986, Dr. John Bailar of the Harvard School of Public Health said that the United States is losing its fight with cancer: "cancer treatment is not getting a whole lot better." However, Dr. Lawrence Garfinkel of the American Cancer Society responded: "There's no doubt that the reason the overall death rate goes up is because of lung cancer. If you take away lung cancer, instead of having an 8 percent increase, you have a 13 percent decrease" ["U.S. Seen as Losing Fight with Cancer," *New York Times,* May 8, 1986, p. A19]. Relate the problems faced by researchers trying to determine the effects of cancer treatments to the problems faced by economists trying to determine the effects of economic policy.

Selected References

Becker, Gary S. "Irrational Behavior and Economic Theory." *Journal of Political Economy* 70 (February 1962), pp. 1–13.

Burtless, Gary, and Larry L. Orr. "Are Classical Experiments Needed for Manpower Policy?" *Journal of Human Resources* 21, no. 4 (Fall 1986), pp. 605–39.

Gujarati, D. *Basic Econometrics*. New York: McGraw-Hill, 1978.

Hausman, Jerry A., and Davis A. Wise, eds. *Social Experimentation*. Chicago: University of Chicago Press, 1985.

Smith, Vernon L. "Microeconomic Systems as an Experimental Science." *American Economic Review* 72, no. 5 (December 1982), pp. 923–55.

CHAPTER 4

Tools of Normative Analysis

The object of government is the welfare of the people. The material progress and prosperity of a nation are desirable chiefly so far as they lead to the moral and material welfare of all good citizens.

THEODORE ROOSEVELT

A s citizens we are called on to react to and evaluate a constant flow of proposals concerning government's role in the economy. Should income taxes be raised? Is it a good idea to change the age at which Social Security payments begin? Should there be stricter controls on auto emissions? The list is virtually endless. Given the enormous diversity of the economic activities undertaken by government, some kind of general framework is needed to organize thoughts about the desirability of various government actions. Without such a systematic framework, each government program would be evaluated on an ad hoc basis, and a coherent economic policy would be impossible to achieve.

Welfare Economics

The framework used by most public finance specialists is **welfare economics,** the branch of economic theory concerned with the social desirability of alternative economic states.[1] In this chapter we sketch the fundamentals of welfare economics. The theory is used to distinguish the circumstances under which markets can be expected to perform well from those under which markets fail to produce desirable results.

---

[1] Welfare economics relies heavily on certain basic economic tools, particularly indifference curves. For a review, see the Appendix at the end of the book.

Figure 4.1
Edgeworth Box

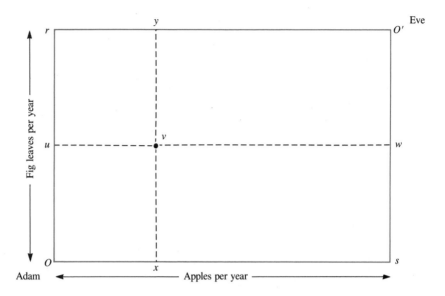

Pure Exchange Economy

We begin by considering a very simple economy: only two people who consume two commodities with fixed supplies. The only economic problem here is to allocate amounts of the two goods between the two people. As simple as this model is, all the important results from the two good–two person case hold in economies with many people and commodities.[2] The two-by-two case is analyzed because of its simplicity.

The two people are Adam and Eve, and the two commodities are apples (food) and fig leaves (clothing). An analytical device known as the **Edgeworth Box** depicts the distribution of apples and fig leaves between Adam and Eve.[3] In Figure 4.1, the length of the Edgeworth Box, *Os,* represents the total number of apples available in the economy; the height, *Or,* is the total number of fig leaves. The amounts of the goods consumed by Adam are measured by distances from point *O;* the quantities consumed by Eve are measured by distances from *O′.* For example, at point *v,* Adam consumes *Ou* fig leaves and *Ox* apples, while Eve consumes *O′y* apples and *O′w* fig leaves. Thus, any point within the Edgeworth Box represents some allocation of apples and fig leaves between Adam and Eve.

Now assume that Adam and Eve each have a set of conventionally shaped indifference curves that depict their preferences for apples and fig leaves. In Figure 4.2, both sets of indifference curves are superimposed onto the Edgeworth Box. Adam's are labeled with *A*'s; Eve's are labeled with *E*'s. The numbering of indifference curves corresponds to higher

---

[2] See Chapter 11 of Henderson and Quandt [1980] where the results are derived using calculus.

[3] Named after the great 19th-century economist F. Y. Edgeworth.

Figure 4.2

Indifference curves
in an Edgeworth
Box

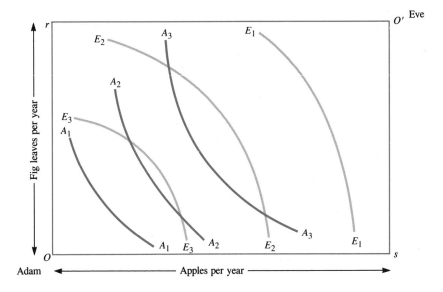

levels of happiness (utility). Adam is happier on indifference curve A_3 than on A_2 or A_1, and Eve is happier on indifference curve E_3 than on E_2 or E_1. In general, Eve's utility increases as her position moves toward the southwest, while Adam's utility increases as he moves toward the northeast.

Suppose that some arbitrary distribution of apples and fig leaves is selected—say point g in Figure 4.3. A_gA_g is Adam's indifference curve that runs through point g, and E_gE_g is Eve's. Now pose the following question: Is it possible to reallocate apples and fig leaves between Adam and Eve in such a way that Adam is made better off, while Eve is made no worse off? A moment's thought suggests such an allocation, at point h. Adam is better off at this point because indifference curve A_hA_h represents a higher utility level for him than A_gA_g. On the other hand, Eve is no worse off at h because she is on her original indifference curve, E_gE_g.

Can Adam's welfare be further increased without doing any harm to Eve? As long as it is possible to move Adam to indifference curves further to the northeast while still remaining on E_gE_g, it is possible. This process can be continued until Adam's indifference curve is just touching E_gE_g, which occurs at point p in Figure 4.3. The only way to put Adam on a higher indifference curve than A_pA_p would be to put Eve on a lower one. An allocation such as point p, at which the only way to make one person better off is to make another person worse off, is called **Pareto efficient**.[4] Pareto efficiency is often used as the standard for evaluating the desirability of an allocation of resources. If the allocation is not Pareto efficient, it is "wasteful" in the sense that it is possible to make someone better off

---

[4] Named after the 19th-century economist Vilfredo Pareto.

Figure 4.3

Making Adam better off without Eve becoming worse off

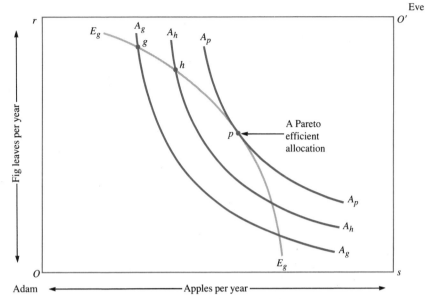

without hurting anybody else. When economists use the word *efficient,* they usually have the notion of Pareto efficiency in mind.

A related notion is that of a **Pareto improvement**—a reallocation of resources that makes one person better off without making anyone else worse off. In Figure 4.3, the move from *g* to *h* is a Pareto improvement, as is the move from *h* to *p*.

Point *p* is not the only Pareto efficient allocation that could have been reached by starting at point *g*. In Figure 4.4 we examine whether it is possible to make Eve better off without lowering the utility of Adam. Logic similar to that surrounding Figure 4.3 suggests moving Eve to indifference curves further to the southwest, provided that the allocation remains on $A_g A_g$. In doing so, a point like p_1 is isolated. At p_1, the only way to improve Eve's welfare is to move Adam to a lower indifference curve. Then, by definition, p_1 is a Pareto efficient allocation.

So far, we have been looking at moves that make one person better off and leave the other at the same level of utility. In Figure 4.5 we consider reallocations from point *g* that make *both* Adam and Eve better off. At p_2, for example, Adam is better off than at point *g* ($A_{p_2} A_{p_2}$ is further to the northeast than $A_g A_g$) and so is Eve ($E_{p_2} E_{p_2}$ is further to the southwest than $E_g E_g$). Point p_2 is Pareto efficient, because at that point it is impossible to make either individual better off without making the other worse off. It should now be clear that starting at point *g*, a whole set of Pareto efficient points can be found. They differ with respect to how much each of the parties gains from the reallocation of resources.

Figure 4.4
Making Eve better
off without Adam's
becoming worse off

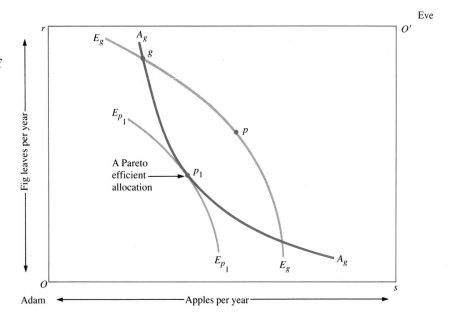

Figure 4.5
Making both Adam
and Eve better off

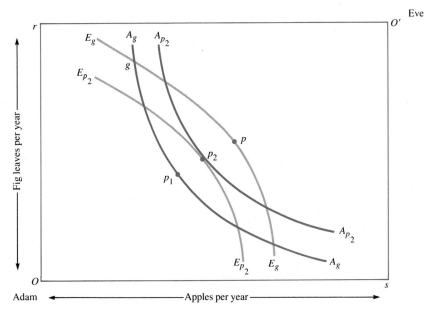

Recall that the initial point *g* was selected arbitrarily. We can repeat the procedure for finding Pareto efficient allocations with any starting point. Had point *k* in Figure 4.6 been the original allocation, Pareto efficient combinations of the commodities like p_3 and p_4 could have been isolated. This exercise reveals a whole set of Pareto efficient points in the

Figure 4.6
Starting from a
different initial point

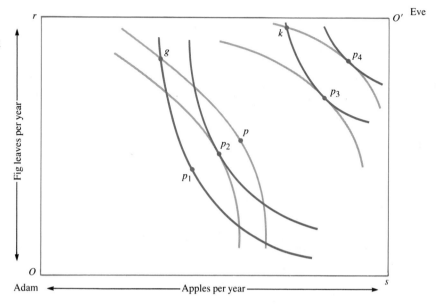

Figure 4.7
The contract curve

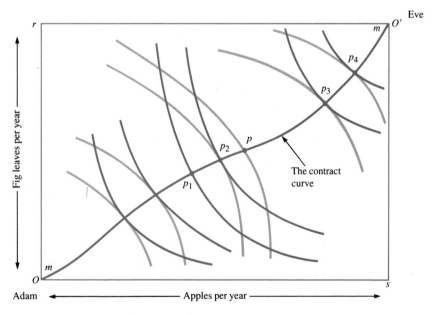

Edgeworth Box. The locus of all the Pareto efficient points is called the
contract curve, and is denoted *mm* in Figure 4.7. Note that for an allocation to be Pareto efficient (to be on *mm*), it must be a point at which the
indifference curves of Adam and Eve are barely touching. In mathematical terms, the indifference curves are tangent—the slopes of the indifference curves are equal.

In economic terms, the absolute value of the slope of the indifference curve indicates the rate at which the individual is willing to trade one good for an additional amount of another, called the marginal rate of substitution (MRS).[5] Hence, a Pareto efficient allocation of resources requires that marginal rates of substitution be equal for all consumers.[6] Algebraically, a necessary condition for Pareto efficiency is

$$MRS_{af}^{\text{Adam}} = MRS_{af}^{\text{Eve}} \tag{4.1}$$

where MRS_{af}^{Adam} is Adam's marginal rate of substitution of apples for fig leaves, and MRS_{af}^{Eve} is defined similarly.

An Economy with Production

The production possibilities curve.   The analysis so far assumes that supplies of all the commodities are fixed. Consider what happens when productive inputs can shift between the production of apples and fig leaves, so that the quantities of the two goods are alterable. Provided that the inputs are efficiently used, if more apples are produced, then fig leaf production must necessarily fall and vice versa. The **production possibilities curve** shows the maximum quantity of fig leaves that can be produced along with any given quantity of apples.[7] A typical production possibilities curve is depicted as *CC* in Figure 4.8. As shown in Figure 4.8, one option available to the economy is to produce *Ow* fig leaves and *Ox* apples. The economy can increase apple production from *Ox* to *Oz*, distance *xz*. To do this, of course, inputs have to be removed from the production of fig leaves and devoted to apples. Fig leaf production must fall by distance *wy* if apple production is to increase by *xz*. The ratio of distance *wy* to distance *xz* is called the **marginal rate of transformation** of apples for fig leaves (MRT_{af}) because it shows the rate at which the economy can transform apples into fig leaves. Just as MRS_{af} measures the absolute value of the slope of an indifference curve, MRT_{af} measures the absolute value of the slope of the production possibilities curve.

It is useful to express the marginal rate of transformation in terms of the notion of **marginal cost** (MC)—the incremental production cost of one more unit of output. To do so, recall that society can increase apple production from *Ox* to *Oz* only by giving up *wy* fig leaves. In effect, then, the distance *wy* represents the incremental cost of producing apples, which we denote MC_a. Similarly, the distance *xz* is the incremental cost of producing fig leaves, MC_f. By definition, the absolute value of the slope

---

[5] The marginal rate of substitution is defined more carefully in the Appendix at the end of the book.

[6] This assumes that a positive quantity of each commodity is consumed, an assumption made throughout.

[7] The production possibilities curve can be derived from an Edgeworth Box whose dimensions represent the quantities of inputs available for production.

Figure 4.8
Production
possibilities curve

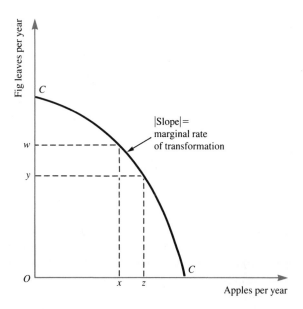

of the production possibilities curve is distance *wy* divided by *xz*, or MC_a/MC_f. But also by definition, the slope of the production possibilities curve is the marginal rate of transformation. Hence, we have shown that

$$MRT_{af} = \frac{MC_a}{MC_f} \tag{4.2}$$

Efficiency conditions with variable production.   When the supplies of apples and fig leaves are variable, the condition for Pareto efficiency in Equation (4.1) must be extended. The necessary condition for Pareto efficiency becomes

$$MRT_{af} = MRS_{af}^{\text{Adam}} = MRS_{af}^{\text{Eve}} \tag{4.3}$$

A simple arithmetic example demonstrates why the first equality in Equation (4.3) must hold. Suppose that at a given allocation Adam's MRS_{af} is ⅓, and the MRT_{af} is ⅔. By the definition of MRT_{af}, at this allocation two additional fig leaves could be produced by giving up three apples. By the definition of MRS_{af}, if Adam lost three extra apples, he would require only *one* fig leaf to maintain his original utility level. Therefore, Adam could be made better off by giving up three apples and having them transformed into *two* fig leaves, and no one else would be made worse off in the process. Such a trade is *always* possible as long as the marginal rate of substitution does not equal the marginal rate of transformation. Only when the slopes of the curves for each are equal is it impossible to make someone better off without making anybody worse off. Hence, $MRT_{af} =$

MRS_{af} is a necessary condition for Pareto efficiency. The rate at which apples can be transformed into fig leaves (MRT_{af}) must equal the rate at which consumers are willing to trade apples for fig leaves (MRS_{af}).

Using Equation (4.2), the conditions for Pareto efficiency can be reinterpreted in terms of marginal cost. Just substitute (4.2) into (4.3), which gives us

$$\frac{MC_a}{MC_f} = MRS_{af}^{\text{Adam}} = MRS_{af}^{\text{Eve}} \tag{4.4}$$

as a necessary condition for Pareto efficiency.

The Fundamental Theorem of Welfare Economics

We have now described the necessary conditions for Pareto efficiency, but have given no indication as to whether or not a real-world economy achieves this apparently desirable state. Will a market system naturally reach the contract curve? The Fundamental Theorem of Welfare Economics provides an answer:

- As long as producers and consumers act as perfect competitors, that is, take prices as given, then under *certain conditions* (discussed later) a Pareto efficient allocation of resources emerges.

Thus, a competitive economy "automatically" allocates resources efficiently, without any need for centralized direction (shades of Adam Smith's "invisible hand"). In a way, the fundamental theorem merely formalizes an insight that social observers have long recognized: When it comes to providing goods and services, the free enterprise system has been amazingly productive.[8]

A rigorous proof of the fundamental theorem requires fairly sophisticated mathematics, but we can provide an intuitive justification. The essence of competition is that all people face the same prices—each consumer and producer is so small relative to the market that his or her actions alone cannot affect prices. In our example, this means that Adam and Eve both pay the same prices for fig leaves (P_f) and apples (P_a). A basic result from the theory of rational choice[9] is that a necessary condition for Adam to maximize utility is

$$MRS_{af}^{\text{Adam}} = \frac{P_a}{P_f} \tag{4.5}$$

---

[8] "The bourgeoisie, during its rule of scarce 100 years, has created more massive and more colossal productive forces than have all preceding generations together," according to Karl Marx and Friedrich Engels in *The Communist Manifesto,* Part I [Tucker, 1978, p. 477].

[9] This result is derived in the Appendix to this book.

Similarly, Eve's utility maximizing bundle is characterized by

$$MRS_{af}^{\text{Eve}} = \frac{P_a}{P_f} \tag{4.6}$$

Equations (4.5) and (4.6) together imply that

$$MRS_{af}^{\text{Adam}} = MRS_{af}^{\text{Eve}}$$

This condition, though, is identical to Equation (4.1), one of the necessary conditions for Pareto efficiency.

However, as emphasized in the preceding section, we must consider the production side as well. A basic result from economic theory is that a profit-maximizing competitive firm produces output up to the point at which marginal cost and price are equal. In our example, this means that $P_a = MC_a$ and $P_f = MC_f$, or

$$\frac{MC_a}{MC_f} = \frac{P_a}{P_f} \tag{4.7}$$

But recall from Equation (4.2) that MC_a/MC_f is just the marginal rate of transformation. Thus, we can rewrite (4.7) as

$$MRT_{af} = \frac{P_a}{P_f} \tag{4.8}$$

Now, consider Equations (4.5), (4.6), and (4.8), and notice that P_a/P_f appears on the right-hand side of each. Hence, these three equations together imply that $MRS_{af}^{\text{Adam}} = MRS_{af}^{\text{Eve}} = MRT_{af}$, which is just the necessary condition for Pareto efficiency. Competition, along with maximizing behavior on the part of all individuals, leads to an efficient outcome.

Finally, we can take advantage of Equation (4.4) to write the conditions for Pareto efficiency in terms of marginal cost. Simply substitute (4.5) or (4.6) into (4.4) to find

$$\frac{P_a}{P_f} = \frac{MC_a}{MC_f} \tag{4.9}$$

A Pareto efficient allocation of resources requires that prices be in the same ratios as marginal costs, and competition guarantees this condition is met. The marginal cost of a commodity represents the additional cost to society of providing it. According to Equation (4.9), efficiency requires that the additional cost of each commodity be reflected in its price.

Choosing among Pareto Efficient Points

If properly functioning competitive markets allocate resources efficiently, what role does the government have to play in the economy? Only a very small government would appear to be appropriate. Its main function would be to establish a setting in which property rights are protected so that competition can work. Government provides law and order, a court

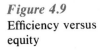

Figure 4.9
Efficiency versus equity

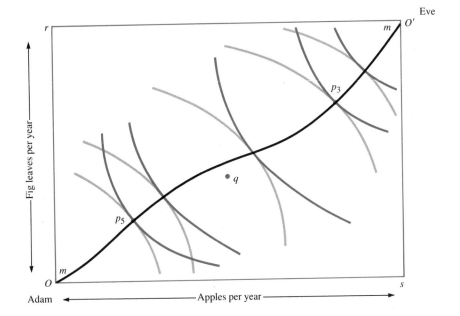

system, and national defense. Anything more is superfluous. However, such reasoning is based on a superficial understanding of the fundamental theorem. Things are really much more complicated. For one thing, it has implicitly been assumed that efficiency is the only criterion for deciding whether or not a given allocation of resources is good. It is not obvious, however, that Pareto efficiency by itself is desirable.

To see why, let us return to the simple model in which the total quantity of each good is fixed. Consider Figure 4.9, which reproduces the contract curve mm derived in Figure 4.7. Compare the two allocations p_5 (at the lower left-hand corner of the box) and q (located near the center). Because p_5 lies on the contract curve, by definition it is Pareto efficient. On the other hand, q is inefficient. Is allocation p_5 therefore better? That depends on what is meant by better. To the extent that society prefers a relatively equal distribution of real income, q might be preferred to p_5, even though q is not Pareto efficient. On the other hand, society might not care about distribution at all, or perhaps care more about Eve than Adam. In this case, p_5 would be preferred to q.

The key point is that the criterion of Pareto efficiency by itself is not enough to determine the desirability of alternative allocations of resources. Rather, explicit value judgments are required on the fairness of the distribution of utility. To formalize this concept, note that the contract curve implicitly defines a relationship between the maximum amount of utility that Adam can attain for each level of Eve's utility. In Figure 4.10, Eve's utility is plotted on the horizontal axis, and Adam's utility is recorded on the vertical axis. Curve UU is the **utility possibilities curve**

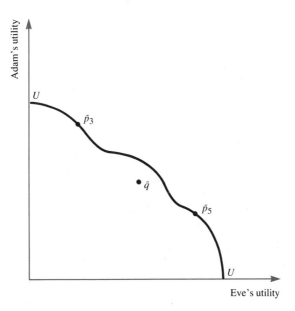

Figure 4.10
Utility possibilities curve

derived from the contract curve.[10] It shows the maximum amount of one person's utility given the utility attained by the other individual. Point $\tilde{p}_5$ corresponds to point p_5 on the contract curve in Figure 4.9. Here, Eve's utility is relatively high compared to Adam's. Point $\tilde{p}_3$ in Figure 4.10 corresponds to p_3 in Figure 4.9. Here, Adam's utility is relatively high, and Eve's relatively low. Point $\tilde{q}$ corresponds to point q in Figure 4.10. Because q is off the contract curve, $\tilde{q}$ must be inside the utility possibilities curve. This reflects the fact that at q, it is possible to increase one person's utility without decreasing the other's.

All points on or below the utility possibilities curve are attainable by society; all points above it are not attainable. By definition, all points on UU are Pareto efficient, but they represent very different distributions of real income between Adam and Eve. Which point is best? The conventional way to answer this question is to postulate a **social welfare function,** which embodies society's views on the relative deservedness of Adam and Eve. Imagine that just as an *individual*'s welfare depends on the quantities of commodities she consumes, *society*'s welfare depends on the utilities of each of its members. Algebraically, social welfare (W) is some function $F(\quad)$ of each individual's utility:

$$W = F(U^{\text{Adam}}, U^{\text{Eve}}) \tag{4.10}$$

---

[10] The production possibilities curve in Figure 4.8 is drawn on the reasonable assumption that the absolute value of its slope continually increases as we move downward along it. The more apples produced, the more fig leaves given up to produce an apple. However, there is no reason to assume that this holds for the trade-off between individuals' utilities. This is why UU in Figure 4.10 is wavy rather than smooth.

Figure 4.11
Social indifference
curves

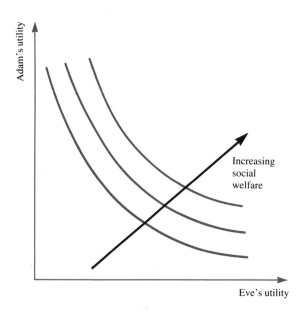

We assume that the value of social welfare increases as either U^{Adam} or U^{Eve} increases.[11] Society is better off when any of its members becomes better off. Note that we have said nothing about how society manifests these preferences. Under some conditions, members of society may not be able to agree on how to rank each other's utilities, and the social welfare function does not even exist. For the moment, we simply assume that it does exist.

Just as an individual's utility function for commodities leads to a set of indifference curves for those commodities, so does a social welfare function lead to a set of indifference curves between people's utilities.

Figure 4.11 depicts a typical set of social indifference curves. The downward slope of the curves indicates that if Eve's utility decreases, the only way to maintain a given level of social welfare is to increase Adam's utility, and vice versa. The level of social welfare increases as we move toward the northeast, reflecting the fact that an increase in any individual's utility increases social welfare, other things being the same.

In Figure 4.12, the social indifference curves are superimposed on the utility possibilities curve from Figure 4.10. Point *i* is not as desirable as point *ii* (point *ii* is on a higher social indifference curve than point *i*) even though point *i* is Pareto efficient and point *ii* is not. Here, society's value judgments, embodied in the social welfare function, favor a more equal distribution of real income, inefficient though it may be. Of course, point *iii* is preferred to either of these. It is both efficient and "fair."

---

[11] We discuss other possible social welfare functions in Chapter 8 under "Rationales for Income Redistribution."

Figure 4.12
Maximizing social
welfare

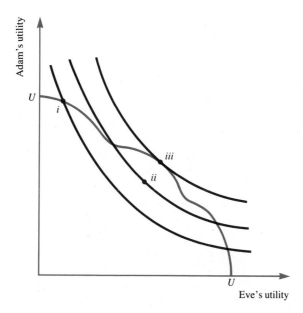

Now, the Fundamental Theorem of Welfare Economics indicates that a properly working competitive system leads to some allocation on the utility possibilities curve. There is no reason, however, that it is the particular point at which social welfare is maximized. We conclude that even if the economy generates a Pareto efficient allocation of resources, government intervention may be necessary to achieve a "fair" distribution of utility.

A second reason the fundamental theorem need not imply a minimal government has to do with the fact that the certain conditions required for its validity may not be satisfied by real-world markets. As we see in the next section of the book, an absence of these conditions may lead free markets to allocate resources inefficiently.

Overview

The Fundamental Theorem of Welfare Economics states that a properly working competitive economy generates a Pareto efficient allocation of resources without any government intervention. However, it is not obvious that an efficient allocation of resources is per se socially desirable; some argue that fairness must also be taken into account. In addition, in certain cases, the real-world economy is not "properly working." Hence, the market-determined allocation of resources is not likely even to be efficient, let alone equitable. There is then an opportunity for government to intervene in the economy to modify the distribution of income and enhance economic efficiency. Even though distributional and market-failure problems provide opportunities for government intervention in the economy, they *do not require it*. The fact that the market-generated allocation of resources is imperfect does not mean that the government is actually capable of doing better. Thus, the fundamental theorem is only helpful in identifying situations in which intervention *may* lead to higher social welfare.

| **Evaluation** | These days, the most dramatic examples of debate over how to organize an economy are taking place in formerly Communist countries. Nevertheless, the same basic issues arise in Western nations as well: How much of national output should be devoted to the public sector, and how should public expenditures be financed? The theory of welfare economics introduced in this chapter provides the standard framework for thinking about these issues. There are, however, some controversies surrounding the theory itself. |

First of all, the underlying outlook is highly individualistic, with a focus on people's utilities and how to maximize them. This is brought out starkly in the formulation of the social welfare function, Equation (4.10). The basic point of view expressed in that equation is that a good society is one in which the members are happy. As suggested in Chapter 1, however, other societal goals are possible—to maximize the power of the state, to glorify God, and so on. Welfare economics does not have much to say to people with such goals.

Because welfare economics puts people's preferences at center stage, it requires that these preferences be taken seriously. People know best what gives them satisfaction. A contrary view, once nicely summarized by Thomas O'Neill, former Speaker of the House of Representatives, is that, "Often what the American people want is not good for them." If one believes that individuals' preferences are ill formed or corrupt, a theory that shows how to maximize their utility is essentially irrelevant.

Richard Musgrave [1959] developed the concept of **merit goods** to describe commodities that ought to be provided even if the members of society do not demand them. Government support of the fine arts is often justified on this basis. Operas and concerts should be provided publicly if individuals are unwilling to pay enough to meet their costs. But as William Baumol and Hilda Baumol [1981] have noted,

> the term *merit good* merely becomes a formal designation for the unadorned value judgment that the arts are good for society and therefore deserve financial support . . . [the] merit good approach is not really a justification for support—it merely invents a bit of terminology to designate the desire to do so. [Pp. 426–427]

Another possible problem with the welfare economics framework is its concern with *results*. Situations are evaluated in terms of the allocation of resources, and not of *how* the allocation was determined. Perhaps a society should be judged by the *processes* used to arrive at the allocation, not the actual results. Are people free to enter contracts? Are public processes democratic? If this view is taken, welfare economics lacks any normative significance.

On the other hand, the great advantage of welfare economics is that it provides a coherent framework for thinking about the appropriateness of various government interventions. Every government intervention, after all, involves a reallocation of resources, and the whole purpose of welfare economics is to evaluate alternative allocations. The framework of welfare economics requires the formation of relevant questions whenever a government activity is proposed:

- Will it have desirable distributional consequences?
- Will it enhance efficiency?
- Can it be done at a reasonable cost?

If the answer to these questions is "no," the market should probably be left alone. Of course, to answer these questions often requires substantial research, and in the case of the first question, value judgments as well. But just asking the right questions imposes a structure on the decision-making process. It forces the investigator to make ethical values explicit, and it facilitates the detection of frivolous or self-serving programs.

Summary

- Welfare economics is the study of the desirability of alternative economic states.

- A Pareto efficient allocation occurs when no person can be made better off without making another person worse off. A necessary condition for Pareto efficiency is that each person's marginal rate of substitution between two commodities equals the marginal rate of transformation. Pareto efficiency is the economist's benchmark of efficient performance for an economy.

- Under certain conditions, competitive market mechanisms lead to Pareto efficient outcomes. This result, the Fundamental Theorem of Welfare Economics, relies on prices reflecting marginal social costs for each commodity.

- Despite its appeal, Pareto efficiency has no obvious claim as an ethical norm. Society may prefer another, inefficient, allocation on the basis of equity, justice, or some other criterion. This provides one possible reason for government intervention in the economy.

- A social welfare function summarizes society's preferences concerning the utility of each of its members. It may be used to find the allocation of resources that maximizes social welfare.

- A second reason for government activity is market failure, violations of the conditions required for the fundamental theorem to hold.

- The fact that the market does not allocate resources perfectly does not necessarily mean that the government can do better. Each case must be evaluated on its own merits.

- Welfare economics is based on an individualistic social philosophy. It does not pay much attention to the processes used to achieve results. Thus, although it provides a coherent and useful framework for analyzing policy, welfare economics is controversial.

Discussion Questions

1. In which of the following markets do you expect efficient outcomes? Why?

   a. Steel.

   b. Highway construction.

   c. Stock market.

   d. Retail food.

2. In 1982, several people died because of poisoned capsules of Tylenol pain reliever. Afterwards, strict government regulations were enacted to control the packaging of retail pharmaceuticals. Would private markets have reached the same result?

3. Hamlet will trade two pizzas for one six-pack of beer and be equally happy. At the same time, Ophelia will gladly exchange two of her six-packs for six pizzas. Is the allocation of beer and pizza Pareto efficient? Illustrate using an Edgeworth Box.

4. Imagine a simple economy with only two people, Augustus and Livia.

   a. Let the social welfare function be

   $$W = U_L + U_A$$

   where U_L and U_A are the utilities of Livia and Augustus, respectively. Graph the social indifference curves. How would you describe the relative importance assigned to their respective well-being?

   b. Repeat *a* when

   $$W = U_L + 2U_A$$

   c. Assume that the utility possibility frontier is as follows:

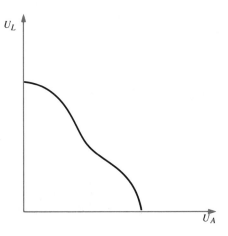

   Graphically show how the optimal solution differs between the welfare functions given in parts *a* and *b*.

5. The French philosopher Simone de Beauvoir said, "No woman should be authorized to stay home to raise her children. . . . Women should not have that choice precisely because if there is such a choice, too many women will make that one" [Schwarzschild, 1986, p. 27]. Is this point of view consistent with conventional welfare economics?

Selected References

Bator, F. M. "The Simple Analytics of Welfare Maximization." *American Economic Review* 47 (March 1957), pp. 22–59.

Baumol, William J. *Economic Theory and Operations Analysis.* 4th ed. Englewood Cliffs, N.J.: Prentice-Hall, 1977, Chapter 21.

Consumer Surplus

This chapter emphasized that reallocations of resources affect individuals' welfare. In many contexts, we want to know not only whether a certain change makes people better or worse off but also by how much. Suppose, for example, that initially the price of apples is P_0, but then it falls to some lower price, P_1. Clearly, apple consumers are better off because of the change. But can we put a dollar figure on the improvement in their welfare? Consumer surplus is a tool for obtaining such a dollar amount.

To begin our discussion of consumer surplus, consider the demand curve for apples, D_a, depicted in Figure 4.A. Assume that consumers can obtain all the apples they demand at the going market price, P_0. Then the supply curve for apples, S_a, is a horizontal line at P_0. According to the diagram, when the price is P_0, the quantity demanded is a_0.

Suppose now that more land is brought into apple production, and the supply curve shifts to S_a'. At the new equilibrium the price falls to P_1, and apple consumption increases to a_1. How much better off are consumers? Another way of stating this question is, "How much would consumers be willing to pay for the privilege of consuming a_1 apples at price P_1 rather than a_0 apples at price P_0?"

Figure 4.A
Measuring
consumer surplus

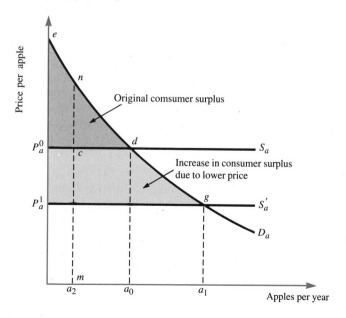

To provide an answer, begin by recalling that the demand curve shows the *maximum* amount that individuals *would be willing* to pay for each apple they consume. Consider some arbitrary amount of apples, a_2. The most people would be willing to pay for the a_2^{th} apple is the vertical distance up to the demand curve, *mn* dollars. At the initial price, consumers in fact had to pay only *mc* per apple. In a sense then, on their purchase of the a_2^{th} apple, consumers enjoyed a surplus of *nc* dollars. The amount by which the sum that individuals would have been *willing* to pay exceeds the sum they *actually* have to pay is called the **consumer surplus.**

Of course, the same exercise could be repeated at any level of consumption, not just at a_2. When the price is P_0 for each level of consumption, the consumer surplus at each output level equals the distance between the demand curve and the horizontal line at P_0. Summing the surpluses for each apple purchased, we find that the total consumer surplus when the price is P_0 is the area P_0ed. More generally, *consumer surplus is measured by the area under the demand curve and above a horizontal line at the market price.*

When the price falls to P_1, consumer surplus is still the area under the demand curve and above a horizontal line at the going price; because the price is now P_1, the relevant area is P_1eg. Consumer surplus has therefore increased by the difference between areas P_1eg and P_0ed—area P_1P_0dg. Thus, the area behind the demand curve between the two prices measures the value to consumers of being able to purchase apples at the lower price.

To implement this procedure for a real-world problem, an investigator needs to know the shape of the demand curve. Generally, this can be obtained by using one or more of the tools of positive analysis discussed in Chapter 3. Hence, consumer surplus is a very practical tool for measuring the changes in welfare induced by changes in the economic environment.

- **A Caveat:** The area under an ordinary demand curve provides only an approximation to the true value of the change in consumer welfare. This is because as price changes, so do people's real incomes, and this may change the value that they place on additions to their income (the marginal utility of income). However, Robert Willig [1976] has shown that measuring consumer surplus by the area under the ordinary demand curve is likely to be a pretty good approximation in most cases, and this approach is used widely in applied work.[12]

---

[12] Alternatively, one can compute welfare changes using areas under a *compensated demand curve*, which holds the individual's utility (as opposed to money income) constant. The Appendix at the end of the book discusses compensated demand curves.

Analysis of
Public Expenditure

Market outcomes need be neither efficient nor fair. This section examines how various "market failures" can be remedied by government intervention. We discuss both the normative question of how the government ought to solve a particular problem and the positive question of how government actually changes the status quo.

The theory of welfare economics focused our attention on the failure of markets to achieve efficient or distributionally acceptable resource allocations as motives for considering government intervention. The chapters in this section illustrate each of these issues. Chapter 5 introduces sources of market failure and examines public goods. Chapter 6 deals with externalities, with special emphasis on environmental issues. In Chapter 7, we discuss whether our political institutions are likely to respond to market failures with the efficiency-enhancing policies derived in Chapters 5 and 6. Chapters 8 and 9 are devoted to income distribution.

Some of the most important cases of market failure occur in the context of insurance. Issues that arise when insurance is provided socially are discussed in Chapters 10 and 11. Our analysis of public expenditure concludes with Chapter 12 on cost-benefit analysis, a theory-based set of practical rules for evaluating public expenditure.

CHAPTER 5

Market Failure and Public Goods

There exists an intrinsic connection between the common good on the one hand and the structure and function of public authority on the other. The moral order, which needs public authority in order to promote the common good in human society, requires also that the authority be effective in attaining that end.

POPE JOHN XXIII

W hich goods and services should the public sector provide, and in what amounts? As the annual debate over the federal budget demonstrates, this question lies at the heart of some of the most important controversies in public policy. In some contexts, the debate reflects a concern with economic efficiency: at what point, for example, do we sacrifice too much elsewhere to justify additional spending on defense? Other issues, such as how much to spend on food stamps, are less concerned with efficiency than with a notion of fairness or decency. In this chapter, we focus on the former set of questions: Under what conditions might the market fail to achieve an efficient allocation of resources, leaving open the possibility that government provision of certain commodities might enhance efficiency? After an overview of the common sources of market failure, we focus on a particular case of market failure, the provision of commodities known as public goods.

Types of Market Failure

In the famous movie *Casablanca,* whenever something seems amiss, the police chief gives an order to "round up the usual suspects." Similarly, whenever markets appear to be failing to allocate resources efficiently, economists round up the same group of possible causes for the supposed failure. Monopoly, public goods, externalities, costly information, and nonexistence of markets are the suspects of market failure. Each may cause an economy with freely operating markets to operate inefficiently. Each type of market failure creates interesting and complicated questions concerning the appropriate governmental remedies discussed in this and subsequent chapters.

Monopoly

When some agents have market power—the ability to affect price—the allocation of resources generally is inefficient. An extreme form of such market power is **monopoly**—only one seller in the market for a given commodity. A monopolist can raise prices above marginal cost by supplying less output than a competitor would. Thus, Equation (4.9), one of the necessary conditions for Pareto efficiency, is violated. An insufficient quantity of resources is devoted to the monopolized good.

Public Goods

Price takers (those who cannot affect the market price) have no incentive to hide true preferences for a good. If bread costs 65 cents per loaf, and I would be willing to pay 68 cents, there is no reason for me to pretend that I do not want to buy it.

The essential characteristic of this example is that bread is consumed privately. When I eat a loaf of bread, no one else can possibly eat it simultaneously. This is sometimes referred to as *rivalness of consumption*. In contrast, a **public good** is not rival in consumption. The classic example of a public good is a lighthouse. When the lighthouse keeper turns on the beacon, it helps to guide all the ships in the vicinity. The fact that one person benefits from the lighthouse's services does not prevent anyone else from doing so simultaneously.

In using the lighthouse, people may have an incentive to hide their true preferences. Suppose that it would be worthwhile to me to have the lighthouse operate. I know, however, that once the beacon is lit, I can enjoy its services whether I pay for them or not. Therefore, I may claim that the lighthouse means nothing to me, hoping that I can get a "free ride" after other people pay for it. Unfortunately, everyone has the same incentive, so the lighthouse may not get built at all, even though its construction could be very beneficial. The market mechanism may fail to force people to reveal their preferences for public goods, and possibly result in insufficient resources being devoted to them.

Externalities

In the basic competitive model, people interact solely by trading with each other in the market. There are situations, however, in which economic agents affect each other in ways outside the market. Returning to the example of Chapter 4, suppose that Eve sets up an apple press to manufacture cider, and the waste products associated with this process are dumped into a stream which flows into Adam's section of the Garden. As a consequence, Adam's drinking water is polluted and his utility declines.

The activity of one person affecting the welfare of another in a way that is outside the market is termed an **externality.** In the presence of an externality, the market may fail to allocate resources efficiently. The problem is Eve's use of a scarce resource, water, in the production of cider. Despite the fact that water is scarce, if no one owns the stream, Eve does not have to pay for the water. Because the price of water (zero) does not reflect the fact that it is scarce, Eve overuses it.

All of this has a simple interpretation in the analytics of welfare economics. In the derivation of Equation (4.9), it was implicitly assumed that marginal cost meant marginal *social* cost—it took into account the incremental value of *all* of society's resources used in production. In this example, however, Eve's marginal private cost is less than the marginal social cost because she does not have to pay for the water she uses. Hence, Equation (4.9) is not satisfied, and the allocation of resources is inefficient. Incidentally, an externality can be positive—confer a benefit—as well as negative. Still, social and private marginal costs are unequal, and the allocation of resources is inefficient. In the case of the positive externality, not enough of the beneficial activity is pursued.

Costly Information

The competitive model assumes that information on existing prices is somehow spread around at no cost, so that everyone can find the best price. In reality, this is not the case. Shopping around to find the lowest price requires time, which is a valuable commodity. Moreover, once information is obtained, it may be imperfect. (Is this car a lemon?) Thus, it is possible that because individuals do not have the necessary information to make the right economic decisions, inefficient patterns of resource allocation emerge.

Nonexistence of Markets

The proof behind the Fundamental Theorem of Welfare Economics assumes that a market exists for each and every good.[1] It seems likely, however, that even if there were no public good or externality problems, markets for certain goods would fail to emerge. Consider, for instance, insurance. In a world of uncertainty, insurance is a "commodity" that is very important. Despite the existence of firms such as Lloyd's of London, there are certain events for which insurance simply cannot be purchased on the private market. For example, suppose that you wanted to purchase insurance against the possibility of becoming poor. Would a firm in a competitive market ever find it profitable to supply poverty insurance? One problem is that people who believed their probability of becoming

---

[1] In a formal sense, several of the previously listed illustrations of market failure are just different manifestations of the nonexistence of markets problem. For example, the public goods problem can be viewed as the failure of markets to emerge because it is too costly (or impossible) to gather information on people's true preferences.

poor was low would not bother to buy such insurance. The purchasers would be mainly people who were actually likely to wind up poor. This phenomenon is known as **adverse selection**—people who buy insurance are more likely to collect it than a typical member of the population. Because only those with a high likelihood of entering poverty would purchase policies, the rates on those policies would have to be quite high. At these high rates, the firm would probably be unable to sell enough policies to stay in business.

An additional problem, known as **moral hazard,** is that the probability of collecting insurance may be influenced by the individual's behavior. Because of costly information, it may be difficult for a private firm to know whether the individual has become poor because of circumstances beyond his or her control.

In short, a commodity that people would be willing to buy is not generally available on the private market, leading to an inefficient allocation of resources. One rationalization for governmental income support programs is that they provide poverty insurance that is unavailable privately. The premium on this insurance policy is the taxes you pay when you are able to earn income. In the event of poverty, your benefit comes in the form of welfare payments.[2]

When the market fails to provide commodities efficiently, it becomes the job of the public finance economist, first, to describe the efficient level of provision and, second, to prescribe public policies that might improve efficiency. The rest of this chapter explores the challenge of providing public goods efficiently.

Public Goods Defined

As we noted earlier, the key feature of a public good is nonrivalness in consumption. This means that once the good is provided, the additional resource cost of another person consuming the good is zero. Consider again the lighthouse example. Once the beacon is lit, no resource cost is incurred when an additional ship uses it for guidance. My consumption of the services provided by the lighthouse does not at all diminish your ability to consume the same services.

Several aspects of our definition of public good are worth noting:

Even though everyone consumes the same quantity of the good, there is *no* requirement that this consumption be valued equally by all.   We expect that owners of ships with relatively valuable cargoes would place a higher value on being guided safely to shore than those with inexpensive cargoes, other things being the same. Indeed, people might differ over

---

[2] Although the government may solve the adverse selection problem by forcing everyone into purchasing the insurance, the moral hazard problem remains unless the government has a better method for monitoring individual behavior than is available to private firms.

whether the value of certain public goods is positive or negative. When a new missile system is constructed, each person has no choice but to consume its services. For those who view the system as an enhancement to their safety, the value is positive. Others believe that additional missiles only escalate the arms race with no increase in national security. Presumably such individuals would value an additional missile negatively. They would be willing to pay not to have it around.

Classification as a public good is not an absolute; it depends on market conditions and the state of technology.   The reading room of a large library can be considered a public good when there are only a few people present. But as the number of users increases, crowding and traffic problems occur that are inimical to serious scholarly research. The same "quantity" of library is being consumed by each person, but because of congestion, its quality can decrease with the number of people. Hence, the nonrivalness criterion is no longer strictly satisfied. (The Library of Congress deals with this problem by severely limiting access to high school students.) In many cases, then, it is useful to think of publicness as a matter of degree. A pure public good satisfies the definition exactly. Consumption of an **impure public good** is to some extent rival. It is difficult to think of many examples of really pure public goods. However, just as analysis of pure competition yields important insights into the operation of actual markets, so the analysis of pure public goods helps us to understand problems confronting public decision makers.

The notion of excludability is often linked to that of public goods.[3]   The consumption of a good is nonexcludable when it is either very expensive or impossible to prevent anyone from consuming the good who is not willing to pay for it. Many goods that are nonrival are also nonexcludable. For example, our lighthouse produces a nonexcludable good, because no particular vessel can be prevented from taking advantage of the signal. However, nonexcludability and nonrivalness do not have to go together. Consider the streets of a downtown urban area during rush hour. In most cases, nonexcludability holds, because it is not feasible to set up enough toll booths to monitor traffic. But consumption is certainly rival, as anyone who has ever been caught in a traffic jam can testify. On the other hand, many people can enjoy a huge seashore area without diminishing the pleasure of others. Despite the fact that individuals do not rival each other in consumption, exclusion is quite possible if there are only a small number of access roads. Note that just like nonrivalness, nonexcludability is not an absolute. It depends on the state of technology and on legal arrangements. Suppose someone invented a jamming device that made it

---

[3] Indeed, in some treatments excludability is made part of the definition of a public good. However, we follow Samuelson [1955] in making nonrivalness the defining characteristic.

possible to prevent ships from obtaining the lighthouse signal unless they purchased a special receiver. Alternatively, imagine that it were legal for the lighthouse to fire an Exocet missile at any ship that failed to purchase a permit to sail within the range of the beacon.[4] In either case, the lighthouse would be excludable.

A number of things that are not conventionally thought of as commodities have public good characteristics.   An important example is honesty. If each citizen is honest in commercial transactions, all of society benefits due to the reduction of the costs of doing business. Such cost reductions are characterized both by nonexcludability and nonrivalness. Similarly, some argue that the income distribution is a public good. (See Thurow [1971].) If income is distributed "fairly," each person gains satisfaction from living in a good society, and no one can be excluded from having that satisfaction. Of course, because of disagreements over notions of fairness, people may differ over how a given income distribution should be valued. Nevertheless, consumption of the income distribution is nonrival, and therefore it is a public good.

Private goods are not necessarily provided exclusively by the private sector.   There are many cases of **publicly provided private goods**—rival commodities that are provided by governments. Medical services and housing are two examples of private goods sometimes provided publicly. Similarly, as we see later, public goods can be provided privately. (Think of an individual donating a park to a community.) In short, the label private or public does not by itself tell us anything about which sector provides the item.

Public provision of a good does not necessarily mean that it is also *produced* by the public sector.   Consider refuse collection. Some communities produce this service themselves—public sector managers purchase garbage trucks, hire workers, and arrange schedules. In other communities, the local government hires a private firm for the job and does not organize production itself.

Efficient Provision of Public Goods

To derive the conditions for efficient provision of a public good, it is useful to begin by reexamining private goods from a slightly different point of view from that used in Chapter 4. Assume again a society populated by two people, Adam and Eve. There are two private goods, apples and fig leaves. In Figure 5.1A, the quantity of fig leaves (f) is measured on the horizontal axis, and the price per fig leaf (P_f) is on the vertical.

---

[4] This example is from Adams and McCormick [undated].

Figure 5.1

Horizontal
summation of
demand curves

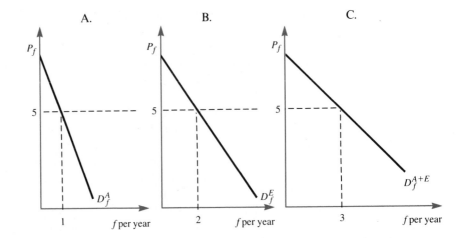

Adam's demand curve for fig leaves is denoted by D_f^A. The demand curve shows the quantity of fig leaves that Adam would be willing to consume at each price, other things being the same.[5] Similarly, D_f^E in Figure 5.1B is Eve's demand curve for fig leaves.

Suppose now that we want to derive the market demand curve for fig leaves. To do so, we simply add together the number of fig leaves each person demands at every price. In Figure 5.1A, at a price of $5, Adam demands one fig leaf, the horizontal distance between D_f^A and the vertical axis. Figure 5.1B indicates that at the same price, Eve demands two fig leaves. The total quantity demanded at a price of $5 is therefore three leaves. The market demand curve for fig leaves is labeled D_f^{A+E} in Figure 5.1C. As we have just shown, the point at which price is $5 and quantity demanded is three lies on the market demand curve. Similarly, finding the market demand at any given price involves summing the horizontal distance between each of the private demand curves and the vertical axis at that price. This process is sometimes called **horizontal summation.**

Figures 5.2A and 5.2B reproduce the private demand curves depicted in Figures 5.1A and 5.1B. Figure 5.2C superimposes the market supply curve, labeled S_f, on the market demand curve D_f^{A+E} from Figure 5.1C. Equilibrium in the market occurs at the price where the quantities demanded and supplied are equal. This occurs at a price of 4 in Figure 5.2C.

At this price, Adam consumes one-and-one-half fig leaves and Eve consumes three. Note that there is no reason to expect Adam's and Eve's consumption levels to be equal. Due to different tastes, incomes, and other characteristics, Adam and Eve demand different quantities of fig leaves.

---

[5] Demand curves are explained in the Appendix to this book.

Figure 5.2
Efficient provision
of a private good

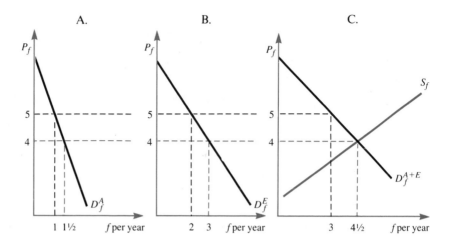

The equilibrium in Figure 5.2C has a significant property: the allocation of fig leaves is Pareto efficient. In consumer theory, a utility-maxi-
mizing individual sets the marginal rate of substitution of fig leaves for
apples (MRS_{fa}) equal to the price of fig leaves (P_f) divided by the price of
apples (P_a): $MRS_{fa} = P_f/P_a$.[6] Because only relative prices matter for
rational choice, the price of apples can be arbitrarily set at any value. For
convenience, set P_a = \$1. Thus, the condition for utility maximization
reduces to $MRS_{fa} = P_f$. The price of fig leaves thus measures the rate at
which an individual is willing to substitute fig leaves for apples. Now,
Adam's demand curve for fig leaves (D_f^A) shows the maximum price per
fig leaf that he would pay at each level of fig leaf consumption. Therefore,
the demand curve also shows the MRS_{fa} at each level of fig leaf consumption. Similarly, D_f^E can be interpreted as Eve's MRS_{fa} schedule.

In the same way, the supply curve S_f in Figure 5.2C shows how the
marginal rate of transformation of fig leaves for apples (MRT_{fa}) varies
with fig leaf production.[7]

At the equilibrium in Figure 5.2C, Adam and Eve both set MRS_{fa}
equal to 4, and the producer also sets MRT_{fa} equal to four. (See Chapter
4.) Hence, at equilibrium

$$MRS_{fa}^{Adam} = MRS_{fa}^{Eve} = MRT_{fa} \qquad (5.1)$$

---

[6] See the Appendix to the book for a proof.

[7] To demonstrate this, note that under competition, firms produce up to the point where price
equals the marginal cost, the incremental cost of the last unit produced. Hence, the supply curve S_f shows
the marginal cost of each level of fig leaf production. As noted in Chapter 4 under "Welfare Economics,"
$MRT_{fa} = MC_f/MC_a$. Because P_a = \$1 and price equals marginal cost, then MC_a = \$1, and $MRT_{fa} = MC_f$.
We can therefore identify the marginal rate of transformation with marginal cost, and hence with the
supply curve.

Equation (5.1) is the necessary condition for Pareto efficiency derived in Chapter 4. As long as the market is competitive and functions properly, the Fundamental Theorem of Welfare Economics guarantees that this condition holds.

Public Good Case

Having now restated the condition for efficient provision of a private good, we turn to the case of a public good. We develop the efficiency condition intuitively before turning to a formal derivation. Suppose that Adam and Eve both enjoy displays of fireworks. Eve's enjoyment of fireworks does not diminish Adam's and vice versa. Hence, a fireworks display is a public good. The size of the fireworks display can be varied, and both Adam and Eve prefer bigger to smaller displays, other things being the same. Suppose that the display currently consists of 19 rockets and can be expanded at a cost of $5 per rocket, that Adam would be willing to pay $6 to expand the display by another rocket, and that Eve would be willing to pay $4. Is it efficient to increase the size of the display by one rocket? As usual, we must compare the marginal benefit to the marginal cost. To compute the marginal benefit, note that because consumption of the display is nonrival, the 20th rocket can be consumed by *both* Adam and Eve. Hence, the marginal benefit of the 20th rocket is the *sum* of what they are willing to pay, which is $10. Because the marginal cost is only $5, it pays to acquire the 20th rocket. More generally, if the sum of individuals' willingness to pay for an additional unit of a public good exceeds its marginal cost, efficiency requires that the unit be purchased; otherwise, it should not. Hence, efficient provision of a public good requires that the sum of each person's marginal valuation on the last unit just equal the marginal cost.

To derive this result graphically, consider panel A of Figure 5.3 in which Adam's consumption of rockets *(r)* is measured on the horizontal axis, and the price per rocket (P_r) is on the vertical. Adam's demand curve for rockets is D_r^A. Similarly, Eve's demand curve for rockets is D_r^E in Figure 5.3B. How do we derive the group willingness to pay for rockets? To find the group demand curve for fig leaves—a private good—we horizontally summed the individual demand curves. That procedure makes it possible for Adam and Eve to consume different quantities of fig leaves at the same price. For a private good, this is fine. However, the services produced by the rockets—a public good—*must* be consumed in *equal* amounts. If Adam consumes a 20-rocket fireworks display, Eve must also consume a 20-rocket fireworks display. It literally makes no sense to try to sum the quantities of a public good that the individual would consume at a given price.

Instead, to find the group willingness to pay for rockets, we add the prices that each would be willing to pay for a given quantity. The demand curve in Figure 5.3A tells us that Adam is willing to pay $6 per rocket when he consumes 20 rockets. Eve is willing to pay $4 when she consumes 20 rockets. Their group willingness to pay for 20 rockets is there-

Figure 5.3

Vertical summation
of demand curves

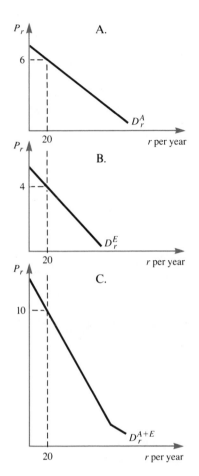

fore $10 per rocket. Thus, if we define D_r^{A+E} in Figure 5.3C to be the group willingness to pay schedule, the vertical distance between D_r^{A+E} and the point $r = 20$ must be 10.[8] Other points on D_r^{A+E} are determined by repeating this procedure for each level of public-good production. For a public good, then, the group willingness to pay is found by **vertical summation** of the individual demand curves.

Note the symmetry between private and public goods. With a private good, everyone has the same *MRS*, but people can consume different quantities. Therefore, demands are summed horizontally over the differing quantities. For public goods, everyone consumes the same quantity, but people can have different *MRS*s. Vertical summation is required to find the group willingness to pay.

---

[8] D_r^{A+E} is not a conventionally defined demand schedule, because it does not show the quantity that would be demanded at each price. However, this notation highlights the similarities to the private good case.

Figure 5.4
Efficient provision
of a public good

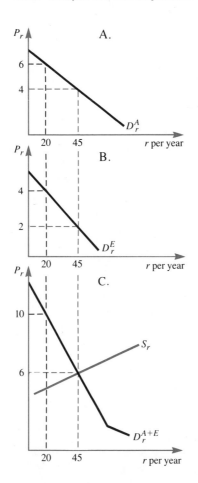

The efficient quantity of rockets is found at the point where Adam's and Eve's willingness to pay for an additional unit just equals the marginal cost of producing a unit. In Figure 5.4C, the marginal cost schedule, S_r, is superimposed on the group willingness to pay curve D_r^{A+E}.[9] The intersection occurs at output 45, where the marginal cost is equal to $6.

Once again, prices can be interpreted in terms of marginal rates of substitution. Reasoning as before, Adam's marginal willingness to pay for rockets is his marginal rate of substitution (MRS_{ra}^{Adam}), and Eve's marginal willingness to pay for rockets is her marginal rate of substitution (MRS_{ra}^{Eve}). Therefore, the sum of the prices they are willing to pay equals

---

[9] This analysis does not consider explicitly the production possibilities frontier which lies behind this supply curve. See Samuelson [1955].

$MRS_{ra}^{Adam} + MRS_{ra}^{Eve}$. From the production point of view, price still represents the marginal rate of transformation, MRT_{ra}. Hence, the equilibrium in Figure 5.4C is characterized by the condition:

$$MRS_{ra}^{Adam} + MRS_{ra}^{Eve} = MRT_{ra} \qquad (5.2)$$

Contrast this with the conditions for efficient provision of a private good described in Equation (5.1). For a private good, efficiency requires that each individual have the same marginal rate of substitution, and that this equal the marginal rate of transformation. For a pure public good, the sum of the marginal rates of substitution must equal the marginal rate of transformation.[10] Because everybody must consume the same amount of the public good, its efficient provision requires that the *total* valuation they place on the last unit provided—the sum of the *MRS*s—equal the incremental cost to society of providing it—the *MRT*.

As stressed in Chapter 4, under a reasonably general set of conditions, one can expect a decentralized market system to provide goods efficiently. In the absence of market imperfections, the efficient quantity of fig leaves in Figure 5.2C will be generated. Will similar forces lead to the efficient output level ($r = 45$) in Figure 5.4? The answer depends in part on the extent to which Adam and Eve reveal their true preferences for fireworks. When a private good is exchanged in a competitive market, an individual has no incentive to lie about how much he or she values it. If Eve is willing to pay the going price for a fig leaf, then she has nothing to gain by failing to make the purchase. This kind of behavior is implicitly assumed in the usual stories of how the forces of supply and demand produce an equilibrium.

For a nonexcludable public good, however, there may be incentives for people to hide their true preferences. Suppose for the moment that rocket displays are nonexcludable. Adam may falsely claim that fireworks mean nothing to him. If he can get Eve to foot the entire bill, he can still enjoy the show and yet have more money to spend on apples and fig leaves. This incentive to let other people pay while you enjoy the benefits is known as the **free rider problem.** Of course, Eve also would like to be a free rider. Where there are public goods, "any one person can hope to snatch some selfish benefit in a way not possible under the self-policing competitive pricing of private goods" [Samuelson, 1955, p. 389]. Hence, there is a good chance that the market will fall short of providing the efficient amount of the public good. No automatic tendency exists for markets to reach the efficient allocation in Figure 5.4.

---

[10] This analysis assumes that the taxes required to finance the public good can be raised without distorting economic decisions in the private sector. When this is not the case, the condition for efficient provision changes. See Atkinson and Stern [1974].

Even if consumption is excludable, market provision of a public good is likely to be inefficient. Suppose now that the fireworks display is excludable; people cannot see the show unless they purchase an admission ticket to a coliseum. A profit-maximizing entrepreneur sells tickets. Recall from Chapter 4 the fact that Pareto efficiency requires that price equal marginal cost. Because a public good is nonrival in consumption by definition, the marginal cost of providing it to another person is zero. Hence, efficiency requires a price of zero. But if the entrepreneur charges everyone a price of zero, then she cannot stay in business.

Is there a way out? Suppose that the following two conditions hold: (1), the entrepreneur knows each person's demand curve for the public good and (2), it is difficult or impossible to transfer the good from one person to another. Under these two conditions, the entrepreneur could charge each person an individual price based on willingness to pay, a procedure known as **perfect price discrimination.** People who valued the rocket display at only a penny would pay exactly that amount; even they would not be excluded from attending. Thus, everyone who put any positive value on the show would attend, an efficient outcome.[11] However, because those who valued the display a lot would pay a very high price, the entrepreneur would still be able to stay in business.

Perfect price discrimination may seem to be the solution until we recall that the first condition requires knowledge of everybody's preferences. But of course, if individuals' demand curves were known, there would be no problem in determining the optimum provision in the first place. We conclude that even if the public good is excludable, private provision is likely to lead to efficiency problems.[12]

The Free Rider Problem

Some suggest that the free rider problem necessarily leads to inefficient levels of nonexcludable public goods; therefore, government provision of such public goods is required for economic efficiency. The argument is that the government can somehow find out everyone's true preferences, and then, using its coercive power, force everybody to pay for public goods. If all this is possible, the government can avoid the free rider problem and ensure that public goods are provided at appropriate levels.

It must be emphasized that free ridership is not a *fact;* it is an implication of the *hypothesis* that people maximize a utility function that depends only on their own consumption of goods. To be sure, one can find examples in which public goods are not provided because people fail to reveal their preferences. On the other hand, much evidence suggests that individuals can and do act collectively without government coercion. Fund

---

[11] In the theory of welfare economics, the outcome is efficient because the price paid by the *marginal* consumer equals marginal cost.

[12] A number of mechanisms have been designed to induce people to reveal their true preferences to a government agency. See the Appendix to this chapter.

drives spearheaded by volunteers have led to the establishment and maintenance of churches, music halls, libraries, scientific laboratories, art museums, hospitals, and other such facilities.[13] One prominent economist has even argued, "I do not know of many historical records or other empirical evidence which show convincingly that the problem of correct revelation of preferences has been of any practical significance" [Johansen, 1977, p. 147].

These observations do not prove that free ridership is irrelevant. Although some goods that appear to have public characteristics are privately provided, others that "ought" to be provided (on grounds of efficiency) may not be. Moreover, the quantity of those public goods that are privately provided may be insufficient. The key point is that the importance of the free rider problem is an empirical question whose answer should not be taken for granted.

Gerald Marwell and Ruth Ames [1981] conducted laboratory experiments to investigate the importance of free rider behavior. Subjects in the experiment were given a number of tokens which they invested in an "individual exchange" or in a "group exchange." Investments in the individual exchange earned a set amount, regardless of the behavior of other group members. The return was excludable in the sense that it neither affected nor was affected by the other members. On the other hand, "The group exchange . . . paid its cash earnings to *all* members of the group by a pre-set formula, regardless of who invested. . . . [It] provided a joint, nonrival, nonexcludable, or *public* form of payoff" [p. 297]. The incentive to free ride was provided by the fact that the group exchange could offer a substantially larger return.

> Under these circumstances, all members of the group would be better off if all the group's resources were invested in the group exchange than if all were invested in the individual exchange. On the other hand, each individual would be best off if she/he invested in the individual exchange while everyone else invested in the group exchange. [P. 297]

What did the results show? On average, people voluntarily contributed 40 to 60 percent of their resources to the provision of the public good. Some free riding therefore was present in the sense that the subjects failed to contribute a substantial portion of their resources. On the other hand, the results flatly contradicted the notion that free riding will lead to zero or trivial amounts of a public good. People's notions of fairness and responsibility may work counter to the pursuit of narrow self-interest.

However, Mark Isaac, Kenneth McCue, and Charles Plott [1985] criticized the structure of this study. They noted that in the Marwell-Ames experiment, the subjects played the game only once. It may be that

---

[13] There is even some evidence of successful private provision of that classic public good, the lighthouse [see Coase, 1974].

as people repeat the game, they begin to realize the advantages of free riding, and start exhibiting that behavior. Isaac, McCue, and Plott ran an experiment in which subjects were allowed to play several times, and they found that the level of public goods provision fell as the number of replications increased.

Presumably, in the future, even more realistic laboratory experiments will be designed to examine the importance of free riding. As was stressed in Chapter 3, caution must be exercised in interpreting the results of such experiments. The setting is artificial and the sample of individuals being observed may not be representative of the population. Still, they are an important tool for investigating the relevance of the free rider problem.

Public versus Private Provision

In some cases, the services provided by publicly provided goods can be obtained privately.[14] The commodity "protection" can be obtained from a publicly provided police force. Alternatively, to some extent protection can also be gained by purchasing strong locks, burglar alarms, and bodyguards, which are obtained privately. A large backyard can serve many of the functions of a public park. Even substitutes for services provided by public courts of law can be obtained privately. For example, because of the enormous costs of using the government's judicial system, companies in Los Angeles sometimes bypass the courts and instead settle their disputes before mutually agreed-upon neutral advisers [Chambers, 1986].

Over time, the mix between public and private modes of provision has changed substantially. During the 19th century, there was much greater private responsibility for education, police protection, libraries, and other functions than there is at present. However, there appears to be a trend back to the private sector for provision of what we have come to consider publicly provided goods and services. For example, in a small number of communities, individual homeowners now contract with private companies to provide protection against fires. At the federal level, thought has been given to selling energy projects, public housing, and even the Postal Service to private entrepreneurs.

The national debate over **privatization** concerns the question of whether society would be better off if more of the goods and services now provided publicly were supplied by the private sector. To analyze the privatization issue, think of publicly and privately provided goods as inputs into the production of some output that people desire. Teachers, classrooms, textbooks, and private tutors are inputs into the production of an output we might call educational quality. Assume that what ultimately matters to people is the level of output, educational quality, not the particular inputs used to produce it. What criteria should be used to select the amount of each input? There are several considerations:

---

[14] As stressed earlier, a publicly provided good need not be a public good—governments also provide goods that are rival in consumption.

Relative wage and materials costs.   If labor and materials cost different amounts for the public and private sector, then *ceteris paribus,* on grounds of efficiency, the less expensive sector is to be preferred. Why should input costs faced by public and private sectors differ? One way this might occur is if public sector employees are unionized while their private sector counterparts are not. We discuss other differences between public and private production in the next section.

Administrative costs.   Under public provision, any fixed administrative costs can be spread over a large group of people. Instead of everyone's having to spend time negotiating an arrangement for garbage collection, the negotiation is done by one office for everybody. The larger the size of the community, the greater the advantage to being able to spread these costs.

Diversity of tastes.   Households with and without children may have very different views about the desirability of high-quality education. People who store jewels in their homes may value property protection more than people who do not. To the extent such diversity is present, it will be efficient to provide the output privately, so that people can tailor their consumption to their own tastes. As President Ronald Reagan put it, "Such a strategy ensures production of services that are demanded by consumers, not those chosen by government bureaucrats" [*Economic Report of the President*, 1986, p. 9]. Clearly, the benefits to allowing for such diversity must be weighed against any possible increases in administrative costs.

Distributional issues.   The community's notions of fairness may require that some commodities be made available to everybody, an idea sometimes referred to as **commodity egalitarianism** [Tobin, 1970]. Commodity egalitarianism may help explain the wide appeal of publicly provided education—people believe that everyone should have access to at least some minimum level of schooling. Public provision of certain private goods such as medical care might also be based on this consideration.

It is one thing to theorize that there is scope for substitution between publicly and privately provided inputs, and another to show that it actually occurs. If we found that states with relatively high costs of privately provided inputs tended to use less of them, *ceteris paribus,* this would provide some support that substitution is possible. Charles Clotfelter [1977] compared various states with respect to their decisions on how to produce the output "personal safety." He estimated a regression equation in which the dependent variable was the state ratio of publicly provided inputs (employment of state and local police) to privately provided inputs (employment in private protective and detective agencies). One of the right-hand side variables was the ratio of public police wages to private protective wages. The parameter estimates implied that a 1 percentage point increase in the ratio of public to private sector wages would lead to about a 2.5 percentage point decrease in the relative employment of publicly and privately provided inputs. At least in the important case of public safety, then, there appears to be scope for substitution, which jurisdictions take into account in their decisions.

Public versus Private Production

In the privatization debate, conservatives want more functions provided by the private sector, while liberals prefer government provision. Moreover, even when it is agreed that certain items should be provided by the public sector, there is disagreement over whether they should be produced publicly or privately. Part of the controversy stems from fundamental differences regarding the extent to which government should intervene in the economy. (See Chapter 1.) Part is due to differences of opinions about the relative costs of public and private production. Some argue that public sector managers, because they do not have to make profits, are less efficient than their private sector counterparts. Anecdotal evidence abounds. One celebrated case involved New York City, which spent $12 million attempting to rebuild the ice-skating rink in Central Park between 1980 and 1986. The main problem was that the contractors were trying to use a new technology for making ice, and it did not work. In 1986, after spending $200,000 on a study to find out what went wrong, city officials learned that they would have to start all over. In June of 1986 a private real estate developer, Donald J. Trump, offered to take over the project, and have it completed by December of that year for about $2.5 million. Trump finished the rink three weeks ahead of schedule and $750,000 under projected cost. On a more mundane level, in 1990 Chicago replaced city crews with private towing companies to haul away 50,000 abandoned cars. The net annual savings were estimated at $2.5 million. In 1991, a private firm announced that, after two years of managing Baltimore's civic arena, a $1.2 million operating deficit had been turned into a modest profit.

Is it true that public sector production is always too expensive? Despite the profusion of horror stories, it is very hard to gather systematic evidence. One reason is that measuring the outputs produced by public sector enterprises tends to be difficult. How does one quantify the amount of education produced by a school? Test scores alone won't be sufficient, because schools are also supposed to encourage creativity and to teach self-discipline and good citizenship. In any case, test scores depend on a multitude of factors outside the school's control, such as family background. Similar problems in measuring outputs arise in comparing public and private costs of producing medical services, police protection, and transportation. But if outputs cannot be measured properly, how can we compare costs of production?

A case study. An important possible exception is refuse collection, for which the output is reasonably well defined and measurable—tons of garbage removed.[15] Peter Kemper and John Quigley [1976] (K&Q) undertook a very careful analysis of refuse collection costs in a number of Connecticut towns. One initial observation was that the public-private dichotomy was too simple to characterize the choices actually available. There are many different organizational types. Among these are *private,* in which refuse collection is left to the free market; *contract,* in which the government engages a private firm to produce a specified level of service; *nonprofit,* in which a nonprofit refuse collection agency independent of the city is created; and *municipal,* in which the service is produced by the town itself.

K&Q estimated a regression in which the dependent variable was cost per ton of collection, and the right-hand side variables included indicators for the type of organization.[16] They found that compared to municipal collection, private collection was about 30 percent *more* expensive, but contract collection was about 30 percent less expensive (p. 64). The finding that contract organization is less expensive than municipal is not too surprising. Presumably, the contractor has incentives to keep down production costs to maximize profits. However, the fact that private organization is more expensive than municipal is rather startling, at least to economists, who believe that competition tends to drive costs down. But K&Q note that private collection does not necessarily imply competition—there is some evidence that the private collectors colluded to keep prices above the competitive level. Indeed, some researchers have suggested that with respect to costs of production, the key issue is not public versus private, but competitive versus noncompetitive: "the oft-noted inefficiency of government enterprises stems from isolation from effective *competition* rather than public ownership *per se*" [Caves and Christensen, 1980, p. 974].[17]

There are a number of reasons why K&Q's results must be interpreted with caution. Their regressions do not control for differences in service quality—litter, noise, dependability, and so forth. These attributes are hard to measure, but potentially important. In addition, their study deals with the experience of towns in only one state. Still, the K&Q study highlights the complexity of the privatization issue. If a community decides that it no longer wants public production of public goods and services, there are a number of alternatives from which it must choose. The choice depends in part on predictions about what kind of market structure will emerge if provision is left to the private market.

---

[15] For a survey of results for other goods and services, see Yarrow [1986].

[16] The other major explanatory variable was population density. *Ceteris paribus,* the closer people live to each other, the cheaper it is to collect a given quantity of garbage.

[17] This result emerges from an analysis of public and private costs of railway operation in Canada.

National Defense

If any commodity is a candidate for public provision, it is national defense. Its consumption is highly nonrival; one can hardly imagine how it could be provided by the private market. Indeed, national defense is recognized even by strict libertarians as being a proper function of government. Nevertheless, the manner in which the government supplies this service is a matter of some controversy.

The national defense budget in 1990 was $330 billion, or 6.2 percent of GNP. Clearly, this is a huge sum. Figure 5.5, which shows defense spending as a percent of GNP for the last quarter century, suggests that big defense budgets are nothing new. As noted in Chapter 2 under "Expenditures," in the early 1960s, the proportion of national output going to defense was higher than it is now.

The U.S. defense establishment rivals in size and complexity the economies of many medium-sized countries. We can deal with only a few issues here, but the discussion should provide a sense of the scope and nature of some of the major problems.

The notion of a production function provides a useful framework for a discussion of defense expenditures. The government purchases capital and labor inputs and uses them to produce defense services. We discuss issues surrounding U.S. Department of Defense expenditures for capital and labor in turn.

Capital: Procurement Contracts

Many of the capital goods demanded by the military are routine—cars, trucks, housing, and so on. An important component of capital spending is for items such as Patriot missiles and communications systems requiring the use of advanced and specialized technologies. Often only a few

Figure 5.5
Outlays for national defense as a percent of GNP

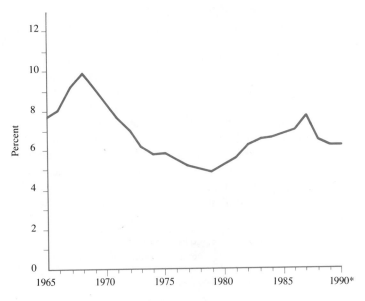

* Estimate based on third quarter activity.

SOURCE: U.S. Department of Commerce. *Survey of Current Business,* June 1989 and October 1990.

firms are capable of producing a given kind of hardware. In addition, the costs associated with such production are likely to be uncertain. Advanced technologies are almost by definition not well understood, so it is hard to predict costs.

Because there are only a few suppliers, the market for military hardware is not competitive. Instead of being a price taker, the Department of Defense (DOD) negotiates prices with supplying firms. Procurement contracts also set forth the specifications of the goods to be produced as well as their prices. In 1989, procurement accounted for $80.7 billion of the defense budget [U.S. Bureau of the Census, 1990, p. 330].

Several different types of contracts are possible.[18] A **fixed price contract** stipulates that the firm will complete the project in return for a fixed price. Once the price is set, it is not renegotiated. This would seem to be a good deal from the point of view of DOD—it knows just what it will have to pay. But there is a rub. Recall that costs of production tend to be highly uncertain. Under a fixed price contract, the firm bears all the consequences if costs are higher than expected. To the extent the firm is averse to risk, it must receive a higher return as compensation for accepting all of this risk—a risk premium. If the firm can make a profit of 10 percent in a relatively safe venture, why should it take a risk unless it can earn more? Hence, the fee that DOD pays under a fixed price contract, although known for certain, may be very high.

A **cost plus contract** does not have this problem. Here, DOD pays a fixed dollar fee plus all additional costs incurred by the firm in completing the project. With cost plus, the firm bears no risk. However, neither does the firm have any incentives to keep costs down. Hence, under cost plus contracts, there is a well-documented tendency for cost overruns. An extreme example is provided by the U.S. Air Force's Advanced Medium Range Air-to-Air Missile (AMRAAM). When the project began in 1977, the cost per missile was estimated at $40,000 to $50,000 (in 1978 dollars). By 1986, the cost per missile was up to $200,000 (in 1978 dollars), and even then, there was a possibility that the price would go higher [McNaugher, 1986].

An **incentive contract** lies in between the extremes of fixed price and cost plus. The contracting firm receives a fixed fee plus some fraction of the costs of the project. Algebraically, if the costs of production are C, then the total cost to the Department of Defense, TC, is

$$TC = F + \lambda C \tag{5.3}$$

where F is the fixed fee and λ is the share of production costs borne by DOD. For example, if the fixed fee for a tank is $5 million, the costs of production are $10 million, and $\lambda = 0.2$, then DOD's bill is $7 million ($= 5 + 0.2 \times 10$).

---

[18] For further details, see Weitzman [1980].

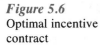

Figure 5.6
Optimal incentive
contract

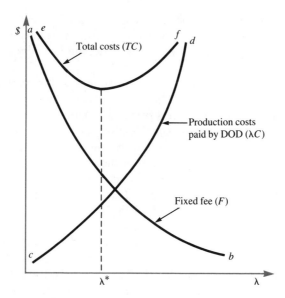

Equation (5.3) makes clear that fixed price and cost plus contracts are special cases of an incentive contract. With fixed price, λ = 0, and with cost plus, λ = 1. Note that both F and C depend on λ. As λ increases from zero to one, incentives to contain costs decrease, but the firm has to assume less risk, so the risk premium embodied in F also falls. In economics, a situation of this kind is referred to as a **principal-agent problem.** A principal (in this case, DOD) wants an agent (the firm) to perform a task. The agent operates in an environment of uncertainty, so if the job is not well done (in this case, if C is too high) the principal cannot know for sure whether or not it is the agent's fault. The principal-agent problem is for the principal to structure the agent's incentives so that the principal's expected net gain is as high as possible.

In our simple model, solving the principal-agent problem amounts to finding the cost-minimizing value of λ. Consider Figure 5.6, in which DOD's share of costs, λ, is on the horizontal axis, and dollars are measured on the vertical. The upward sloping curve *cd* reflects the fact that production costs increase with λ, and the downward sloping curve *ab* reflects the decline in the fixed fee as the risk premium falls. Curve *ef* is the sum of the two schedules. The cost minimizing value of λ, λ*, is associated with the lowest point on *ef*. The value of λ* depends on, among other things, how averse to risk the firm is (which determines the shape of the *ab* curve), and the rate at which costs fall as the firm has to bear a higher proportion of the costs (which determines the shape of the *cd* curve). Unfortunately, not much is known about the actual shapes of these curves. On the basis of some fragmentary evidence, Martin Weitzman [1980] estimates that for a typical defense project, the optimal λ is below one half, and in some cases, below 10 percent. If this result is correct, then DOD does not have to do too much cost sharing in order to minimize its total costs.

Historically, the defense contractor who successfully bid to develop a weapons system could expect to be a monopolist in supplying that system. In the 1980s, DOD introduced increased competition into capital procurement by allowing competitive bidding for the production of weapons systems. By removing monopoly rights to weapons production from the companies that designed them, DOD achieved significant cost savings in several cases. For example, the price of the Army's Hellfire missile fell from $43,000 in 1983 to $28,000 five years later [Stevenson, 1988]. It may be, however, that monopoly profits in production have sometimes been relied on to recoup losses incurred in research and development (R&D). If so, increased competition for production contracts may reduce companies' willingness to pursue R&D or, perhaps, increase the degree of cost-sharing demanded in contracts for weapons development.

Finally, we note that the model of optimal incentive contracts ignores the important question of how the quality of the work can be monitored. Equally important, the model does not consider whether DOD acts in the public interest when making its capital purchases. Newspapers are full of accusations of "gold-plating"—purchasing weapons that are more complicated and expensive than is really necessary. In short, another principal-agent problem is lurking in the background. This time the principal is the public, and the agent is DOD. We take up the question of why there may be a conflict of interest between citizens and their governments in Chapter 7.

Labor: The All Volunteer Force

The United States has 2.1 million men and women on active military duty; payments to military personnel account for about 27 percent of the defense budget [U.S. Bureau of the Census, 1990, pp. 330, 339]. Since the 1970s the United States has had no draft; members of the armed forces serve voluntarily.

To understand the budgetary consequences of an all volunteer force, it is useful to consider a supply and demand model of military personnel.[19] In Figure 5.7, S_m is the supply of people to the military, D_m is the demand. For simplicity, it is assumed that defense personnel requirements are fixed at level $\overline{M}$, at least in the short run. Hence, the demand curve is perfectly vertical at $\overline{M}$. Supply and demand intersect at point E which is associated with wage level w_m. The budgetary cost for personnel is thus w_m times $\overline{M}$. Geometrically, w_m is the length of rectangle $w_m 0\overline{M}E$; $\overline{M}$ is that rectangle's width; so their product, the military wage bill, is its area.

---

[19] Much of this argument is based on Olvey et al. [1984].

Figure 5.7
Supply and demand
of military
personnel

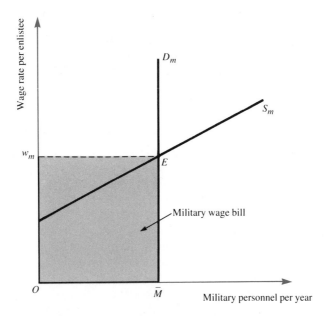

Now suppose that there is a decrease in the supply of labor to the military because of a reduction in the size of the pool of young people. (According to demographic projections, such a reduction will occur in the 1990s.) In Figure 5.8, the reduction in the potential number of enlistees is reflected as a shift of the supply curve S_m to S'_m. Supply and demand now intersect at wage w'_m, so that to obtain $\overline{M}$ recruits the wage bill must increase to $w'_m 0 \overline{M} E'$. Suppose, however, that DOD is not authorized to increase the wage rate. If the wage rate stays at w_m, the quantity demanded, $w_m E$, exceeds the quantity supplied, $w_m A$—there is a shortage of AE.

What can be done to deal with the shortage? One possibility is to adopt policies to shift S'_m back toward S_m. This might be done via advertising, adding more benefits such as job-training programs. Of course, such measures would add to the defense budget; presumably the reason that w_m was not allowed to rise in the first place was to keep down expenditures. Another possibility is to enact a draft, that is, simply force AE people to join the military at wage w_m. To assess the consequences of a draft, assume that the army manages to conscript only those individuals who would have been willing to enter the service if the wage were w'_m, that is, the individuals who lie along the supply curve from A to E'. In this case, everyone in the conscription army would have been willing to receive w'_m, but as a consequence of the draft, they receive only w_m. In effect, then, the draft is a tax that reduces each enlistee's wage from w'_m to w_m. The total "draftee tax" is $\overline{M}$ times the wage reduction (distance $w_m w'_m$), or rectangle $w'_m w_m E E'$. Thus, under a draft, part of the military personnel budget is financed by taxes on society as a whole (area

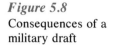

Figure 5.8
Consequences of a
military draft

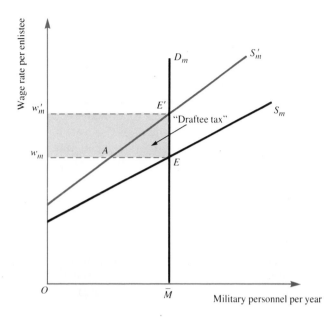

$w_m O\overline{M}E$) and part by a special draftee tax (area $w'_m w_m E E'$).[20] However,
the draftee tax does not appear on the budget, so the cost to society of
maintaining the military is underestimated.

In addition, a draft may induce the military to use an inefficient mix of
capital and labor. Although in the short run the demand curve for military
personnel may be vertical as in our figures, in the long run capital can be
substituted for labor. Some empirical studies suggest that when the price
of labor decreases, the military employs more of it, *ceteris paribus* (see
Olvey, Golden, and Kelly, 1984). Under the draft, the military perceives
the cost of labor to be w_m, while its social cost is w'_m—the amount that
enlistees could earn in alternative employment. Because the military
faces an artificially low price for labor, it uses an inefficiently large
amount.

None of this is meant to imply that a peacetime draft is necessarily a
bad thing. There are reasonable arguments on both sides. Opponents of
the draft dislike the restrictions that it puts on individuals' freedom of
choice. Proponents sensibly emphasize that all citizens are obliged to bear
arms, not just those willing to accept military pay. However, some supporters of the draft argue that it is desirable because it is less costly than a
volunteer army: "[I]f the volunteer system now in use continues, the
Defense Department will find it continually more expensive to recruit a
shrinking number of insufficiently skilled volunteers. In such circum-

---

[20] The draftee tax is increased to the extent that individuals to the right of E' on the supply curve S'_m
are drafted.

stances some form of draft deserves careful thought'' [Davis, 1987, p. A27]. This argument is highly misleading. A draft hides some of the costs of obtaining military personnel; it does not eliminate them.

Public Goods and Public Choice

The use of the word *public* to describe commodities that are nonrival in consumption almost seems to prejudge the question of whether they ought to be provided by the public sector. Indeed, we have shown that it is unlikely that private markets will generate pure public goods in Pareto efficient quantities. Some collective decision must be made regarding the quantity to be supplied. As we saw in our discussion of national defense, collective decisions regarding *how* the public good is to be produced are also required. In contrast to national defense, sometimes there may be private substitutes for the services produced by a public good. But community decision making is also needed in these cases, this time to choose the extent to which public provision will be used. Thus, the subjects of public goods and public choice are closely linked. In Chapter 7 we discuss and evaluate a number of mechanisms for making collective decisions.

Summary

- Prominent causes of market failure are monopoly, public goods, externalities, costly information, and nonexistent markets.

- Public goods are characterized by nonrivalness in consumption. Each person consumes the same amount, but not necessarily the preferred amount, of the public good.

- Consumption of a good is nonexcludable when it is either very expensive or impossible to prevent anyone from consuming the good. Many public goods are also nonexcludable.

- Efficient provision of public goods requires that the sum of the individual *MRS*s equal the *MRT*, unlike private goods where each *MRS* equals the *MRT*.

- Market mechanisms are unlikely to provide public goods efficiently, even if they are excludable in consumption.

- Casual observation and laboratory studies indicate that people do not fully exploit free riding possibilities. Nonetheless, in certain cases, free riding is likely to be a significant problem.

- Public goods can be provided privately, and private goods can be provided publicly. The choice between public and private provision should depend on relative wage and materials costs, administrative costs, diversity of tastes for the good, and distributional issues.

- Even in cases where public provision of a good is selected, a choice between public and private production must be made. Although there is much anecdotal evidence suggesting that public production is relatively expensive, it is hard to establish this fact statistically.

- National defense is a clear example of a public good. Defense services are produced using capital and labor. Capital acquisition decisions are complicated by the fact that certain types of military equipment are based on new technologies whose costs are highly uncertain. In the defense labor market, the key question is the extent to which conscription should be used to meet personnel needs.

Discussion Questions

1. There is substantial government intervention in the U.S. economy. In each of the following cases, can you rationalize the government's policy? If not, explain why each exists.

    a. Agricultural price supports (the government buys enough of a crop to ensure a minimum price).
    b. Maximum price laws for gasoline.
    c. Product safety standards.
    d. Zoning and land use laws.

2. Which of the following do you consider public goods? Private goods? Why?

    a. Wilderness areas.
    b. Roads.
    c. Invasion of Kuwait to displace Iraqi occupiers.
    d. Public television programs.
    e. Private television programs.
    f. Cable television programs.

3. Tarzan and Jane live alone in the jungle and have trained Cheetah to both patrol the perimeter of their clearing and to harvest tropical fruits. Cheetah can collect three pounds of fruit an hour and currently spends 6 hours patroling, 8 hours picking, and 10 hours sleeping.

    a. What are the public and private goods in this example?

    b. If Tarzan and Jane are each currently willing to give up one hour of patrol for two pounds of fruit, is the current allocation of Cheetah's time Pareto efficient? Should he patrol more or less?

4. Suppose you are asked to determine whether public or private hospitals produce at lower cost. What kind of data would you need? Suggest an econometric strategy.

5. In which of the following situations do you expect principal-agent problems to be most severe?

    a. A community arranges for refuse collection with a local company.
    b. The Congress asks the Joint Chiefs of Staff to modernize the armed forces.
    c. The Board of Education wants to increase the quality of education by improving teachers' wages.

6. Frank Lichtenberg [1989] has estimated that the price elasticity of the U.S. government's demand for weapons is roughly -0.55. Suppose that this estimate is approximately accurate. Suppose further that increased competition in weapons production brings substantial price reductions. Do you expect the price fall and resulting increase in quantity demanded to increase or to decrease the amount DOD spends on weapons procurement?

Selected References

Bator, F. M. "The Anatomy of Market Failure." *Quarterly Journal of Economics* 72 (August 1958), pp. 351–79.

Coase, Ronald H. "The Lighthouse in Economics." *Journal of Law and Economics,* October 1974, pp. 357–76.

Marwell, Gerald, and Ruth E. Ames. "Economists Free Ride, Does Anyone Else? Experiments on the Provision of Public Goods, IV." *Journal of Public Economics* 15, no. 3 (June 1981), pp. 295–310.

Olvey, Lee D., James R. Golden, and Robert C. Kelly. *Economics of National Security.* Wayne, N.J.: Avery Publishing Group, 1984.

Samuelson, Paul A. "Diagrammatic Exposition of a Theory of Public Expenditure." *Review of Economics and Statistics* 37 (1955), pp. 350–56.

Yarrow, George. "Privatization in Theory and Practice." *Economic Policy: A European Forum* 1, no. 2 (April 1986), pp. 324–77.

APPENDIX 5   Preference Revelation Mechanisms

We have seen that markets generally fail to induce individuals to reveal their true preferences for nonexcludable public goods, and hence, a price system does not provide them in efficient amounts. Is there any other way, short of forcing everyone to take a lie detector test, to get people to tell the truth? A number of writers have suggested procedures for inducing people to reveal their true preferences. We now describe one based on the work of Theodore Groves and Martin Loeb [1975].[21]

Imagine that a government agent approaches Eve and says, "Please tell me your demand curve for rocket displays. I will use this information plus the information I receive from Adam to select a Pareto efficient quantity of rockets, and to assign each of you a tax. But before you give me your answer, I want you to realize that you will be taxed in the following way: Whenever the level of public good provision increases by a unit, the change in your tax bill will be the incremental cost of that unit, minus the value that everyone else puts on the increase."

After the agent departs, the first thing Eve does is to represent the tax structure algebraically. If ΔT^{Eve} is the change in her tax bill when provision of the public good is expanded by one unit; MRT_{ra} is the incremental resource cost of the one unit; MRS_{ra}^{Total} is the marginal value of one more unit to Adam and Eve; and MRS_{ra}^{Eve} is the marginal value to Eve alone; then

$$\Delta T^{\text{Eve}} = MRT_{ra} - (MRS_{ra}^{\text{Total}} - MRS_{ra}^{\text{Eve}}) \tag{5A.1}$$

Faced with Equation (5A.1), Eve has to decide whether or not to tell the truth, that is, to reveal her true marginal valuation for every level of rocket display provision. She knows that from her selfish point of view, production should continue up to the point where the marginal benefit of consuming one more unit, MRS_{ra}^{Eve}, equals the marginal cost to her, which is just the increase in her tax bill. Thus, Eve would like to see the public good provided in an amount such that

$$\Delta T^{\text{Eve}} = MRS_{ra}^{\text{Eve}} \tag{5A.2}$$

---

[21] See also Groves and Ledyard [1977] and Tideman and Tullock [1976].

Substituting from Equation (5A.1) for ΔT^{Eve} gives us

$$MRT_{ra} - (MRS_{ra}^{\text{Total}} - MRS_{ra}^{\text{Eve}}) = MRS_{ra}^{\text{Eve}}$$

Adding $(MRS_{ra}^{\text{Total}} - MRS_{ra}^{\text{Eve}})$ to both sides of the equation yields

$$MRT_{ra} = MRS_{ra}^{\text{Total}} \qquad\qquad\qquad\qquad (5A.3)$$

Because conditions (5A.2) and (5A.3) are equivalent, it would be in Eve's interest to tell the truth if she knew that the government would use her information to achieve the allocation corresponding to Equation (5A.3).

But then she realizes that this is exactly what the government agent will do. Why? Remember that the agent promised to select a Pareto efficient provision given the information he receives. Such a provision is characterized by Equation (5.2) in the text. Since, by definition, $MRS_{ra}^{\text{Total}} = MRS_{ra}^{\text{Adam}} + MRS_{ra}^{\text{Eve}}$, equations (5A.3) and (5.2) are identical. Thus, the government's provision of rocket displays will satisfy equation (5A.3), and Eve has an incentive to tell the truth. Provided that Adam is confronted with the same kind of tax structure, he too has an incentive to be truthful. The free rider problem appears to have been solved.

To see intuitively why the system works, consider the right-hand side of Equation (5A.1), which shows how Eve's tax bill is determined. Note that $(MRS_{ra}^{\text{Total}} - MRS_{ra}^{\text{Eve}})$ is the sum of everyone's marginal benefit but Eve's. Hence, the increase in Eve's tax bill when output expands does not depend on her own marginal benefit, and therefore she has no incentive to lie about it.

There are several problems with this mechanism, many of which are shared by other devices to solve the free rider problem. First, taxpayers may not be able to figure out how the system works. (If you don't think this is a problem, try to explain the system to a friend who has not had any economics courses.) Second, even if the scheme can be made comprehensible, taxpayers have to be willing to make the effort to compute their entire demand curves and report them to the government. People may feel that it is not worth their time. Third, given that millions of people are involved in governmental decisions, the costs of gathering and assimilating all the information would be prohibitive.[22] (For relatively small groups like social clubs, this would not be as much of a problem.) We conclude that although preference revelation mechanisms of this kind provide interesting insights into the structure of the free rider problem, they are not a practical way for resolving it, at least for public sector decision making.

---

[22] There are some additional technical problems. There is no guarantee that the taxes collected will balance the budget, and it may be possible for coalitions to form and thwart the system. See Tideman and Tullock [1976].

CHAPTER 6 Externalities

We have always known that heedless self-interest was bad morals; we know now that it is bad economics.

FRANKLIN D. ROOSEVELT

A common observation is that the world is becoming an ever more interdependent place. The notion of interdependence occupies a central position in economics. After all, that is what markets are all about—people interacting as they trade goods and services.

Simple supply and demand models make it clear that people's actions have consequences for the welfare of others. Suppose large numbers of suburbanites decide that they want to live in an urban setting. As they move to the city, the price of urban land increases. Urban property owners are better off, but the welfare of tenants already there is lowered. Merchants in the city benefit from increased demand for their products, while their suburban counterparts are worse off. By the time the economy settles into a new equilibrium, the distribution of real income has changed substantially.

In this example, all the effects are transmitted *via changes in market prices*. Suppose that prior to the change in tastes, the allocation of resources was Pareto efficient. The shifts in supply and demand curves change relative prices, but the Fundamental Theorem of Welfare Economics guarantees that these will be brought into equality with the relevant marginal rates of substitution. Thus, the fact that the behavior of some people can affect the welfare of others does *not* necessarily cause market failure. As long as the effects are transmitted via prices, there are no adverse consequences for economic efficiency.[1]

---

[1] Of course, the new pattern of prices may be more or less desirable from a distributional point of view, depending on one's ethical judgments as embodied in the social welfare function. Effects on

However, people also affect each other in direct ways external to the market, often as the unintended by-product of some activity. Suppose that Sluggo operates a factory that dumps its garbage into a river nobody owns. Bill makes his living by fishing from the river. Sluggo's activities make Bill worse off in a direct way that is not the result of price changes. An **externality** occurs when the activity of one entity affects the welfare of another in a way that is outside the market. Unlike effects that are transmitted through market prices, externalities adversely affect economic efficiency.

In this chapter we analyze these inefficiencies and possible remedies for them. One of the most important applications of externality theory has been the debate over environmental quality, and much of the discussion focuses on this issue.

The Nature of Externalities

In the pollution example just given, clean water is an input to Sluggo's production process. Clean water gets used up just like all other inputs: land, labor, capital, and materials. Clean water is also a scarce resource with alternative uses, such as fishing by Bill and swimming. As such, efficiency requires that for the water he uses, Sluggo should pay a price that reflects the fact that water is a scarce resource valued for other activities. Instead, Sluggo pays a zero price and, as a consequence, uses the water in inefficiently large quantities.

Posing the externality problem this way allows us to expose its source. Sluggo uses his other inputs efficiently because he must pay their owners prices that reflect their value for alternative uses.[2] Otherwise, the owners of the inputs simply sell them elsewhere. However, if no one owns the river, everyone can use it for free. An externality, then, is a consequence of the failure or inability to establish property rights. If someone owned the river, a price would have to be paid for its use, and the externality would not materialize.

Suppose that Bill owned the stream. He could charge Sluggo a fee for polluting that reflected the damage done to his catch. Sluggo would take these charges into account when making his production decisions and no longer use the water inefficiently. On the other hand, if Sluggo owned the stream, he could make money by charging Bill for the privilege of fishing in it. The amount of money that Bill would be willing to pay Sluggo for the

---

welfare that are transmitted via prices are sometimes referred to as **pecuniary externalities.** Mishan [1971a] argues convincingly that because such effects are part of the normal functioning of a market, this is a confusing appellation. It is mentioned here only for the sake of completeness and is ignored henceforth.

[2] The situation is no different if Sluggo owns some of the inputs himself. In that case, the price paid by Sluggo is the income forgone by not selling those inputs to other producers.

right to fish in the stream would depend on the amount of pollution present. Hence, Sluggo would have an incentive not to pollute too much. Otherwise, he could not make much money from Bill.

The point is that as long as someone owns a resource, its price reflects the value for alternative uses, and the resource is therefore used efficiently.[3] In contrast, resources that are owned in common are abused because no one has an incentive to economize in their use.

To expand on the subject, note the following characteristics of externalities:

1. They can be produced by consumers as well as firms. Just think of the person who smokes a cigar in a crowded room, lowering the welfare of others by using up the common resource, fresh air.

2. The costliness of externalities depends on what is around to be damaged. In our example, it seems natural to refer to Sluggo as the ''polluter.'' However, we could just as well think of Bill as ''polluting'' the river with fishermen, increasing the social cost of Sluggo's waste disposal. As an alternative to fishing, using the river for waste disposal is not obviously worse from a social point of view. As we show later, it depends on the costs of alternatives for both activities.

3. Externalities can be positive or negative. If I spray my trees to kill gypsy moths, my neighbors benefit directly by my actions. If there is no way to get my neighbors to pay me for these benefits, I do not consider them when deciding how much to spray. Therefore, I do less spraying than is justified by the beneficial spillovers I create. In the case of a positive externality, an inefficiently low level of the activity is undertaken.

4. Public goods can be viewed as a special kind of externality. Specifically, when an individual creates an externality with full effects felt by every person in the economy, the externality is a pure public good. At times, the boundary between public goods and externalities is a bit fuzzy. In the tree-spraying example, for instance, the classification would depend on the distance at which the effects of the insecticide dissipated. If I kill the whole community's gypsy moths, then I have, in effect, created a pure public good. If only a few neighbors are affected, then it is an externality. Although externalities and public goods are quite similar from a formal point of view, in practice it is usually useful to distinguish between them.

---

[3] This assumes the absence of any other ''market failures'' such as the existence of monopoly.

Figure 6.1
An externality
problem

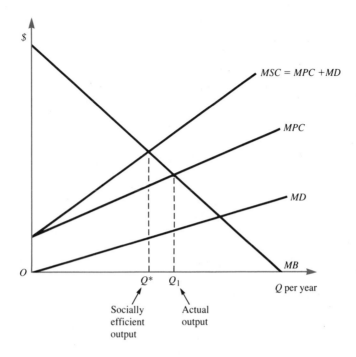

**Graphical
Analysis**

Figure 6.1 analyzes the Sluggo-Bill example described earlier. The horizontal axis measures the amount of output, *Q*, produced by Sluggo's
factory, and the vertical axis measures dollars.[4] The curve labeled *MB*
indicates the marginal benefit to Sluggo of each level of output; it is
assumed to decline as output increases.[5] Also associated with each level
of output is some marginal *private* cost, *MPC*. Marginal private costs
reflect payments made by Sluggo to the factors of production, and are
assumed here to increase with output. As a by-product of its activities,
the factory produces pollution that makes Bill worse off. Assume that as
the factory's output increases, so does the amount of pollution it creates.
The marginal damage inflicted on Bill by the pollution at each level of
output is denoted by *MD*. *MD* is drawn sloping upward, reflecting the
assumption that as Bill is subjected to additional pollution, he becomes
worse off at an increasing rate.

   If Sluggo is interested in maximizing profits, how much output does
he produce? Sluggo produces each unit of output for which the marginal
benefit *to him* exceeds the marginal cost *to him*. In Figure 6.1, he pro-

---

[4] It is assumed throughout this section that there are no other inefficiencies in the economy.

[5] If Sluggo consumes all the output of his factory, then the declining MB reflects the diminishing
marginal utility of the output. If Sluggo sold his output in a competitive market, MB would be constant at
the market price.

duces all levels of output for which *MB* exceeds *MPC*, but does not produce where *MPC* exceeds *MB*. Thus, he produces up to the output at which *MPC* intersects *MB*, at output Q_1.

From the point of view of society, production should take place as long as the marginal benefit *to society* exceeds the marginal cost to society. The marginal cost to society has two components: First are the inputs purchased by Sluggo. Their value is reflected in *MPC*. Second is the marginal damage done to Bill as reflected in *MD*. Hence, marginal social cost is *MPC plus MD*. Graphically, the marginal social cost schedule is found by adding together the heights of *MPC* and *MD* at each level of output. It is depicted in Figure 6.1 as *MSC*. Note that, by construction, the vertical distance between *MSC* and *MPC* is *MD*. (Because *MSC* = *MPC* + *MD*, it follows that *MSC* − *MPC* = *MD*.)

Efficiency from a social point of view requires production of only those units of output for which *MSC* exceeds *MB*. Thus, output should be produced just up to the point at which the schedules intersect, at Q^*.

Implications

This analysis suggests the following observations: First, unlike the case in which externalities are absent, there is no reason to expect private markets to produce the socially efficient level of output. In particular, when a good is associated with a negative externality, too much of it is produced relative to the efficient output.[6]

Second, the model not only shows that efficiency would be enhanced by a move from Q_1 to Q^* but also provides a way to measure the benefits from doing so. Figure 6.2 replicates from Figure 6.1 the marginal benefit (*MB*), marginal private cost (*MPC*), marginal damage (*MD*), and marginal social cost (*MSC*) schedules. When output is cut from Q_1 to Q^*, Sluggo loses profits. To calculate the precise size of his loss, recall that the marginal profit associated with any unit of output is the difference between marginal benefit and marginal private cost. If the marginal private cost of the eighth unit is $10 and its marginal benefit is $12, the marginal profit is $2. Geometrically, the marginal profit on a given unit of output is the vertical distance between *MB* and *MPC*. If Sluggo is forced to cut back from Q_1 to Q^*, he therefore loses the difference between the *MB* and *MPC* curves for each unit of production between Q_1 and Q^*. In Figure 6.2, this is represented as area *dcg*.

At the same time, however, Bill becomes better off because the less Sluggo produces, the smaller the damages done to Bill's fishery. For each unit that Sluggo's output is reduced, Bill gains an amount equal to the marginal damage associated with the unit of output. In Figure 6.2, Bill's

---

[6] Note that this model assumes the only way to reduce pollution is to reduce output. If antipollution technology is available, it may be possible to maintain output and still reduce pollution. However, the analysis is basically the same, because the adoption of the technology requires the use of resources.

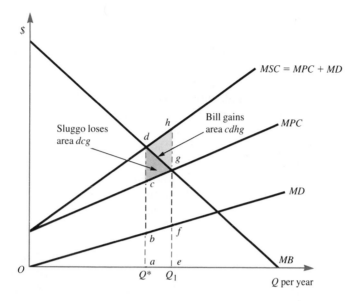

Figure 6.2

Gains and losses from moving to an efficient level of output

gain for each unit of output reduction is the vertical distance between *MD* and the horizontal axis. Therefore, Bill's gain when output is reduced from Q_1 to Q^* is the area under the marginal damage curve between Q^* and Q_1, *abfe*. Now note that *abfe* equals area *cdhg*. This is by construction—the vertical distance between *MSC* and *MPC* is *MD*, which is the same as the vertical distance between *MD* and the horizontal axis.

In sum, if output were reduced from Q_1 to Q^*, Sluggo would lose area *dcg* and Bill would gain area *cdhg*. If from society's point of view, a dollar to Sluggo is equivalent to a dollar to Bill, then moving from Q_1 to Q^* yields a net gain to society equal to the difference between *cdhg* and *dcg*, which is *dhg*.

Third, the analysis implies that zero pollution is not socially desirable as a general rule. Finding the right amount of pollution requires trading off its benefits and costs, and this generally occurs at some positive level of pollution. Because virtually all productive activity involves some pollution, the requirement that pollution be set at zero would be equivalent to no production whatsoever, clearly an inefficient solution. If all this seems only like common sense, it is. But note that the U.S. Congress once set as a national goal that "the discharge of pollutants into the navigable waters be eliminated by 1985" [Baumol and Oates, 1979, p. 211]. The adoption of such infeasible and inefficient objectives is not only silly but, as shall be argued later, may also actually hinder *any* movement away from points like Q_1.

Finally, to implement the framework of Figure 6.2, it is not enough to be able to draw some hypothetical marginal damage and benefit curves.

Their actual shapes for any given pollutant must be determined, at least approximately. However, difficult practical questions arise when it comes to identifying and valuing the damage done by pollution.

What activities produce pollutants?   The types and quantities of pollution associated with various production processes must be identified. Consider acid rain, a phenomenon that has caused widespread concern. Scientists have shown that acid rain forms when sulfur oxides and nitrogen oxides emitted into the air react with water vapor to create acids. These acids fall to earth in rain and snow, increasing the general level of acidity with potentially harmful effects on plant and animal life.

However, it is not known just how much of acid rain is associated with productive activities and how much with natural activities such as plant decay and volcanic eruptions. Moreover, it is hard to determine what amounts of nitrogen and sulfur emissions generated in a given region eventually become acid rain. It depends in part on local weather conditions and in part on the extent to which other pollutants such as nonmethane hydrocarbons are present. Finally, some scientific studies have indicated there is no strong evidence that acidification has been getting worse over time [Funkhauser, 1983, p. A27].

Which pollutants do harm?   The ability of health practitioners and ecologists to conduct large-scale controlled experiments on the effects of pollution is severely limited. Hence, it is often difficult to pinpoint just what effect a given pollutant has. Acid rain may be a case in point: Preliminary results from the federal government's 10-year, $500 million National Acid Precipitation Assessment Program "suggests that acid rain is having virtually no effect on agricultural output, and that its effects on forests are limited to mountain tops in the northeastern United States" [Portney, 1990, p. 175]. This finding has led some scientists to disagree with the consensus that acid rain causes great damage in the United States. This kind of uncertainty can obviously lead to serious problems in formulating environmental policy. Lester Lave and Gilbert Omenn [1981, p. 45] argue that some of the air pollutants that have been the focus of U.S. environmental policy are considerably less dangerous than other pollutants that are officially ignored.

What is the value of the damage done?   Even if the physical damage a pollutant creates is determined, the value of getting rid of it must be calculated. When economists think about measuring the value of something, typically they think of people's willingness to pay for it. If you are willing to pay $162 for a bicycle, that is its value to you.

Unlike bicycles, there is no explicit market in which pollution is bought and sold. How then can people's marginal willingness to pay for pollution removal be measured? Some attempts have been made to infer it indirectly by studying housing prices. When people shop for houses, they consider both the quality of the house itself and the characteristics of the neighborhood, such as cleanliness of the streets and quality of schools. Suppose in addition that families care about the level of air pollution in the neighborhoods. Consider two identical houses situated in two identical neighborhoods, except that the first is in an unpolluted area, and the second is in a polluted area. We expect that the house in the unpolluted area has a higher price. This price differential measures people's willingness to pay for clean air.

These observations suggest a natural strategy for estimating people's willingness to pay for clean air. Examine houses identical in all respects except for the surrounding air quality and compare their prices. The apparent problem is to find such houses. Luckily, the necessity of doing so can be avoided if the statistical technique of multiple regression analysis is used (see Chapter 3). David Harrison and Daniel Rubinfeld [1978] estimate a regression equation in which the left-hand variable is the value of owner-occupied homes in a given community. The right-hand variables include the factors that should influence house value: number of rooms, age of house, crime rate in the town, and so forth. The right-hand side also includes a measure of air pollution, the concentration of nitrogen oxide measured in parts per hundred million.

If the equation is specified correctly, the parameter multiplying the nitrogen oxide variable indicates the *independent* effect of the pollutants on house values, and hence, people's willingness to pay for their removal. Harrison and Rubinfeld's estimates [1978, p. 91] suggest that when the annual average concentration of nitrogen oxide is about five parts per hundred million, a middle-income family would be willing to pay an amount equal to about 6 percent of their house value in return for a one part per hundred million improvement.

As stressed in Chapter 3, the validity of econometric analysis depends in part on the completeness with which the model is specified. If there are important determinants of housing prices omitted by Harrison and Rubinfeld, their estimate of the pollution effect may be unreliable. More fundamentally, the use of a willingness-to-pay measure can be questioned. People may be ignorant about the effects of air pollution on their health, and hence underestimate the value of reducing it. The econometric approach is promising, but it does not close the debate.

Conclusion

We conclude that implementing the framework of Figure 6.2 requires the skills of biologists, engineers, ecologists, and health practitioners, among others. A resolutely interdisciplinary approach to investigating the pollution problem is needed. Having said this, however, we emphasize that even with superb engineering and biological data, efficient decisions simply cannot be reached without applying the economist's tool of marginal analysis.

Possible Remedies

A number of alternative solutions for achieving the efficient level of output Q^* have been proposed, as follows:[7]

Taxes

Sluggo produces inefficiently because the prices he faces for inputs incorrectly signal social costs. Specifically, because his input prices are too low, the price of his output is too low. A natural solution, suggested by the British economist A. C. Pigou, is to levy a tax on the polluter that makes up for the fact that some of his inputs are priced too low. A **Pigouvian tax** is a tax levied on each unit of a polluter's output in an amount just equal to the marginal damage it inflicts *at the efficient level of output*. Figure 6.3 reproduces the example of Figures 6.1 and 6.2. In this case, the marginal damage done at the efficient output Q^* is distance cd. This is the Pigouvian tax. (Remember that the vertical distance between MSC and MPC is MD.)

How does Sluggo react if a tax of cd dollars per unit of output is imposed? The tax raises Sluggo's effective marginal cost. For each unit he produces, Sluggo has to make payments both to the suppliers of his inputs (measured by MPC) *and* to the tax collector (measured by cd). Geometrically, Sluggo's new marginal cost schedule is found by adding cd to MPC at each level of output. This is done by shifting up MPC by a vertical distance equal to cd.

Profit maximization requires that Sluggo produce up to the output at which marginal benefit equals marginal cost. This now occurs at the intersection of MB and $MPC + cd$ which is at the efficient output Q^*. In effect, the tax forces Sluggo to take into account the costs of the externality that he generates, and hence, induces him to produce efficiently. Note that the tax generates revenue of cd dollars for each of the id units produced ($id = OQ^*$). Hence, tax revenue is $cd \times id,$ which is equal to the area of rectangle $ijcd$ in Figure 6.3.[8] It would be tempting to use these revenues to compensate Bill, who still is being hurt by Sluggo's activities, although to a lesser extent than before the tax. However, caution must be exercised. If it becomes known that anyone who fishes along the river receives compensation for fishing there, then some people may choose to fish there who otherwise would not have done so. Then an inefficiently large amount of fishing would be done in the river. The key point is that compensation to the victim of the pollution is not necessary to achieve efficiency.

---

[7] The list of possibilities considered here is by no means exhaustive. See Baumol and Oates [1979] for a careful discussion of several alternatives.

[8] It is assumed that these tax revenues are spent by the government in such a way that none of the schedules in Figure 6.3 changes position.

Figure 6.3
Analysis of a
Pigouvian tax

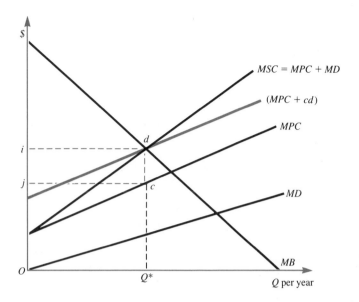

There are practical problems in implementing a Pigouvian tax scheme. In light of the previously mentioned difficulties in estimating the marginal damage function, it is bound to be hard to find the correct tax rate. Still, sensible compromises can be made. Suppose that a certain type of automobile produces noxious fumes. In theory, a tax based on the number of miles driven enhances efficiency. But a tax based on mileage might be so cumbersome to administer as to be infeasible. The government might instead consider levying a special sales tax on the car, even though it is not ownership of the car per se that determines the size of the externality, but the amount it is driven. The sales tax would not lead to the most efficient possible result, but it still might lead to a substantial improvement over the status quo.

More generally, the tax approach assumes that it is known who is doing the polluting and in what quantities. In many cases, these questions are very hard to answer. Of course, the relevant issue is not whether Pigouvian taxes are a perfect method of dealing with externalities, but whether or not they are likely to be better than the other alternatives.

Although we have been discussing Pigouvian taxation in the context of environmental damage, it is equally relevant for dealing with other externalities. Heavy trucks, for example, create externalities by damaging highways. The marginal damage depends on the weight of the truck and the number of axles. Kenneth Small and Clifford Winston [1986] estimate that if trucking firms were forced to pay a tax equal to the marginal damage caused by their vehicles, the welfare gain to society— area *dhg* in Figure 6.2—would be $1.2 billion per year.

Figure 6.4

Analysis of a
Pigouvian subsidy

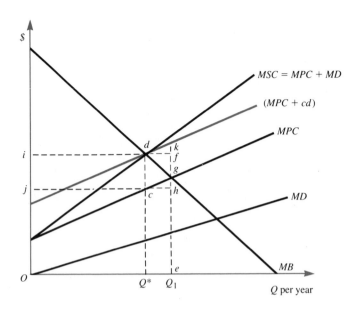

Subsidies

Under the assumption that the number of polluting firms is fixed, the efficient level of production can be obtained by paying the polluter not to pollute. Although this notion may at first seem peculiar, it works much like the tax scheme. This is because a subsidy for not polluting is simply another method of raising the polluter's effective cost of production.

Suppose that the government announces that it will pay Sluggo a subsidy of cd for each unit of output that he does *not* produce. What will Sluggo do? In Figure 6.4, Sluggo's marginal benefit at output level Q_1 is measured by the distance between *MB* and the horizontal axis, ge. The marginal cost of producing at Q_1 is the sum of the amount that Sluggo pays for his inputs (which we read off the *MPC* curve), *and* the subsidy of cd which he forgoes by producing. Once again, then, the perceived marginal cost schedule is $MPC + cd$. At output Q_1, this is distance $ek (= eg + gk)$. But ek exceeds the marginal benefit, ge. As long as the marginal cost exceeds the marginal benefit, it does not make sense for Sluggo to produce the Q_1st unit of output. Instead, he should forgo its production and accept the subsidy. The same line of reasoning indicates that Sluggo will choose not to produce any output in excess of Q^*. At all output levels to the right of Q^*, the sum of the marginal private cost and the subsidy exceeds the marginal benefit. On the other hand, at all points to the left of Q^*, it is worthwhile for Sluggo to produce even though he has to give up the subsidy. For these output levels, the total opportunity cost, $MPC + cd$, is less than the marginal benefit. Hence, the subsidy induces Sluggo to produce just to Q^*, the efficient output.

The distributional consequences of the tax and subsidy schemes differ dramatically. Instead of having to pay the tax of *idcj,* Sluggo receives a payment equal to the number of units of forgone production, *ch,* times the subsidy per unit, *cd,* which equals rectangle *dfhc* in Figure 6.4.[9] That an efficient solution can be associated with different income distributions is no surprise. It is analogous to the result from Chapter 4; there is an infinite number of efficient allocations in the Edgeworth Box, each of which is associated with its own distribution of real income.

In addition to the problems associated with the Pigouvian tax scheme, the subsidy program has a few of its own. First, recall that the analysis of Figure 6.4 is based on the assumption of a fixed number of firms. The subsidy leads to higher profits, so in the long run, firms that would not have located along the river may be induced to do so by the lure of these profits. Hence, the subsidy may cause so many new firms to relocate on the river that total pollution actually increases.

Second, the subsidy payments have to be raised by taxes levied somewhere in the economy. In general, taxation distorts people's incentives. And it is not obvious that these distortion effects would be less costly than the externality itself. (The efficiency costs of taxation are discussed in detail in Chapter 14.)

Finally, subsidies may be undesirable from a moral perspective. As E. J. Mishan [1971a, p. 25] notes:

> It may be argued [that] the freedom to operate noisy vehicles, or pollutive plant, does incidentally damage the welfare of others, while the freedom desired by members of the public to live in clean and quiet surroundings does not, of itself, reduce the welfare of others. If such arguments can be sustained, there is a case . . . for making polluters legally liable.

Auction Pollution Permits

Another method of achieving Q^* is to sell producers permits to pollute. The government announces that it will sell permits to dump into the river the amount of garbage associated with output Q^*. Firms bid for the right to own these permissions to pollute, and the permissions go to the firms with the highest bids. The fee charged is that which "clears the market"—the amount of pollution equals the level set by the government.

In the simple model, the pollution permit and the Pigouvian tax are identical. Both achieve the efficient level of pollution. Implementing both requires knowledge of who is polluting and in what quantities. Baumol and Oates [1979, p. 251] argue that pollution permits have some advantages over the tax scheme from a practical point of view. One of the most

---

[9] In Figure 6.4, Q_1 is the baseline from which Sluggo's reduction in output is measured. In principle, any baseline to the right of Q^* would do.

important is that the permit scheme reduces uncertainty about the ultimate level of pollution. If the government is certain about the shapes of the marginal private cost and marginal benefit schedules of Figure 6.3, it can safely predict how a Pigouvian tax will affect behavior. But if there is poor information about these schedules, it is hard to know for sure how much a particular tax will reduce pollution. If lack of information forces policymakers to choose the pollution standard arbitrarily, with a system of permits, there is more certainty that this level will be obtained. In addition, under the assumption that firms are profit-maximizers, they will find the cost minimizing technology to attain the standard.

Moreover, when the economy is experiencing inflation, the market price of pollution rights would be expected to keep pace automatically, while changing the tax rate could require a lengthy administrative procedure. On the other hand, one possible problem with the auctioning scheme is that large firms might be able to buy up pollution licenses in excess of the firms' cost-minimizing requirements to deter other firms from entering the market. Whether such strategic behavior is likely to occur is hard to predict.

Establish Property Rights

If the root cause of an externality is the absence of property rights, perhaps the most straightforward way to cure the problem is to put the resource in question into private hands. Suppose that property rights to the river are assigned to Sluggo. Assume further that it is costless for Bill and Sluggo to bargain with each other. Is it possible for the two parties to strike a bargain which will result in output being reduced from Q_1?

Sluggo would be willing to not produce a given unit of output as long as he received a payment which exceeded his net incremental gain from producing that unit ($MB - MPC$). On the other hand, Bill would be willing to pay Sluggo not to produce a given unit as long as the payment were less than the marginal damage done to him, MD. As long as the amount that Bill is willing to pay Sluggo exceeds the cost to Sluggo of not producing, the opportunity for a bargain exists. Algebraically, the requirement is that $MD > (MB - MPC)$. Figure 6.5 (which reproduces the information from Figure 6.1) indicates that at output Q_1, $MB - MPC$ is zero, while MD is positive. Hence, MD exceeds $MB - MPC$, and there is scope for a bargain.

Similar reasoning indicates that the payment Bill would be willing to make exceeds $MB - MPC$ at every output level to the right of Q^*. In contrast, to the left of Q^*, the amount of money that Sluggo would demand to reduce his output would exceed what Bill would be willing to pay. Hence, Bill pays Sluggo to reduce output just to Q^*, the efficient level. We cannot tell without more information exactly how much Bill will end up paying Sluggo. This depends on the relative bargaining strengths of the two parties. Regardless of how the gains from the bargain are divided, however, production ends up at Q^*.

Figure 6.5
Coase theorem

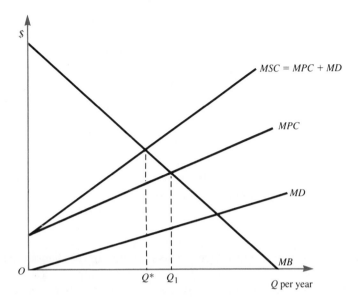

Now suppose that the shoe is put on the other foot, and Bill is assigned the property rights to the stream. The bargaining process now consists in Sluggo's paying for Bill's permission to pollute. Bill is willing to accept some pollution as long as the payment is greater than the marginal damage (*MD*) to his fishing enterprise. Sluggo finds it worthwhile to pay for the privilege of producing as long as the amount is less than the value of *MB* − *MPC* for that unit of output. Reasoning similar to the foregoing suggests that they have every incentive to reach an agreement whereby Bill sells Sluggo the right to produce at *Q**.

The conclusion is that the efficient solution will be achieved *independently* of who is assigned the property rights, as long as *someone* is assigned those rights. This result, known as the **Coase Theorem,** implies that once property rights are established, no government intervention is required to deal with externalities [Coase, 1960]. The Coase Theorem is especially attractive to those who are predisposed against government intervention in the economy. However, there are at least two reasons society cannot always depend on the Coase Theorem to solve externality problems.

First, the theorem requires that the costs of bargaining do not deter the parties from finding their way to the efficient solution. However, externalities such as air pollution involve literally millions of people (both polluters and pollutees). It is difficult to imagine them getting together for negotiations at a sufficiently low cost.[10]

---

[10] As we have emphasized earlier, there is no guarantee that the transactions costs of implementing a government solution will be less.

Second, the theorem assumes that resource owners can identify the source of damages to their property and legally prevent the damages. Consider again the important case of air pollution. Even if property rights to air were established, it is not clear how owners would be able to identify which of thousands of potential polluters was responsible for dirtying their air space and for what proportion of the damage each was liable.

The Coase Theorem, then, is most relevant for cases in which there are a few parties involved and the sources of the externality are well defined. Of course, even when these conditions hold, the assignment of property rights *is* relevant from the point of view of income distribution. Property rights are valuable; if Bill owns the stream it will increase his income relative to Sluggo's, and vice versa.

Regulation

Under regulation, each polluter is told to reduce pollution by a certain amount or else face legal sanctions. In the diagrammatic analysis, Sluggo would simply be ordered to reduce output to Q^*.

Regulation is likely to be inefficient when there is more than one firm. To see this, assume that there are two firms, X and Z, which generate the same externality. In Figure 6.6, output of firms X and Z is measured on the horizontal axis and dollars on the vertical. MB_X is the marginal benefit schedule for X and MB_Z the schedule for Z. For expositional ease only, X and Z are assumed to have identical MPC schedules and profit-maximizing outputs $X_1 = Z_1$.

Suppose it is known that the marginal damage at the efficient level of total output is d dollars. Then efficiency requires that each firm produce at the point of intersection of its marginal benefit curve with the sum of its marginal private cost curve and d. The efficient outputs are denoted X^* and Z^* in Figure 6.6. The crucial thing to observe is that efficiency does *not* require the firms to reduce pollution equally. The efficient reduction in production of Z is much greater than that of X. Here this is due to different MB schedules, but in general, each firm's appropriate reduction in output depends on the shapes of its marginal benefit and marginal private cost curves. Hence, a regulatory rule that mandates all firms to cut back by equal amounts (either in absolute or proportional terms) leads to some firms producing too much and others too little.

Intuitively, this analysis simply illustrates that the costs and benefits of pollution reduction are likely to differ from case to case. A car that operates in a relatively uninhabited area creates less damage than one that operates in a heavily populated area. What sense does it make for both cars to have exactly the same emissions standard? Under U.S. policy, all cars must meet standards that were set to improve the air quality in just a half dozen heavily polluted cities. Clearly the policy is inefficient. Of course, the regulatory body could assign each polluter its specially designed production quota. But in the presence of a large number of polluters, this is administratively infeasible.

Figure 6.6
Two polluting firms

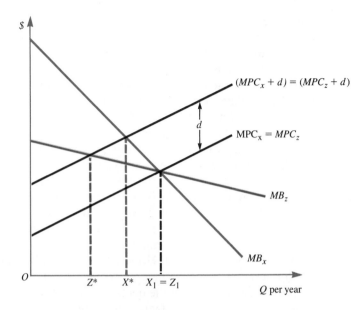

A number of empirical studies have sought to compare the costs of obtaining a given reduction in pollution using economic incentives and regulations. The particular results depend on the type of pollution being considered and the site of the pollution. In every case, though, economic incentives provide a much cheaper solution; in some instances, the incentive approach is only one-tenth the cost of regulation. (See Oates [1985, p. 332].)

Evaluation

Except in cases where the Coase Theorem is likely to be relevant, the presence of externalities requires some kind of intervention to achieve efficiency. Implementing any environmental policy entails a host of difficult technical issues. No policy is likely to do a perfect job. However, of the options available, most economists prefer Pigouvian taxes or the sale of pollution permits. Generally, these are more likely to achieve efficient outcomes than either subsidies or direct regulation.

The U.S. Response

How do real-world responses to externality problems compare to the solutions suggested by theory? The main federal law dealing with air pollution is the Clean Air Act of 1963 and subsequent amendments. In the clean air amendments passed in 1970, Congress set national air quality standards that were to be met independent of the costs of doing so. An Environmental Protection Agency (EPA) was established to set the standards, and ensure that the states attained the standards by 1975. Major additions to the Clean Air Act were introduced in 1990. One provision mandated that by 1995 all gasoline sold in the country's nine smoggiest cities had to be reformulated to cut emissions by 15 percent. Another provision required automakers to produce 150,000 super-clean cars annually, beginning with the 1996 model year. These examples illustrate the general U.S. tendency to rely on regulation rather than market incentives.[11] As stressed above, this is a costly approach to correcting externalities. According to estimates by Paul Portney [1990], as a consequence of the 1990 additions to the Clean Air Act, by the year 2005 the United States will increase its spending on pollution control by about $30 billion in return for benefits that range from $6 to $25 billion dollars.

While it is obviously too early to determine the efficacy of the 1990 laws, one can ask whether the earlier Clean Air legislation accomplished its goals. Even ignoring the issue of costs, the record is mixed and difficult to interpret. Certain types of air pollution such as nitrogen oxides have actually increased since the original Clean Air Act passed. On the other hand, the presence of a number of dangerous substances such as particulate matter has decreased. However, one must be cautious in attributing such decreases to environmental regulation. Perhaps, for example, the improvement was due to the decline in industrial activity associated with a generally sluggish manufacturing sector, and not to the EPA at all. Paul MacAvoy [1984] estimated a regression in which the amount of pollution in a given year was the dependent variable, and various measures of business conditions were used as regressors. He found that decreases in pollution were due to the economic variables; regulation was irrelevant. Although some other analysts of the data have given the EPA a bit more credit [Oates, 1985], there is little disagreement that the performance of regulation has been disappointing. Indeed, as of 1990, 96 areas had missed regulatory deadlines for meeting EPA health standards for ozone, a major component of smog.

We have already shown why a regulatory approach like the Clean Air Act is likely to be inefficient. Why has it been so ineffectual as well? William Baumol [1976] emphasizes how the efficacy of regulation depends on the vigilance of the regulator, that is:

> the promptness with which orders are issued, the severity of their provisions, the strength of the regulator's resistance to demands for modifications, his effectiveness in detecting and documenting violations, his vigor and success in prosecuting them, and the severity of the penalties imposed by the judicial mechanism. [P. 445]

This is a tall order, especially considering the political pressures under which the regulator is likely to be acting. In contrast, Pigouvian taxes "depend not on the watchfulness of the regulator but on the reliable tenacity of the tax collector. They work by inviting the polluter to avoid

---

[11] Excellent summaries of the act's provisions are Portney [1990], and Oates [1985]. Oates also discusses the Clean Water Act, which takes the same general regulatory approach as the Clean Air Act.

his payments through the loophole deliberately left to him—the reduction of his emissions'' [Baumol, 1976, p. 446].

In addition, Lawrence White [1976] has documented how the ''or else'' approach of regulation often backfires. The ultimate threat is to close down the polluting factory. In many cases, however, such closure would create major dislocations among workers and/or consumers and is therefore politically difficult. Consider the case of Olean, New York, a factory town with a dangerously polluted water supply. In 1985 the EPA ordered the polluting firms to pay millions of dollars to finance a clean-up. Many residents believed that this would be tantamount to forcing the firms to close, and therefore decided to support the corporations in their battle against the EPA. Indeed, the City Council voted to defy the EPA's rulings [Perlez, 1985].

White's analysis is also consistent with a rather bizarre political situation that developed during the first Reagan administration. Environmentalists accused the head of the EPA, Ann Gorsuch, of trying to gut the Clean Air Act and thus expose the environment to damage. What action prompted these charges? All she did was announce her intention to stringently carry out the provisions of the act! Gorsuch threatened to impose the statutory sanctions for areas that did not meet air quality standards. The sanctions included withholding federal highway funds and federal grants. Presumably, both Gorsuch and the environmentalists realized that actually enforcing the law would lead to a public outcry and perhaps an eventual change in the statute.

This is not to say that direct regulation is never useful. When very toxic substances are involved, it might be the best solution. But in general, the regulatory approach is probably the source of much of the failure in environmental policy. Why then is it so popular? Perhaps legislators like the immediate sense of doing something that enacting regulations gives them, even though more passive measures like Pigouvian taxes would probably do the job better. A cynic would argue that the regulatory solution is the result of politicians' desire to have it both ways: Pass noble sounding legislation to please environmentalists, but make it unworkable to keep business happy.

Implications for Income Distribution

Our main focus so far has been on the efficiency aspects of externalities. Welfare economics indicates that to maximize social welfare requires taking distributional as well as efficiency considerations into account. However, attempts to assess the distributional implications of environmental improvement raise a number of difficult questions.

Who Benefits?

In our simple model, the distribution of benefits is a trivial issue because there is only one type of pollution and one pollution victim. In reality, there are many different types of individuals who suffer differently from various externalities. Some evidence suggests that poor neighborhoods tend to have more exposure to air pollution than high-income neighborhoods [Baumol and Oates, 1979, p. 178]. If this is true, lowering the level of air pollution might make the distribution of real income more equal, other things being the same. On the other hand, the benefits of environmental programs that enhance the quality of recreational areas such as national parks probably benefit mainly high-income families, who tend to be their main users [Baumol and Oates, 1979, pp. 178, 180].

Even knowledge of who is suffering from a given externality does not tell us how much it is worth to them to have it removed. Accounting for willingness to pay can have a major impact on conclusions about the distribution of benefits. Suppose that a high-income family would be willing to pay more for a given improvement in air quality than a low-income family. Then even if a cleanup program reduces more of the *physical* amount of pollution for low- than for high-income families, in *dollar* terms the program can end up favoring those with high incomes.

Who Bears the Costs?

Suppose that large numbers of polluting firms are induced to reduce output by government policy. As these firms contract, the demand for the inputs they employ falls, which tends to make the owners of these inputs worse off.[12] Some of the polluters' former workers may suffer unemployment in the short run and be forced to work at lower wages in the long run. If these workers have low incomes, environmental cleanup makes the distribution of real income more unequal.

The extent to which the poor bear the costs of environmental protection is a source of bitter public controversy. A critic of environmentalism argued, "Let's face it, a family in Harlem or the Texas barrio is a lot more concerned about jobs and cheap electricity than in visiting the beautiful wilderness. . . . Where's the sensitivity and concern to those people by all these organizations and groups litigating in the District of Columbia?"[13] Environmentalists have labeled such assertions "job blackmail" and argue that there is no good evidence that the poor are really hurt.

Another consideration is that if polluting firms are forced to take into account marginal social costs, their products will tend to become more expensive. From an efficiency point of view, this is totally desirable, because otherwise prices give incorrect signals concerning full resource costs. Nevertheless, there will be a tendency for buyers of these commod-

---

[12] More specifically, under certain conditions, those inputs used relatively intensively in the production of the polluting good will suffer income losses. See Chapter 13 under "General Equilibrium Models."

[13] Dan M. Burt, quoted in "In Watt's Corner," *San Francisco Chronicle,* October 1, 1981, p. 18. For further argument along these lines, see Tucker [1982].

ities to be made worse off.[14] If the commodities so affected tend to be consumed primarily by high-income groups, the distribution of real income becomes more equal, other things being the same. Thus, to assess the distributional implications of reducing pollution, we also need to know the pattern of demand for the goods produced by polluting companies.

It is obviously a formidable task to determine how the costs of pollution control have been distributed. In one careful study, David Robison [1985] estimated that the higher a family's income, the *smaller* the proportion of its income reduced by antipollution measures. He calculated that for an individual at the bottom of the income distribution, existing pollution controls cost about 1 percent of family income. For a household at the top of the income distribution, the figure was closer to 0.22 percent. If these results are correct, they pose a serious dilemma for those who favor both a more equal income distribution and a cleaner environment.

Positive Externalities

Most of the focus in this chapter has been on negative externalities. We did observe, however, that spillover effects could just as well be positive. The formal analysis of this case is symmetrical. Suppose that when a scientist does research, the marginal private benefit *(MPB)* and marginal cost *(MC)* schedules are as depicted in Figure 6.7. The scientist chooses

Figure 6.7
Positive externality

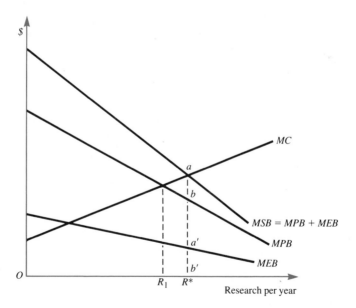

---

[14] One cannot know a priori how high consumer prices will rise. It depends on the shapes of the supply and demand schedules. See Chapter 13 under "Tax Incidence: General Remarks."

research output R_1, where $MC = MPB$. Assume further that the scientist's work enables industrial firms to produce their products more cheaply, but that the firms do not have to pay for using scientific results because these are part of general knowledge.[15] In Figure 6.7, the marginal benefit to other firms of each quantity of research is denoted MEB (for marginal external benefit). The marginal *social* benefit of research is the sum of MPB and MEB, which is depicted as schedule MSB.

Efficiency requires the equality of marginal cost and marginal *social* benefit, which occurs at R^*. Hence, an insufficient quantity of research is done. Just as a negative externality can be corrected by a Pigouvian tax, a positive externality can be corrected by a Pigouvian subsidy. Specifically, if the scientist is given a subsidy equal to the marginal external benefit at the optimum—distance ab in Figure 6.7—the scientist will be induced to produce efficiently.[16] The lesson is clear: When an individual or firm produces positive externalities, the market will underprovide the activity or good, but an appropriate subsidy can remedy the situation. Of course, all the difficulties concerning problems in measuring the quantity and value of the externality are still relevant.

A Cautionary Note

Many people who have never heard the term *positive externality* nevertheless have a good intuitive grasp of the concept and its policy implications. They understand that if they can convince the government their activities create beneficial spillovers, they may be able to dip into the treasury for a subsidy. Requests for such subsidies must be viewed with caution for two reasons:

- One way or another, the subsidy has to come from resources extracted from taxpayers. Hence, implicit in all subsidies is a redistribution of income from taxpayers as a whole to the particular recipients. Even if the efficiency consequences of the subsidy are desirable, the distributional implications may not be. This depends on the value judgments embodied in the social welfare function.

- When the presence of a beneficial externality is claimed, its precise nature must be determined. The fact that an activity is socially desirable per se does *not* mean that a subsidy is required for efficiency. A subsidy is appropriate only if the market does not allow those performing the activity to capture the full marginal return. For example, a brilliant surgeon who does much good for humanity creates no positive externality as long as the

---

[15] If the scientist produces an invention, then this type of situation can partially be avoided by patent laws. But in many cases, the results of pure research are not patentable, even though they may be used for commercial purposes.

[16] Note that by construction, $ab = a'b'$.

surgeon's salary reflects the incremental value of his or her services.

We illustrate these points with two examples.

Owner-occupied housing.   Through a variety of provisions in the U.S. federal income tax code, owner-occupied housing receives a substantial subsidy. (These provisions are detailed in Chapter 16.) This subsidy was worth almost $43 billion in 1989 [U.S. Bureau of the Census, 1990, p. 314]. How can this subsidy be justified? Arguments usually boil down to an assertion that homeownership creates positive externalities. Homeowners take good care of their property and keep it clean, which makes the other people in their neighborhoods better off; hence, the externality. In addition, homeownership provides an individual with a stake in the nation. This tends to increase social stability, another desirable spillover effect.

It is indisputable that careful maintenance of property creates positive externalities. But is it home ownership as such that induces this desirable behavior? Henry Aaron [1972] argues that the beneficial side effects associated with homeownership are probably a consequence of the fact that the 65 percent of American families who are homeowners tend to have relatively high incomes. (The median income of homeowners is almost twice that of renters [U.S. Bureau of the Census, 1990, p. 445].) Neither is there any evidence that low ownership rates necessarily contribute to social instability. In Switzerland, which is not known for its revolutionary tendencies, only about 28 percent of the dwellings are owner occupied [Melton, 1979, p. 4].

Of course, even if the subsidy does not contribute to correcting an inefficiency, it might be justifiable on equity grounds. But as just noted, homeowners tend to have higher incomes than renters. Thus, only if the distributional objective is to increase income inequality does a subsidy for homeownership make sense from this point of view.

Higher education.   The federal government has been supporting higher education on a large scale since the mid-1960s.[17] In 1965, outlays for direct loans, grants, and work-study programs amounted to $250 million. This figure reached $19.1 billion by 1990. As of the mid-1980s, the most extensive program was the guaranteed student loan program which covered about 3.5 million students. Under this program, the federal government guarantees private lenders that it will repay loans on which students default and subsidizes the difference between the rates charged and the market rate of interest. The role of outright grants has decreased since

---

[17] For further details, see Congressional Budget Office [1991]. There is also substantial support for higher education from the states.

the 1970s, although the amounts involved—$4.6 billion in 1990—are not trivial.

One rationalization for subsidizing higher education is that it produces externalities.[18] This argument is quite convincing for primary and secondary schooling. Such schooling not only increases an individual's earning capacity, it also contributes to the literate and well-informed populace that is generally agreed to be necessary for a smoothly functioning modern democracy.[19] Some argue that college education should be subsidized because it increases productivity. That college increases productivity may be true,[20] but *as long as the earnings of college graduates reflect their higher productivity, there is no externality*. In fact, the earnings of college graduates are substantially higher than their counterparts who have not attended college. Labor economists estimate that other things being the same, each year of schooling increases annual earnings between roughly 5 and 11 percent.[21] For the externality argument to be convincing, a case has to be made that the productivity gain *exceeds* this differential.

Even if such evidence were produced, it would not justify the form of current programs which subsidize all eligible students at the same rate. Are the external benefits of all kinds of college training equal? Do art history, accounting, and premedical courses all produce the same externalities? If not, efficiency requires that they be subsidized differentially.

It is observed that if the subsidies were cut, fewer people would attend college. This is probably true, but alone is no justification for the subsidy. If there were subsidies for young people who wanted to open auto repair shops and these were cut, then the number of auto repair shops would also decline. Why should a potential car mechanic be treated differently from a potential classicist?

Some argue that if government subsidies for college students were removed, students from poorer families would bear the brunt of the burden, because they find it especially difficult to obtain loans from the private sector. This argument has considerable merit. By their very nature, it is difficult to provide collateral for loans for "human capital" investments, so markets for these loans may not materialize. One possible remedy for this market failure is for the government to make loans available at the going rate of interest. Unless the existence of a positive externality can be established, there is no efficiency basis for subsidizing the interest rate. What about the problem of paying back the debt after graduation? As Peter Passell [1985] notes, "The prospect of heavy debt after graduation would no doubt discourage some students from borrowing.

---

[18] We discuss aspects of educational policy other than externalities in Chapter 21.

[19] Bowen [1964] provides further details.

[20] There is some controversy with respect to whether the higher incomes associated with more education are actually due to enhanced productivity, or to the fact that college is a screening device that identifies for prospective employers those individuals with high ability. [See Aaron, 1978, Chapter 3.]

[21] See, for example, Card and Krueger [1990].

But that may be the wisest form of restraint. Someone finally has to pay the bill, and it is hard to see why that should be the taxpayers rather than the direct beneficiary of the schooling.''

The theory of welfare economics recognizes that it is possible to justify an inefficient program if it produces "desirable" effects on income distribution. Subsidies for college students represent a transfer from taxpayers as a whole to college goers. Looking at the student as part of the family he or she has grown up in, it seems that educational aid programs are indeed aimed at increasing income equality. Eighty percent of full-time undergraduates from families with incomes below $11,000 receive federal student aid, while only fifteen percent of students from families with incomes above $50,000 get federal help [Congressional Budget Office, 1991, p. 95]. Remember, though, that most college students are individuals about to form their own households, and that the lifetime incomes of college graduates are higher than those of the population as a whole. Such a transfer policy, by subsidizing individuals with college educations, could actually lead to greater inequality in the income distribution.[22]

When subsidies for college students came under attack in 1981, the president of the Association of Student Loan Funds argued "The government is spending about $2 billion a year [under the guaranteed student loan program] to support $20 billion in credit to students. . . . That's an outstanding bargain for the government, the students and the institutions" ["Cuts in Federal Aid," 1981, p. 67]. To be sure, the subsidized loans are a great deal for students and colleges, both of whom have lobbied intensely for their maintenance. In the absence of persuasive evidence on externalities, however, the benefit to society as a whole is less clear.

New Directions in Environmental Policy

The presence of externalities creates problems that are as complicated as they are important. It would not be surprising to find a great deal of disagreement among economists on how public policy should be designed. In the case of externalities, however, this is generally not true. To be sure, there has been some wrangling about the extent to which private individuals can be relied on to bargain their way to efficient solutions without government intervention. In general, though, for cases in which externalities affect large numbers of people, economists agree that intervention is appropriate, and that it should take the form of market incentives to produce efficiently.

As we have seen, for the most part this approach has been rejected in the United States, and progress in improving the environment has been less than satisfactory. However, economists' arguments are beginning to

---

[22] However, to the extent that the loans go to people who would not otherwise have gone to college, the program may increase income equality.

have at least some influence. In 1986 the Environmental Protection Agency issued guidelines for trading allowances to pollute the air. Under this program, the EPA sets a basic limit to overall emissions from a given industrial plant. If a firm's emissions are below its limit, it receives a credit. The credit can be used by the firm to increase its emissions at a later date, or it can be sold to another firm, which can use the credit to increase its own emissions. In effect, there is a market in entitlements to pollute, much along the lines described earlier in this chapter. However, unlike that model, this market is "embodied in a broader body of regulations, some of which prescribe technology-based standards and place obstacles in the way of cost-saving trades" [Oates, 1985, p. 337]. The 1990 revisions to the Clean Air Act also include some market incentives within a regulatory framework. The legislation targets 107 utility plants in the Midwest and Southeast, requiring them to cut their emissions of sulfur dioxide in half by the year 2000. Plants that cannot meet the targets will be allowed to buy pollution credits from plants that have cut back by more than the required amount. This emissions trading program is an important and interesting experiment in the use of market-oriented approaches to deal with externalities.

Summary

- An externality occurs when the activity of one person affects another person outside the market mechanism. Externalities may generally be traced to the absence of property rights.

- Externalities cause market price to diverge from social costs and benefits. This generally brings about an inefficient allocation of resources.

- A Pigouvian tax is a tax levied on the polluters' output in an amount equal to the marginal social damage at the efficient output. Such a tax gives the producer a private incentive to produce the efficient output.

- A subsidy for output not produced can induce polluters to produce at the efficient level. However, subsidies can lead to too much production, are administratively difficult, and are regarded by some as ethically unappealing.

- Pollution rights may be auctioned off to individual polluters. This fixes the total level of pollution, an advantage when administrators are uncertain how polluters will respond to Pigouvian taxes.

- The Coase Theorem indicates that private parties may bargain toward the efficient output if property rights are established. However, bargaining costs must be low and the source of the externality easily identified.

- Regulation is likely to be inefficient because the social value of pollution reduction varies across firms, locations, and the populace. Nevertheless, this is the most widespread form of environmental policy—a source of dismay to economists. A prime example is the U.S. Clean Air Act, including the changes enacted in 1990.

- Each approach to the externality problem has different implications for the distribution of income. As always, the social welfare function may indicate that the most efficient solution is not the most desirable.

- Positive externalities generally lead to underprovision of an activity. A subsidy can correct the problem, but care must be taken to avoid wasteful subsidies.

Figure 6.A
Private marginal
costs and benefits

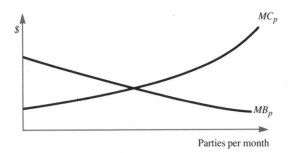

Discussion Questions

1. Which of the following are examples of an externality?

   a. After a heavy snowfall, I shovel the sidewalk in front of my house.

   b. Due to an impending war in the Mideast, motorists begin panic-buying gasoline. The price of gasoline increases, which increases profits of oil companies.

   c. Madonna plays an outdoor concert at the local football stadium.

2. In Figure 6.A, the number of parties that Cassanova gives per month is measured on the horizontal axis, and dollars are measured on the vertical. MC_p is the marginal cost of providing parties and MB_p is Cassanova's marginal benefit schedule from having parties.

   a. Graphically, show how many parties Cassanova will host.

   b. Suppose there is a fixed marginal benefit, b, per party to Cassanova's friends. Illustrate this on your graph.

   c. What is the socially (no pun intended) optimal level of parties? How could the Social Committee induce Cassanova to throw this number?

   d. On your graph, show the optimal subsidy per party and the total amount paid to Cassanova. Who gains and loses under this plan?

3. For each of the following situations, is the Coase Theorem applicable? Why or why not?

   a. Two cottages share a small pond. One cottager fishes, while the other prefers to hold games of water polo.

   b. The heat from a copper smelter interferes with the neighboring ice company, but aids an adjacent dry cleaner.

   c. The pollution from a copper smelter drifts out over a surrounding residential area.

4. In 1990, the Japanese government announced a plan to impose a tax on gasoline and coal, with the intention of reducing carbon dioxide emissions, which are thought to influence global warming. Is this a sensible policy? How should the tax be structured?

5. In 1983, the EPA asked the citizens of Tacoma, Washington, to decide whether they wanted "to accept some risk of cancer from arsenic in the air rather than face the probable closing of a copper smelter that provide[d] 800 jobs" [Shabecoff, 1983]. Is this a good policy, or should the EPA simply make the decision on its own?

Selected References

Coase, Ronald H. "The Problem of Social Cost." *Journal of Law and Economics* (October 1960), pp. 1–44.

Oates, Wallace E. "The Environment and the Economy: Environmental Policy at the Crossroads." In *American Domestic Priorities: An Economic Ap-*

praisal, ed. John M. Quigley and Daniel L. Rubinfeld. Berkeley: University of California Press, 1985, pp. 311–45.

Portney, Paul R. "Policy Watch: Economics and the Clean Air Act." *Journal of Economic Perspectives* 4, no. 4 (Fall 1990), pp. 173–182.

White, Lawrence J. "Effluent Charges as a Faster Means of Achieving Pollution Abatement." *Public Policy* 24, no. 1 (Winter 1976), pp. 111–25.

CHAPTER 7 Public Choice

Monarchy is like a sleek craft, it sails along well until some bumbling captain runs it into the rocks; democracy, on the other hand, is like a raft. It never goes down but, dammit, your feet are always wet.

FISHER AMES

Textbook discussions of market failures and their remedies tend to convey a rather rosy view of government. With a tax here, an expenditure there, the state can readily correct all market imperfections, meanwhile seeing to it that incomes are distributed in a way that reflects the community's ethical judgments. Such a view is at variance with apparent widespread public dissatisfaction with government performance. Public opinion polls, for example, consistently report that under 40 percent of the people have much confidence in Congress. Former President Ronald Reagan probably summarized the sentiments of many when he quipped, "When you get in bed with the government, you're going to get more than a good night's sleep."

It is possible that this is merely gratuitous whining on the part of individuals. As a matter of definition, in a democracy we get the government we want. Another possibility, however, is that it is inherently difficult for even democratically elected governments to respond to the national interest.

This chapter discusses and evaluates various mechanisms for making public choices. At the outset, we examine direct democracies, and how well they translate the preferences of their members into collective action. We then turn to the complications that arise when decisions are made not by individuals themselves, but by their elected representatives.

Direct Democracy

As we saw in Chapter 5, the extent to which certain goods should be provided collectively is controversial. However, for at least some important public goods such as national defense, it is hard to imagine a decentralized market system. A public decision has to be made. In democratic societies, various voting procedures are used to decide what quantities of public goods to provide. This section looks at some of these procedures.

Unanimity Rules

The irony of the free rider problem is that everyone could be better off if the public good were provided efficiently, but because people act in their narrow self-interest, not enough is provided. This suggests that in principle, if a vote were taken on whether to provide the good in an efficient quantity, consent would be unanimous as long as there was a suitable tax system to finance it. A procedure designed to elicit such unanimous agreement was proposed in the early 20th century by Erik Lindahl [1919/1958].

To understand Lindahl's procedure, assume again that there are two individuals, Adam and Eve, and one public good, rockets for fireworks *(r)*. Suppose Adam is told that his share of the cost of rocket provision will be 30 percent. Then if the market price per rocket is P_r, Adam's price per rocket is $.30 \times P_r$. Given this price, the prices of other goods, his tastes, and his income, there is some quantity of rockets that Adam will want to consume. More generally, let S^A denote Adam's share of the cost of rocket provision. For any particular value of S^A, Adam demands some quantity of rockets. As his tax share increases and it becomes more expensive for him to obtain rockets, he demands a smaller quantity.

In Figure 7.1, the horizontal axis measures the quantity of rockets. Adam's tax share is measured by the vertical distance from point O. The curve D_r^A shows how the quantity of rockets demanded by Adam decreases as his tax share increases.

In the same way, define S^E as Eve's share of the cost of rocket provision. (By definition, $S^A + S^E = 1$.) When S^E goes up, the quantity demanded by Eve decreases. In Figure 7.1, Eve's tax share increases as we move down along the vertical axis from O'. (Thus, the distance OO' is 1.) Her demand schedule is denoted D_r^E. It slopes upward because upward movements along the vertical axis represent a lower price to her.

An obvious similarity exists between the role of tax shares in the Lindahl model and market prices in the usual theory of demand. But there is an important difference. Instead of each individual facing the same price, each faces a personalized price per unit of public good, which depends on his or her tax share. The tax shares are referred to as **Lindahl prices.**

An equilibrium in the model is a set of Lindahl prices such that at those prices each person votes for the same quantity of the public good. In Figure 7.1, this occurs when Adam's tax share is OS^* and Eve's tax share is $O'S^*$. At these Lindahl prices, both parties agree that r_* rockets should be provided.

Figure 7.1
Lindahl's model

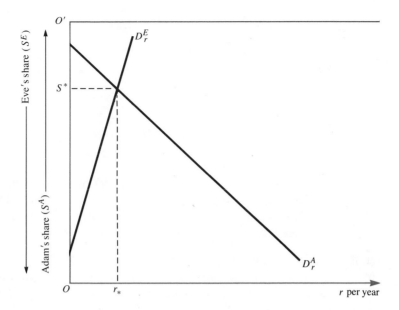

Feasibility of unanimity rules. The Lindahl model shows the existence of tax shares and a level of public good provision that is agreeable to all members of society. The big question is how the economy reaches the equilibrium. Imagine that an auctioneer announces some initial set of tax shares. On the basis of their respective demand schedules, Adam and Eve vote for the number of rockets they want. If agreement is not unanimous, the auctioneer announces another set of tax shares. The process continues until Adam and Eve unanimously agree upon the quantity of rockets (r_* in Figure 7.1). The determination of the quantity of public goods, then, is quite similar to the market process. Like the outcome of a market process, it can be shown that the allocation is Pareto efficient.[1]

As a practical method for providing public goods, there are two main problems with Lindahl's procedure. First, it assumes that people vote sincerely. If Adam can guess the maximum amount that Eve would spend for rockets rather than do without them, he can try to force her to that allocation. Eve has the same incentives. Strategic behavior may prevent Adam and Eve from reaching the Lindahl equilibrium.

Second, it may take a lot of time to find the set of tax shares agreed on by everyone. In this example, there are only two parties. In most important cases, many people are likely to be involved. To get everyone to agree is likely to involve very high decision-making costs. Indeed, al-

---

[1] Intuitively, assume that $P_r = 1$. Then Eve sets $S^E P_r = MRS_{ra}^{Eve}$, and Adam sets $S^A P_r = MRS_{ra}^{Adam}$. Therefore $MRS_{ra}^{Eve} + MRS_{ra}^{Adam} = S^E P_r + S^A P_r = P_r(S^E + S^A) = P_r$. But P_r represents MRT_{ra}, so $MRS_{ra}^{Eve} + MRS_{ra}^{Adam} = MRT_{ra}$, which is the necessary condition for Pareto efficiency of Equation (5.2). For further details, see Mueller [1976].

Table 7.1   **Voter preferences that lead to an equilibrium**

	Voter		
Choice	*Denise*	*Rudy*	*Theo*
First	A	C	B
Second	B	B	C
Third	C	A	A

though unanimity rules guarantee that no one will be "exploited," they often lead to situations in which *no* decisions are made. Historically, when organizations adopted a unanimity rule, it was often expressly because the participants wanted to make sure that no actions were taken![2]

Majority Voting Rules

Unanimity is clearly a difficult state to reach. As a result, voting systems not requiring unanimity may be desirable. With a **majority voting rule,** one more than half of the voters must favor a measure for it to be approved.

Although the mechanics of majority voting are familiar, it is useful to review them carefully. Consider a community with three voters, Denise, Rudy, and Theo, who have to choose among three levels of missile provision, A, B, and C. Level A is small, level B is moderate, and level C is large. The voters' preferences are depicted in Table 7.1. Each column shows how the voter ranks the choices. For example, Rudy most prefers level C, but given a choice between B and A, would prefer B.

Suppose that an election were held on whether to adopt A or B. Denise would vote for A while Rudy and Theo would vote for B. Hence, B would win by a vote of 2 to 1. Similarly, if an election were held between B and C, B would win by a vote of 2 to 1. Level B wins any election against its opposition, and thus is the option selected by majority rule. Note that the selection of B is independent of the order in which the votes are taken.

Do we always expect majority decision rules to yield such clear-cut results? Not necessarily. Suppose that the preferences for various levels of missile provision are as depicted in Table 7.2. Again, imagine a series of paired elections to determine the most preferred level. In an election between A and B, A would win by a vote of 2 to 1. If an election were held between B and C, B would win by a vote of 2 to 1. Finally, in an election between A and C, C would win by the same margin. This is a disconcerting result. The first election suggests that A is preferred to B; the second that B is preferred to C. Conventional notions of consistency suggest that A should therefore be preferred to C. But in the third election, just the

---

[2] In 17th-century Poland, the structure of government was essentially feudal. None of the nobles wanted to lose any power to the monarch. Hence, the monarch had to promise to take no actions unless he received the unanimous consent of the Polish parliament [see Massie, 1980, p. 228].

Table 7.2   **Voter preferences that lead to cycling**

Choice	Voter		
	Denise	*Rudy*	*Theo*
First	A	C	B
Second	B	A	C
Third	C	B	A

opposite occurs. Although each individual voter's preferences are consistent, the community's are not. This phenomenon is referred to as the **voting paradox.**

Moreover, in the situation depicted in Table 7.2, the ultimate outcome depends crucially on the order in which the votes are taken. If the first election is between propositions A and B and the winner (A) runs against C, then C is the ultimate choice. On the other hand, if the first election is B versus C, and the winner (B) runs against A, then A is chosen. Under such circumstances, the ability to control the order of voting—the agenda—confers great power. **Agenda manipulation** is the process of organizing the order of votes to assure a favorable outcome.

A related problem is that paired voting can go on forever without a decision being reached. After the election between A and B, A wins. If C challenges A, then C wins. If B then challenges C, B wins. The process can continue indefinitely, a phenomenon called **cycling.** Many important historical cases of cycling have been identified. A good example concerns the 17th Amendment to the U.S. Constitution, which provides for direct election of U.S. senators. Adoption "was delayed for 10 years by parliamentary maneuvers that depended on voting cycles involving the status quo (the appointment of senators by the state legislature) and two versions of the amendment" [Blair and Pollak, 1983, p. 88].

Clearly, the majority rule does not have to suffer from these problems. After all, the elections associated with Table 7.1 went perfectly smoothly. What is the source of the difference? It turns on the structure of individual preferences for various levels of missile procurement. Consider again the people in Table 7.2. Because Denise prefers A to B to C, it follows that A gives Denise more utility than B, and B more than C. The schedule denoted Denise in Figure 7.2 depicts this relationship. The schedules labeled Rudy and Theo do the same for the other voters.

We define a **peak** in an individual's preferences as a point at which all the neighboring points are lower.[3] A voter has **single-peaked preferences** if, as he moves away from his most preferred outcome in any and all

---

[3] For this analysis, the absolute amount of utility associated with each alternative is irrelevant. The vertical distances could change, but as long as the pattern of peaks stays unchanged, so does the outcome of the election.

Figure 7.2

Graphing the
preferences from
Table 7.2

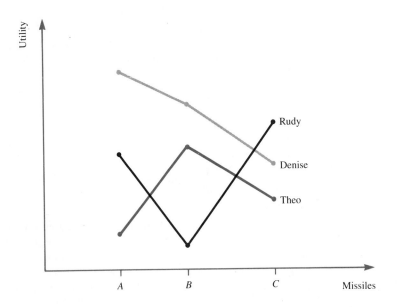

directions, his utility consistently falls. He has **double-peaked preferences**
if, as he moves away from the most preferred outcome, utility goes down,
but then goes up again. Thus, Denise has a single peak at point A; Theo
has a single peak at point B; and Rudy has two peaks, one at A and one at
C. It turns out that Rudy's preferences are the ones that lead to the voting
paradox. If Rudy had *any* set of single-peaked preferences, majority voting would lead to a consistent decision. This is why no voting paradox
emerges from Figure 7.2. There, each voter has single-peaked preferences. More generally, if all voters' preferences are single peaked, no
voting paradox occurs.

Because multipeaked preferences can throw a wrench into majority
voting, it is important to know whether they are likely to be important as a
practical matter. Consider again in Table 7.2 Rudy, whose preferences
have two peaks. She prefers either very large or very small missile expenditures to a quantity in the middle. Although such preferences are not
necessarily "irrational," they do seem a bit peculiar.[4]

Suppose, however, that instead of missiles, voters are choosing
among expenditure levels for a public park—a good for which there are
private substitutes. Assume that in the presence of small or medium public park expenditures, voter Smith will join a private country club, but
given large expenditures, he will use the public park. Provided that
Smith's tax burden increases with park expenditure, he prefers a small to
a medium park—since neither of these options benefits Smith, he prefers

---

[4] Perhaps Rudy believes that moderate numbers of missiles will provide little if any real protection,
so that unless expenditures are large, they might as well be close to nothing.

the one with the smaller tax burden. But his most preferred outcome might be the large expenditure public park. (This depends in part on the associated tax burden compared to the country club membership fee.) In short, Smith may prefer either the small or large public park to the medium-sized one. Thus, when there are private substitutes for a publicly provided good, a multipeaked pattern like Rudy's in Figure 7.2 can easily emerge.

Moreover, when issues are not based on a single dimension, multipeaked preferences are also a serious possibility.[5] Suppose that a community is trying to decide how to use a vacant building. Choice A is an abortion clinic, choice B is an adult book store, and choice C is an Army recruitment office. Unlike the choice between different levels of missile expenditure, here the alternatives do not represent more or less of a single characteristic. It is easy to imagine multipeaked preferences emerging.

The median voter theorem.   Let us now return to the simple case in which all alternatives being considered represent smaller or greater amounts of a single characteristic. People rank each alternative on the basis of this single characteristic. An example is how much of some public good to acquire. Define the **median voter** as the voter whose preferences lie in the middle of the set of all voters' preferences; half the voters want more of the good than the median voter, and half want less. The **median voter theorem** states that as long as all preferences are single peaked, the outcome of majority voting reflects the preferences of the median voter.[6]

To demonstrate the median voter theorem, assume that there are five voters: Donald, Daisy, Huey, Dewey, and Louie. They are deciding how large a party to give together, and each of them has single-peaked preferences for party sizes. The most preferred level for each voter is noted in Table 7.3. *Because preferences are single peaked,* the closer an expenditure level is to a given voter's peak, the more he or she prefers it. A movement from zero party expenditure to $5 would be preferred to no money for parties by all voters. A movement from $5 to $100 would be approved by Daisy, Huey, Dewey, and Louie, and from $100 to $150 by Huey, Dewey, and Louie. Any increase beyond $150, however, would be blocked by at least three voters: Donald, Daisy, and Huey. Hence, the majority votes for $150. But this is just the amount preferred by Huey, the median voter. The election results mirror the median voter's preferences.

To summarize: when all preferences are single peaked, majority voting yields a stable result, and the choice selected reflects the preferences of the median voter. However, when all voters' preferences are not single

---

[5] Atkinson and Stiglitz [1980, p. 306] explain how the notion of a "peak" is generalized to a multidimensional setting.

[6] See Black [1948]. When there is an even number of voters, there may be a tie between two median voters which must be broken arbitrarily.

Table 7.3   **Preferred level of party expenditure**

Voter	Expenditure
Donald	$ 5
Daisy	100
Huey	150
Dewey	160
Louie	700

peaked, a voting paradox may emerge.[7] Because multipeaked preferences may be important in many realistic situations, majority voting cannot be depended on to yield consistent public choices. Moreover, as we shall see next, even when majority voting leads to consistent decisions, it may not be efficient in the sense that overall benefits exceed costs.

Econometric application of the median voter theorem.   Despite its imperfections, the median voter theorem provides a useful framework for empirical investigation of the demand for public goods. Assume that each community's preferences for public goods coincide with the preferences of its median voter. Suppose that for a sample of communities we have data on the quantity of public goods (G), the relative price per unit of public good (P), and the median voter's income (I). Then by examining how G depends on P and I, we can in effect compute the demand curve for public goods. Specifically, we can estimate a regression equation in which the quantity of some public good, G, is the dependent variable, and P and I appear as explanatory variables. The responsiveness of public goods demand to changes in price and income can then be inferred from the coefficients on P and I, respectively.[8]

Several problems arise in implementing this procedure. First, standard data sources do not reveal the identity of the voter with median preferences for the public good; hence, we do not know her income. The typical procedure is to assume that the median income in the community is also the income of the median voter. While in many cases this is probably a pretty good assumption, it need not always be correct. To see why, suppose that poor people have a relatively low demand for public education, and that as income increases, the demand goes up. However, suppose further that as people's incomes become very high, they choose to

[7] The presence of one or more voters with multipeaked preferences does not *necessarily* lead to a voting paradox. It depends on the number of voters and the structure of their preferences. See Question 1 at the end of this chapter.

[8] Note that it is necessary to include on the right-hand side variables that might affect the community's tastes for public goods. For example, the size of the school-aged population influences preferences for education.

send their children to private schools, so that the demand for *public* education falls with income. Thus, both high- and low-income people have relatively low demands for education, and the demand for public education by the person with median income might exceed the demand of the person with median preferences for education.

A second problem is measuring the price of the public good. Think of P as the median voter's cost of purchasing an additional unit of G. This depends on the resource cost of purchasing an additional unit of G, and the share of the cost which must be paid by the median voter. The share, in turn, depends on how taxes are raised in the community.[9] For example, assume that all community revenues are raised by proportional taxes on housing. Thus, if the median voter's house is worth V and the tax rate is t, then her tax liability is tV. Her share of total community taxes is $tV/t\hat{V}$ where $\hat{V}$ is the total value of all houses in the community. Because the t's divide out, the median voter's share of the resource cost is simply the value of her house relative to the value of all houses in the community. Thus, information on the tax system together with data on the community's resource cost for public goods can be used to construct P.

Many econometric studies have taken advantage of this framework. The demands for education, hospitals, parks, police protection, and public works have been analyzed. Naturally, the results differ depending on the particular item being studied. In general, however, both the implied income and price elasticities tend to be small. For example, in his survey of results on the demand for education, Rubinfeld [1985] reports that most studies find income elasticities that are less than one, and price elasticities in the range of -0.2 to -0.4. Thus, demands for education (as well as most other public goods) are relatively unresponsive to changes in their prices. Results such as these are helpful in answering a number of policy questions, such as how the provision of local public goods might change if their prices were subsidized by the federal government.

Logrolling

Some argue that an important problem with simple majority voting is that it does not allow people to register how strongly they feel about the issues. Whether a particular voter just barely prefers A to B or has an enormous preference for A has no influence on the outcome. **Logrolling** systems allow people to trade votes and hence register how strongly they feel about various issues. Suppose that voters Smith and Jones prefer not to have more missiles, but this preference is not strongly felt. Brown, on the other hand, definitely wants more missiles. With a logrolling system, Brown may be able to convince Jones to vote for more missiles if Brown promises to vote for a new road to go by Jones's factory.

---

[9] Things are complicated further by the fact that some other levels of government may pay some share of the cost via grants-in-aid. See Chapter 21 under "Intergovernmental Grants."

Table 7.4   **Logrolling can improve welfare**

| | Voter | | | |
Project	Bart	Lisa	Maggie	Total Net Benefits
Hospital	200	−50	−55	95
Library	−40	150	−30	80
Pool	−120	−60	400	200

Vote trading is controversial. Its proponents argue that trading votes leads to efficient provision of public goods, just as trading in commodities leads to efficient provision of private goods. Proponents also emphasize its potential for revealing the intensity of preferences and establishing a stable equilibrium. Moreover, the compromises implicit in vote trading are necessary for a democratic system to function. As the English statesman Edmund Burke noted, "All government—indeed, every human benefit and enjoyment, every virtue and every prudent act—is founded on compromise and barter." (Married readers will believe this!)

A numerical example helps illustrate these advantages of logrolling. Suppose that a community is considering three projects, a hospital, a library, and a swimming pool. The community has three voters, Bart, Lisa, and Maggie. Table 7.4 shows their benefits for each project. (A minus sign indicates a net loss; that is, the costs exceed the benefits.)

The first thing to notice about the table is that the total net benefit for each project is positive. Thus, by definition, the community as a whole would be better off if each project were adopted.[10] But what would happen if the projects were voted on *one at a time?* Bart would vote for the hospital because his net benefit is positive, but Lisa and Maggie would vote against it because their benefits are negative. The hospital would therefore lose. Similarly, the library and the swimming pool would go down in defeat.

Vote trading can remedy this situation. Suppose Bart agrees to vote for the library if Lisa consents to vote for the hospital. Bart comes out ahead by 160 (= 200 − 40) with such a trade; Lisa comes out ahead by 100 (= 150 − 50). They therefore strike the deal, and the hospital and library pass. In the same way, Bart and Maggie can make a deal in which Bart's support for the pool is given in return for Maggie's vote for the hospital. Thus logrolling allows all three measures to pass, a desirable outcome.

On the other hand, opponents of logrolling stress that it is likely to result in special-interest gains not sufficient to outweigh general losses.

---

[10] We assume the absence of externalities or any other considerations which would make private costs and benefits unequal to their social counterparts.

"At last! A weapons system absolutely impervious to attack: it has components manufactured in all 435 congressional districts!''

By John Trever © by permission of North American Syndicate, Inc., 1985.

Large amounts of waste can be incurred. For example, in the midst of negotiations to reduce spending and the deficit in 1990, Congress earmarked millions of dollars for water projects, highway construction, and airport improvements in Mississippi, despite the fact that the projects generally were believed to have little value. Why? One important reason was that the projects were located in the district of Representative Jamie L. Whitten, chairman of the House Appropriations Committee; his vote would be important on a number of Congress members' pet projects [Pear, 1990, p. A16].

Other anecdotal reports of the effects of logrolling often are heard in the context of military spending. As the cartoon indicates, some observers believe that when Pentagon money is being distributed, members of Congress seem less concerned with obtaining efficient weapons systems than with getting a lot of money spent in their home states. The late Senator John Tower of Texas once suggested that each senator submit a list with the military projects in his state that could be eliminated to cut the defense budget. In response, the audience in the hearing room rocked with laughter.[11]

A numerical example can be used to illustrate situations in which logrolling leads to such undesirable outcomes.[12] Assume we have the same three voters and three projects under consideration as in Table 7.4, but now the various net benefits are as depicted in Table 7.5. Every project has a negative net benefit. Each should therefore be rejected, as would be the case if the projects were voted on one at a time.

However, with logrolling, some or all of these inefficient projects could pass. Suppose that Bart offers to support the library in return for Lisa's vote for the hospital. The deal is consummated because both of

---

[11] "Weaning Congress from the Pork Barrel," *New York Times,* March 23, 1986, p. E5.

[12] For further details, see Buchanan and Tullock [1962].

Table 7.5   **Logrolling can also lower welfare**

| | Voter | | | |
Project	Bart	Lisa	Maggie	Total Net Benefits
Hospital	200	−110	−105	−15
Library	−40	150	−120	−10
Pool	−270	−140	400	−10

them come out ahead—Bart by 160 (=200 − 40) and Lisa by 40 (=150 − 110). With the support of Bart and Lisa together, both projects pass. In the same way, Lisa and Maggie can trade votes for the pool and the library, so that both of those projects are adopted.

To understand the source of this outcome, consider again Bart and Lisa's vote trading over the hospital and the library. Note that Maggie comes out behind on both projects. This demonstrates how with logrolling, a majority of voters can form a coalition to vote for projects that serve their interests, but whose costs are borne to a large extent by the minority. Hence, despite the fact that the benefits of the projects to the majority exceed the costs, this is not true for society as a whole. We conclude that although under some circumstances logrolling can improve on the results from simple majority voting, this is not necessarily the case.

Arrow's Impossibility Theorem

We have shown that neither simple majority voting nor logrolling has entirely desirable properties. Many other voting schemes have also been considered, and they, too, are flawed.[13] An important question is whether *any* ethically acceptable method for translating individual preferences into collective preferences escapes from these problems. It depends on what you mean by ethically acceptable. Kenneth Arrow [1951] proposed that in a democratic society, a collective decision-making rule should satisfy the following criteria:[14]

1. It can produce a decision whatever the configuration of voters' preferences. Thus, for example, the procedure must not fall apart if some people have multipeaked preferences.

---

[13] These include point voting (each person is given a fixed number of points which are cast for the different alternatives), plurality voting (the alternative with the most votes wins), Borda counts (each alternative is ranked by each voter, and the ranks are totaled to choose), Condorcet elections (the alternative that defeats the rest in paired elections wins), and exhaustive voting (the proposal favored least by the largest number of voters is repeatedly removed until only one remains). See Mueller [1976] for further details.

[14] Arrow's requirements have been stated in a number of different ways. Here we follow the treatment of Blair and Pollak [1983].

2. It must be able to rank all possible outcomes.

3. It must be responsive to individuals' preferences. Specifically, if every individual prefers A to B, then society's ranking must prefer A to B.

4. It must be consistent in the sense that if A is preferred to B and B is preferred to C, then A is preferred to C.[15]

5. Society's ranking of A and B depends only on individuals' rankings of A and B. Thus, the collective ranking of defense expenditures and foreign aid does not depend on how individuals rank either of them relative to research on a cure for AIDS. This assumption is sometimes called the **independence of irrelevant alternatives.**

6. Dictatorship is ruled out. Social preferences must not reflect the preferences of only a single individual.

Taken together, these criteria seem quite reasonable. Basically, they say that society's choice mechanism should be logical and respect the preferences of individuals. Unfortunately, the stunning conclusion of Arrow's analysis is that in general it is *impossible* to find a rule that satisfies all these criteria.[16] A democratic society cannot be expected to be able to make consistent decisions.

This result, sometimes called Arrow's Impossibility Theorem, thus casts doubt on the very ability of democracies to function. Naturally, the theorem has generated a great deal of debate, much of which has focused on whether other sets of criteria might allow formation of a social decision-making rule. It turns out that if any of the six criteria is dropped, a decision-making rule that satisfies the other five *can* be constructed. But whether or not it is permissible to drop any of the criteria depends on one's views of their ethical validity.

Arrow's theorem does not state that it is *necessarily* impossible to find a consistent decision-making rule. Rather, the theorem only says that it cannot be guaranteed that society will be able to do so. For certain patterns of individual preferences, no problems arise. An obvious example is when members of society have identical preferences. Some radical theorists have suggested that the real significance of Arrow's theorem is that it shows the need for a virtual uniformity of tastes if a democracy is to function. They then argue that many capitalist institutions have the express purpose of molding people's tastes to make sure that uniformity emerges. An example is mandatory public education. (We discuss the role of education further in Chapter 21.)

---

[15] More precisely, in this context *preferred to* means *better than or just as good as.*

[16] The proof involves fairly sophisticated mathematics. The procedure of proof is to show that if all six conditions are imposed, phenomena like the voting paradox can arise.

Others have argued that Arrow's theorem does not really have much to say about the viability of democratic processes. James Buchanan [1960] views the inconsistencies of majority voting as having beneficial aspects:

> Majority rule is acceptable in a free society precisely because it allows a sort of jockeying back and forth among alternatives, upon none of which relative unanimity can be obtained. . . . It serves to insure that competing alternatives may be experimentally and provisionally adopted, tested, and replaced by new compromise alternatives approved by a majority group of ever-changing composition. This is [the] democratic choice process. [P. 83]

Another important question raised by Arrow's theorem concerns use of a social welfare function in economic analysis. Recall from Chapter 4 that a social welfare function is a rule that evaluates the desirability of any given configuration of individuals' utilities. In a democratic society, choosing the social welfare function must be done collectively. But Arrow's theorem says that it may be impossible to make such decisions, and hence we cannot assume that a social welfare function really exists. However, if it does not exist, how can economists use the social welfare function to rank alternative states? A number of economists have therefore rejected the function's use. They argue that it is merely a way of introducing ethical views about the desirability of various economic states and not a representation of "society's" preferences. As such, a social welfare function does not isolate the correct allocation of resources. However, most economists believe that the function is an important tool. It may not provide "the" answer, but it can be used to draw out the implications of alternative sets of value judgments. As long as this interpretation is kept in mind, the social welfare function can provide valuable insights.

Representative Democracy

Although the discussion of public decision making thus far sheds light on some important questions, it is based on a very unrealistic view of government. In this view, government is essentially a big computer that elicits from citizens their preferences and uses this information to produce social decisions. The state has no interests of its own; it is neutral and benign.

In fact, of course, government is done by people—politicians, judges, bureaucrats, and others. To understand the realities of public choice, one must study the goals and behavior of the people who govern. The remainder of this chapter discusses some theories of government action based on these individuals' motivations and behavior. The results are used to examine the important and perplexing question of the rapid growth of the public sector. We also discuss some institutional reforms to improve government performance.

The Cast of Characters

The process of political decision making is clearly very complicated. We examine it using simple economic models of the behavior of some of the key people involved. These models typically assume that people in government attempt to maximize their self interest. Two points are important regarding this assumption:

- Selfishness does not necessarily lead to inefficient outcomes. As we saw in Chapter 4, under certain conditions the marketplace harnesses greed to serve a social end. The question is what, if anything, performs that role in the "political market."
- While the maximization assumption may not be totally accurate, just as in more conventional settings, it provides a good starting point for analysis.

Elected Politicians

Our earlier discussion of direct democracy led to the median voter theorem: If individual preferences are single peaked and can be represented along a single dimension, the outcome of majority voting reflects the preferences of the median voter. In reality, direct referenda on fiscal matters are most unusual. More commonly, citizens elect representatives who make decisions on their behalf. Nevertheless, under certain assumptions, the median voter theory can help explain how these representatives set their positions.

Consider an election between two candidates, Smith and Jones. Assume that voters have single-peaked preferences along the spectrum of political views. Voters cast ballots to maximize their own utility, and candidates seek to maximize the number of votes received.

What happens? Anthony Downs [1957] argues that under these conditions, a vote-maximizing politician adopts the preferred program of the median voter—the voter whose preferences are exactly in the middle of the distribution of preferences. To see this, assume that voters rank all positions on the basis of whether they are "conservative" or "liberal." Figure 7.3 shows a hypothetical distribution of voters who most prefer each point in the political spectrum. Suppose that Candidate Jones adopts position M, at the median, and Candidate Smith chooses position S to the right of center. Because all voters have single-peaked preferences and want to maximize utility, each supports the candidate whose views lie closest to his or her own. Smith will win all the votes to the right of S, as well as some of the votes between S and M. Because M is the median, one-half of the voters lie to the left of M. Jones will receive all of these votes and some of those to the right of M, guaranteeing him a majority. The only way for Smith to prevent himself from being "outflanked" is to move to position M himself. Therefore, it pays both candidates to position themselves as close as possible to the position of the median voter.

Figure 7.3
Median voter
theorem for
elections

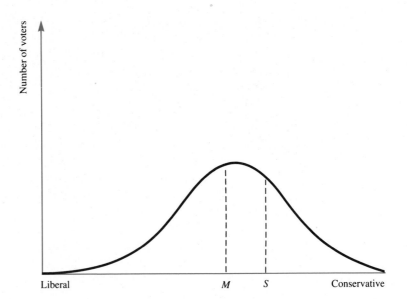

This model has two striking implications: First, two-party systems tend to be stable in the sense that both parties stake out positions near the "center." In some respects, this is a good description of American political life. It appears, for example, that presidential candidates who are perceived as too far from the middle-of-the-road (Barry Goldwater in 1964 and George McGovern in 1972) do not fare well with the electorate.[17] In the 1988 election, candidates George Bush and Michael Dukakis appear to have behaved consistently with the median voter model. Each tried to portray himself as a moderate, so much so that one commentator wrote that on the major issues they "are in fundamental accord: Lower the Federal and the trade deficits, halt crime and drugs, improve education, be more 'competitive' in the world market, maintain a strong military posture while negotiating arms reduction with the Soviets. . . . [T]hey have not as yet been sufficiently specific to distinguish themselves dramatically from one another" [Tyler, 1988, p. 10].

Second, the replacement of direct referenda by a representative system will have *no* effect on the outcome. Both simply mirror the preferences of the median voter. Thus, government spending cannot be "excessive" because political competition for votes leads to an expenditure level that is exactly in accord with the median voter's wishes.

Before taking these rather optimistic results too much to heart, however, several aspects of the analysis require careful examination.

---

[17] One of Goldwater's campaign slogans was "A choice, not an echo." The median voter theorem helps to explain why echoes are so prevalent.

Single dimensional rankings.   If all political beliefs cannot be ranked along a single spectrum, the median voter theorem falls apart because the identity of the median voter then depends on the particular issue actually being considered. The median voter with respect to feminist questions may not be the same person as the median voter on atomic energy issues. Similarly, just as in the case of direct referenda, if preferences are not single peaked, there may not be a stable voting equilibrium at all.

Ideology.   While it is assumed that politicians are simple vote maximizers, they may care about more than just winning elections. Ideology can play an important role. After all, in 1850 Henry Clay said, "Sir, I would rather be right than be president."

Issues alone?   The assumption that voters' utilities depend only on issues may be unrealistic. In some cases, personalities may be more important in determining election outcomes. Some have argued, for example, that much of President Dwight D. Eisenhower's appeal was his fatherly personality.

Leadership.   In the model, politicians passively respond to voters' preferences. But these preferences may be influenced by the politicians themselves. This is just another way of saying that politicians provide leadership. Indeed, at times in history, rational calculations of voter self-interest have apparently given way altogether to the appeals of charismatic politicians. "Politics is magic. He who knows how to summon forces from the deep, him they will follow."[18]

Decision to vote.   The analysis assumes that every eligible citizen chooses to exercise his or her franchise. If the candidates' positions are too close, however, some people may become too apathetic to vote. Individuals with extreme views may fail to vote out of alienation. The model also ignores the costs of acquiring information and voting. A rational voter must make a determination on the suitability of a candidate's platform, the probability that the candidate will be able and willing to keep his or her promises, and so forth. The fact that these costs may be high, together with the perception that a single vote will not influence the outcome anyway, may induce a self-interested citizen to abstain from voting. A free rider problem emerges—each individual has an incentive not to vote but unless a sizable number of people exercise their franchise, a democracy cannot function [see Downs, 1957]. Although low voter-participation rates are often bemoaned (for example, in the 1988 presidential election, only 50 percent of the voting-age population cast a vote), in a

---

[18] Hugo von Hofmannsthal quoted in Schorske [1981, p. 172].

way it is puzzling that the percentage is as high as it is. Part of the answer may be the success with which the educational system instills the idea that the citizen's obligation to vote transcends narrow self-interest.

Voting and economic performance.   As just noted, the median voter model does not consider how voters obtain information about the political candidates and their parties. One obvious way is by watching candidates' performance while in office. If the performance is satisfactory, then vote to reelect them. Otherwise, "throw the rascals out."

Ray Fair [1982] based an econometric study of presidential election results on the notion that good economic performance enhances the probability that the incumbent party will remain in office. He estimated a regression equation in which the Democratic proportion of the two-party presidential vote (which we denote D) depends on the following explanatory variables:[19]

g =   growth rate of real per capita gross national product in the second and third quarters of the year of the election, multiplied by -1 if the incumbent party is Republican. If voters reward parties whose presidents are associated with high growth rates, this variable should have a positive coefficient. The reason for the -1 is that if the Republicans do well, this should *decrease* the number of Democratic votes, other things being the same.

INF =   rate of inflation, measured as the absolute value of the average growth rate of prices in the two-year period before the election multiplied by -1 if the incumbent party is Republican. If voters punish parties whose incumbents are associated with inflation, the coefficient on this variable should be negative.

DEM =   1 if there is a Democratic incumbent *and* he or she is running for reelection; -1 if there is a Republican incumbent who is running for reelection; zero otherwise. If incumbency produces an electoral advantage, the coefficient of this variable should be positive.

$INCUM$ =   1 if there is a Democratic incumbent; -1 if there is a Republican incumbent. If having a member of your party in office during the election helps (even if the incumbent is not seeking reelection), the coefficient of this variable should be positive.

---

[19] Fair estimated a number of equations with other variables, as well. He also included in his equations a complicated measure of vote-getting ability which is not described here, and which is suppressed in reporting the results below. See Fair [1982] and [1978] for more details.

When Fair estimated the regression using data from the presidential elections of 1916 to 1980, he obtained the following result:

$$D = .478 + .0080\ g - .0096\ INF + .0479\ DEM + .0230\ INCUM \quad (7.1)$$

The signs of the estimated parameters conform to expectations. The positive sign on g shows that a party associated with a high economic growth rate has enhanced prospects for capturing the White House. (Each percentage point increase in the growth rate increases the proportion of the votes cast for Democrats by .008.) Inflation, on the other hand, diminishes a party's share of the vote. The coefficient on DEM indicates that merely by virtue of being an incumbent, a Democratic candidate can increase his or her fraction of the vote by about .047. The coefficient on $INCUM$ suggests that the party with the incumbent (even if he or she is not running) enjoys an advantage of 0.0230. Except for the coefficient on $INCUM$, all are statistically significant, that is, it is unlikely that the results are a random fluke.

An interesting test of the equation's usefulness is to see how well it does predicting election results after 1980, the last presidential election included in Fair's study. Consider the Bush–Dukakis contest in 1988. In that year, the absolute values of g and INF were 2.75 and 4.4, respectively; DEM equaled 0, and $INCUM$ equaled −1.0 because there was a Republican incumbent (Reagan) who was not running for office. Substituting these values into Equation (7.1), we obtain a prediction for Dukakis' fraction of the two-party vote of 0.475.[20] In fact, Dukakis received 0.461. Thus, the equation's prediction is off by only 0.014.

Some comments about Fair's choices of variables to represent economic performance are required. First, despite the fact that the unemployment rate is a widely quoted statistic, Fair finds that it has little or no explanatory power. The implication is that people's perceptions of economic performance are based more on the growth of income than on unemployment. Perhaps this is because unemployment is concentrated in a relatively small part of the population.

Second, note that g measures the income growth rate for only the six months preceding the election. Given that the incumbent party has held the presidency for almost four years by election time, one might guess that the growth rate measured over a longer period would be more appropriate. But this turns out not to be the case. Growth rates computed over longer horizons do a *worse* job of predicting election results. If this result is correct, it suggests that voters are extremely shortsighted; all they care about is the economy's behavior in the very recent past. This may help explain the often observed tendency of incumbents to increase government spending before elections to "pump up" the economy.[21] More gen-

---

[20] $0.475 = .478 + 0.0080 \times (-2.75) - .0096 \times (-4.4) + .0479 \times (0) + 0.0230 \times (-1.0)$.

[21] Tufte [1978] argues that such behavior is an important cause of the business cycle.

erally, this finding is consistent with the notion that political decision making is inherently myopic. Politicians who are under pressure to produce favorable results by the next election have incentives to take actions that have high short-run payoffs but possibly detrimental long-run effects.

Finally, Fair's model does not include personalities, social issues, campaign spending, or foreign affairs. The fact that such a simple economic model can do so well at predicting elections is impressive. Nevertheless, other variables may also be important, and their inclusion could affect the results.[22] In any case, the use of economic models and econometrics to explain the behavior of voters and politicians is an active area of research that promises to provide many interesting insights.

Public Employees

The next group we consider is public employees, also referred to as bureaucrats. To understand their role, note that the legislation enacted by elected politicians is often vague. The precise way a program is run is in the hands of public employees. A classic example is the Internal Revenue Service, which makes rulings on hundreds of aspects of tax-code administration not considered by lawmakers. Similarly, important details in administration of welfare programs are often unspecified, so matters such as eligibility are left up to bureaucrats in the Department of Health and Human Services and other agencies. As Table 7.6 shows, the number of public employees is large and has been growing over time. Lately, bureaucrats have been the target of much bitter criticism. They are blamed for being unresponsive, creating excessive red tape, and intruding too much into the private affairs of citizens. Even a new-wave rock group joined in the attack:

> Red tape, I can see can't you see
> Red tape, do'in to you, do'in to me
> Red tape, bureaucracy in D.C.
> Red tape, killing you and killing me.
> Tax this, tax that, tax this, tax that.
> NO MORE RED TAPE.[23]

Remember, however, that a modern government simply cannot function without bureaucracy. Bureaucrats provide valuable technical expertise in the design and execution of programs. Moreover, the fact that their tenures in office often exceed those of elected officials provides a continuity in government that would otherwise be lacking.

On the other hand, it would be naive to assume a government bureaucrat's only aim is to interpret and passively fulfill the wishes of the electorate and its representatives. Having said this, we are still left with the

---

[22] For example, many believe that Carter lost the 1980 election because of the Iranian hostage crisis.

[23] From "Red Tape," words and music by Keith Morris and Greg Hetson of the Circle Jerks. © 1980, Irving Music, Inc., and Plagued Music (BMI). All rights reserved. International copyright secured.

Table 7.6 **Government versus private-sector employees (thousands)**

Year	All Governments*	Federal*	State and Local†	All Private Industries
1942	5,915	2,664	3,251	53,570
1949	6,203	2,047	4,156	58,710
1959	8,487	2,399	6,088	65,581
1969	12,685	2,969	9,716	77,902
1979	15,971	2,869	13,102	98,824
1988	17,588	3,112	14,476	106,551

* Does not include military.

† Includes education.

Source: U.S. Department of Commerce, Bureau of the Census, *Statistical Abstract of the United States* (Washington, D.C.: U.S. Government Printing Office), various editions, and Advisory Commission on Intergovernmental Relations [1990, p. 176].

problem of specifying the bureaucrat's goals. William Niskanen [1971] argued that in the market-oriented private sector, an individual who wants to "get ahead" will do so by making his or her company as profitable as possible. When the firm's profits go up, so will the individual's salary. In contrast, bureaucrats tend to focus on such items as perquisites of office, public reputation, power, and patronage because opportunities for monetary gains are minimal.[24] Niskanen suggested that all of these objectives are positively correlated with the size of the bureaucrat's budget, and hence concluded that the bureaucrat's objective is to maximize his or her budget.

To assess the implications of this hypothesis, consider Figure 7.4. The output of a bureaucracy, Q, is measured on the horizontal axis. Q might represent the number of units of public housing managed by the Department of Housing and Urban Development, or the quantity of missiles stockpiled by the Department of Defense. Dollars are measured on the vertical axis. The curve VV represents the total value placed on each level of Q by the legislative sponsor who controls the budget. The slope of VV is the marginal social benefit of the output; it is drawn on the reasonable assumption of diminishing marginal benefit. The total cost of providing each output level is given by CC. Its slope measures the marginal cost of each unit of output. CC is drawn on the assumption of increasing marginal cost.

Suppose the bureaucrat knows that the sponsor will accept any project whose total benefits exceed total costs. Then the bureaucrat (bc) proposes Q_{bc}, the output level that maximizes the size of the bureau subject to the constraint that CC not be above VV. Q_{bc}, however, is an inefficient level of output. Efficiency requires that a unit of output be

---

[24] Obviously, this distinction is blurred in the real world. Firm executives care about power and job perks as well as money. Nevertheless, the distinction is useful for analytical purposes.

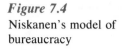

Figure 7.4
Niskanen's model of
bureaucracy

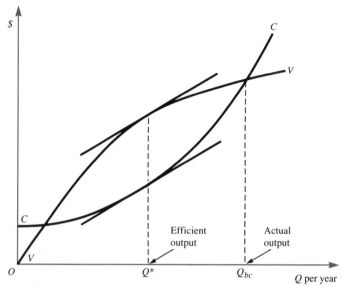

produced only as long as the additional benefit from that output exceeds
the additional cost. Hence, the efficient output is that at which marginal
cost equals marginal benefit, *not* total cost equals total benefit. In Figure
7.4 the efficient level is Q^*, where the *slopes* of VV and CC are equal.
Thus, the bureaucrat's desire to build as large an "empire" as possible
leads to an inefficiently large bureaucracy.

An important implication of Niskanen's model is that bureaucrats
have incentives to expend effort on promotional activities to increase the
sponsor's perceptions of the benefits of the bureau's output—to shift up
the VV curve. This is analogous to the use of advertising in the private
sector. If such efforts succeed, the equilibrium value of Q_{bc} moves to the
right. Hence, Defense Department officials are expected to emphasize
security threats, and their counterparts in Health and Human Services to
promote awareness of the poverty problem. Note also that an unscrupu-
lous bureaucrat may ask for more funds than needed to achieve a given
output level and/or to overstate the benefits of the program. However, the
tendency of bureaucracies to exceed their efficient size does not depend
on such outright trickery.

An obvious question is why the sponsor allows the bureaucrat to
operate at Q_{bc} rather than Q^*. In essence, Niskanen assumes that the
bureaucrat can present his output to the sponsor as an all-or-nothing
proposition: take Q_{bc} or none at all. But, if the sponsor is well informed
and cares about efficiency, she should require output Q^* and insist that it
be produced at minimum cost. One impediment is that it may be difficult
for the sponsor to know just what is going on. The process of producing
the bureaucratic output is likely to be complicated and require specialized

Table 7.7 **Average monthly earnings per employee in public and private sectors**

Year	All Government*	Federal*	State and Local*	All Private Industries†
1942	$ 149	$ 183	$ 121	$ 147
1949	227	263	209	220
1959	367	447	335	353
1969	600	793	541	518
1979	1,132	1,648	1,019	1,077
1985	1,734	2,509	1,563	1,544
1988	1,945	2,563	1,812	1,985

* Computed as monthly payroll divided by monthly employment.

† Computed as four times average weekly earnings or, for 1988, one-twelfth average annual earnings.

SOURCE: U.S. Department of Commerce, Bureau of the Census, *Statistical Abstract of the United States* (Washington, D.C.: U.S. Government Printing Office), various editions, and Tax Foundation, *Facts and Figures on Government Finance, 1991*, pp. 24–25.

information that is not easily obtainable by the sponsor. Just consider the technical expertise required to monitor production of electronic guidance systems for missiles.

Are government bureaucracies more likely to operate at points Q_{bc} or Q^*? One way to find out would be to compare the costs and outputs of a government bureau to a private firm producing the same product. For example, hospital services are provided by both public and private institutions. Unfortunately, in many important cases like the Department of Defense, there is no private operation that corresponds to the public bureau. Moreover, as noted in Chapter 5, government bureaucracies tend to produce outputs that are very hard to measure. (How can the quantity and quality of health care produced by a public or private hospital be measured?) Thus, the widespread suspicion that bureaucrats' main concern is empire building is hard to confirm or deny.

Bureaucrats' salaries.   Another complaint about bureaucrats is that they are overpaid. It is argued that because government agencies are not subject to competitive pressures to minimize their costs, they pay more than private sector firms. According to this view, overpayment is also encouraged by the fact that public employees and their families vote for politicians who grant them big raises.

Table 7.7 provides some data on the salaries of public sector employees and those in the private sector. Both federal and state and local pay levels exceed those in the private sector, although the margin is substantially greater for federal employees. It would be erroneous to conclude immediately from these figures that federal employees are overpaid, because it may be that federal employment requires more skills (such as higher levels of education) than private employment. For the same reason, one cannot jump to the conclusion that state and local workers are paid approximately equivalently to private sector workers. The salaries of public- and private-sector workers *with similar qualifications* must be compared.

Richard Freeman [1985] analyzed the salaries of employees in both sectors, taking into account differences in education, work experience, marital status, sex, race, and so on.[25] He found that government workers as a whole have wages only 2 percent higher than equally qualified private sector workers. But this figure masks considerable differences among various types of jobs. Workers in federal public administration enjoy a 19 percent higher wage rate than their private sector counterparts; for state and local public administrators, this figure is about 5 percent, and for postal workers it is 26 percent. On the other hand, public school teachers earn about 6 percent *less* than comparable private sector workers.

Freeman's figures, however, do not take into account the different pension benefits received by public and private sector employees. Again, there are large differences by level of government and occupation. But the general result seems to be that public sector plans are more generous. For example, Howard Frant and Herman Leonard [1984] estimate that among state and local workers, the percentage of average final earnings that a worker receives per year of service is 1.9 percent; the comparable private sector figure is about 1.0 percent.

Special Interests

We have been assuming so far that citizens who seek to influence government policy can act only as individual voters.[26] In fact, people with common interests can exercise disproportionate power by acting together. The source of the group's power might be that its members tend to have higher voter participation rates than the population as a whole. Alternatively, members might be willing to use their incomes to make campaign contributions and/or pay bribes. As an example, in 1987–88, members of the House and Senate received $476.5 million in campaign contributions [U.S. Bureau of the Census, 1990, p. 269].

On what bases are these power groups established? There are many possibilities.

Source of income: Capital or labor.   According to orthodox Marxism, people's political interests are determined by whether they are capitalists or laborers. This view is too simple to explain interest-group formation in the contemporary United States. Even though there is a tendency for

---

[25] Freeman estimated a regression equation in which the dependent variable is the logarithm of the wage, and the explanatory variables include various worker characteristics and a public-employment variable. The public-employment variable is equal to one if the individual is employed in the public sector and is zero otherwise. The coefficient on this variable therefore gives the public-sector wage differential.

[26] Much of this section is based on the excellent treatment by Musgrave [1980].

those with high incomes to receive a disproportionate share of their income from capital, much of the income of the rich is also derived from labor. Thus, it is difficult even to identify who are the capitalists and the laborers. Indeed, in the United States more than half of the inequality in total income is due to inequality in labor income, and only about 10 percent due to inequality in capital income [Lerman and Yitzhaki, 1985].

Size of income. On many economic policy issues, the rich and the poor have different views, independent of the sources of their incomes. The poor favor redistributive spending programs and the rich oppose them. Similarly, each group supports implicit or explicit subsidies for goods they tend to consume intensively. Hence, the rich support subsidies for owner-occupied housing, while the poor favor special treatment for rental housing.

Source of income: Industry of employment. Both workers and owners have a common interest in government support for their industry. A good example is provided by the efforts of the textile industry to erect trade barriers: "Labor and management have fought a number of brushfire wars across the South in recent years over the unionization of textile mills. But on Capitol Hill these days, the old antagonists are working closely together on a common problem: protecting the textile industry from a flood of foreign imports" [Roberts, 1985, p. A14].

Region. Residents of geographical regions often share common interests. Citizens of the Sun Belt are interested in favorable tax treatment of oil; midwesterners care about agricultural subsidies; and northeasterners lobby for expenditures on urban development.

Demographic and personal characteristics. The aged favor subsidized health care and generous retirement programs; young married couples are interested in good schools and low payroll taxes. Religious beliefs play a major role in debates over the funding of abortion and state aid to private schools. Ethnic groups differ on the propriety of government expenditure for bilingual education programs. Some analysts argue that gender is beginning to be an important basis for interest-group formation; in the 1990 congressional elections, women voted in disproportionately large numbers for Democrats, and much concern was expressed by Republicans over the gender gap.

The list could go on indefinitely. Given the numerous bases on which interest groups can be established, it is no surprise that people who are in opposition on one issue may be in agreement on another; "politics makes strange bedfellows" is more or less the order of the day.

This discussion has ignored the question of how individuals with common interests actually manage to organize themselves. Belonging to a group may require membership fees, donation of time, and so forth. Each individual has an incentive to let others do the work while he or she reaps the benefits, becoming a free rider. George Stigler [1974] suggests that the probability that a group will actually form increases when the number of individuals is small, and it is possible to levy sanctions against nonjoiners. But perhaps the role of rational financial self-interest should not be relied on too heavily as an explanation in this context. It is only necessary to observe the debate over the public funding of abortion to realize the influence of ideology and emotion on the decision to join a group.

The iron triangle.   Let us now consider the interaction of interest groups with bureaucrats and elected representatives. In the view of some social commentators, this three-sided relationship—the **iron triangle**—is the most important aspect of modern American politics [Will, 1981, p. 120]. The idea is that the members of Congress who authorize a given program, the bureaucrats who administer it, and the special interests who benefit from it all tend to coalesce behind the program. Thus, we observe members of the construction, lumber, and electrical machinery industries joining with bureaucrats from the Department of Housing and Urban Development and members of Congress with urban constituents to support public housing.

The obvious question to ask is how such bills are passed by a majority if they benefit only members of an iron triangle. There are two possible explanations: One reason is that interest groups and bureaucrats may be well organized and armed with information, while those who will bear the costs are not organized and may not even be aware of what is going on. Even if those citizens who will bear the costs are well informed, it may not be worth their while to fight back. Because the costs of the program are spread over the population as a whole, any given citizen's share is low, and even if total costs exceed total benefits, it would not be worth the time and effort to organize opposition. In contrast, the benefits are relatively concentrated, making political organization worthwhile for potential beneficiaries. (See Olson [1982].)

The other reason for the success of such bills is that other representatives may be involved in their *own* iron triangles and therefore willing to trade votes to gain support for their pet projects. According to one member of the House of Representatives, the system works this way: each member brings his or her pet project to the chairman of the relevant committee, who incorporates it into a giant appropriations bill. "But there's one rule of thumb . . . You keep your mouth shut on all other projects in the bill" ["How Congress Slices the Pork," 1982, p. 18].

As usual, it is not clear how much weight should be given to anecdotes. Determining the actual importance of the iron triangle phenomenon is a difficult task.

Other Actors   Without attempting to be exhaustive, we list a few other parties who affect government fiscal decisions.

The judiciary.   Court decisions on the legality of various taxes have major effects on government finance. One of the most famous Supreme Court rulings on taxation was the 1895 decision that a federal tax on personal incomes was unconstitutional. This was circumvented in 1913 by the 16th Amendment to the Constitution. The judiciary also affects the expenditure side of the account. Judges have mandated public expenditures on items as diverse as bilingual education in the public schools and prison remodeling.

A fascinating question is how far the judiciary can go in seeing that judicially mandated spending is carried out. In 1987, a federal district court judge ordered a property tax increase for Kansas City after voters had repeatedly rejected tax increases necessary to fund mandated improvements to the city's decaying public schools. In defense of his action, Judge Russell Clark wrote, "A majority has no right to deny others the constitutional guarantees to which they are entitled" [Seligmann and Hammill, 1987, p. 98]. Judge Clark's ruling was upheld by the U.S. Court of Appeals.

Journalists.   The ability to bring certain issues to public attention gives the press considerable influence. For example, the widespread publicity given to certain parts of the Reagan administration's plan to cut school lunches helped lead to their defeat in Congress. Politicians, bureaucrats, and special-interest groups often try to use the media to influence the outcome of debates on fiscal issues. For example, in recent years the advocates of AIDS victims have brought their plight to public attention by numerous media events. This attention contributed to the enactment of increased federal subsidies for research on AIDS.

Experts.   Information is potentially an important source of power. Legislative aides who gain expertise on certain programs often play important roles in drafting statutes. They can also affect outcomes by virtue of their ability to influence which items are put on the legislative agenda. Of course, there are also experts outside the government. Many academic social scientists have sought to use their expertise to influence economic policy. Economists love to quote John Maynard Keynes' [1965/1936, p. 383] famous dictum "the ideas of economists and political philosophers, both when they are right and when they are wrong, are more powerful than is commonly understood. Indeed, the world is ruled by little else." However, it is extremely difficult to determine whether social science research influences policy, and if so, through what channels this influence operates. In his careful study of the relationship between academic research and the formulation of Great Society programs during the administration of Lyndon Johnson, Henry Aaron [1978, p. 9] observed that "in many cases, the findings of social science seemed to come after, rather than before, changes in policy, which suggests that political events may influence scholars more than research influences policy."

Explaining Government Growth

Much of the concern about whether government operates efficiently has been stimulated by the rate of growth in government. As documented in Chapter 2, over the long run, both defense and nondefense expenditures in the United States have grown enormously, both in absolute terms and proportionately. A growing public sector is not unique to the United States, as the figures for a few other Western countries in Table 7.8 indicate. Thus, as we search for explanations for the growth in government, care must be taken not to rely too heavily on events and institutions that are peculiar to the U.S. experience. Also, the various explanations are not necessarily mutually exclusive. No single theory accounts for the whole phenomenon. Indeed, even taken together, they still leave much unexplained. Some of the most prominent theories follow:

Citizen preferences.   Growth in government expenditure is an expression of the preferences of the citizenry. Suppose that the median voter's demand for public sector goods and services (G) can be written as some function (f) of the relative price of public sector goods and services (P) and income (I):

$$G = f(P,I) \qquad (7.2)$$

Table 7.8   **Ratio of government expenditures to GNP in selected countries** *(selected years)*

Year	Canada	Switzerland	United Kingdom
1900	9.5	n.a.	14.4
1910	11.4	n.a.	12.7
1920	16.1	n.a.	26.2
1930	18.9	15.9	26.1
1940	23.1	19.2	30.0
1950	22.1	19.9	39.0
1960	29.7	17.7	31.9
1970	31.2	21.3	33.2
1980	37.8	29.3	41.8
1987	44.2	28.8	39.0

n.a.   Not available.

SOURCE: Years prior to 1970 from Pommerehne, "Quantitative Aspects of Federalism: A Study of Six Countries," in *The Political Economy of Fiscal Federalism,* ed. Wallace Oates (Lexington, Mass.: D. C. Heath, 1977), p. 310. Years 1970, 1980, and 1987 computed from *National Accounts,* vol. 2 (Paris: Organization for Economic Cooperation and Development, 1989), pp. 13, 480, 507.

There are many different ways such a demand function can lead to an increasing proportion of income spent on public-sector goods and services.[27] Suppose that when income increases by a given percentage, the quantity demanded of public goods and services increases by a greater percentage—the income elasticity of demand is greater than one. If this is the case, the process of income growth by itself leads to an ever-increasing share of income going to the public sector, other things being the same.[28] Similarly, if the elasticity of G with respect to I is less than one but P falls fast enough over time, an increase in government's share of income may also occur.

The important point is that the relative increase in the size of the public sector does not necessarily imply that something is "wrong" with the political process. Government growth could well be a consequence of the wishes of voters, who rationally take into account its opportunity cost in forgone consumption in the private sector. The question then becomes whether the actual changes in P and I over time could have accounted for the actual historical changes in G. To answer this question, Thomas Borcherding [1985] begins by computing the actual percentage changes in P and I that have taken place over time. He then multiplies the percentage change in P by the elasticity of G with respect to P, and the percentage change in I by the elasticity with respect to I.[29] This calculation yields the percentage change in G attributable solely to changes in P and I. Borcherding then compares this figure with the actual change in G, and finds that only about 38 percent of the growth in U.S. public budgets can be explained by Equation (7.2). While this is an admittedly rough calculation, it does suggest that more is going on than a simple median voter story can explain.

Political-economic interaction.   According to some Marxist theories, the rise of state expenditure is viewed as inherent to the political-economic system.[30] In the Marxist model, the private sector tends to overproduce, so the capitalist-controlled government must expand expenditures to absorb this production. Typically, this is accomplished by augmenting military spending. At the same time, the state attempts to decrease worker discontent by increasing spending for social services. Eventually, rising expenditures outpace tax revenue capacity, and the government collapses.

Richard Musgrave [1980] argues that the historical facts are inconsistent with this analysis. "There is little evidence . . . [that] expenses

---

[27] In this context, income redistribution should be thought of as a government service.

[28] The hypothesis that government services rise at a faster rate than income is often called **Wagner's Law,** after Adolph Wagner, the 19th-century economist who formulated it.

[29] These elasticities come from econometric studies of the demand for public goods of the kind discussed earlier in this chapter.

[30] These theories are surveyed by Musgrave [1980], on which this discussion is based.

directed at appeasing social unrest [have] continuously increased'' [p. 388]. It is also noteworthy that in Western Europe, the enormous increase in the size and scope of government in the post–World War II era has been accompanied by anything but a resurgence in militarism. The main contribution of this Marxist analysis is its explicit recognition of the links between the economic and political systems as sources of government growth.

Chance events.   In contrast to the theories that view government growth as inevitable are those which consider it as the consequence of chance events. In ''normal'' periods there is only moderate growth in public expenditure. Occasionally, however, external shocks to the economic and social system ''require'' higher levels of government expenditure and novel methods of financing. Even after the shock disappears, higher levels continue to prevail because of inertia. A. T. Peacock and J. Wiseman [1967] call this the *displacement effect*. Examples of shocks are the Great Depression, World War II, the Great Society, and the Vietnam War.

Societal attitudes.   In popular discussions, it is sometimes suggested that specific changes in societal attitudes have encouraged government growth. Robert Lubar [1980] argued that social trends encouraging personal self-assertiveness lead people to make extravagant demands on the political system. At the same time, widespread television advertising has created unrealistically high expectations, leading to a ''Santa Claus mentality'' that causes people to lose track of the fact that government programs do have an opportunity cost.

However, it could just as well be argued that people misperceive the benefits of government projects instead of their costs. In this case, there would be a tendency for the public sector to be too small, not too big. More generally, although recent social phenomena might account for some movement in the growth of government expenditure, this growth has been going on for too many years and in too many places for this explanation to have much credibility.

Income redistribution.   Government grows because low-income individuals use the political system to redistribute income toward themselves [see Meltzer & Richard, 1981]. The idea is that politicians can attract voters whose incomes are at or below the median by offering benefits that impose a net cost on those whose incomes are above the median. As long as average income exceeds the median, and the mechanisms used to bring about redistribution are not too detrimental to incentives, politicians have an incentive to increase the scope of government-sponsored income distribution. Suppose, for example, that there are five voters whose incomes are $5,000; $10,000; $15,000; $25,000; and $40,000. The median income is

$15,000 and the average income is $19,000. A politician who supports government programs that transfer income to those with less than $25,000 will win in majority voting.

If this is the case, it must still be explained why the share of public expenditures increases *gradually* (as in Table 2.1). Why not a huge once-and-for-all transfer as the poor confiscate the incomes of the rich? Because in Western countries, property and/or status requirements for voting have *gradually* been abolished during the last century. In the United States, many of the remaining barriers to voting were removed by civil rights laws passed in the 1960s. Extension of the right to vote to those at the bottom of the income scale increases the proportion of voters likely to support politicians promising redistribution. Hence, it is the gradual extension of the franchise that leads to continuous growth in government, rather than a once-and-for-all increase.

One problem with this theory is that it fails to explain the methods used by government to redistribute income. If it is correct, most income transfers should go to the poor and should take the form that would maximize their welfare, that is, direct cash transfers. Instead, as we see in Chapter 8, transfers in the United States are often given in kind and many benefit those in the middle- and upper-income classes.

An alternate view of the role of income redistribution focuses not on the poor, but on middle-income individuals. As George Stigler [1970] argues, "Public expenditures are made for the benefit primarily of the middle classes, and financed by taxes which are borne in considerable part by the poor and the rich."[31] But there are also government transfer programs with rich beneficiaries; see, for example, the discussion of Medicare in Chapter 11.

Transfer programs that benefit different income classes can exist simultaneously, so these various views of government redistribution are not necessarily mutually exclusive. The important point here is their common theme. Government growth is a consequence of individuals attempting to use the political system to redistribute income toward themselves. Generically, these activities are called **rent-seeking**—using the government to obtain higher than normal returns ("rents"). Via the iron triangle discussed previously, coalitions of politicians, rent-seeking special-interest groups, and bureaucrats vote themselves programs of ever-increasing size.

There are very different hypotheses for explaining the growth of the state's economic role. Unfortunately, the chances for testing them econometrically seem remote. To begin with, it is very difficult to measure the

---

[31] Stigler dubs this proposition **Director's Law,** after economist Aaron Director, an economist who made this observation.

size of government (see Chapter 2). In addition, it is hard to quantify many of the variables that are important in the politically oriented theories—how, for example, can "bureaucratic power" be measured? Thus, the relative importance of each theory is likely to remain open to question.

Bringing Government under Control

As we have seen, substantial growth in the public sector need not imply that there is anything wrong with the political budgetary process. For those who believe that public sector fiscal behavior is more or less at the size desired by the median voter, bringing government under control is a nonissue.[32] On the other hand, for those who perceive growth in government as a symptom of flaws in the political process, bringing government under control is very much a problem.

Two types of argument are made in the controllability debate. One view is that the basic problem results from commitments made by government in the past, so there is very little current legislators and executives can do to change the rate of growth or composition of government expenditures. Entitlement programs that provide benefits to the retired, disabled, unemployed, sick, and others are the largest category of uncontrollable expenditures. When we add in other items such as payments on the national debt, farm support programs, and certain defense expenditures, it turns out that about 75 percent of the federal budget is uncontrollable.

There is some controversy over how uncontrollable these expenditures really are. If legislation created entitlement programs, it can take them away. In theory, then, many of the programs can be reduced or even removed. In reality, both moral and political considerations work against reneging on past promises to various groups in the population. Any serious reductions are likely to be scheduled sufficiently far into the future so that people who have made commitments based on current programs will not be affected.

According to the second argument, our political institutions are fundamentally flawed, and bringing things under control is more than just a matter of changing the entitlement programs. A number of remedies have been proposed.

Change bureaucratic incentives.   Niskanen, who views bureaucracy as a cause of unwarranted government growth, suggests that financial incentives be created to mitigate bureaucrats' empire-building tendencies. For example, the salary of a government manager could be made to depend negatively on changes in the size of his or her agency. A bureaucrat who cut the agency's budget would get a raise. (Similar rewards could be offered to budget-cutting legislators.) However, it is easy to imagine such

---

[32] Of course, the composition of government expenditure is at issue, not just its total size. Some believe that defense expenditures are out of control, and social welfare expenditures are too small. Others argue to the contrary.

a system's leading to some undesirable results. To increase his or her salary, the bureaucrat might reduce the budget beyond the point at which marginal benefits equal marginal costs.

Niskanen also suggests expanding the use of private firms to produce public goods and services, although the public sector would continue to finance them. The question of whether privatization is likely to reduce the costs of services that are currently produced by the government was already discussed in Chapter 5.

Change the budget process.   Most of the focus on bringing government spending under control has been on the budget-making process itself. Prior to the 1970s, the congressional procedure lacked coherence. The president submitted a budget message to Congress. Subcommittees concerned with different types of expenditure examined the budget independently. There was little coordination among committees, and decisions were made without considering a common budget total. It was as if a husband would make food decisions and a wife housing decisions, neither consulting the other or taking into account the size of the family income.

The Congressional Budget and Impoundment Control Act of 1974 was an attempt to improve this situation. A special budget committee was formed in each house, and a detailed calendar for the budget process was established. The act also created a budgetary bureaucracy for the Congress, the Congressional Budget Office, with the job of providing the technical skill required to estimate costs of proposed legislation so that legislators can make sensible decisions.

Essentially, the purpose of the 1974 reform was to add some rationality to the budget process by forcing Congress to vote on totals, instead of just on individual items. However, critics of the reform argued that it left the spending process about as undisciplined as ever, citing as evidence the existence of large federal deficits. Of course, the presence of a deficit is not by itself evidence that spending is "too high." Perhaps it means that taxes are "too low." Or a deficit may not be a social problem in any case. (This possibility is discussed in Chapter 18.) Nevertheless, the existence of large and persistent deficits is commonly viewed as a failure in the U.S. system of public choice.

By the mid-1980s, congressional frustration over its inability to reduce the federal deficit (which was $212 billion in 1985) set the stage for a dramatic change in the budgetary process. In 1985 Congress passed and President Reagan signed the Balanced Budget and Emergency Deficit Control Act, better known as **Gramm-Rudman-Hollings (GRH),** after its legislative sponsors, Phil Gramm, Warren B. Rudman, and Ernest F. Hollings. The original GRH legislation, which has since been amended, established a set of steadily declining deficit targets after 1986, culminating in a balanced budget in 1991. The crucial feature of the original GRH legislation was that if Congress failed to reduce the deficit to the target level prior to the start of the fiscal year, the excess deficit was *automati-*

cally removed by cutting budget outlays. The process of making such automatic cuts was referred to as a **sequester.** Thus, through GRH, the Congress bound itself to a rule to reduce the deficit.

According to GRH, half the mandatory cuts had to come from defense and half from nondefense spending. But some programs were totally exempt, including Social Security, interest payments on the national debt, most Medicare payments, and Pentagon multi-year contracts. Every nondefense program that was not exempted had to be cut by the *same* proportion.

At the time of its passage, GRH was very controversial. It was variously described as "an act of legislative desperation," "clumsy and cowardly," and "an important and innovative political experiment." Those who favored GRH believed that logrolling and special interest politics lead to irresistible incentives to increase government spending beyond the optimal amount. GRH allows legislators to tell their constituencies that spending cuts are not their fault—GRH is the villain.

To the criticism that it is cowardly for the Congress to evade its responsibility to make hard budgetary decisions, one proponent argued, "In personal life as in political life, it is wise and important that we can sometimes borrow courage by resorting to strategems and formulas and tricks that will make it easier to do what is right" [Bator, 1986, p. 12]. In the jargon of economics, this argument views GRH as the solution to a principal-agent problem. (See Chapter 5.) The principal, P (the public, as represented by the current Congress) must rely on an agent, A (future Congresses) to perform various tasks. However, P cannot know for sure whether A is acting in P's interest. P therefore puts constraints on A's behavior to produce a desirable outcome.

Critics of GRH focused their attention on the automatic across-the-board cutting procedure. If spending is to be reduced, it should be done in such a way that the marginal social benefit of the last dollar spent on each program is the same. In general, taking the same percentage out of each program's budget will not be consistent with this rule. Thus, GRH does not allow priorities to be set rationally. For example, the Drug Enforcement Agency would have its budget cut in the midst of a serious upsurge in the use of crack and other illegal substances. In the words of one critic, "Gramm-Rudman outlaws choice, discretion, thought" [Will, 1986, p. 80]. Keynesian macroeconomists also argued that GRH would make it more difficult for the federal government to conduct an effective stabilization policy because deficit spending to fight recessions was allowed only under certain very stringent conditions.

So, who turned out to be right, the critics or proponents of GRH? The GRH has not led to traumatic across-the-board cuts in spending, in spite of persistently large budget deficits. In some years, legislators used gimmicks to meet the GRH targets and avoid sequester. In its first year of operation, for example, one trick was to backdate "revenue-sharing and Medicare checks, so that hundreds of millions of [the current] year's expenditures [could] be counted against [the] last year's budget" [O'Connor, 1986, p. 35]. Such "smoke and mirrors" gimmickry subsequently was forbidden, but to little avail. To reduce the 1990 deficit, for example, telephone companies were told to pay their taxes a week early, adding $102 million in revenues that otherwise would have accrued in 1991 [Kenworthy, 1989, p. 14A].

In addition to trickery, legislators simply changed the GRH legislation. For example, the original GRH legislation called for a balanced budget in 1991. The targets for 1988 onward were then amended, raising the 1991 deficit target to $64 billion. The budget eventually passed for 1991 contained a deficit estimated at $260 billion; nonetheless, GRH spending cuts were not invoked.

The original GRH target for 1990 was $36 billion. The actual figure was $220 billion. This led to a widespread feeling that something new had to be tried, and two major changes in GRH were enacted in 1990. First, instead of making failure to reach arbitrary *deficit* targets the action-forcing events, the focus was shifted to *spending* targets. Specifically, for 1991 through 1994, the new law set separate caps on three categories of spending programs: defense, domestic discretionary, and international. The second major change concerned the consequences of exceeding spending targets. If the targets are exceeded, the administration is authorized to make across-the-board cuts in all programs *within the same category*. Under the previous version of the law, *all* categories of spending were cut if the target was exceeded. The reason for the change was the belief that the previous GRH law had failed because the threat of across-the-board cuts was so draconian that no one took it seriously. The hope was that a "mini-sequester" for each category would be more efficacious because it was a more credible threat.

Institute constitutional limitations.   Some commentators believe that the weakness of Gramm-Rudman-Hollings is that it is simply a piece of legislation and as such readily can be amended, suspended, or repealed by a majority vote of both houses of Congress. They would go further, and put budgetary rules into the Constitution itself. In the early 1980s, a proposed constitutional amendment with the following provisions received much public attention:

1. Congress must adopt a budget statement "in which total outlays are no greater than total receipts."
2. Total receipts may not increase "by a rate greater than the rate of increase in national income."
3. "The Congress and President shall . . . ensure that actual outlays do not exceed the outlays set forth in the budget statement."
4. The provisions can be overridden in times of war.

Although the amendment received a lot of political support (including the president's), after a lengthy debate, it failed to get through Congress.

Most economists of both liberal and conservative political persuasions believe that for several reasons the amendment was ill conceived.[33]

First, adopting a statement of outlays and revenues requires making forecasts about how the economy will perform. This problem is sufficiently difficult that forecasters with complete integrity can arrive at very different estimates. How does the Congress choose among forecasts? If an incorrect forecast is chosen, Congress may be in violation of the law without realizing it! Things become even murkier when it is realized that some forecasts will be biased by political considerations. Those who want to expand expenditures, for example, would encourage forecasts that indicated a high rate of growth of tax revenues during the coming year and vice versa.

Second, the amendment fails to define outlays and receipts. By using suitable accounting methods, Congress could easily circumvent the law. For example, the government could simply create various agencies and corporations that were authorized to make expenditures and borrow. As noted in Chapter 2 under "The Size of Government," such off-budget credit activity is already an important way of concealing the actual size of the budget. More generally, the experience with GRH discussed earlier indicates that if politicians have incentives to increase spending, they find ways to do so regardless of the budgetary rules.

Finally, legal scholars have noted some important questions. What happens if there is a deficit? Is the entire Congress put in jail? Could Congress be sued for spending too much? Could a single citizen go to court and obtain an injunction to stop all government activity in the event of a deficit? Again, the experience with GRH seems informative. When various deadlines stated in the law were missed, nothing happened. And when the consequences of complying with the law seemed worse than ignoring the law, the law was ignored.

Conclusions

Public choices are made in a complicated fashion that is not well understood. Contrary to simple models of democracy, there appear to be forces pulling government expenditures away from levels that would be preferred by the median voter. However, critics of the current budgetary process have not come up with a satisfactory alternative. The formulation of meaningful rules and constraints for the budgetary process, either at the constitutional or statutory level, is an important item on both the academic and political agendas for the years ahead. In this context it should be stressed that the judgment that government currently may be inequitable or inefficient does not necessarily imply that government as an institution is "bad." People who like market-oriented approaches to resource allocation can nevertheless seek to improve markets. The same goes for government.

---

[33] See Penner [1982], and Suits and Fisher [1985].

Summary

This chapter examines the problems of public choice in the contexts of both direct and representative democracy.

Direct Democracy

- Economists have studied several methods of providing public goods:

  Lindahl pricing results in a unanimous decision to provide an efficient quantity of public goods, but relies on honest revelation of preferences.

  Majority voting may lead to inconsistent decisions regarding public goods if some people's preferences are not single peaked.

  Logrolling allows voters to express the intensity of their preferences by trading votes. However, minority gains may come at the expense of greater general losses.

- Arrow's Impossibility Theorem states that in general it is impossible to find a decision-making rule that simultaneously satisfies a number of apparently reasonable criteria. The implication is that democracies are inherently prone to inconsistency regarding public goods and other decisions.

Representative Democracy

- Explanations of actual government performance require studying the interaction of elected officials, public employees, and special-interest groups.

- Under restrictive assumptions, the actions of elected officials mimic the wishes of the median voter.

- Voters may respond to recent economic performance. If they do, the actions of elected politicians are focused on favorably influencing the economy. Recent research indicates that near-term economic conditions are powerful predictors of voting behavior in presidential elections.

- Public employees have an important impact on the development and implementation of economic policy. One theory predicts that bureaucrats will attempt to maximize the size of their agency's budget, resulting in oversupply of the service.

- Rent-seeking private citizens form groups to influence government activity. Special interests can form on the basis of income source, income size, industry, region, or personal characteristics.

- The growth of government has been rapid by any measure. Explanations of this phenomenon include:

  Citizen preferences.

  Marxist theories. Simple Marxism predicts that the public sector must expand to absorb private excess production.

  Chance. Random events (such as wars) increase the growth of government, while inertia prevents a return to previous levels.

  Societal attitudes. Unrealistic expectations have resulted in increasing demands that ignore the opportunity costs of public programs.

  Income redistribution. Two theories are popular. One predicts that politicians form a coalition of the poor and redistribute in their favor. Another suggests that middle- and upper-income groups employ the iron triangle to increase their shares of income.

- Proposals to control the growth in government include decentralization to reduce bureaucratic power, encouraging private-sector competition, reforming the budget process, and direct legislative restrictions.

  As amended in 1990, the Gramm-Rudman-Hollings Act requires the Congress to meet certain spending targets each year. If these targets are not met, then automatic spending cuts are mandated. However, large automatic spending costs are too draconian a threat to be credible.

Discussion Questions

1. Suppose that there are five people—1, 2, 3, 4, and 5—who rank projects A, B, C, and D as follows:

1	2	3	4	5
A	A	D	C	B
D	C	B	B	C
C	B	C	D	D
B	D	A	A	A

   a. Sketch the preferences, as in Figure 7.2.
   b. Will any project be chosen by a majority vote rule? If so, which one? If not, explain why.

2. Suppose that in a given referendum, the conditions required for the median voter rule are satisfied. Construct an example to demonstrate that the outcome can be inefficient, that is, that Equation (5.2) is violated. (Hint: Write down marginal benefits and marginal costs for each voter, and remember that the marginal costs [tax burdens] can differ across voters.)

3. Industries in the country of Technologia invest in new equipment that annually increases productivity of private workers by 3 percent. Government employees do not benefit from similar technical advances.

   a. If wages in the private sector are set equal to the value of the marginal product, how much will they rise yearly?
   b. Government workers annually receive increases so that wages remain comparable to those in the private sector. What happens to the price of public services relative to privately produced goods?
   c. If the same quantity of public services is produced each year, what happens to the size of the government (measured by spending)?

4. In 1990, California's voters passed a referendum limiting to 12 the number of years an individual could serve in the state legislature. If the assumptions of the median voter model hold, how would term limitations affect the level of state expenditures? If the "iron triangle" model holds, how would expenditures be affected?

5. In 1990, the Congress proposed a $500,000 appropriation to build a museum in North Dakota dedicated to the performer Lawrence Welk. What theory of government spending discussed in this chapter might explain this proposed appropriation?

Selected References

Blair, Douglas H., and Robert A. Pollak. "Rational Collective Choice." *Scientific American* 249, no. 2 (August 1983), pp. 88–95.

Borcherding, Thomas E. "The Causes of Government Expenditure Growth: A Survey of the U.S. Evidence." *Journal of Public Economics* 28, no. 3 (December 1985), pp. 359–82.

Congressional Budget Office. *Balancing the Federal Budget and Limiting Federal Spending: Constitutional and Statutory Approaches.* Washington, D.C.: U.S. Government Printing Office, 1982.

Fair, Ray C. "The Effect of Economic Events on Votes for President: 1980 Results." *Review of Economics and Statistics* 64, no. 2 (May 1982), pp. 322–24.

Greider, William. "The Education of David Stockman." *The Atlantic Monthly,* December 1981, pp. 27–54.

CHAPTER 8

Income Redistribution: Conceptual Issues

A decent provision for the poor is the true test of civilization.

SAMUEL JOHNSON

"In general, the art of government consists in taking as much money as possible from one class of citizens to give to the other." While Voltaire's assertion is an overstatement, it is true that virtually every important political issue has implications for the distribution of income. Even when they are not explicit, questions of who will gain and who will lose lurk in the background of most public policy debates. This chapter presents a framework for thinking about the normative and positive aspects of government income redistribution policy. The next chapter then uses this framework to analyze major government programs for maintaining the incomes of the poor.

At the outset, note that not everybody agrees that economists should consider distributional effects in their policy analyses. Notions concerning the "right" income distribution are value judgments and there is no "scientific" way to resolve differences in matters of ethics. Therefore, some argue that discussion of distributional issues is detrimental to objectivity in economics and that economists should restrict themselves to analyzing only the efficiency aspects of social issues.[1]

This view has two problems. The first is that, as emphasized in Chapter 4, the theory of welfare economics indicates that efficiency by itself cannot be used to judge the desirability of a given situation. Criteria other

---

[1] For additional arguments that economists should put distributional matters in the background, see Kristol [1980].

than efficiency must be brought to bear on questions that involve comparing alternative allocations of resources. Of course, it can be asserted that only efficiency matters, but this in itself is a value judgment.

In addition, decision makers care about the distributional implications of policy. If economists ignore distribution, then policymakers will ignore economists. Policymakers may thus end up focusing only on distributional issues and pay no attention at all to efficiency. The economist who systematically takes distribution into account can keep policymakers aware of both efficiency and distributional issues. In sum, although training in economics certainly does not confer a superior ability to make ethical judgments, economists *are* skilled at drawing out the implications of alternative sets of values and measuring the costs of achieving various ethical goals.

A related question is whether government ought to be involved in changing the income distribution. As noted in Chapter 1, some important traditions of political philosophy suggest that government should play no redistributive role. However, even the most minimal government conceivable influences income distribution. For example, when the government purchases materials for public goods, some firms receive contracts and others do not; presumably the owners of the firms receiving the contracts enjoy increases in their relative incomes. More generally, both the taxing and spending activities of government are bound to change the distribution of real income. Distributional issues are part and parcel of the government's functioning.

Distribution of Income

To begin, it is useful to get some sense of what the present distribution of income actually looks like. Table 8.1 shows the U.S. income distribution for selected years since World War II. The figures in this table include cash transfers from the government, but exclude **in-kind transfers**—payments to individuals in commodities or services as opposed to cash. The table suggests the presence of a lot of inequality. In 1989, the richest fifth of the population received almost 45 percent of total income, while the share of the poorest fifth was less than 5 percent. The table also suggests that the income distribution has remained rather stable over time, although in recent years there has been an increase in inequality as measured by these data. The share of family income going to the richest fifth of families in 1989 was the highest ever recorded; the share going to the poorest fifth of families was the lowest since 1954, and the share going to the second poorest fifth was the lowest ever recorded.

Some very important qualifications must be kept in mind when interpreting such changes in the official income data. Recall that the data measure before-tax money incomes of households, so that any changes in tax burdens, in nonmonetary sources of economic support, or in the composition of households can affect the distribution of real resources in a way that may not be adequately reflected. In the 1980s, for example,

Table 8.1   **The distribution of money income among families** *(selected years)*

Year	Lowest Fifth	Second Fifth	Middle Fifth	Fourth Fifth	Highest Fifth	Top 5 Percent
			Percentage Share			
1947	5.0%	11.9%	17.0%	23.1%	43.0%	17.5%
1952	4.9	12.3	17.4	23.4	41.9	17.4
1957	5.1	12.7	18.1	23.8	40.4	15.6
1962	5.0	12.1	17.6	24.0	41.3	15.7
1967	5.5	12.4	17.9	23.9	40.4	15.2
1972	5.4	11.9	17.5	23.9	41.4	15.9
1977	5.2	11.6	17.5	24.2	41.5	15.7
1981	5.0	11.3	17.4	24.4	41.9	15.4
1984	4.7	11.0	17.0	24.4	42.9	16.0
1989	4.6	10.6	16.5	23.7	44.6	17.9

SOURCE: U.S. Bureau of the Census, *Current Population Reports*, series P-60 (Washington, D.C.: U.S. Government Printing Office), various issues. These figures do not include the value of in-kind transfers.

income taxes fell for most of the working poor, but Social Security payroll taxes rose. While both affected the purchasing power of the poor, these changes are not taken into account in the data. Neither do the data include the value of the future Social Security benefits to which the payroll taxes entitle people. Moreover, the data ignore resources that households receive in kind. In-kind transfers from the government, such as the provision of medical care, have increased in recent years. Another major in-kind resource is the value of time adults devote to their households; the official data miss important differences in the levels of economic resources available to single-parent versus two-parent families and between two-parent families with both parents working versus those with one parent at home. Finally, income is often shared across certain kinds of households. Changes in divorce rates or in the propensity of young or elderly adults to form their own households, for example, all have repercussions for the measured income distribution. We discuss these and other problems in income measurement later in this chapter.

Another way to get a sense of the problems associated with the income distribution is to compute the number of people below the **poverty line,** a fixed level of real income considered enough to provide a minimally adequate standard of living.[2] While there is clearly some abitrariness in determining what is adequate, the notion of a poverty line still provides a useful benchmark. The poverty line for a family of four in 1989 was

[2] To compute the poverty line, the first step is to estimate the minimum cost of a diet that meets adequate nutritional standards. The second step is to find the proportion of income spent on food in families of different sizes. The poverty line is then found by multiplying the reciprocal of this proportion by the cost of the ''adequate'' diet.

Table 8.2   **Who is poor? (1989)**

Group	Poverty Rate	Group	Poverty Rate
All persons	12.8%	Under 15 years	19.6%
White	10.0	65 years and older	11.4
Black	30.7	Female households,	
Spanish origin	26.2	no husband present	32.2

SOURCE: U.S. Bureau of the Census, "Money Income and Poverty Status of Families and Persons in the United States: 1989," *Current Population Reports*, series P-60, no. 168 (Washington, D.C.: U.S. Government Printing Office, 1990).

Table 8.3   **Poverty rate** *(selected years)*

Year	Poverty Rate	Year	Poverty Rate
1959	22.4%	1976	11.8%
1960	22.2	1979	11.7
1965	17.3	1982	15.0
1970	12.6	1985	14.0
1973	11.1	1989	12.8

SOURCE: U.S. Bureau of the Census, *Current Population Reports*, series P-60 (Washington, D.C.: U.S. Government Printing Office), various issues.

$12,675; during the same year, the median income—the level half the families were above and half below—was $32,640. In 1989, 31.5 million people were below the poverty line, 12.8 percent of the population [U.S. Department of Commerce, 1990].[3]

Table 8.2 shows the proportion of people below the poverty line for various demographic groups. Poverty is particularly widespread among female-headed households in which no husband is present—32 percent of such families are below the poverty line. Blacks and individuals of Spanish origin also have poverty rates substantially above that for the population as a whole.

Table 8.3 depicts changes in the poverty rate over time.[4] The figures suggest that the incidence of poverty in the United States is considerably lower now than it was three decades ago. However, the trend has not been steadily downward; during the 1970s the poverty rate was lower than it was in the 1980s.

In contemplating policies that might alleviate poverty, it is sometimes helpful to know how far the poverty population lies below the poverty

---

[3] These figures take into account money income only; the cash value of in-kind transfers is not included.

[4] For a discussion of the economic factors affecting the poverty rate, see Sawhill [1988].

line. The **poverty gap** measures how much income would have to be transferred to the poverty population to lift every household's income to the poverty line (assuming that the transfers had no effects on the recipients' work effort). In 1989, the poverty gap stood at $54.3 billion [Center for Budget and Policy Priorities, 1990, p. 7].

The question of why there are large disparities in income has long occupied a central place in economics and is far from definitively settled.[5] In the United States, the most important reason for inequality in family incomes appears to be differences in the wages and salaries of the family heads. Differences in property income (interest, dividends, etc.) account for only about 10 percent of income inequality [Lerman and Yitzhaki, 1985]. While very important, this observation does not explain income inequality—one must still account for the large differences in earnings. Earned income depends on items as diverse as physical strength, intelligence, effort, health, education, marriage decisions, the existence of race and sex discrimination, the presence of public welfare programs, and luck. No single item can account for every case of poverty. As we see later, this fact has bedeviled attempts to formulate sensible policies for redistributing income.

Rationales for Income Redistribution

As just shown, there is no doubt that income is distributed unequally. But there is a lot of controversy concerning whether the government is justified in undertaking policies to change that distribution. This section discusses several different views regarding whether the government should redistribute income, and, if so, to what extent.

Simple Utilitarianism

Conventional welfare economics posits that the welfare of society is defined by how well off its members are. Algebraically, if there are n individuals in society and the ith individual's utility is U_i, then social welfare, W, is some function $F(\cdot)$ of individuals' utilities:[6]

$$W = F(U_1, U_2, \ldots, U_n). \tag{8.1}$$

Equation (8.1) is sometimes referred to as a **utilitarian social welfare function** because of its association with the utilitarian social philosophers of the 19th century.[7] It is assumed that an increase in any of the U_is, other things being the same, increases W. A change that makes someone better off without making anyone worse off increases social welfare.

---

[5] For an excellent survey of alternative theories, see Atkinson [1983].

[6] This discussion ignores the problems that arise if the members of a society cannot agree on a social welfare function. See Chapter 7 under "Direct Democracy."

[7] Actually, the utilitarians postulated that social welfare was the sum of utilities, Equation (8.2), but the label is now often used to describe the more general formulation of Equation (8.1).

What does utilitarianism say about whether the government should redistribute income? The answer is straightforward—redistribute income as long as such a policy increases W. To obtain more specific guidance, it is useful to consider an important special case of Equation (8.1):

$$W = U_1 + U_2 + \ldots + U_N \tag{8.2}$$

Here social welfare is simply the sum of individuals' utilities. This is referred to as an **additive social welfare function.**

Suppose that the government's goal is to maximize the value of W given in Equation (8.2). Alone, this social welfare function tells us little about the appropriate governmental redistribution policy. If a few assumptions are made strong results can be obtained. Assume that:

1. Individuals have identical utility functions that depend only on their levels of income.
2. These utility functions exhibit diminishing marginal utility of income—as individuals' incomes increase, they become better off, but at a decreasing rate.
3. The total amount of income available is fixed.

Under these assumptions and the additive social welfare function of Equation (8.2), the government should redistribute income so that *complete equality* is obtained. To prove this, assume that the society consists of only two people, Peter and Paul. (It is easy to generalize the argument to cases where there is an arbitrary number of people.)

In Figure 8.1, the horizontal distance OO' measures the total amount of income available in society. Paul's income is measured by the distance to the right of point O; Peter's income is measured by the distance to the left of point O'. Thus, any point along OO' represents some distribution of income between Paul and Peter. The problem is to find the "best" point.

Paul's marginal utility of income is measured vertically, beginning at point O. Following assumption 2, the schedule relating Paul's marginal utility of income to his level of income is downward sloping. It is labeled MU_{Paul} in Figure 8.1. Peter's marginal utility of income is measured vertically, beginning at point O'. His marginal utility of income schedule is denoted MU_{Peter}. (Remember that movements to the left on the horizontal axis represent *increases* in Peter's income.) Because Peter and Paul have identical utility functions, MU_{Peter} is a mirror image of MU_{Paul}.

Assume that initially Paul's income is Oa and Peter's is $O'a$. Is social welfare as high as possible, or could the sum of utilities be increased if income were somehow redistributed between Paul and Peter? Suppose that ab dollars are taken from Peter and given to Paul. Obviously, this makes Peter worse off and Paul better off. However, the crucial question is what happens to the *sum* of their utilities. Because Peter is richer than Paul, Peter's loss in utility is smaller than Paul's gain, so that the sum of

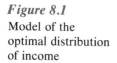

Figure 8.1

Model of the optimal distribution of income

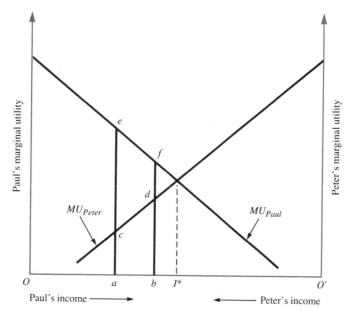

their utilities goes up. Geometrically, the area under each person's marginal utility of income schedule measures the change in his utility induced by the income change. Distributing *ab* dollars to Paul increases his utility by area *abfe*. Taking the *ab* dollars from Peter decreases his utility by area *abdc*. The sum of their utility therefore increases by *cefd*.

Similar reasoning suggests that as long as incomes are unequal, marginal utilities will be unequal, and the *sum* of utilities can be increased by distributing income to the poorer individual. Only at point *I**, where incomes and marginal utilities are equal, is social welfare maximized. Full income equality should be pursued.

The policy implications of this result are breathtaking, so the assumptions behind it require careful scrutiny.

Assumption 1. The validity of assuming that individuals have identical utility functions is fundamentally impossible to determine. It simply cannot be known whether individuals derive the same amount of satisfaction from the consumption of goods, because satisfaction cannot be objectively measured. There are, however, two possible defenses for the assumption. First, although it cannot be *proved* that people derive the same utility from equal amounts of income, it is a reasonable guess. After all, if people generally do not vary wildly in their observable characteristics—weight, height, and so on—why should their utility functions differ? Second, one can interpret the assumption not as a psychological statement, but as an *ethical* one. Specifically, in designing a redistributional policy, government ought to act *as if* all people have the same utility functions, whether they do or not.

Clearly, neither of these defenses would convince a skeptic, and the assumption remains troublesome.

Assumption 2.   A more technical, but equally important objection concerns the assumption of decreasing marginal utility of income. While it may be that the marginal utility of any given *good* decreases with its consumption, it is not clear that this is true for *income* as a whole. In Figure 8.1, the results change drastically if the marginal utility of income schedules fails to slope down. Suppose that the marginal utility of income is constant at all levels of income. Then MU_{Peter} and MU_{Paul} are represented by an identical horizontal line. Whenever a dollar is taken from Peter, the loss in his utility is exactly equal to Paul's gain. Thus, the value of the sum of their utilities is independent of the income distribution. Government redistributive policy cannot change social welfare.

Assumption 3.   By this assumption, the total amount of income in the society, distance OO', is totally fixed. The size of the pie does not change as the government redistributes its pieces. Suppose, however, that individuals' utilities depend not only on income but also on leisure. Each individual chooses how much leisure to surrender (how much to work) to maximize his utility. The taxes and subsidies enacted to redistribute income generally change people's work decisions and diminish total real income.[8] Thus, a society whose goal is to maximize the sum of utilities faces an inescapable dilemma. On one hand, it prefers to equalize the distribution of income. However, in the process of doing so, it reduces the total amount of income available. The optimal income distribution must take into account the costs (in lost real income) of achieving more equality. Some studies suggest that these costs may indeed be quite substantial. Charles Ballard [1985] estimated that each dollar increase in the disposable incomes of the lowest 20 percent of the income distribution requires a reduction of $1.40 to $1.90 in the disposable income of the highest 20 percent. However, research on this topic is still at a formative stage.[9]

Thus, even if we are willing to accept the assumption of identical utility functions, we cannot conclude that the goal of government distributional policy should be to obtain complete equality. The answer depends on the methods used to redistribute income and their effects on people's behavior.

The Maximin Criterion

In the utilitarian framework, the form of the social welfare function plays a crucial role in determining the appropriate governmental redistribution policy. So far, we have examined the simple additive social welfare func-

---

[8] It is possible that taxes and subsidies induce people to work more hours. However, even if their *money* incomes are higher, their real incomes (measured in utility) are lower because the taxes and subsidies distort their behavior patterns. See Chapter 14.

[9] See also Browning and Johnson [1984].

tion of Equation (8.2), according to which society is indifferent to the distribution of utilities.[10] If a unit of utility (or "util") is taken away from one individual and given to another, the sum of utilities is unchanged, and by definition, so is the level of social welfare.

Other kinds of utilitarian social welfare functions do not carry this implication, and hence yield different policy prescriptions. Consider the following social welfare function:

$$W = \text{Minimum}(U_1, U_2, \cdots, U_n) \tag{8.3}$$

According to Equation (8.3), social welfare depends only on the utility of the person who has the lowest utility. This social objective is often called the **maximin criterion** because the objective is to maximize the utility of the person with the minimum utility.[11] The maximin criterion implies that the income distribution should be perfectly equal, *except* to the extent that departures from equality increase the welfare of the worst-off person. Consider a society with a rich person, Peter, who employs a poor person, Paul. The government levies a tax on Peter, and distributes the proceeds to Paul. However, when Peter is taxed, he cuts production and fires Paul. Moreover, the income that Paul receives from the government is less than his job-related income loss. In this hypothetical economy, satisfaction of the maximin criterion would still allow for income disparities.

The maximin criterion has received considerable attention, principally because of philosopher John Rawls's [1971] assertion that it has a special claim to ethical validity. Rawls's argument relies on his notion of the **original position,** an imaginary situation in which people have no knowledge of what their place in society is to be. Because of this ignorance as to whether ultimately they will be rich or poor, Rawls believes that in the original position, people's opinions concerning distributional goals are impartial and fair. Rawls then argues that in the original position, people adopt the maximin social welfare function because of the insurance it provides against disastrous outcomes. People are frightened that they may end up at the bottom of the income distribution, and therefore want the level at the bottom as high as possible.

Rawls's analysis has raised considerable controversy. One important issue is whether decisions that people would make in the hypothetical original position have any superior claim to ethical validity. Why should the amoral and selfish views that individuals have in the original position be given special moral significance? Further, granted Rawls's view on the ethical validity of the original position, it is not obvious that rational self-interest would lead to the maximin criterion. Rawls's decision makers are

---

[10] Equation (8.2) does *not* imply that society is indifferent to the distribution of *incomes,* as was proved in the preceding section.

[11] The maximin criterion can be regarded as a special case of Equation (8.1). The function F(·) takes the minimum of all the utilities.

so averse to risk that they are unwilling to take any chances whatsoever. However, people might be willing to accept a small probability of being very poor in return for a good chance of receiving a high income.

Finally, critics have noted that the maximin criterion has some peculiar implications. Martin Feldstein [1976a, p. 84] considers the following scenario: "A new opportunity arises to raise the welfare of the least advantaged by a slight amount, but almost everyone else must be made substantially worse off, except for a few individuals who would become extremely wealthy." Because *all* that is relevant is the welfare of the worst-off person, the maximin criterion indicates that society should pursue this opportunity. Intuitively, however, such a course seems quite unappealing.

**Pareto Efficient
Income
Redistribution**

In our discussion of both additive and maximin social welfare functions, we assumed that redistribution makes some people better off and others worse off. Redistribution was never a Pareto improvement—a change that allowed all individuals to be at least as well off as under the status quo. This is a consequence of the assumption that each individual's utility depends on his or her income only. In contrast, imagine that high-income individuals are altruistic, so that their utilities depend not only on their own incomes but those of the poor as well. Under such circumstances, redistribution can actually be a Pareto improvement.

Assume that if (rich) Peter were to give a dollar of income to (poor) Paul, then Peter's increase in satisfaction from doing a good deed would outweigh the loss of his own consumption. At the same time, assume that Paul's utility would increase if he received the dollar. Both individuals would be made better off by the transfer. Indeed, efficiency requires that income be redistributed until Peter's gain in utility from giving a dollar to Paul just equals the loss in Peter's utility caused by lower consumption.[12] Suppose that it is difficult for Peter to bring about the income transfer on his own, perhaps because he lacks enough information to know just who is really poor. Then if the government costlessly does the transfer for Peter, efficiency is enhanced.

In a formal sense, this is just an externality problem. Paul's behavior (his consumption) affects Peter's welfare in a way that is external to the market. As usual in such cases, government may be able to increase efficiency.

Pushing this line of reasoning to its logical extreme, the income distribution can be regarded as a public good, because everyone's utility is affected by the degree of inequality.[13] Suppose that each person would feel better off if the income distribution were more equal. No individual

---

[12] See Hochman and Rodgers [1969].
[13] See Thurow [1971].

acting alone, however, is willing to transfer income to the poor. If the government uses its coercive power to force *everyone* who is wealthy to redistribute income to the poor, economic efficiency increases.

Although altruism doubtless plays an important part in human behavior, it does not follow that altruistic motives explain the majority of government income redistribution programs.[14] This argument *assumes* that in the absence of coercion, people will contribute less than an efficient amount to the poor. Some argue, however, that if people really want to give to the poor, they do so—witness the billions of dollars in charitable contributions made each year.

There are other reasons self-interest might favor income redistribution. For one, there is always some chance that through circumstances beyond your control, you will become poor. An income distribution policy is a bit like insurance. When you are well off, you pay ''premiums'' in the form of tax payments to those who are currently poor. If bad times hit, the ''policy'' pays off, and you receive relief. The idea that government should provide a safety net is an old one. The 17th-century political philosopher Thomas Hobbes [1963/1651, pp. 303–4] noted, ''And whereas many men, by *accident* become unable to maintain themselves by their labour; they ought not to be left to the charity of private persons; but to be provided for, as far forth as the necessities of nature require, by the laws of the Commonwealth'' [emphasis added].

In addition, some believe that income distribution programs help purchase social stability. If poor people become *too* poor, they may engage in antisocial activities such as crime and rioting. The link between social stability and changes in income distribution is not totally clear, however. It may be that some improvement in the well-being of the poor increases their aspirations and leads to demands for more radical change.

Nonindividualistic Views

The views of income distribution discussed so far have quite different implications, but they share a utilitarian outlook. In each, social welfare is some function of individuals' utilities, and the properties of the optimal redistribution policy are *derived* from the social welfare function. Some thinkers have approached the problem by specifying what the income distribution should look like independent of individuals' tastes. As Ray Fair [1971, p. 552] notes, Plato argued that in a good society the ratio of the richest to the poorest person's income should be at the most four to one. Others have suggested that as a first principle, incomes should be distributed equally.[15]

---

[14] See Becker [1976].

[15] This view is considerably stronger than that of Rawls, who allows inequality as long as it raises the welfare of the worst-off individual.

In a less extreme proposal, James Tobin [1970] suggested that only special commodities should be distributed equally, a position sometimes called **commodity egalitarianism.** In some cases, this view has considerable appeal. Most people believe that the right to vote should be distributed equally to all, as should the consumption of certain essential foodstuffs during times of war. Other types of commodity egalitarianism are more controversial. Should all American children consume the same quality of primary school education, or should richer communities be allowed to purchase more? Should everyone receive the same type of health care? Clearly, limiting the range of the "special" commodities is a difficult problem.

Interestingly, a position that bears at least a close resemblance to commodity egalitarianism can be rationalized on the basis of conventional welfare economics. Assume that Henry cares about Catherine's welfare. Specifically, Henry's utility depends on his own income as well as Catherine's level of *food consumption,* as opposed to her *income.* (This might be due to the fact that Henry does not approve of the other commodities that Catherine might consume.) In effect, then, Catherine's food consumption generates a positive externality. Following the logic developed in Chapter 6, efficiency may be enhanced if Catherine's food consumption is subsidized, or perhaps if food is provided to her directly. In short, when donors care about recipients' consumption of certain commodities, a policy of redistributing income via these commodities can be viewed as an attempt to enhance efficiency by correcting an externality.

Other Considerations

The positions discussed earlier take for granted that individuals' incomes are common property that can be redistributed as "society" sees fit. No attention is given to the fairness of either the processes by which the initial income distribution is determined or of the procedures used to redistribute it. In contrast, some argue that a just distribution of income is defined by the *process* that generated it. For example, it is a popular belief in the United States that if "equal opportunity" (somehow defined) were available to all, then the ensuing outcome would be fair, *regardless* of the particular income distribution it happened to entail. Hence, if the process generating income is fair, there is no scope for government-sponsored income redistribution.

Arguing along these lines, the philosopher Robert Nozick [1974] has attacked the use of utilitarian principles to justify changes in the distribution of income. He argues that how "society" should redistribute its income is a meaningless question because "society" per se has no income to distribute. Only *people* receive income, and the sole possible justification for government redistributive activity is when the pattern of property holdings is somehow improper. Nozick's approach shifts emphasis from the search for a "good" social welfare function to a "good" set of rules to govern society's operation. The problem is how to evaluate social processes. It is hard to judge a process independent of the results generated. If a "good" set of rules consistently generates outcomes that are undesirable, how can the rules be considered good?

Irving Kristol [1980] offers an alternative argument against the government undertaking redistribution policies. He suggests that with sufficient social mobility, the distribution of income is of no particular ethical interest. Suppose that those at the bottom of the income distribution (or their children) will occupy higher rungs on the economic ladder in future years. At the same time, some other people will move down, at least in relative terms. Then, even distributional statistics that remain relatively constant over time will conceal quite a bit of churning *within* the income distribution. Even if people at the bottom are quite poor, it may not be a major social problem if the people who are there change over time.

There have been several studies of income mobility. Mary Jo Bane and David Ellwood [1986] examined the American poverty population over an eight-year period in the 1970s. They found that only a small proportion of people who enter poverty in a particular year are chronically poor. Nearly 40 percent exit from poverty within a year, and two-thirds of poverty spells are over within three years. As Alan Blinder [1980] notes, "While ghetto dwellers rarely trade places with Rockefellers, ours is not a stratified society" [p. 452]. On the other hand, there is probably not sufficient mobility to convince utilitarians and those of related philosophies that income inequality is unimportant.

Expenditure Incidence

We turn now from a discussion of whether the government *ought* to redistribute income to analytical problems in assessing the effects of *actual* government redistributive programs. The way in which expenditure policy influences the distribution of real income is referred to as **expenditure incidence.** The government influences income distribution through its taxation as well as its expenditure policies. (We defer a discussion of the tax side to Chapter 13.) Expenditure incidence is difficult to determine for several reasons, which follow.

Problems in Income Measurement

Discussing how government expenditure policy changes income distribution presupposes that we can measure income in the first place.[16] In principle, a person's income during a given period is defined as the sum of the amount he or she consumes during that period and the amount he or she saves. In practice, it is difficult to obtain good measures of people's initial incomes for at least two reasons.

First, as we saw earlier in this chapter, some forms of nonmonetary income are hard to value. An important example is housework. Clearly, people who work within the home produce valuable services for them-

---

[16] A more detailed discussion of these issues is included in Chapter 16 under "Defining Income."

selves and their families, but it is not clear how these services should be valued. Another example is the income provided by durable goods. A house provides its owner with a flow of housing services. The value of these services is the cost to the homeowner of renting a comparable dwelling. Again, however, it is often difficult to make such valuations. Moreover, it is not clear where to stop: should one impute income flows to stereo equipment, furniture, and food processors? Finally, some income is earned in the "underground economy," which includes illegal activities as well as legal transactions that are not reported to the government to evade taxation. Clearly, this is difficult to measure.

As well, the definition of income indicates that the concept makes sense only if it is measured over some period of time.[17] But it is not obvious what the time frame should be. A daily or weekly measure would be absurd, because even rich individuals could very well have zero incomes during some short periods of time. It makes much more sense to measure the flow of income over a year, as is customarily done. However, even annual measures may not reflect an individual's true economic position. After all, there can be unexpected fluctuations in income from year to year. From a theoretical point of view, lifetime income would be ideal, but the practical problems in estimating it are enormous.

Although distinguishing between different time periods may seem a mere academic quibble, it is really quite important. People tend to have low incomes when they are young, more when they are middle-aged, and less again when they are old and in retirement. Therefore, people who have *identical* lifetime incomes but are in different stages of the life cycle can show up in the annual data as having *unequal* incomes. Measures based on annual income, such as those in Tables 8.1 through 8.3, suggest more inequality than those constructed on the more appropriate lifetime basis.

Unit of Observation

Most people live with others, and at least to some extent make their economic decisions jointly. Should income distribution be measured over individuals or households? If there are economies achieved by living together, should they be taken into account in computing an individual's income? For example, are the members of a two-person household with total income of $30,000 as well off as a single individual with $15,000? Although two may not be able to live as cheaply as one, they may be able to live as cheaply as 1.5. If this is true, the members of the couple are better off in real terms. But finding just the right adjustment factor is not easy.

---

[17] In contrast, wealth measures the value of an individual's stock of assets at any point in time. Problems in measuring and taxing wealth are discussed in Chapter 20.

A related problem crops up when the structure of household formation changes over time. Consider what happens

> when higher living standards and/or more generous public transfer programs enable junior, or grandma and grandpa, to move into an apartment of their own. A new economic unit is formed, with a rather low income, thus bringing down the average level of income and raising its inequality. Both economic indicators will therefore signal a deterioration in welfare, though we may presume that these changes in living arrangements actually make the parties involved better off [Blinder, 1980, p. 418].

Thus, especially when distributional comparisons are being made across time, changes in household composition must be taken into account.

Estimating Effects on Relative Prices

Suppose that the government decides to help the poor by subsidizing the consumption of low-income housing. How does this affect the distribution of income? A first guess would be that the people who get the subsidy gain and those who pay the taxes lose. If those who pay the taxes have higher incomes than the subsidy recipients, the distribution of income tends to become more equal.

Unfortunately, this simple story is likely to be misleading. If the subsidy induces poor people to demand more housing, then the *pre*subsidy cost of housing may rise. Therefore, the subsidy recipients do not benefit to the full extent of the subsidy; the landlords reap part of the gain. However, on theoretical grounds alone it cannot be determined how much, if at all, housing prices are bid up. As shown in Chapter 13, this depends on the shapes of the supply and demand curves for housing.

A housing subsidy program also affects the incomes of people who supply the inputs used in its construction. Thus, wages of workers in the building trades increase, as do prices of construction materials. If the owners of these factors of production are in the middle- and upper-income classes, there will be a tendency to make the distribution more unequal.

More generally, any government program sets off a chain of price changes that affects the incomes of people both in their roles as consumers of goods and as suppliers of inputs. A spending program that raises the relative price of a good you consume intensively makes you worse off, other things being the same. Similarly, a program that raises the relative price of a factor you supply makes you better off. The problem is that it is very hard to trace all the price changes generated by a particular policy. As a practical matter, economists are usually forced to assume that a given policy benefits the recipients only and that the effects of other price changes on income distribution are minor. In many cases, this is probably a good assumption.

Public Goods

Substantial government expenditure is for public goods—goods that may be consumed simultaneously by more than one person. As noted in Chapter 5, the market does not force people to reveal how much they value public goods. But if we do not know how much each family values a public good, how can we determine its impact on income distribution? The government spent about $300 billion on defense in 1990 [Office of Management and Budget, 1990, p. 78]. How much in dollar terms did this increase the real income of each family? Did each benefit by the same amount? If not, did the poor benefit less than the rich, or vice versa?

It is impossible to answer questions like these definitively. Unfortunately, alternative answers based on equally plausible assumptions can have very different implications. R. A. Musgrave, K. E. Case, and H. Leonard [1974] examined the distributional implications of expenditures on all pure public goods (such as defense) using three different assumptions: *(a)* a family's share of the benefit is in proportion to its total income; *(b)* its share is in proportion to the amount of taxes it pays; and *(c)* its share is proportional to the number of people in the family. Under assumption *(a)*, public good expenditures increase the incomes of the poorest group[18] by 16.7 percent; under *(b)*, by 13.2 percent; and under *(c)*, by about 70 percent. The average percentage increase for all income groups was 16.7 percent. Thus, depending on the assumptions, pure public goods expenditures have a very great redistributive impact, or none whatsoever.

Valuing In-Kind Transfers

In 1982, headlines were made when the Agriculture Department began offering surplus cheese, butter, and dried milk to poor Americans. More than 3 billion pounds of food have been given away since then. The surplus food program is just one example of an in-kind transfer program. We often think of in-kind transfers as being directed toward lower-income individuals: food stamps, Medicaid, and public housing come to mind. However, middle- and upper-income people are also the beneficiaries of in-kind transfers. A prominent example is education.

Unlike pure public goods, in-kind transfers are not consumed by everyone. Nevertheless, it is difficult to estimate their value to beneficiaries. A convenient assumption is that a dollar spent by the government on an in-kind transfer is equivalent to a dollar increase in the recipient's income. Unfortunately, there is no reason to believe that in-kind transfers are valued by beneficiaries on a dollar per dollar basis.

To see why, consider Jones, a typical welfare recipient who divides her monthly income of $300 between cheese and "all other goods." The market price of cheese is $2 per pound, and the units of "all other goods" are measured so that the price per unit is $1. In Figure 8.2, Jones's consumption of cheese is measured on the horizontal axis, and her consumption of all other goods on the vertical. Jones's budget constraint is line AB.[19] Assuming that Jones is interested in maximizing utility, she consumes bundle E_1, which consists of OG_1 units of all other goods and OC_1 units of cheese.

---

[18] Less than $4,000 in 1968.

[19] For details on how to construct budget lines, see the Appendix at the end of the book.

Figure 8.2
An in-kind transfer
results in a lower
utility level than a
cash transfer

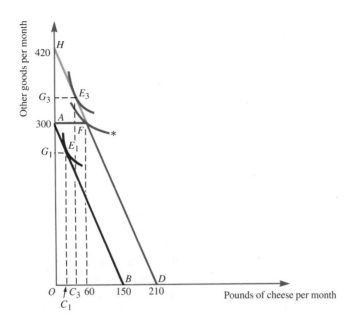

Now suppose the government provides Jones with 60 pounds of cheese per month, which she is prohibited from reselling on the market. How does introduction of the cheese program change her situation? At any level of consumption of all other goods, Jones can now consume 60 more pounds of cheese than previously. Geometrically, her new budget constraint is found by moving 60 units to the right of each point on *AB*, yielding *AFD*. The highest indifference curve that can be reached subject to constraint *AFD* is marked with a (*) in Figure 8.2. It touches the constraint at its "corner"—at point *F*, where Jones's consumption of cheese is 60 and her consumption of all other goods is 300.

Compared to her original consumption bundle, Jones's consumption of both cheese and all other goods has gone up. Because the government provides her with free cheese, Jones can devote to all other goods money that otherwise would have been spent on cheese.

Now suppose that instead of giving Jones 60 pounds of cheese, the government gives her cash equal to its market value, $120 (= 60 pounds × $2 per pound). An increase in income of $120 leads to a budget line that is exactly 120 units above *AB* at every point. This is represented in Figure 8.2 as line *HD*. Note that the cash transfer allows Jones to consume along segment *HF*. This opportunity was not available under the cheese program because Jones was not allowed to trade government cheese for any other goods.

Facing budget line *HD*, Jones maximizes utility at point E_3, where she consumes OG_3 of all other goods and OC_3 pounds of cheese. Comparing points E_3 and *F* we can conclude that: (1) under the cash transfer program, Jones consumes less cheese and more of all other goods than under the cheese giveaway program; and (2) $120 worth of cheese does *not* make Jones as well off as $120 of income. Because E_3 is on a higher indifference curve than point *F*, the cash transfer makes her *better* off. Intuitively, the problem with the cheese program is that it forces Jones to consume the full 60 pounds of cheese. She would prefer to sell some of the cheese and spend the proceeds on other goods.

Is an in-kind transfer always worse than the cash equivalent? Not necessarily. Figure 8.3 depicts the situation of Smith, whose income is identical to Jones's, and who therefore faces exactly the same budget constraints (*AB* before the cheese program, and *AFD* afterwards). However, Smith has different tastes and thus a different set of indifference curves. Before the subsidy, he maximizes utility at point E_4, consuming OG_4 units of all other goods and OC_4 pounds of cheese. After the subsidy, he consumes OG_5 units of all other goods and OC_5 pounds of cheese. Smith would not be better off with a cash transfer because his most preferred point along *HD* is available under the cheese subsidy anyway. Because Smith is happy to consume more than 60 pounds of cheese, the restriction that he consume at least 60 pounds does him no harm.

Thus, it cannot be known for certain whether an in-kind transfer will be valued less than a direct income transfer. Ultimately, the answer has to be found by empirical analysis. For example, several studies of the consumption patterns of the poor suggest that a dollar received in public housing is worth only about 80 cents received in cash [Smeeding, 1982, p. 65].[20]

Another problem with in-kind transfer programs is that they often entail substantial administrative costs. In the cheese program just discussed, costs are incurred for storage, transportation, and distribution of the cheese. (Indeed, the costs are so large that some communities choose not to participate.) Lois Blanchard et al. [1982, p. ii] estimated that administrative costs of the food stamp program could be reduced by about 36 percent if beneficiaries simply received checks instead of coupons redeemable for food.

As we show in the next chapter, in-kind transfers involving food, housing, and medical care play an important role in the U.S. income maintenance policy. If in-kind transfers are less satisfactory than cash from the point of view of the recipients *and* entail more administrative costs, how can we account for their presence? There are a number of possible explanations. Several relate to our earlier discussion of normative issues. In particular, there is some evidence that commodity egalitarianism is an important factor in distributional policy. For instance, in 1949 the U.S. Congress explicitly set as a national goal "a decent home and a

---

[20] The structure of public housing programs differs somewhat from the cheese program just analyzed because recipients have to pay some price for the housing. But the basic idea is the same. For further details, see the next chapter.

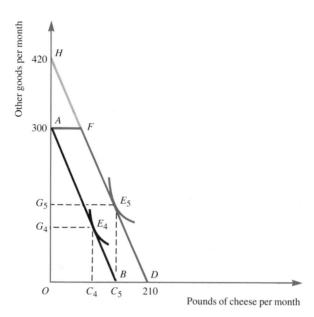

Figure 8.3
An in-kind transfer results in the same utility level as a cash transfer

suitable living environment for every American family'' [Weicher, 1979, p. 470]. Note the distinction between this goal and "enough income so that every American family can live in a decent home, if it chooses."

Moreover, in-kind transfers may also help curb welfare fraud. The discussion so far has assumed that in programs for the poor, there are no problems in identifying who is eligible and who is not. In reality, this is not the case, and people who do not qualify are sometimes able to obtain benefits. Albert Nichols and Richard Zeckhauser [1982] suggest that in-kind transfers may discourage ineligible persons from applying because some middle-class people may be quite willing to lie to receive cash, but less willing to commit fraud to obtain a commodity they do not really want. This is especially true if the commodity is difficult to resell, like an apartment in a public housing project. In the same way, creating hassles for welfare recipients (waiting in line, filling out a lot of forms) may discourage those who are not "truly needy" from applying. Thus, there is a trade-off. On one hand, a poor person would prefer $500 in cash to $500 worth of public housing. But if the in-kind program leads to less fraud, more resources can be channeled to those who really need them. However, many would argue that the government has created far more than the optimal number of administrative hurdles for welfare recipients. In some communities, for example, children who receive free school lunches have to obtain and submit the Social Security numbers of each adult who lives at home. This is felt by many to be an unfair burden on the children.

Finally, in-kind transfers are attractive politically because they help not only the beneficiary but also the producers of the favored commodity. A transfer program that increases the demand for housing benefits the building industry, which therefore becomes willing to lend its support to a political coalition in favor of the program. Similarly, the agricultural interests have always been avid supporters of food stamps. In the same way, the public employees who administer the various in-kind transfer programs can be expected to put their political support behind them. In 1977, when welfare reformers proposed that subsidized housing be phased out and replaced with cash grants, the Department of Housing and Urban Development registered vigorous opposition [Weicher, 1980, p. 51].

These explanations for in-kind transfers are not mutually exclusive, and they probably have all influenced policy design.

Overview

We began by surveying a very wide range of opinions concerning whether the government should adopt explicit policies to redistribute income. The various views run the gamut from engineering complete equality to permitting the status quo. The scope of disagreement should not be surprising. Setting a distributional objective is no less than formalizing one's views of what a good society should look like, and this is an issue about which there will always be controversy. Theories on the optimal income distribution are normative rather than positive. Actual government redistributive policies may be guided by a number of these considerations, but it is not obvious that this is the case. As we see in the next chapter, finding a coherent explanation of U.S. income distribution practices is not easy.

We also stressed the difficulties involved in defining income and determining how government policy affects each person's income. Measures of income before intervention are calculated on an annual rather than a lifetime basis. Many important types of income are ignored because of measurement difficulties. Calculating the effect of government spending programs is no easier. These programs change relative prices and therefore real incomes in ways that are hard to discern. Transfers often take the form of public goods and in-kind payments on which it is difficult to put a dollar value. Thus, any evidence on how government programs change the distribution of income should be interpreted with caution.

Summary

- Economists analyze distributional issues to determine the consequences of alternative government policies on the distribution of income and to draw out the implications of various ethical goals.

- If (1) social welfare is the sum of identical utility functions that depend only on income; (2) there is decreasing marginal utility of income; and (3) the total amount of income is fixed, then income should be equally distributed. These are quite strong assumptions, and weakening them gives radically different results.

- The maximin criterion states that the best income distribution maximizes the utility of the member of society who has the lowest utility. Rawls has argued that the maximin criterion has a compelling ethical justification, but his argument has been criticized.

- It is possible that income distribution is much like a public good—everyone derives utility from the fact that income is equitably distributed, but government coercion is needed to accomplish redistribution. Pareto efficient redistribution occurs when no one is made worse off as a result of the redistributive activity.

- Other views of income distribution do not follow the utilitarian framework. Some believe that it is a first principle that income, or at least certain goods, be distributed equally. Others argue that the distribution of income is not a relevant question. As long as the distribution arises from a "fair" process, the actual income distribution is irrelevant. These views sidestep the problem of how to judge the "fairness" of a process without looking at its results.

- Income before transfers is hard to measure correctly. Some goods and services are not marketed, and the values of the services provided by durable goods are not observed. Moreover, it is not clear what time period— month, year, lifetime—or what unit of observation—individual, household, family—is appropriate.

- A government program can change the entire set of relative prices in the economy, creating losses and gains for various individuals. It is difficult to trace out all of these price changes, so economists generally focus only on the prices in the markets directly affected.

- Because people do not reveal how they value public goods, it is difficult to determine how real incomes are affected.

- Many government programs provide goods and services (in-kind transfers) instead of cash. Recipients are not legally allowed to sell the goods and services so received. If recipients would prefer to consume less, the value of the in-kind transfer is less than the market price, but exactly how much less is hard to determine.

- In general, beneficiaries would prefer cash to in-kind transfers. The prevalence of in-kind transfer programs may be due to paternalism, commodity egalitarianism, administrative feasibility, or political attractiveness.

Discussion Questions

1. Are the concepts of *fairness* and *equality* in the distribution of income synonymous? To what extent is income inequality consistent with fairness? What are the implications of your answer for government expenditure policy?

2. Suppose that there are only two people, Simon and Charity, who must split a fixed income of $100. For Simon, the marginal utility of income is:

$$MU_s = 400 - 2I_s$$

while for Charity, marginal utility is:

$$MU_c = 400 - 6I_c$$

where I_c, I_s are the amounts of income to Charity and Simon, respectively.

   a. What is the optimal distribution of income if the social welfare function is additive?

   b. What is the optimal distribution if society values only the utility of Charity? What if the reverse is true? Comment on your answers.

   c. Finally, comment on how your answers change if the marginal utility of income for both Simon and Charity is constant:

$$MU_c = 400$$
$$MU_s = 400$$

3. Affirmative action programs give preferential treatment in job hiring to members of groups that have suffered from past discrimination. Which, if any, of the rationales for income redistribution could be used to rationalize this policy?

4. Consider the following government programs:
   a. Subsidies to opera companies.
   b. Purchase of helicopters for the Air Force.
   How might each program affect the distribution of income?

Selected References

Atkinson, A. B. *The Economics of Inequality.* Oxford: Oxford University Press, 1983.

Hochman, H. M., and J. D. Rodgers. "Pareto Optimal Redistribution." *American Economic Review* 59 (1969), pp. 542–57.

Kristol, Irving. "Some Personal Reflections on Economic Well-Being and Income Distribution." In *The American Economy in Transition,* ed. Martin Feldstein. Chicago: University of Chicago Press, 1980, pp. 479–86.

Sawhill, Isabel. "Poverty in the U.S.: Why Is It So Persistent?" *Journal of Economic Literature* 56 (1988), pp. 1073–1119.

Expenditure Programs for the Poor

And distribution was made to each as had need.

Acts 4:35

The last chapter documented that the distribution of income in the United States is highly unequal and indicated that whether or not this is a problem depends on your political and ethical views. Regardless, there does appear to be a strong consensus that at least some government intervention is required to increase the material well-being of those at the bottom of the income distribution. This chapter discusses the major expenditure programs in the United States aimed at maintaining the incomes of the poor.

A Quick Look at Welfare Spending

The spending programs that constitute welfare are **means-tested**—only individuals whose financial resources fall below a certain level can receive benefits. In 1965, government means-tested assistance accounted for about 1.2 percent of the gross national product (GNP). By 1988, the figure had tripled, to 3.6 percent. Most of the growth in government transfer programs has been in the form of in-kind assistance. In 1988, cash assistance was 1.1 percent of GNP, the same percentage observed in 1965 [Burtless, 1986, p. 24, and Congressional Research Service, 1989, p. 1].

The importance of in-kind transfers is reflected in Table 9.1, which lists federal government outlays for the most important programs that are designed to help the poor.[1] Although the table provides an adequate over-

---

[1] The role of states and localities in distributional policy is discussed in Chapter 21 under "Optimal Federalism."

Table 9.1   **Some federal programs for low-income individuals, 1991** *($ billions)*

Cash transfers:	
Aid to Families with Dependent Children (AFDC)	$14.1
Supplemental Security Income (SSI)	15.7
In-kind transfers:	
Medicaid	51.6
Food stamps	18.3
Child nutrition	5.7
Housing assistance	17.6
Employment and training	5.8
Compensatory education	6.2

SOURCE: Projections from Executive Office of the President—Office of Management and Budget, *Budget of the United States Government, Fiscal Year 1991,* Washington, D.C.: U.S. Government Printing Office, 1991, pp. 4–8, 4–9, 7–129.

view, there are several reasons why it is not a comprehensive "poverty budget." First, there is some arbitrariness in deciding whether certain programs are for the poor. Some programs that are not explicitly redistributional end up transferring considerable sums to the poor. Social Security is usually considered an insurance program rather than a distributional program (see Chapter 10). Yet about 40 percent of Social Security payments go to low-income households [Committee on Ways and Means, 1990, p. 19]. Similarly, the poor receive some unemployment insurance payments and veterans' pensions. In addition, many families that are not below the poverty line receive some sort of assistance from programs listed in the table.[2] For example, about 6 percent of the households receiving food stamps are above the poverty level [Committee on Ways and Means, 1990, p. 1267].

With these caveats in mind, we now discuss and evaluate the major programs.

Aid to Families with Dependent Children

Aid to Families with Dependent Children (AFDC), perhaps the most controversial of U.S. welfare programs, provides cash to families with dependent children and an absent, incapacitated, or unemployed parent.[3] The great majority of AFDC families are headed by women. In 1989, about 3.8 million families participated in the program. About 54 percent of the money for AFDC is provided by the federal government, and the rest by

[2] When *all* federal cash and in-kind transfer payments are considered, only 43 percent go to households with incomes in the bottom fifth of the income distribution [Executive Office of the President, 1991, pp. 2–137].

[3] Needy two-parent families in which the primary worker is employed less than 100 hours a month are covered through AFDC–UP (Unemployed Parents).

state and local governments. It is administered jointly by the federal government and the states. Each state determines its own benefit levels, subject only to broad federal guidelines. As a consequence, there are large interstate differences in benefits. For example, in January 1989 the maximum monthly AFDC payment for a family of three in Alabama was $118; in California it was $694.

Each state also determines its own eligibility standards. A family is ineligible if its income exceeds 185 percent of the state's "standard of need," a figure which is supposed to reflect the cost of basic expenses such as rent, food, clothing, and utilities. Twenty-two states have a payment standard below their own needs standard [Levitan, 1990, p. 49]. Moreover, participating families' assets (excluding an owner-occupied home and an automobile) cannot exceed $1,000.

Prior to 1967, when an AFDC recipient earned any income, her assistance was reduced by exactly that amount. A law passed in 1967 allowed a deduction for reasonable work expenses, including child care. In addition, the first $30 of earnings per month as well as one-third of any additional earnings were disregarded in the computation of the welfare benefit. Hence, if a recipient earned $90 per month after expenses, her aid would be reduced not by the full $90 but by only $40 [= 2/3 × (90 − 30)]. However, the Reagan administration limited the $30 earned income disregard to only the first 12 months of work, and the additional one-third disregard was limited to only the first four months. Thus, the United States is now essentially back to the pre-1967 system, in which every additional dollar of earnings reduces welfare by a dollar.

Work Incentives and AFDC

The fact that welfare benefits react sharply to earnings suggests that incentives to work may be reduced. The question of whether welfare adversely affects participation in the labor market and increases dependence on the government has dominated discussions of income maintenance policy for years. Indifference curve analysis of the individual's labor supply choice sheds some light on this issue.[4] Consider Smith, who is trying to decide how much of her time to devote each month to work and how much to leisure. In Figure 9.1, the horizontal axis measures the number of hours devoted to leisure. Even if Smith does not work at all, there is an upper limit to the amount of leisure she can consume, because there are just so many hours in a month. This number of hours, referred to as the **time endowment,** is shown by the distance *OT* in Figure 9.1. We assume that all time not spent on leisure is devoted to work in the market.[5] Any point on the horizontal axis therefore simultaneously indicates hours of

---

[4] A verbal discussion of the theory of labor supply was provided in Chapter 3 under "The Role of Theory." The reader may want to consult that discussion before proceeding with the graphical exposition provided here.

[5] A more general model allows for three uses of time: leisure, work in the market, and housework.

Figure 9.1
Budget constraint
for the
leisure/income
choice

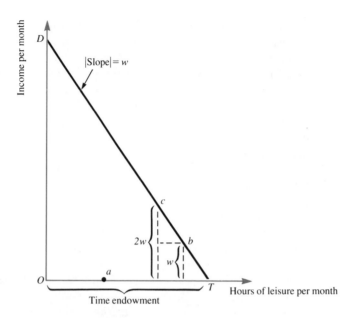

leisure and hours of work. For example, at point *a, Oa* hours are devoted to leisure, and the difference between that and the time endowment, *OT,* represents time spent at work, *aT.*

Our first problem is to illustrate how Smith's income, which is measured on the vertical axis, varies with her hours of work. Assume that she can earn a wage of $\$w$ per hour. Also, for the moment, assume that no welfare is available. Then her income for any number of hours worked is just the product of $\$w$ and the number of hours.[6] Suppose, for example, Smith does not work at all. If labor is her only source of income, her income is simply zero. This option of zero work and zero income is represented by point *T.*

If Smith works one hour each week, by definition she consumes leisure equal to her time endowment minus one hour. This point is one hour to the left of *T* on the horizontal axis. Working one hour gives her a total of $\$w$. The combination of one hour of work with a total income of $\$w$ is labeled point *b.* If Smith works two hours—moves two hours to the left of *T*—her total income is $2 \times \$w$ that is labeled point *c.* Continuing to compute the income associated with each number of hours of work, we trace out all the leisure/income combinations that are available to Smith—the straight line *TD,* whose slope, in absolute value, is the wage rate. *TD* is the analog of the budget constraint in the usual analysis of the choice between two goods. (See the Appendix to the book.) Here, however, the

---

[6] Assume for simplicity that the hourly wage does not depend on the number of hours worked—there is no overtime.

Figure 9.2
Utility maximizing
choice of leisure
and income

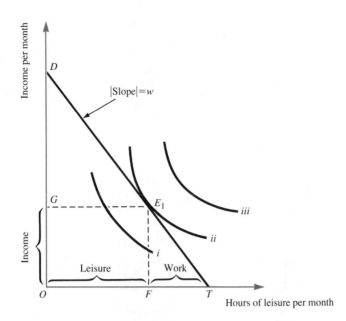

goods are income and leisure. The price of an hour of leisure is its opportunity cost (the income forgone by not working that hour), which is just the wage.

To know which point on *TD* Smith chooses, we need information on her tastes. In Figure 9.2 we reproduce the budget constraint *TD*. Assume that preferences for leisure and income can be represented by normal, convex-to-the-origin indifference curves. Three such curves are labeled *i*, *ii*, and *iii* in Figure 9.2. Utility is maximized at point E_1, where Smith devotes *OF* hours to leisure, works *FT* hours, and earns income *OG*.

Suppose now that the welfare authorities announce that Smith is eligible to receive a grant of $200 per month. However, as noted earlier, the law requires that the grant be reduced by $1 for each dollar she earns. How does introduction of the program modify the budget constraint?

In Figure 9.3, clearly one option that AFDC makes available to Smith is point *P*, which is associated with zero hours of work and an income of $200 from welfare. Now suppose that Smith works one hour. Graphically, this is represented by a one-hour movement to the left from *P*. When Smith works one hour, she receives a wage of $*w* from her employer, *but* simultaneously her welfare is reduced by the same amount. The hour of work has netted her nothing—her total income is still $200. This is shown by point P_1, where there is one hour of work and total income is still $200. In effect, Smith's earnings are being taxed at a rate of 100 percent. Additional hours of work continue to produce no net gain in income, so the budget constraint is flat. This continues until point *R*, at which point Smith's earnings exceed $200, so that she is out of the welfare system

Figure 9.3
Budget constraint under a welfare system with a 100 percent tax rate on additional earnings

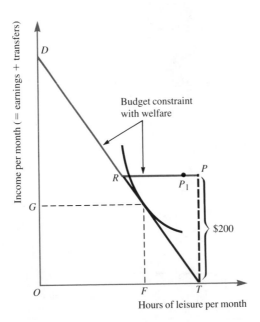

altogether. Beyond that point, each hour of work raises her income by w.[7] Thus, the budget constraint is the kinked line *PRD*, whose segment *PR* has zero slope, and the absolute value of the slope of segment *RD* is w.

How will Smith respond to such incentives? Figure 9.4 shows one distinct possibility: she maximizes utility at point *P,* at which no labor is supplied. In no case will a rational person work between zero and *PR* hours. This should come as no surprise. Why should someone work if she can receive the same income by not working?[8]

Of course, the welfare system does not necessarily induce an individual to stop working. If the indifference curves are flat enough, a point along segment *RD* may be chosen. Figure 9.5 depicts the leisure/income choice of Jones, who faces exactly the same budget constraint as Smith in Figure 9.4. However, Jones maximizes utility at point E_2, where she works *MT* hours per month. Moreover, for many recipients, the welfare system is less extreme than depicted in Figures 9.4 and 9.5—the implicit tax rate on additional earnings is less than 100 percent. Nevertheless, there is considerable evidence that the welfare system has substantially reduced the labor supply of recipients. For example, Rebecca Blank [1985] found that each dollar decrease in the effective wage rate due to AFDC induces a decline in labor supply of about one hour per week.

---

[7] If Smith becomes subject to the income tax, her take-home wage will be less than w. This consideration is unimportant in the current context, and is discussed in Chapter 17 under "Labor Supply."

[8] In a more complicated model, an individual might select a point along segment *RD* to develop her skills or to signal her quality to future employers by maintaining a continuous work history.

Figure 9.4
Work decision
under a welfare
system with a 100
percent tax rate on
additional earnings

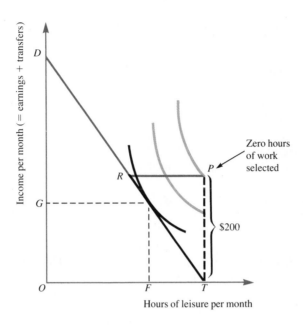

Figure 9.5
An individual
chooses to work in
the presence of a
welfare system

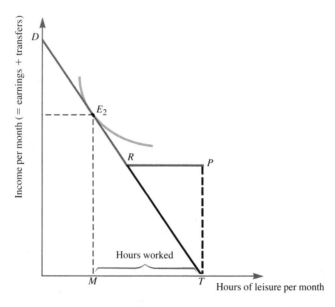

**Welfare
Dependence**

The public debate on AFDC's incentives has encompassed broader issues
than just hours of work per month. One such issue is whether receipt of
AFDC payments (and payments from other programs as well) creates a
welfare mentality that reduces the chances the recipient will ever become
self-supporting (see Murray [1984]). In terms of the economist's standard
framework for analyzing work decisions, the question is whether the
receipt of welfare changes the slopes of an individual's leisure/income

indifference curves. Do people become "lazy," so that for any given set of earnings opportunities, they work less than they would have prior to being introduced to welfare?

To be sure, many families do receive welfare payments over long periods of time [Sawhill, 1988]. However, it does not follow that the welfare system has changed the preferences of such families. It is just as likely that the family stays on welfare simply because its earnings opportunities continue to be meager. So far, no empirical studies have succeeded in distinguishing between the two possibilities. Thus, the notion that AFDC changes the preferences of its recipients remains a conjecture.

Another way that AFDC might create long-term welfare dependence is through its effects on family structure. As noted earlier, AFDC is generally only for one-parent families. The argument is that this induces fathers to leave their families. Mothers left to fend for themselves can neither earn enough money to bring the family out of poverty, nor provide a proper environment for raising children. Hence, welfare dependency is transmitted across generations.

It is well documented that the family structure of the poor has become less cohesive relative to what it was prior to the 1960s. Is this the fault of AFDC? Ellwood and Crane [1990] note that between 1960 and the mid-1970s, welfare benefits have fallen in real terms, yet the proportion of children not living with two parents has continued to increase. If welfare were a major determinant of family structure, one would have expected to see the trend reverse itself when benefits fell, but this did not occur. Of course, such simple comparisons do not take into account other variables that might have been influencing family structure simultaneously. However, econometric studies that attempt to take such factors into account generally find little or no link between welfare and family structure. The data hardly justify the conventional assumption that welfare is the driving force behind the break-up of poor families. In fact, the reasons for changes in family structure are not well understood.

Nevertheless, the concerns about the incentive effects of the current system are of sufficient seriousness that a number of alternative approaches have been considered. We discuss two of these next: the negative income tax and workfare.

Negative Income Tax

The negative income tax is a **noncategorical welfare program**—the benefit depends only on income, and not whether the person is in a particular category (single parent, disabled, etc.). Under this scheme, individuals who do not work receive some basic grant. But welfare recipients who enter the labor market have their grants reduced only by some fraction of their earnings, rather than by 100 percent. For example, suppose that the basic monthly grant is $100 and the system has a tax rate on additional earnings of 25 percent. If Smith earns $40, the basic grant is reduced by $10 (= .25 × $40), to $90. Total monthly income is then the sum of $90 (from relief) plus $40 (from earnings), or $130.

Figure 9.6

Budget constraint under a negative income tax

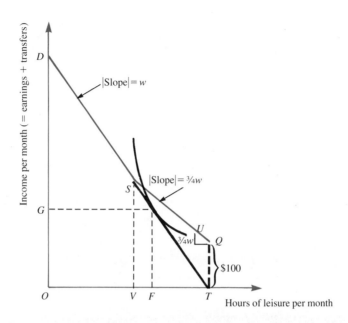

Figure 9.6 illustrates this program. As before, in the absence of welfare, Smith works *FT* hours and earns *OG*. In the presence of the negative income tax, one option is point *Q*, where no labor is supplied and Smith receives $100 from welfare. If Smith works one hour, she receives *w* from her employer. Simultaneously, her grant is reduced by ¼*w*, still leaving her ahead by ¾*w*. Thus, another point on the budget constraint is *U*, which is one hour to the left of *Q*, and ¾*w* above it. Similarly, Smith continues to receive an effective hourly wage of ¾*w* until she works *VT* hours, at which point her earnings are high enough that she receives no welfare.[9] Thus, the budget constraint is the kinked line *QSD*. Segment *QS* has a slope in absolute value of ¾*w*, segment *SD* a slope of *w*.

As usual, the ultimate work decision depends on the shapes of the individual's indifference curves. As drawn in Figure 9.7, Smith works less than she did before the negative income tax (*KT* hours, as opposed to *FT* before). However, unlike the situation depicted in Figure 9.4, she does not opt out of the labor force altogether. To be sure, we could also draw

---

[9] At point *S*, Smith is earning $400 monthly. She receives no welfare at this, or any higher, level of earnings because the amount taxed away exhausts the basic grant of $100. Algebraically, the benefit received (*B*) is related to the basic grant (*G*), tax rate (*t*), and level of earnings (*E*) by:

$$B = G - tE$$

Using this, it follows that the benefit is zero (*B* = 0) when:

$$E = G/t$$

or at any higher level of *E*.

Figure 9.7
Labor supply
decision under a
negative income tax

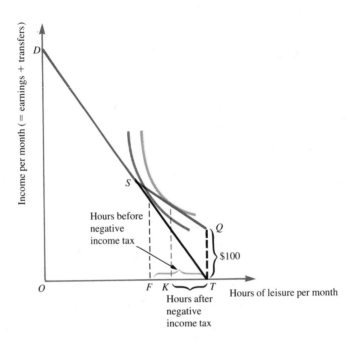

indifference curves at which the maximum utility is reached at zero hours of work. But because the implicit tax rate is less than 100 percent, this outcome is less likely under the negative income tax.

The fundamental dilemma in designing a negative income tax is the trade-off between the size of the basic grant and the tax rate on additional earnings. For a given program cost, the larger the basic grant, the larger must be the tax rate. A system with good work incentives might provide little money for those who are unable to work, such as the severely disabled.[10]

Proponents of the negative income tax like its noncategorical nature. Since everyone is eligible, recipients do not have to submit to humiliating procedures to prove they qualify. At the same time, because there is no need for a bureaucracy to verify that a claimant really is a single parent or disabled, administrative costs are cut. However, a major concern about a noncategorical system is that it would lead to widespread withdrawals from the labor force.[11] To investigate this possibility, the federal government sponsored a series of social experiments in the 1960s and 1970s. In

---

[10] The negative income tax could be supplemented with a system of special grants for such individuals. This would, of course, complicate administration considerably.

[11] "We categorically reject the notion of a guaranteed annual income, no matter how it may be disguised, which would destroy the fiber of our economy and doom the poor to perpetual dependence" (1980 platform of the Republican party).

each, a sample of low-income individuals participated in a negative income tax program. The behavior of members of a control group who did not participate was also monitored. Henry Aaron's [1984, p. 13] analysis of the results suggests that "few men who were offered cash assistance actually quit their jobs and that the reduction in the number of hours they worked was under 10 percent. But the tests also suggested that for every $100 provided to male-headed families, earnings would fall $25 to $50." In short, while the labor supply responses are not huge, neither are they small enough to ignore.

Of course, such results must be interpreted cautiously, due to the problems with social experiments discussed in Chapter 3. They do suggest, however, that constructing a noncategorical welfare system that provides adequate support *and* good work incentives might be an expensive proposition.

Workfare

So far, our labor supply analysis has assumed that the welfare recipient is free to choose her hours of work subject only to her budget constraint. The welfare authorities do not tell a recipient to work or not; it is her decision. An alternative scheme is **workfare.** Able-bodied individuals receive transfer payments only if they agree to participate in a work-related activity and accept employment, if offered. Legislation passed by the Congress in 1988 requires AFDC recipients whose youngest child is at least three to register for education, training, or employment, depending on the recipient's skills.

A number of skeptical questions have been raised about workfare: Is such a system an affront to the dignity of the poor? Can useful jobs be found for recipients? In light of the huge caseloads that welfare administrators have to handle, can they differentiate between people who are able-bodied and those who are not? Are the costs of administering workfare prohibitive?

Daniel Friedlander et al. [1986] report on the results of an interesting social experiment designed to answer some of these questions. Over a five-year period, AFDC applicants in a number of communities were randomly assigned to experimental treatment and control groups. Members of the experimental groups entered workfare programs; the control groups received conventional AFDC.

The specific results differed from site to site, which is to be expected since employment conditions, welfare benefits, and so forth vary across communities. A general conclusion was that workfare was more expensive than conventional AFDC, by amounts running from $158 to $909 per participant. However, after nine months of workfare participation, the number of individuals who were still receiving welfare was 0.8 to 6.9 percent lower than for the AFDC group. The general conclusion was that mandatory programs of job search, short-duration unpaid work experience, and training can be implemented for AFDC clients, and they can be operated at relatively low cost, and that they can have some short-run effect on employment. [Friedlander et al., 1986, p. 228]

As experience with workfare programs accumulates, more will be learned about their effects.

Putting Work Incentives in Perspective

Public concern over how much welfare recipients work may be somewhat misplaced. True, an important aspect of any welfare system is the incentive structure it creates. But if the goal of welfare policy were only to maximize work effort, the government could simply force the poor into workhouses, as was done under the English Poor Law of 1834. Designing good transfer systems requires a careful balancing of incentive and equity considerations.

Supplemental Security Income

Supplemental Security Income (SSI), enacted in 1972, is a federal program that provides a basic monthly benefit for the aged, blind, or disabled. In 1989, the federal benefit was $368 per month for an individual having no other income, and $553 for a couple. Assets of SSI recipients cannot exceed certain limits: $2,000 for an individual, $3,000 for a couple.[12] SSI recipients are allowed to receive $65 per month before there is any reduction in their payments. After that, the implicit tax rate on additional earnings is 50 percent; that is, benefits are reduced by 50 cents for each dollar earned.

There are a number of striking contrasts between AFDC and SSI. First, there is a uniform minimum federal guarantee for SSI, and none for AFDC.[13] Second, SSI benefits are considerably higher than the average AFDC rate. Third, work incentives under SSI are much better than under AFDC. The earned income disregarded is $65 per month for SSI instead of AFDC's $30, and the implicit tax rate on additional earnings is 50 percent instead of AFDC's 100 percent.

Why is SSI more generous than AFDC? Most observers agree that the public's perceptions of the two groups are quite different. SSI recipients are thought to be in poverty through no fault of their own, and therefore "truly needy." In contrast, many people suspect that AFDC recipients are poor as a consequence of their own decisions, and hence not as deserving.

---

[12] This excludes small amounts for the value of home, automobile, and life insurance policies.

[13] However, at their option, states can supplement the federal benefits.

Medicaid

As Table 9.1 indicates, Medicaid is by far the largest spending program for low-income individuals.[14] Enacted in 1965 to pay for the medical care of certain low-income individuals, Medicaid covers a broad range of benefits, including hospital inpatient and outpatient care, laboratory and X-ray fees, physicians' services, and so forth. Most of these services are provided free of charge to the recipients. In addition, some states include optional services such as dental care and eyeglasses. Total Medicaid payments have grown rapidly over time. In 1975 total (federal and state) Medicaid payments were $12.6 billion; by 1990 they were about $71 billion [Committee on Ways and Means, 1990, p. 1291]. Even after accounting for changes in the price level, this represents more than a doubling.

In light of last chapter's discussion of cash versus in-kind payments, we might ask why society has chosen to make transfers in the form of medical services such an important component of the welfare system. One explanation is commodity egalitarianism. There appears to be a strong societal consensus that everyone should have access to basic medical services. Elements of paternalism may also be present. Some believe that even if affordable insurance policies were available to poor people, they would lack the foresight to purchase adequate coverage.

Administration

Medicaid is administered by the states, and funded by both the federal government and the states. Legislation passed in 1981 had two important effects on the administration of Medicaid. First, it reduced the federal payments made to each state. Second, it gave states increased flexibility in the administration of the program. In particular, prior to 1981 Medicaid systems were always characterized by **cost-based reimbursements**—health-care providers reported their costs to the government and received a check in that amount. Under the 1981 legislation, states can try other methods. One of these is a **capitation fee** system under which medical care is provided for a particular individual or set of individuals for a fixed monthly fee.

Eligibility

To receive Medicaid, an individual must receive or be eligible for federally assisted cash welfare payments, that is, AFDC or SSI. Thus, needy people in the 21- to-64-year-old age range cannot receive Medicaid unless they are in families with dependent children or are disabled. As we noted earlier, AFDC eligibility criteria vary considerably across states. It follows that there are also considerable variations in Medicaid eligibility. To make things even more complicated, states have the option of covering

---

[14] Medicaid should not be confused with Medicare, which provides health care insurance to the aged. Medicare is not means-tested. See Chapter 11 under "Medicare."

specific groups of people who do not participate in AFDC or SSI. Nevertheless, about 90 percent of the Medicaid caseload consists of people who qualify because of AFDC or SSI eligibility.

In the decade after Medicaid was established, the number of beneficiaries increased dramatically. By 1973 there were 19.6 million recipients; in 1976 there were 22.8 million. Interestingly, since then the number has essentially leveled off; there were 22.9 million recipients in 1989. Thus, if we seek to explain the growth in total Medicaid costs in recent years, it would appear that the chief factor is increases in the cost per recipient.

The largest number of Medicaid recipients—about 70 percent of them—are on AFDC. However, most of the Medicaid money—about two thirds of it—goes to those on SSI. This reflects the fact that the SSI population is in poorer health than the AFDC population, and hence the medical expenditures per capita are higher.

Valuing Medicaid Payments

The previous chapter explained the difficulties in assigning money values to in-kind transfers. These difficulties are compounded in Medicaid because of the nature of the benefit it provides. Consider an individual who is eligible for Medicaid during a given year, but who happens to enjoy perfect health that year. No payments are made on that individual's behalf. Do we want to say that the individual has received no benefit from the existence of Medicaid? Probably not. If the individual had become ill, he would have received benefits. The Medicaid program provides insurance against this outcome, and owning such insurance is valuable. Note, however, that the market value of such an insurance policy is not the value to the recipient. As we saw in the last chapter, the market value of an in-kind transfer may be greater than the value to a recipient if the program induces him to consume "too much" of the commodity; that is, if he would have preferred to spend the money on other commodities. Timothy Smeeding's [1982, p. 67] analysis of the medical expenditures of low-income individuals suggested that the value to recipients of Medicaid is only about 44 percent of the market value. While any specific number must be taken with a grain of salt, it does seem pretty clear that if Medicaid were "cashed-out"—the recipients were simply given the market value of the Medicaid insurance policy as a lump sum—they would consume considerably fewer medical services.

Has Medicaid Succeeded?

A primary reason for initiating Medicaid was to increase the access of the poor to medical services. By some measures, it seems to have worked. In the early 1960s, about 71 percent of high-income individuals saw a physician during a year; for low-income people, the figure was 56 percent. By 1980, the proportions had more or less equalized at about 75 percent for all income groups.

Such figures, of course, do not tell us much about the quality of care being received by the poor—does it indeed improve their health? There seems to be some evidence that the health of the poor has improved since the start of Medicaid. For example, in the decade before the introduction of Medicaid, life expectancy increased by only about a year. Since 1970, however, it has increased by about five years [Committee on Ways and Means, 1990, p. 995]. Similarly, infant mortality rates halved between 1970 and 1987. Of course, much of this improvement could have been due to other factors, such as changes in lifestyle. Although it is difficult to sort out the contribution of various factors, there seems to be a consensus that Medicaid expenditures played an important role.

On the other hand, due to the nature of the eligibility requirements, about one in seven Americans has neither public nor private health coverage at any point in time; about 30 percent of these are below the poverty level [Short, 1990, pp. 4–7]. Hence, if universal health care coverage is the goal, we are still a long way from achieving it.

Reforming Medicaid

The public debate about Medicaid has been dominated by its costs. As noted earlier, cost increases appear to be due to rising costs per patient rather than an increasing number of patients. It is generally agreed that the cost-based reimbursement system is a major contributor to the problem.[15] Under this system, neither the physician nor the patient has any incentive to minimize the costs of health services.

One possible alternative would be cost-sharing, an arrangement under which the patient pays some portion of the fee. This gives the patient an incentive to request less expensive treatments. At the same time, if the health-care provider is aware that the patient is paying part of the bill, he or she may be less likely to request expensive procedures whose expected benefits are small. The big problem with cost-sharing in the context of Medicaid is that the recipients are so poor that they might not be able to afford even a small share of their expenses. Hence, their health might suffer.

An alternative to cost-sharing is for the government to contract with certain hospitals on a competitive basis to provide health care for a given population of the poor. The government would pay a fixed fee in return for the provision of health care services. This would give the health care provider an incentive to economize. Critics of such proposals object to the restrictions they place on poor people's freedom of choice. They cannot choose their health provider, but must go to the health center

---

[15] But other factors are also at work. For example, a number of modern medical procedures require the use of advanced and expensive technologies. See Chapter 11 under "Medicare" for a further discussion of the rise in the costs of health care.

selected by the government. But Starr [1986, p. 126] argues that the scope of choice of the poor under the status quo is already limited—the payments allowed by Medicaid are so low that many doctors do not accept Medicaid patients. Currently, California is experimenting with contract systems, and they are under consideration in a number of other states as well. The results from these experiments should help inform future debates about the best way to deliver health care to the poor.

Food Stamps and Child Nutrition

A food stamp is a government-issued voucher that can be used only for the purchase of food. (Animal food, alcohol, tobacco, and imported food are not allowed.) In 1989 the food stamp program increased the purchasing power of more than 20.2 million people by $13.8 billion [Committee on Ways and Means, 1990, p. 1275].[16] The direct cost of the food stamps is paid by the federal government. However, the administration of the program, including distribution of the stamps, is done by the states.

Most public assistance recipients are eligible to receive food stamps, as are other households with net incomes at or below the poverty line. A household's monthly food stamp allotment is based on its size and income. In 1989, for a family of four the maximum monthly food stamp allotment was $300 [Committee on Ways and Means, 1990, p. 1275]. As is the case with AFDC, the allotment is reduced when the household's income increases, but the implicit tax on food stamps is only 30 cents on the dollar.[17] In effect, then, the food stamp program operates a lot like a negative income tax, albeit one where the minimum guarantee is very low.

Of course, there is one crucial difference—unlike cash, food stamps cannot be used to buy anything except food. Thus, we expect food stamps to be worth less to consumers than the same amount of cash. However, unlike Medicaid, the difference between the market value of food stamps and the value placed on them by recipients is not large. One analysis of the food consumption patterns of low-income individuals suggested that a dollar of food stamps was worth about 97 cents to a recipient [Smeeding, 1982, p. 63].

Additional evidence on the near equivalence of food stamps and cash comes from a social experiment conducted in the early 1980s. Elderly food stamp recipients in one group were given checks instead of food stamps, while a control group received food stamps. When the two groups were compared, it was found that the cash-out of food stamps had virtually no effect on the food consumption of the recipients [Blanchard et al., 1982, p. viii].[18]

---

[16] See U.S. Department of Agriculture [1989, p. 500].

[17] In addition, the law allows certain deductions to be made before applying the 30 percent tax.

[18] For additional evidence along these lines, see Fraker, Devaney, and Cavin [1986].

The near equivalence of food stamps and cash raises a puzzle. Only about 40 percent of families eligible for food stamps actually participate in the program [Moffitt, 1983, p. 1023]. If food stamps are just as good as cash, it would appear that nonparticipation is tantamount to throwing away money. Why do people fail to take advantage of the program? One possibility is that individuals are unaware that they are eligible. Another is that there is some stigma associated with participation in the program; that is, the process of participation per se causes some reduction in utility. In one survey of low-income individuals, 32 percent of nonparticipants indicated that they considered receiving food stamps embarrassing, as opposed to 19 percent of participants [Blanchard et al., 1982, p. vi].

Indeed, the presence of stigma may be one reason why the government has chosen not to cash-out food stamps. If there is some embarrassment to enrolling in the program, then people may be less likely to participate, and hence costs can be kept down. Of course, there are other reasons why the government might prefer food stamps to cash. The usual justification of paternalism is one. Despite evidence to the contrary, legislators may fear that the poor will waste cash instead of spending it on food. Alternatively, from a political point of view, it may be easier to get support for a program to abolish hunger than to simply pay cash.

Child Nutrition Programs

These programs are targeted at nursing mothers, infants, children under five years old, and school-children. In 1989, 4.1 million women, infants, and children benefited from these programs [Committee on Ways and Means, 1990, p. 1319]. As with food stamps, there does appear to be some stigma associated with the program. For example, children who qualify for subsidized lunches often are singled out by having to stand in special lines or eat at special tables. To the extent this discourages participation, there are eligible children who receive no benefits [Levitan, 1990, pp. 105–6].

Housing Assistance

In the United States, subsidies for the provision of housing to the poor began in 1937. Until very recently, the largest program was public housing. Public housing units are developed, owned, and run by local authorities which operate within a municipality, county, or several counties as a group. The federal government subsidizes both the costs of construction and a portion of the operating costs paid by the tenants. In 1988, there were 1.5 million public housing units [U.S. Bureau of the Census, 1990, p. 726].

The average monthly value of public housing to a recipient has been estimated at about 80 percent of the cash value. The income limits for participation in public housing are locally established. Unlike other welfare programs, satisfying the means test does not automatically entitle a family to participate in public housing. As noted previously, there are only 1.5 million public housing units, while there are more than 31 million people whose incomes fall beneath the poverty line. Many more people desire entry into public housing than it is possible to accommodate. In short, public housing confers a relatively large value per recipient, but most poor people receive nothing from the program at all.

Such inequities are one reason many economists have suggested that if there are to be subsidies to housing for the poor, their link to the public provision of housing should be broken. If the subsidy could be applied to private sector housing, it would no longer be necessary for the public sector to get involved in apartment construction and management. In addition, recipients of aid would no longer be geographically concentrated and marked publicly.

There is indeed a federal housing program organized somewhat along these lines, created as part of Section 8 of the Housing Act of 1974. Under this program, which involved expenditures of about $1.2 billion in 1992, eligible households search on the private market for housing units [Executive Office of the President, 1991, p. 4-103]. If the dwelling meets certain quality standards and the rent is deemed fair by the government, it subsidizes the rent with payments directly to the landlord. (The tenant's rent payment is a fixed proportion of family income, currently set at 30 percent.) Unlike traditional public housing, Section 8 attempts to give the poor access to the existing stock of housing, instead of trying to add to the stock. However, Section 8 recipients are limited in their choice of dwellings, cannot spend more than 30 percent of their incomes on rent, and can choose only from landlords who participate in the program.

A demand-oriented subsidy program that has received a good deal of attention is housing allowances.[19] Under this scheme, each qualified individual would receive from the government a payment equal to the difference between the cost of standard housing established by the program and some fraction of income. The allowance could be spent on any housing on the private market, providing that it met certain quality standards. In the late 1970s, a major social experiment (the Experimental Housing Allowance Program) was conducted in several cities to determine how housing allowances would affect people's behavior. Analysis of the data by Eric Hanushek and John Quigley [1981, p. 204] suggests a moderate effect on housing consumption; income increases of 10 percent led to housing expenditures going up by about 5 percent. Interestingly, the increased demand generated by the housing allowances does not seem to have had much effect on housing prices in the communities where the experiment was conducted. This is probably because the supply of housing services is fairly elastic and the response to the increased allowance takes place

---

[19] A number of alternative policy approaches are discussed in Congressional Budget Office [1982].

gradually over time. It was also found that the stipulation that the dwellings meet various quality standards reduced participation in the program significantly [Allen, Pitts, and Glatt, 1981, p. 26].

In 1985, the Department of Housing and Urban Development began a housing voucher plan similar in many respects to the housing allowance experiment. Participants receive vouchers for the difference between fair market rent and 30 percent of family income. Participants are free to choose whatever housing suits them, as long as it meets certain quality standards. The voucher program is still relatively small; in 1991, about $449 million was appropriated for housing vouchers [Executive Office of the President, 1990, p. A-744].

Programs to Enhance Earnings

Most expenditures for the poor are designed to increase their current consumption levels. In contrast, some programs have been designed to enhance their ability to support themselves in the future. These include educational and job training programs.

Education

A popular theory is that much poverty in the United States is due to lack of education. The argument is that with more and better education, individuals can earn more money and, hence, are less likely to end up in poverty. Under legislation passed in 1965, the federal government provides funds to individual school districts for compensatory education at the elementary and secondary levels for disadvantaged students. The most famous example is the Head Start Program, which provides pre-school activities for four- and five-year-old children from disadvantaged backgrounds. The idea is to assure that by the time they start kindergarten, they can achieve at the same level as children from more affluent families.

Have compensatory education programs eliminated disparities in educational achievement between poor and middle-class children? It appears that at least in the short run, the programs do eliminate part of the gap. However, some studies suggest that the gains from compensatory education are not sustained—although the participants seem to do better in the short run, the advantage disappears in the long run [Jencks, 1986]. The point, of course, is not that poor children are unable to learn more than they do now. Rather, it is that our understanding of the educational process is not well enough developed to determine what works. In short, "the gaps in our understanding of the effects of compensatory education remain enormous" [Jencks, 1986, p. 178]. More generally, there is less optimism now than there was in the 1960s that education is the cure for poverty. To be sure, there is a positive correlation between years of education and earnings. But it is not clear what aspects of education increase wage rates, or whether the relationship is causal at all. (See Aaron [1978].) Until more is known about the causes of poverty, programs to eliminate its roots can be of only limited efficacy.

Employment and Job Training

Federal job training programs address another possible cause of poverty—lack of job market skills. Suppose that poor people are not able to obtain jobs that provide good training because of discrimination, or because no such jobs are located in their neighborhoods. The idea behind these programs is that the government will provide opportunities to develop marketable skills.

The government runs a variety of programs of this kind. Recently, there has been an emphasis on providing job-related training to welfare recipients. The Family Support Act of 1988 created the Job Opportunities and Basic Skills (JOBS) program, a nationwide education, training, and employment program for AFDC parents whose youngest child is at least three years old.

Many econometric studies have been done to assess the impact of government programs on the subsequent earnings and employment of participants. Laurie Bassi and Orley Ashenfelter [1986] argue that, taken together, the results of all these studies are largely inconclusive. An important reason for this disappointing situation is the fact that in most cases, individuals themselves decide whether or not to participate in job training programs. To see why this is a problem, suppose we observe that subsequent to participating in a job training program, on average the participants experience increases in their wage rates. We cannot infer that the program would have the same effect on any group of low earners, because the people who chose to enroll may have been more energetic or ambitious than those who did not enroll. This phenomenon is referred to as *self-selection bias*. Bassi and Ashenfelter argue that until job training effects are evaluated in comparison to a similarly selected control group, it will be impossible to assess job training programs.

Have Welfare Programs Helped?

A reasonable way to begin an evaluation of the welfare system is to examine its impact on poverty rates. The impact is actually quite substantial. In 1988, for example, cash plus food and housing transfers reduced the poverty rate by about 43 percent.[20] This figure, of course, does not take into account the fact that in the absence of welfare, people's earnings might have been higher. Still, in terms of the popular metaphor of government welfare programs as a safety net, it appears that although many people have slipped through the holes, many others also have been caught.

---

[20] Computed from Committee on Ways and Means [1990, p. 1042].

Academic economists—both liberals and conservatives—have focused much of their criticism on the messiness of the current system. It certainly is a hodgepodge of programs. Some programs give cash assistance; some are in-kind. Administrative responsibilities and financing are split in a haphazard way among federal, state and local governments. Each program has its own eligibility requirements, and for any given program, eligibility differs across jurisdictions. Why not cash-out in-kind programs, and replace both them and the various cash assistance programs with a single noncategorical negative income tax [Mills, 1986, p. 61]?

Other economists are beginning to reject this position for several reasons. First of all, it appears to be totally infeasible politically:

> The American public has declared unmistakably that it is willing to provide those in need of aid such commodities as basic housing, food, and health care, but it is unwilling to give poor people the cash to buy these items themselves. This attitude has persisted long enough to be taken as a constant on the welfare scene. Further efforts to modify the welfare system should treat it as a reality rather than try to explain why it does not make sense. [Aaron, 1984, p. 16]

Secondly, from an efficiency point of view, a system of categorical programs may have some merit. Specifically, if relatively large amounts of aid can be targeted at groups for whom labor supply incentives are not very important (for example, the disabled), then the overall efficiency of the system may be enhanced. Thus, while the current system is by no means ideal, its categorical structure is not necessarily a fatal flaw.

Of course, the most controversial aspect of the current system is not its messy structure, but whether it is too generous or not generous enough. In standard welfare economics, the correct answer depends on the strength of one's preferences for income equality, and the distortions in incentives induced by the system. However, some critics have suggested that any welfare system, regardless of its structure, is likely to be a bad idea:

> Welfare, like many other expressions of noble intentions, has a seed of corruption in it. You might, at first, accept charity because you really need it. But if you don't stop accepting it the very moment you can make a living on your own—even a modest living—then you lose your soul. [Kenan, 1982, p. A29]

Proponents of transfers to the poor are quick to point out that they are not the only beneficiaries of public "charity." A number of government expenditure and tax programs benefit middle- and upper-income people. Spending by the National Science Foundation increases the incomes of scientists; subsidies for the production of energy increase the incomes of the owners of oil wells; and defense programs increase the incomes of munitions manufacturers. Indeed, sometimes programs that are ostensibly for other purposes are actually nothing more than income distribution programs favoring various groups. For example, most economists believe that farm price supports have a negligible efficiency purpose and are only a veiled way of transferring income to the politically powerful agricultural interests. (These programs cost about $30 billion, and thousands of farmers receive payments in excess of $500,000 [Schneider, 1986, p. A15]). Similarly, the location of certain U.S. military bases may serve only to raise incomes in key legislative districts.

However, "welfare to the rich" does not carry that label. Perhaps that is why no one worries about their losing *their* souls.

Summary

- Means-tested programs transfer income to people whose resources fall below a certain level. Government means-tested programs are about 3.6 percent of GNP.

- Aid to Families with Dependent Children (AFDC) provides cash to families with dependent children. Benefit levels vary widely across states.

- For many welfare recipients, AFDC in effect creates a 100 percent tax on earnings. Economic theory suggests that this may discourage work, and this hypothesis is confirmed by most empirical research.

- AFDC is also accused of creating long-term welfare dependence. However, the evidence for this contention is weak.

- An alternative to AFDC would be a negative income tax—a noncategorical program in which benefits received depend only on income, and benefits are reduced only by a fraction of incremental earnings. For a given program cost, the main problem in designing a negative income tax is to choose the trade-off between adequate support and good work incentives.

- Under workfare, able-bodied individuals receive transfer payments only when they agree to accept employment if offered. States have the option to make AFDC recipients participate in workfare programs. Preliminary evidence suggests that workfare reduces AFDC caseloads.

- Supplemental Security Income (SSI) provides cash grants to the aged, blind, or disabled.

- Medicaid, the largest spending program for the poor, provides certain medical services at no charge. The market value of Medicaid is the cost of obtaining a comparable insurance policy. Empirical work suggests that the value placed on Medicaid by recipients is considerably below its market value.

- Recent discussions concerning the reform of Medicaid have focused on containing its costs. The problem is to do so without impairing the quality of care.

- A food stamp is a voucher that can be used only for the purchase of food. Food stamps appear to be almost equivalent to cash.

- Housing assistance in the United States has traditionally focused on the creation of public housing for the poor. Some economists favor breaking the link between housing subsidies and public housing. A small program now provides recipients with housing vouchers to pay the rent on the dwellings of their choice.

- The goal of education and job training programs is to enhance the ability of the poor to support themselves in the future. The efficacy of such programs is very controversial. Part of the reason is self-selection bias—individuals who choose to participate in the programs may not be representative of the poor population as a whole.

- Many economists argue that both efficiency and equity would be enhanced if current programs were consolidated and cashed-out. However, this appears to be politically infeasible. Also, a categorical system can be justified on efficiency grounds, because it allows transfers to be targeted at individuals for whom work incentives are not very important.

Discussion Questions

1. Elizabeth's wage rate is $5 per hour. She faces a welfare system that pays a monthly benefit of $150. The benefit is reduced by 25 cents for each dollar of earnings.

   a. Sketch the budget constraint in a leisure/income diagram.

   b. Sketch a set of indifference curves consistent with Elizabeth's participating in the labor market.

   c. Draw your diagram for part *a* again, and now sketch a set of indifference curves consistent with Elizabeth's *not* participating in the market.

2. Suppose you wanted to conduct an econometric study of the impact of the AFDC program on marriage rates. What data would you need? Suggest a specific estimating equation.

3. Discuss: "Workfare is an efficient way to transfer income if the quantity of leisure consumed by the recipient appears in the utility function of the donor."

4. Philip's demand curve for housing is shown in Figure 9.A. (Assume that quantity of housing is measured simply by the number of square feet. Other aspects of quality are ignored.) The market price of housing is P_1; Philip can purchase as much housing as he desires at that price. Alternatively, Philip can live in public housing for a price of P_2 per square foot, but the only apartment available to him has H_2 square feet.

   Will Philip choose public housing or rent on the private market? Explain carefully. (Hint: Compare consumer surplus [appendix to Chapter 4] under both possibilities.)

Figure 9.A

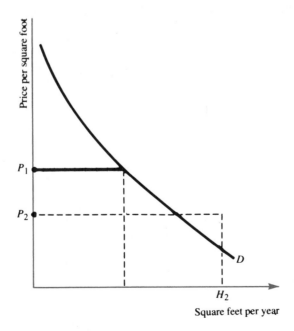

Square feet per year

5. Evaluate: "To win the War on Poverty does not require more government expenditures. What is needed is more sensible use of expenditures already being made." Base your answer not only on historical experience but also on the relevant economic arguments.

Selected References

Aaron, Henry J. "Six Welfare Questions Still Searching for Answers." *Brookings Review* 3, no. 1 (Fall 1984), pp. 12–17.

Ellwood, David T. *Poor Support: Poverty in the American Family.* New York: Basic Books, 1988.

Levitan, Sar. *Programs in Aid of the Poor.* 6th ed. Baltimore: Johns Hopkins University Press, 1990.

Murray, Charles A. *Losing Ground, American Social Policy, 1950–1980.* New York: Basic Books, 1984.

10

Social Insurance I: Social Security

It is easier for a mother to take care of 10 children than for 10 children to take care of a mother.

YIDDISH PROVERB

Life is full of uncertainties. Unexpected events such as fires or illness can dramatically lower people's well-being. One way to gain some protection against such eventualities is to purchase insurance. In return for paying premiums to the insurance company, an individual is guaranteed benefits in the event of certain losses. Several federal government programs also replace income losses that are consequences of events at least in part outside personal control. These programs, collectively referred to as **social insurance,** are listed in Table 10.1. As the table indicates, expenditures on social insurance are a large proportion of both federal government expenditures and gross national product.

Although the various programs serve quite different functions, several share these common characteristics:

- Participation is compulsory.
- Eligibility and benefit levels depend, in part, on past contributions made by the worker.
- Benefit payments begin with some identifiable occurrence such as unemployment, illness, or retirement.
- The programs are not means-tested—financial distress need not be established to receive benefits.

We begin by discussing possible rationales for social insurance. The rest of this chapter is devoted to the largest social insurance program,

Table 10.1   **Major social insurance programs** *(billions of 1992 dollars)*

Program	Date Enacted	1965	1992*
Social Security (OASDI)	1935	69.1	282.8
Medicare	1965	0	74.5
Unemployment Insurance	1935	10.5	25.4
Veterans' Disability Compensation	1917	9.2	12.3
Railroad Retirement	1937	4.6	7.9
Black Lung	1969	0	1.4
Total as percent of federal expenditure		18.9%	28.0%
Total as percent of GNP		3.3%	6.8%

* Estimates.

SOURCE: Figures for 1965 are based on S. Danziger, R. Haveman, and R. Plotnick, "How Income Transfers Affect Work, Savings, and the Income Distribution," *Journal of Economic Literature* 19, no. 3 (September 1981), p. 977. Figures for 1992 are computed from projections in Executive Office of the President, Office of Management and Budget, *The Budget of the United States Government, for Fiscal Year 1992* (Washington, D.C.: U.S. Government Printing Office, 1991).

Social Security. The next chapter takes up two of the very important programs that have been studied intensively by economists, unemployment insurance and Medicare.

Why Have Social Insurance?

Adverse Selection

According to the Fundamental Theorem of Welfare Economics, private markets generally provide commodities in efficient quantities. What is special about the commodity insurance?

Some argue that private markets for certain kinds of insurance will fail to emerge [see Diamond, 1977]. Consider the problem of obtaining insurance against loss of income in case you become disabled due to illness or age. Private insurance companies do indeed sell policies that provide a fixed annual income in the event of disablement. However, such policies—called annuities—are normally sold only to fairly large *groups* of people. Employers with many workers can make collective purchases for their employees, as can unions for their members. Insurance companies usually do not sell these annuities to individuals or very small groups.

To see why, consider a company selling annuities to a large group in which some members are prone to heart disease and others are not. As long as the group is reasonably large, the insurance company can make a good guess as to how many heart attacks will occur, even though it does not know exactly who the victims will be. It can then use this information to set the premium for the policy.

The situation of an insurance company contemplating selling such a policy to an individual is quite different. We can expect an individual who knows he is especially likely to collect benefits to have an especially high demand for insurance, a phenomenon known as **adverse selection.** However, even if the insurance company requires a physical examination, chances are that the individual will know more about his health status than the company does. Due to adverse selection and the fact that the individual has better information about his health, the insurance company must charge a higher premium for individual coverage than for group coverage to break even. These higher premiums exacerbate the adverse selection problem. Only individuals who know that they are at great risk will pay the high prices. This, in turn, requires a further increase in premiums, and the pattern continues. Thus, many people who are not part of some large group find the cost of insurance so high that they choose not to insure. The market fails to provide an efficient amount of insurance. In essence, mandatory social insurance solves this problem by forcing everybody into one big group—the country.

Is adverse selection empirically important enough to justify the provision of social insurance? It depends on the particular program being considered. On one hand, there are well-developed markets for health insurance, and policies can be obtained by most people either as part of a group or on an individual basis. In contrast, there is not much of a market for insurance against losses caused by unemployment brought about by the business cycle.

Other Justifications

We have seen that to beat the adverse selection problem, participation in social insurance programs must be compulsory. However, considerations other than adverse selection can be used to rationalize the compulsory nature of social insurance programs.

Paternalism.   The usual argument is that individuals are not farsighted enough to buy sufficient insurance for their own good and therefore the government must force them to. For example, it is popularly believed that in the absence of the program, most people would not accumulate enough assets to finance an adequate level of consumption during their retirement. This argument raises two issues. First, is it true that people really would fail to provide for themselves adequately without Social Security? To find out would require estimating how people would behave in the absence of the program. As noted later, this is very difficult to do. Second, even if it is true, it does not necessarily follow that the government should step in. Those with a highly individualistic philosophical framework believe that people should be left to make their own decisions, even if this occasionally results in mistakes.

A related consideration is that individuals who can opt out of a social insurance program may believe that if they put themselves in a sufficiently desperate situation, society will feel obliged to come to their aid. For example, society may feel it intolerable to have destitute elderly citizens around. Realizing this, some younger people may not bother to save for their old age, gambling that they will be bailed out. Part of the justification for a compulsory system may be to eliminate such games.

Economize on decision-making costs.   Insurance and annuity markets are complicated, and it is likely to involve quite a bit of time and effort for an individual to choose the right policy. If public decision makers can select an appropriate program for everybody, individuals do not have to waste resources on making their own decisions. A clear criticism here is that there is no reason to believe the government would necessarily choose the right kind of policy. After all, different people have different needs, so it might be better to let people shop around on their own.

Income distribution.   We noted earlier that benefits from social insurance programs are determined *in part* by past contributions. In fact, for some of the programs, the link between benefits and earlier contributions is quite weak. Some people do better than they would have if they had purchased private insurance, and some do worse. To an extent, then, social insurance programs are also income redistribution programs. This helps explain why the programs are compulsory. Otherwise, those who lose might opt out of them.

Regardless of the rationale, however, the United States does provide several forms of social insurance. The rest of this chapter explores the best known, Social Security.

Structure of Social Security

Social Security—officially, Old Age, Survivors, and Disability Insurance (OASDI)—is the largest single domestic spending program. In brief, the system works as follows: During their working lives members of the system and their employers make contributions via a tax on payrolls. On retirement, members are eligible for payments based in part on their contributions. Social Security also provides benefits for disabled workers and for dependents and survivors of disabled and retired workers. Today, virtually every member of the population who works is covered either by Social Security or by some other government retirement program.

Basic Components

Partially funded financing.   Originally, the Social Security program (begun in 1935) was broadly similar to a private insurance system. During their working lives, individuals deposited some portion of their salaries into a fund. Over time, the fund would accumulate interest, and on retirement, the principal and accrued interest would be used to pay benefits. Such a scheme is characterized as **fully funded.** This plan was scrapped almost immediately. In 1939 the system was converted to a **pay-as-you-go** basis, meaning that the benefits paid to current retirees come from payments made by those who are presently working. Each generation of retirees is supported by payments made by the current generation of workers, *not* by drawing down an accumulated fund. An important reason for the switch to pay-as-you-go was the perception that the savings of many of the elderly had been wiped out by the Great Depression, and they deserved to be supported at a level higher than that possible with only a few years of contributions.

The early Social Security recipients received very high returns on their contributions. An extreme case is that of Ida Fuller, the first beneficiary, who paid about $22 in Social Security taxes. She lived until the age of 99 and collected about $20,000 in benefits ["Your Stake in the Fight," September 1981, p. 504].

The prospect of supporting the post–World War II baby boom's retirement led to a decision to modify the pay-as-you-go financing strategy. As a consequence of changes introduced in 1983, the system is now building up substantial surpluses in the **Social Security Trust Fund.** These funds are being accumulated to support the baby boom in retirement without having to raise future payroll tax rates. In effect, then, the current system is neither fully funded nor pay-as-you-go. For current retirees, the system is pay-as-you-go: their benefits are paid almost entirely by taxes from current workers. For future retirees, some of the benefits will be paid by the then current workers and some out of the Social Security Trust Fund. For want of a better label, we characterize this system as partially funded financing.

Explicit transfers.   Another key change in the 1939 legislation was a broadening of the scope of the program. The 1935 act provided primarily for monthly retirement benefits for insured workers aged 65 and over. In 1939, monthly benefits for dependents and survivors of insured workers were introduced. Thus, Social Security not only provides insurance but it also transfers income between individuals. The transfer function has grown in importance over time, and culminated in the enactment of **Supplemental Security Income (SSI)** in 1972. SSI, although administered by the Social Security Administration, is not insurance by the conventional definition.[1] It is a welfare program which provides a federal minimum income guarantee for the aged and disabled. SSI is discussed with other welfare programs in Chapter 9.

---

[1] There is a broader sense in which any transfer program can be considered insurance. See Chapter 8 under "Rationales for Income Redistribution."

Benefit structure.   An individual's Social Security benefits depend on his or her earnings history, age, and other personal circumstances. The first stage is to calculate the **average indexed monthly earnings (AIME).** This represents the individual's average wages in covered employment over the length of his or her working life.[2] Not all years of work are included. (For example, for a worker reaching 62 years of age in 1987, just the highest 31 years of indexed wages were included.) Only annual wages up to a given ceiling are included in the calculation. This ceiling is the same as the maximum amount of wages subject to the Social Security payroll tax (discussed in the following section on financing). In addition, if the individual elects to work after age 62, years of higher earnings after that age can be substituted for years of lower earnings before it.

The next step is to substitute the AIME into a benefit formula to find the individual's **primary insurance amount (PIA),** which is the basic benefit payable to a worker who retires at age 65 or who becomes disabled. The benefits formula is structured so that the PIA increases with the AIME but at a slower rate. For a person turning 65 in 1990, the PIA was calculated as

90 percent of the first $356 of AIME, plus

32 percent of AIME between $357 and $2,145, plus

15 percent of AIME above $2,145.

Thus, for a retiree with an AIME of $200, the PIA was $180; while for a retiree with an AIME of $1,600, the PIA was about $718. Note that workers with low AIMEs are entitled to benefits that are a higher proportion of their earnings than those with high AIMEs.[3] The amount of an individual's actual benefit depends not only on the PIA but also on two factors.

Age at which benefit is drawn.   Currently, a worker can retire as early as age 62, but if he or she does so, benefits are reduced. For example, a worker who retires at age 62 instead of 65 receives a 20 percent reduction. If retirement is delayed past 65, benefits are increased. Currently, the credit for delayed retirement is 3 percent for each year past 65. Legislation passed in 1983 gradually increases the age at which future retirees will be able to receive full benefits. By 2022, the age will be 67. In the future, retirement benefits will still be available at age 62, but there will be a greater benefit reduction for electing to retire early.

---

[2] Wages earned over different years are not directly comparable because of changes in the price level over time. To correct for this, wages are indexed by the percentage increase in all workers' wages.

[3] The law specifies a maximum PIA as well as a special minimum benefit that provides long-term low-paid workers with a higher benefit than the regular formula permits.

Recipient's family status.   When a fully insured single worker retires at 65, the actual monthly benefit is just equal to the primary insurance amount. A worker with a dependent wife, husband, or child, receives an additional 50 percent of the PIA. In 1990, the average monthly benefit for a retired couple was $966.

Three additional rules have an important effect on the benefit structure:

1. The amount that an individual can earn and still receive full benefits is strictly limited by the **earnings test.** In 1990, the initial earnings level for retirees between the ages of 65 and 70 was $9,360 annually. For each dollar earned in excess of $9,360, 33⅓ cents of benefits were withheld. The earnings test does not apply to capital and rental incomes or to other pensions.

2. Up to one-half of the benefits received by individuals whose incomes exceed certain base amounts are subject to the federal personal income tax. These base amounts are $25,000 for a single taxpayer, and $32,000 for married taxpayers.

3. Benefits are corrected for inflation. As already noted, the computation of AIME includes an adjustment of past earnings by an index of wage growth. Moreover, once a person becomes eligible for a Social Security benefit, the purchasing power of the benefit is maintained through annual cost-of-living increases based on the minimum of *(a)* the increase in prices as measured by the consumer price index; and *(b)* the increase in wages as measured for purposes of defining the benefit base.[4]

Financing.   The payroll tax is a flat percentage of an employee's annual gross wages up to a certain amount. Half the tax is paid by employers and half by employees. The legislative intention was apparently that the cost of the program be shared equally by workers and employees. However, it may be the case that employers can "shift" part or all of their share to employees in the form of a lower pretax wage. Whether such shifting occurs is a complicated question discussed in Chapter 13. For now, we merely note that it is highly unlikely that the true division of the costs of the program is really 50–50.

As benefits have grown over time, so have the payroll tax rates. The current tax rate, 6.2 percent (on the employer and employee *each*), is more than six times its original level. (See Table 10.2.) Legislation passed in 1977 mandated that maximum taxable earnings rise automatically with future increases in average wages.

---

[4] The minimum rule is in effect only when the ratio of the assets in the Social Security Trust Fund to estimated outgo falls below a certain percentage.

Table 10.2   **Social security tax rates*** *(selected years)*

Year	Maximum Taxable Earnings (dollars)	Employer and Employee, Each (percent)
1937	$ 3,000	1.000%
1950	3,000	1.500
1955	4,200	2.000
1960	4,800	3.000
1965	4,800	3.625
1970	7,800	4.200
1975	14,100	4.950
1980	29,700	5.080
1986	42,000	5.700
1991	53,400	6.200

* These rates do *not* include the payroll tax used to finance Medicare. See Chapter 11 under "Medicare".
Source: Committee on Ways and Means [1990, p. 71].

Note that the figures in Table 10.2 do not include an additional payroll tax that finances the Medicare program, which is discussed in the next chapter. That tax is currently 1.45 percent on the employee and employer each and, with legislation passed in 1990, its base is the first $125,000 of earnings in 1991, and indexed thereafter. Thus, for an individual whose earnings are below the maximum taxed for Social Security, the payroll tax rate to finance both Social Security and Medicare is 15.3 [$= 2 \times (6.2 + 1.45)$] percent.

Distributional Issues

Our description of Social Security indicates that it serves as much more than a corrective for the nonavailability of certain types of insurance. If providing insurance were the only objective, individuals would receive approximately the same return on their contributions. Specifically, each individual would receive an actuarially fair return, meaning that on average, the benefits received would equal the premiums paid. (The calculation must be made on average because total benefits depend on the length of the individual's life, which cannot be known in advance with certainty.) In fact, some people earn higher returns than others. Implicitly, the people who earn low returns are taxed to subsidize those who receive high returns.

Due to the complexity of the Social Security law, it is difficult to make many general statements concerning who gains and who loses. The most straightforward way to explore distributional issues is to actually compute the expected lifetime net benefits from Social Security for several representative individuals and see which ones come out ahead. The first step in this computation is to estimate the expected lifetime value of the Social

Table 10.3   **Estimated benefits and costs of Social Security by age and earnings, 1985** *(single earner couples)*

Year of Birth		Earnings Level		
		$10,000	$30,000	$50,000
1915	Social Security wealth	$92,277	$144,845	$133,969
	Lifetime payroll taxes	36,280	68,340	72,205
	Gain (loss)	55,997	76,505	61,764
1945	Social Security wealth	62,679	109,128	100,503
	Lifetime payroll taxes	48,951	136,498	140,253
	Gain (loss)	13,727	(27,370)	(39,750)
1975	Social Security wealth	37,774	67,464	63,051
	Lifetime payroll taxes	33,273	99,819	112,081
	Gain (loss)	4,501	(32,355)	(49,030)

SOURCE: Boskin et al. [1986, p. 11]. The calculations assume a real interest rate of 3 percent.

Security benefits to which the worker is entitled.[5] Although the Supreme Court has ruled that Congress has the power to reduce Social Security benefits, past experience and the current political environment suggest that these benefits will continue to be paid. The value of future Social Security payments is an important part of a family's assets and is often referred to as **Social Security wealth.**

The second step in the net benefit calculation is to find the expected lifetime value of the costs of being in the system—the payroll taxes collected from the individual. Of course, both an individual's Social Security wealth and future payroll taxes depend on wage growth over time. The calculations following are for "representative" individuals whose wages over time are related to the economy-wide growth in wages.

Table 10.3 shows how Social Security affects single earner couples of different earnings levels and different ages.[6] The computations are done for the year 1985, as the law stood in that year. Each cell of the table gives the following information:

1. Social Security wealth;
2. Lifetime value of payroll taxes;

---

[5] Because Social Security benefits received depend on the length of life, the actual value is uncertain, and actuarial tables must be used to compute the value "on average," or the "expected" value. Because benefits and costs occur over time, lifetime magnitudes must be computed as "present values." Those unfamiliar with this concept should consult Chapter 12.

[6] All of the results in Tables 10.3 and 10.4 ignore possible effects that Social Security might have on before-tax prices. See Chapter 13. Note also that the earnings figures for each cohort give their earnings at age 25.

3. The net gain from the Social Security system, calculated simply as (1) minus (2). (When the difference is negative, the figure shows the individual's *loss* from the system. Losses are surrounded by parentheses.)

Thus, an individual born in 1915 who had $30,000 earnings can expect Social Security wealth of $144,845. Lifetime payroll taxes for this person are $68,340, so his net benefit from the system is $76,505.

Reading across Table 10.3 illustrates how Social Security redistributes income across income classes. For individuals of the same age, generally the higher the earnings, the smaller the gain (or the larger the loss) from Social Security. Reading down the table shows how Social Security redistributes income toward older generations. Consider two individuals with $30,000 earnings, one who was born in 1915, and the other in 1975. For the first, the net benefit of Social Security is $76,505; for the second, a net loss of $32,355. In general, Social Security is very generous to the current generation of the elderly.

Social Security also redistributes income across different types of households. As Table 10.4 indicates, at all earnings levels, women gain more (or lose less) than men. This is a consequence of the well-known fact that females have longer life expectancies than males, and hence collect benefits over a longer period of time.

Social Security redistributes income from single individuals to married persons with uncovered spouses. Consider a man earning $10,000. According to Table 10.4, if he is single, his net benefit from Social Security is minus $19,038. If married, he receives an extra benefit for his wife equal to 50 percent of his own benefit. Moreover, if he dies, the wife is entitled to his full benefit as a surviving spouse. These extra benefits raise his net gain from Social Security to $13,727.

Finally, Social Security distributes income from two-earner to one-earner couples. Consider a family in which the wife has higher lifetime covered earnings than the husband. (The qualitative results are the same when the roles are reversed.) If the benefit the husband would receive on the basis of his earnings history turns out to be less than 50 percent of his wife's benefit, the husband is entitled to *no more* than the 50 percent of his wife's benefit which he would have received even without working. If his benefit is more than 50 percent of hers, he gains only the difference between his benefit and 50 percent of hers. Thus, even though the spouse with lower earnings is subject to the payroll tax during his or her working life, he or she does not gain very much in Social Security wealth. This effect shows up quite dramatically in Table 10.4. A one-earner family with $50,000 earnings has a loss of $39,750; the loss for a two-earner family with the same income is $109,691.[7]

---

[7] See Congressional Budget Office [1986] for further discussion of how Social Security treats different types of families.

Table 10.4   **Estimated benefits and costs of Social Security by family type and earnings, 1985** *(individuals born in 1945)*

	Earnings Level		
	$10,000	*$30,000*	*$50,000*
Single-earner couple:			
Social Security wealth	$62,679	$109,128	$100,503
Lifetime payroll taxes	48,951	136,498	140,253
Gain (loss)	13,727	(27,370)	(39,750)
Single male:			
Social Security wealth	29,913	52,282	48,532
Lifetime payroll taxes	48,951	136,498	140,253
Gain (loss)	(19,038)	(84,216)	(91,721)
Single female:			
Social Security wealth	40,306	71,715	69,590
Lifetime payroll taxes	46,901	130,802	144,723
Gain (loss)	(6,595)	(59,087)	(75,133)
Two-earner* couple:			
Social Security wealth	53,293	96,044	108,428
Lifetime payroll taxes	48,264	144,760	218,119
Gain (loss)	5,029	(48,715)	(109,691)

* Calculations assume that the husband's earnings are twice the wife's.

SOURCE: Boskin et al. [1986, p. 19]. These calculations assume a real interest rate of 3 percent.

Are the redistributive patterns illustrated in Tables 10.3 and 10.4 desirable? As usual, the answer depends in part on value judgments. It could be argued, for example, that the people who lost both labor income and financial wealth during the Great Depression were unfairly treated by fate, and therefore deserve to be compensated by younger generations. If so, the intergenerational transfers shown in Table 10.3 might be appropriate. On the other hand, it is not clear what principle of equity would justify the results in Table 10.4, where families with the same income and age are treated differently by tens of thousands of dollars.

Although there has been some public discussion of the transfers implicit in Social Security, one is struck by the relative lack of attention they have received. The sums involved are huge; if such amounts were being transferred via a direct expenditure program there would probably be an ongoing major debate. However, the workings of the Social Security system are sufficiently obscure that public awareness of this situation is low.

Economic Status of the Aged

As we noted toward the beginning of this chapter, one of the main purposes of Social Security is to maintain the incomes of the elderly. Has the program achieved this goal? The numbers seem to tell a pretty upbeat story. Just a few decades ago the elderly were a relatively disadvantaged group. In 1970, about one in four elderly households was below the poverty line. Over the last 20 years, the incomes of the elderly have increased at a faster rate than the rest of the population. Currently, per capita incomes of elderly and nonelderly families are just about equal. Not only has the poverty rate for the elderly fallen; it is now below the rate for the population as a whole. In 1989, 11.4 percent of the population over 65 was poor, while for the population as a whole, the rate was 12.8 percent.

Remarkably, this increase in the incomes of the elderly took place at the same time as a dramatic decrease in their labor force participation. In 1970, 26.8 percent of elderly males worked in the market; by 1991 the figure was 14.8 percent [U.S. Bureau of Labor Statistics, 1991, p. 12]. The associated decreases in wage earnings were largely offset by increases in Social Security benefits. Currently, about 38 percent of all of the income going to elderly households is from Social Security. For elderly recipients in the lowest fifth of the family income distribution, Social Security comprises about 80 percent of income [U.S. Department of Health and Human Services, 1989, p. 205].

Two caveats are in order. First, although Social Security has doubtless reduced poverty among the elderly, it has not eliminated it. Michael Boskin and John Shoven [1986] document that in this age group females, particularly widows, are especially likely to experience economic distress. Second, Social Security benefits do not necessarily represent a *net* addition to the resources available to retirees. Perhaps individuals save less in anticipation of receiving Social Security. Or they may leave the work force to qualify for benefits. The question of how Social Security influences individuals' decisions is thus central to assessing the system's impact. We turn now to this topic.

Effects on Economic Behavior

In recent years, several investigators have argued that the Social Security system influences people's economic decisions in a way that is detrimental to the economy's efficient operation. Most of the discussion has focused on the impact of Social Security on saving behavior and labor supply decisions.[8] As we shall see, all the difficulties in doing empirical work that were explained in Chapter 3 arise here with a vengeance. The impact of Social Security on behavior remains a controversial subject, so this section is best regarded as a report on research in progress, rather than a compendium of definitive conclusions.

---

[8] These issues are discussed here because they are important and have been the subject of much research. Some fascinating questions which have not received as much attention surround the impact of Social Security on family structure. For example, how has decreased parental need for children's support in old age changed family relationships?

Savings Behavior   The starting point for most work on Social Security and savings is the life-cycle theory of savings, which suggests that individuals' consumption and saving decisions are based on lifetime considerations. During their working lives, individuals save some portion of their incomes to accumulate wealth from which they can finance consumption during retirement.[9] Such funds can be invested until they are needed, thus increasing society's capital stock.

The introduction of a Social Security system can substantially alter the amount of lifetime saving. Such changes are the consequences of three effects: First, workers realize that in exchange for their Social Security contributions, they will receive a guaranteed retirement income. If they view Social Security taxes as a means of "saving" for these future benefits, they will tend to save less on their own. But as emphasized earlier, with a partially funded system, the contributions are not all saved—part is paid out immediately to the current beneficiaries. Thus, there is no public saving to correspond to some of the loss of private saving, which means a reduction in the total amount of capital accumulation. This phenomenon is referred to as the **wealth substitution effect.**

Second, Social Security may induce people to retire earlier than they would have, because to receive benefits, they have to reduce their participation in the labor force. However, if the length of retirement increases, the individual has more nonworking years during which consumption must be financed, but fewer working years to accumulate funds. This **retirement effect** tends to increase saving.

Finally, suppose that an important reason for saving is the bequest motive—people want to leave an inheritance for their children. Suppose further that people realize that, as noted in Table 10.3, the Social Security system tends to shift income from children (worker/taxpayers) to parents (retiree/benefit recipients). Then parents may save more to increase bequests to their children, and hence offset the distributional effect of Social Security. In essence, people increase their saving to undo the impact of Social Security on their children's incomes. This is referred to as the **bequest effect.**

Given that the three effects work in different directions, on the basis of theory alone it cannot be known how Social Security affects saving. Econometric analysis is necessary. The first step is to specify a mathematical relationship that shows how the amount of saving depends on Social Security wealth and other variables that might plausibly have an effect. Alternatively, an investigator can just as well posit a relation that explains the amount of *consumption* as a function of the same variables,

---

[9] Of course, savings are also accumulated for other reasons as well: to finance the purchase of durables, to use in case of a rainy day, and so forth. For a more complete discussion of the life-cycle theory, see Modigliani [1986].

because by definition, saving and consumption are opposite sides of the same coin—anything that raises consumption by a dollar must lower saving by the same amount.

In a controversial study, Martin Feldstein [1974a] assumed that consumption during a given year is a function of private wealth at the beginning of the year, disposable income during the year and during the previous year, corporate retained earnings, and Social Security wealth. Income and private wealth are included because they are measures of the individual's capacity to consume. The previous year's disposable income is included to allow for the possibility that people may take a while to adjust their saving habits to changes in their incomes—they react to last year's as well as this year's income. Retained earnings are corporation profits that are not distributed to shareholders. Although technically held by the corporations, these sums represent income to the stockholders, and, hence, should influence their level of saving.

Feldstein estimated the regression equation with annual U.S. data from 1929 to 1976, using statistical methods similar to those described in Chapter 3. For our purposes, the key question is the sign and magnitude of the parameter multiplying the Social Security wealth variable. Feldstein found a positive and statistically significant value of 0.018.[10] This positive sign suggests that increases in Social Security wealth increase consumption and, hence, decrease saving. Thus, the wealth substitution effect dominates the retirement and bequest effects.

To assess the quantitative importance of the coefficient, consider a rough estimate of the value of Social Security wealth in 1990, $7,000 billion. A coefficient of .018 implies that Social Security reduced personal saving in 1990 by $126 billion (= .018 × $7,000). In comparison, during 1990 personal saving was $179 billion. The $126 billion is thus 41 percent of the potential personal saving of $305 billion (the sum of $126 billion and $179 billion). Thus, if Feldstein's calculations are correct, the pay-as-you-go nature of the Social Security system has had a huge negative impact on capital accumulation in the United States. Given the current concern that some of America's "productivity crisis" is due to insufficient capital, this is a serious matter indeed.[11]

Feldstein's study has spawned a considerable amount of controversy, much of which has centered on whether his equation contains all the explanatory variables that it should. Alicia Munnell [1977] has suggested that the rate of unemployment is an important determinant of the aggregate amount of saving, because during years of high unemployment, people are likely to draw down their savings to maintain their standard of

---

[10] This estimate is from a revision and update of the 1974 paper. See Feldstein [1982a].

[11] Interestingly, when Social Security was introduced during the 1930s, the perception that it decreased saving was regarded as a virtue. This was because of the belief that a major cause of the Great Depression was the failure of people to consume enough.

living. She argued further that Feldstein's failure to include the unemployment rate in the equation tends to make his coefficient on the Social Security wealth variable appear higher than it actually is. This is because through time, Social Security wealth and unemployment have tended to move in opposite directions. (During the decade of the 1930s, Social Security wealth was zero for most of the years, and the unemployment rate was very high. Later on, Social Security wealth increased while the unemployment rate came down.) Thus, part of the variation in saving that might be caused by fluctuations in unemployment is reflected in the coefficient of the Social Security wealth variable. When Munnell estimated an equation similar to Feldstein's, but included the rate of unemployment, she found that Social Security wealth still reduces personal saving, but the magnitude is only about 10 percent of that found by Feldstein. Obviously, the implications for capital accumulation are much less portentous.

Other studies have used different data sets and methods of estimation. Dean Leimer and Selig Lesnoy [1982] found evidence that Social Security might even have *increased* saving. In their survey of the available evidence, Sheldon Danziger, Robert Haveman, and Robert Plotnick [1981, p. 1006] concluded that Social Security has a negative effect on savings, but it is probably not very large.

Retirement Decisions

For those over 62 years of age, Social Security provides some incentives for partial or complete retirement. In 1930, 54 percent of the men over 65 participated in the labor force. By 1950, the participation rate for this group was 41.4 percent, and by 1991, it was 14.8 percent.[12] A number of factors have doubtless contributed to this phenomenon: rising incomes, changing life expectancies, and differences in occupations. Many investigators believe that Social Security has played a key role in this dramatic change in retirement patterns.

The retirement incentive is illustrated nicely by a numerical example. Consider Mr. Hooper, a man who earned about the average wage throughout his life and turned 65 in 1990. Hooper could retire at age 65 with benefits equal to approximately 42 percent of his preretirement gross earnings [Committee on Ways and Means, 1990, p. 118]. If he had a nonworking wife, Hooper received a dependent's benefit equal to one half of his own, making the total benefit about 62 percent of former gross earnings. Assume that Hooper's earnings were taxed at a rate of 15 percent, but his Social Security benefits were untaxed.[13] Because of the 15 percent tax rate, for every dollar earned, Hooper could keep only 85 cents. Thus, the percent of *after*-tax earnings replaced by Social Security was 73 percent (=62/85). Earning a dollar generated a gain of only 23

---

[12] See U.S. Bureau of the Census [1975, p. 132] and U.S. Bureau of the Census [1990].

[13] As noted earlier, for high-income individuals, a half of Social Security benefits are subject to tax.

cents ($=1.0-.62-.15$) over what Hooper would have gotten with no work at all. Hence, Social Security weakens the incentive to continue participation in the work force past the age of 65.

For workers who wish to participate in the labor market on a full-time basis, Social Security puts a high implicit tax on earnings via the earnings test. Those receiving Social Security are permitted to earn only a small amount of money in the market without having their benefits reduced. In 1990, retirees between the ages of 65 and 70 could earn no more than $9,360 without suffering a reduction of benefits. For each dollar earned above this amount, benefits are reduced by 33⅓ cents—in effect, a 33⅓ percent rate of taxation.[14]

A number of econometric studies have assessed the impact of Social Security on retirement decisions. Many of them are consistent with the hypothesis that the system increases the likelihood of retirement and reduces the amount of labor supplied by those who continue to work. Danziger, Haveman, and Plotnick [1981, p. 966] argue that Social Security may have accounted for about half of the increase since 1950 in the retirement rate for older men. However, this estimate is much in doubt. One important reason for the uncertainty is the fact that many of the variables influencing labor supply decisions of the aged are difficult to measure and sometimes unavailable altogether. These include: health status, local labor market conditions, and the amount of wealth accumulated in private pensions. As better data become available, more reliable answers will be obtained.

Implications

Many economists believe that Social Security depresses both work effort and saving. However, the evidence is murky, and many others are unconvinced. Even if future research establishes more firmly that the system does distort economic decisions, this is not necessarily a bad thing. If society wants to achieve some level of income security for its members, then presumably it should be willing to pay for that security in terms of some loss of efficiency. On the other hand, efforts should be made to structure the system so that labor and savings incentives are adversely affected as little as possible.

The Importance of the Trust Fund

The management of the Social Security Trust Fund has become a major political and economic issue. As noted earlier, the 1983 decision to build up the fund was made with the future retirement of the baby boom generation in mind. These 74 million people, born between 1946 and 1964, make up roughly 30 percent of the country's population. Currently, there are

---

[14] For recipients between the ages of 62 and 65 who lose some benefits because of the earnings test, there is an upward adjustment of benefits they can receive after age 65. In some cases, this adjustment is so large that it actually creates an incentive to work more. See Blinder, Gordon, and Wise [1980].

about 3.3 workers for every retiree; when the baby boomers are retiring in the 2030s, that number is expected to fall to 1.9. Hence, the baby boom's retirement will leave a smaller proportion of the population working to produce the output that must be shared by workers and retirees alike. If their retirement were to be financed on a pay-as-you-go basis, by the year 2030, Social Security taxes would absorb one third of the nation's payroll [King, 1987, p. A18].

To avoid such a dramatic rise in payroll tax rates, the 1983 Social Security reforms raised current taxes in anticipation of the baby boom's retirement. Social Security tax revenues currently exceed benefit payments. In contrast, when the baby boom generation is retired, tax revenues will fall below benefit payments. The shortfall will be financed by drawing down the trust fund balance. Present forecasts indicate that the trust fund will grow until roughly 2035. Its assets will be exhausted by the year 2055.

The size of the trust fund to be accumulated under this scenario is substantial. As early as 2015, the annual Social Security surplus is projected to be about $500 billion. Assets of the trust fund ultimately will reach almost $7 trillion [Kilborn, 1988, p. 1].

Perhaps the most important question surrounding such a large trust fund is whether its assets will be used to finance investment or consumption. If the trust fund's assets are directed toward productivity-enhancing investments, future output per worker can be increased. Present consumption will fall as the payroll tax diverts dollars to investment purposes; future consumption will rise. Thus, a trust fund that leads to increased investment, in a real sense, shifts some of the burden of the baby boom's future retirement into the present. If, on the other hand, the trust fund's assets finance current consumption (for example, they are borrowed to finance government transfer programs), the existence of a Social Security trust fund will do nothing to ease the future strain of an economy trying to support a large nonworking population. The trust fund will transfer purchasing power to the elderly without having increased the total amount of consumption goods available to be purchased, in much the same way a 33 percent payroll tax would do under pay-as-you-go financing. The key is not just amassing a trust fund, but increasing the capital stock so that there will be a greater productive capacity to support a large generation of retirees. (See Aaron [1989].)

Our focus has been on the importance of the effect of the trust fund on capital accumulation. However, by law, the trust fund is required to invest its money only in federal debt—it cannot, for example, buy stock in firms that invest in plant and equipment. Does this mean that the trust fund cannot engender increased capital accumulation? Certainly not. For a given level of total government debt, the more of it held by the trust fund, the less private sector money is required to finance the debt. This private sector money consequently is freed up for investment in the private sector. Thus, provided that the trust fund is not "borrowed" to increase current government consumption, the existence of the fund increases capital accumulation. Put another way, the resources available for capital accumulation must equal public saving plus private saving. Provided that increases in the trust fund lead to increases in public saving (or equivalently, decreases in dissaving), then capital accumulates, just as if the fund were being invested directly.

The recognition of the link between the trust fund and total saving was part of the reason for a recent change in the U.S. government's system of computing the deficit. Before 1990, Social Security taxes were counted as revenues for purposes of computing the official deficit. In effect, accumulations to the trust fund were masking the size of the difference between current revenues and current expenditures. There were fears that with a smaller official deficit, government expenditures would increase and that the Social Security Trust Fund, in effect, would be spent to finance current consumption. Hence, in 1990, Social Security taxes (and expenditures) were removed from the computation of the federal deficit. More discussion of issues involved in computing the deficit is included in Chapter 18.

Social Security Reform

Social Security is a complex system, and almost any of its specific provisions are potential targets for reform. For example, since the benefit formula redistributes income, some critics suggest that this welfare component of Social Security should be funded from general revenues rather than through a payroll tax. In practice, this means financing Social Security from federal personal income tax collections. Those who regard the Social Security system mainly as a transfer program often favor this method of finance. Under the income tax, the average rate of taxation tends to increase with income. Hence, those with high incomes bear a disproportionately high share of the burden, which is desirable if the goal is to equalize the distribution of income.[15]

However, for those who view Social Security primarily as an insurance program, the payroll tax is more appropriate because it maintains the link between contributions and benefits. Some proponents of Social Security favor payroll tax finance because it insulates the system from political pressures to emasculate it. The idea is that a link between taxes and benefits—no matter how tenuous—creates an obligation on the part of the government to maintain the system that promised the benefits. Franklin Roosevelt articulated this position with typical eloquence:

---

[15] This statement assumes that those who pay the income tax are unable to shift its burden. That this might not be the case is shown in Chapter 13. The structure of the federal income tax is described in detail in Chapter 16.

> Those taxes were never a problem of economics. They are politics all the way through. We put those payroll contributions there so as to give the contributors a legal, moral, and political right to collect their pensions. With these taxes in there, no damn politician can ever scrap my Social Security Program. ["Your Stake in the Fight," 1981, p. 504]

The reforms mentioned so far keep intact the basic structure of the Social Security system. Thinking about a major overhaul requires a careful statement of the goals of the program. As already noted, although Social Security is called social insurance, apparently one of its important objectives is to redistribute income. Thus, there are really two distinct goals: to force individuals to insure themselves by reallocating income from their working years to their retirements, and to distribute income to those elderly citizens who would otherwise lack a "socially adequate" level of support. Many of the problems with Social Security stem from the fact that it attempts to meet both objectives through a single structure of benefits and taxes. Several economists have suggested that the system be restructured to meet the two objectives separately.[16]

Under this separation proposal, the compulsory saving aspect of Social Security would continue to be funded out of earmarked payroll taxes. Each individual would have the *same* rate of return on his or her contributions. This is in marked contrast to the current system, which gives different people very different rates of return. (Recall the discussion surrounding Tables 10.3 and 10.4.)

Of course, for many people who had low earnings during their working lives, the return on their lifetime contributions might not provide a level of support considered adequate by society. Under the separation proposal, the retirement incomes of such people would be supplemented by direct transfers, the amounts of which would be based on personal circumstances. Supplemental Security Income, which is funded out of general revenues, is a mechanism already in place for making such transfers. Presumably, it could be expanded to allow for as much redistribution to the elderly poor as society desired.

This proposal has two implications: First, family status would no longer have a major effect on the value of a person's Social Security wealth. If a one-earner couple and a two-earner couple paid the same amount into the system, they would receive the same benefits. The problem of supporting nonworking spouses could be dealt with by crediting each spouse with half of the total taxes paid by the couple. In this way, even if a divorce occurred, each spouse would carry with him or her a given balance on which retirement payments would be based.

Second, the earnings test would be eliminated. Because benefits would be the returns from what an individual had already paid into the system, there would be no reason for benefits to be limited by the amount

---

[16] See, for example, Munnell [1977].

of other income. Presumably, elimination of the earnings test would diminish some of the work disincentives already discussed. However, under the reform, all Social Security benefits would be subject to income tax—just like any form of ordinary income.

Of course, general financing of the transfer part of Social Security would require it to compete openly with other government priorities. Policymakers and the public would have to determine explicitly the value of transfers to the elderly relative to other social objectives.

Other aspects of Social Security that have prompted criticism are its compulsory nature and its partial reliance on pay-as-you-go funding. Fearing that people in some generations may be compelled to contribute to the system only to have benefits cut back or dismantled when they retire, it has been suggested that participation in the system should be voluntary or, alternatively, that fully funded individual accounts be established.

Social Security is an emotional political issue, and any attempts to tinker with the system—let alone overhaul it—will be met with fierce resistance. A cliché in Washington is that Social Security is the third rail of politics—touch it and you die. The changes of 1983 came only after they were recommended by a bipartisan commission, and they probably would not have been implemented without the pressure of the short-term financial crisis. At this time, it is unlikely that any major changes will be made in the system.

Summary

- Social insurance programs replace income lost due to different events. They share characteristics of private insurance, but participation is mandatory.

- Public provision of social insurance may be justified on grounds of adverse selection, decision-making costs, income distribution, or paternalism.

- Social Security (OASDI) is the largest social insurance program, indeed the largest domestic spending program. It provides retirement incomes and minimum incomes for the aged (Supplemental Security Income—SSI).

- Social Security benefits are calculated in two steps. Average indexed monthly earnings (AIME) are derived from the worker's earnings history and determine the primary insurance amount (PIA). To compute actual benefits, the PIA is adjusted according to retirement age, family status, and other earnings.

- The Social Security system is partially funded. While current benefits are being financed mostly by taxes on current workers, in the future benefits will be paid out of accumulations in the Social Security Trust Fund.

- Broadly speaking, Social Security redistributes incomes from high- to low-income individuals, from men to women, and from young to old. Married couples with one earner in the family tend to gain relative to either two-earner couples or individuals.

- Over the past several decades, there has been a major improvement in the economic status of the elderly. Increasing Social Security benefits have played an important role in this development.

- Social Security may reduce private savings—the *wealth substitution effect*—or increase savings—the *retirement* and *bequest* effects. Numerous studies have produced conflicting results. A general conclusion is that savings have been reduced, but the magnitude of this effect is not clear.

■ The percentage of retired older workers has increased dramatically since the introduction of Social Security and much evidence indicates that this is the result of disincentives in the system.

■ The Social Security Trust Fund is expected to accumulate $7 trillion before baby boomers retire. The fund can ease the problem of financing their retirement to the extent that it fosters capital accumulation.

Discussion Questions

1. "Social Security improves economic welfare. Because the system distributes current earnings of the young (which they would save anyway) to the old, the old are better off and the young unaffected." Discuss carefully.

2. In 1991, New York's Senator Moynihan argued that since the rest of the budget was in deficit, the Social Security surpluses were in effect being used to fund other federal expenditures rather than providing saving for investment. He therefore proposed cutting Social Security payroll taxes and putting the system back on a pay-as-you-go basis. Evaluate this proposal and the reasoning behind it.

3. Suppose that participation in the current Social Security program were made optional. What do you expect would happen to aggregate private saving?

Selected References

Aaron, Henry J. *Can America Afford to Grow Old? Financing Social Security.* Washington, D.C.: The Brookings Institution, 1989.

Danziger, Sheldon; Robert Haveman; and Robert Plotnick. "How Income Transfers Affect Work, Savings, and the Income Distribution." *Journal of* *Economic Literature* 19, no. 3 (September 1981), pp. 975–1028.

Economic Report of the President 1985. "Economic Status of the Elderly." Washington, D.C.: U.S. Government Printing Office, 1985, Chapter 5.

Social Insurance II: Unemployment Insurance and Medicare

If you fall—I will catch you
I'll be waiting
*Time after time**

CYNDI LAUPER

T his chapter continues our discussion of U.S. social insurance programs, examining the systems for insuring against unemployment and ill health. As in the case of Social Security, the goal is to understand the relevant institutions, and then to evaluate them using the tools of positive and normative analysis.

Unemployment Insurance

Congress passed the federal legislation that led states to establish unemployment insurance (UI) programs in 1935, the same year as Social Security. The purpose of the program is to replace income lost due to unemployment. About 97 percent of all wage earners are covered, and in mid-1990, about 2.4 million workers received UI benefits each week. The average weekly UI benefit was $162.

Why should insurance against the possibility of unemployment be provided socially? Recall from Chapter 5 that private markets fail to provide adequate amounts of insurance in situations where adverse selection and moral hazard are important. This is certainly the case in the context of unemployment. Those workers who have the highest probability of becoming unemployed have the highest demand for unemployment insurance (adverse selection). Therefore, private firms that attempted to

---

* "Time after Time," by Cyndi Lauper and Rob Hyman © 1983 Rellla Music Corp. (BMI) and Dub Notes (ASCAP).

provide such insurance would have to charge relatively high premiums to make a profit, which would exclude many people from making purchases. At the same time, those workers who did manage to obtain insurance might experience more unemployment than otherwise would have been the case (moral hazard). Because it is difficult for the insurer to determine whether or not a layoff is the fault of a worker, a private unemployment insurance company might find itself having to pay out large amounts of money for false claims. In short, it is hard to imagine that it would be a profitable venture for private insurance companies to provide unemployment insurance. Adverse selection would similarly discourage employers from providing UI benefits to their own employees, because offering UI as a fringe benefit might attract workers who were not interested in staying with the firm for a long time.

However, a compulsory government program avoids the problem of adverse selection. Hence, government provision of UI has the potential to increase efficiency. Note, however, that government provision does *not* eliminate the moral hazard problem. As we see later, this complicates the problem of designing a UI system. We now discuss how the UI program works in practice.

Benefits

The number of weeks for which an individual can receive unemployment compensation is determined by a complicated formula that depends on work history and the state in which the person works. In most states, the regular maximum length of time is 26 weeks. However, this period can be extended if the state unemployment rate exceeds certain levels.

In most states, the benefit formula is designed so that the **gross replacement rate**—the proportion of pretax earnings replaced by UI—is about 50 percent.[1] Consider Smith, who makes $300 a week before taxes. Given a 50 percent gross replacement rate, if Smith becomes unemployed, he receives a weekly benefit of $150. It would seem, then, that Smith loses half his income when he becomes unemployed. However, since Smith's earnings are subject to both income and payroll taxes whereas his UI benefits are subject only to income taxes, the proportion of after-tax earnings replaced by UI—the **net replacement rate**—is somewhat larger than the gross replacement rate. The difference between net and gross replacement rates was more dramatic in the past, when UI benefits were exempted from income taxation.

Financing

UI is financed by a payroll tax. Unlike the Social Security system, in most states this tax is paid by employers only, not jointly by employers and employees.[2] The employer's UI tax liability for a given worker is the

---

[1] However, there is a maximum benefit level that cannot be exceeded.

[2] As emphasized in Chapter 13, despite the fact that the statute requires the tax to be paid by employers, some or all of it may be shifted to employees.

product of the employer's UI tax rate, t_u, and the worker's annual earnings up to the UI tax ceiling. Federal law dictates that the UI tax base include at least the first $7,000 of each covered worker's annual earnings. More than two-thirds of the states currently have UI tax bases above the federal base, with taxed earnings running as high as $21,300 in Alaska [U.S. Department of Labor, 1990, pp. 2-23 to 2-24].

An important feature of the payroll tax is that t_u is not the same for all employees. Rather, UI is **experience rated**—t_u depends on the firm's layoff experience. Firms that lay off relatively large numbers of employees generate a lot of demands on the UI system. Therefore, such firms are assigned a relatively high t_u. However, if a worker is laid off, generally the increased costs to the employer due to the higher value of t_u are less than the UI benefits received by the worker. For this reason, the experience rating system is described as "imperfect."

Effects on Unemployment

Ever since its inception, there have been concerns that the UI system increases unemployment. One possible reason is imperfect experience rating. To see why, suppose that the demand for a firm's product is temporarily slack, so the firm is considering temporary layoffs for some of its workers. Under imperfect experience rating, the cost to the employer in increased UI taxes is less than the UI benefit to the worker. Hence, it may be mutually beneficial for the worker to be laid off temporarily. If the system were characterized by perfect experience rating, UI would provide no such incentive for temporary layoffs.

Much of the academic and political discussion of UI's incentives has focused on the impact of relatively high net replacement rates on unemployment. As we already suggested, in many cases an individual's employment status is under his or her control. A worker's behavior on the job can influence the probability that he or she will lose it. Similarly, an unemployed worker can control the intensity with which he or she seeks a new job. The high net replacement rates of UI may make workers more likely to accept employment in industries where the probability of future layoffs is great. In addition, UI may induce the unemployed to spend more time looking for work than otherwise would have been the case.

Is this moral hazard problem empirically important? This question has been the subject of many econometric studies. Typically, investigators estimate regressions in which the variable on the left-hand side is the number of weeks unemployment insurance is received. The explanatory variables include personal characteristics of the worker such as sex and marital status, as well as the UI weekly benefit amount. If UI encourages unemployment, the coefficient on the weekly benefit amount should be positive; higher benefits lead to a longer duration of unemployment. A recent study suggests that a 10 percentage point increase in the net replacement rate of UI—increasing the ratio of weekly benefits to weekly wages from 45 percent to 55 percent, for instance—increases the duration of unemployment by about 1½ weeks [Meyer, 1990].

The fact that UI extends the duration of unemployment is not necessarily undesirable. If workers take more time to search, they may find jobs that are more appropriate for their skills, which enhances efficiency.[3] More generally, a society that believes it is worthwhile to maintain income levels for those who are involuntarily unemployed may be willing to pay the price in terms of some increased voluntary unemployment.

Medicare

The Medicare program, enacted in 1965, provides health insurance for people aged 65 and older. Its purpose is to increase the access to quality health care by the elderly and reduce their financial burden. Expenditures on Medicare in 1990 were $107.4 billion, or 2.0 percent of gross national product [Congressional Budget Office, 1991, pp. 152, 154]. It is the second largest domestic spending program; only Social Security is larger.

Before discussing the details of the Medicare program, we might ask why there should be such massive government involvement in the market for health insurance for the elderly. After all, it is foreseeable that eventually both earnings capacity and health are likely to decline. Why not simply purchase health insurance when young to cover these eventualities?

Most of the general arguments made in the last chapter for rationalizing the existence of social insurance apply to the specific case of Medicare. First, due to adverse selection, private insurance tends to be purchased by those individuals at highest risk. As noted earlier, this drives up premiums, and the market is likely to underprovide health insurance. Second, purchase of health insurance involves high administrative and sales costs. People have to search for the right policy, potential purchasers may have to be given physical exams, and so on. By forming the aged into a single group, a government program may economize on such costs. Finally, people may not understand how insurance works, or they may lack the foresight to purchase it. Paternalistic arguments suggest that people should be forced into a medical insurance system for their own good.

Would the elderly really be underinsured if left to their own devices? In 1963, prior to the introduction of Medicare, only about 56 percent of the population aged 65 and older had health insurance [Gornick et al., 1985, p. 14]. While one cannot prove that this figure is too low, it does suggest that there is some scope for government intervention in the market for health insurance for the elderly. Whether the Medicare system has been a sensible form of intervention is the subject to which we now turn.

---

[3] This argument assumes that in the absence of UI, the amount of time devoted to search would be suboptimal. Such might be the case if unemployed workers could not borrow to maintain their consumption levels while looking for jobs.

The Structure of Medicare

Medicare covers nearly the entire population aged 65 and older. In 1989 there were about 33 million enrollees [Department of Labor, 1990].[4] The program is administered by the federal government, and eligibility standards are uniform across the states. Unlike Medicaid, the program of health care for the poor which was discussed in Chapter 9, Medicare is *not* means-tested. There is no need for claimants to establish that their incomes fall below a certain level to participate.

Benefits.   The Medicare program is divided into two parts, A and B. Part A, which accounted for $60.8 billion in expenditures in 1989, is **Hospital Insurance (HI).** Participation in HI is compulsory. It covers 90 days of inpatient medical care per year.[5] Once the patient is out of the hospital, HI pays for 100 days of care in a skilled nursing facility. Thus, HI does not cover long-term institutional services. If a chronic illness occurs, Medicare is of relatively little help. After Medicare stops paying an individual's bills, the government steps in again only after the individual has become impoverished, and hence qualifies for Medicaid.

Part B of Medicare is **Supplementary Medical Insurance (SMI),** which pays for physicians, supplies ordered by physicians, and medical services rendered outside the hospital. Unlike HI, SMI is voluntary. Enrollees must pay a monthly premium, equal to $29.90 in 1991 and scheduled to rise to $46.10 by 1996. However, about 99 percent of the eligible population chooses to enroll in SMI.

Taken together, HI and SMI account for about 45 percent of health-care expenditures for persons 65 and older. Of the remainder, 18 percent is from other public sources (mostly Medicaid), and 37 percent from private sources (out-of-pocket payments and private insurance).[6]

Financing.   HI is financed by a payroll tax on the earnings of current workers. In 1991, the rate was 1.45 percent on the employer and employee each, for a total of 2.90 percent. The tax is applied up to a ceiling of $125,000. (The ceiling is indexed to increases in wages.) The tax proceeds are deposited in the HI Trust Fund, from which disbursements to health care providers are made. Note that Medicare runs on a pay-as-you-go basis. The medical bills of the present generation of retirees are paid by today's workers, not by drawing on money accumulated in the HI Trust Fund.

Medicare recipients must finance some hospital expenses out of their own resources. First is the annual **deductible**—the amount the patient must pay before Medicare makes any contribution. In 1989, the Medicare

---

[4] Most of the institutional material in this section is from Marian Gornick et al. [1985].

[5] HI will pay benefits for another 90-day spell only after the individual is out of the hospital for 60 days.

[6] Committee on Ways and Means [1990, p. 241].

Table 11.1   **Federal government outlays for Medicare**
           (selected years)

Year	Outlays (in billions)	Outlays as Percent of GNP
1967	$ 3.4	0.4%
1970	7.1	0.7
1975	14.8	1.0
1980	34.2	1.3
1983	55.9	1.7
1985	69.0	1.8
1993*	143.7	2.2

* Projections.

SOURCE: Congressional Budget Office [1985, pp. 165, 166] and Executive Office of the President [1991], pp. 4–97 and historical tables, p. 15.

deductible was $560. Secondly, the patient is liable for a certain proportion of bills above the deductible. This proportion, called the **coinsurance rate,** is one quarter of the expenses incurred during days 60 through 90 of a hospital stay. Moreover, more than three quarters of Medicare enrollees purchase on the private market so-called "Medigap" policies to cover some or all of the deductible and coinsurance payments [Committee on Ways and Means, 1990, p. 239].

Unlike HI, SMI relies on general revenues for financing, not on a payroll tax. In addition, SMI receives funds from the monthly premium mentioned earlier. Currently, about three quarters of SMI finance is from general revenues and one fourth from premiums, so the federal subsidy is heavy. The SMI deductible is $100 per year, and the coinsurance rate is 25 percent.

Forebodings of Bankruptcy

Table 11.1 shows Medicare expenditures over time, both in dollars and as a proportion of GNP. In 1967, Medicare outlays were $3.4 billion, or about 0.4 percent of GNP. By 1990, the figure was $106.6 billion, or 2.0 percent of GNP. The Congressional Budget Office [1991] projects that by 1994, the Medicare program will absorb 2.2 percent of GNP. Table 11.2 helps put the increase in Medicare costs in the context of soaring health-care costs in general. In 1960, health care accounted for 5.3 percent of GNP; by 1989, the proportion had more than doubled, to 11.6 percent; one projection is that by the year 2000 it will reach 17 percent of GNP [Darman, 1991]. The last column of Table 11.2 documents the increasing role of government in the health care sector. It accounted for 20.8 percent of health expenditures in 1960, and more than 41 percent by 1989. The general picture painted by Tables 11.1 and 11.2 is pretty clear. Health care expenditures, and Medicare outlays in particular, are enormous and growing at a rate that is not sustainable in the long run.

Table 11.2   **National health expenditures** *(selected years)*

Year	Total Expenditures (in billions)	Percent of GNP	Public Share as Percent of Total Health Expenditure*
1960	$ 26.9	5.3%	20.8%
1965	41.9	6.1	21.3
1970	75.0	7.4	33.2
1975	132.7	8.3	38.6
1980	248.1	9.1	39.3
1985	425.0	10.7	38.9
1989	604.1	11.6	41.9

* Includes Medicare, Medicaid, and public assistance.

SOURCE: U.S. Bureau of the Census, *Statistical Abstract of the United States.* (Washington, D.C., 1990) p. 92, and *Economic Report of the President 1991*, p. 135.

In contrast, payments into the HI trust fund have not increased at anything like the rate of Medicare costs. Although legislation passed in 1990 increased the HI payroll tax base to include annual earnings of up to $125,000 per worker, it is likely that without further restructuring, Part A of Medicare is headed for bankruptcy. Note that "bankruptcy," though, does not mean the same thing for a government operation as for a firm. After all, the government can use its coercive power to raise taxes. However, eliminating the HI deficit would require a substantial increase in the HI payroll tax rate, which currently appears to be politically infeasible. Because SMI is financed out of general revenues rather than the payroll tax, concerns about its solvency do not have the same kind of urgency. Given that SMI outlays contribute to the federal deficit, however, there will be pressure to lower them as well.

How did we get into this situation? A number of interrelated explanations for increasing Medicare costs have been suggested.

Demographic trends. In the 1980s, the population aged 65 and older grew at more than twice the rate of the overall population, and the age group 85 years and older grew at more than three times the overall rate. As the number of aged persons increases, so does the number of Medicare enrollees and hence the number of potential beneficiaries. In 1960, 9.2 percent of the population was 65 and older. By 1990, this figure was 12.5 percent. Moreover, the Medicare population itself is getting older—in 1965, 37 percent of the people over 65 were also older than 75, but by 1990 this figure had grown to 41 percent [Bureau of the Census, 1990, p. 2].

Despite common stereotypes, "old" and "sick" do not necessarily go together. Studies of the elderly by health care professionals indicate a wide range of physical and mental abilities. Still, the use of medical services does increase considerably with age, so as the population continues to "gray," Medicare expenditures will increase.[7]

Retrospective cost-based reimbursements.   For most of the history of Medicare, hospitals were reimbursed on the basis of reasonable costs incurred for a patient during his or her stay. A system that computes payments by looking back at the actual costs incurred is called *retrospective*. Under a retrospective system, there is little incentive to economize on methods for delivering health care; to the contrary, the more resources devoted to a patient, the more money the health-care provider receives.

In 1983, a revolutionary change was introduced—*prospective* cost-based reimbursements. Under this system, HI pays to a hospital an amount per patient that depends on his or her illness and is determined *before* treatment is received. Specifically, each patient is classified into one of 468 **diagnosis related groups (DRGs).** The payment from Medicare depends only on the patient's DRG; the hospital's actual costs are irrelevant. Under a prospective system, the hospital has a clear incentive to be more efficient in the treatment of each case.

Critics have noted several problems with the DRG system. First, the hospital receives its payment whenever a patient is discharged; the payment does not depend on the length of the stay. This would seem to encourage shorter hospital stays, and perhaps even excessive admissions—get a patient out of the hospital quickly, collect the payment from HI, and then readmit him or her soon. Early evidence indicates that the DRG system is indeed related to shorter hospital stays. Admission rates, however, have actually fallen as treatment once administered during a hospital stay is now provided by outpatient services or care in other institutions not subject to Medicare's prospective payment schedule [Russell, 1989, p. 83].

The second and more vexing problem with any prospective payment system is that it creates incentives for the health-care provider to skimp on the quality of care. After all, the same payment is received regardless of the services provided. The government has tried to deal with this problem by instituting "Peer Review Organizations" (PROs). Hospitals involved in prospective-based payment systems must contract with a PRO to monitor their behavior and assure that they are delivering proper care. Does the system work? One review of the early evidence concludes that "indirect measures of quality, such as readmissions to hospitals or transfers to other institutions, offer no clear-cut signals that prospective payment has brought ill effects." [Russell, 1989, p. 84].

---

[7] Victor Fuchs [1984] argues that much of the correlation between age and health care is due to the fact that the great bulk of these expenditures occur in the last year before dying.

Third-party payment.   So far, our focus has been on the hospital's incentives to contain costs. Under normal circumstances, consumers also desire the services they purchase to be provided as efficiently as possible. However, both Medicare and typical private insurance plans largely insulate consumers of medical services from the financial consequences of their health-care decisions. Instead, a third party (the government or the insurance company) pays, and the patient need not be concerned with the bill. Third-party payments are an important feature of the U.S. health-care system. In 1989, consumers' out-of-pocket spending covered only 23 percent of personal health-care costs. With third-party payments, not only does the patient face incentives to demand the very best care; he or she has little if any motivation to seek this care from an efficient supplier.

The effects of such a system on health-care costs can be analyzed using a conventional supply-and-demand diagram. In Figure 11.1, the market demand curve for medical services in the absence of insurance is labeled D_m. For simplicity, assume that the marginal cost of producing medical services is a constant, P_0. Hence, the supply curve, S_m, is a horizontal line at P_0. As usual, equilibrium is at the intersection of supply and demand; the equilibrium price and quantity are P_0 and M_0, respectively. Total expenditure in the market is the product of the price per unit times number of units, that is, OP_0 times OM_0, or rectangle $P_0 OM_0 a$ (the area in the diagram with the color added).

Before proceeding, we should note one possible objection to Figure 11.1—the downward-sloping demand curve. When people are sick, don't they just follow the doctor's orders, regardless of price? Would you haggle with your surgeon in the midst of an appendicitis attack? The implication of this view is that the demand curve for medical services is perfectly vertical, not downward sloping. Such reasoning ignores the fact that many medical procedures are discretionary. Patients make the initial decision whether to seek health care, and do not always comply with the doctor's advice. Mark Pauly [1986] surveyed a number of empirical studies suggesting that when the price of medical services goes down, the quantity demanded does indeed increase.

Now, how does the introduction of a system such as Medicare affect the market? To keep things simple, assume that all Medicare patients are subject to a 20 percent coinsurance rate. The key to analyzing the impact of Medicare is to realize that this is equivalent to an 80 percent reduction in the price facing patients—if the incremental cost to the hospital for a day's stay is $500, the patient pays only $100. In Figure 11.1, the price confronted by the patient is no longer P_0, but only .2 times P_0. Given this lower price, the quantity demanded increases to M_1.

Note that at the new equilibrium, although the patient is paying $.2P_0$ per unit, the marginal cost of providing health services is still P_0; the difference $(.8P_0)$ is paid by Medicare. Hence, *total* expenditures are OP_0 times OM_1, or the rectangle P_0OM_1b. Thus, as a consequence of the

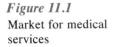

Figure 11.1

Market for medical services

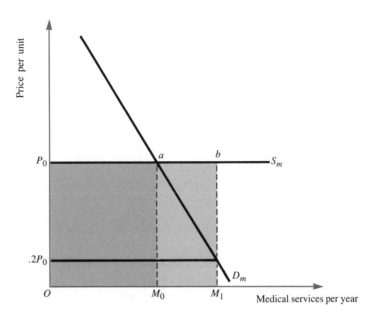

insurance, health-care expenditures increase from P_0OM_0a to P_0OM_1b, or the gray area aM_0M_1b.

Of course, the actual amount by which expenditures increase depends on the shape of the demand curve, the precise deductible and coinsurance rates, and so on.[8] But the general point is clear—systems that fail to confront consumers with the full marginal cost of medical services lead to increases in quantity demanded and total expenditure.

Improvements in quality.   Physician training, medical techniques, and equipment have all improved over time. Indeed, the last several decades have witnessed breathtaking developments in medical technology. As a result, the quality of health care has improved—the treatment of kidney stones today is not the same "commodity" as treatment of kidney stones in 1960. But these improvements are costly. For example, it costs in excess of $1 million dollars to acquire a magnetic resonance imaging (MRI) scanner, a device that uses computers to examine internal organs with much greater detail than is possible with traditional X-rays. Hence, even in the absence of the factors already noted above, medical treatments would be growing more expensive.[9]

---

[8] Moreover, if the supply curve is not horizontal, the result depends on its elasticity as well. See problem 2 at the end of the chapter.

[9] One interesting question is how much the growth of expensive medical technologies has been fueled by the existence of third-party schemes like Medicare. Would the development of such technologies have been profitable if doctors and patients had to confront their full costs? See Joseph Newhouse [1978, p. 64].

**Reforming
Medicare**

Recent policy discussions about Medicare and health care in general have been dominated by their large and increasing costs. Hence, most "reforms" are viewed with an eye toward what they can do to reduce expenses. Before proceeding to a discussion of such reforms, we might pause for a moment to ask how we know that Medicare expenditures really are "too high." What is the "correct" level of health-care expenditures?

The theory of welfare economics (Chapter 4) gives us one answer—the correct level of health care is that at which social marginal cost equals social marginal benefit. Since third-party payment systems do not force individuals to confront the social marginal costs of their treatments, it would seem that there is indeed "too much" health care.

However, some economists argue that the health-care market does not function well in the welfare economics sense, and hence this conclusion is misleading. The standard model assumes that consumers come to the market with good information about the commodities they consume, or else they can learn quickly.[10] Either you know how much you are willing to pay for a fudge ripple ice cream cone, or at relatively little expense, you can purchase one and find out if it is to your liking. In contrast, medical care is generally used infrequently, it can be obtained in a variety of forms, and it is hard for laypersons to judge its quality. In addition, health-care decisions sometimes must be made at times of serious emotional stress.

Things are complicated by the fact that the person on whom the consumer relies for advice on how much to consume, the physician, is also the person who supplies the commodity. This is another example of the principal-agent problem described in Chapter 5. The principal (the patient) desires the agent (the physician) to provide appropriate health care. Due to the fact that the physician's income depends partly on the treatment prescribed, there is a potential conflict of interest with the patient. And because there is substantial uncertainty in the technology of health-care provision, it is hard to know whether unhappy outcomes (high medical bills and/or continued sickness) are the consequences of bad luck or incompetent care.

Poor information and principal-agent problems are not unique to the health-care sector. Such phenomena also are present in markets for commodities as diverse as higher education, used cars, funerals, and child care. The argument is that in the health-care sector these factors are so pervasive and loom so large that the standard model provides very little normative guidance. In short, Figure 11.1 might play a useful role in

---

[10] Another possible source of market failure in the health-care market is externalities. Some medical treatments such as inoculations against contagious diseases may produce benefits for other people. However, in the context of the health-care market as a whole, such externalities do not seem very important.

helping us understand the *positive* question of how health-care expenditures are determined. However, because consumers are so poorly informed, their decisions as embodied in the demand curve lack any *normative* significance.

It is not clear where this line of reasoning leaves us. Apparently, the "political process" must decide on the appropriate amount of health care, and then design a system for delivering it efficiently. But how is one supposed to know what is "appropriate" without reference to its effect on the individual's utility? And how is one to judge whether the government can do better than individuals' admittedly imperfect decisions?

In any case, the political process does seem to have determined that the costs of Medicare, or at least their rate of growth, should be reduced. Several suggestions for doing so have been made.

Reduce the number of beneficiaries.   One way to reduce the number of claimants would be to raise the eligibility age from 65 to, say, 70. Proponents of this view observe that 65-year-olds are now healthier than they used to be; therefore, it would not be a great burden to remove their eligibility for Medicare. This observation highlights an important point. Medicare cannot be evaluated in isolation from other policies that affect the elderly. For example, if the eligibility age for receiving Social Security were raised, presumably more people would stay in the work force. They would therefore have more access to employer-provided health insurance, and have less need of Medicare. Thus, the merits of a given change in Medicare cannot be determined unless the relevant provisions of the Social Security system are also brought into the picture.

Another way to reduce Medicare beneficiaries would be to means-test the program—allow participation only if an individual's financial resources fall below a certain level. Proponents of means-testing argue that it would allow the government to target resources at the people who need them most. However, means-testing would reflect a fundamental philosophical shift in Medicare. It is currently perceived to be an insurance program—you pay your premiums when young, and receive benefits when old. Means-testing would make the program more like welfare, and hence encounter serious political resistance.

Increase cost sharing.   As noted previously, under Medicare there are relatively modest deductibles and coinsurance rates, and patients have little incentive to find cost-effective treatments. If more cost sharing were introduced, such incentives could be improved.[11] Proposals to increase

---

[11] Presumably, however, some restrictions on the use of Medigap policies would have to be implemented for this to work.

cost sharing often include a **catastrophic cap**—an upper limit on the amount of an individual's out-of-pocket costs for an illness. For example, the Reagan administration proposed increasing the coinsurance rate for the early days of a spell of hospitalization, but eliminating any cost sharing after the sixtieth day. Some economists have argued that reforms should go even further in this direction. Make patients pay most of the costs for all routine procedures, but provide virtually complete insurance against catastrophes. The hope is that this would cut the costs of the program, yet provide individuals with the kind of insurance they really need. However, it is hard to know whether such a system would in fact reduce program costs. After all, once the catastrophic cap is reached, the sky is the limit. Very expensive treatments, albeit for a relatively small proportion of patients, could increase overall Medicare costs.

Encourage capitated systems.   A capitated system is a contract to provide medical care on a per-person basis. Thus, Medicare might pay a fixed annual fee to a health-care provider to meet a person's medical needs during that year. Currently, the use of capitated systems is growing in the private sector. The best known examples are Health Maintenance Organizations (HMOs).

Capitated systems provide an obvious incentive for the health-care provider to minimize costs. Skeptics about the use of capitated systems for Medicare worry that individuals who are at high risk may have trouble gaining access to health care. Why accept a patient if he or she will lead to a loss in profits? More generally, like other prospective payment methods, capitated systems induce conflicts of interest between providers and patients. As in other contexts, the question is whether a monitoring mechanism can be developed that would mitigate this problem.

Vouchers.   Some argue that the best way to bring government health-care costs under control would be to enhance the role of market forces in the health-care sector. One popular proposal for doing this is to replace Medicare with a system of vouchers—coupons that could be used by the recipient to pay for a certain dollar amount of medical services at the institution of his or her choice. An individual could use the voucher to purchase a conventional insurance policy, or participate in an HMO, and so forth.[12] Individuals would be made aware of the various options and their costs via both government-provided information and private advertising; presumably, the government could monitor for truth in advertising. The value of the voucher would be set to cover the cost of an efficient health plan. If an individual participated in a more expensive plan, he or

---

[12] Under some versions of the voucher scheme, participation in the current Medicare system is an option. In others, Medicare is eliminated.

she would have to pay the incremental cost. Thus, competition among health-care providers for customers would help keep down costs in the conventional manner.

Proponents of vouchers stress that they would increase the scope of consumer choice, and hence better allow individuals to enroll in health-care systems that met their particular needs. Moreover, it would remove government from its current deep involvement and responsibility for health-care costs. To be sure, the government would have to monitor the market to prevent unfair practices and fraudulent behavior, but the cost-minimizing outcome would be generated by the invisible hand of competition, not by regulation.

Critics of vouchers have argued that this scenario is much too rosy. Harold Luft [1984], for example, stresses that vouchers may not work because of adverse selection—individuals who know themselves to be at high risk for illness tend to concentrate in certain types of plans. For example, they might prefer plans with a relatively high entrance fee, but a relatively low or zero coinsurance rate, like an HMO. However, as more high-risk people enter such organizations, they have to raise their fees to break even. The higher fee exacerbates the problem, because now only individuals at even higher risk will participate. This in turn leads to another increase in fees, and the process continues. Thus, because of adverse selection, the market may not provide the "right" mix of health-care alternatives.

One possible solution would be for the value of the voucher to depend on the individual's risk class. If certain characteristics (such as age and sex) were positively correlated with the probability of illness, people with those characteristics would receive relatively large vouchers. The problem is that even a large number of *observable* characteristics does not provide as much information about a person's health status as that person has about him- or herself. And as long as the risk ratings are imperfect, adverse selection is a potential problem. Of course, theory by itself cannot tell us just how important adverse selection would be. But given its potentially devastating impact, voucher schemes must be approached with caution.

Voucher critics also argue that the scheme overestimates the ability of people to seek out and assimilate information on various health-care options. This brings us back yet again to the question of whether the health-care market operates more or less like markets for other goods and services. To the extent that one believes that the usual supply and demand framework of Figure 11.1 has normative significance, vouchers will be attractive. If one believes that individuals are not capable of making sensible health-care decisions *and* the government can do better, the *status quo* may be preferred. Most economists believe that the current system could be improved by the introduction of more market forces. But there is great controversy over just how much reliance on the market is optimal.

Conclusions

A thought suggested by this chapter and the one before it is that social insurance programs have had unintended consequences. It is hard to imagine that the designers of the Social Security program really wanted to generate huge income redistributions based on marital status. Similarly, no one wanted to design an unemployment insurance system that increased unemployment, or to create a medical insurance system that contributed to an explosion of health-care costs.

The extent to which social insurance actually is responsible for current economic problems is unknown. There does seem to be a widespread consensus, however, that U.S. social insurance policy fails to operate in a fair and efficient way. This is partly due to the fact that our social insurance programs are largely an inheritance from earlier times when economic and demographic conditions were different than they are today. Part is also due to the failure of policymakers to fully think through the implications of their programs and to define their goals precisely. Unfortunately, prospects for serious reform are remote because the current forms of social insurance have become almost sacrosanct.

Having said this, we should emphasize that designing "good" social insurance systems is not easy. As stressed throughout the chapter, moral hazard complicates the design of both private and social insurance plans. The presence of UI induces workers to spend "too much" time in between jobs, just as Medicare induces patients to demand "too much" medical care. Mitigating such incentives through lower replacement ratios, copayments, and the like reduces the scope of the insurance provided. But the whole reason for introducing the programs in the first place was to provide insurance. Finding the right tradeoff between incentives and adequate insurance is a problem for which the solution is not transparent.

Summary

- Unemployment Insurance (UI) replaces a portion of income lost due to unemployment.
- The UI system has imperfect experience ratings for employers. In addition, UI benefits frequently offer net replacement rates that are relatively high. Both these phenomena increase unemployment.
- The Medicare program provides health insurance for people aged 65 and older. Medicare has two parts. Hospital Insurance (HI) covers inpatient medical care. Supplementary Medical Insurance (SMI) pays for physicians.
- HI is financed by a payroll tax on the earnings of current workers. SMI relies mostly on general revenues, although it also receives funds from monthly premiums paid by the elderly.
- Medicare costs have increased for a number of reasons. These include demographic trends, retrospective cost-based reimbursement systems, third-party payments, and the introduction of expensive new technologies.
- There are several ways in which Medicare costs, or at least their rate of growth, might be reduced. One of these, a prospective payment system, has been adopted for the hospital insurance part of Medicare. Other possible cost-cutting measures include reducing the

number of beneficiaries, increasing the role of cost sharing, encouraging the use of capitated systems, and introducing vouchers. In each case, the problem is to reduce costs without impairing the quality of health care received.

■ Many economists favor reforms that would strengthen the role of market forces in health-care provision. However, others believe that unique characteristics of this market require substantial government intervention.

Discussion Questions

1. Some states pay unemployment insurance to those who quit their jobs as well as to those who are laid off. Does this improve or impair economic efficiency? Should these benefits be subject to the personal income tax?

2. Proposals are always arising to modify social insurance policies. Discuss these two ideas which came up in 1991:

    a. In light of the recession that was then occurring, some congressional Democrats suggested that the length of time that unemployment benefits could be received should be extended.

    b. The Bush administration proposed that Medicare premiums should be increased for people with incomes over $125,000.

3. Figure 11.1 analyzes the impact of insurance on health-care expenditures assuming that the supply curve of medical services is horizontal. Repeat the analysis with an upward-sloping supply curve.

4. Hospitals in New York State are required to file reports with the State Health Department documenting all cases in which patients are harmed or jeopardized because of hospitals' mistakes or negligence. The hospital industry successfully lobbied to prevent these documents from being released to the public under the Freedom of Information Act. How would you account for the hospital industry's behavior? Relate your answer to the issue of whether the health-care market is "properly functioning."

Selected References

Congressional Budget Office. *Promoting Employment and Maintaining Incomes with Unemployment Insurance.* Washington, D.C.: U.S. Government Printing Office, March 1985b.

Luft, Harold S. "On the Use of Vouchers for Medicare." *Milbank Memorial Fund Quarterly* 62, no. 2 (Spring 1984), 237–50.

Pauly, Mark V. "Taxation, Health Insurance, and Market Failure in the Medical Economy." *Journal of Economic Literature* XXIV, no. 2 (June 1986), 629–75.

Russell, Louise. *Medicare's New Hospital Payment System: Is It Working?* Washington, D.C.: The Brookings Institution, 1989.

CHAPTER 12 Cost-Benefit Analysis

Paris is well worth a Mass.

<small>ATTRIBUTED TO HENRI IV OF FRANCE</small>

S uppose that the government is presented with a project—building a road, starting a job-training program, or organizing a parade—and must determine whether to pursue it. The theory of welfare economics provides an approach for answering this kind of question: Evaluate the social welfare function before and after the project, and see whether social welfare increases. If it does, then do the project.

This methodology is correct, but not very useful. The amount of information required to specify and evaluate a social welfare function is enormous. While social welfare functions are valuable for thinking through certain conceptual problems, they are generally not much help for the day-to-day problems of project evaluation. However, welfare economics does provide the basis for **cost-benefit analysis**—a set of practical procedures for guiding public expenditure decisions.[1]

Most government projects and policies result in the private sector having more of some scarce commodities and less of others. At the core of cost-benefit analysis is a set of systematic procedures for valuing these commodities. However, cost-benefit analysis is not a panacea that provides a definitive "scientific" answer to every question. For example, when it comes to assigning dollar values to such intangibles as national security or environmental purity, the tools of cost-benefit analysis provide no easy solutions. Nevertheless, using a cost-benefit analysis helps to ensure consistent decision making that focuses on the appropriate issues.

---

[1] The links between theoretical welfare economics and cost-benefit analysis are discussed by Dreze and Stern [1985].

Present Value

Project evaluation usually requires comparing costs and benefits that occur in different time periods. For example, a program of preschool education for poor children may require substantial expenditures in the present and then yield returns many years into the future. In this section we discuss problems that arise in comparing dollar amounts from different time periods. Initially, we assume that no price inflation occurs over time. We show later how expected changes in the price level affect the results.

Suppose that you take $100 to the bank and deposit it in an account that yields 5 percent interest after taxes. At the end of one year, you will have $(1 + .05) \times \$100 = \$105$ in the account—the $100 initially deposited, plus $5 in interest. Suppose further that you let the money sit in the account for another year. At the end of the second year, you will have $(1 + .05) \times \$105 = \$110.25$. This can also be written as $(1 + .05) \times (1 + .05) \times 100 = (1 + .05)^2 \times 100$. Similarly, if the money is put in an account for three years, it will be worth $(1 + .05)^3 \times \$100$ by the end of the third year. More generally, if R are invested for T years at an interest rate of r, at the end of T years, it will be worth $\$R \times (1 + r)^T$. This formula shows the future value of money invested in the present.

Now suppose that someone offers a contract that promises to pay you $100 *one year from now*. The person is entirely trustworthy, so you do not have to worry about default. (Also, remember that there is no inflation.) What is the maximum amount that you should be willing to pay *today* for this promise? It is tempting to say that a promise to pay $100 is worth $100. But this neglects the fact that the $100 of the promise is not payable for a year, and that in the meantime you are forgoing the interest that could be earned on the money. Why should you pay $100 today to receive $100 a year from now, if you can receive $105 a year from now simply by putting the $100 in the bank today? Thus, the value today of $100 payable one year from now is *less* than $100. The **present value** of an amount of money in the future is the maximum amount you would be willing to pay today for the right to receive the money in the future.

To find the very most you would be willing to give up now in exchange for $100 payable one year in the future, you must find that number which, when multiplied by $(1 + .05)$, just equals $100. By definition, this is $100/(1 + .05)$, or approximately $95.24. Thus, when the interest rate is 5 percent, the present value of $100 payable one year from now is $100/$(1 + .05)$. Note the symmetry with the familiar problem of projecting money into the future that we discussed already. To find the value of money today one year in the future, you *multiply* by one plus the interest rate; to find the value of money one year in the future today, you *divide* by one plus the interest rate.

Next consider a promise to pay $100 *two* years from now. In this case, the calculation has to take into account the fact that if you invested $100 yourself for two years, at the end it would be worth $100 \times$

Table 12.1   **Calculating present value**

Dollars Payable	*Years in Future*	*Discount Factor*	*Present Value*
R_0	0	1	R_0
R_1	1	$(1 + r)$	$R_1/(1 + r)$
R_2	2	$(1 + r)^2$	$R_2/(1 + r)^2$
.	.	.	.
.	.	.	.
.	.	.	.
R_T	T	$(1 + r)^T$	$R_T/(1 + r)^T$

$(1 + .05)^2$. The most you would be willing to pay today for $100 in two years is that amount which when multiplied by $(1 + .05)^2$ yields exactly $100—$100/$(1 + .05)^2$, or about $90.70.

In general, when the interest rate is *r*, the present value of a promise to pay *$R* in *T* years is simply *$R*/$(1 + r)^T$.[2] Thus, even in the absence of inflation, a dollar in the future is worth less than a dollar today and must be "discounted" by an amount that depends on the interest rate and when the money is receivable. For this reason, *r* is often referred to as the **discount rate.** Similarly, $(1 + r)^T$ is called the **discount factor** for money *T* periods into the future. Note that the further into the future the promise is payable (the larger is *T*), the smaller is the present value. Intuitively, the longer you have to wait for a sum to be paid, the less you are willing to pay for it today, other things being the same.

Finally, consider a promise to pay *$R_0* today, *and $R_1* one year from now, *and $R_2* two years from now, and so on for *T* years. How much is this deal worth? By now, it is clear that the naive answer (*$R_0* + *$R_1* + · · · + *$R_T*) is wrong because it assumes that a dollar in the future is exactly equivalent to a dollar in the present. Without dividing by the discount factor, adding up dollars from different points in time is like adding up apples and oranges. The correct approach is to convert each year's amount to its present value and *then* add them up.

Table 12.1 shows the present value of each year's payment. To find the present value *(PV)* of the income stream *$R_0*, *$R_1*, *$R_2*, . . . , *$R_T*, we simply add the figures in the last column:

$$PV = R_0 + \frac{R_1}{(1 + r)} + \frac{R_2}{(1 + r)^2} + \cdots + \frac{R_T}{(1 + r)^T} \tag{12.1}$$

The importance of computing present values is hard to overestimate. Serious errors can be made if it is ignored. In particular, failure to discount will make ventures that yield returns in the future appear more

---

[2] This assumes that the interest rate is constant at *r*. Suppose that the interest rate changes over time, so that in year 1 it is r_1, in year 2, r_2, and so on. Then the present value of a sum R_T payable *T* years from now is $R_T/[(1 + r_1) \times (1 + r_2) \times \cdots \times (1 + r_T)]$.

valuable than they really are. For example, consider a project that yields a return of $1 million 20 years from now. If the interest rate is 5 percent, the present value is $376,889 [$=$1,000,000/(1.05)^{20}$]. If $r = 10\%$, the present value is only $148,644 [$=$1,000,000/(1.10)^{20}$].

Inflation

We now consider how to modify the procedure when the price level is expected to increase in the future. To begin, consider a project that, in present prices, yields the same return each year. Call this return $\$R_0$. Now, assume that inflation occurs at a rate of 7 percent per year. The dollar value of the return will increase along with all prices. Therefore, the dollar value of the return one year from now, $\$\tilde{R}_1$, is $(1.07) \times \$R_0$. Similarly, two years into the future, the dollar value is $\$\tilde{R}_2 = (1.07)^2 R_0$. In general, this same return has a dollar value in year T of $\$\tilde{R}_T = (1 + .07)^T R_0$.

The dollar values $\$\tilde{R}_0, \$\tilde{R}_1, \$\tilde{R}_2, \ldots, \$\tilde{R}_T$ are referred to as **nominal amounts.** Nominal amounts are valued according to the level of prices in the year the return occurs. It is possible to measure these returns in the prices that exist in a single year. These are called **real amounts** because they do not reflect changes that are due merely to alterations in the price level. In our example, the real amount was assumed to be a constant $\$R_0$ measured in present prices. More generally, if the real returns in present year prices are $\$R_0, \$R_1, \$R_2, \ldots, \$R_T$, and inflation occurs at a rate of π per year, then the nominal returns are: $\$R_0, \$R_1 \times (1 + \pi), \$R_2 \times (1 + \pi)^2, \ldots, \$R_T \times (1 + \pi)^T$.

But this is not the end of the story. When prices are expected to rise, lenders are no longer willing to make loans at the interest rate r that prevailed when prices were stable. Lenders realize they are going to be paid back in depreciated dollars, and to keep even in real terms, their first year's payment must also be inflated by $(1 + \pi)$. Similarly, the second year's payment must be inflated by $(1 + \pi)^2$. In other words, the market interest rate may be expected to increase by an amount approximately equal to the expected rate of inflation, from r percent to $r + \pi$ percent.[3]

We see, then, that when inflation is anticipated, *both* the stream of returns and the discount rate are increased. When expressed in *nominal* terms, the present value of the income stream is thus

$$PV = R_0 + \frac{(1 + \pi)R_1}{(1 + \pi)(1 + r)} + \frac{(1 + \pi)^2 R_2}{(1 + \pi)^2(1 + r)^2} + \cdots$$
$$+ \frac{(1 + \pi)^T R_T}{(1 + \pi)^T(1 + r)^T}$$

(12.2)

---

[3] The product of $(1 + r)$ and $(1 + \pi)$ is $1 + r + \pi + r\pi$. Thus, the nominal rate actually exceeds the real rate by $\pi + r\pi$. However, for numbers of reasonable magnitude, $r\pi$ is negligible in size, so $r + \pi$ is a good approximation of the nominal rate. There are circumstances under which nominal interest rates may fail to rise by exactly the rate of inflation. See Chapter 16 under "Taxes and Inflation."

A glance at Equation (12.2) indicates that it is equivalent to Equation (12.1) because all the terms involving $(1 + \pi)$ cancel out. The moral of the story is that the *same answer* is obtained whether real or nominal magnitudes are used. It is crucial, however, that dollar magnitudes and discount rates be measured consistently. If real values are used for the Rs, the discount rate must also be measured in real terms—the market rate of interest *minus* the expected inflation rate. Alternatively, if the market rate of interest is used for discounting, returns should be measured in nominal terms.

Private Sector: Project Evaluation

As we noted at the beginning of the chapter, the central problem in cost-benefit analysis is valuing the inputs and outputs of government projects. A useful starting point is to consider the same problem from the point of view of a private firm.

Suppose that a firm is considering two mutually exclusive projects, X and Y. The real benefits and costs of project X are B^X and C^X, respectively; and those for project Y are B^Y and C^Y. For both projects, the benefits and costs are realized immediately. The firm's decision maker must answer two questions: First, should either project be done at all; are the projects **admissible?** (The firm has the option of doing neither project.) Second, if both projects are admissible, which is **preferable?** Because both benefits and costs occur immediately, answering these questions is simple. Compute the net return to project X, $B^X - C^X$, and compare it to the net return to Y, $B^Y - C^Y$. A project is admissible only if its net return is positive, that is, the benefits exceed the costs. If both projects are admissible, the firm should choose the project with the higher net return.

In reality, most projects involve a stream of real benefits and returns that occur over time rather than instantaneously. Suppose that the initial benefits and costs of project X are B_0^X and C_0^X, those at the end of the first year are B_1^X and C_1^X, and those at the end of the last year are B_T^X and C_T^X. We can characterize project X as a stream of net returns (some of which may be negative):

$$(B_0^X - C_0^X), (B_1^X - C_1^X), (B_2^X - C_2^X), \ldots , (B_T^X - C_T^X)$$

The present value of this income stream (PV^X) is

$$PV^X = B_0^X - C_0^X + \frac{B_1^X - C_1^X}{(1 + r)} + \frac{B_2^X - C_2^X}{(1 + r)^2} + \cdots + \frac{B_T^X - C_T^X}{(1 + r)^T}$$

where r represents the real rate of return that is generally available to the owners of the firm, the opportunity cost of their funds.

Similarly, suppose that project Y generates streams of costs and benefits B^Y and C^Y over a period of T' years. (There is no reason for T and T' to be the same.) Project Y's present value is:

$$PV^Y = B_0^Y - C_0^Y + \frac{B_1^Y - C_1^Y}{1 + r} + \frac{B_2^Y - C_2^Y}{(1 + r)^2} + \cdots + \frac{B_{T'}^Y - C_{T'}^Y}{(1 + r)^{T'}}$$

Table 12.2   **Comparing the present values of two projects**

	Annual Net Return			PV	
Year	*R&D*	*Oil Well*	*r =*	*R&D*	*Oil Well*
0	−$1,000	−$1,000	0	$150	$200
1	600	−0−	.01	128	165
2	−0−	−0−	.03	86	98
3	550	1,200	.05	46	37
			.07	10	−21

Since both projects are now evaluated in present value terms, we can use the same rules that were applied to the instantaneous project described earlier. The **present value criteria** for project evaluation are that:

- A project is admissible only if its present value is positive.
- When two projects are mutually exclusive, the preferred project is the one with the higher present value.

The discount rate plays a key role in the analysis. Different values of *r* can lead to very different conclusions concerning the admissibility and comparability of projects.

Consider the two projects shown in Table 12.2, a research and development program (R&D) and drilling a new oil well. Both require an initial outlay of $1,000. The R&D program produces a return of $600 at the end of the first year and $550 at the end of the third year. The well, on the other hand, has a single large payoff of $1,200 in three years.

The calculations show that the discount rate chosen is important. For low values of *r*, the oil well is preferred to R&D. However, higher discount rates weigh against the oil drilling project (where the returns are concentrated further into the future) and may even make the project inadmissible.

Thus, one must take considerable care that the value of *r* represents as closely as possible the firm's actual opportunity cost of funds. If the discount rate chosen is too high, it tends to discriminate against projects with returns that come in the relatively distant future and vice versa. The firm's tax situation is relevant in this context. If the going market rate of return is 10 percent, but the firm's tax rate is 25 percent, its after-tax return is only 7.5 percent. Because the after-tax return represents the firm's opportunity cost, it should be used for *r*.

Several criteria other than present value are often used for project evaluation. As we see, they can sometimes give misleading answers, and therefore, the present value criteria are preferable. However, these other methods are popular, so it is necessary to understand them, and to be aware of the problems their use entails.

**Internal Rate
of Return**

A firm is considering the following project: It spends $1 million today on an advertising campaign and reaps a benefit of $1.04 million in increased profits a year from now. If you were asked to compute the advertising campaign's "rate of return," you would probably respond, "4 percent." Implicitly, you calculated that figure by finding the value of ρ that solves the following equation:

$$-\$1,000,000 + \frac{\$1,040,000}{(1 + \rho)} = 0$$

We can generalize this procedure as follows: If a project yields a stream of benefits *(B)* and costs *(C)* over *T* periods, the **internal rate of return** *(ρ)* is defined as the ρ that solves the equation

$$B_0 - C_0 + \frac{B_1 - C_1}{1 + \rho} + \frac{B_2 - C_2}{(1 + \rho)^2} + \cdots + \frac{B_T - C_T}{(1 + \rho)^T} = 0 \qquad (12.3)$$

The internal rate of return is that discount rate that would make the present value of the project just equal to zero.

An obvious admissibility criterion is to accept a project if ρ exceeds the firm's opportunity cost of funds, *r*. For example, if the project earns 4 percent while the firm can obtain 3 percent on other investments, the project should be done. The corresponding comparability criterion is that if two mutually exclusive projects are both admissible, the one with the higher value of ρ should be chosen.

Project selection on the basis of the internal rate of return can, however, lead to bad decisions. Consider project *X* that requires the expenditure of $100 today and yields $110 a year from now, so that its internal rate of return is 10 percent. Project *Y* requires $1,000 today, and yields $1,080 in a year, generating an internal rate of return of 8 percent. (Neither project can be duplicated.) Assume that the firm can borrow and lend freely at a 6 percent rate of interest.

On the basis of internal rate of return, *X* is clearly preferred to *Y*. However, the firm makes only $4 profit on *X* ($10 minus $6 in interest costs), while it makes a $20 profit on *Y* ($80 minus $60 in interest costs). Contrary to the conclusion implied by the internal rate of return, the firm should prefer *Y*, the project with the higher profit. In short, when projects are of different sizes, the internal rate of return can give poor guidance. In contrast, the present value rule gives correct answers even when the projects differ in scale. The present value of *X* is $-100 + 110/1.06 = 3.77$, while that of *Y* is $-1,000 + 1080/1.06 = 18.87$. The present value criterion says that *Y* is preferable, as it should.

Sometimes it is impossible even to find a unique value of the internal rate of return. Consider the following three-period project:

Period	B − C
0	100
1	−260
2	165

Using Equation (12.3), we find this project's internal rate of return by solving:

$$100 - \frac{260}{1 + \rho} + \frac{165}{(1 + \rho)^2} = 0$$

This is a quadratic equation in ρ, and has *two* roots, $\rho = .1$ and $\rho = .5$.[4] The two values have quite different implications, and there is no obvious way to choose between them.

Benefit-Cost Ratio

Suppose that a project yields a stream of benefits $B_0, B_1, B_2, \ldots, B_T$, and a stream of costs $C_0, C_1, C_2, \ldots, C_T$. Then the present value of the benefits, B, is

$$B = B_0 + \frac{B_1}{1 + r} + \frac{B_2}{(1 + r)^2} + \cdots + \frac{B_T}{(1 + r)^T}$$

and the present value of the costs, C, is

$$C = C_0 + \frac{C_1}{1 + r} + \frac{C_2}{(1 + r)^2} + \cdots + \frac{C_T}{(1 + r)^T}$$

The **benefit-cost ratio** is defined as B/C.

Admissibility requires that a project's benefit-cost ratio exceed one. Application of this rule always gives correct guidance. To see why, note simply that $B/C > 1$ implies that $B - C > 0$, which is equivalent to the present value criterion for admissibility.

As a basis for comparing admissible projects, however, the benefit-cost ratio is virtually useless. Consider a community that is considering two methods for disposing of toxic wastes. Method I is a toxic waste dump with $B = \$250$ million, $C = \$100$ million, and therefore a benefit-cost ratio of 2.5. Method II involves sending the wastes in a rocket to Saturn, which has $B = \$200$ million, $C = \$100$ million, and therefore a benefit-cost ratio of 2. The town's leaders choose the dump because it has the higher value of B/C. Now suppose that in calculating the benefits and costs of the dump, the analysts inadvertently neglected to take into account seepage-induced crop damage of $40 million. If the $40 million is viewed as a reduction in the dump's benefits, its B/C becomes $\$210/\$100 = 2.1$, and the dump is still preferred to the rocket. However, the $40 million can just as well be viewed as an increase in costs, in which case $B/C = \$250/\$140 = 1.79$. Now the rocket looks better than the dump!

We have illustrated that there is an inherent ambiguity in computing benefit-cost ratios because benefits can always be counted as "negative costs" and vice versa. Thus, by judicious classification of benefits and

---

[4] Multiplying the equation through by $(1 + \rho)^2$ yields $100(1 + \rho)^2 - 260(1 + \rho) + 165 = 0$ which is equivalent to $\rho^2 - 0.6\rho + 0.05 = 0$. Applying the quadratic formula, $\rho = (.6 \pm \sqrt{.36 - .2})/2 = (.6 \pm .4)/2 = .1$ or $.5$.

costs, any admissible project's benefit-cost ratio can be made arbitrarily high. In contrast, a glance at Equation (12.1) indicates that such shenanigans have no effect whatsoever on the present value criterion because it is based on the *difference* between benefits and costs rather than their *ratio*.

- We conclude that the internal rate of return and the benefit-cost ratio can lead to incorrect inferences. The present value criterion is the most reliable guide.

Public Sector Discount Rate

Sensible decision making by the government also requires present value calculations. However, the way in which the public sector should compute costs, benefits, and discount rates differs from that used in the private sector. This section discusses problems in the selection of a public sector discount rate. In the next, we turn to problems in evaluating costs and benefits.

As suggested previously, the discount rate chosen by private individuals should reflect the rate of return available on alternative investments. Although in practice it may be difficult to pinpoint this rate, from a conceptual point of view there is agreement that the opportunity cost of funds to the firm gives the correct value of r.[5]

There is less consensus on the conceptually appropriate discount rate for government projects. Several possibilities have been proposed, some of which are discussed next.[6]

Rates Based on Returns in the Private Sector

Suppose that the last $1,000 of private investment in the economy yields an annual rate of return of 16 percent. If the government extracts $1,000 from the private sector for a project, and the $1,000 is entirely at the expense of private sector investment, society loses the $160 that would have been generated by the private sector project. Thus, the opportunity cost of the government project is the 16 percent rate of return in the private sector. Because it measures the opportunity cost, the 16 percent should be used as the discount rate. Note that it is irrelevant whether or not this return is taxed. Whether it all stays with the investor or part goes to the government, the before-tax rate of return measures the value of output that the funds would have made available to society.

Contrary to the assumption made earlier, it is likely that some of the funds for the government project would come at the expense of consumption as well as investment. As just argued, for those funds coming out of investment, the before-tax rate of return is the opportunity cost and there-

[5] One reason for the practical difficulties is the fact that there are hundreds of different types of securities on the market, many of which offer different returns and which are taxed at different rates. See Chapter 16 under "Excludable Forms of Money Income."

[6] See Richard Tresch [1981, Chapter 24] for further discussion of the alternative views.

fore the appropriate discount rate. But this is not the case for funds that come at the expense of consumption. Consider Nelson, who is deciding how much to consume and how much to save this year. For each dollar Nelson consumes this year, he gives up one dollar of consumption next year *plus* the rate of return he would have earned on the dollar saved. Hence, the opportunity cost to Nelson of a dollar of consumption now is measured by the rate of return he would have received if he had saved the dollar. Suppose that the before-tax yield on a project available to Nelson is 16 percent, but he must pay 50 percent of the return to the government in the form of taxes. All that Nelson gives up when he consumes an additional dollar today is the *after*-tax rate of return of 8 percent. Because the after-tax rate of return measures what an *individual* loses when consumption is reduced, the opportunity cost of dollars comes at the expense of consumption. In short, dollars that come at the expense of consumption should be discounted by the after-tax rate of return.

Because funds for the public sector come at the expense of both private sector consumption and investment, a natural solution is to use a weighted average of the before- and after-tax rates of return, with the weight on the before-tax rate equal to the proportion of funds that comes from investment, and that on the after-tax rate the proportion that comes from consumption [see Harberger, 1974a]. In the preceding example, if one-quarter of the funds came at the expense of investment and three-quarters at the expense of consumption, then the public sector discount rate would be 10 percent (¼ × 16 percent + ¾ × 8 percent). Unfortunately, in practice it is hard to determine what the proportions of sacrificed consumption and investment actually are for a given government project. The funds are collected from a variety of taxes, each of which has a different effect on consumption and investment. And even with information on the impact of each tax on consumption and investment, it is difficult in practice to determine which tax is used to finance which project.

None of this is very important if the magnitudes of pre- and post-tax rates of return are fairly close. In fact, there are large differences. Martin Feldstein, Louis Dicks-Mireaux, and James Poterba [1983] estimated that the before-tax nominal rate of return in the post–World War II period was about 12 percent, and the after-tax rate only 5 percent. Therefore, the inability to reliably determine a set of weights lessens the usefulness of this approach as a practical guide to determining discount rates.

Social Discount Rate

An alternative view is that public expenditure evaluation should involve a **social rate of discount,** which measures the valuation that *society* places on consumption that is sacrificed in the present.[7] But why should

---

[7] Complications arise in implementing this approach when public funds come at the expense of private investment. See R. C. Lind [1982].

society's view of the opportunity cost of forgoing consumption differ from the opportunity cost revealed in market rates of return? Several reasons have been suggested for believing that the social discount rate is lower.

Concern for future generations.   It is the duty of public sector decision makers to care about the welfare not only of the current generation of citizens but of future generations as well. The private sector, on the other hand, is concerned only with its own welfare. Hence, from a social point of view, the private sector devotes too few resources to saving—it applies too high a discount rate to returns in the future. As Edward Gramlich [1981, p. 97] notes, the idea of government as the guardian of the interests of future generations may be appealing, but it assumes a degree of omni-science and benevolence that is unrealistic. Moreover, even totally selfish individuals often find it in their personal interest to engage in projects that will benefit future generations. If future generations are expected to bene-fit from some project, the anticipated profitability will be high, which encourages investment today. Private firms plant trees today in return for profits on wood sales that may not be realized for many years.[8]

Paternalism.   Even from the point of view of their own narrow self-interest, people may not be farsighted enough to weigh adequately bene-fits in the future; they therefore discount such benefits at too high a rate. A. C. Pigou [1932, Chapter 2] described this problem as a "defective telescopic faculty." The government should use the discount rate that individuals *would* use if they knew their own good. This is, of course, a paternalistic argument—government forces citizens to consume less in the present, and in return, they have more in the future, at which time they presumably thank the government for its foresight. Like all paternal-istic arguments, it raises the fundamental philosophical question of when public preferences should be imposed on individuals.

Market inefficiency.   When a firm undertakes an investment, it generates knowledge and technological know-how that can benefit other firms. This process has been called **learning by doing** [Arrow, 1962]. In a sense, then, investment creates positive externalities, and by the usual kinds of argu-ments, investment is underprovided by private markets (see Chapter 6 under "Positive Externalities"). By applying a discount rate lower than the market's, the government can correct this inefficiency. The enormous practical problem here is measuring the actual size of the externality. Moreover, the theory of externalities suggests that a more appropriate remedy would be to determine the size of the marginal external benefit at the optimum, and grant a subsidy of that amount (see again Chapter 6).

---

[8] Why should people invest in a project whose returns may not be realized until after they are dead? Investors can always sell the rights to future profits to members of the younger generation and hence consume their share of the anticipated profits during their lifetimes.

It appears, then, that none of the arguments concerning the inadequacy of market rates provides much specific guidance with respect to the choice of a public sector discount rate. Where does this leave us? It would be difficult to argue very strongly against any public rate of discount in a range between the before- and after-tax rates of return in the private sector. One practical procedure is to evaluate the present value of a project over a range of discount rates and see whether or not the present value stays positive for all reasonable values of r. If it does, the analyst can feel some confidence that the conclusion is not sensitive to the discount rate.

Valuing Public Benefits and Costs

The next step in project evaluation is computing benefits and costs. From a private firm's point of view, their computation is relatively straightforward. The benefits from a project are the revenues received; the costs are the firm's payments for inputs; and both are measured by market prices. The evaluation problem is more complicated for the government because *social* benefits and costs may not be reflected in market prices. There are several possibilities for measuring the benefits and costs of public sector projects.

Market Prices

As noted in Chapter 4, in a properly functioning competitive economy, the price of a good simultaneously reflects marginal social costs of its production and its marginal value to consumers. It would appear that if the government uses inputs and/or produces outputs that are traded in private markets, then market prices should be used for valuation.

The problem is that real-world markets have many imperfections, such as monopoly, externalities, and uncertain information. In such a world, prices do not necessarily reflect marginal social costs and benefits. As R. N. McKean [1977, p. 123] has suggested, "There are enough things wrong with observed market prices to make one's hair stand on end."

The relevant question, however, is not whether market prices are perfect, but whether they are likely to be superior to alternative measures of value. Such measures would either have to be made up or derived from highly complicated—and questionable—models of the economy. And, whatever their problems, market prices provide plenty of information at a low cost. Most economists believe that in the absence of any glaring imperfections, market prices should be used to compute public benefits and costs.

Adjusted Market Prices

The prices of goods traded in imperfect markets generally do not reflect their marginal social cost.[9] The **shadow price** of such a commodity is its underlying social marginal cost. Although market prices of goods in im-

---

[9] This section is based on Richard Layard [1977, pp. 18–22].

perfect markets diverge from shadow prices, in some cases the market prices can be used to *estimate* the shadow prices. We discuss the relevant circumstances next. In each case, the key insight is that the shadow price depends on how the economy responds to the government intervention.

Monopoly.   Suppose that a public project uses a monopolistically produced input. In contrast to perfect competition under which price is equal to marginal cost, a monopolist's price is above marginal cost (see Chapter 5). Should the government value the input at its market price (which measures its value to consumers) or at its marginal production cost (which measures the incremental value of the resources used in its production)?

The answer depends on the impact of the government purchase on the market. If production of the input is expected to increase by the exact amount used by the project, the social opportunity cost is the value of the resources used in the extra production—the marginal production cost. On the other hand, if no more of the input will be produced, the government's use comes at the expense of private consumers, whose value of the input is measured by the demand price. If some combination of the two responses is expected, a weighted average of price and marginal cost is appropriate. (Note the similarity to the previous discount rate problem.)

Taxes.   If an input is subject to a sales tax, the price received by the producer of the input is less than the price paid by the purchaser. This is because some portion of the purchase price goes to the tax collector. When the government purchases an input subject to sales tax, should the producer's or purchaser's price be used in the cost calculations? The basic principle is the same as that for the monopoly case. If production is expected to expand, then the producer's supply price is appropriate. If production is expected to stay constant, the purchaser's price should be used. For a combination of responses, a weighted average is required.

Unemployment.   Like most microeconomic tools, cost-benefit analysis generally assumes that all resources are fully employed. Nevertheless, a project may involve hiring workers who are currently involuntarily unemployed. Because hiring an unemployed worker does not lower output elsewhere in the economy, the wage the worker is paid does not represent an opportunity cost. All that is forgone when the worker is hired is the leisure he or she was consuming, the value of which is presumably low if the unemployment is involuntary. There are two complications, however: (1) If the government is running its stabilization policy to maintain a constant rate of employment, hiring an unemployed worker may mean reducing employment and output elsewhere in the economy. In this case, the social cost of the worker is his or her wage. (2) Even if the worker is involuntarily unemployed when the project begins, she will not necessar-

Figure 12.1
Measuring the
change in consumer
surplus

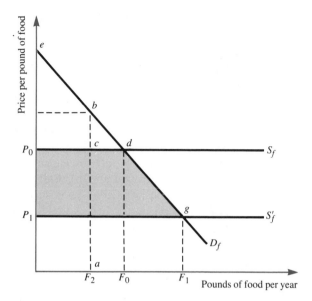

ily continue to be so during its entire duration. But forecasting an individual's future employment prospects is a difficult problem indeed. In light of
the current lack of consensus on the causes and nature of unemployment,
the pricing of unemployed resources remains a problem with no agreed-on
solution. In the absence of a major depression, valuation of unemployed
labor at the going wage is probably a good approximation for practical
purposes.

**Consumer
Surplus**

In many cases, private firms are small relative to the economy. Therefore,
they do not have to be concerned that changes in the amount they produce will affect the market price of their product. In contrast, public-
sector projects can be so large that they induce changes in market prices.
For example, a government irrigation project could lower the marginal
cost of agricultural production so much that the market price of food falls.
But if the market price changes, how should the additional amount of food
be valued—at its original price, at its price after the project, or at some
price in-between?

   The situation is depicted in Figure 12.1. Pounds of food are measured
on the horizontal axis, the price per pound is measured on the vertical,
and D_f is the demand schedule for food. Prior to the irrigation project, the
supply curve is labeled S_f, and market price and quantity are P_0 and F_0,
respectively. (The supply curve is drawn horizontally for convenience.
The main points would still hold even if it sloped upward.)

   Suppose that after more land is brought into production by the irrigation project, the supply curve for food shifts to S_f'. At the new equilibrium, the price falls to P_1, and food consumption increases to F_1. How

much better off are consumers? Another way of stating this question is, "How much would consumers be willing to pay for the privilege of consuming F_1 pounds of food at price P_1 rather than F_0 pounds at price P_0?"

The economic tool for answering this question is **consumer surplus**—the amount by which the sum that individuals would have been willing to pay exceeds the sum they actually have to pay. As shown in the Appendix to Chapter 4, consumer surplus is measured by the area under the demand curve and above a horizontal line at the market price. Thus, when price is P_0, consumer surplus is P_0ed.

When the price of food falls to P_1 because of the irrigation project, consumer surplus is still the area under the demand curve and above a horizontal line at the going price, but because the price is now P_1, the relevant area is P_1eg. Consumer surplus has therefore increased by the difference between areas P_1eg and P_0ed—area P_1P_0dg. Thus, the area behind the demand curve between the two prices measures the value to consumers of being able to purchase food at the lower price. Provided that the planner can estimate the shape of the demand curve, the benefit of the project can be measured.

Inferences from Economic Behavior

We have so far been dealing with cases in which market data can serve as a starting point for valuing the costs and benefits of government projects. Sometimes the good in question is not explicitly traded, so no market price exists. We discuss two examples of how people's willingness to pay for such commodities can be estimated.

The value of time.   Suppose that if the government builds a road it will save each traveler half an hour a day. While it is true that "time is money," to do cost-benefit analysis we need to know *how much* money. A common way to estimate the value of time is to take advantage of the theory of leisure-income choice. When people have control over the amount they work, they work just until the point where the subjective value of leisure is equal to the income they gain from one more hour of work—the after-tax wage rate. Thus, the after-tax wage can be used to value the time that is saved.[10]

Although this approach is useful, it has two major problems: (1) Some people cannot choose their hours of work. Involuntary unemployment represents an extreme but common case. (2) Not all uses of time away from the job are equivalent. For example, to avoid spending time on the road, a person who hated driving might be willing to pay at a rate exceeding his wage. On the other hand, a person who used the road for

---

[10] For further details, see Chapter 17 under "Labor Supply."

pleasure drives on weekends might not care very much about the opportunity cost of time, particularly if she could not work on weekends anyway.

Several investigators have estimated the value of time by looking at people's choices between modes of transportation that involve different traveling times. Suppose that in a given community people can commute to work either by bus or by train. The train takes less time, but is more expensive. By seeing how much extra money people are willing to pay for the train, we can infer how much they are willing to pay to reduce their commuting time, and hence how they value that time. Of course, other characteristics of people, such as their incomes, affect their choice of travel mode. Statistical techniques similar to those described in Chapter 3 can be used to take these other variables into account. On the basis of several such studies, a reasonable estimate of the effective cost of traveling time is about 60 percent of the before-tax wage rate. (See Small [1983].)

The value of life.   A newspaper reporter once asked the head of the Federal Occupational Safety and Health Administration: "How do you place dollar values on human life or health?" [Shabecoff, 1981, p. E9]. It's a hard question. Our religious and cultural values suggest that life is priceless. Consider the events that transpired when a construction crane fell on Brigitte Gerney as she walked along a Manhattan street in 1985:

> Hundreds of police officers rerouted traffic . . . Two cranes were brought
> from other boroughs to lift the one that had fallen. Doctors . . . set up a
> mobile hospital at the construction site. Emergency Service rescue work-
> ers risked their own lives to save hers. Once she was freed, the police
> halted traffic for 30 blocks . . . to speed her trip to the emergency room.
>
> No city official questioned how much the rescue effort cost the city, or
> whether saving Mrs. Gerney's life was worth the price. To do so would
> have been unthinkable. "There's no point where you say that's too expen-
> sive," said [a spokesman] for the New York City Police Department.
> [Greer, 1985]

Similarly, if a person were asked to value his or her own life, it would not be surprising if the response indicated that the sky was the limit.

Such a position presents obvious difficulties for cost-benefit analysis. If the value of life is infinite, any project that leads even to a single life being saved has an infinitely high present value. This leaves no sensible way to determine the admissibility of projects. If *every* road in America were a divided four-lane highway, it is doubtless true that traffic fatalities would decrease. Would this be a good project?

Economists have considered two methods for assigning finite values to human life. The first requires measuring the individual's lost earnings; the second requires estimating the value the individual puts on changes in the probability of death.

Lost earnings. The value of life is the present value of the individual's net earnings over a lifetime.[11] If an individual dies as a consequence of a given project, the cost to society is just the expected present value of the output that person would have produced. This approach is often used in law courts to determine how much compensation the relatives of accident fatalities should receive. However, taken literally, this approach means that society would suffer no loss if the aged, infirm, or severely handicapped were summarily executed. This implication is sufficiently bizarre that the method is rejected by many economists.

Probability of death. A second approach has as its starting point the notion that most projects do not actually affect with *certainty* a given individual's prospects for living. Rather, it is more typical for a change in the *probability* of a person's death to be involved. (See Viscusi [1983].) For example, you do not know that cancer research will save *your* life. All that can be determined is that it may reduce the probability of your death. The reason this distinction is so important is that even if people view their lives as having infinite value, they very often accept increases in the probability of death for finite amounts of money. An individual driving a light car is subject to a greater probability of death in an auto accident than a counterpart in a heavy car, other things being the same. People are willing to accept the increased risk of death because of the money they can save by purchasing lighter cars.

Another way that people reveal their risk preferences is by their occupational choices. Some jobs involve a higher probability of death than others. Suppose we compare two workers who have identical job qualifications (education, experience, etc.), but one is in a riskier job than the other. The individual in the riskier job is expected to have a higher wage to compensate for the higher probability of death. The difference between the two wages provides an estimate of the value that people place on a decreased probability of death. John Garen [1988] estimated that increasing by one the number of fatalities per 100,000 workers in an occupation increases the yearly earnings in the occupation by about 0.55 percent.[12]

An appealing aspect of this approach is that it puts the analysis on the same willingness to pay basis that is so fruitful in other contexts. It remains highly controversial, however. J. Broome [1978] has argued that the probabilistic approach is irrelevant once it is conceded that *some* people's lives are *certainly* going to be at stake. The fact that we happen

---

[11] See Herbert Klarman [1965] for an example using this approach.

[12] See Kip Viscusi [1983] for further discussion of such estimates. Note that the cost-benefit analyst should also consider the psychological cost of bereavement to families and friends, and the changes in financial status of relatives.

to be ignorant of just who will die is beside the point. If this position is taken, we are back where we started, with no way at all to value projects that involve human life.

This academic controversy has become a matter of public concern because of various proposals to subject government safety regulations to cost-benefit analysis. In an attack on one proposal, the president of the Amalgamated Clothing and Textiles Workers Union said, "It seems incredible that . . . anyone could seriously suggest trading lives for dollars" [Finley, 1981, p. A23]. Unfortunately, in a world of scarce resources, we have no choice in the matter. The only question is whether or not sensible ways for making the trade are used.

Valuing Intangibles

No matter how ingenious the investigator, some benefits and costs seem impossible to value: One of the benefits of the space program is increased national prestige. Creating national parks gives people the thrill of enjoying beautiful scenery. The mind boggles at putting a dollar value on these "commodities." Three points must be kept in mind when intangible items might be important.

First, intangibles can subvert the entire cost-benefit exercise. By claiming that they are large enough, *any* project can be made admissible. A journalist commenting on Britain's deliberations about whether to construct a tunnel below the English channel gave this advice: "Build it, not because dreary cost-benefit analysis says it will pay but because Britain needs a big project to arouse it" (Will [1985]). However, presumably anyone who favors a particular project can make a case on the basis of its ability to "arouse." How does one then choose among projects?

Second, the tools of cost-benefit analysis can sometimes be used to force planners to reveal limits on how they value intangibles. Suppose that a space program's measurable costs and benefits are C and B, respectively, and its intangible benefits, such as national prestige, are an unknown amount X. Then if the measured costs are greater than measured benefits, X must exceed $(C - B)$ for the program to be admissible.[13] With this information, it may become clear that the intangible is not valuable enough to merit doing the project. If $(C - B)$ for the space program were $10 million per year, people might agree that its contribution to national prestige was worth it. But if the figure were $10 billion, a different conclusion might emerge.

Finally, even if it is impossible to measure certain benefits, there may be alternative methods of attaining them. If so, systematic study of the costs of the various alternatives should be done to find the cheapest way possible. This is sometimes called **cost-effectiveness analysis.** Thus, while

---

[13] A similar strategy can be applied to intangible costs.

it may be impossible to put a dollar value on national security, it still may be feasible to subject the costs of alternative weapons systems to careful scrutiny.

Some Pitfalls

In addition to the problems we have already discussed, Tresch [1981] has noted a number of common errors in cost-benefit analysis.

The Chain-Reaction Game

The idea is to make a proposal look especially attractive by counting secondary profits arising from it as part of the benefits. If the government builds a road, the primary benefits are the reductions in transportation costs for individuals and firms. At the same time, though, profits of local restaurants, motels, and gas stations probably increase. This leads to increased profits in the local food, bed-linen, and gasoline-production industries. If enough of such secondary effects are added to the benefit side, eventually a positive present value can be obtained for practically any project.

This procedure ignores the fact that there may be losses as well as profits induced by the project. After the road is built, the profits of train operators would decrease as some of their customers turn to cars for transportation. Increased auto use may bid up the price of gasoline, decreasing the welfare of many gasoline consumers.

In short, the problem with the chain-reaction game is that it counts as benefits changes that are merely transfers. The increase in the price of gasoline, for example, transfers income from gasoline consumers to gasoline producers, but it does not represent a net benefit of the project. As noted later, distributional considerations may indeed be relevant to the decision maker. But if this is the case, consistency requires that if secondary benefits are counted, so must be secondary losses.

The Labor Game

In 1982, the Congress debated and eventually passed a multibillion dollar bill to improve the quality of the nation's roads. Although some of the public debate concerned the benefits that would follow from improved highways, proponents of the bill emphasized that the project would employ a lot of labor. Indeed, the measure was often referred to as a "highway repair and job-creation bill."

This is a typical example of the argument that a given project should be implemented because of all the employment that it "creates." Essentially, the wages of the workers employed are viewed as *benefits* of the project. This is absurd, because wages belong on the cost, not the benefit side of the calculation. Of course, as already suggested, it is true that if workers are involuntarily unemployed, their social cost is less than their wage. Even in an area with high unemployment, it is unlikely that all the labor used in the project would have been unemployed, or that all those who were unemployed would have remained so for a long time.

**The
Double-Counting
Game**

Suppose that the government is considering irrigating some land that currently cannot be cultivated. It counts as the project's benefits the sum of (1) the increase in value of the land, *and* (2) the present value of the stream of net income obtained from farming it. The problem here is that a farmer can *either* farm the land and take as gains the net income stream, *or* sell the land to someone else. Under competition, the sales price of the land just equals the present value of the net income from farming it. Because the farmer cannot do both simultaneously, counting both (1) and (2) represents a doubling of the true benefits.

This error may seem so silly that no one would ever commit it. However, Tresch [1981, p. 561] points out that at one time double counting was the official policy of the Bureau of Reclamation within the U.S. Department of the Interior. The bureau's instructions for cost-benefit analysts stipulated that the benefits of land irrigation be computed as the *sum* of the increase in land value and the present value of the net income from farming it.

**Distributional
Considerations**

So far, we have not taken into account the distributional effects of public projects. In the private sector, normally no consideration is given to the question of who receives the benefits and bears the costs of a project. A dollar is a dollar, regardless of who is involved. Some economists have argued that the same view be taken in public-project analysis. If the present value of a project is positive, it should be undertaken regardless of who gains and loses. This is because as long as the present value is positive, the gainers *could* compensate the losers and still enjoy a net increase in utility. This notion, sometimes called the **Hicks-Kaldor criterion,** thus bases project selection on *potential* gains in social welfare. (See Hicks [1940] and Kaldor [1939].) The actual compensation does not have to take place. That is, it is permissible to impose costs on some members of society if that provides greater net benefits to someone else.

Others believe that because the goal of government is to maximize social welfare (not profit), the distributional implications of a project should be taken into account. Moreover, because it is the actual pattern of benefits and costs that really matters, the Hicks-Kaldor criterion does not provide a satisfactory escape from grappling with distributional issues.

One way to avoid the distributional problem is to assume that the government can and will costlessly correct any undesirable distributional aspects of a project by making the appropriate transfers between gainers and losers.[14] The government works continually in the background to ensure that income stays optimally distributed, so that the cost-benefit

---

[14] *Costlessly* in this context means that the transfer system costs nothing to administer, and the transfers are done in such a way that they do not distort people's economic behavior. See Chapter 14.

analyst need only be concerned with computing present values. Again, reality gets in the way. The government may have neither the power nor the ability to distribute income optimally.[15] (See Chapter 8.)

Suppose the cost-benefit analyst believes that some group in the population is especially deserving. This distributional preference can be taken into account by assuming that a dollar benefit to a member of this group is worth more than a dollar going to others in the population. This, of course, tends to bias the selection of projects in favor of those that especially benefit the preferred group. Although much of the discussion of distributional considerations has focused on income as the basis for classifying people, presumably characteristics like race, ethnicity, and sex can be used, as well.

Suppose that the policymaker who actually has to make the decision supplies the cost-benefit analyst with the criteria for membership in the preferred group. The analyst still faces the question of precisely how to weight benefits to members of that group relative to the rest of society. It matters a lot whether a dollar to a poor person is counted as twice a dollar to a rich person, or 50 times as much. As usual, the resolution of such issues depends on value judgments. All the analyst can do is induce the policymaker to state explicitly his or her value judgments and understand their implications.

A potential hazard of introducing distributional considerations is that political concerns come to dominate the entire cost-benefit exercise. Depending on how weights are chosen, any project can generate a positive present value, regardless of how inefficient it is. In addition, incorporating distributional considerations substantially increases the information requirements of cost-benefit analysis. The analyst needs to estimate not only benefits and costs but also how they are distributed across the population. As noted in Chapter 8 under "Expenditure Incidence," it is difficult indeed to assess the distributional implications of government fiscal activities.

Uncertainty

On January 28, 1986, the space shuttle *Challenger* exploded within minutes of liftoff from the Kennedy Space Center. About two months later, a nuclear disaster occurred at the Chernobyl power plant in the U.S.S.R. Both events are dramatic reminders of the fact that the outcomes of public projects often cannot be predicted with certainty. Indeed, many important debates over project proposals center around the fact that their outcomes are not known for sure. How much will a job-training program increase the earnings of trainees? Will a high-tech weapons system function properly under combat conditions?

---

[15] Moreover, as the government works behind the scenes to modify income distribution, relative prices probably change. But as relative prices change, so do the benefit and cost calculations. Hence, efficiency and equity issues cannot be separated as neatly as suggested here.

Suppose that two projects are being considered. They have identical costs, and both affect only one citizen, Smith. Project X guarantees a benefit of $1,000 with certainty. Project Y creates a benefit of zero dollars with a probability of one in two, and a benefit of $2,000 with a probability of one in two. Which project does Smith prefer?

Note that on average, the benefit from Y is equal to that from X. This is because the expected benefit from Y is $\frac{1}{2} \times \$0 + \frac{1}{2} \times \$2,000 = \$1,000$. Nevertheless, if Smith is risk averse, she prefers X to Y. This is because project Y subjects Smith to risk, while X is a sure thing. In other words, if Smith is risk averse, she would be willing to trade project Y for a *certain* amount of money less than $1,000—she is willing to give up some income in return for gaining some security. The most obvious evidence that people are in fact willing to pay to avoid risk is the widespread holding of insurance policies of various kinds.

Therefore, when the benefits or costs of a project are risky, they must be converted into **certainty equivalents**—the amount of *certain* income that the individual would be willing to trade for the set of uncertain outcomes generated by the project. The computation of certainty equivalents requires information on both the distribution of returns from the project and how risk averse the people involved are. The method of calculation is described in the Appendix to this chapter.

The calculation of certainty equivalents presupposes that the random distribution of costs and benefits is known in advance. In some cases, this is a reasonable assumption. For example, in estimating the benefits from a dam, engineering and weather data could be used to estimate how it would reduce the probability of flood destruction. In many important cases, however, it is hard to assign probabilities to various outcomes. There is not enough experience with nuclear reactors to gauge the likelihood of various malfunctions. Similarly, how do you estimate the probability that a given weapons system will deter foreign aggression? As usual, the best the analyst can do is to make explicit his or her assumptions, and determine the extent to which substantive findings change when these assumptions are modified.

An Application

The White Cloud Peaks lie about 30 miles north of Sun Valley, Idaho.[16] This public area occupies about 20,000 acres, supports a large variety of wildlife, and with some development could provide excellent opportunities for hiking, camping, fishing, and hunting. The White Cloud Peaks also appear to have substantial deposits of the valuable metal, molybdenum, and in the late 1960s, a company requested permission to mine these deposits. The land cannot be used for mining and for recreation simulta-

---

[16] This section is based on Krutilla and Fisher [1975, chap. 7].

neously. Should the White Cloud Peaks be developed for recreational purposes? Should the area be mined instead? Or should it be left alone altogether?

John Krutilla and Anthony Fisher [1975] (K&F) employed the tools of cost-benefit analysis to answer these questions. We discuss here only one component of K&F's study—an examination of whether the incremental costs of developing the White Cloud Peaks for recreational use would exceed the incremental benefits. The analysis well illustrates several of the issues raised in this chapter.

Estimating the costs and benefits of developing the White Cloud Peaks for recreation requires specifying just what *kind* of recreation. Constructing roads for Jeeps has very different costs and benefits than extending hiking trails. K&F assumed that the land would be used in such a way that its basic ecology would be preserved. Specifically, they assumed that development would take the form of creating four additional trails, which would allow more access for visitors.

Earlier sections of this chapter indicated that cost-benefit analysis entails selecting a discount rate and specifying the costs and benefits for each year. We now discuss these in turn.

Discount Rate

As usual, theoretical considerations do not pin down one particular discount rate, so K&F followed the sensible practice of selecting several and seeing whether the substantive results are sensitive to the differences. Next, we report their results for discount rates of 7 and 10 percent.[17]

Costs

Creating additional trails requires immediate outlays for equipment and labor, estimated to be $23,000 in 1971. This figure is recorded in row *1* of Table 12.3. Because these capital outlays are made immediately, their present value is also $23,000, regardless of the discount rate.

After the trails are put in, yearly expenditures must be made for their maintenance. The estimated annual cost is $12,092. Because these costs are incurred over time, however, they must be discounted. Row *2* of Table 12.3 shows the discounted present value of these maintenance expenditures over a 50-year period for both $r = 7$ percent and $r = 10$ percent. Note how the present value of maintenance is smaller with the higher discount rate. The total cost of extending the trails, given in row *3*, is the present value of the capital and maintenance outlays.

If the goal is to expand recreational use *while maintaining the quality of the environment,* appropriate sanitation facilities are required. K&F estimated that initially nine toilets, at a cost of $750 per toilet, are needed.

---

[17] K&F do not indicate whether these are intended to be real or nominal discount rates. Given their magnitudes, they appear to be nominal. However, as noted later, the benefits and costs are in real terms. As an exercise, students might want to explain what problems this creates.

Table 12.3 **Incremental costs for expanded recreational use of White Cloud Peaks**

	Present Value	
Trail Extensions	r = 7%	r = 10%
(1) Initial outlays: $23,000	$ 23,000	$ 23,000
(2) Maintenance outlays per year: $12,092	170,981	119,835
(3) Total present value of trail extensions costs (sum of rows *1* and *2*)	193,981	142,835
Sanitary Facilities		
Outlays for equipment:		
(4) In year 1, nine toilets at a cost of $750 per toilet	$ 6,750	$ 6,750
(5) In year 30, nine toilets	887	387
(6) In year 60, nine toilets	114	20
(7) Maintenance and operation outlays per year: $100	1,414	990
(8) Total present value of sanitation costs (sum of rows *4, 5, 6,* and *7*)	$ 9,165	$ 8,147
(9) Present value of all costs (sum of rows *3* and *8*)	$203,146	$150,982

SOURCE: Computations based on Krutilla and Fisher [1975, p. 163].

The total expenditure, $6,750, is recorded in row *4*. The toilets have to be replaced at 30-year intervals. Rows *5* and *6* show the present value of the same $6,750 toilet expenditure made 30 and 60 years in the future, respectively. In addition, the sanitation facilities have to be maintained at an annual cost of $100. The present value of this stream of expenditures at the two discount rates is recorded in row *7*. Row *8* gives the sum of all the sanitation costs, and row *9* adds these to the costs of extending the trails. In our earlier notation (p. 247), the figures in row *9* represent *C*, the present value of the project's costs, at each discount rate.

Benefits

A key piece of information is required: how much would people be willing to pay for the privilege of using the new trails? To answer this question, K&F took advantage of a regression equation that was computed by other analysts of recreational demand for wilderness areas. The dependent variable was the willingness to pay for a wilderness trip as expressed by individuals in a survey. The right-hand side variables included the length of the trip, congestion at the camp site, and various socioeconomic characteristics of the respondents. On the basis of this regression, K&F estimated that in the initial year (1971), a typical user would be willing to pay $10 per day. They further estimated that the area would be used 4,600 recreation-days that year, making the first year's benefit $46,000.

Table 12.4   **Incremental benefits for expanded recreational use of White Cloud Peaks**

Present Value	
$r = 7\%$	$r = 10\%$
$991,000	$390,000

SOURCE: Krutilla and Fisher [1975, p. 171].

The analysis required estimates of benefits in future years as well. K&F assumed that use of the area would grow initially by 10 percent per year, and that willingness to pay would increase by 4 percent per year.[18] Of course, an uninterrupted growth rate of 10 percent a year over a long time would result in the area being overrun by visitors. On the basis of discussions with district rangers and other experts, K&F postulated a maximum number of possible users consistent with maintaining environmental quality. After this figure is reached, the annual number of visits is not allowed to grow.

On the basis of K&F's willingness-to-pay calculations, the benefits flowing from the increased expenditures for recreational use are as shown in Table 12.4. In our earlier notation, Table 12.4 gives the value of B, the present value of the benefits, for each discount rate.

Computation of the net present value of the project is now straightforward. For each discount rate, take the benefit value from Table 12.4, and subtract from it the cost figure from row 9 of Table 12.3. This computation reveals that when $r = 7$ percent, benefits minus costs are $787,854, and when $r = 10$ percent, benefits minus costs are $239,018. Thus, for either choice of discount rate, $(B - C)$ exceeds zero, and by the present value criterion, the project is admissible. This does not complete the analysis, however, because we still have to find out whether the net present value exceeds that of the alternative project, molybdenum mining. However, discussion of that part of the study would take us too far afield. Interested readers should consult Krutilla and Fisher [1975] for further details.

Comments

This White Cloud Peaks analysis illustrates some important aspects of practical cost-benefit studies:

1. The analysis is often interdisciplinary because economists alone do not have the technical expertise to evaluate all costs and benefits. Thus, engineers were required to predict construction costs of the trails, wilderness-use experts to estimate the maximum number of campers the area can support, and so forth.

---

[18] As use increases, some congestion occurs, which tends to lower people's willingness to pay. (A visit to a crowded wilderness area isn't as pleasant as a visit to a quiet one.) K&F estimated the dampening effect of increased congestion costs and factored it into their willingness-to-pay calculations.

2. Evaluation of costs and benefits, especially those arising in the future, is likely to require some ad hoc assumptions. As just shown, it is difficult enough to estimate *current* willingness to pay for a commodity that is not priced on the market; projecting such figures decades into the future is even tougher. In most cases, all the analyst can do is assume that willingness to pay follows some pattern of growth, and see whether the substantive results change when alternative reasonable patterns are postulated. Moreover, in situations characterized by so much uncertainty, it may overburden the analysis to include distributional considerations. An investigator who can barely predict the total number of users two decades in the future can hardly be expected to estimate the distribution of their incomes as well.

3. For all its limitations, cost-benefit analysis is a remarkably useful way of summarizing information. It also forces analysts to make explicit their assumptions so that the reasons for their ultimate recommendation are clear. Indeed, any other way of making decisions is implicitly just a cost-benefit analysis without its assumptions explicitly stated.

Use by Government

Much effort has been devoted to refining the techniques of cost-benefit analysis. Have these methods been put to work by the government? Stipulations that certain kinds of federal projects be subjected to cost-benefit analysis began appearing in the late 1930s.[19] However, not until the mid-1960s did such analysis receive major public interest. At that time, President Lyndon Johnson's Great Society (a catchall term for a number of social programs) was leading to a tremendous expansion in the scope and magnitude of government programs. With so many new projects being proposed, some kind of systematic evaluation procedure was needed.

Thus was born the *Planning Programming Budget System* (PPBS) adopted by the federal government in 1965. It mandated that each program's costs and benefits be computed, and that they be compared to the returns of relevant alternatives. Furthermore, common analytic techniques were to be used throughout the government, where possible.

However, PPBS does not appear to have induced major changes in the style of government project selection; there are several probable reasons for its failure. This was partly due to the many practical difficulties in implementing cost-benefit analysis, particularly when there is no consensus as to what the government's objectives are. In addition, many bureaucrats lacked either the ability or the temperament to perform the

---

[19] Edward Gramlich [1981, pp. 7–11] provides a concise and useful discussion of the history of cost-benefit analysis in the United States up to the early 1980s.

analysis—particularly when it came to their own programs. And neither were politicians particularly eager to see their pet projects subjected to careful scrutiny. Nevertheless, PPBS did introduce some tendency toward more systematic evaluation of government projects. Many government bureaucracies have created planning and analysis units and hired social scientists to staff them.

The use of cost-benefit analysis received further encouragement in 1981, when President Ronald Reagan issued an executive order requiring that all new regulations had to pass a cost-benefit test. As a consequence, the preparation of analyses of the costs and benefits of regulation has become standard operating procedure, particularly in the environmental area. Although there have been defects in some of these analyses, the policy of requiring them seems to be a desirable step.[20]

On the other hand, in certain vital areas not only has cost-benefit analysis failed to take hold, it has been expressly forbidden. For example, the Clean Air Act prohibits costs from being taken into account when air quality standards are being set. Similarly, the Occupational Safety and Health Act of 1970 states that the Secretary of Labor "shall set the standard which most adequately assures, *to the extent feasible . . .* that no employee will suffer material impairment of health or functional capacity" ["A High Court Win for OSHA," 1981, p. 59; italics added]. In 1981, a Supreme Court majority interpreted this as meaning that the costs of achieving a given improvement in health are strictly irrelevant. Justice William Brennan wrote, "Congress itself defined the basic relationship between costs and benefits by placing the 'benefit' of worker health above all other considerations save those making attainment of this 'benefit' unachievable" ["A High Court Win," 1981, p. 59].

However, as Justice William Rehnquist pointed out, feasibility is really "no standard at all"—the only perfectly safe factory is an empty factory [MacAvoy, 1981, p. F3]. Although cost-benefit analysis is surely an imperfect tool, it is the only analytical framework available for making consistent decisions. Forbidding cost-benefit analysis amounts to outlawing sensible decision making.

Summary

- Cost-benefit analysis is the practical use of welfare economics to evaluate potential projects.
- Cost-benefit analyses consider net benefits received over time. To make these compara-ble, the present value of all future net benefits must be computed.
- Other methods—internal rate of return, bene-fit-cost ratio—can lead to incorrect decisions.

---

[20] See the essays in V. Kerry Smith [1984].

The present value criterion is superior in this context.

■ Choosing the discount rate is critical in cost-benefit analyses. In public sector analyses three possible measures are the before-tax private rate of return, a weighted average of before- and after-tax private rates of return, and the social discount rate. Choosing among them depends on the type of private activity displaced—investment or consumption—and the degree to which private markets are believed to reflect society's preferences.

■ The benefits and costs of public projects may be measured in several ways:

Market prices serve well if there is no strong reason to believe that they depart from social marginal costs.

Shadow prices adjust market prices for deviations from social marginal costs due to market imperfections. In each case, the investigator must determine the value of resources in their alternative uses. This may be the market price, including the distortion if production is constant and consumption is displaced, or the cost of inputs if production increases and private consumption is unchanged.

If labor is currently unemployed and will remain so for the duration of the project, the opportunity cost is small. However, forecasting unemployment is quite difficult.

Consumer surplus measures the benefit to consumers of changes in market prices. If large government projects change equilibrium prices, analysts may measure consumer surplus by estimating the shape of the demand curve.

For nonmarketed commodities, no prices are available. In some instances, the values of these commodities can be inferred by observing people's behavior. Two examples are computing the benefits of saving time and the benefits of a reduced probability of death.

■ Certain intangible benefits and costs simply cannot be measured. The safest approach is to exclude these in a cost-benefit analysis and then calculate how large intangibles must be to reverse the decision.

■ Cost-benefit analyses sometimes fall prey to several pitfalls:

Chain-reaction game—secondary benefits are included to make a proposal appear more favorable, without including the corresponding secondary costs.

Labor game—wages are viewed as *benefits* rather than *costs* of the project.

Double-counting game—benefits are mistakenly counted twice.

■ Whether distributional considerations belong in cost-benefit analysis is controversial. Some analysts count dollars equally for all persons, while others apply weights that favor projects for selected population groups. Because of the potential for political manipulation, distributional weights must be introduced explicitly.

■ In uncertain situations, individuals favor less risky projects, other things being the same. In general, the costs and benefits of uncertain projects must be adjusted to reflect this.

Discussion Questions

1. The Army Corps of Engineers frequently employs the cost-benefit ratio for evaluating public projects. In Senate hearings on a breakwater project, one senator was impressed that the project had "an amazingly high 17 to 1 benefit-cost ratio" [U.S. Congress, 1973, p. 1]. If you were on the senator's staff, what would you have said?

2. The city of Sundown is considering a plan to build a convention center to revitalize the downtown area. The project requires hiring workers in the construction union. Because of unionization, the workers' wage rate is above the value that would be determined by supply and demand. However, city analysts have econometrically estimated the wage that

would prevail if the labor market were competitive.

   a. If the convention center increases the total number of construction workers employed, what is the appropriate cost of labor?

   b. Suppose instead that total employment is unaffected; workers leave private projects to work in the convention center. Does your answer to (*a*) change? Why?

3. A project yields an annual benefit of $25 a year, starting next year and continuing forever. What is the present value of the benefits if the interest rate is 10 percent? [HINT: The infinite sum $x + x^2 + x^3 + \ldots$ is equal to $x/(1 - x)$, where x is a number less than 1.]

4. An outlay of $1,000 today yields an annual benefit of $80 beginning next year and continuing forever. There is no inflation and the market interest rate is 10 percent before taxes and 5 percent after taxes.

   a. What is the internal rate of return?

   b. Taxes levied to fund the project come entirely from consumer spending. Is the project admissible? Why? Suppose instead that taxes are collected by reducing private firms' investments. Is the project admissible in this case? Finally, suppose that consumers spend 60 cents of their last dollar and save 40 cents. Is the project admissible now? Explain your calculations.

   c. Suppose that the social discount rate is 4 percent. What is the present value of the project?

   d. Now suppose that 10 percent annual inflation is anticipated over the next 10 years. How are your answers to (*a*), (*b*), and (*c*) affected?

5. Bill rides the subway at a cost of 75 cents per trip, but would switch if the price were any higher. His only alternative is a bus which takes five minutes longer, but costs only 50 cents. He makes 10 trips per year. The city is considering renovations of the subway system that would reduce the trip by 10 minutes, but fares would rise by 40 cents per trip to cover the costs. The fare increase and reduced travel time both take effect in one year and last forever. The interest rate is 25 percent.

   a. As far as Bill is concerned, what are the present values of the project's benefits and costs?

   b. The city's population consists of 55,000 middle-class people, all of whom are identical to Bill, and 5,000 poor people. Poor people are either unemployed or have jobs close to their homes, so they do not use any form of public transportation. What are the total benefits and costs of the project for the city as a whole? What is the net present value of the project?

   c. Some members of the city council propose an alternative project which consists of an immediate tax of $1.25 per middle-class person to provide "free" legal services for the poor in both of the following two years. The legal services are valued by the poor at a total of $62,500 per year. (Assume this amount is received at the end of each of the two years.) What is the present value of the project?

   d. If the city must choose between the subway project and the legal services project, which should it select?

  *e. What is the "distributional weight" of each dollar received by a poor person that would make the present values of the two projects just equal? That is, how much must each dollar of income to a poor person be weighted relative to that of a middle-class person? Interpret your answer.

_____

   * Difficult.

Selected References

Broome, J. "Trying to Value a Life." *Journal of Public Economics,* February 1978, pp. 91–100.

Lind, R. C. "A Primer on the Major Issues Relating to the Discount Rate for Evaluating National Energy Options." In *Discounting for Time and Risk in Energy Policy,* R. C. Lind et al. Washington, D.C.: Resources for the Future, 1982, pp. 21–114.

McKean, R. N. "The Use of Shadow Prices." In *Cost-Benefit Analysis,* ed. Richard Layard. New York: Penguin Books, 1977, pp. 119–39.

Viscusi, W. Kip. *Risk By Choice.* Cambridge, Mass.: Harvard University Press, 1983.

A P P E N D I X   **Calculating the Certainty Equivalent Value**

This appendix shows how to calculate the certainty equivalent value of an uncertain project.

Consider Jones, whose current earnings are E dollars. He enters a job-training program with an unpredictable effect on his future earnings. The program will leave his annual earnings unchanged with a probability of ½, or it will increase his earnings by y dollars, also with a probability of ½.[21] The benefit of the program is the amount that Jones would be willing to pay for it, so the key problem here is to determine that amount. A natural answer is $y/2$ dollars, the expected increase in his earnings.[22] However, this value is too high, because it neglects the fact that the outcome is uncertain and therefore subjects Jones to risk. As long as Jones does not like risk, he would give up some income in return for gaining some security. When the benefits or costs of a project are risky, they must be converted into **certainty equivalents,** the amounts of *certain* income that the individual would be willing to trade for the set of uncertain outcomes generated by the project.

The notion of certainty equivalence is illustrated in Figure 12.A. The horizontal axis measures Jones's income, and the vertical axis indicates the amount of his utility. Schedule OU is Jones's utility function, which shows the total amount of utility associated with each income level. Algebraically, the amount of utility associated with a given income level, I, is

---

[21] In this analysis, probabilities of ½ are used for simplicity. The general results hold regardless of the probabilities chosen.

[22] Expected earnings are found simply by multiplying each possible outcome by the associated probability and then adding: $(½ \times 0) + (½ \times y) = y/2$.

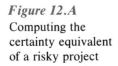

Figure 12.A
Computing the
certainty equivalent
of a risky project

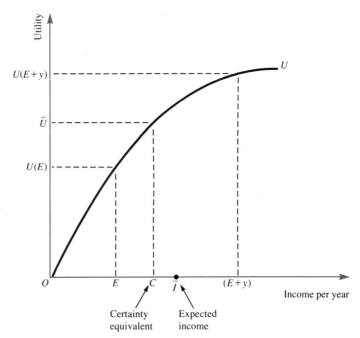

$U(I)$. The shape of the schedule indicates that as income increases, utility also increases, but at a declining rate—there is diminishing marginal utility of income.[23]

To find the amount of utility associated with any income level, simply go from the horizontal axis up to OU, and then off to the vertical axis. For example, if the training project yields no return so that Jones's income is E, then his utility is $U(E)$, as indicated on the vertical axis. Similarly, if the project succeeds so that Jones's income increases by y, his total income is $(E + y)$, and his utility is $U(E + y)$.

Because each outcome occurs with a probability of ½, Jones's average or expected *income* is $E + y/2$, which lies halfway between E and $(E + y)$ and is denoted $\bar{I}$. However, what Jones really cares about is not expected income, but expected *utility*.[24] Expected utility is just the average of the utilities of the two outcomes, or $½U(E) + ½U(E + y)$. Geometrically, expected utility is halfway between $U(E)$ and $U(E + y)$, and is denoted by $\bar{U}$.

---

[23] If marginal utility were increasing, all the derived results would be reversed. Practically all economists believe that the assumption of diminishing marginal utility is more plausible.

[24] Those who are familiar with the theory of uncertainty will recognize the implicit assumption that individuals have "Von Neumann-Morgenstern utility functions." See Henderson and Quandt [1980].

We are now in a position to find out exactly how much certain money the job-training program is worth to Jones. All we have to do is find the amount of income that corresponds to utility level $\bar{U}$. This is shown on the horizontal axis as C, which is by definition the certainty equivalent. It is crucial to note that C is less than $\bar{I}$—the certainty equivalent of the job training program is *less* than the expected income. This is consistent with the intuition developed earlier. Jones is willing to pay a premium of $(\bar{I} - C)$ in exchange for the security of a sure thing.

We have shown, then, that proper evaluation of the costs and benefits of an uncertain project requires more than finding the project's expected value. The latter must be reduced by a risk premium which depends on the shape of the individual's utility function.

In a way, this is a disappointing outcome, because the computation of an expected value is much simpler than that of a certainty equivalent. Fortunately, it turns out that in many cases the expected value is enough. Suppose that a new bomber is being considered, and because the technology is not completely understood, analysts are unsure of its eventual cost. The cost will be either $15 per family or $25, each with probability ½. Although in the aggregate a large amount of money is at stake, on a per-*family* basis, the sums involved are quite small compared to income. In terms of Figure 12.A, the two outcomes are very close to each other on curve OU. As points on OU get closer and closer together, the expected value and certainty equivalent become virtually identical, other things being the same. Intuitively, people do not require a risk premium to accept a gamble that involves only a small amount of income.[25]

Thus, for projects that spread risk over large numbers of people, expected values can provide good measures of uncertain benefits and costs. But for cases in which risks are large relative to individuals' incomes, certainty equivalents must be computed.

---

[25] As the points on OU come closer together, the shape of the curve between them becomes approximately linear. When the utility function is linear, the risk premium is always zero, a fact that is easily verifiable diagrammatically. See Kenneth Arrow and R. C. Lind [1970].

P A R T 4

A Framework for Tax Analysis

B oth politicians and economists have long searched for a set of principles to guide tax policy. Several centuries ago, the French statesman Jean-Baptiste Colbert suggested that "the art of taxation is the art of plucking the goose so as to get the largest possible amount of feathers with the least possible squealing" [Armitage-Smith, 1907, p. 36]. Modern economics takes a somewhat less cynical approach, emphasizing how taxes should be levied to enhance economic efficiency and to promote a "fair" distribution of income. These are the topics of the next three chapters. Although the discussion is illustrated with examples from the U.S. tax system, the main focus is a theoretical framework for thinking about tax policy. A more thorough discussion of U.S. tax institutions is deferred to Part Five.

CHAPTER 13

Taxation and Income Distribution

Struggle and contrive as you will, lay your taxes as you please, the traders will shift it off from their own gain.

JOHN LOCKE

In recent years, American policy debates about the tax system have been dominated by the question of whether its burden is distributed fairly. A sensible discussion of this normative issue requires some understanding of the positive question of how taxes affect the distribution of income. A simple way to determine how taxes change the income distribution would be to conduct a survey in which each person is asked how many dollars he or she pays to the tax collector each year. Simple— but usually wrong. An example demonstrates that assessing correctly the burden of taxation is a complicated problem.

Suppose that the price of a bottle of wine is $10. The government imposes a tax of $1 per bottle, to be collected in the following way: every time a bottle is purchased, the tax collector (who is lurking about the store) takes a dollar out of the wine seller's hand before the money is put into the cash register. A casual observer might conclude that the wine seller is paying the tax.

However, suppose that a few weeks after its imposition, the tax induces a price rise to $11 per bottle. Clearly, the proprietor is receiving the same amount per bottle as he did before the tax. The tax has apparently made him no worse off. The entire amount of the tax is being paid by consumers in the form of higher prices. On the other hand, suppose that after the tax the price only increases to $10.30. In this case, the proprietor keeps only $9.30 for each bottle sold; he is worse off by 70 cents per bottle. Consumers are also worse off, however, because they have to pay

30 cents more per bottle.[1] In this case, producers and consumers share the burden of the tax. Yet another possibility is that after the tax is imposed, the price stays at $10. If this happens, the consumer is no worse off, while the seller bears the full burden of the tax.

The **statutory incidence** of a tax indicates who is legally responsible for the tax. All three cases in the preceding paragraph are identical in the sense that the statutory incidence is on the seller. But the situations differ drastically with respect to who is really bearing the burden. Because prices may change in response to the tax, knowledge of statutory incidence tells us *essentially nothing* about who is really paying the tax. In contrast, the **economic incidence** of a tax is the change in the distribution of private real income brought about by a tax.[2] Our focus in this chapter is on the forces that determine the extent to which statutory and economic incidence differ—the amount of **tax shifting.**

Tax Incidence: General Remarks

Several observations should be kept in mind in any discussion of how taxes affect the distribution of income.

Only People Can Bear Taxes

Under the U.S. legal system, certain institutions are treated as if they were people. The most prominent example is the corporation. Although for many purposes this is a convenient fiction, it sometimes creates confusion. From an economist's point of view, people—stockholders, workers, landlords, consumers—bear taxes. A corporation cannot. Thus, when some politicians declare that "business must pay its fair share of taxes," it is not clear what, if anything, this means.

Given that only people can bear taxes, how should they be classified for purposes of incidence analysis? Often their role in production—what inputs they supply to the production process—is used. (Inputs are often referred to as *factors of production*.) Attention then focuses on how the tax system changes the distribution of income among capitalists, laborers, and landlords. This is referred to as the **functional distribution of income.**

Basing the analysis this way may seem a bit old-fashioned. In 18th-century England, it may have been the case that property owners never worked and workers owned no property. But in the contemporary United States, many people who derive most of their income from labor also have savings accounts and/or common stocks. (Often, these assets are held for individuals in pensions.) Similarly, some people own huge amounts of

---

[1] Actually, the change in the prices faced by consumers and producers is only part of the story. There is also a burden due to the tax-induced distortion of choice. See Chapter 14.

[2] Note the similarity to the problem of *expenditure incidence* introduced in Chapter 8.

capital and also work full time. Thus it seems more relevant to study how taxes affect the way in which total income is distributed among people: the **size distribution of income.** Given information on what proportion of people's income is from capital, land, and labor, changes in the factor distribution can be translated into changes in the size distribution. For example, a tax that lowers the relative return on capital tends to hurt those at the top of the income distribution because a relatively high proportion of the incomes of the rich is from capital.[3]

Other classification schemes might be interesting for particular problems. In the analysis of energy taxation, incidence by region is important. (Are people from the Northeast or the Sun Belt hurt more by a tax on fuel oil?) Alternatively, in a study of taxation of land in urban areas, it might be useful to look at incidence by race. It is easy to think of further examples based on sex, age, and so forth.

Both Sources and Uses of Income Should Be Considered

In the previous wine tax example, it is natural to assume that the distributional effects of the tax depend crucially on people's spending patterns. To the extent that the price of wine increases, the people who tend to consume a lot of wine are made worse off. Further thought suggests, however, that if the tax reduces the demand for wine, the factors employed in wine production may suffer income losses. Thus, the tax may also change the income distribution by affecting the sources of income. Suppose that poor people spend a relatively large proportion of their incomes on wine, but that vineyards tend to be owned by the rich. Then on the uses of income side, the tax redistributes income away from the poor, but on the sources side, it redistributes income away from the rich. The overall incidence depends on how both the sources and uses of income are affected.

In practice, it is common for economists to ignore effects on the sources side when considering a tax on a commodity, and to ignore the uses side when analyzing a tax on an input. This procedure is appropriate if the most *systematic* changes of a commodity tax are on the uses of income and those of a factor tax on the sources of income. The assumption simplifies analyses, but its correctness must be considered for each case.

Incidence Depends on How Prices Are Determined

We have emphasized that the incidence problem is fundamentally one of determining how taxes change prices. Clearly, different models of price determination may give quite different answers to the question of who really bears a tax. This chapter considers several different models, and compares the results.

---

[3] However, some low-income retirees also derive the bulk of their income from capital.

A closely related issue is the time dimension of the analysis. Incidence depends on changes in prices, but change takes time. In most cases, it is expected that responses are larger in the long run than the short run. Thus, the short- and long-run incidence of a tax may differ, and the time frame that is relevant for a given policy question must be specified.

Incidence Depends on the Disposition of Tax Revenues

Balanced-budget incidence computes the combined effects of levying taxes *and* government spending financed by those taxes. In general, the distributional effect of a tax depends on how the government spends the money. As an example, expenditures on missiles have a very different distributional impact than spending on hot lunches for schoolchildren. Some studies assume that the government spends the tax revenue exactly as the consumers would if they had received the money. This is equivalent to returning the revenue as a lump sum and letting consumers spend it.

In most cases, tax revenues are not earmarked for particular expenditures. It is then desirable to be able to abstract from the question of how the government spends the money. The idea is to examine how incidence differs when one tax is replaced with another, holding the government budget constant. This is called **differential tax incidence.** Because differential incidence looks at changes in taxes, it is useful to have a reference point. The hypothetical "other tax" used as the basis of comparison is often assumed to be a **lump sum tax**—a tax for which the individual's liability does not depend upon behavior. (For example, a 10 percent income tax is *not* a lump sum tax because it depends on how much the individual earns. But a head tax of $500 independent of earnings *is* a lump sum tax.)

Finally, **absolute tax incidence** examines the effects of a tax when there is no change in either other taxes or government expenditure. Absolute incidence is of most interest for macroeconomic models in which tax levels are changed to achieve some stabilization goal.

Tax Progressiveness Can Be Measured in Several Ways

Suppose that an investigator has managed to calculate every person's real share of a particular tax—the economic incidence as defined above. The bottom line of such an exercise is often a characterization of the tax as proportional, progressive, or regressive. The definition of **proportional** is straightforward; it describes a situation in which the ratio of taxes paid to income is constant regardless of income level.[4]

----

[4] However, the definition of income is not straightforward; see Chapter 16.

Table 13.1   **Tax liabilities under a hypothetical tax system**

Income	Tax Liability	Average Tax Rate	Marginal Tax Rate
$ 2,000	$-200	-0.10	0.2
3,000	0	0	0.2
5,000	400	0.08	0.2
10,000	1,400	0.14	0.2
30,000	5,400	0.18	0.2

Defining progressive and regressive is not easy and, unfortunately, ambiguities in definition sometimes confuse public debate. A natural way to define these words is in terms of the **average tax rate,** the ratio of taxes paid to income. If the average tax rate increases with income, the system is **progressive;** if it falls, the tax is **regressive.**

Confusion arises because some people think of progressiveness in terms of the **marginal tax rate**—the *change* in taxes paid with respect to a change in income. To illustrate the distinction, consider the following very simple income tax structure. Each individual computes his or her tax bill by subtracting $3,000 from income and paying an amount equal to 20 percent of the remainder. (If the difference is negative, the individual gets a subsidy equal to 20 percent of the figure.) Table 13.1 shows the amount of tax paid, the average tax rate, and the marginal tax rate for each of several income levels. The average rates increase with income. However, the marginal tax rate is constant at 0.2 because for each additional dollar earned, the individual pays an additional 20 cents, regardless of income level. People could disagree about the progressiveness of this tax system and each be right according to his or her own definition. It is therefore very important to make the definition clear when using the terms *regressive* and *progressive*. In the remainder of this book, we assume that they are defined in average tax rates.

Measuring *how* progressive a tax system is presents an even harder task than defining progressiveness. Many reasonable alternatives have been proposed, and we consider two simple ones.[5] The first says that the greater the increase in average tax rates as income increases, the more progressive the system. Algebraically, let T_0 and T_1 be the tax liabilities at income levels I_0 and I_1, respectively (I_1 is greater than I_0). The measurement of progressiveness, ν_1, is

$$\nu_1 = \frac{\dfrac{T_1}{I_1} - \dfrac{T_0}{I_0}}{I_1 - I_0}.$$

(13.1)

---

[5] See John Formby, James Smith, and David Sykes [1986].

Once the analyst has found the economic incidence of the tax as embodied in T_1 and T_0, the tax system with the higher value of ν_1 is said to be more progressive.

The second possibility is to say that one tax system is more progressive than another if its elasticity of tax revenues with respect to income (i.e., the percentage change in tax revenues divided by percentage change in income) is higher. Here the expression to be evaluated is ν_2, defined as

$$\nu_2 = \frac{(T_1 - T_0)}{T_0} \div \frac{(I_1 - I_0)}{I_0} \tag{13.2}$$

Now consider the following proposal: everyone's tax liability is to be increased by 20 percent of the amount of tax he or she currently pays. This proposal would increase the tax liability of a person who formerly paid T_0 to $1.2 \times T_0$, and the liability that was formerly T_1 to $1.2 \times T_1$. Member of Congress A says the proposal will make the tax system more progressive, while member of Congress B says that it has no effect on progressiveness whatsoever. Who is right? It depends on the progressivity measure. Substituting the expressions $1.2 \times T_0$ and $1.2 \times T_1$ for T_0 and T_1, respectively, in Equation (13.1), ν_1 increases by 20 percent. The proposal thus increases progressiveness. On the other hand, if the same substitution is done in Equation (13.2), the value of ν_2 is unchanged. (Both the numerator and denominator are multiplied by 1.2, which cancels out the effect.) The lesson here is that even very intuitively appealing measures of progressiveness can give different answers.[6] Again, intelligent public debate requires that people make their definitions clear.

Partial Equilibrium Models

With preliminaries out of the way, we turn now to the fundamental issue of this chapter: how taxes affect the income distribution. We have argued that the essence of the problem is that taxes induce changes in relative prices. Knowing how prices are determined is therefore a key ingredient in the analysis. In this section we analyze **partial equilibrium models** of price determination—models that study only the market in which the tax is imposed and ignore the ramifications in other markets. This kind of analysis is most appropriate when the market for the commodity taxed is relatively small compared to the economy as a whole.

Unit Taxes on Commodities

We study first the incidence of a **unit tax,** so named because it is levied as a fixed amount per unit of a commodity sold. For example, the federal government imposes a tax on champagne of $3.40 per wine gallon and a

---

[6] Note also that ν_1 and ν_2, in general, depend on the level of income. That is, even a single tax system does not usually have a constant ν_1 and ν_2. This further complicates discussions of the degree of progressiveness.

Figure 13.1
Price and quantity
prior to taxation

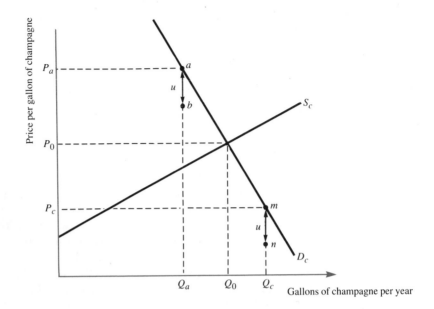

tax on cigarettes of \$0.24 per pack.[7] Suppose that the price and quantity of
champagne are determined competitively by supply (S_c) and demand (D_c)
as in Figure 13.1. Prior to imposition of the tax, the quantity demanded
and price are Q_0 and P_0, respectively. Now suppose that a unit tax of $\$u$
per gallon is imposed on each purchase, and the statutory incidence is on
buyers.

A key step in incidence analysis is to recognize that in the presence of
a tax, the price paid by consumers and the price received by suppliers
differs. Previously, we could use a supply-demand analysis to determine
the *single* market price. Now, this analysis must be modified to accommodate two different prices, one for buyers and one for sellers.

We begin by determining how the tax affects the demand schedule.
Consider an arbitrary point *a* on the demand curve. Recall that this point
indicates that the *maximum* price per gallon that people would be willing
to pay for Q_a gallons is P_a. After the unit tax of *u* is imposed, the most that
people would be willing to spend for Q_a is *still* P_a. There is no reason to
believe that the tax affects the underlying valuation people place on champagne. However, when people pay P_a per gallon, producers no longer
receive the whole amount. Instead, they receive only $(P_a - u)$, an amount
that is indicated as point *b* in Figure 13.1. In other words, after the unit
tax is imposed, *a* is no longer a point on the demand curve as *perceived by* suppliers. Point *b* *is* on the demand curve as perceived by
suppliers, because they realize that if Q_a is supplied, they receive only

---

[7] The cigarette tax figure assumes a pack of 20 small cigarettes.

Figure 13.2
Incidence of a unit
tax imposed on the
demand side

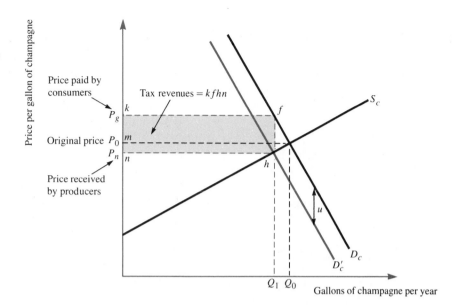

$(P_a - u)$ per gallon. It is irrelevant to the suppliers how much consumers
pay per gallon; all that matters to suppliers is the amount they receive
per gallon.

Of course, point a was chosen arbitrarily. At any other point on the
demand curve, the story is just the same. Thus, for example, after the tax
is imposed, the price received by suppliers for output Q_c is at point n,
which is found by subtracting the distance u from point m. If we repeat
this process at every point along the demand curve, we generate a new
demand curve located exactly u dollars below the old one. In Figure 13.2,
the demand curve so constructed is labeled D'_c. Schedule D'_c is relevant to
suppliers because it shows how much they receive for each unit sold.

We are now in a position to find the equilibrium quantity of champagne after the unit tax is imposed. The equilibrium is where the supply
equals demand as perceived by suppliers. In Figure 13.2, this takes place
at output Q_1. Thus, the tax lowers the quantity sold from Q_0 to Q_1.

The next step is to find the new equilibrium price. As noted earlier,
there are really two prices at the new equilibrium: the price received by
producers, and the price paid by consumers. The price received by producers is at the intersection of their effective demand and supply curves,
which occurs at P_n. The price paid by consumers is P_n *plus* u, the unit tax.
To find this price geometrically, we must go up from P_n a vertical distance
exactly equal to u. But by construction, the distance between schedules
D_c and D'_c is equal to u. Hence, to find the price paid by consumers, we
simply go up from the intersection of D'_c and S_c to the original demand
curve D_c. The price so determined is P_g. Because P_g includes the tax, it is
often referred to as the price *gross* of tax. On the other hand, P_n is the
price *net* of tax.

Consumers are made worse off by the tax because P_g, the new price they face, is higher than the original price P_0. But the consumers' price has not increased by the full amount of the tax—$(P_g - P_0)$ is less than u. Producers also pay part of the tax in the form of a lower price received per gallon. Producers now receive only P_n, while before the tax they received P_0. Thus, both producers and consumers are made worse off by the tax.[8] Notice that consumers and producers "split" the tax in the sense that the increase in the consumer price $(P_g - P_0)$ and the decrease in the producer price $(P_0 - P_n)$ just add up to $\$u$.

By definition, revenues collected are the product of the number of units purchased, Q_1, and the tax per unit, u. Geometrically, Q_1 is the width of rectangle $kfhn$ and u is its height, so tax revenues are the area of this rectangle. This analysis has two important implications:

The incidence of a unit tax is independent of whether it is levied on consumers or producers.   Suppose the same tax u had been levied on the suppliers of champagne instead of the consumers. Consider an arbitrary price P_i on the original supply curve in Figure 13.3. The supply curve indicates that for suppliers to produce Q_i units, they must receive at least P_i per unit. After the unit tax, suppliers still must receive P_i per unit. For them to do so, however, consumers must pay price $P_i + u$ per unit, which is shown geometrically as point j. It should now be clear where the argument is heading. To find the supply curve as it is perceived by consumers, S_c must be shifted up by the amount of the unit tax. This new supply curve is labeled S_c'. The post-tax equilibrium is at Q_1', where the schedules S_c' and D_c intersect. The price at the intersection, P_g', is the price paid by consumers. To find the price received by producers, we must *subtract u* from P_g', giving us P_n'. A glance at Figure 13.2 indicates that $Q_1' = Q_1$, $P_g' = P_g$, and $P_n' = P_n$. Thus, the incidence of the unit tax is independent of the side of the market on which it is levied.

This is the same as our statement that the statutory incidence of a tax tells us nothing of the economic incidence of the tax. It is irrelevant whether the tax collector (figuratively) stands next to consumers and takes u dollars every time they pay for gallons of champagne, or stands next to sellers and collects u dollars from them whenever they sell a gallon. Figures 13.2 and 13.3 prove that what matters is the size of the disparity the tax introduces between the price paid by consumers and the price received by producers, and not on which side of the market the

---

[8] In terms of surplus measures, consumers are worse off by area $mkfg$ and producers are worse off by $mghn$. The loss of total surplus exceeds the tax revenues by triangle fhg; this is the *excess burden* of the tax, as explained in Chapter 14. Area $mghn$ is the loss in producer surplus. Just as consumer surplus is the area between the demand curve and a horizontal line at the going price, producer surplus is the area between the supply curve and a horizontal line at the going price. For a review of consumer surplus, see the Appendix to Chapter 4.

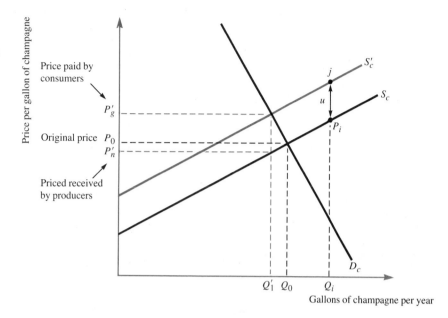

Figure 13.3
Incidence of a unit tax imposed on the supply side

disparity is introduced. The tax-induced difference between the price paid by consumers and the price received by producers is referred to as the **tax wedge**.

The incidence of the unit tax depends on the elasticities of supply and demand. In Figure 13.2, consumers bear the brunt of the tax—the amount that they pay goes up much more than the amount received by producers goes down. This result is strictly a consequence of the way in which the demand and supply curves are drawn. In general, the more elastic the demand curve, the less the tax borne by consumers, *ceteris paribus*. Similarly, the more elastic the supply curve, the less the tax borne by producers, *ceteris paribus*. Intuitively, elasticity provides a rough measure of an economic agent's ability to escape the tax. The more elastic the demand, the easier it is for consumers to turn to other products when the price goes up, and therefore more of the tax must be borne by suppliers. Conversely, if consumers purchase the same amount regardless of price, the whole burden can be shifted to them. Similar considerations apply to the supply side.

Two illustrations of extreme cases are provided in Figures 13.4 and 13.5. In Figure 13.4, commodity X is supplied perfectly inelastically. When a unit tax is imposed, the effective demand curve becomes D_X'. As before, the price received by producers is at the intersection of S_X and D_X', which is P_n. Note that P_n is exactly u less than P_0. Thus, the price received by producers falls by exactly the amount of the tax. At the same time, the price paid by consumers, P_g ($= P_n + u$), remains at P_0. When

Figure 13.4

Tax incidence when supply is perfectly inelastic

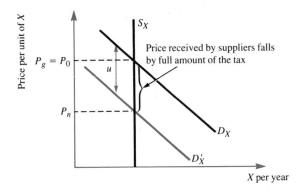

Figure 13.5

Tax incidence when supply is perfectly elastic

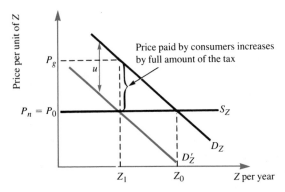

supply is perfectly inelastic, producers bear the entire burden. Figure 13.5 represents an opposite extreme. The supply of commodity Z is perfectly elastic. Imposition of a unit tax leads to demand curve D_Z'. At the new equilibrium, quantity demanded is Z_1 and the price received by producers, P_n, is still P_0. The price paid by consumers, P_g, is therefore $P_0 + u$. In this case, consumers bear the entire burden of the tax.[9]

Ad Valorem Taxes

We now turn to the incidence of an **ad valorem** tax, which is one with a rate given as a *proportion* of the price. Ad valorem taxes are quite common; for example, state and local taxes on food and clothing are usually levied as some proportion of sales price.

Luckily, the analysis of ad valorem taxes is very similar to that of unit taxes. The basic strategy is still to find out how the tax changes the effective demand curve and compute the new equilibrium. However, instead of moving the curve down by the same absolute amount for each

---

[9] Note that as long as input costs are constant, the *long-run* supply curve for a competitive market is horizontal as in Figure 13.5. Hence, under these conditions, in the long run consumers bear the entire burden of the tax.

Figure 13.6

Introducing an ad valorem tax

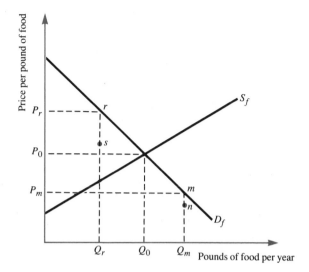

quantity, the ad valorem tax lowers it in the same *proportion*. To show this, consider the demand (D_f) and supply (S_f) curves for food in Figure 13.6. In the absence of taxation, the equilibrium price and quantity are P_0 and Q_0, respectively. Now suppose that a tax of 25 percent of the gross price is levied on the consumption of food.[10] Consider point m on D_f. After the tax is imposed, P_m is still the most that consumers will pay for Q_m pounds of food; the amount that producers will receive is 75 percent of the vertical distance between point m and the horizontal axis, which is labeled point n. Hence, point n is one point on the demand curve perceived by producers. Similarly, the price at point r migrates down one quarter of the way between it and the horizontal axis to point s. When this exercise is repeated for every point on D_f, the effective demand curve facing suppliers is determined as D'_f in Figure 13.7. From here, the analysis proceeds in exactly the same way as in the unit tax case: The equilibrium is at the intersection of S_f and D'_f, with the quantity exchanged Q_1, the price received by food producers P_n, and the price paid by consumers P_g. As before, the extent to which the prices paid by consumers and received by producers rise and fall, respectively, is determined by the elasticities of supply and demand.

---

[10] There is a fundamental ambiguity involved in measuring ad valorem tax rates. Is the tax to be measured as a percentage of the net or gross price? In this example, the tax is 25 percent of the gross price, which is equivalent to a rate of 33 percent of net price. To see this, note that if the price paid by the consumer were $1, the tax paid would be 25 cents, and the price received by producers would be 75 cents. Expressing the 25 cents tax bill as a fraction of 75 cents gives us a 33 percent rate as a proportion of the net price.

Figure 13.7
Incidence of an ad
valorem tax

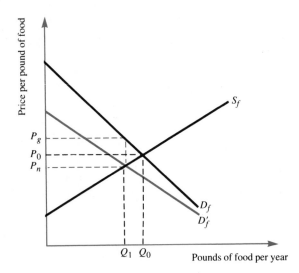

Taxes on Factors   So far we have discussed taxes on goods, but the analysis can also be applied to factors of production.

The Payroll Tax.   Consider the payroll tax used to finance the Social Security system. As noted in Chapter 10 under "Structure of Social Security," a tax equal to 7.65 percent of workers' earnings must be paid by their employers, and a tax at the same rate paid by the workers themselves—a total of 15.3 percent.[11] This division has a long history and is a consequence of our lawmakers' feeling that the payroll tax should be shared equally by employers and employees. It is important to realize that the *statutory distinction between workers and bosses is irrelevant*. As noted earlier, the incidence of this tax on labor is determined only by the wedge that the tax puts between what employees receive and employers pay.

This point is illustrated in Figure 13.8, where D_L is the demand for labor and S_L is the supply of labor. For purposes of illustration, assume S_L to be perfectly inelastic. Prior to taxation, the wage is w_0. The ad valorem tax on labor moves the effective demand curve to D_L'. As usual, the distance between D_L' and D_L reflects the difference between what is paid for an item and what is received by those who supply it. After the tax is imposed, the wage received by workers falls to w_n. On the other hand, w_g, the price paid by employers, stays at w_0. In this example, despite the statutory division of the tax, the wage rate received by workers falls by exactly the amount of the tax—they bear the entire burden.

---

[11] After earnings exceed a certain level, the payroll tax rate becomes zero. See Chapter 10.

Figure 13.8

Incidence of a
payroll tax with an
inelastic supply of
labor

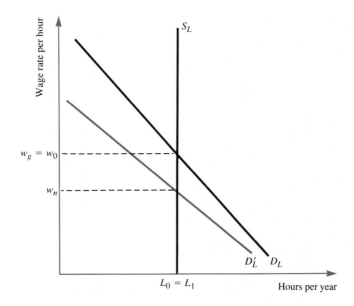

Of course, we could have gotten just the opposite result by drawing
the supply curve as perfectly elastic. The key point to remember is that
nothing about the incidence of a tax can be known without information on
the relevant behavioral elasticities. In fact, there is some evidence that
the elasticity of the total supply of hours of work in the United States is
about zero.[12] At least in the short run, labor probably bears most of the
payroll tax, despite the intense congressional debates on the "fair" distribution of the burden.

Capital taxation in an open economy.   The strategy for analyzing a tax
on capital is essentially the same as that for analyzing a tax on labor—
draw the supply and demand curves, shift or pivot the relevant curve by
an amount depending on the size of the tax, and see how the after-tax
equilibrium compares with the original one. In an economy that is closed
to trade, it is reasonable to assume that the demand curve will slope
downward (firms demand less capital when its price goes up), and that the
supply of capital will slope upward (people supply more capital, i.e., save
more, when the return to saving increases).[13] In this case, the owners of
capital will bear some of the burden of the tax, the precise amount depending on the supply and demand elasticities.

---

[12] See Richard Quandt and Harvey Rosen [1986].

[13] However, saving need not increase with the rate of return. See Chapter 17.

Now suppose that the economy is open and capital is perfectly mobile across countries. In effect, there is a single world market for capital, and if suppliers of capital cannot earn the going world rate of return in a particular country, they will take it out of that country and put it in another. In terms of a supply and demand diagram, the supply of capital to a particular country is perfectly elastic—its citizens can purchase all the capital they want at the going rate of return, but none whatsoever at a lower rate. The implications for the incidence of a tax on capital are striking. As in Figure 13.5, the before-tax price paid by the users of capital rises by exactly the amount of the tax, and the suppliers of capital bear no burden whatsoever. Intuitively, capital will simply move abroad if it has to bear any of the tax; hence, the rate of return has to rise.

Now, even in our highly integrated world economy, capital is not perfectly mobile across countries. Moreover, for a country like the United States whose capital market is large relative to the world market, it is doubtful that the supply curve is perfectly horizontal. Nevertheless, policymakers who ignore the fact that the economy is open will tend to overestimate their ability to place the burden of taxation on owners of capital. To the extent that capital is internationally mobile, taxes on capitalists will be shifted to others, and the apparent progressivity of taxes on capital will prove to be illusory.

Commodity Taxation without Competition

The assumption of competitive markets has played a major role in our analysis. We now discuss how the results might change under alternative market structures.

Monopoly.   The polar opposite of competition is monopoly—one seller.[14] Figure 13.9 depicts a monopolist that produces commodity X. Prior to any taxation, the demand curve facing the monopolist is D_X, and the associated marginal revenue curve is MR_X. The marginal cost curve for the production of X is MC_X, and the average total cost curve, ATC_X. As usual, the condition for profit maximization is that production be carried to the point where marginal revenue equals marginal cost. This occurs at output X_0 where the price charged is P_0. Economic profit per unit is the difference between average revenue and average total cost, distance ab. The number of units sold is db. Hence, total profit is ab times db, which is the area of rectangle $abdc$.

Now suppose that a unit tax of u is levied on X. For exactly the same reasons as before, the effective demand curve facing the producer shifts down by a vertical distance equal to u.[15] In Figure 13.10, this demand

---

[14] See William Baumol and Alan Blinder [1982, Chapter 25] for a review of price and output determination under monopoly.

[15] Alternatively, we could shift the marginal cost curve *up* by u. The final outcomes are identical.

Figure 13.9
Equilibrium of a
monopolist

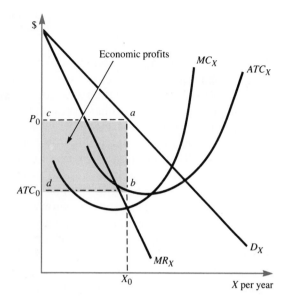

Figure 13.10
Imposition of a unit
tax on a monopolist

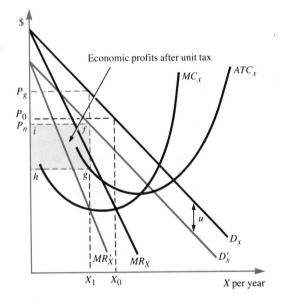

curve is labeled D'_X. At the same time, the marginal revenue curve facing
the firm also shifts down by distance u because the firm's incremental
revenue for each unit sold is reduced by the amount of the tax. The new
effective marginal revenue curve is labeled MR'_X.

The profit-maximizing output is found at the intersection of MR'_X and
MC_X, which occurs at output X_1. Using output X_1, we find the price
received by the monopolist by going up to D'_X, the demand curve facing

him, and locate price P_n. The price paid by consumers is determined by adding u to P_n, which is shown as price P_g on the diagram. After-tax profit per unit is the difference between the price *received by the monopolist* and average total cost, distance *fg*. Number of units sold is *if*. Therefore, monopoly economic profits after tax are measured by area *fghi*.

What are the effects of the tax? Quantity demanded goes down $(X_1 < X_0)$; the price paid by consumers goes up $(P_g > P_0)$; and the price received by the monopolist goes down $(P_n < P_0)$. Note that monopoly profits are lower under the tax—area *fghi* in Figure 13.10 is smaller than area *abdc* in Figure 13.9. Despite its market power, a monopolist is in general made worse off by a unit tax on the product it sells. In public debate it is often assumed that a firm with market power can simply pass on all taxes to consumers. This analysis shows that even a completely greedy and grasping monopolist must bear some of the burden. As before, the precise share of the burden borne by consumers depends on the elasticity of the demand schedule.

It is straightforward to repeat the exercise for an ad valorem tax on the monopolist (D_X and MR_X pivot instead of moving down in a parallel fashion); this is left as an exercise for the reader.

Oligopoly.   Between the polar extremes of perfect competition and monopoly is the oligopoly market structure in which there are a "few" sellers. Unfortunately, there is no well-developed theory of tax incidence in oligopoly. The reason for this embarrassing fact is simple: incidence depends primarily on how relative prices change when taxes are imposed, but there is no generally accepted theory of how oligopolistic prices are determined. Depending on your view of how oligopolists function, practically anything can happen when a tax is imposed.

Suppose first that any single oligopolist believes that if she raises her price in response to a tax, the other firms in the industry will not follow. According to this belief, raising her price leads to a substantial loss of customers to the other firms [see Musgrave, 1959, p. 281]. If every oligopolist shares the same belief, then none will raise price in response to the tax. The price paid by the consumer remains constant, and the entire burden of the tax falls on producers.

However, a different story about oligopoly behavior can lead to the opposite prediction. Suppose that the imposition of a tax serves as a signal to the members of the oligopoly that they can all raise prices together, without having to fear that any one firm will leave its price low. In this case, much of the tax might be shifted to consumers. Yet another possibility is that oligopolistic firms engage in *markup pricing*—they set their prices as some fixed percentage in excess of their costs. To the extent that taxes on their output are regarded as part of costs, they are reflected in higher prices paid by consumers.

As economic behavior under oligopoly becomes better understood, improved models of incidence will be developed. In the meantime, most economists feel fairly comfortable in relying on the predictions produced by competitive models, although they realize that these are only approximations.

Profits Taxes

So far we have been discussing taxes based on sales. Firms can also be taxed on their **economic profits,** defined as the return to owners of the firm in excess of the opportunity costs of the factors used in production. (Economic profits are also referred to as *supranormal* or *excess* profits.) We now show that as long as firms are profit maximizing, a tax on economic profits cannot be shifted—it is borne only by the owners of the firm.

Consider first a perfectly competitive firm in short-run equilibrium. The firm's output is determined by the intersection of its marginal cost and marginal revenue schedules. A tax of a given rate on economic profits changes neither marginal cost nor marginal revenue. Therefore, no firm has the incentive to change its output decision. Because output does not change, neither does the price paid by consumers, so they are no worse off. The tax is completely absorbed by the firms. Another way to get to the same result is this: If the tax rate on economic profits is t_p, the firm's objective is to maximize after-tax profits, $(1 - t_p)\Pi$, where Π is the pretax level of economic profits. But it is just a matter of arithmetic that whatever strategy maximizes Π is identical to the one that maximizes $(1 - t_p)\Pi$. Hence, output and price faced by consumers stay the same, and the firm bears the whole tax.

In long-run competitive equilibrium, a tax on economic profits has no yield, because economic profits are zero—they are all competed away. For a monopolist, there may be economic profits even in the long run. But for reasons exactly the same as those given in the preceding paragraph, the tax is borne by the owners of the monopoly. If a firm is maximizing profits before the profits tax is imposed, the tax cannot be shifted.[16]

Because they distort no economic decisions, taxes on economic profits might appear to be very attractive policy alternatives. However, they have received very little support from public finance specialists. Probably the main reason is the tremendous problems in making the theoretical notion of economic profits operational. For example, excess profits are often computed by examining the rate of return that a firm makes on its capital stock and comparing it to some "basic" rate of return set by the government. Clearly, how the capital stock is measured is important.

---

[16] On the other hand, if the firm is following some other goal, it may raise the price in response to a profits tax. One alternative to profit maximization is revenue maximization; firms try to make their sales as large as possible, subject to the constraint that they earn a "reasonable" rate of return.

Should the original cost be used, or the cost of replacing it? And what if the rate of return is high not because of excess profits, but because the enterprise is very risky and investors have to be compensated for this risk? Considerations like these lead to major difficulties in administration and compliance.[17]

In this context, note that many taxes popularly referred to as "profits taxes" *do not in any way* resemble taxes on economic profits. For example, the so-called windfall profits tax on oil that created so much controversy when introduced during the Carter administration is essentially a complicated *sales tax* on crude oil.[18] Unlike a tax on economic profits, such a tax would certainly be expected to affect production incentives and to be shifted (by an amount determined by the relevant elasticities) to consumers.

Tax Incidence and Capitalization

We now consider special issues that arise when land is taxed. For these purposes, the distinctive characteristics of land are that it is fixed in supply and it is durable.[19] Suppose the annual rental rate on land is $\$R_0$ this year. It is known that the rental will be $\$R_1$ next year, $\$R_2$ two years from now, and so on. How much should someone be willing to pay for the land? If the market for land is competitive, the price of land is just equal to the present discounted value of the stream of the rents. Thus, if the interest rate is r, the price of land (P_R) is

$$P_R = \$R_0 + \frac{\$R_1}{(1 + r)} + \frac{\$R_2}{(1 + r)^2} + \cdots + \frac{\$R_T}{(1 + r)^T} \qquad (13.3)$$

where T is the last year the land yields its services (possibly infinity).

Assume that it is announced that a tax of $\$u_0$ will be imposed on land now, $\$u_1$ next year, $\$u_2$ two years from now, and so forth. From Figure 13.4 we know that because land is fixed in supply, the annual rental received by the owner falls by the full amount of the tax. That means that the landlord's return initially falls to $\$(R_0 - u_0)$, in year 1 to $\$(R_1 - u_1)$, and in year 2 to $\$(R_2 - u_2)$. Prospective purchasers of the land take into account the fact that if they purchase the land, they buy a future stream of tax liabilities as well as a future stream of returns. Therefore, the most a purchaser is willing to pay for the land after the tax is announced (P_R'), is

$$P_R' = \$(R_0 - u_0) + \frac{\$(R_1 - u_1)}{1 + r} + \frac{\$(R_2 - u_2)}{(1 + r)^2} + \cdots$$
$$+ \frac{\$(R_T - u_T)}{(1 + r)^T} \qquad (13.4)$$

---

[17] See Malcolm Gillis and Charles McLure [1979] for further details.

[18] See David Meiselman [1979]. The tax has now been repealed, but whenever oil prices increase, attempts are made to reintroduce it.

[19] Hence, the analysis of this section applies to any commodity or input with these characteristics.

Comparing Equations (13.4) and (13.3), we see that as a consequence of the tax, the price of land falls by an amount equal to

$$
u_0 + \frac{u_1}{1 + r} + \frac{u_2}{(1 + r)^2} + \cdots + \frac{u_T}{(1 + r)^T}
$$

Thus, at the time the tax is imposed, the price of the land falls by the present value of *all future tax payments*. This process by which a stream of taxes becomes incorporated into the price of an asset is referred to as **capitalization.**[20]

As a consequence of capitalization, the person who bears the full burden of the tax *forever* is the landlord at the time the tax is levied. To be sure, *future* landlords make payments to the tax authorities, but such payments are not really a "burden" because they just balance the lower price paid at purchase. Capitalization complicates attempts to assess the incidence of a tax on a durable item that is fixed in supply. Knowing the identities of current owners is not sufficient—one must know who the landlords *were* at the time the tax was imposed.[21]

To the extent that land is *not* fixed in supply, the preceding analysis must be qualified. For example, at the fringes of urban areas that are adjacent to farmland, the supply of urban land can be extended. Similarly, in some areas the amount of land can be increased by landfills. In such cases, the tax on land is borne both by landlords and the users of land, in proportions that depend on the elasticities of demand and supply.[22]

General Equilibrium Models

A great attraction of partial equilibrium models is their simplicity—examining only one market at a time is a relatively uncomplicated affair. In some cases, however, ignoring feedback into other markets leads to an incomplete picture of a tax's incidence. Suppose, for example, that a tax is levied on all capital used in the construction of housing. Partial equilibrium analysis of this tax would involve analyzing only the supply and demand curves for housing capital. But suppose that the tax induces some people who formerly invested in housing to invest their capital in the manufacturing sector instead. As new capital flows into the manufacturing sector, the rate of return to capital employed there will fall. Thus, capitalists in the manufacturing sector may end up bearing part of the burden of a tax imposed on the housing sector.

---

[20] More generally, capitalization refers to the incorporation of any change in the revenue stream into the price.

[21] If a land tax is anticipated before it is levied, then presumably it is borne at least in part by the owner at the time the anticipation becomes widespread. In theory, then, even finding out the identity of the landowner at the time the tax was imposed may not be enough.

[22] In the same way, if imposition of the land tax somehow leads to changes in the discount rate, r, then the results will change.

More generally, when a tax is imposed on a sector that is "large" relative to the economy, looking only at the market where the tax is imposed may not be enough. The purpose of **general equilibrium analysis** is to take into account the ways in which various markets are interrelated.

Another problem with partial equilibrium analysis is that it gives insufficient attention to the question of just who the "producers" of a taxed commodity are. The "producer" is a composite of entrepreneurs, capitalists, and workers. In many cases the division of the tax burden among these groups is of some importance. General equilibrium analysis provides a framework for investigating it.

Before turning to the specifics of general equilibrium analysis, note that the fundamental lesson from partial equilibrium models still holds: because of relative price adjustments, the statutory incidence of a tax generally tells *nothing* about who is really bearing its burden.

Tax Equivalence Relations

The idea of dealing with tax incidence in a general equilibrium framework at first appears daunting. After all, thousands of different commodities and inputs are traded in the economy. How can we keep track of all of their complicated interrelations? Luckily, it turns out that for many purposes useful general equilibrium results can be obtained from models in which there are only two commodities, two factors of production, and no savings. For illustration, call the two commodities food *(F)* and manufactures *(M)*, and the two factors capital *(K)* and labor *(L)*. There are nine possible ad valorem taxes in such a model:

t_{KF} = a tax on capital used in the production of food.

t_{KM} = a tax on capital used in the production of manufactures.

t_{LF} = a tax on labor used in the production of food.

t_{LM} = a tax on labor used in the production of manufactures.

t_F = a tax on the consumption of food.

t_M = a tax on consumption of manufactures.

t_K = a tax on capital in both sectors.

t_L = a tax on labor in both sectors.

t = a general income tax.

The first four taxes, which are levied on a factor in only some of its uses, are referred to as **partial factor taxes.**

Certain combinations of these taxes are equivalent to others. One of these equivalences is already familiar from the theory of the consumer.[23] Taxes on food (t_F) and manufactures (t_M) at the same rate are equivalent

---

[23] The theory of the consumer is outlined in the Appendix at the end of the book.

Table 13.2 **Tax equivalence relations**

t_{KF}	and	t_{LF}	are equivalent to		t_F
and		and			and
t_{KM}	and	t_{LM}	are equivalent to		t_M
are equivalent to		are equivalent to			are equivalent to
t_K	and	t_L	are equivalent to		t

SOURCE: Charles E. McLure, Jr., "The Theory of Tax Incidence with Imperfect Factor Mobility," *Finanzarchiv* 30 (1971), p. 29.

to an income tax (t).[24] To see this, just note that equiproportional taxes on all commodities have the same effect on the consumer's budget constraint as a proportional income tax. Both create a parallel shift inward.

Now consider a proportional tax on both capital (t_K) and labor (t_L). Because in this model all income is derived from either capital or labor, it is a simple matter of arithmetic that taxing both factors at the same rate is also equivalent to an income tax (t).

Perhaps not so obvious is the fact that partial taxes on both capital and labor in the food sector at a given rate $(t_{KF} = t_{LF})$ are equivalent to a tax on food (t_F) at the same rate. Because capital and labor are the only inputs to the production of food, making each of them more expensive by a certain proportion is equivalent to making the food itself more expensive in the same proportion.

More generally, any two sets of taxes that generate the same changes in relative prices have equivalent incidence effects. All the equivalence relations that can be derived using similar logic are summarized in Table 13.2. For a given ad valorem tax rate, the equivalences are shown by reading across the rows or down the columns. To determine the incidence of all three taxes in any row or column, only two have to be analyzed in detail. The third can be determined by addition or subtraction. For example, from the third row, if we know the incidence of taxes on capital and labor, then we also know the incidence of a tax on income.

In the next section, we discuss the incidence of four taxes: a food tax (t_F), an income tax (t), a general tax on labor (t_L), and a partial tax on capital in manufacturing (t_{KM}). With results on these four taxes in hand, the incidence of the other five can be determined by using Table 13.2.

---

[24] Note that given the assumption that all income is consumed, an income tax is also equivalent to a tax on consumption expenditure.

Assumptions of the Harberger Model

The pioneering work in applying general equilibrium models to tax incidence is Arnold Harberger's [1974c]. The principal assumptions of his model are as follows:

1. *Technology.* Firms in each sector use capital and labor to produce their outputs. The technologies in each sector are such that a simultaneous doubling of both inputs leads to a doubling of output, *constant returns to scale.*[25] However, there is no requirement that the production technologies be the same in each sector. In general, the production technologies differ with respect to the ease with which capital can be substituted for labor (the **elasticity of substitution**) and the ratios in which capital and labor are employed. For example, it has been calculated that the capital-labor ratio in the production of food is about 1.3 times that used in the production of appliances.[26] The industry in which the capital-labor ratio is relatively high is characterized as **capital intensive;** the other is **labor intensive.**

2. *Behavior of Factor Suppliers.* Suppliers of both capital and labor maximize total returns. Moreover, capital and labor are perfectly mobile—they can freely move across sectors according to the wishes of their owners. Consequently, the net marginal return to capital must be the same in each sector, and so must the net marginal return to labor. Otherwise, it would be possible to reallocate capital and labor in such a way that total net returns could be increased.[27]

3. *Market Structure.* Firms are competitive and maximize profits, and all prices (including the wage rate) are perfectly flexible. Therefore, factors are fully employed, and the return paid to each factor of production is the value of its marginal product—the value to the firm of the output produced by the last unit of the input.

4. *Total Factor Supplies.* The total amounts of capital and labor available to the economy are fixed. But, as already suggested, both factors are perfectly free to move between sectors.

5. *Consumer Preferences.* All consumers have identical preferences. A tax therefore cannot generate any distributional effects by affecting people's uses of income. This assumption allows us to concentrate on the effect of taxes on the sources of income.

---

[25] It is also assumed that the production function is homogeneous, a technical condition which means that each ratio of factor prices is uniquely associated with a given ratio of capital to labor.

[26] See S. Devarajan, D. Fullerton, and R. Musgrave [1980, p. 167].

[27] To see why maximizing behavior results in an allocation in which marginal returns are equal, see the Appendix to this book.

6. ***Tax Incidence Framework.*** The framework for the analysis is differential tax incidence: we consider the substitution of one tax for another. Therefore, approximately the same amount of income is available before and after the tax, so it is unnecessary to consider how changes in aggregate income may change demand and factor prices.

Clearly, these assumptions are somewhat restrictive but they serve to simplify the analysis considerably. Later in this chapter, we consider the consequences of dropping some of them. We now employ Harberger's assumptions to analyze several different taxes.

Analysis of Various Taxes

A commodity tax (t_F).   When a tax on food is imposed, its relative price increases (although not necessarily by the amount of the tax). Consumers are thereby induced to substitute manufactures for food. Consequently, less food and more manufactures are produced. As food production falls, some of the capital and labor formerly used in food production are forced to find employment in manufacturing. Because the capital-labor ratios probably differ between the two sectors, the relative prices of capital and labor have to change for manufacturing to be willing to absorb the unemployed factors from food production. For example, assume that food is the capital-intensive sector. (U.S. agriculture does, in fact, use relatively more capital equipment—tractors, combines, and so forth—than many types of manufacturing.) Therefore, relatively large amounts of capital must be absorbed in manufacturing. The only way for all of this capital to find employment in the manufacturing sector is for the relative price of capital to fall—including capital already in use in the manufacturing sector. In the new equilibrium, then, *all* capital is relatively worse off, not just capital in the food sector. More generally, a tax on the *output* of a particular sector induces a decline in the relative price of the *input* used intensively in that sector.

To go beyond such qualitative statements, additional information is needed. The greater the elasticity of demand for food, the more dramatic will be the change in consumption from food to manufactures, which ultimately induces a greater decline in the return to capital. The greater the difference in factor proportions between food and manufactures, the greater must be the decrease in capital's price for it to be absorbed into the manufacturing sector. (If the capital-labor ratios for food and manufactured goods were identical, neither factor would suffer relative to the other.) Finally, the harder it is to substitute capital for labor in the production of manufactures, the greater the decline in the rate of return to capital needed to absorb the additional capital.

Thus, on the sources side of the budget, the food tax tends to hurt people who receive a proportionately large share of their incomes from capital. Given that all individuals are identical (assumption 5), there are no interesting effects on the uses side. However, were we to drop this assumption, then clearly those people who consumed proportionately large amounts of food would tend to bear relatively larger burdens. The total incidence of the food tax then depends on both the sources and uses sides. For example, a capitalist who eats a lot of food is worse off on both counts. On the other hand, a laborer who eats a lot of food is better off from the point of view of the sources of income, but worse off on the uses side.

An income tax (t).   As already noted, an income tax is equivalent to a set of taxes on capital and labor at the same rate. Since factor supplies are completely fixed (assumption 4), this tax cannot be shifted. It is borne in proportion to people's initial incomes. The intuition behind this result is similar to the analogous case in the partial equilibrium model; since the factors cannot "escape" the tax (by opting out of production), they bear the full burden.

A general tax on labor (t_L).   A general tax on labor is a tax on labor in *all* its uses, in the production of both food and manufactures. As a result, there are no incentives to switch labor use between sectors. Further, the assumption of fixed factor supplies implies that labor must bear the entire burden.

A partial factor tax (t_{KM}).   When capital used in the manufacturing sector *only* is taxed, there are two initial effects:

1. The price of manufactures tends to rise, which decreases the quantity demanded by consumers.
2. As capital becomes more expensive in the manufacturing sector, producers there use less capital and more labor.

Peter Mieszkowski [1969] refers to the first as the **output effect,** and the second as the **factor substitution effect.** A flow chart for tracing the implications of these two effects is presented in Figure 13.11.

The output effect is described on the left side. As its name suggests, the output effect is a consequence of reductions in the production of manufactures. When the price of manufactures increases and less is demanded, capital and labor are released from manufacturing and must find employment in the production of food. If the manufacturing sector is labor intensive, then (relatively) large amounts of labor have to be absorbed in the food sector, and the relative price of capital increases. If, on the other hand, the manufacturing sector is capital intensive, the relative price of capital falls. Thus, the output effect is ambiguous with respect to the final effect on the relative prices of capital and labor.

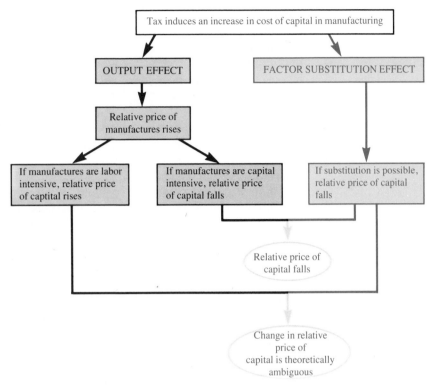

Figure 13.11
Incidence of a
partial factor tax
(t_{KM}) in a general
equilibrium model

SOURCE: Adapted from Anthony B. Atkinson and Joseph E. Stiglitz, *Lectures on Public Economics* (New York: McGraw-Hill, 1980), p. 173.

This ambiguity is not present with the factor substitution effect, as depicted in the right-hand side of Figure 13.11. As long as substitution between capital and labor is possible, an increase in the price of capital induces manufacturers to use less capital and more labor, tending to decrease the demand for capital and its relative price.

Putting the two effects together, we see that if manufacturing is capital intensive, both effects work in the same direction, and the relative price of capital must fall. But if the manufacturing sector is labor intensive, the final outcome is theoretically ambiguous. Even though the tax is levied on capital, it can make labor worse off! More generally, as long as factors are mobile between uses, a tax on a given factor in *one* sector ultimately affects the return to *both* factors in *both* sectors. Such results cannot be obtained with the partial equilibrium models discussed earlier in this chapter.

Much of the applied research on incidence in general equilibrium models has focused on the corporation income tax. Such work assumes that the two sectors are "corporate" and "noncorporate," and that the corporation income tax is an ad valorem tax on capital only on its use in the corporate sector.[28] Given the theoretical ambiguity of the effect of a partial factor tax on the demand for capital, empirical work is required to find its incidence. Using plausible values for the key parameters of the model, John Shoven [1976] estimated that capital bears the full burden of the corporation tax.

**Some
Qualifications**

Changes in the assumptions underlying the general equilibrium model can modify its implications for tax incidence in the following ways:

Differences in individuals' tastes.   By assumption 5, all consumers have the same preferences for the two goods. When they do not, tax-induced changes in the distribution of income change aggregate spending decisions and hence relative prices and incomes. Consider a general tax on labor. As noted, in the model with fixed factor supplies, this is borne entirely by laborers. However, if laborers consume different commodities from capitalists, those commodities favored by laborers face a decrease in demand. Resources are then allocated away from these commodities, and the factor used intensively in their production receives a lower return. If laborers tend to consume capital-intensive goods disproportionately, capital can end up bearing part of the burden of a general tax on labor.

More than two sectors.   The division of the economy into two sectors is an enormously useful abstraction that keeps the analysis both conceptually and mathematically tractable. Nevertheless, this assumption can lead to misleading results. For example, the noncorporate sector lumps together such diverse enterprises as agriculture, real estate, crude oil, and gas. To the extent that taxes induce substitutions *within* each of the two sectors, potentially important effects on the income distribution are ignored in the two-sector model. Shoven [1976] analyzed corporation tax incidence for the United States in a model with 12 sectors. Interestingly, he found results quite similar to those obtained in the two-sector case.[29] There is currently a good deal of research in progress to refine the computation of incidence in general equilibrium models.

Immobile factors.   By assumption 2, resources are free to flow between sectors, seeking the highest rate of return possible. However, for institutional or technological reasons, some factors may be immobile. For example, if certain land is zoned for residential use, it cannot be used in manufacturing, no matter what the rate of return. Abandoning perfect mobility

---

[28] Specifically, it is assumed that the capital is financed by selling shares of stock as opposed to borrowing. As we see in Chapter 19, this is a somewhat controversial view.

[29] However, there have also been studies in which multisector approaches yield significantly different results. See Shoven and Whalley [1984].

can dramatically affect the incidence implications of a tax. For example, earlier we showed that if factors are mobile, the incidence of a partial factor tax is ambiguous, depending on the outcome of several conflicting effects. If the factor is immobile, however, the incidence result is clear-cut: the taxed factor bears the whole burden. Intuitively, this is because the factor cannot "escape" taxation by migrating to the other sector. Note also that because the return to the taxed immobile factor falls by just the amount of the tax, the prices of capital and labor in the untaxed sectors are unchanged, as is the price of the good in the taxed sector.

Variable factor supplies.   By assumption 4, the total supplies of both factors are fixed. In the long run, however, the supplies of both capital and labor to the economy are variable. Allowing for growth can turn conclusions from the static model completely on their heads. Consider a general factor tax on capital. When the capital stock is fixed, this tax is borne entirely by the capital's owners. In the long run, however, less capital may be supplied due to the tax.[30] To the extent this occurs, the economy's capital-labor ratio decreases, and the return to labor falls. (The wage falls because labor has less capital with which to work, and hence is less productive, *ceteris paribus*.) Thus, labor can be made worse off as a result of a general tax on capital.

Because the amount of calendar time that must elapse before the long run is reached may be substantial, short-run effects should not be regarded as inconsequential. On the other hand, intelligent policy also requires consideration of the long-run consequences of taxation.

An Applied Incidence Study

In an influential study, Joseph Pechman [1985] used the theory of tax incidence as a framework to estimate how the U.S. system of federal, state, and local taxation affects the distribution of income. It should by now be clear that all incidence results depend crucially on the underlying models. Pechman examined tax burdens using several alternative models and compared the results. Some of his computations, for example, assumed that markets are competitive, and capital flows freely between sectors. Other variants assumed that capital is essentially immobile between sectors, so that, for example, corporate capital bears the entire burden of the corporation income tax.

Pechman found that in 1985, the tax system as a whole was roughly proportional over much of the income range. Hence, the tax system does not have much of an effect on the distribution of income. This is even true under the assumption that the corporation tax is borne by the owners of capital, which would be expected to generate a progressive outcome.

---

[30] However, the supply of capital does not necessarily decrease. See Chapter 17.

Note that in *all* his analyses, Pechman assumes (1) no shifting of the personal income tax and (2) general commodity taxes are borne by consumers in proportion to their consumption of the taxed items. These assumptions help simplify the problem considerably. But the theory of tax incidence suggests that they are extremely questionable, especially in the long run.

Another problem with Pechman's analysis is that it is based on individuals' annual incomes. Using some measure of lifetime income would be more appropriate and could change the results importantly. To see why, we begin by noting that a substantial amount of empirical research suggests people's consumption decisions are more closely related to some lifetime income measure than the value of income in any particular year. Just because a person's income is *temporarily* high or low in a year does not have that great an impact on consumption decisions (see Friedman [1957]).

Assume that the consumption of commodity X is proportional to lifetime income. Assume further that the supply curve for X is horizontal, so that consumers bear the entire burden of any tax on X. Then a tax on X would be proportional with respect to lifetime income. However, in any particular year, some people have incomes that are temporarily higher than their permanent values, and some lower. A person with a temporarily high income spends a relatively small proportion of his annual income on X because he does not increase his consumption of X due to the temporary increase in income. Similarly, a person with a temporarily low income devotes a relatively high proportion of her income to good X. In short, based on annual income, good X's budget share appears to fall with income, and a tax on X looks regressive. Consistent with this theory, several investigators have found that incidence results are very sensitive to whether lifetime or annual measures are employed. For example, in their analysis of Canadian data, James Davies, France St.-Hilaire, and John Whalley [1984] find that sales taxes in Canada are 27.2 percent of the *annual* incomes of the lowest income decile, and 8.5 percent in the highest decile—a decidedly regressive pattern. Using lifetime income, however, the pattern is closer to proportional, with sales taxes taking 15.0 percent of lifetime income in the lowest decile, and 12.4 percent in the highest decile. We conclude that even though empirical work of the sort done by Pechman is suggestive, the results should be viewed with some caution.

Conclusions

We began this chapter with an innocent question: "Who bears the burden of a tax?" It led us to an analysis of the sometimes complicated relationships between various markets. We have seen that price changes are the key to finding the burden of a tax, but that price changes depend on a lot of things: market structure, elasticities of supply and demand, movements of factors of production, and so on. At this stage, an obvious question is: "What do we really know?"

For taxes that may reasonably be analyzed in isolation, the answer is "Quite a bit." To do a partial equilibrium incidence analysis, the economist needs only to know the market structure and the shapes of the supply and demand curves. In cases other than a clear-cut monopoly, the competitive market paradigm has proved to be a sensible choice of market structure. Estimates of supply and demand curves can be obtained using the empirical methods discussed in Chapter 3. Incidence analysis is on firm ground.

Even in general equilibrium models, incidence analysis is equally suitable for analyzing taxes on immobile factors. Here the incidence of the tax is straightforward—it is borne entirely by the taxed factor. More generally, though, if a tax affects many markets, incidence depends on the reactions of numerous supply and demand curves for goods and inputs. The answers are correspondingly less clear.

Unfortunately, it seems that many important taxes such as the corporate tax fall into the last category. Why is this? It may be for the very reason that the incidence is hard to find. (What are the political chances of a tax that clearly hurts some important group in the population?) Complicated taxes may actually be simpler for a politician because no one is sure who actually ends up paying them.

In any case, the models in this chapter tell us exactly what information is needed to understand the incidence even of very complex taxes. To the extent that this information is currently unavailable, the models serve as a measure of our ignorance. This is not altogether undesirable. As St. Jerome noted, "It is worse still to be ignorant of your ignorance."

Summary

- Statutory incidence refers to the legal liability for a tax, while economic incidence shows the actual sacrifice of income due to the tax. Knowledge of the legal incidence usually tells us little about economic incidence.

- Economic incidence is determined by the way price changes when a tax is imposed. The incidence of a tax ultimately falls on individuals via both their sources and uses of income.

- Neither incidence nor progressiveness are unambiguous concepts. Depending on the policy being considered, it may be appropriate to examine balanced budget, differential, or absolute incidence. Similarly, progressiveness may be measured in reference to either the average or the marginal tax rate.

- Most partial equilibrium incidence studies assume that markets are competitive. In these models, tax incidence depends on the elasticities of supply and demand. The same general approach can be used to study incidence in a monopolized market. For oligopoly, however, there is no single accepted framework for tax analysis.

- Due to capitalization, the burden of future taxes may be borne by *current* owners of an inelastically supplied durable commodity such as land.

- General equilibrium incidence analysis is often conducted using a two-sector, two-factor model. In this framework are nine possible taxes. Certain combinations of these taxes are equivalent to others.

- Taxing a single factor in its use only in a particular sector changes relative factor prices, and hence, the distribution of income. The particular outcome depends on factor intensities, ease of substitution in production, mobility of factors, and elasticities of demand for outputs.

Discussion Questions

1. In January 1991, the federal unit tax on beer doubled from 16 cents to 32 cents per six-pack. Many stores advertised the approaching tax increase and urged customers to stock up in advance of the impending 16 cent price increase. Under what circumstances would a 16 cent tax increase actually lead to a 16 cent price hike for consumers?

2. Suppose that the citizens of Hungary can purchase all the oil they desire at the going international price. If the Hungarian government levies a tax on oil, who bears the burden? Illustrate your answer with a supply and demand diagram.

3. For commodity X, average cost is equal to marginal cost at every level of output. Assuming that the market for X is competitive, analyze the effects when a unit tax of u dollars is imposed. Now analyze the effects of the same tax assuming that the market for X is a monopoly. Discuss the differences.

4. Assume that the capital-labor ratios are identical in all sectors of the economy. What determines the incidence of a tax on the output of any single sector?

Selected References

Devarajan, S., D. Fullerton, and R. Musgrave. "Estimating the Distribution of Tax Burdens: A Comparison of Alternative Approaches." *Journal of Public Economics* 13 (1980), pp. 155–82.

Kotlikoff, Laurence, and Lawrence Summers. "Tax Incidence." In *Handbook of Public Economics,* *Volume II,* ed. Alan J. Auerbach and Martin Feldstein. Amsterdam: North Holland, 1987, Chapter 16.

Pechman, Joseph A. *Who Paid the Taxes, 1966–85?* Washington, D.C.: Brookings Institution, 1985.

Taxation and Efficiency

Waste always makes me angry.

RHETT BUTLER
in *Gone With the Wind*

T
axes impose a cost on the taxpayer. It is tempting to view the cost as simply the amount of money that individuals hand over to the tax collector. However, an example indicates that this is just part of the story.

Consider Breyer Dazs, a citizen who typically consumes 10 ice cream cones each week, at a price of 80 cents per cone. The government levies a 25 percent tax on his consumption of ice cream cones, so that Dazs now faces a price of $1.[1] In response to the price hike, Dazs reduces his ice cream cone consumption to zero, and he spends the $8 per week on other goods and services. Obviously, because Dazs consumes no ice cream cones, the ice cream tax yields zero revenue. Do we want to say that Dazs is unaffected by the tax? The answer is no. Dazs is worse off because the tax has induced him to consume a less desirable bundle of goods than previously. We know that the after-tax bundle is less desirable because, prior to tax, Dazs had the option of consuming no ice cream cones. Since he chose to buy 10 cones weekly, this must have been preferred to spending the money on other items. Thus, despite the fact that the tax raised zero revenue, it made Dazs worse off.

This example is a bit extreme. Normally, we expect that an increase in price diminishes the quantity demanded but does not drive it all the way to zero. Nevertheless, the basic result holds: because a tax distorts

---

[1] As emphasized in Chapter 13, the price paid by the consumer generally does not rise by the full amount of the tax. This assumption, which is strictly correct only if the supply curve is horizontal, is made here only for convenience.

economic decisions, it brings about an **excess burden**—a loss of welfare above and beyond the tax revenues collected. Excess burden is sometimes referred to as *welfare cost* or *deadweight loss*. In this chapter we discuss the theory and measurement of excess burden, and explain why it is an important concept for evaluating actual tax systems.

Excess Burden

Ruth has a fixed income of I dollars, which she spends on only two commodities: barley and corn. The price per pound of barley is P_b and the price per pound of corn is P_c. There are no taxes or "distortions" such as externalities or monopoly in the economy, so the prices of the goods reflect their social marginal costs. For convenience, these social marginal costs are assumed to be constant with respect to output. In Figure 14.1, Ruth's consumption of barley is measured on the horizontal axis and her consumption of corn on the vertical. Her budget constraint is the line AD, which has slope $-P_b/P_c$ and horizontal intercept I/P_b.[2] Assuming that Ruth maximizes a utility function characterized by standard indifference curves (convex to the origin), she chooses a point like E_1 on indifference curve i, where she consumes B_1 pounds of barley and C_1 pounds of corn.

Now suppose that the government levies a tax at a percentage rate of t_b on barley so that the price Ruth faces becomes $(1 + t_b)P_b$. (The before-tax price is unchanged because of our assumption of constant marginal social costs.) Imposition of the tax changes Ruth's budget constraint. It now has a slope of $-[(1 + t_b)P_b/P_c]$ and horizontal intercept $I/[(1 + t_b)P_b]$. This is represented in Figure 14.1 as line AF. (Because the price of corn is still P_c, lines AF and AD have the same vertical intercept.)

Note that for any given consumption level of barley, the vertical distance between AD and AF shows Ruth's tax payments measured in corn. To see this, consider an arbitrary quantity of barley $\tilde{B}$ on the horizontal axis. Before the tax was imposed, Ruth could have both $\tilde{B}$ pounds of barley and $\tilde{C}$ pounds of corn. After the tax, however, if she consumed $\tilde{B}$ pounds of barley, the most corn she could afford would be $\hat{C}$ pounds. The difference (distance) between $\tilde{C}$ and $\hat{C}$ must therefore represent the amount of tax collected by the government measured in pounds of corn. If we choose, we can convert tax receipts to dollars by multiplying the distance $\tilde{C}\hat{C}$ by the price per pound of corn, P_c. For convenience, we can choose to measure corn in units such that $P_c = 1$. In this case, the distance $\tilde{C}\hat{C}$ measures tax receipts in corn *or* dollars.

So far, we have not indicated which point Ruth chooses on her new budget constraint, AF. Figure 14.2 shows that her most preferred bundle is at E_2 on indifference curve ii, where her consumption of barley is B_2,

---

[2] The construction of budget constraints and the interpretation of their slopes and intercepts are discussed in the Appendix at the end of the book.

Figure 14.1
Effect of a tax on
the budget
constraint

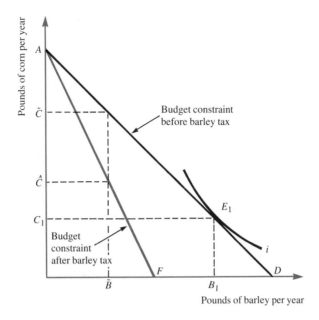

Figure 14.2
Effect of a tax on
the consumption
bundle

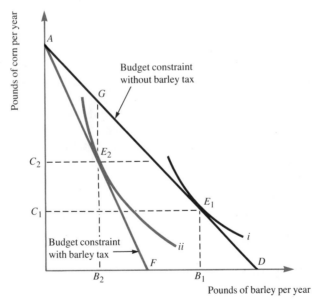

her consumption of corn is C_2, and her tax bill is the associated vertical distance between AD and AF, GE_2. Note that if the tax authorities had erroneously assumed that Ruth would maintain her barley consumption at B_1 after the tax, they would have estimated tax receipts greater than the amount actually collected. In general, failure to account for the fact that taxes affect economic behavior leads to incorrect revenue predictions.

Clearly, Ruth is worse off at E_2 than she was at E_1. However, *any* tax would have put her on a lower indifference curve.[3] The important question is whether the barley tax inflicts on Ruth a greater utility loss than is necessary to raise revenue GE_2. Alternatively, is there some other way of raising revenue GE_2 that would cause a smaller utility loss to Ruth? If so, the barley tax has an excess burden.

To investigate this issue, we need to find a dollar equivalent of the loss that Ruth suffers by having to move from indifference curve *i* to *ii*. One way to measure this is the **equivalent variation**—the amount of income we would have to take away from Ruth (before the barley tax was levied) to induce her to move from *i* and *ii*. Essentially, the equivalent variation measures the loss inflicted by the tax as the size of the reduction in income that would induce the same decrease in utility as the tax.

To depict the equivalent variation graphically, recall that taking away income from an individual is represented simply by a parallel movement inward of her budget line. Hence, to find the equivalent variation, all we have to do is shift AD inward, until it is tangent to indifference curve *ii*. The amount by which we have to shift AD is the equivalent variation. In Figure 14.3, budget line HI is parallel to AD and tangent to indifference curve *ii*. Hence, the vertical distance between AD and HI, ME_3, is the equivalent variation. Ruth is indifferent between losing this much income and facing the barley tax.

Note that the equivalent variation ME_3 exceeds the barley tax revenues of GE_2. To see why, just observe that ME_3 equals GN, because both measure the distance between the parallel lines AD and HI. Hence, ME_3 exceeds GE_2 by distance E_2N. This is really quite a remarkable result. It means that the barley tax makes Ruth worse off by an amount that actually exceeds the revenues it generates. In Figure 14.3, the amount by which the loss in welfare (measured by the equivalent variation) exceeds the taxes collected—the excess burden—is distance E_2N.[4]

Does *every* tax entail an excess burden? Define a **lump sum tax** as a certain amount that must be paid regardless of the taxpayer's behavior. If the government levies a $100 lump sum tax on Ruth, there is nothing she can do to avoid paying the $100, other than to leave the country or die. In contrast, the barley tax is not a lump sum tax, because the revenue yield ultimately depends on Ruth's barley consumption.

Let us analyze a lump sum tax that leaves Ruth as well off as the barley tax. To begin, we must sketch the associated budget line. It must have two characteristics. First, it must be parallel to AD. (Because a lump

---

[3] This ignores benefits that might be obtained from the expenditures financed by the tax.

[4] The alternative ways of defining excess burden are all very similar conceptually. See Alan Auerbach and Harvey Rosen [1980].

Figure 14.3

Excess burden of
the barley tax

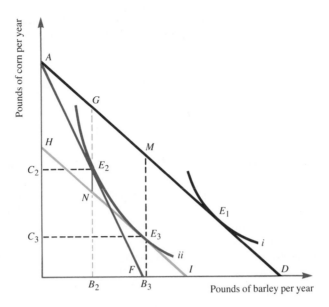

sum tax simply takes away money from Ruth, it does not change the
relative prices of barley and corn; two budget lines embodying the same
price ratio must be parallel.) Second, because of the stipulation that Ruth
attain the same utility level as under the barley tax, the budget line must
be tangent to indifference curve *ii*.

Budget line *HI* in Figure 14.3, which is tangent to indifference curve *ii*
at point E_3, satisfies both these criteria. If confronted with this budget
line, Ruth would consume B_3 pounds of barley and C_3 pounds of corn.
The revenue yield of the lump sum tax is the vertical distance between E_3
and the before-tax budget constraint, or distance ME_3. But we showed
earlier that ME_3 is also the equivalent variation of the move from indifference curve *i* to *ii*. This comes as no surprise, since a lump sum tax is just
a parallel shift of the budget line. Because the revenue yield of a lump
sum tax equals its equivalent variation, *a lump sum tax has no excess
burden*.

In short, a lump sum tax that leaves Ruth on the *same indifference
curve* as the barley tax generates more revenue for the government. Alternatively, if we compared a lump sum tax and a barley tax that raised the
same revenue, the lump sum tax would leave Ruth on a higher indifference curve.

The skeptical reader may suspect that this result is merely an artifact
of the particular way the indifference curves are drawn in Figure 14.3.
This is not the case. It can be shown that as long as the indifference
curves have the usual shape, a tax that changes relative prices generates

an excess burden.[5] Alternatively, a tax that changes relative prices is inefficient in the sense that it lowers individual utility more than is necessary to raise a given amount of revenue.

Excess Burden: Questions and Answers

The previous section's discussion of excess burden raises some important questions.

If lump sum taxes are so efficient, why aren't they widely used?   Lump sum taxation is an unattractive policy tool for several reasons. Suppose the government announced that every person's tax liability was $2,000 per year. This is a lump sum tax, but most people would consider it unfair for everyone to pay the same tax regardless of their economic circumstances. In 1990, the government of British Prime Minister Margaret Thatcher implemented a tax that in some ways resembled a lump sum tax. The property tax that had financed local government was replaced by a head tax; in each local jurisdiction the amount depended on that jurisdiction's per capita revenue needs. The tax was lump sum to the extent that a person's tax liability did not vary with the amount of income earned or property owned; it did vary, however, with a person's choice of where to live. The perceived unfairness of that tax was one of the factors that led to Mrs. Thatcher's downfall in 1990, and it was repealed in 1991 by her successor, John Major.

As a way of producing more equitable results, one might consider making people pay different lump sum taxes based on their incomes. A rich person might be required to pay $20,000 annually, independent of his or her economic decisions, while a poor person would pay only $500. The problem with this proposal is that people entering the work force would soon realize that their eventual tax burden depended on their incomes. They would then adjust their work and savings decisions accordingly. In short, because the amount of income individuals earn, and hence their tax liabilities, are at least in part under their control, the income-based tax is not a lump sum tax.

Ultimately, to achieve an equitable system of lump sum taxes, it would be necessary to base the tax on some underlying "ability" characteristic that measured individuals' *potential* to earn income. In this way, high- and low-potential people could be taxed differently. Because the base is potential, an individual's tax burden would not depend on behavior. Even if such an ability measure existed, however, it could not possibly be observed by the taxing authority. Thus, individual lump sum taxes are best viewed as standards of efficiency, but not as major policy options in a modern economy.

[5] For a proof see Peter Diamond and Daniel McFadden [1974]. For the more general case in which marginal social costs are not constant, the analogous result is that any tax that creates an inequality between the ratio of prices and the ratio of marginal social costs generates an excess burden.

Are there any results from welfare economics that would help us understand why excess burdens arise?   Recall from Chapter 4 that a necessary condition for a Pareto efficient allocation of resources is that the marginal rate of substitution of barley for corn in consumption (MRS_{bc}) equals the marginal rate of transformation of barley for corn in production (MRT_{bc}). Under the barley tax, consumers face a price of barley of $(1 + t_b)P_b$. Therefore, they set

$$MRS_{bc} = \frac{(1 + t_b)P_b}{P_c} \tag{14.1}$$

Equation (14.1) is the algebraic representation of the equilibrium point E_2 in Figure 14.3.

Producers make their decisions by setting the marginal rate of transformation equal to the ratio of the prices *they receive*. Even though Ruth pays $(1 + t_b)P_b$ per pound of barley, the barley producers receive only P_b—the difference goes to the tax collector. Hence, profit-maximizing producers set

$$MRT_{bc} = \frac{P_b}{P_c} \tag{14.2}$$

Clearly, as long as t_b is not zero, MRS_{bc} exceeds MRT_{bc}, and the necessary condition for an efficient allocation of resources is violated.

Intuitively, when MRS_{bc} is greater than MRT_{bc}, the marginal utility of substituting barley consumption for corn consumption exceeds the change in production costs necessary to do so. Thus, utility would be raised if such an adjustment were made. However, in the presence of the barley tax there is no *financial* incentive to do so. The excess burden is just a measure of the utility loss. The loss arises because the barley tax creates a disparity between what the consumer pays and what the producer receives (i.e., a tax wedge). In contrast, under a lump sum tax, the price ratios faced by consumers and producers are equal. There is no wedge, so the necessary conditions for Pareto efficiency are satisfied.

Does an income tax entail an excess burden?   Figure 14.3 showed the imposition of a lump sum tax as a downward parallel movement from *AD* to *HI*. This movement could just as well have arisen via a tax that took some proportion of Ruth's income. Like the lump sum tax, an income reduction moves the intercepts of the budget constraint closer to the origin but leaves its slope unchanged. Perhaps, then, lump sum taxation and income taxation are equivalent. In fact, if income were fixed, an income tax *would* be a lump sum tax. However, once we explicitly consider choices with respect to income, it becomes clear that an income tax is *not* generally equivalent to a lump sum tax.

Think of Ruth as consuming *three* commodities, barley, corn, and leisure time, *l*. (We could draw indifference surfaces in three dimensions, but this is not essential for our argument.) Ruth gives up leisure (supplies labor) to earn income which is spent on barley and corn. In the production sector, Ruth's leisure is an input to the production of the two goods. The rate at which her leisure time can be transformed into barley is MRT_{lb}, and into corn MRT_{lc}. Just as a utility maximizing individual sets the marginal rate of substitution between two commodities equal to their price ratio, the *MRS* between leisure and a given commodity is set equal to the ratio of the wage (the price of leisure) and the price of that commodity.

Again appealing to the theory of welfare economics, the necessary conditions for a Pareto efficient allocation of resources in this three-commodity case are

$$MRS_{lb} = MRT_{lb}$$

$$MRS_{lc} = MRT_{lc}$$

$$MRS_{bc} = MRT_{bc}$$

A proportional income tax, which is equivalent to a tax at the same rate on barley and corn, leaves the third equality unchanged, because producers and consumers still face the same *relative* prices for barley and corn. However, it introduces a tax wedge in the first two conditions. To see why, suppose that Ruth's employer pays her a before-tax wage of *w*, and the income tax rate is *t*. Ruth's decisions depend on her after-tax wage, $(1 - t)w$. Hence, she sets $MRS_{lb} = (1 - t)w/P_b$. On the other hand, the producer's decisions are based on the wage rate he or she pays, the before-tax wage, *w*. Hence, the producer sets $MRT_{lb} = w/P_b$. Consequently, $MRS_{lb} \neq MRT_{lb}$. Similarly, $MRS_{lc} \neq MRT_{lc}$. In contrast, a lump sum tax leaves all three equalities intact. Thus, income and lump sum taxation are generally not equivalent.

The fact that the income tax breaks up two equalities while taxes on barley and corn at different rates break up all three is in itself irrelevant for determining which system is more efficient. Once *any* of the equalities fails to hold, a loss of efficiency results, and the sizes of the welfare losses cannot be compared merely by counting wedges. Rather, the excess burdens associated with each tax regime must be computed and then compared. There is no presumption that income taxation is more efficient than a system of commodity taxes at different rates—differential commodity taxation. It *may* be true, but this is an empirical question that cannot be answered on the basis of theory alone.[6]

---

[6] It turns out that income taxation is necessarily more efficient than differential commodity taxation only when the underlying structure of consumer preferences has a very particular property. See Agnar Sandmo [1976].

Figure 14.4

Excess burden of a
tax on a commodity
whose ordinary
demand curve is
perfectly inelastic

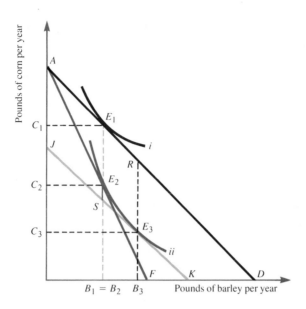

**If the demand for a commodity does not change when it is taxed, does this
mean that there is no excess burden?**   The intuition behind excess burden
is that it results from distorted decisions. If there is no change in the
demand for the good being taxed, one might conclude that there is no
excess burden. This conjecture is examined in Figure 14.4. Naomi, the
individual under consideration, begins with the same income as Ruth and
faces the same prices and taxes. Hence, her initial budget constraint is
AD, and after the barley tax, it is AF. However, as was not true in Ruth's
case, the quantity of barley demanded by Naomi is unchanged by the
barley tax; that is, $B_1 = B_2$. The barley tax revenues are E_1E_2. Is there an
excess burden? The equivalent variation of the barley tax is RE_3. This
exceeds the barley tax revenues of E_1E_2 by E_2S. Hence, even though
Naomi's barley consumption is unchanged by the barley tax, it still creates an excess burden of E_2S.

The explanation of this paradox begins with the observation that even
though Naomi's barley consumption doesn't change, her corn consumption does (from C_1 to C_2). When the barley tax changes the relative price,
the marginal rate of substitution is affected, and the composition of the
commodity *bundle* is distorted.

A more rigorous explanation requires that we distinguish between
two types of responses to the barley tax. The movement from E_1 to E_2 is
the **uncompensated response.** It shows how consumption changes because
of the tax and incorporates effects due to both losing income and the tax-
induced change in relative prices. Now, we can imagine decomposing the
move from E_1 to E_2 into a move from E_1 to E_3, and then from E_3 to E_2. The
movement from E_1 to E_3 shows the effect on consumption of a lump sum

tax. This change, called the **income effect,** is due solely to the loss of income because relative prices are unaffected. In effect, then, the movement from E_3 to E_2 is strictly due to the change in relative prices. It is generated by giving Naomi enough income to maintain her utility level even as barley's price rises due to the tax. Because Naomi is being compensated for the rising price of barley with additional income, the movement from E_3 to E_2 is called the **compensated response.** The compensated response is sometimes referred to as the **substitution effect.**[7]

The compensated response is the important one for calculating excess burden. Why? By construction, the computation of excess burden involves comparison of tax collections at points E_2 and E_3 on indifference curve *ii*. But the movement from E_3 to E_2 along indifference curve *ii* is precisely the compensated response. Note also that it is only in moving from E_3 to E_2 that the marginal rate of substitution is affected. As shown earlier, this change violates the necessary conditions for a Pareto efficient allocation of commodities.

An ordinary demand curve depicts the uncompensated change in the quantity of a commodity demanded when price changes. A **compensated demand curve** shows how the quantity demanded changes when price changes *and* simultaneously income is compensated so that the individual's commodity bundle stays on the same indifference curve. A way of summarizing this discussion is to say that excess burden depends on movements along the compensated rather than the ordinary demand curve.

Although these observations may seem like theoretical nit-picking, they are actually quite important. In many policy discussions, attention is focused on whether or not a given tax influences observed behavior, with the assumption that if it does not, there is necessarily no serious efficiency problem. For example, some would argue that if hours of work do not change when an income tax is imposed, then the tax has no adverse efficiency consequences. We have shown that such a notion is fallacious. A substantial excess burden may be incurred even if the uncompensated response of the taxed commodity is zero.

Excess Burden Measurement with Demand Curves	The concept of excess burden can be reinterpreted using (compensated) demand curves.[8] This interpretation relies heavily on the notion of consumer surplus—the difference between what people would be *willing* to pay for a commodity and the amount they actually have to pay. As shown in the Appendix to Chapter 4, consumer surplus is measured by the area between the demand curve and the horizontal line at the market price.

---

[7] See the Appendix to the book for further discussion of income and substitution effects.

[8] This discussion is based on Arnold Harberger [1974a]. Compensated demand curves are explained in the Appendix at the end of the book.

Figure 14.5

Excess burden of a commodity tax

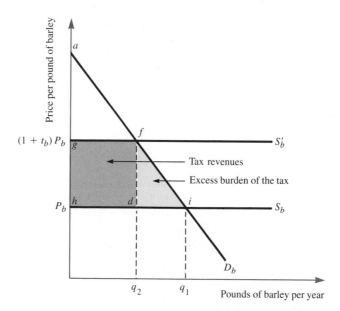

Assume that the compensated demand curve for barley can be represented by the straight line D_b in Figure 14.5. For convenience, we continue to assume that the social marginal cost of barley is constant at P_b, so that the supply curve is the horizontal line marked S_b.[9] In equilibrium, q_1 pounds of barley are consumed. Consumer surplus, the area between the price and the demand curve, is *aih*.

Again suppose that a tax at percentage rate t_b is levied on barley, so the new price, $(1 + t_b)P_b$, is associated with supply curve S_b'. Supply and demand now intersect at output q_2. Observe the following characteristics of the new equilibrium:

1. Consumer surplus is reduced to the area between the demand curve and S_b', *agf*.

2. The revenue yield of the barley tax is rectangle *gfdh*. This is because tax revenues are equal to the product of the number of units purchased *(hd)* and the tax paid on each unit: $(1 + t_b)P_b - P_b = gh$. But *hd* and *gh* are just the base and height, respectively, of rectangle *gfdh,* and hence their product is its area.

3. The sum of post-tax consumer surplus and tax revenues collected (area *hafd*) is less than the original consumer surplus *(ahi)* by area *fid*. In effect, even if we returned the tax revenues to barley consumers as a lump sum, they would still be worse off by triangle *fid*. The triangle, then, is the excess burden of the tax.

---

[9] The analysis is easily generalized to the case when the supply curve slopes upward. See footnote 10.

This analysis provides a convenient framework for computing an actual dollar measure of excess burden. The area of triangle *fid* is one-half the product of its base (the tax-induced change in the quantity of barley) and height (the tax per pound). Some simple algebra leads to the conclusion that this product can be written:

$$\tfrac{1}{2}\eta P_b q_1 t_b^2 \tag{14.3}$$

where η is the absolute value of the compensated price elasticity of demand for barley.[10] (A proof is provided in Appendix A at the end of this chapter.)

A high (absolute) value of η indicates that the compensated quantity demanded is quite sensitive to changes in price. Thus, the presence of η in Equation (14.3) makes intuitive sense—the more the tax distorts the (compensated) consumption decision, the higher the excess burden. $P_b \times q_1$ is the total revenue expended on barley initially. Its inclusion in the formula shows that the greater the initial expenditure on the taxed commodity, the greater the excess burden.

Finally, the presence of t_b^2 suggests that as the tax rate increases, excess burden goes up with its square. Doubling a tax quadruples its excess burden, other things being the same. Because excess burden increases with the square of the tax rate, the *marginal* excess burden from raising one more dollar of revenue exceeds the *average* excess burden. That is, the incremental excess burden of raising one *more* dollar of revenue exceeds the ratio of total excess burden to total revenues. This fact has important implications for cost-benefit analysis. Suppose, for example, that the average excess burden per dollar of tax revenue is 18 cents, but the marginal excess burden per additional dollar of tax revenue is 38 cents. (These are plausible figures according to calculations by Dale Jorgenson and Kun-Young Yun [1990].) The social cost of each dollar raised for a given public project is the dollar *plus* the incremental excess burden of 38 cents. Thus, a public project must produce marginal benefits of more than $1.38 per dollar of explicit cost if it is to improve welfare.

---

[10] The formula holds strictly only for an infinitesimally small tax levied in the absence of any other distortions. Therefore, it should be viewed only as an approximation. When the supply curve is upward sloping rather than horizontal, the excess-burden triangle contains some producer surplus as well as consumer surplus. The formula for excess burden then depends on the elasticity of supply as well as the elasticity of demand. Robert Bishop [1968] shows that in this case, the excess burden is

$$\tfrac{1}{2}\frac{P_b q}{\dfrac{1}{\eta}+\dfrac{1}{\varepsilon}}\, t_b^2$$

where ε is the elasticity of supply. Note that as ε approaches infinity, this expression collapses to Equation (14.3). This is because an ε of infinity corresponds to a horizontal supply curve as in Figure 14.5.

Preexisting Distortions

This analysis has assumed no distortions in the economy other than the tax under consideration. In reality, when a new tax is introduced, there are already other distortions: monopolies, externalities, and preexisting taxes. In such a situation, the analysis of excess burden becomes more complicated.

Suppose that consumers regard gin and rum as substitutes. Suppose further that rum is currently being taxed, creating an excess burden "triangle" similar to that depicted in Figure 14.5. Now the government decides to impose a tax on gin. What is the excess burden of the gin tax? In the gin market, the gin tax creates a wedge between what gin consumers pay and gin producers receive. As usual, this creates an excess burden. But the story is not over. If gin and rum are substitutes, the rise in the consumers' price of gin induced by the gin tax increases the demand for rum. As a consequence, the quantity of rum demanded increases. Now, because rum was taxed under the status quo, "too little" of it was being consumed. The increase in rum consumption induced by the gin tax helps move rum consumption back toward its efficient level. There is thus an efficiency gain in the rum market that helps offset the excess burden imposed in the gin market. In theory, the gin tax could actually lower the overall excess burden. (A more rigorous graphical discussion of this phenomenon is contained in Appendix B at the end of this chapter.)

We have shown, then, that the efficiency impact of a given tax or subsidy cannot be considered in isolation. To the extent that there are other markets with distortions, and the goods in these markets are related (either substitutes or complements), then the overall efficiency impact depends on what is going on in all the markets. To compute the overall efficiency impact of a set of taxes and subsidies, it is generally incorrect to calculate separately the excess burdens in each market and then add them up. The aggregate efficiency loss is not equal to the "sum of its parts."

This result can be quite discomfiting because strictly speaking, it means that *every* market in the economy must be studied to assess the efficiency implications of *any* tax or subsidy. In most cases, practitioners simply assume that the amount of interrelatedness between the market of their concern and other markets is sufficiently small that cross-effects can safely be ignored.[11] Although this is clearly a convenient assumption, its reasonableness must be evaluated in each particular case.

The Excess Burden of a Subsidy

Commodity subsidies are important components of the fiscal systems of many countries. In effect, a subsidy is just a negative tax, and like a tax, it is associated with an excess burden. To illustrate the calculation of the

---

[11] There are exceptions. See, for example, Charles Ballard, John Shoven, and John Whalley [1985b].

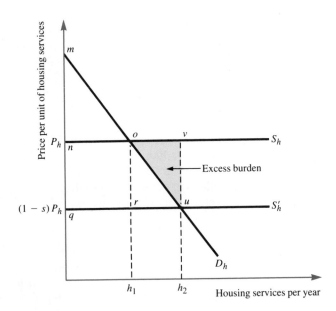

Figure 14.6

Excess burden of a housing subsidy

excess burden of a subsidy, we consider the subsidy for owner-occupied housing provided by the federal government via certain provisions of the personal income tax. (See Chapter 17 for details of the law.)

Assume that the demand for owner-occupied housing services is the straight line D_h in Figure 14.6. Supply is horizontal at price P_h, which measures the marginal social cost of producing housing services. Behind the horizontal supply curve, then, is the assumption that the marginal social cost is constant. Initially, the equilibrium quantity is h_1. Now suppose that the government provides a subsidy of s percent to housing producers. The new price for housing services is then $(1 - s)P_h$ and the associated supply curve is S_h'. The subsidy increases the quantity of housing services consumed to h_2. If the purpose of the subsidy was to increase housing consumption, then it has succeeded. But if its goal was to maximize social welfare, is it an appropriate policy?

Prior to the subsidy, consumer surplus was area *mno*. After the subsidy, consumer surplus is *mqu*. The benefit to housing consumers is the increase in their surplus, area *nouq*. But at what cost is this benefit obtained? The cost of the subsidy program is the quantity of housing services consumed, *qu*, times the subsidy per unit, *nq*, or rectangle *nvuq*.[12] Thus, the cost of the subsidy actually exceeds the benefit—there is an excess burden equal to the difference between areas *nvuq* and *nouq*, which is the shaded area *ovu*.

---

[12] It is assumed that the funds for the subsidy are raised with lump sum taxes. As noted earlier, if this is not the case, the cost is even greater because raising the funds to provide the subsidy creates another excess burden. In addition, this analysis ignores any administrative costs of the program. For further details, see David Laidler [1969].

Figure 14.7
Excess burden of a
tax on labor

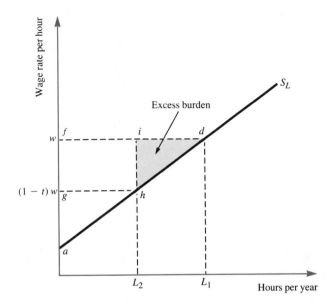

How can a "good thing" such as a subsidy be inefficient? Recall that any point on the demand curve for housing services measures how much people value that particular level of consumption. To the right of h_1, although individuals do derive utility from consuming more housing, its value is less than P_h, the marginal cost to society of providing it. In other words, the subsidy induces people to consume housing services that are valued at less than their cost—hence, the inefficiency.[13]

A very important policy implication follows from this analysis. It is often proposed that some group be helped by subsidizing a commodity that its members tend to consume heavily. We have shown that this is an inefficient way to aid people. Less money could raise them to the same utility level if it were given to them as a direct grant. In Figure 14.6, people would be indifferent between a housing subsidy program costing *nvuq* and a direct grant of *nouq*, even though the subsidy program costs the government more money.[14] This is one of the reasons many economists prefer direct income transfers to commodity subsidies.

**The Excess
Burden of
Income Taxation**

The theory of excess burden that we have developed for taxing commodities applies just as well to factors of production. In Figure 14.7, Jacob's hours of work are plotted on the horizontal axis and his hourly wage on

---

[13] Another way to look at this is that after the subsidy, the marginal rate of substitution in consumption depends on $(1 - s)P_h$, while the marginal rate of transformation in production depends on P_h. Hence, the marginal rate of transformation is not equal to the marginal rate of substitution, and the allocation of resources cannot be efficient. Of course, if there were a positive externality associated with housing, a subsidy might enhance efficiency. See Chapter 6 under "Positive Externalities."

[14] This result is very similar to that obtained when we examined in-kind subsidy programs in Chapter 8. That chapter also discusses why commodity subsidies nevertheless remain politically popular.

American Way of Tax*

Humorist Russell Baker never uses the term excess burden *in the column reproduced below. Nevertheless, he gives an excellent description of the phenomenon.*

NEW YORK—The tax man was very cross about Figg. Figg's way of life did not conform to the way of life several governments wanted Figg to pursue. Nothing inflamed the tax man more than insolent and capricious disdain for governmental desires. He summoned Figg to the temple of taxation.

"What's the idea of living in a rental apartment over a delicatessen in the city, Figg?" he inquired. Figg explained that he liked urban life. In that case, said the tax man, he was raising Figg's city sales and income taxes. "If you want them cut, you'll have to move out to the suburbs," he said.

To satisfy his local government, Figg gave up the city and rented a suburban house. The tax man summoned him back to the temple.

"Figg," he said, "you have made me sore wroth with your way of life. Therefore, I am going to soak you for more federal income taxes." And he squeezed Figg until beads of blood popped out along the seams of Figg's wallet.

"Mercy, good tax man," Figg gasped. "Tell me how to live so that I may please my government, and I shall obey."

The tax man told Figg to quit renting and buy a house. The government wanted everyone to accept large mortgage loans from bankers. If Figg complied, it would cut his taxes.

Figg bought a house, which he did not want, in a suburb where he did not want to live, and he invited his friends and relatives to attend a party celebrating his surrender to a way of life that pleased his government.

The tax man was so furious that he showed up at the party with bloodshot eyes. "I have had enough of this, Figg," he declared. "Your government doesn't want you entertaining

the vertical. Jacob's compensated labor supply curve, which shows the smallest wage that would be required to induce him to work each additional hour, is labeled S_L. Initially, Jacob's wage is w and the associated hours of work L_1. In the same way that consumer surplus is measured as the area between the demand curve and the market price, worker surplus is the area between the supply curve and the market wage rate. When the wage is w, Jacob's surplus is therefore area *adf*.

Now assume that an income tax at a rate t is imposed. The after-tax wage is then $(1 - t)w$, and given supply curve S_L, the quantity of labor supplied falls to L_2 hours. Jacob's surplus after the tax is *agh*, and the government collects revenues equal to *fihg*. The excess burden due to the tax-induced distortion of the work choice is the amount by which Jacob's

friends and relatives. This will cost you plenty.''

Figg immediately threw out all his friends and relatives, then asked the tax man what sort of people his government wished him to entertain. ''Business associates,'' said the tax man. ''Entertain plenty of business associates, and I shall cut your taxes.''

To make the tax man and his government happy, Figg began entertaining people he didn't like in the house he didn't want in the suburb where he didn't want to live.

Then was the tax man enraged indeed. ''Figg,'' he thundered, ''I will not cut your taxes for entertaining straw bosses, truck drivers, and pothole fillers.''

''Why not?'' said Figg. ''These are the people I associate with in my business.''

''Which is what?'' asked the tax man.

''Earning my pay by the sweat of my brow,'' said Figg.

''Your government is not going to bribe you for performing salaried labor,'' said the tax man. ''Don't you know, you imbecile, that tax rates on salaried income are higher than on any other kind?''

And he taxed the sweat of Figg's brow at a rate that drew exquisite shrieks of agony from Figg and little cries of joy from Washington, which already had more sweated brows than it needed to sustain the federally approved way of life.

''Get into business, or minerals, or international oil,'' warned the tax man, ''or I shall make your taxes as the taxes of 10.''

Figg went into business, which he hated, and entertained people he didn't like in the house he didn't want in the suburb where he did not want to live.

At length the tax man summoned Figg for an angry lecture. He demanded to know why Figg had not bought a new plastic factory to replace his old metal and wooden plant. ''I hate plastic,'' said Figg. ''Your government is sick and tired of metal, wood, and everything else that smacks of the real stuff, Figg,'' roared the tax man, seizing Figg's purse. ''Your depreciation is all used up.''

There was nothing for Figg to do but go to plastic, and the tax man rewarded him with a brand new depreciation schedule plus an investment credit deduction from the bottom line.

* By Russell Baker, *International Herald Tribune*, April 13, 1977, page 14. © 1977 by The New York Times Company. Reprinted by permission.

loss of welfare *(fdhg)* exceeds the tax collected: area *hid (=fdhg − fihg)*. In analogy to Equation (14.3), area *hid* is approximately

$$\tfrac{1}{2}\varepsilon w L_1 t^2 \tag{14.4}$$

where ε is the compensated elasticity of hours of work with respect to the wage.

Recent calculations suggest that for an American married male, a reasonable value for ε is about 0.2.[15] For illustrative purposes, suppose

[15] See Edgar Browning [1985], who provides an edifying discussion of the pitfalls involved in the calculation of excess burdens.

that prior to taxation, Jacob works 2,000 hours per year at a wage of $20 per hour. A tax on earnings of 40 percent is then imposed. Substituting these figures into Equation (14.4), the excess burden of the tax is about $640 annually. One way to put this figure into perspective is to note that it is approximately 4 percent of tax revenues. Thus, on average, each dollar of tax collected creates an excess burden of 4 cents.

Of course, wage rates, tax rates, and elasticities vary across members of the population, so different people are subject to different excess burdens. Moreover, the excess burden of taxing labor also depends on tax rates levied on other factors of production. Jorgenson and Yun [1990] estimated that for plausible values of the relevant elasticities, the excess burden of labor income taxation in the United States is about 30 percent of the revenues raised. As we show in Chapter 17, however, there is considerable uncertainty about the values of some of the key elasticities. Hence, this particular estimate must be regarded cautiously. Still, it probably provides a good sense of the magnitudes involved.

Differential Taxation of Inputs

In the income tax example just discussed, we assumed that labor income was taxed at the same rate regardless of the market to which the labor was supplied.[16] But sometimes the tax levied on a factor of production depends on where it is employed. For instance, because of the corporate income tax, some argue that capital employed in the corporate sector faces a higher rate than capital in the noncorporate sector. Another example is the differential taxation of labor in the household and market sectors. If an individual does housework, valuable services are produced but not taxed.[17] On the other hand, if the same individual works in the market, the services are subject to the income and payroll taxes. The fact that labor is taxed in one sector and untaxed in another distorts people's decisions on how much time to spend on each. The efficiency cost can be measured using a model developed by Harberger [1974b]. In Figure 14.8A, hours of work in the household sector are measured on the horizontal axis, and dollars are measured on the vertical. Now define the **value of the marginal product** *(VMP)* of hours worked in the household sector as the dollar value of the *additional* output produced for each hour worked. The schedule VMP_x in Figure 14.8A represents the value of the marginal product of household work. It is drawn sloping downward,

---

[16] This section can be skipped without loss of continuity.

[17] The value of housework was expressed nicely by a biblical author who wrote during an era in which it was assumed that homes were managed only by females. In Proverbs 31, he discusses in detail the many tasks performed by the woman who "looketh well to the ways of her household" (*v.* 27). His general conclusion is that "her price is far above rubies" (*v.* 10). Unfortunately, price data on rubies during the biblical era are unavailable.

Figure 14.8

The allocation of time between housework and market work

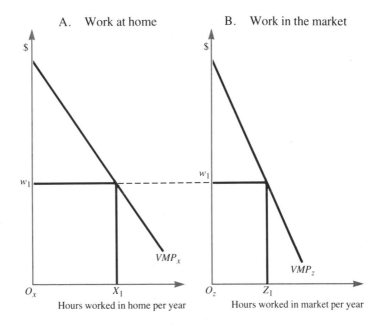

A.   Work at home   B.   Work in the market

Hours worked in home per year   *Hours worked in market per year*

reflecting the reasonable assumption that as more hours are spent in the home, the incremental value of those hours decreases. This is just an example of the law of diminishing marginal returns.

Similarly, schedule VMP_z in Figure 14.8B shows the value of the marginal product of hours worked in the market sector. Although we also expect VMP_z to slope downward, there is no reason to expect that its shape should be identical to that of VMP_x.

For simplicity, assume that the total number of hours of work available is fixed, so that the only question is how to divide the work between the market and household sectors. Assume further that individuals allocate their time between housework and market work to maximize their total incomes. As a result of this allocation process, the value of the marginal product of labor is the same in both sectors. If it were not, it would be possible for people to reallocate labor between the sectors to increase their incomes.[18] In Figure 14.8, the initial equilibrium occurs where X_1 hours are devoted to housework and Z_1 hours to market work. The value of the marginal product of labor in both sectors is w_1 dollars. Competitive pricing ensures that the wage in the market sector is equal to the value of the marginal product.

Now assume that a tax of t is levied on income from market work, but the return to housework is untaxed. Immediately after the tax is levied, the net return to market work declines to $(1 - t)w_1$. The original allocation

---

[18] For further discussion of why this must be true, see the Appendix at the end of the book.

Figure 14.9
Differential factor
taxation

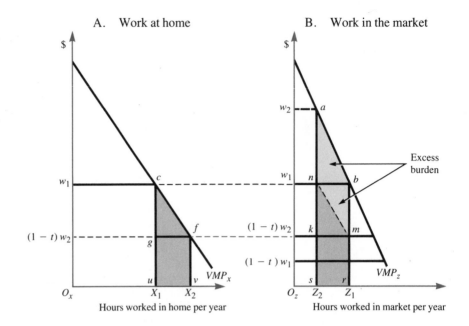

A.   Work at home   B.   Work in the market

Hours worked in home per year   Hours worked in market per year

is no longer desirable to individuals because the return to the last hour of work in the household (w_1) exceeds the comparable rate in the market, $(1 - t)w_1$. As a result, people begin working less in the market and more at home. As individuals devote less time to the market sector, VMP_z begins to rise; as they enter the household sector, VMP_x falls. Equilibrium is reached when the *after-tax* value of marginal product in the market sector equals the value of marginal product in the household sector. In Figure 14.9, this occurs when people work X_2 hours in the home and Z_2 hours in the market. Because the *total* hours of work are fixed, the increase in hours in the household sector exactly equals the decrease in the market sector—distance $X_1 X_2$ equals distance $Z_2 Z_1$.

At the new equilibrium, the after-tax VMPs in the two sectors are both equal to $(1 - t)w_2$. However, the *before-tax* VMP in the market sector, w_2, is greater than the *VMP* in the household sector $(1 - t)w_2$. This means that if more labor were supplied to the market sector, the increase in income there (w_2) would exceed the loss of income in the household sector, $(1 - t)w_2$. But there is no incentive for this reallocation to occur, because individuals are sensitive to the returns they receive *after tax,* and these are already equal. The tax thus creates a situation in which there is "too much" housework being done, and "not enough" work in the market. In short, the tax leads to an inefficient allocation of resources in the sense that it distorts incentives to employ inputs in their most productive uses. The resulting decrease in real income is the excess burden of the tax.

To measure the excess burden, we must analyze Figure 14.9 closely. Begin by observing that as a result of the exodus of labor from the market, output there goes down by an amount whose value is area *abrs,* the area under VMP_z between Z_1 and Z_2.[19] On the other hand, as labor enters the household sector, output increases by an amount whose value is *cfvu,* the area under the VMP_x curve between X_1 and X_2. Therefore the excess burden is area *abrs* minus area *cfvu*. Because $X_1 X_2 = Z_2 Z_1$ (remember, the total supply of hours is fixed), it follows that area *cfvu* equals area *nmrs.* Hence, the difference between *abrs* and *cfvu* is simply *abmn*. This area, which is the excess burden of the tax, has a convenient algebraic representation:

$$\tfrac{1}{2}(\Delta Z)tw_2$$

where ΔZ is the change in hours worked in the market sector.[20] The greater the change in the allocation of labor (ΔZ) and the greater the tax wedge (tw_2), the greater the excess burden.

In general, whenever a factor is fixed in total supply and is taxed differently in different uses, a misallocation of factors between sectors and hence an efficiency loss is generated. In the case of housework versus market work just discussed, Michael Boskin [1975] estimated the cost of the distortion as between 6 and 13 percent of tax revenues.

Does Efficient Taxation Matter?

·

Every year both public- and private-sector organizations publish dozens of documents relating to the details of government spending and taxation. You would look in vain, however, for an "excess burden budget," detailing the distortionary impact of government fiscal policies. The reason for this is not hard to understand. Excess burden does not appear in anyone's bookkeeping system. It is conceptually a rather subtle notion and is not easy to make operational. Nevertheless, although the losses in real income associated with tax-induced changes in behavior are hidden, they are real, and according to some estimates, they are very large. We have emphasized repeatedly that efficiency considerations alone are never enough to determine policy. As Chief Justice Warren Burger remarked in a different context, "Convenience and efficiency are not the primary objectives—or the hallmarks—of democratic government." Still, it is unfortunate that policymakers often seem to ignore efficiency altogether.

---

[19] The vertical distance between *VMP* and the horizontal axis at any level of input gives the value of *marginal* product for that level of input. Adding up all these distances gives the value of the *total* product. Thus, the area under *VMP* gives the value of total product.

[20] Proof: Area *abmn* is the sum of two triangles *abn* and *nbm*. Triangle $abn = \tfrac{1}{2}(nb)(an) = \tfrac{1}{2}\Delta Z(an)$. Triangle $nbm = \tfrac{1}{2}(nb)(bm) = \tfrac{1}{2}(\Delta Z)(bm)$. Their sum is $\tfrac{1}{2}(\Delta Z)(an + bm) = \tfrac{1}{2}(\Delta Z)tw_2$.

The fact that a tax generates an excess burden is not necessarily morally evil. One hopes, after all, that the tax will be used to obtain something beneficial for society either in purchase of public goods or income redistribution. But to determine whether or not the supposed benefits are large enough to justify the costs, intelligent policy requires that excess burden be included in the calculation as a social cost. Moreover, as we see in the next chapter, excess burden is extremely useful in evaluating the relative desirability of alternative tax systems. Providing estimates of excess burden is an important role for the economist.

Summary

- Taxes generally impose an excess burden—a cost beyond the tax revenue collected.

- Excess burden is caused by tax-induced distortions in behavior. It may be examined using either indifference curves or compensated demand curves.

- Lump sum taxes do not cause distortions but are unattractive as policy tools. Nevertheless, they are an important standard against which the excess burdens of other taxes can be compared.

- Excess burden may result even if observed behavior is unaffected, because it is the compensated response to a tax that determines its excess burden.

- When a single tax is imposed, the excess burden is proportional to the compensated elasticity of demand, and to the square of the tax rate.

- In cost-benefit analysis, the marginal excess burden of raising funds by taxation should be included as a cost.

- Excess-burden calculations typically assume no other distortions. If other distortions exist, the incremental excess burden of a new tax depends on its effects in other markets.

- Subsidies also create excess burdens because they encourage people to consume goods valued less than the marginal social cost of production.

- An important application of excess-burden analysis is the impact on efficiency of differential taxation of inputs. In this instance, inputs are used "too little" in taxed activities and "too much" in untaxed activities.

Discussion Questions

1. a. Using a simple example with only two goods, sketch a set of indifference curves which exhibit the property that the income-compensated effect of taxing one of the goods is zero.

   b. Draw the compensated demand curve corresponding to your answer to part (a) and contrast it with a situation in which there is a large compensated response. Be sure to show the equilibrium before and after the tax, the tax revenues, and the excess burden. Can you relate your results to Equation (14.3)?

2. Which of the following is likely to impose a large excess burden?

   a. A tax on land.

   b. A subsidy for personal computers.

   c. A tax on interest from accounts at savings and loan associations only.

d. A subsidy for food consumption.

e. A tax on economic profits.

3. "In the formula for excess burden given in Equation (14.3), the tax is less than one. When it is squared, the result is smaller, not bigger. Thus, having t^2 instead of t in the formula makes the tax less important." Comment.

4. In 1991 the federal tax on airline tickets was increased from 8 to 10 percent. Use a diagram to illustrate the total excess burden of the air travel tax, and the incremental effect of the 1991 increase.

5. Recall Harberger's general equilibrium model presented in Chapter 13 under "General Equilibrium Models." In that model, there are two commodities and two factors of production, and the total supply of each factor of production is fixed. What is the excess burden of a proportional income tax? What is the excess burden of a proportional tax on one of the two factors?

6. Suppose there are two commodities, R and S. When a tax on R alone is imposed, the excess burden is χ_R. When a tax on S alone is imposed, the excess burden is χ_S. When the two taxes are imposed simultaneously, the overall excess burden is *greater* than $\chi_R + \chi_S$. Explain how this might happen.

Selected References

Browning, Edgar K. "A Critical Appraisal of Hausman's Welfare Cost Estimates." *Journal of Political Economy* (1985), pp. 1025–34.

Harberger, Arnold C. "Taxation, Resource Allocation, and Welfare." In *Taxation and Welfare,* ed. Arnold

C. Harberger. Boston: Little, Brown, 1974, pp. 25–62.

Sandmo, Agnar. "Optimal Taxation—An Introduction to the Literature." *Journal of Public Economics* 6 (1976), pp. 37–54.

A P P  D I X   **Formula for Excess Burden**

This appendix shows how the excess burden triangle *fdi* of Figure 14.5 may be written in terms of the compensated demand elasticity. The triangle's area, A, is given by the formula:

$$A = \tfrac{1}{2} \times base \times height$$
$$= \tfrac{1}{2} \times (di) \times (fd) \tag{14A.1}$$

fd is just the difference between the gross and net prices (ΔP_b) due to the tax:

$$fd = \Delta P_b = (1 + t_b) \times P_b - P_b = t_b \times P_b \tag{14A.2}$$

di is the change in the quantity (Δq) as a result of the price rise:

$$di = \Delta q \tag{14A.3}$$

Now, note that the definition of the price elasticity, η, is:

$$\eta \equiv \frac{\Delta q}{\Delta P_b} \frac{P_b}{q}$$

so that

$$\frac{\Delta q}{\Delta P_b} = \eta \left(\frac{q}{P_b}\right) \qquad (14A.4)$$

We saw in (14A.2) that $\Delta P_b = t_b \times P_b$, so that (14A.4) yields:

$$di = \Delta q = \eta \times \frac{q}{P_b} \times (t_b P_b) = \eta \times q \times t_b \qquad (14A.5)$$

Finally, substitute both (14A.5) and (14A.2) into (14A.1) to obtain:

$$A = \frac{1}{2}(di)(fd)$$
$$= \frac{1}{2}(\eta q t_b) \times (t_b P_b)$$
$$= \frac{1}{2} \times \eta \times P_b \times q \times (t_b)^2,$$

as in the text.

 A P P E N D I X   # Multiple Taxes and the Theory of the Second Best

This appendix discusses the measurement of excess burden when a tax is imposed in the presence of a preexisting distortion. The analysis is based on Harberger [1974a].

In Figure 14.B we consider two goods, gin and rum, whose demand schedules are D_g and D_r, and whose before-tax prices are P_g and P_r, respectively. (The prices represent marginal social costs and are assumed to be constant.) Rum is currently being taxed at a percentage rate t_r so its price is $(1 + t_r)P_r$. This creates an excess burden in the rum market, triangle abc. Now suppose that a tax on gin at rate t_g is introduced, creating a wedge between what gin consumers pay and gin producers receive. This creates an excess burden in the gin market of efd. But this is not the end of the story. If gin and rum are substitutes, the increase in the consumers' price of gin induced by the gin tax shifts the demand curve for rum to the right, say to D_r'. As a consequence, the quantity of rum demanded increases from r_2 to r_3, distance cg. For each bottle of rum

Figure 14.B

Excess burden of a
tax in the presence
of an existing tax

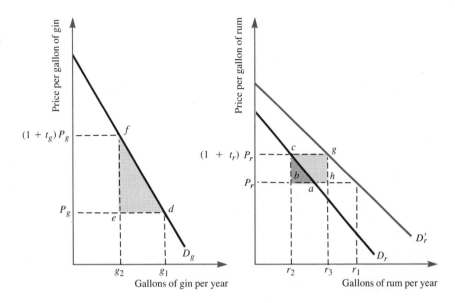

purchased between r_2 and r_3, the amount that people pay $[(1 + t_r)P_r]$
exceeds the social cost (P_r) by distance cb. Hence, there is a social gain of
cb per bottle of rum times cg bottles, or area $cbhg$.

To summarize: given that the tax on rum was already in place, the tax
on gin creates an excess burden of *efd* in the gin market *and* simultaneously decreases excess burden by *cbhg* in the rum market. If *cbhg* is
sufficiently large, the tax can actually reduce overall excess burden. This
is an example of the **theory of the second best**: in the presence of existing
distortions, policies that in isolation would increase efficiency can decrease it and vice versa.

This discussion is a special case of the result that the excess burden of
a *set* of taxes generally depends on the whole set of tax rates, as well as on
the degree of substitutability and complementarity between the various
commodities. Specifically, suppose that n commodities are subject to
taxation. Let P_i be the before-tax price of the ith commodity; t_i the ad
valorem tax on i^{th} commodity; and S_{ij}, the compensated response in the
demand of the ith good with respect to a change in the price of the jth good.
Then it can be shown [see Tresch, 1981, Chapter 15] that the overall
excess burden is

$$-\tfrac{1}{2} \sum_{i=1}^{n} \sum_{j=1}^{n} t_i P_i t_j P_j S_{ij}$$

For example, in the two-good case just discussed, where the goods are g
and r, the overall excess burden is

$$-\tfrac{1}{2}(t_r^2 P_r^2 S_{rr} + 2t_r P_r t_g P_g S_{rg} + t_g^2 P_g^2 S_{gg}).$$

Efficient and Equitable Taxation

A nation may fall into decay through taxation in two ways. In the first case, when the amount of the taxes exceeds the powers of the nation and is not proportioned to the general wealth. In the second case, when an amount of taxation, proportioned on the whole to the powers of the nation, is viciously distributed.

PIETRO VERRI

T he last two chapters have focused on the positive questions: "How do taxes affect the distribution of income and economic efficiency?" We turn now to the normative question: "How should a tax system be designed if it is to yield efficient and fair outcomes?" Our goal is to establish a set of criteria that can be used to evaluate real-world tax systems.

Optimal Commodity Taxation

Consider a simple society composed of a group of identical taxpayers. Assume that government spending decisions have been made. As a result, the government requires a certain amount of revenue. Suppose further that the revenue must be raised by taxes on various commodities—lump sum levies are ruled out. The theory of optimal commodity taxation outlines how these taxes should be imposed to minimize excess burden.

Several important insights about optimal commodity taxation can be obtained from a careful analysis of the taxpayer's budget constraint. To formulate an algebraic representation of the budget constraint, assume for simplicity that each individual consumes only two commodities, X and Y, as well as leisure, l. The price of X is P_x, the price of Y is P_y, and the wage rate (which is the price of leisure) is w. The maximum number of hours per year that the individual can work—his or her **time endowment**—is fixed at $\overline{T}$. (Think of $\overline{T}$ as the amount of time left over after sleep.) It follows that hours of work are $(\overline{T} - l)$—whatever time is not spent on leisure is devoted to work. Income is the product of the wage rate and hours of work—$w(\overline{T} - l)$. Assuming that all income is spent on commodities X and Y (there is no saving), the budget constraint is

$$w(\overline{T} - l) = P_x X + P_y Y \tag{15.1}$$

The left-hand side gives total earnings, and the right-hand side shows how the earnings are spent.

Equation (15.1) can be rewritten as

$$w\overline{T} = P_x X + P_y Y + wl \tag{15.2}$$

The left-hand side of (15.2) is the value of the time endowment. It shows the income that could be earned if the individual worked every waking hour.

Now, suppose that it is possible to tax X, Y, and l at the same ad valorem rate, t. The tax raises the effective price of X to $(1 + t)P_x$, of Y to $(1 + t)P_y$, and of l to $(1 + t)w$. Thus, the individual's after-tax budget constraint is

$$w\overline{T} = (1 + t)P_x X + (1 + t)P_y Y + (1 + t)wl \tag{15.3}$$

Dividing through Equation (15.3) by $(1 + t)$, we have

$$\frac{1}{1 + t} w\overline{T} = P_x X + P_y Y + wl \tag{15.4}$$

Comparison of (15.3) and (15.4) points out the following fact: a tax on all commodities *including leisure*, at the same percentage rate, t, is equivalent to reducing the value of the time endowment from $w\overline{T}$ to $[1/(1 + t)] \times w\overline{T}$. For example, a 25 percent tax on X, Y, and l is equivalent to a reduction of the value of the time endowment by 20 percent. However, because w and $\overline{T}$ are fixed, their product, $w\overline{T}$, is also fixed; for any value of the wage rate, the individual cannot change the value of the time endowment. Therefore, a tax that reduces the value of the time endowment is in effect a lump sum tax. From Chapter 14 we know that lump sum taxes have no excess burden. We conclude that a tax at the same rate on all commodities, *including leisure*, is equivalent to a lump sum tax and has no excess burden.

In practice, putting a tax on leisure time is impossible (see Chapter 14). The only *available* tax instruments are taxes on commodities X and Y. Therefore, *some* excess burden generally is inevitable. The goal of optimal commodity taxation is to select tax rates on X and Y in such a way that the excess burden of raising the required tax revenue is as low as

Figure 15.1
Marginal excess
burden

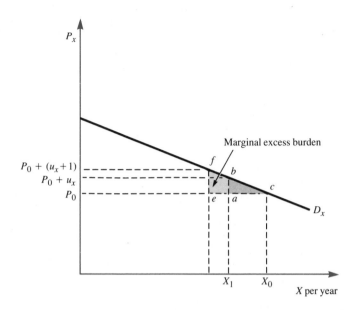

possible. It is popular to suggest that the solution to this problem is to tax *X* and *Y* at the same rate—so-called **neutral taxation.**[1] We see that, in general, neutral taxation is *not* efficient.

The Ramsey Rule

To raise the revenue with the least excess burden possible, how should the tax rates on *X* and *Y* be set? To minimize *overall* excess burden, the marginal excess burden of the last dollar of revenue raised from each commodity must be the same. Otherwise, it would be possible to lower overall excess burden by raising the rate on the commodity with the smaller marginal excess burden, and vice versa.

To explore the consequences of this typical example of marginal analysis in economics, suppose for simplicity that *X* and *Y* are unrelated commodities—they are neither substitutes nor complements for each other. Hence, a change in the price of either commodity affects its own demand and not the demand for the other. Figure 15.1 shows the compensated demand for *X*, D_x. Assume that the consumer can buy all the *X* she wants at the price P_0, so the supply curve of *X* is horizontal.

Suppose that a small unit tax of u_x is levied on *X*. As proven in the last chapter, the excess burden of the tax is the area of triangle *abc*. The height of the triangle is the change in the price induced by the tax, u_x, and the base is the change in the (compensated) demand for *X*, which we denote ΔX. Hence, the excess burden is

$$\tfrac{1}{2} u_x \Delta X \tag{15.5}$$

---

[1] In light of the tax equivalence relations in Table 13.2, in this model, a tax on *X* and *Y* at the same rate is equivalent to an income tax.

The revenues raised by the tax are found by multiplying the tax per unit (u_x) by the number of units sold (X_1), or

$$u_x X_1 \qquad\qquad (15.6)$$

Recall that excess burden minimization requires information on the *marginal* excess burden on the last dollar of revenue collected. To derive an explicit expression for this, our strategy is to imagine increasing the unit tax rate by a dollar. Step 1 is to find the marginal excess burden induced by the tax increase. Step 2 is to compute the associated increase in revenues. Step 3 is simply to divide the step 1 result by that from step 2. By definition, this gives us the marginal excess burden per incremental dollar of revenue collected.

Step 1.   If the unit tax increases from u_x to ($u_x + 1$), then according to Equation (15.5), excess burden increases to approximately $\frac{1}{2}(u_x + 1)\, \Delta X$. The marginal excess burden is just the difference between the excess burdens before and after the tax increase. Thus, we subtract $\frac{1}{2}\, u_x \Delta X$ from $\frac{1}{2}(u_x + 1)\, \Delta X$, which gives us

$$\tfrac{1}{2}\Delta X = \text{marginal excess burden} \qquad\qquad (15.7)$$

Graphically, this is approximately the difference between the excess burden associated with the tax rate ($u_x + 1$) (triangle *fec* in Figure 15.1), and the original excess burden (*abc*), or trapezoid *feab*.

Step 2.   Note from Equation (15.6) that when the unit tax increases from u_x to ($u_x + 1$), revenues increase approximately from $u_x X_1$ to ($u_x + 1$) X_1. Therefore, marginal tax revenues are just ($u_x + 1$) X_1 minus $u_x X_1$, or

$$X_1 = \text{marginal tax revenue} \qquad\qquad (15.8)$$

Step 3.   Marginal excess burden per additional dollar of tax revenue is expression (15.7) divided by (15.8) or

$$\frac{\tfrac{1}{2}\Delta X}{X_1}$$

Exactly the same reasoning indicates that if a unit tax of u_y is levied on Y, the marginal excess burden per last dollar of revenue is

$$\frac{\tfrac{1}{2}\Delta Y}{Y_1}$$

Because the condition for minimizing overall excess burden is that the marginal excess burden per last dollar of revenue be the same for each commodity, we must set

$$\frac{\tfrac{1}{2}\Delta X}{X_1} = \frac{\tfrac{1}{2}\Delta Y}{Y_1}$$

Multiplying both sides of the equation by two yields

$$\frac{\Delta X}{X_1} = \frac{\Delta Y}{Y_1} \tag{15.9}$$

To interpret Equation (15.9), note that the *change* in a variable divided by its *total* value is just the percentage change in the variable. Hence, Equation (15.9) says that *to minimize total excess burden, tax rates should be set so that the percentage reduction in the quantity demanded of each commodity is the same.*[2] This result, called the **Ramsey rule** (after its discoverer, Frank Ramsey [1927]), also holds even for cases when *X, Y,* and *l* are related goods—substitutes or complements.

But why should efficient taxation induce equiproportional changes in quantities demanded rather than equiproportional changes in price? Because excess burden is a consequence of distortions in *quantities*. To minimize total excess burden requires that all these changes be in the same proportion.

A reinterpretation of the Ramsey rule.   It is useful to explore the relationship between the Ramsey rule and demand elasticities. Let η_x be the compensated elasticity of demand for X. Let t_x be the tax rate on X, this time expressed as an ad valorem rate rather than a unit tax.[3] Now, by definition of an ad valorem tax, t_x is the percentage increase in the price induced by the tax. Hence, $t_x\eta_x$ is the percentage change in the price times the percentage change in quantity demanded when the price increases by 1 percent. This is just the percentage reduction in the demand for X induced by the tax. Similarly, defining t_y and η_y analogously to t_x and η_x, then $t_y\eta_y$ is the proportional reduction in Y induced by the tax. The Ramsey rule says that to minimize excess burden, these percentage reductions in quantity demanded must be equal:

$$t_x\eta_x = t_y\eta_y \tag{15.10}$$

Now divide both sides of the equation by $t_y\eta_x$ to obtain

$$\frac{t_x}{t_y} = \frac{\eta_y}{\eta_x} \tag{15.11}$$

Equation (15.11) is the **inverse elasticity rule:** As long as goods are unrelated in consumption, tax rates should be inversely proportional

---

[2] The result holds strictly only for infinitesimal taxes.

[3] In a competitive market, any unit tax can be represented by a suitably chosen ad valorem tax, and vice versa. For example, suppose that a commodity is subject to a unit tax of 5 cents, and the price paid by consumers is 50 cents. Then the resulting excess burden is the same as that which would be induced by an ad valorem tax at a rate of 10 percent of the after-tax price.

to elasticities. That is, the higher is η_y relative to η_x, the lower should be t_y relative to t_x.[4] Efficiency does *not* require that all rates be set uniformly.

The intuition behind the inverse elasticity rule is straightforward. An efficient set of taxes should distort decisions as little as possible. The potential for distortion is greater the more elastic the demand for a commodity. Therefore, efficient taxation requires that relatively high rates of taxation be levied on relatively inelastic goods. Indeed, if the compensated demand for a commodity were perfectly inelastic, efficient taxation would require that all revenues be raised by taxes on that good, since no distortion would arise at all.[5]

The Corlett-Hague rule.   W. J. Corlett and D. C. Hague [1953] proved an interesting implication of the Ramsey rule: When there are two commodities, efficient taxation requires taxing the commodity that is complementary to leisure at a relatively high rate. To understand this result intuitively, recall that *if* it were possible to tax leisure, a "first-best" result would be obtainable—revenues could be raised with no excess burden. Although the tax authorities cannot tax leisure, they *can* tax goods that tend to be consumed jointly *with* leisure, indirectly lowering the demand for leisure. If yachts are taxed at a very high rate, people consume fewer yachts and spend less time at leisure. In effect, then, taxing complements to leisure at high rates provides an indirect way to "get at" leisure, and, hence, move closer to the perfectly efficient outcome that would be possible if leisure were taxable.[6]

Equity Considerations   At this point the reader may suspect that efficient tax theory has unpleasant policy implications. For example, the inverse elasticity rule says that

---

[4] A more careful demonstration requires a little calculus. Recall from Equation (14.3) that the excess burden on commodity X is $\frac{1}{2}\eta_x P_x X t_x^2$. Similarly, the excess burden on Y is $\frac{1}{2}\eta_y P_y Y t_y^2$. Then the total excess burden is $\frac{1}{2}\eta_x P_x X t_x^2 + \frac{1}{2}\eta_y P_y Y t_y^2$. (We can just add up the two expressions because by assumption, X and Y are unrelated.) Now, suppose the required tax revenue is R. Then t_x and t_y must satisfy the relation $P_x X t_x + P_y Y t_y = R$. Our problem is to choose t_x and t_y to minimize $\frac{1}{2}\eta_x P_x X t_x^2 + \frac{1}{2}\eta_y P_y Y t_y^2$ subject to $R - P_x X t_x - P_y Y t_y = 0$. Set up the Lagrangian expression

$$\mathcal{L} = \frac{1}{2}\eta_x P_x X t_x^2 + \frac{1}{2}\eta_y P_y Y t_y^2 + \lambda[R - P_x X t_x - P_y Y t_y]$$

where λ is the Lagrange multiplier. (The method of Lagrangian multipliers is reviewed in James Henderson and Richard Quandt [1980, pp. 381–83].) Taking $\partial\mathcal{L}/\partial t_x$ yields $\eta_x t_x = \lambda$ and $\partial\mathcal{L}/\partial t_y$ yields $\eta_y t_y = \lambda$. Hence, $\eta_x t_x = \eta_y t_y$, and Equation (15.11) follows immediately. For a more rigorous proof that also allows goods to be substitutes and/or complements, see Agnar Sandmo [1976].

[5] In indifference curve analysis, a perfectly inelastic compensated demand curve means that the "substitution effect" is zero. See the Appendix to the book.

[6] As Alan Auerbach [1985] notes, what is "special" about leisure in this model is that it is the only good with an endowment $(\bar{T})$ that cannot be taxed independently of its consumption.

inelastically demanded goods should be taxed at relatively high rates. Is this fair? Do we really want a tax system that collects the bulk of its revenue from taxes on insulin?

Of course not. Unlike the model discussed so far, in the real world, people are not all the same. Efficiency thus becomes only one criterion for evaluating a tax system; fairness is just as important. In particular, it is widely agreed that a tax system should have **vertical equity:** it should distribute burdens fairly across people with different abilities to pay. The Ramsey rule has been modified to consider the distributional consequences of taxation. Suppose, for example, that the poor spend a greater proportion of their income on commodity X than do the rich, and vice versa for commodity Y. X might be bread, and Y caviar. Suppose further that the social welfare function puts a higher weight on the utilities of the poor than on those of the rich. Then even if X is more inelastically demanded than Y, optimal taxation may require a higher rate of tax on Y than X [Diamond, 1975]. True, a high tax rate on Y creates a relatively large excess burden, but it also tends to redistribute income toward the poor. Society may be willing to pay the price of a higher excess burden in return for a more equal distribution of income. In general, the extent to which it makes sense to depart from the Ramsey rule depends on:

1. The strength of society's egalitarian preferences. If society cares only about efficiency—a dollar to one person is the same as a dollar to another, rich or poor—then it may as well strictly follow the Ramsey rule.
2. The extent to which the consumption patterns of the rich and poor differ. If the rich and the poor consume both goods in the same proportion, taxing the goods at different rates can have no effect on the distribution of income. Even if society *has* a distributional goal, it cannot be achieved by differential taxation of X and Y.

Overview

If lump sum taxation were available, taxes could be raised without any excess burden at all. Optimal taxation would need to focus only on distributional issues. Lump sum taxes are not available, however, so the problem becomes how to collect a given amount of tax revenue with as small an excess burden as possible. In general, minimizing excess burden requires that taxes be set so that the (compensated) demands for all commodities are reduced in the same proportion. For unrelated goods, this implies that tax rates should be set in inverse proportion to the demand elasticities. However, if society has distributional goals, departures from efficient taxation rules may be appropriate.

Application to Taxation of the Family

Under current federal income tax law, the fundamental unit of income taxation is the family.[7] A husband and wife are taxed on the sum of their incomes. Regardless of whether the wife or the husband earns an extra dollar, it is taxed at the same rate. Is this efficient? In other words, is the family's excess burden minimized by taxing each spouse's income at the same rate?

Imagine the family as a unit whose utility depends on the quantities of three "commodities": total family consumption, husband's hours of work, and wife's hours of work. Family utility increases with family consumption, but decreases with each spouse's hours of work. Each spouse's hours of work depend on his or her wage rate, among other variables. A tax on earnings distorts the work decision, creating an excess burden. (See Chapter 14, Figure 14.7.) How should tax rates be set so that the family's excess burden is as small as possible?

Assume for simplicity that the husband's and wife's hours of work are approximately "unrelated goods"—an increase in the husband's wage rate has very little impact on the wife's work decision and vice versa. This assumption is consistent with much empirical research. Then application of the inverse elasticity rule suggests that a higher tax should be levied on the commodity which is relatively inelastically supplied. To enhance efficiency, whoever's labor supply is relatively inelastic should bear a relatively high tax rate. Numerous econometric studies suggest that the husband's supply of labor is considerably less elastic than that of the wife. Efficiency could therefore be gained if the current tax law were modified to give husbands higher marginal tax rates than wives.[8]

Again, we emphasize that efficiency is only one consideration in tax design. However, it is interesting that this result is consistent with the claims of some who have argued that on equity grounds the relative tax rate on the earnings of working wives should be lowered.[9]

Optimal User Fees

So far we have assumed that all production takes place in the private sector. The government's only problem is to set the tax rates that determine consumer prices. Sometimes, the government itself is the producer of a good or service. In such cases, the government must directly choose a **user fee**—a price paid by users of a good or service provided by the

---

[7] This section is based on Michael Boskin and Eytan Sheshinski [1979].

[8] See Charles Ballard, John Shoven, and John Whalley [1985a, p. 131] for a review of several econometric studies on labor supply. Note that the important distinction here is not between *husband* and *wife,* but between *primary earner* and *secondary earner.* In families where the wife has the lower supply elasticity, efficiency requires that she have the higher tax rate.

[9] See, for example, Alicia Munnell [1980], and Chapter 16 under "Choice of Unit."

government. As usual, we would like to determine the "best" possible user fee. Analytically, the optimal tax and user fee problems are closely related. In both cases, the government sets the final price paid by consumers. In the optimal tax problem, this is done indirectly by choice of the tax rate, while in the optimal user fee problem, it is done directly.

When does the government choose to produce a good instead of purchasing it from the private sector? Government production is likely when the production of some good or service is subject to continually decreasing average costs—the greater the level of output, the lower the cost per unit. Under such circumstances, it is unlikely that the market for the service is competitive. A single firm can take advantage of economies of scale and supply the entire industry output, at least for a sizable region. This phenomenon is often called **natural monopoly.**[10] Examples are highways, bridges, electricity, and television. In some cases, these commodities are produced by the private sector and regulated by the government (electricity); and in others they are produced by the public sector (highways). Although we study public production here, many of the important insights apply to regulation of private monopolies.

Figure 15.2 measures the output of the natural monopoly, Z, on the horizontal axis, and dollars on the vertical. The average cost schedule is denoted AC_Z. By assumption, it decreases continuously over all relevant ranges of output. Because average cost is decreasing, marginal cost must be less than average. Therefore, the marginal cost (MC_Z) curve, which shows the incremental cost of providing each unit of Z, lies below AC_Z. The demand curve for Z is represented by D_Z. The associated marginal revenue curve is MR_Z. It shows the incremental revenue associated with each level of output of Z.

To illustrate why decreasing average costs often lead to public sector production or regulated private sector production, consider what would happen if Z were produced by an unregulated monopolist. The monopolist seeking to maximize profits produces up to the point that marginal revenue equals marginal cost. In Figure 15.3, this occurs at output level Z_m. The associated price, P_m, is found by going up to the demand curve, D_Z. Monopoly profits are equal to the product of number of units sold times the profit per unit, and are represented geometrically by the light colored rectangle.

Is output Z_m efficient? According to the theory of welfare economics, efficiency requires that price equal marginal cost—the value that people place on the good must equal the incremental cost to society of producing it. At Z_m, price is *greater* than marginal cost. Hence, Z_m is inefficient.

---

[10] It is also possible that the industry can end up as an oligopoly (few sellers). We focus on the analytically simpler case of monopoly.

Figure 15.2
A natural monopoly

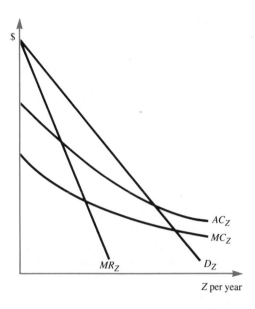

Figure 15.3
Alternative pricing
schemes for a
natural monopoly

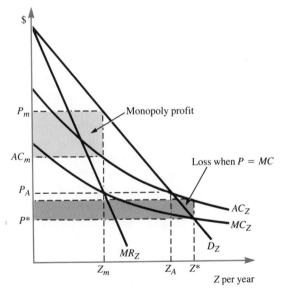

This inefficiency, plus the fact that society may not approve of the existence of the monopoly profits, provide a possible justification for government taking over the production of Z.[11]

----

[11] The usual caveat applies: just because government intervention can improve the status quo does not mean that it will.

The obvious policy prescription seems to be for the government to produce up to the point where price equals marginal cost. In Figure 15.3, the output at which $P = MC$ is denoted Z^*, and the associated price is P^*. There is a problem, however: at output Z^*, the price is less than the average cost. Price P^* is so low that the operation cannot cover its costs, and it continually suffers losses. The total loss is equal to the product of the number of units sold, Z^*, times the loss per unit, measured as the vertical distance between the demand curve and AC_Z at Z^*. Geometrically, the loss is the darker colored rectangle in Figure 15.3.

How should the government confront this dilemma? Several solutions have been proposed.

Average cost pricing.   To set price equal to average cost, find the intersection of the demand and average cost schedules. At this point, output is Z_A in Figure 15.3 and price is P_A. By definition, when price equals average cost, there are neither profits nor losses—the enterprise just "breaks even." The operation no longer has to worry about a deficit. However, note that Z_A is less than Z^*. Although average cost pricing leads to more output than at the profit-maximizing level, it still falls short of the efficient amount.

Marginal cost pricing with lump sum taxes.   Charge $P = MC$, and make up the deficit by levying lump sum taxes. Charging $P = MC$ ensures efficiency in the market for Z; financing the deficit with lump sum taxes on the rest of society guarantees that no new inefficiencies are generated by meeting the deficit. However, there are two problems with this solution:

First, as previously noted, lump sum taxes are generally unavailable. It is more likely that the deficit will have to be financed by distorting taxes, such as income or commodity taxes. If so, it is possible that the distortion in the market where the tax is levied will more than outweigh the efficiency gain in the market for Z.

Second, there is also a widespread belief that fairness requires consumers of a publicly provided service to pay for it—the so-called **benefits-received principle.** If this principle is taken seriously, it is unfair to make up the deficit by general taxation. Why should people who don't use a bridge have to pay for it?

Two-part tariff.   A **two-part tariff** involves a lump sum charge to gain permission to use the service, plus a price equal to marginal cost for each unit of the service consumed. To see how this works, suppose there are 1,000 users of service Z. Under the simplest version of the scheme, each user would be charged $1/1,000$ of the deficit just for the privilege of having the option to purchase Z. Once this lump sum entrance fee was paid, Z could be freely purchased at a price equal to its marginal cost. Hence, the deficit is made up by a nondistorting tax on the users of the service, who are then given incentives to consume it in efficient quantities. Two-part tariffs may seem like a peculiar idea, but they are really fairly common. Just think of your telephone company, which charges each user a monthly fee plus an additional fee for each minute of calling time.[12]

The two-part tariff is not a perfect solution, however, because having to pay the entrance fee may deter some users so that consumption falls below the efficient level. Whether this is an empirically important problem depends on the commodity in question. In a country such as the United States, it is not likely to be important for natural monopolies like water and electricity.

Another problem is that the entrance fee is essentially an equal lump sum tax on all users, rich and poor alike. If society cares about income distribution, this will be undesirable. Martin Feldstein [1972] shows how the two-part tariff can be modified when society has distributional objectives. Suppose that Z is consumed in disproportionately high amounts by the rich and that society places a relatively high weight on the welfare of the poor. Then it is optimal to set the price per each unit of Z above marginal cost. When the price is greater than marginal cost, the deficit is less than the darker colored area in Figure 15.3. Because the rich consume Z in proportionately large amounts, they account for the bulk of the reduction of the deficit. Thus, by charging a price above marginal cost, some efficiency is lost, but some equity is gained. There is an obvious similarity to the optimal tax problem discussed earlier. In both cases, departures from full efficiency may be appropriate in the presence of distributional objectives.

Overview

Of the various possibilities for dealing with decreasing costs, which has the United States chosen? In most cases, average cost pricing has been selected whether for a publicly owned or a regulated private enterprise. Richard Tresch [1981, pp. 203–6] argues that although average cost pricing is inefficient, it is probably a reasonable compromise. It has the virtue of being fairly simple and adheres to the popular benefits-received principle.[13] Some economists, however, argue that more reliance on two-part tariffs would be desirable.

Optimal Income Taxation

Thus far, we have assumed that a government can levy taxes on all commodities and factors of production. We now turn to the question of how to design systems in which tax liabilities are based on people's incomes. Income taxation is an obvious candidate for special attention because of its importance in the revenue structures of most developed countries. In addition, some argue that income is an especially appropri-

---

[12] This is not to imply that the structure of telephone companies' two-part tariffs are necessarily optimal.

[13] There are problems in administering average cost pricing in regulated industries. See Tresch [1981, Chapter 10].

ate tax base because it is the best measure of an individual's ability to pay. For the moment, we merely assume that society has somehow decided that income taxation is desirable, and ask what is the optimal way to structure an income tax. In subsequent chapters, we discuss whether income really is a particularly desirable tax base.

Edgeworth's Model

At the end of the 19th century, F. Y. Edgeworth [1957/1897] examined the question of optimal income taxation using a simple model based on the following assumptions.

1. Subject to the revenues required, the goal is to make the sum of individuals' utilities as high as possible. Algebraically, if U_i is the utility of the ith individual and W is social welfare, the tax system should maximize

$$W = U_1 + U_2 + \cdots + U_n \tag{15.12}$$

where n is the number of people in the society.

2. Individuals have identical utility functions which depend only on their levels of income. These utility functions exhibit diminishing marginal utility of income; as income increases, an individual becomes better off, but at a decreasing rate.

3. The total amount of income available is fixed.

Edgeworth's assumptions are virtually identical to the assumptions behind the optimal income distribution model presented in Chapter 8 under "Rationales for Income Redistribution." There we showed that with these assumptions, maximization of social welfare requires that each person's marginal utility of income be the same. When utility functions are identical, equal marginal utilities of income occur only at equal levels of income. The implications for tax policy are clear: Taxes should be set in such a way that the after-tax distribution of income is as equal as possible. In particular, income should be taken first from the rich because the marginal utility lost is smaller than that of the poor. If the government requires more revenue even after complete equality has been reached, the additional tax burden should be evenly distributed.

Edgeworth's model, then, implies a radically progressive tax structure—incomes are leveled off from the top until complete equality is reached. In effect, marginal tax rates on high income individuals are 100 percent. However, as stressed in Chapter 8, each of the assumptions underlying this analysis is subject to question. Beginning in the 1970s, a number of studies were done to ascertain how Edgeworth's results change when certain of the assumptions are relaxed.

Modern Studies

One of the most vexing problems with Edgeworth's analysis is the assumption that the total amount of income available to society is fixed. Confiscatory tax rates are assumed to have no effect on the amount of

Figure 15.4
A linear income tax

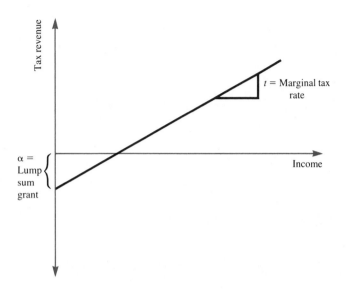

output produced. More realistically, suppose that individuals' utilities depend not only on income but on leisure, as well. Then income taxes distort work decisions and create excess burdens (Chapter 14). A society with a utilitarian social welfare function thus faces an inescapable dilemma. On the one hand, it desires to allocate the tax burden to equalize the after-tax distribution of income. However, in the process of doing so, it reduces the total amount of real income available. Design of an optimal income tax system must take into account the costs (in excess burden) of achieving more equality. In Edgeworth's model, the cost of obtaining more equality is zero, which explains the prescription for a perfectly egalitarian outcome.

How much is Edgeworth's result changed when work incentives are taken into account? Nicholas Stern [1976] studied a model similar to Edgeworth's, except that individuals make choices between income and leisure. To simplify the analysis, Stern assumed that the amount of tax revenues collected from a person is given by

$$\text{Revenues} = -\alpha + t \times \text{Income} \qquad (15.13)$$

where α and t are positive numbers. For example, suppose that $\alpha = \$3,000$ and $t = .25$. Then a person with income of $20,000 would have a tax liability of $2,000 ($= -\$3,000 + .25 \times \$20,000$). A person with an income of $6,000 would have a tax liability of *minus* $1,500 ($= -\$3,000 + .25 \times \$6,000$). Such a person would receive a $1,500 grant from the government.

The significance of Equation (15.13) is best understood by graphing it. In Figure 15.4, income is measured on the horizontal axis and tax revenues on the vertical. When income is zero, the tax burden is negative—the individual receives a lump sum grant from the government of α dollars. Then, for each dollar of income, the individual must pay t dollars to the government. Thus, t is the *marginal* tax rate, the proportion of an additional dollar that must be paid in tax. Because the geometric interpretation of (15.13) is a straight line, it is referred to as a **linear income tax schedule.** In popular discussions, a linear income tax schedule is often referred to as a **flat tax.** Note that even though the marginal tax rate for a linear tax schedule is constant, the schedule is progressive in the sense that the higher an individual's income, the higher the proportion of income paid in taxes.[14] Just how progressive depends on the precise values of α and t. Greater values of t are associated with more progressive tax systems. However, at the same time that high values of t lead to more progressiveness, they create larger excess burdens. The optimal income tax problem is to find the "best" combination of α and t—the values that maximize social welfare [Equation (15.12)] subject to the constraint that a given amount of revenue (above the required transfers) be collected.

Stern [1976] finds that allowing for a modest amount of substitution between leisure and income, and with required government revenues equal to about 20 percent of income, a value of t of about 19 percent maximizes social welfare.[15] This is considerably less than the value of 100 percent implied by Edgeworth's analysis. It is, incidentally, also much smaller than the actual marginal tax rates found in many Western countries. Even quite modest incentive effects appear to have important implications for optimal marginal tax rates.

More generally, Stern showed that the more elastic the supply of labor, the lower the optimal value of t, other things being the same. Intuitively, the cost of redistribution is the excess burden it creates. The more elastic the supply of labor, the greater the excess burden from taxing it. [See Equation (14.4).] More elastic labor supply therefore means a higher cost to redistribution, so that less should be done.

Stern also investigated how alternative social welfare functions affect the results, focusing on the impact of giving different social weights to the utilities of the rich and the poor. In Equation (15.12), more egalitarian preferences are represented by assigning the utilities of poor people higher weights than utilities of the rich. An interesting extreme case is the maximin criterion, according to which the only individual who receives any weight in the social welfare function is the person with the minimum utility (see Chapter 8). Stern found that the maximin criterion calls for a marginal tax rate of about 80 percent. Not surprisingly, if society has extremely egalitarian objectives, high tax rates are called for. Even here, though, the rates fall short of 100 percent.

---

[14] See the discussion of the definition of "progressive" in Chapter 13.

[15] Specifically, the result reported here assumes that the elasticity of substitution between leisure and income is 0.6. In Stern's model, this corresponds to a small positive elasticity of labor supply with respect to the net wage, about 0.1.

This cataloging of Stern's results may convey a somewhat false sense of precision as to what economists really know about the optimal tax system. After all, there are many controversial value judgments behind the utilitarian social welfare that the optimal tax system seeks to maximize. Moreover, as explained in Chapter 17, there is substantial uncertainty about the behavioral elasticities that are crucial to measuring the tradeoff between efficiency and equity. Nevertheless, it is extremely informative to have explicit calculations of what the optimal tax rates would be under alternative sets of assumptions.

We noted earlier that Stern restricted himself to studying linear income tax schedules. There have also been analyses of general tax schedules that allow nonconstant marginal tax rates; t can either increase or decrease with income. One of the most surprising results is that maximization of social welfare requires the marginal tax rate to be *zero* at the very top of the income scale [Seade, 1977].

To see why, suppose that the richest person is Homer Hughes, who currently has an income of exactly $1 billion and faces a positive marginal tax rate on his billion-and-first dollar. Now suppose the marginal tax rate on the billion-and-first dollar is reduced to zero. Knowing that if he earns another dollar he will get to keep it all, Hughes may decide to do so. If he does, it makes him better off. The government is no worse off, because it still collects the same amount of revenue as before. Similarly, no other taxpayer is made worse off. In short, Hughes is better off, and no one else's welfare has decreased. Social welfare, which is the sum of utilities, has therefore increased. Of course, Hughes may choose not to earn the extra dollar. In that case, no harm is done—the status quo is simply maintained.

One must be very cautious in drawing policy implications from this result. The individual at the very top of the income scale may have a very high income even compared to other rich people. Hence, zero is probably a poor approximation to the optimal marginal income tax rate even for most people in the highest 1 percent of the income distribution. Moreover, note that this result pertains to the *marginal* tax rate facing the richest individual. It says nothing about the *average* tax rate. It is possible to collect very high taxes from an individual on income earned before the last dollar, and thus have a high average rate even though the marginal rate is very low.

The contrast between this result and real-world income tax systems is striking. Far from having zero marginal tax rates at the highest incomes, actual tax systems tend to tax these incomes at the highest rates. Under the U.S. federal personal income tax, the highest statutory marginal income tax rate is 31 percent as of 1991; at times it has been 90 percent.

The theory and computation of optimal tax rates continues to be of great interest to economists. The basic models have been expanded to see how optimal tax rates are affected by new complications.[16] This literature cannot be expected to produce a blueprint of the optimal tax system. As has been stressed, the answer depends to a large extent on value judgments, and economics does not provide definitive answers to ethical questions. The contribution of the literature on optimal taxation is systematically to draw out the implications of alternative ethical and behavioral assumptions, thus allowing coherent discussions of tax policy.

Politics and the Time Inconsistency Problem

Optimal taxation is a purely normative theory. It does not purport to predict what real-world tax systems look like, or to explain how these tax systems emerge. The theory pays little attention to the institutional and political setting in which tax policy is made. Geoffrey Brennan and James Buchanan [1977] argued that actual tax systems may look more reasonable when political realities are taken into account than they do from an optimal tax point of view.

Assume that in a certain society, there are three commodities, X, Y, and leisure. Labor is totally fixed in supply, and therefore, income is fixed. Currently, this society levies a tax on X, but its constitution forbids taxing Y. Viewing this situation, a student of optimal tax theory might say something like: "You are running an inefficient tax system. Because labor is fixed in supply, you could have no excess burden if you taxed X and Y at equal rates—an income tax. I recommend that you lower the tax on X and impose a tax at the same rate on Y. Set the rates so that the same amount of revenue is collected as before."

Suppose, however, that the citizens suspect that if they allow Y to be taxed, their politicians and bureaucrats will *not* lower the tax rate on X. Rather, they will simply take advantage of the opportunity to tax something new to make tax revenues as large as possible. As we saw in Chapter 7 under "Explaining Government Growth," certain theories of the public sector suggest that those who run the government can and will maximize tax revenues despite the wishes of the citizenry. Therefore, by constitutionally precluding the taxation of Y, the citizens may be rationally protecting themselves against an inefficiently large public sector. In other words, if citizens do not trust the government, what looks inefficient from the point of view of optimal commodity taxation may be efficient in a larger setting.[17]

---

[16] Boskin and Sheshinski [1978] examined the implications of *interdependent utilities*, i.e., the utility of each individual depends not only on his own income but also on the incomes of other individuals. Jonathan Eaton and Harvey Rosen [1980a] studied how people's uncertainties about their future incomes affect optimal tax rates.

[17] Walter Hettich and Stanley Winer [1985] provide further comparison between optimal tax theory and the Buchanan-Brennan approach.

This situation is related to a more general phenomenon called the **time inconsistency of optimal policy.** Suppose that the government announces that it will place a 10 percent tax on the value of capital in place today, but promises that no tax on capital will be levied at any time in the future. While capitalists presumably would not be pleased to pay the tax, it would appear to have no impact on their current incentives to save for the future. Such a tax is in effect a lump sum levy and therefore fully efficient.

There is a problem, however. The government has an incentive to renege on its promise and pull exactly the same trick next year. That way the government can again attempt to raise revenue without an excess burden. Thus, the stated tax policy will be inconsistent with the government's incentives over time. Even worse, the capitalists realize that the government has an incentive to renege. They will change their saving behavior to reflect the expectation that the more they save now, the more they will be taxed next year. Because the expected tax changes behavior, it introduces an inefficiency.

In short, unless the government can *credibly* promise not to renege, it cannot conduct the fully efficient tax policy. To avoid this time inconsistency problem, the government must be able to commit itself to behave in certain ways in the future. How can this be done? One possible approach is to enact constitutional provisions that would forbid the government to go back on its promises. However, as long as the government has an underlying incentive to renege, suspicions will remain, frustrating attempts to run an efficient policy. These considerations suggest that the credibility of the political system must be taken into account before making recommendations based on optimal tax theory.

Other Criteria for Tax Design

As we have seen, optimal taxation depends on the trade-off between "efficiency" and "fairness." However, the use of these concepts in optimal tax theory does not always correspond closely to lay usage. In the context of optimal tax theory, a fair tax is one that guarantees a socially desirable distribution of the tax burden; an efficient tax is one with a small excess burden. In public discussion, on the other hand, a fair tax is often one that imposes equal liabilities on people who have the same ability to pay, and an efficient tax system is one that keeps down administrative and compliance expenses. These alternative notions of fairness and efficiency in taxation are the subject of this section.

Horizontal Equity

A traditional criterion for good tax design is **horizontal equity:** "people in equal positions should be treated equally" [Musgrave, 1959, p. 160]. Horizontal equity appeals to a fundamental sense of justice. However, to use this notion, *equal position* must be defined. Customarily, some observable index of ability to pay, such as income, expenditure, or wealth, defines equal position.

Unfortunately, these measures represent the *outcomes* of people's decisions, and are not really suitable measures of equal position. Consider two individuals, both of whom can earn $10 per hour. Mr. A chooses to work 1,500 hours each year, while Ms. B works 2,200 hours each year. A's income is $15,000 and B's is $22,000, so that in terms of income, A and B are not in "equal positions." In an important sense, however, A and B *are* the same, because their earning capacities are identical—B just happens to work harder. Thus, because work effort is at least to some extent under people's control, two individuals with different incomes may actually be in equal positions. Similar criticism would apply to expenditure or wealth as a criterion for measuring equal positions.

These arguments suggest that the individual's wage *rate* rather than income be considered as a candidate for measuring equal positions, but there are two major problems with this idea.

First, investments in human capital—education, on-the-job training, and health care—can influence the wage rate. If Mr. A had to go to college to earn the same wage that Ms. B is able to earn with only a high school degree, is it fair to treat them the same?

Second, computation of the wage rate requires division of total earnings by hours of work, but the latter is not easy to measure. (How should time spent on coffee breaks be counted?) Indeed, for a given income, it would be worthwhile for a worker to exaggerate hours of work to be able to report a lower wage rate and pay fewer taxes. Presumably, bosses could be induced to collaborate with their employees in return for a share of the tax savings.

As an alternative to measuring equal position either in incomes or wage rates, Feldstein [1976a] suggests that it be defined in utilities. Hence, the **utility definition of horizontal equity:** *(a)* if two individuals would be equally well off (have the same utility level) in the absence of taxation, they should also be equally well off if there is taxation; and *(b)* taxes should not alter the utility ordering—if A is better off than B before taxation, he should be better off after.

To assess the implications of Feldstein's definition, first assume that all individuals have the same preferences, that is, identical utility functions. In this case, individuals who consume the same commodities (including leisure) should pay the same tax, or, equivalently, all individuals should face the same tax schedule. Otherwise, individuals with equal before-tax utility levels would have different after-tax utilities.

Now assume that people have diverse tastes. For example, let there be two types of individuals, Gourmets and Sunbathers. Both groups consume food (which is purchased using income) and leisure, but Gourmets put a relatively high value on food, as do Sunbathers on leisure time. Assume further that prior to any taxation, Gourmets and Sunbathers have identical utility levels. If the same proportional income tax is imposed on everybody, Gourmets are necessarily made worse off than Sunbathers, because the former need relatively large amounts of income to support their food habits. Thus, even though this income tax is perfectly fair judged by the traditional definition of horizontal equity, it is not fair according to the utility definition. Indeed, as long as tastes for leisure differ, *any* income tax violates the utility definition of horizontal equity.

Of course, the practical difficulties involved in measuring individuals' utilities preclude the possibility of having a utility tax. Nevertheless, the utility definition of horizontal equity has some provocative policy implications. Assume again that all individuals have the same preferences. Then it can be shown that *any* existing tax structure does not violate the utility definition of horizontal equity *if* individuals are free to choose their activities and expenditures.

To see why, suppose that in one type of job a large part of compensation is in the form of amenities that are not taxable. These might include pleasant offices, access to a swimming pool, and so forth. In another occupation, compensation is exclusively monetary, all of which is subject to income tax. According to the traditional definition, this situation is a violation of horizontal equity, because a person in the job with a lot of amenities has too small a tax burden. But, if both arrangements coexist and individuals are free to choose, then the net after-tax rewards (including amenities) must be the same in both jobs. Why? Suppose that the net after-tax reward is greater in the jobs with amenities. Then individuals migrate to these jobs to take advantage of them. But the increased supply of workers in these jobs depresses their wages. The process continues until the *net* returns are equal. In short, although people in the different occupations pay unequal taxes, there is no horizontal inequity because of adjustments in the *before-tax* wage.

Some suggest that certain tax advantages available only to the rich are sources of horizontal inequity.[18] According to the utility definition, this notion is wrong. If these advantages are open to everyone with high income, and all high-income people have identical tastes, then the advantages may indeed reduce tax progressiveness, but they have no effect whatsoever on horizontal equity.

We are led to a striking conclusion: Given common tastes, a preexisting tax structure cannot involve horizontal inequity. Rather, all horizontal inequities arise from *changes* in tax laws. This is because individuals make commitments based on the existing tax laws which are difficult or impossible to reverse. For example, people may buy larger houses because of the preferred tax treatment for owner-occupied housing.[19] When

---

[18] A number of such tax provisions are discussed in Chapter 16.

[19] See Chapter 17.

the tax laws are changed, their welfare goes down, and horizontal equity is violated. As one congressman put it, "It seems unfair to people who have done something in good faith to change the law on them."[20] These observations give new meaning to the dictum, "The only good tax is an old tax."

The fact that tax changes may generate horizontal inequities does not necessarily imply that they should not be undertaken. After all, tax changes may lead to improvements from the points of view of efficiency and/or vertical equity. However, the arguments suggest that it might be appropriate somehow to ease the transition to the new tax system. For example, if it is announced that a given tax reform is not to go into effect until a few years subsequent to its passage, people who have based their behavior on the old tax structure will be able to make at least some adjustments to the new regime. The problem of finding fair processes for changing tax regimes **(transitional equity)** is very difficult and not many results are available on the subject.

The very conservative implications of the utility definition of horizontal equity should come as no great surprise, because implicit in the definition is the notion that the pre-tax status quo has special ethical validity. (Otherwise, why be concerned about changes in the ordering of utilities?) However, it is not at all obvious why the status quo deserves to be defended. A more general feature of the utility definition is its focus on the *outcomes* of taxation. In contrast, some have suggested that the essence of horizontal equity is to put constraints on the *rules* that govern the selection of taxes, rather than to provide criteria for judging their effects. Thus, horizontal equity excludes capricious taxes, or taxes based on irrelevant characteristics. For example, we can imagine the government levying special lump sum taxes on people with red hair, or putting very different taxes on angel food and chocolate cakes. The **rule definition** of horizontal equity would presumably exclude such taxes from consideration, even if they somehow had desirable efficiency or distributional effects. In this sense, provisions in the U.S. Constitution that rule out certain kinds of taxes can be interpreted as an attempt to guarantee horizontal equity. (See Chapter 2.)

However, identifying the permissible set of characteristics on which to base taxation is a problem. Most people would agree that religion and race should be irrelevant for purposes of determining tax liability. On the other hand, there is considerable disagreement as to whether or not marital status should influence tax burdens (see Chapter 16 under "Choice of Unit"). And even once there is agreement that certain characteristics are legitimate bases for discrimination, the problem of how much

---

[20] "Changes in Tax Bill Expected," *New York Times*, May 26, 1986, p. 31.

discrimination is appropriate still remains. Everyone agrees that serious physical impairment should be taken into account in determining personal tax liability. But how much must your vision be impaired before you are eligible for special tax treatment as blind? And by what amount should your tax bill be reduced?

We are forced to conclude that horizontal equity, however defined, is a rather amorphous concept. Yet it continues to have enormous appeal as a principle of tax design. Notions of fairness among equals, regardless of their vagueness, will continue to play an important role in the implementation of tax policy.

Costs of Running the Tax System

The 1984 debate between vice presidential candidates George Bush and Geraldine Ferraro included a discussion of their respective tax problems. At one point, the following exchange occurred:

Bush: "I notice she [Ferraro] said she has a new good accountant. I'd like to get his name and phone number because I think I've paid too much in the way of taxes."

Ferraro: "Let me just say that I'd be happy to give the vice president the name of my accountant, but I warn you, he's expensive." [21]

This rare moment of comradery between the candidates illustrates an important point. Contrary to what most optimal tax models assume, collecting taxes is *not* a costless activity. Rather, gathering taxes requires the consumption of resources by the taxing authorities. At the same time, taxpayers incur costs in complying with the tax system. These include outlays for accountants and tax lawyers, as well as the value of taxpayers' time spent on filling out tax returns and keeping records.

The costs of administering the income tax in the United States are fairly low. For example, the Internal Revenue Service spends only about 51 cents to raise each $100 in taxes [Commissioner of Internal Revenue, 1990]. However, the compliance costs of personal income taxation are quite substantial. On the basis of survey evidence, Joel Slemrod and Nikki Sorum [1983] estimated that in 1982, the average U.S. household devoted about 29 hours to state and federal tax preparation, and spent about $53 for professional advice. If the value of time is approximated at about $10.70 per hour, then the total resource cost per household is about $364. Multiplying this by the 97 million taxpaying units in 1982 gives a total resource cost of $35.3 billion, about 9 percent of total federal and state income tax revenue. The desire to reduce the costs of federal income tax compliance was one of the important motivations for the tax reform bill passed in 1986. However, it is still too early to estimate the effect that this tax "simplification" has had on compliance costs.

---

[21] "The Candidates' Finances," *New York Times,* October 12, 1984, p. B5.

Clearly, the choice of tax and subsidy systems should take account of administrative and compliance costs. Even systems that appear fair and efficient (in the excess burden sense) might be undesirable because they are excessively complicated and expensive to administer. Consider the possibility of taxing output produced in the home—housecleaning, child care, and so on. As suggested in Chapter 14, the fact that market work is taxed but housework is not creates a sizable distortion in the allocation of labor. Moreover, an argument could be made that taxing differentially on the basis of choice of workplace violates some notions of horizontal equity. Nevertheless, the difficulties involved in valuing household production would create such huge administrative costs that the idea is infeasible.

Unfortunately, in many cases, administrative problems receive insufficient attention. A classic case is the federal luxury tax on new jewelry enacted in 1990. The tax applies only to the portion of the price that exceeds $10,000, and only items worn for adornment are subject to the tax. As *The Wall Street Journal* noted, the tax is an administrative nightmare: "loose gems and repairs aren't taxed; market value after a major modification is. Thus, . . . you may be taxed if you have gems from your grandma's brooch put in a new setting. But you won't be if you replace a $30,000 diamond lost from a ring; that's a repair."[22] Some commentators predicted that the costs to the Internal Revenue Service of collecting the luxury tax would exceed the revenues collected!

Obviously, no tax system is costless to administer; the trick is to think carefully about whether or not the administrative costs are worth the benefits. To make this notion more concrete, assume that the government can potentially levy a large number of commodity taxes, some of which are more costly to administer than others.[23] Now, the more of the taxes that the government levies, the smaller the excess burden of collecting a given amount of tax revenue. This is due to the fact that when a commodity is excluded from taxation, in effect its tax rate is set as zero. In general, however, we expect the Ramsey rule to imply nonzero tax rates on each commodity. Hence, as each commodity becomes subject to taxation, its tax rate can be set at the efficient level, and excess burden decreases.[24] Intuitively, excess burden decreases because the tax burden is "spread over" more commodities.

On the other hand, as more taxes are levied, the costs of administration increase. The optimal size of tax administration is the number of tax instruments for which the *total* costs of tax collection—excess burden

---

[22] Schmedel, Scott R., "Tax Report," *The Wall Street Journal,* January 9, 1991, p. A1.

[23] This analysis is based on Shlomo Yitzhaki [1979].

[24] More precisely, the excess burden cannot increase with the number of possible taxes provided that as more taxes are introduced, each tax rate is reset so that the Ramsey rule holds.

plus administrative costs—is at a minimum. Thus, when administrative costs are included, the efficient tax system may involve a zero tax rate on many commodities. For such commodities, any reductions in excess burden that arise from spreading the tax burden are more than offset by the associated administrative costs.

Tax Evasion

We now turn to one of the most important problems facing any tax administration—cheating. First, it is important to distinguish between tax avoidance and tax evasion. **Tax avoidance** is changing your behavior in such a way as to reduce your legal tax liability. There is nothing illegal about tax avoidance:

> Over and over again courts have said that there is nothing sinister in so arranging one's affairs so as to keep taxes as low as possible. Everybody does so, rich or poor; and all do right, for nobody owes any public duty to pay more than the law demands. . . . To demand more in the name of morals is mere cant. [Judge Learned Hand, *Commissioner* v. *Newman,* 1947].

In contrast, **tax evasion** is failing to pay legally due taxes. If a tax on mushrooms is levied and you sell fewer mushrooms, it is tax avoidance. If you fail to report your sales of mushrooms to the government, it is tax evasion. Tax evasion is not a new problem. Centuries ago Plato observed, "When there is an income tax, the just man will pay more and the unjust less on the same amount of income." In recent years, however, the phenomenon of tax evasion has received an especially large amount of public attention. A case that received a lot of publicity was that of Leona Helmsley, the New York "hotel queen." In 1989, she was convicted of evading more than $1 million in federal income taxes. As punishment, Helmsley was sentenced to four years in jail and ordered to pay a $7.1 million fine in addition to the taxes she owed.

Tax cheating is extremely difficult to measure. The Internal Revenue Service estimated that in 1987, the difference between the amount of income tax owed by taxpayers and the amount they voluntarily paid was about $85 billion [U.S. General Accounting Office, 1990]. If this estimate is even roughly accurate, it suggests that evasion is a very important issue.

There are several common ways to commit tax fraud:

1. Keep two sets of books to record business transactions. One records the actual business and the other is shown to the tax authorities. Some evaders use two cash registers.

2. Moonlight for cash. Of course, there is nothing illegal in working an extra job. In many cases, however, the income received on such jobs is paid in cash rather than by check. Hence, there is no legal record, and the income is not reported to the tax authorities.

3. Barter. "I'll fix your car if you bake me five loaves of bread." When you receive payment in kind instead of money, it is legally a taxable transaction. However, such income is seldom reported.

4. Underreport tips. Tips paid to hotel and restaurant workers, parking lot attendants, and the like are subject to taxation. Only the recipient knows for sure how much is received, however, and underreporting is common.

5. Deal in cash. Paying for goods and services with cash and checks made out to "cash" makes it very difficult for the Internal Revenue Service to trace transactions.[25]

Public perception of the tax evader has changed over time. As Agnar Sandmo [1981] notes, whereas previously tax evasion was associated with income from capital hidden in Swiss bank accounts, the current image of a tax evader may well be a repairer who gets a substantial amount of income from "unofficial" work not reported for tax purposes. There is widespread feeling that "everyone is doing it."

We first discuss the positive theory of tax evasion, and then turn to the normative question of how public policy should deal with it.

Positive analysis of tax evasion.   Assume that Al cares only about maximizing his expected income.[26] He has a given amount of earnings and is trying to choose R, the amount that he hides from the tax authorities. Suppose that Al's marginal income tax rate is 0.3; for each dollar shielded from taxable income, his tax bill falls by 30 cents. This is the marginal benefit to him of hiding a dollar of income from the tax authorities. More generally, when Al faces a marginal income tax rate t, the marginal benefit of each dollar shielded from taxation is t.

The tax authority does not know Al's true income, but it randomly audits all taxpayers' returns. As a result, there is some probability, π, that Al will be audited. If he is caught cheating, Al pays a penalty which increases with R at an increasing rate. Note that if it were costless to monitor Al every second of every day, there would be no opportunities for evasion. The fact that such monitoring is infeasible is the fundamental source of the problem.

Assuming that Al knows the value of π and the penalty schedule, he makes his decision by comparing the marginal costs and benefits of cheating. In Figure 15.5 the amount of income not reported is measured on the horizontal axis, and dollars on the vertical. The marginal benefit *(MB)* for each dollar not reported is t, the amount of tax saved. The expected

---

[25] For further examples, see Steve Lohr [1981, p. 1].

[26] This model is similar in structure to those that have been used to describe criminal behavior in general. See Gary Becker [1968] and Frank Cowell [1985].

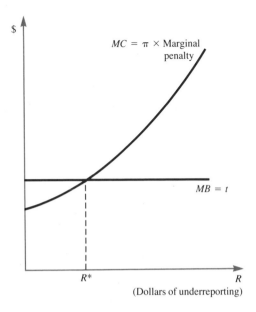

Figure 15.5
Optimal tax evasion
is positive

marginal cost *(MC)* is the amount by which the penalty goes up for each dollar of cheating (the marginal penalty) times the probability of detection. For example, if the additional penalty for hiding the thousandth dollar is \$1.50 and the probability of detection is 1 in 3, then the *expected* marginal penalty is 50 cents. The "optimal" amount of cheating is where the two schedules cross, at R^*. R^* is optimal in the sense that *on average* it is the policy that maximizes Al's income. In a world of uncertainty, finding the best policy in this "expected value" sense is a reasonable way to proceed. It is possible, of course, that it will be optimal not to cheat at all. For the individual in Figure 15.6, the marginal cost of cheating exceeds the marginal benefit for all positive values of R, so the optimum is equal to zero.

The model implies that cheating increases when marginal tax rates go up. This is because a higher value of t increases the marginal benefit of evasion, shifting up the marginal benefit schedule so that the intersection with marginal cost occurs at a higher value of R.[27] On the basis of such reasoning, many people expect the reduction of marginal income tax rates enacted in 1986 to reduce cheating. A further implication of the model is that cheating decreases when the probability of detection goes up and when the marginal penalty rate increases. Both of these steps raise the expected marginal cost of cheating.

Although this model yields useful insights, it ignores some potentially important considerations.

---

[27] This prediction is borne out by the econometric work of Charles Clotfelter [1983], who estimated that the elasticity of underreported income with respect to the marginal tax rate is about 0.84.

Figure 15.6
Optimal tax evasion
is zero

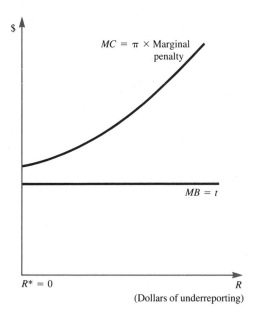

(Dollars of underreporting)

Psychic costs of cheating.   Simply put, tax evasion may make people feel guilty. One way to model this phenomenon is by adding psychic costs to the marginal cost schedule. For some very honest people, the psychic costs are so high that they would not cheat even if the expected marginal penalty were zero.

Risk aversion.   Figures 15.5 and 15.6 assume that people care only about expected income, and that risk per se does not bother them. To the extent that individuals are risk averse, their decisions to engage in what is essentially a gamble may be modified. (See the Appendix to Chapter 12 for a discussion of choice under uncertainty.)

Work choices.   The model assumes that the only decision is how much income to report. The type of job and the amount of before-tax income are taken as given. In reality, the tax system may affect hours of work and what kinds of jobs people take. For example, high marginal tax rates might induce people to choose occupations that provide substantial opportunities for evading taxation, the so-called **underground economy**.[28] This includes economic activities that are legal but easy to hide from the tax authorities (home repairs) as well as work that is criminal per se (prostitution, selling drugs). Some estimates place the size of the underground economy at 5 to 10 percent of gross national product [Cowell, 1985]. One of the few econometric analyses of an underground economy

---

[28] However, this is not necessarily the case. See Sandmo [1981].

is a study by Bernard Fortin, Thomas Lemieux, and Pierre Frechette [1990] on data from a random survey carried out in the region of Quebec City, Canada. They found that when marginal tax rates increase, so does the probability of participating in the underground sector.

Changing probabilities of audit.   In our simple analysis, the probability of an audit is independent of both the amount evaded and the size of income reported. However, in the United States audit probabilities depend on occupation and the size of reported income. This complicates the model but does not change its essential aspects.

It is clear that cheating is a more complicated phenomenon than Figures 15.5 and 15.6 suggest. Nevertheless, the model provides us with a useful framework for thinking about the factors that influence the decision to evade. Unfortunately, by its very nature, it is difficult to do empirical work on tax evasion. Consequently, it is not known whether high fines or frequent audits are more effective ways of deterring cheating. One tentative result that emerges from several econometric studies is that for most groups, audits do increase the probability of subsequent compliance, but the magnitude of the effect is small [Beron, Tauchen, and Witte, 1990].

Normative analysis of tax evasion.   An assumption in much public discussion is that the existence of the underground economy is a bad thing and that policy should be designed to reduce its size. Although possibly correct, this proposition is worth careful scrutiny.

An important question in this context is whether or not we care about the welfare of tax evaders. In the jargon of welfare economics, are the utilities of participants in the underground economy to be included in the social welfare function? Assume for the moment that they are. Then under certain conditions, the existence of an underground economy raises social welfare. For example, if the supply of labor is more elastic to the underground economy than to the regular economy, optimal tax theory suggests that the former be taxed at a relatively low rate. This is simply an application of the inverse elasticity rule, Equation (15.11). Alternatively, suppose that participants in the underground economy tend to be poorer than those in the regular economy. Then to the extent society has egalitarian income redistribution objectives, leaving the underground economy intact might be desirable.

Of course, there is no proof that either of these assertions is correct. The important point is that analysis of the usual utilitarian welfare criteria leads to ambiguous results about the desirability of an underground economy.[29]

---

[29] For further discussion along these lines, see Sandmo [1981].

Consider now the policy implications when evaders are not given any weight in the social welfare function, and the goal is simply to eliminate cheating at the lowest administrative cost possible. Figure 15.5 suggests a fairly straightforward way to accomplish this objective. The expected marginal cost of cheating is the product of the penalty rate and the probability of detection. The probability of detection depends on the amount of resources devoted to tax administration; if the Internal Revenue Service has a big budget, it can catch a lot of cheaters. However, even if the tax authorities have a small budget so that the probability of detection is low, the marginal cost of cheating can still be made arbitrarily high if the penalty is large enough. If only one tax evader were caught each year, but he or she were publicly hanged for the crime, the *expected* cost of tax evasion would deter many people. The fact that such a draconian policy has never been seriously proposed in the United States is indicative of the fact that existing penalty systems try to take into account the notion of *just retribution*.[30] Contrary to the assumptions of the utilitarian framework, society cares not only about the end result (getting rid of cheaters) but also the processes by which the result is achieved.

In their search for a socially acceptable way to deal with tax evaders, many state governments have declared periods of **tax amnesty.** During a tax amnesty, people can pay delinquent taxes without facing criminal charges for their previous tax evasion. From 1981 to 1990, 31 states and the District of Columbia conducted tax amnesties [Graetz, 1990], and the possibility of declaring a federal tax amnesty has been suggested.

There are several difficulties involved in trying to assess the likely impact on tax collections of a federal tax amnesty. In many cases, state tax amnesties have been accompanied by the state's announced intention to increase its enforcement efforts. The success of many tax amnesty programs, then, is really due not just to the amnesty but rather to a tax amnesty combined with increased enforcement. This makes it difficult to extrapolate from the experience of state governments to the potential success of a federal tax amnesty, since federal tax enforcement standards are already quite strict. A further problem in assessing the success of tax amnesty programs lies in the long-term effects of tax amnesties on tax compliance. Three states have held more than one tax amnesty; when tax amnesties are declared repeatedly, the knowledge that an amnesty is forthcoming can lower taxpayers' perceived chances of being prosecuted for future tax evasion. By lowering the expected costs of future tax evasion, an amnesty program that brings with it an expectation of future amnesties may actually *increase* tax evasion. Because

---

[30] Other nations have not been so constrained in enforcing economic honesty. In China, for example, embezzlement can be a capital offense.

state amnesty programs began in the 1980s, it is too early to assess such long-term consequences. In light of these considerations, several investigators have estimated that a federal tax amnesty would raise very little net revenue, about $1 billion [Lerman, 1986, pp. 325–26].

The development of the underground economy raises several broader issues for society. Some have argued, for example, that cheating is habit-forming; once people become accustomed to evading taxation, they continue to do so, even if marginal tax rates are lowered in the future [see Lindbeck, 1980b]. There is no econometric evidence for this assertion, but it is very troubling. There are also fears that growth of the underground economy will force some people into cheating. Suppose that tax evasion becomes prevalent in sectors of the economy dominated by small businesses whose activities are particularly difficult to monitor. Then firms that eschew cheating are at a competitive disadvantage because of higher costs. The only choices for these firms are to cheat or to go out of business.

More generally, in a system that relies to an important extent on self-assessment by taxpayers, a high marginal tax rate is in some sense a tax on honesty. Honesty is obviously a desirable quality for ethical reasons. It is also important for the functioning of the economy. Just imagine what would happen to efficiency if for every economic transaction, you had to take precautions against being cheated. The fact that our tax system makes it expensive to be honest has consequences that are impossible to quantify, but which may be significant.

Optimal Taxation and the Global Economy

So far, our analysis of optimal tax theory has been in a national context. Given the huge volume of world trade and its importance to the U.S. economy (exports were over $600 billion in 1990), the optimal tax treatment of international transactions is of some interest. This section discusses the efficiency and equity aspects of taxing income earned abroad. In addition to being of independent interest, this topic allows us to apply in a new setting the approach to optimal taxation discussed in this chapter. We first discuss tax issues for individuals and then turn to businesses. In both cases, the design of an equitable and efficient tax system requires consideration of issues not present in a purely domestic setting.

Individuals

U.S. provisions.   Income earned by an individual outside his or her nation of citizenship is potentially of interest to the tax authorities of the citizen's home and host governments. U.S. law recognizes the principle that the host country has the primary right to tax income earned within its borders. At the same time, the United States adheres to the notion that an American citizen, wherever he or she earns money, has a tax obligation to the native land. To avoid double taxation of foreign source income, the

United States taxes income earned abroad, but allows a credit for tax paid to foreign governments.[31] Suppose that Smith's U.S. tax liability on her income earned in Germany is $7,000, and she had paid $5,500 in German income taxes. Then $5,500 can be taken as a credit on Smith's U.S. tax return, so that she need pay only $1,500 to the Internal Revenue Service. A U.S. citizen's total tax liability, then, is based on *global* income.

Global versus territorial systems.   The philosophical premise of the U.S. system is that equity in taxation is defined on a citizenship basis.[32] If you are a U.S. citizen, the total amount of tax you pay should be roughly independent of whether you earn your income at home or abroad. We refer to this as a **global system.** In contrast, virtually every other country adheres to a **territorial system**—a citizen earning income abroad need pay tax only to the host government. (See Bhagwati [1982, p. 286].) Which system is better? It is hard to build a case for the superiority of one system over the other on either equity or efficiency grounds. The following paragraphs expand on the problem.

Equity.   John, a citizen of the United Kingdom, and Sam, a U.S. citizen, both work in Hong Kong and have identical incomes. Because the United Kingdom has a territorial system, John pays tax only to Hong Kong. Sam, on the other hand, also owes money to the United States (provided that his U.S. tax bill is higher than his Hong Kong tax payment). Thus, Sam pays more tax than John, even though they have the same income. Although a global system produces equal treatment for citizens of the same country, it can lead to substantially different treatments for citizens of different countries. Should horizontal equity be defined on a national or world basis? Each principle has some merit, but in general, no system of international tax coordination can satisfy both.

Efficiency.   The global system may distort international production decisions. Suppose that American firms operating abroad have to pay the U.S. income tax for their American employees. French firms, which operate under the territorial system, have no analogous obligation. Other things being the same, then, the U.S. companies may end up paying more for their labor, and hence be at a cost disadvantage.[33] French firms could conceivably win more contracts than the American firms, even if the latter are more technologically efficient.

---

[31] The credit cannot exceed what the U.S. tax on the foreign income would have been.

[32] Much of this discussion is based on Jagdish Bhagwati [1982, pp. 286–87].

[33] This assumes that: *(a)* the incidence of the U.S. tax falls on employers rather than employees, and *(b)* American companies cannot respond simply by hiring French workers. The validity of assumption *(a)* depends on the elasticity of supply of U.S. workers to U.S. firms abroad. To the extent the supply curve is not horizontal, employees bear part of the tax. See Chapter 13.

On the other hand, a territorial system can produce a different distortion—in people's locational decisions. Citizens of a given country may find their decision to work abroad influenced by the fact that their tax liability depends on where they live. Under a global regime, you cannot escape your country's tax collector unless you change citizenship. Hence, there is less incentive to relocate just for tax purposes.

Thus, the global system may distort production decisions, and the territorial system residential decisions. It is hard to know which distortion creates a larger efficiency cost.

Relation to the brain drain.   In the United States, the tax treatment of personal foreign-source income has not been a prominent issue in public policy debates. In contrast, the problem occupies center stage in many less-developed countries. It arises in discussions of the **brain drain,** the emigration of highly skilled citizens of these nations to more developed countries.

Because the less-developed countries tend to use the territorial system, once a citizen of such a nation leaves, the country has no claim on the citizen's earnings. Some argue that less-developed countries should tax the incomes of their citizens who are successful abroad. Doing so might discourage some of the society's more productive members from leaving. And the taxes collected from those who still chose to emigrate could be used to benefit those left behind. The basic justification is that "one should reject . . . citizenship without the obligation to pay the income tax" [Bhagwati, 1982, p. 285].

The idea of taxing citizens employed abroad raises a number of difficult philosophical questions. What relationship is there between social responsibilities and place of birth? Why should an Indian practicing medicine in Chicago owe more to India than an American practicing medicine in Chicago? Does the answer hinge on the amount of Indian resources that were devoted to the Indian's education? Should citizens who wish to leave a country be required to pay back the money that the country has invested in them? What is the trade-off between the personal freedom to move and social responsibility?

Let us assume that the government of a less-developed country has somehow worked its way through these questions and come to the conclusion that taxing emigrants on their foreign earnings is justifiable. Assume further that it is administratively feasible for that country to collect the tax. The country must then reformulate its optimal income tax schedule in light of this new opportunity.

In the standard optimal income tax problem, higher tax rates allow more income redistribution, but they lower economic efficiency. The idea is to find the tax schedule associated with just the right combination of efficiency and equity. Here, the basic setup is the same, but for a country on the territorial system, "efficiency" must include not only distortions in work decisions but also losses to the nation when highly productive people emigrate to escape taxation.

Bhagwati and Hamada [1982] showed that under reasonable conditions, the opportunity to tax emigrants raises the optimal tax rate. Allowing the taxation of emigrants puts more resources at the less-developed country's disposal, so that it can pursue a more redistributive policy than would otherwise have been possible. Alternatively, the ability to tax emigrants makes the effective labor supply in the home country more inelastic, because workers cannot escape tax by moving abroad. As shown earlier, the more inelastic the supply of labor, the higher the optimal marginal tax rate, other things being the same.

We observed at the outset that the entire argument rests on the assumption that it is administratively feasible to tax emigrants. Earlier sections of this chapter stressed that the problem of enforcing tax compliance is never easy, and it is much harder when the taxpayers are abroad. Even if an effective method were somehow devised, some emigrants might respond by changing their citizenship. The possibility that a country may create a class of tax exiles needs to be taken into account in determining the optimal tax schedule.

Corporate Income

U.S. tax treatment of foreign-source corporate income is similar to the treatment of individuals. U.S. multinational corporations are subject to tax at the standard rate on total taxable income, including income earned abroad. A credit is then allowed for foreign taxes paid—for each dollar of tax paid to the foreign government, U.S. tax liability is reduced by a dollar. The credit cannot exceed the amount that would have been owed under U.S. tax law.

An evaluation of the U.S. tax treatment of multinational firms requires a careful statement of the policy goal. One possible objective is to maximize worldwide income, another is to maximize national income. A system that is optimal given one goal may not be optimal given another.

Maximization of world income.   The maximization of world income requires that the before-tax rate of return on the last dollar invested in each country—the marginal rate of return—be the same.[34] To see why, imagine a situation in which marginal returns are not equal. Then it would be possible to increase world income simply by taking capital from a country where its marginal return was low and moving it to one where the

---

[34] As usual, we refer here to rates of return after differences in risk are taken into account.

marginal return was high.[35] Algebraically, if $r_{U.S.}$ is the marginal rate of return in the United States and r_f is the marginal rate of return in a given foreign country, then worldwide efficiency requires

$$r_f = r_{U.S.} \qquad\qquad (15.14)$$

What kind of tax system induces profit-maximizing firms to allocate their capital so that the outcome is consistent with Equation (15.14)? The answer hinges on the fact that investors make their decisions on the basis of after-tax returns. They therefore allocate their capital across countries so that the after-tax marginal return in each country is equal. If $t_{U.S.}$ is the U.S. tax rate and t_f is the foreign tax rate, a firm allocates its capital so that

$$(1 - t_f)r_f = (1 - t_{U.S.})r_{U.S.} \qquad\qquad (15.15)$$

Clearly, condition (15.15) is satisfied if and only if t_f equals $t_{U.S.}$. Intuitively, if we want capital allocated efficiently from a global point of view, capital must be taxed at the same rate wherever it is located.

The policy implication seems to be that if the United States cares about maximizing world income, it should devise a system that makes its firms' tax liabilities independent of their location. A *full* credit against foreign taxes paid would do the trick. However, as already noted, the U.S. system allows a tax credit *only* up to the amount that U.S. tax on the foreign earnings would have been.

Why is the credit limit present? Our model implicitly assumes that the behavior of foreign governments is independent of U.S. government actions. Suppose that the United States announces it will pursue a policy of allowing a full foreign tax credit to its multinational firms. Then foreign governments have an incentive to raise their own tax rates on U.S. corporations virtually without limit. Doing so will not drive out the foreign countries' American firms, because the tax liability for their domestic operations is reduced by a dollar for every dollar foreign taxes are increased.[36] Essentially, the program turns into a transfer from the United States to foreign treasuries. Limiting the credit is an obvious way to prevent this from happening.

Maximization of national income.   At the outset, we noted the importance of defining the objectives of tax policy on foreign source corporate income. Some have argued that tax policy should be set to maximize not

---

[35] For further discussion of this principle, see the Appendix at the end of the book.

[36] The amount the foreign government can extract in this way is limited to the firm's tax liability to the United States on its domestic operations. Suppose that the firm's tax liability on its U.S. operations is $1,000. If the foreign government levies a tax of $1,000, under a full credit, the firm's U.S. tax liability is zero. If the foreign government raises the tax to $1,001, the firm's domestic tax liability cannot be reduced any further (assuming that there is no negative income tax for corporations).

world income, but national income.[37] Some care must be taken in defining national income here. It is the sum of *before*-tax domestically produced income and foreign-source income *after* foreign taxes are paid. This is because taxes paid by U.S. firms to the U.S. government, although not available to the firms themselves, are still part of U.S. income. Thus, domestic income is counted before tax. However, taxes paid to foreign governments are not available to U.S. citizens, so foreign income is counted after tax.

National income maximization requires a different condition than that shown in Equation (15.14). The difference arises because marginal rates of return must now be measured from the U.S. point of view. According to the U.S. perspective, the marginal rate of return abroad is $(1 - t_f)r_f$—foreign taxes represent a cost from the U.S. point of view and hence are excluded in valuing the rate of return. The marginal return on investments in the United States is measured at the before-tax rate, $r_{U.S.}$. Hence, maximization of national income requires

$$(1 - t_f)r_f = r_{U.S.} \tag{15.16}$$

A comparison with Equation (15.14) suggests that under a regime of world income maximization, investments are made abroad until $r_f = r_{U.S.}$, while if national income maximization is the goal, foreign investment is made until $r_f = r_{U.S.}/(1 - t_f)$. In words, if national income maximization is the goal, the before-tax marginal rate of return on foreign investment is higher than it would be if global income maximization were the goal. [As long as t_f is less than one, $r_{U.S.} < r_{U.S.}/(1 - t_f)$.] But under the reasonable assumption that the marginal return to investment decreases with the amount of investment, a higher before-tax rate of return means less investment. In short, from a national point of view, world income maximization results in "too much" investment abroad.

What kind of tax system induces American firms to allocate their capital so that Equation (15.16) is satisfied? Suppose that multinational firms are allowed to *deduct* foreign tax payments from their U.S. taxable income. (For example, a firm with domestic income of $1,000 and foreign taxes of $200 would have a U.S. taxable income of $800.) Given that foreign tax payments are deductible, a firm's overseas return of r_f increases its taxable U.S. income by $r_f(1 - t_f)$. Therefore, after U.S. taxes, the return on the foreign investment is $r_f(1 - t_f)(1 - t_{U.S.})$. At the same time, the after-tax return on investments in the United States is $r_{U.S.}(1 - t_{U.S.})$. Assuming that the investors equalize after-tax marginal returns at home and abroad,

$$r_f(1 - t_f)(1 - t_{U.S.}) = r_{U.S.}(1 - t_{U.S.}) \tag{15.17}$$

---

[37] In our normative framework, this view implies that only the utilities of U.S. citizens appear in the relevant social welfare function. The conflict between a world and a national point of view is analogous to the clash of national and community perspectives that arises in federal systems. See Chapter 21.

Clearly, Equations (15.17) and (15.16) are equivalent. [Just divide both sides of (15.17) by $(1 - t_{U.S.})$.] Because Equation (15.16) is the condition for national income maximization, this implies that deduction of foreign tax payments leads to a pattern of investment that maximizes U.S. income.

Such reasoning has led to some political support for replacing credits for foreign taxes paid with deductions. One important problem with the case for deductions is that the analysis assumes that the capital-exporting country can impose the tax rate that maximizes its income, while the capital-importing foreign countries passively keep their own tax rates constant. Martin Feldstein and David Hartman [1977] analyzed a model in which the capital-exporting country takes into account the possibility that changes in its tax rate may induce changes in the host countries' tax rates. Suppose, for example, that if the United States lowers its tax rate on capital invested abroad, host governments do the same. In this case, it may be worthwhile for the United States to tax preferentially income earned abroad. Of course, it is also possible that host governments could choose to raise their tax rates when the U.S. rate goes down. The point is that when interdependent behavior is allowed, the national income-maximizing tax system generally does not consist of a simple deduction for foreign taxes paid. The effective tax rate on foreign-source income can be either larger or smaller than that associated with deductibility. We conclude that just as in the strictly domestic context, optimal tax theory shows that simple rules of thumb for tax policy do not necessarily achieve a given goal.

Overview

Traditional analysis of tax systems elucidated several "principles" of tax design: taxes should have horizontal and vertical equity, be "neutral" with respect to economic incentives, be administratively easy, and so on. In recent years, public finance economists have integrated these somewhat ad hoc guidelines with the principles of welfare economics. The optimal tax literature *derives* the criteria for a good tax using an underlying social welfare function.

On some occasions, optimal tax analysis has corrected previous errors. For example, it may *not* be efficient for all tax rates to be the same (neutral). More frequently, however, the benefit has been to clarify the trade-offs between efficiency and equity in tax design. As a by-product, the various definitions of "equity" have been scrutinized carefully.

The result of this work is not a blueprint for building a tax system, if for no other reason than the economic theory forming the basis for optimal tax theory has its own problems (see Chapter 4). In this context two comments are cogent: (1) Optimal tax theory generally ignores political and social institutions. An "optimal" tax may easily be ruined by politicians or be overly costly to administer. (2) While the optimal tax approach points out that the concept of horizontal equity is difficult to make operational, the fact remains that *equal treatment of equals* is an appealing ethical concept. Horizontal equity is difficult to integrate with optimal tax theory because of the latter's focus on outcomes rather than processes.

Thus, optimal tax theory has used the tools of welfare economics to add analytical strength to the traditional discussion of the goals of tax design. Nevertheless, it is wedded to the utilitarian welfare approach in economics. As such, it is open to criticisms concerning the adequacy of this description of the world.

Summary

- Efficient commodity tax theory studies the methods by which a given amount of revenue may be raised while creating a minimum excess burden.

- The Ramsey rule stipulates that to minimize excess burden, tax rates should be set so that the proportional reduction in the quantity demanded of each good is the same.

- When goods are unrelated in consumption, the Ramsey rule implies that relative tax rates should be inversely related to compensated demand elasticities.

- Choosing optimal user fees for government-produced services is quite similar to choosing optimal taxes. In particular, there are efficiency and distributional considerations in choosing an optimal two-part tariff.

- Income taxation is a major source of revenue in developed countries. Edgeworth's early study of optimal income taxes stipulated that after-tax incomes be equal. However, when the excess burden of distorting the leisure-income trade-off is included, marginal tax rates of far less than 100 percent are optimal. A surprising result of optimal income tax theory is that if marginal tax rates are allowed to vary, in general, the marginal tax rate on the highest income should be zero.

- Tax systems may be evaluated by standards other than those of optimal tax theory. Horizontal equity, the costs of administration, incentives for tax evasion, and political constraints all affect the design of tax systems.

- Traditional definitions of horizontal equity rely on income as a measure of "equal position" in society. However, it is not clear that income as conventionally measured does an adequate job. The utility definition is more precise, but leads to radically different policy provisions and contains an inherent bias toward the pre-tax status quo. Other definitions of horizontal equity focus on the rules by which taxes are chosen.

- The costs of running a tax system are ignored in most theoretical analyses. However, administrative and compliance costs affect the choice of tax base, tax rates, and the amount of tax evasion.

- The general approach of this chapter can also be applied to international tax policy. For example, the brain drain problem faced by many less-developed countries can be analyzed using the same basic model employed to explore optimal income taxation.

Discussion Questions

1. "If the compensated demand for a single commodity is completely inelastic, the most socially desirable ad valorem tax rate on this commodity will be higher than the tax rates on other commodities." Comment.

2. In 1991, the federal government introduced a tax of 10 percent on that part of a car's price exceeding $30,000. (For example, the tax liability on a $45,000 car would be 0.10 × ($45,000 − $30,000), or $1,500.) Discuss the efficiency, equity, and administrability of this "luxury car tax."

3. Give an example of a tax schedule with high average tax rates on high incomes and with a zero marginal tax rate on the last dollar earned.

4. "If tips must be reported as taxable income, restaurants will go out of business, costing jobs. In addition, it's too hard to find out how much in tips waiters and waitresses actually receive. Besides, most of the people who earn tips have low incomes and shouldn't be taxed anyway." Discuss the equity and efficiency aspects of the problem of taxing tips.

5. Explain: "The choice between deductions and credits for taxes paid to foreign governments by multinational corporations depends on the choice between national and global income maximization."

Selected References

Aaron, H. "Politics and the Professors Revisited." *American Economic Review*, May 1989, pp. 1–15.

Sandmo, Agnar. "Optimal Taxation—An Introduction to the Literature." *Journal of Public Economics* 6 (1976), pp. 37–54.

Simon, Carl P., and Ann D. Witte. "The Underground Economy: Estimates of Size, Structure and Trends." In *Special Study on Economic Change*, vol. 5, *Government Regulation: Achieving Social and Economic Balance*. Washington, D.C.: U.S. Government Printing Office, 1980, pp. 70–120.

Slemrod, Joel. "Do We Know How Progressive the Income Tax System Should Be?" *National Tax Journal* 36, no. 3 (September 1983), pp. 361–70.

5

The United States Revenue System

The next five chapters are devoted to description and analysis of the major sources of revenue in the U.S. fiscal system. This involves some bad news and some good news. The bad news is that it is hard to know just how long the descriptive material will be correct. Despite the fact that there were major changes in the tax system in 1986 and 1990, important modifications are under consideration, and it is likely that a number of "reforms" will be made in the future. The good news is that after seeing the tools of public finance applied to the existing tax institutions, the reader will be in a position to analyze any new taxes that may arise. Moreover, for each tax we discuss some of the major proposed modifications.

Describing each tax individually seems to be the only feasible expositional technique. Nevertheless, keep in mind that the various taxes do interact. For example, your federal income tax liability depends in part on the amount of property tax paid to local government. More generally, failure to consider more than one tax at a time gives a misleading picture of the overall magnitude of the tax burden.

CHAPTER 16

The Personal Income Tax

It was true as taxes is. And nothing's truer than them.

CHARLES DICKENS
David Copperfield

The personal income tax is the workhorse of the federal revenue system. In 1990, about 100 million tax returns were filed, which generated $476 billion in revenue, and accounted for 46 percent of federal budget receipts.[1] This chapter discusses problems associated with designing a personal income tax system, how the United States has dealt with them, and the efficiency and equity of the results.

Since its inception in 1913, the income tax code has been revised several times. Recently, the **Tax Reform Act of 1986** (which we refer to as **TRA86**) and the **Omnibus Budget Reconciliation Act of 1990** (**OBRA90,** for short) created sweeping changes. Our discussion devotes special attention to explaining and evaluating these changes.

Basic Structure

Americans file an annual tax return that computes their previous year's tax liability. The return is due every April 15. As the cartoon indicates, this date is emblazoned in the minds of most taxpayers. The calculation of tax liability requires a series of steps summarized in Figure 16.1.[2] The first step is to compute **Adjusted Gross Income (AGI).** AGI is defined as total income from all taxable sources less certain expenses incurred in earning that income. Taxable sources include (but are not limited to) wages, dividends, interest, business and farm profits, rents, royalties, prizes, and even the proceeds from embezzlement.

---

[1] Computed from Office of Management and Budget [1990].

[2] Our exposition of legal issues is necessarily sketchy. For details, see Michael Graetz [1988].

370

Drawing by M. Stevens;
© 1986 The New Yorker
Magazine, Inc.

Not all of AGI is subject to tax. The second step is to convert AGI to **taxable income**—the amount of income subject to tax. This is done by subtracting various amounts called **exemptions** and **deductions** from AGI. Deductions and exemptions are discussed more carefully later.

The final step is to calculate the amount of tax due. A **rate schedule** indicates the tax liability associated with each level of taxable income. Different types of taxpayers face different rate schedules. For example, husbands and wives who file tax returns together—joint returns—have different rates than single people.

For most taxpayers, during the year some tax is withheld out of each paycheck. The amount that actually has to be paid on April 15 is the difference between the tax liability and the accumulated withholding payments. If more has been withheld than is owed, the taxpayer is entitled to a refund.

It sounds pretty straightforward, but in reality, complications arise in every step of the process. We now discuss some of the major problems.

Defining Income

Clearly, the ability to identify "income" is necessary to operate an income tax.[3] A natural way to begin this section would be to discuss and evaluate the tax code's definition of income. However, the law provides no definition. The constitutional amendment that introduced the tax merely says "The Congress shall have power to lay and collect taxes on incomes, from whatever source derived." While the tax law does provide examples of items that should be classified as income—wages and salaries, rents, dividends, and so on—the words "from whatever source derived" do not really provide a standard that can be used to decide whether or not the exclusion of certain items from taxation is appropriate.

---

[3] See David Bradford [1986] for further discussion of the material in this section.

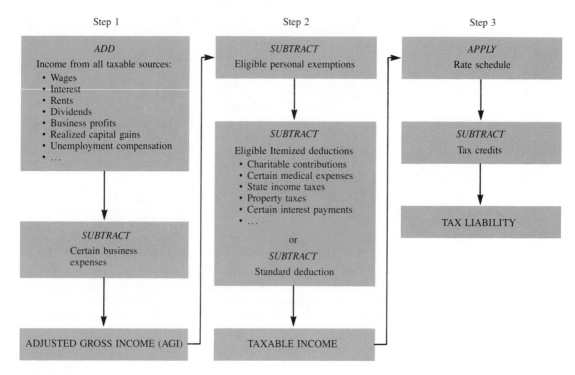

Figure 16.1
Computation of
federal personal
income tax liability

Public finance economists have traditionally used their own standard, the so-called **Haig-Simons (H-S) definition:** income is the money value of the net increase to an individual's power to consume during a period.[4] This is equal to the amount actually consumed during the period plus net additions to wealth. Net additions to wealth—saving—must be included in income because they represent an increase in *potential* consumption.

Importantly, the H-S criterion requires the inclusion of *all* sources of potential increases in consumption, regardless of whether the actual consumption takes place, and regardless of the form in which the consumption occurs. At the same time, the H-S criterion implies that any decreases in an individual's potential to consume should be subtracted in determining income. An example is expenses that have to be incurred to earn income. If the gross revenues from an individual's business are $100,000, but business expenses are $95,000, the individual's potential consumption has only increased by $5,000.

---

[4] Named after Robert M. Haig and Henry C. Simons, economists who wrote in the first half of the 20th century. Richard Goode [1977] discusses some alternative income definitions.

The H-S definition encompasses those items ordinarily thought of as income: wages and salaries, business profits, rents, royalties, dividends, and interest.[5] However, the criterion also includes certain unconventional items:

Employer contributions to pensions and other retirement plans.   Such payments, even though not made directly to the recipient, represent an increase in an individual's potential to consume.

Employer contributions for employees' insurance.   Even if compensation is paid to an employee in the form of a certain commodity (in this case, an insurance policy) instead of cash, it is still income.

Transfer payments, including Social Security retirement benefits, unemployment compensation, and aid to families with dependent children. Any receipt, be it from the government or an employer, is income.

Capital gains.   Increases in the value of an asset are referred to as **capital gains,** decreases as **capital losses.** Suppose Brutus owns some shares of IBM stock that increase in value from $10,000 to $12,500 over the course of a year. Then he has enjoyed a capital gain of $2,500. This $2,500 represents an increase in potential consumption, and hence, belongs in income.[6] If Brutus sells the IBM stock at the end of the year, the capital gain is said to be **realized;** otherwise it is **unrealized.** From the H-S point of view, it is absolutely irrelevant whether a capital gain is realized or unrealized. It represents potential to consume and hence, is income. If Brutus does not sell his IBM stock, in effect he chooses to save by reinvesting the capital gain in IBM. Because the H-S criterion does not distinguish between different uses of income, the fact that Brutus happens to reinvest is irrelevant. All the arguments for adding in capital gains apply to subtracting capital losses. If Casca's Eastman Kodak stock decreases in value by $4,200 during a given year, this $4,200 should be subtracted from other sources of income.

Income in kind.   Some people receive part or all of their incomes in kind—in the form of goods and services rather than cash. Farmers provide field hands with food; corporations give employees subsidized lunches or access to company cars. One important form of income in kind

---

[5] Again, these must all be measured after the expenses required to earn them are deducted.

[6] It is the real value of capital gains that constitutes income, not gains due merely to inflation. This issue is discussed later.

is the annual rental value of owner-occupied homes. A homeowner receives a stream of services from a dwelling. The net monetary value of these services—**imputed rent**—is equal to the rental payments that would have been received had the owner chosen to rent the house out, after subtracting maintenance expenses, taxes, and so so.

In all these cases, from the H-S point of view, it makes no difference whether benefits are received in monetary form, or in the form of goods and services. They are all income.

Some Practical and Conceptual Problems

A number of difficulties arise in attempts to use the Haig-Simons criterion as a basis for constructing a tax system.

1. The criterion makes it clear that only income *net of business expenses* increases potential consumption power. But it is often hard to distinguish between expenditures that are made for consumption and those that are costs of obtaining income. If Calpurnia buys a desk to use while working at home, but the desk is also a beautiful piece of furniture, to what extent is the desk a business expense? What portion of a "three-martini lunch" designed to woo a client is consumption and what portion is business? (According to current law, the answer to the latter question is that 20 percent is consumption. Eighty percent of business meal expenses are deductible.)

2. Capital gains and losses may be very difficult to measure, particularly when they are unrealized. For assets that are traded in active markets, the problem is fairly manageable. Even if Brutus does not sell his shares of IBM common stock, it is easy to determine their value at any time by consulting the financial section of the newspaper. It is not nearly as easy to measure the capital gain on a piece of art that has appreciated in value. One possibility would be to find a comparable piece that had recently been sold, a task that would be difficult if only a few sales were being made. Alternatively, art owners could be required to hire professional appraisers to value their collections each year, but this would be expensive and different appraisers might produce different estimates.

3. Imputed income from durables also presents measurement difficulties. For example, it may be hard to estimate the market rent of a particular owner-occupied dwelling. Similarly, measuring the imputed rental streams generated by other durables such as cars, compact disk players, and motor boats is not feasible.

4. In-kind services are hard to value. One important example is the income produced by people who do housework rather than participate in the market. These services—housecleaning, cooking, child care, and so forth—are clearly valuable. However,

even though markets exist for purchasing these services, it would be difficult to estimate whether a given homemaker's services were equal to the market value.

Evaluation of H-S Criterion

Numerous additional examples of the difficulties involved in implementing the H-S criterion can be provided, but the main point is clear. No definition of income can make the administration of an income tax simple and straightforward. Arbitrary decisions about what should be included in income are inevitable. Nevertheless, the Haig-Simons criterion has often been regarded as an ideal toward which policymakers should strive: Income should be defined as broadly as is feasible, and all sources of income received by a particular person should be taxed at the same rate. The U.S. Treasury suggested a tax reform proposal based on these principles in 1984.[7] Although not adopted, it was viewed very favorably by many academics and other commentators.

Why is the H-S criterion so attractive? There are two reasons: First, the criterion appeals to a sense of justice. Recall the traditional definition of horizontal equity from Chapter 15—people with equal incomes should pay equal taxes. For this dictum to make any sense, *all* sources of income must be included in the tax base. Otherwise, two people with identical abilities to pay could end up with different tax liabilities.

On the other hand, Martin Feldstein [1976a] has argued that as long as people's abilities to earn income differ, the H-S criterion cannot produce fair outcomes. Suppose that Popeye is endowed with a lot of brains, and Bluto with a lot of brawn. Suppose further that the work done by brawny people is less pleasant than that available to brainy individuals. In that case, if Bluto and Popeye have the same *income,* then Popeye has more *utility.* Is it fair to tax them as equals?

The second reason for the appeal of the Haig-Simons criterion is efficiency. Defenders of the criterion argue that it has the virtue of *neutrality*—it treats all forms of income the same, and hence, does not distort the pattern of economic activity. Following this reasoning, it is argued that the failure to tax imputed rent from owner-occupied housing leads to excessive investment in housing, other things being the same.

It is doubtless true that many departures from the Haig-Simons criterion have led to inefficiencies. But it does *not* follow that equal tax rates on all income, regardless of source, would be most efficient. Consider income from rent on unimproved land. The supply of such land is perfectly inelastic, and hence, no excess burden would be created by taxing it at a very high rate.[8] An efficient tax system would tax the returns to such land at higher rates than other sources of income, and *not* tax all sources

---

[7] See U.S. Department of the Treasury [1984].

[8] This fact has long been recognized. See Henry George [1914].

at the same rate, as dictated by the Haig-Simons criterion. More generally, the optimal tax literature discussed in Chapter 15 suggests that as long as lump sum taxes are ruled out, efficiency is enhanced when relatively high tax rates are imposed on those activities with relatively inelastic supply. "Neutrality," in the sense of equal tax rates on all types of income, generally does *not* minimize excess burden.

Where does this leave us? Emil Sunley [1977, p. 272] points out that we cannot be sanguine about the possibilities for using optimal tax theory as a framework for designing the tax base: "If one follows this efficiency logic, . . . one would end up with a highly differentiated tax system that would strike most people as unjust, unworkable, and having no obvious appeal." It would be unwise, therefore, to abandon the Haig-Simons criterion altogether. On the other hand, there is no reason to regard the criterion as sacred. Departures from it should be considered on their merits, and should not be viewed prima facie as unfair and inefficient.

Excludable Forms of Money Income

We have seen that some income sources that would be taxable according to the Haig-Simons criterion are omitted from the tax base for practical reasons. In addition, several forms of income that would be administratively relatively easy to tax are partially or altogether excluded from Adjusted Gross Income.

Interest on State and Local Bonds

The interest earned by individuals on bonds issued by states and localities is not subject to federal tax. From the H-S point of view, this exclusion makes no sense—interest from these bonds represents no less an addition to potential consumption than any other form of income. The exclusion originally followed from the view that it would be unconstitutional for one level of government to levy taxes on the securities issued by another level of government. However, many constitutional experts now believe that such taxation would be permissible [see Pechman, 1977b, p. 115].

In the absence of legal restrictions, the exclusion of state and local interest might be justified as a powerful tool for helping states and localities to raise revenues. If investors do not have to pay federal tax on interest from state and local bonds, they should be willing to accept a lower before-tax rate of return than they receive on taxable bonds. Suppose that Caesar faces a tax rate of 31 percent on additional income, and that the rate of return on taxable securities is 15 percent. Then as long as the rate of return on state and local securities exceeds about 10.4 percent, Caesar prefers them to taxable securities, other things being the same.[9]

---

[9] In particular, it is assumed that the two types of securities are perceived as being equally risky. The demand for assets whose risks differ is discussed in the next chapter.

More generally, if t is an individual's marginal tax rate and i is the rate of return on taxable securities, he will be willing to purchase nontaxable securities as long as their return exceeds $(1 - t)i$. Hence, state and local governments can borrow funds at rates lower than those prevailing on the market. In effect, the revenue forgone by the Treasury subsidizes borrowing by states and localities.

Unfortunately, tax-exempt bonds are an expensive way to help state and local governments. To see why, assume there are two taxpayers, Caesar, who faces a 31 percent tax rate on additional income, and Brutus, who faces a 15 percent rate. If the market rate of return on taxable bonds is 15 percent, Caesar's after-tax return is about 10.4 percent and Brutus' is 12.75 percent. To induce *both* Caesar and Brutus to buy something other than taxable bonds, the net rate of return must therefore be at least 12.75 percent. Suppose a town issues tax-exempt bonds yielding just slightly more than 12.75 percent, and both Caesar and Brutus purchase the bonds. The key thing to note is that some of the tax break is wasted on Caesar—he would have been willing to buy the bond at any yield greater than 10.4 percent, yet he receives 12.75 percent.[10]

What is the net effect on government revenues? Suppose that the town borrows $100 from Brutus at the interest rate of 12.75 percent instead of the market rate of 15 percent. This saves the town $2.25 in interest payments. On the other hand, the U.S. Treasury loses $2.25 (= .15 × $15) in income tax revenue. In effect, the Treasury has provided a $2.25 subsidy to the town. Now, if the town borrows $100 from Caesar it still saves only $2.25. But the Treasury loses about $4.65 (= .31 × 15) in tax revenues. Thus, about $2.40 of the tax break is wasted.

In short, the net effect of tax-exempt bonds is zero only for those investors who are just on the margin of choosing tax-exempt versus taxable securities. For all others, the subsidy to the state and local borrower is outweighed by the revenue lost at the federal level.

Why not eliminate the interest exclusion and subsidize states and localities with direct grants from the federal government? The main reason such a proposal has little support is political. A direct subsidy to states and localities would be just another item in the federal budget, an item whose existence might be jeopardized by the vagaries of the political climate. Indeed, if the subsidy were made explicit, rather than buried in the tax law, voters might decide that it was not worthwhile. Hence, state and local officials have lobbied intensively—and successfully—to maintain this exclusion.

---

[10] Note that the individual with the higher tax rate enjoys a greater increase in income due to the tax-exempt status of the state and local bonds. As we argued in Chapter 15, this is not necessarily a violation of horizontal equity, although it has implications for vertical equity.

Capital Gains

Prior to TRA86, only 40 percent of realized capital gains were taxed.[11] Currently, however, for most taxpayers all realized capital gains are taxed as ordinary income.[12] As with the old law, capital losses—decreases in the value of an asset—can be offset against capital gains. Suppose that Antony realizes a gain of $6,000 on asset A, but a loss of $2,000 on asset B. Then Antony is treated as if his capital gains are only $4,000. Moreover, capital losses in excess of capital gains (up to a limit of $3,000) can be subtracted from ordinary income. Suppose that in the example just given, asset B had lost $8,200. Then Antony could reduce his capital gains liability to zero and still have $2,200 in losses left over. He could subtract this amount from his ordinary income.

Although these provisions are pretty much in line with the Haig-Simons criterion, other aspects of the tax treatment of capital gains depart from it in important ways.

Only realizations taxed.   Unless a capital gain is actually realized—the asset is sold—no tax is levied. In effect, the tax on a capital gain is deferred until the gain is realized. The mere ability to postpone taxes may not seem all that important, but its consequences are enormous.[13] Consider Cassius, who purchases an asset for $100,000 that increases in value by 12 percent each year. After the first year, it is worth $100,000 × (1 + .12) = $112,000. After the second year, it is worth $112,000 × (1 + .12) = $100,000 × (1 + .12)^2 = $125,440. Similarly, by the end of 20 years, it is worth $100,000 × (1 + .12)^{20} = $964,629. If the asset is sold at the end of 20 years, Cassius realizes a capital gain of $864,629 (= $964,629 − $100,000). Assume that the tax rate applied to *realized* capital gains is 28 percent. Then Cassius' tax liability is $242,096 (= $864,629 × .28), and his net gain (measured in dollars 20 years from now) is $622,533 (= $864,629 − $242,096).

Now assume that the 28 percent capital gains tax is levied *as the capital gains accrue,* regardless of whether they are realized. At the end of the first year, Cassius has $108,600 [= $100,000 × (1 + .086)]. (Remember, about $3,360 of the $12,000 gain goes to the tax collector.) Assuming that the $8,640 after-tax gain is reinvested in the asset, at the end of two years, Cassius has $108,600 × (1 + .086) = $100,000 × (1.086)^2 = $118,026. Similarly, by the end of 20 years, he has $100,000 × (1.086)^{20} = $524,560. Cassius' after-tax capital gain is $424,560 (= $524,560 −

---

[11] The 60 percent exclusion applied only if the asset had been held for a specified time which depended on the type of asset.

[12] Under OBRA90, the maximum statutory tax rate applicable to capital gains is 28 percent. Hence, for individuals in the 31 percent bracket, there is a slight break for capital gains.

[13] At this point, it may be useful to review the discussion of interest compounding from Chapter 12 under "Present Value."

$100,000). Comparing this to the previous amount of $622,533 makes clear that the seemingly innocent device of letting the gains accrue without tax makes a big difference. This is because the deferral allows the investment to grow geometrically at the before-tax rather than the after-tax rate of interest. In effect, the government gives the investor an interest-free loan on taxes due.

It should now be clear why a favorite slogan among tax accountants is "taxes deferred are taxes saved." Many very complicated tax shelter plans are nothing more than devices for deferring payment of taxes.

Because only realized capital gains are subject to tax, taxpayers who are considering switching or selling capital assets must take into account that doing so will create a tax liability. As a consequence, they may be less likely to make changes in their portfolios. This phenomenon is referred to as the **lock-in effect,** because the tax system tends to lock investors into their current portfolios.[14] There have been several econometric studies of the tax treatment of capital gains realizations. A number of these have found that cuts in capital gains tax rates would significantly increase the realization of long-term capital gains, although the magnitude of the response is controversial (see Auten and Cordes [1991]).

Gains not realized at death.   Capital gains are not taxed at death. Suppose Octavius purchases an asset for $1,000. During Octavius' lifetime, he never sells the asset, and when he dies, it is worth $1,200. Under U.S. law, the $200 capital gain is not subject to tax when Octavius dies. Moreover, when Octavius, Jr. (Octavius' heir) gets around to selling the asset, his computation of capital gains is made as if the purchase price were $1,200, not $1,000. In effect, then, capital gains on assets held to death of the owner are never taxed. Death and taxes may both be inevitable, but death does help your heirs escape taxes.

Evaluation of capital gains rules.   We conclude that in terms of the Haig-Simons criterion, TRA86 improved the tax treatment of capital gains, but many problems remain. The criterion requires that all capital gains be taxed, whether realized or unrealized. As a consequence of the 1986 changes, the tax system generally does indeed tax realized gains as ordinary income. But unrealized capital gains can accrue without taxation, and if the asset is held until death of the owner, capital gains escape taxation altogether.

---

[14] Note that while the deferral of taxes lowers the effective tax rate on capital gains, this is somewhat offset by the fact that the lock-in effect prevents investors from reallocating their portfolio optimally when economic conditions change. See Daniel Kovenock and Michael Rothschild [1985].

The optimal tax literature does not provide any more justification for preferential treatment of capital gains than the Haig-Simons criterion.[15] However, a number of rationalizations have been proposed for preferential treatment of this form of capital income. Some argue that capital gains are not regular income, but rather windfalls that occur unexpectedly. Fairness requires that such unexpected gains not create a tax liability. Moreover, because investing requires the sacrifice of abstaining from consumption, it is only fair to reward this sacrifice. However, it could just as well be asserted that *labor* income should be treated preferentially, because it involves the unpleasantness of work, while those who receive capital gains need only relax and wait for their money to flow in. Ultimately, it is impossible to argue convincingly that production of one source of income or another requires more sacrifice and should therefore be treated preferentially.

Another justification for preferential taxation of capital gains is that it is needed to stimulate capital accumulation and risk taking. This was the rationale provided by the Bush administration in 1989 and 1990 when it urged Congress to restore special tax treatment of capital gains. In the next chapter, we deal at some length with the question of how taxation affects saving and risk-taking incentives. For now, we merely note that it is not at all clear that special treatment for capital gains does increase saving and risk taking. If the goal is to stimulate these activities, there are probably more efficient ways to do so.

Some promote preferential treatment of capital gains because it helps counterbalance inflation's tendency to increase the effective rate at which capital gains are taxed. As we see later, under existing tax rules, inflation does indeed produce an especially heavy burden on capital income. But arbitrarily taxing capital gains at a different rate is not the best way to deal with this problem.

Finally, we stress that a full picture of the tax treatment of capital income requires taking into account that much of this income is generated by corporations, and corporations are subject to a separate tax system of their own. The overall rate of tax on capital income thus depends on the personal *and* corporate rates. We discuss the effect of the corporation tax on the return to capital in Chapter 19.

In 1990, the tax treatment of capital gains was the center of a bitter political dispute. President George Bush wanted to exclude 30 percent of realized capital gains from taxable income (provided that the asset was held three years or longer). Arguing that capital gains relief would

---

[15] However, under certain conditions, optimal tax theory suggests that *no* forms of capital income should be taxed. See Chapter 20 under "Personal Consumption Tax."

primarily benefit the rich, congressional Democrats fought against a differential tax rate. The Democrats ultimately won, but this controversy is likely to surface again in the future.[16]

Employer Contributions to Benefit Plans

Income paid by an employer that is put into an employee's retirement fund is not subject to tax. Neither does the government tax the interest that accrues on the pension contributions over time. Only when the pension is paid out at retirement are the principal and interest subject to taxation. Similarly, employer contributions to medical insurance plans are not included in income.

As already argued, pensions and health insurance represent additions to potential consumption, and hence, should be counted as income according to the Haig-Simons criterion. Similarly, the interest on pension funds should be taxable as it accrues. However, the inclusion of such items in the tax base appears to be politically infeasible. A 1984 Treasury proposal to tax health insurance benefits created a political furor, and the idea was quickly dropped.

Some Employee Saving for Retirement

Under certain circumstances, workers can engage in tax-favored saving for their retirement. Between 1982 and 1986, the law was quite liberal in this regard. Using an **individual retirement account (IRA),** *any* worker could deposit up to $2,000 per year in a **qualified account.** (A qualified account includes most of the usual forms of saving: savings accounts, money market funds, etc.) The money so deposited was deductible from Adjusted Gross Income. Just as in an employer-managed pension fund, the interest that accrued was untaxed. Tax was due only when the money was paid out at retirement.[17] Penalties were imposed if money was withdrawn early.

After an acrimonious debate, the qualifications for deducting IRA contributions from AGI were tightened drastically in 1986. For individuals without pension plans at work, the rules are as before. But for a single worker whose employer sponsors a retirement plan, IRA contributions are fully deductible only if his or her AGI is less than $25,000. The portion of the IRA that is deductible is reduced proportionately as AGI increases from $25,000 to $35,000, and when AGI exceeds $35,000, none of the contribution is deductible. (For married couples filing joint returns, the phaseout occurs between $40,000 and $50,000 of AGI.) Note, however, that even in cases where the IRA contribution itself is partially or

---

[16] For further discussion of issues in the capital gains debate, see Gerald Auten and Joseph Cordes [1991].

[17] Figures on various deductions used in this chapter are from Internal Revenue Service [1990].

totally nondeductible, the *earnings* on the entire IRA contribution are exempt from tax until they are withdrawn. As noted, the advantages to such a postponement of taxes can be substantial. In any case, the restrictions on their use severely reduced the attractiveness of IRAs. In 1985, IRA contributions were $39 billion; in 1988, they were only $11.9 billion.

Another tax-favored method of saving is a **401(k) plan,** named for the section of the Internal Revenue Code that authorizes it. With a 401(k) plan, an employee can earmark a portion of his or her salary each year, and no income tax liability is incurred on that portion. Under TRA86, employees can contribute up to 20 percent of their salaries, with a maximum deposit of $7,000. (Under the old law, the cap was a much higher figure of $30,000.)

A third type of retirement account, a **Keogh plan,** is available only to self-employed individuals.[18] Such individuals can exclude from taxation 15 percent of their net business income (up to $15,000) if the money is deposited into a qualified account. Again, participants are allowed the powerful advantage of tax-free accrual of interest. In 1988, $6.8 billion were contributed to Keogh plans.

IRAs, 401(k)s, and Keogh plans were introduced partly to give more people the option to accumulate retirement wealth in tax-favored funds. Part of the motivation was also to stimulate saving. However, it is not clear how aggregate saving is affected. People may merely shuffle around their portfolios, reducing their holdings of some assets and depositing them into retirement accounts. This is indeed the principal finding in a careful econometric analysis of IRAs and saving by W. G. Gale and J. K. Scholz [1990], although other studies claim that IRAs induced substantial new saving [Venti and Wise, 1987]. In any case, it is clear that even in their present scaled-down incarnation, the existence of plans for the preferential treatment of retirement saving represents another important departure from the H-S criterion.

Gifts and Inheritances

Although gifts and inheritances represent increases in the beneficiaries' potential consumption, these items are not subject to the federal income tax. Instead, separate tax systems cover gifts and estates (see Chapter 20 under "Estate and Gift Taxes").

Exemptions and Deductions

In terms of Figure 16.1, we have now completed the first step in the computation of income taxes, figuring Adjusted Gross Income. Once Adjusted Gross Income is determined, certain subtractions are made to find taxable income. The two principal subtractions are exemptions and deductions, which we discuss in turn.

---

[18] Named after Congressman Eugene Keogh of New York.

Exemptions

Basically, a family is allowed an exemption for each of its members. The exemption—$2,150 in 1991—is adjusted annually for inflation. For example, in 1991 a husband and wife with three dependent children could claim five exemptions and subtract $10,750 from AGI. However, exemptions are phased out for people with AGIs above certain levels. For joint returns, personal exemptions are reduced by 2 percentage points for each $2,500 (or fraction thereof) by which AGI exceeds $150,000.[19] Suppose, for example, that our family of five has an AGI of $157,600. Subtracting $150,000 from $157,600, dividing the result by $2,500, and rounding up to the nearest whole number gives us 4. Hence, the family loses 8 percent (= 4 × 2 percent) of its exemptions. Because 8 percent of $10,750 is $860, the family can subtract only $9,890 in determining its taxable income.

Why are there exemptions? Some argue that they adjust ability to pay for the presence of children. Raising children involves certain nondiscretionary expenses, and taxable income should be adjusted accordingly. However, this view of the personal exemption has some problems. As most parents can tell you, if the exemption is really there to compensate for the expenses of child rearing (including parents' time), $2,150 is much too little. Moreover, it is not clear why expenses involving children should be considered nondiscretionary in the first place. Given the wide availability of contraceptive methods, many would argue that raising children is undertaken as the result of conscious choice [see Becker and Lewis, 1973]. If one couple wishes to spend its money on European vacations while another chooses to raise a family, why should the tax system reward the latter?[20] On the other hand, the religions of certain people rule out effective birth-control methods, and for them, children are not a *choice* as the term is conventionally defined.

Although exemptions are sometimes viewed as a kind of child allowance, they can also be thought of as a method of providing tax relief for low-income families. The higher the exemption, the greater Adjusted Gross Income must be before *any* income tax is due. Consider a family of four with an AGI of $8,600 or less. When this family's $8,600 in exemptions is subtracted from AGI, the family is left with zero taxable income, and hence, no tax liability. More generally, the greater the exemption level, the greater is the progressivity with respect to average tax rates. This effect is reinforced when exemptions are phased out for high-income families.

---

[19] For singles, the beginning of the phaseout range is $100,000. The beginnings for the phaseouts are adjusted annually for inflation.

[20] If there are positive externalities involved in raising children, then a subsidy might be appropriate [see Chapter 6]. Some would argue that because the world is overcrowded, additional children create negative externalities, and hence, should be *taxed*. In China, families with more than one child forfeit certain government benefits. In effect, this is a tax on children.

Deductions

The other subtraction allowed from AGI is a deduction. There are two kinds: **Itemized deductions** are subtractions for specific expenditures cited in the law. The taxpayer must list each item separately on the tax return and be able to prove (at least in principle) that the expenditures have been made. In lieu of itemizing deductions, the taxpayer can take a **standard deduction,** which is a fixed amount, and which does not require documentation. The taxpayer can choose whichever deduction minimizes his or her tax liability.

Deductibility and relative prices.   Before cataloging the expenditures that can be itemized, let us consider the relationship between deductibility of expenditures on an item and its relative price. Suppose that expenditures on commodity Z are tax deductible. The price of Z is $10 per unit. Suppose further that Cleopatra's marginal tax rate is 31 percent. Then, whenever Cleopatra purchases a unit of Z, it only costs her $6.90. Why? Because expenditures on Z are deductible, purchasing a unit lowers Cleopatra's taxable income by $10. Given a 31 percent marginal tax rate, $10 less of taxable income saves Cleopatra $3.10 in taxes. Hence, her effective price of a unit Z is $10 minus $3.10, or $6.90.

More generally, if the price of Z is P_Z and the individual's marginal tax rate is t, allowing deduction of expenses on Z lowers Z's effective price from P_Z to $(1 - t)P_Z$. This analysis brings out two important facts:

- Because deductibility changes the relative price of the commodity involved, in general, we expect the quantity demanded to change.
- The higher the individual's value of t, the greater the value to the individual of a given dollar amount of deductions and the lower the effective price of the good.[21]

Itemized deductions.   We now discuss some of the major itemized deductions. The list is far from inclusive, and the tax code should be consulted for further details.

Unreimbursed medical expenses that exceed 7.5 percent of AGI.   The justification is that large medical expenses are nondiscretionary and therefore do not really contribute to an individual's ability to pay. It is hard to say to what extent health-care expenditures are under an individual's control. A person suffering a heart attack does not have much in the way of choice. On the other hand, individuals can choose how often to visit their doctors, whether to visit expensive or moderately priced practition-

---

[21] Note that these observations apply more generally to expenditures on any items that are excluded from the tax base, not just deductions. For example, the value of excluding interest from municipal bonds increases with the marginal tax rate, other things being the same. So do the values of fringe benefits such as employer provided health insurance.

ers, and whether or not to have elective surgery. Moreover, it may be possible for individuals to substitute preventive health care (good diet, exercise, etc.) for formal medical services.

Finally, insurance to pay for medical care can often be obtained on the private market. Under typical private insurance plans, the first portion of medical expenses is met entirely by the insured, but after a point, some proportion is paid by the insurance company and the rest by the individual. In effect, by allowing deduction of some medical expenses, the tax system provides a kind of social health-care insurance. The terms of this "policy" are that the amount that the individual pays entirely on his or her own is 7.5 percent of AGI, and after that the Treasury pays a share equal to the marginal tax rate. The pros and cons of providing social insurance were already discussed in Chapter 10.

State and local income and property taxes.   In the two-year debate that preceded the Tax Reform Act of 1986, one of the most contentious issues was the treatment of state and local taxes. From the beginning of the federal income tax, state and local income taxes, property taxes, and general sales taxes had been deductible. In the fall of 1984, the U.S. Treasury recommended that these deductions be totally eliminated. So did President Ronald Reagan in 1985. However, state and local public-sector leaders were adamantly opposed because they believed that eliminating deductibility would make it more difficult to obtain voter support for public expenditures. The compromise embodied in TRA86 eliminated sales tax deductibility, but left the deductibility of state and local income and property taxes intact. Such payments accounted for $120 billion worth of deductions in 1988.

Those who support deductibility argue that state and local taxes represent nondiscretionary decreases in ability to pay. An alternative view is that they are simply user fees. A person pays state and local taxes in return for benefits such as public schools, police protection, and so forth. Some people choose to live in jurisdictions that provide a lot of such services, and they pay relatively high amounts of tax; others opt for low-service, low-tax jurisdictions. To the extent this description of reality is accurate, there is no particular reason to allow deductibility of state and local taxes. If some people want to purchase a lot of state and local public services while others choose to buy privately provided goods, why should the former receive a deduction?

On the other hand, if state and local taxes are not user fees, it may be appropriate to regard them as decreases in ability to pay.[22] Unfortunately, it is very difficult to determine what proportion of state and local taxes are best viewed as user fees for public services.

---

[22] But not necessarily! If the taxes are capitalized into the value of property, the current owners may not be bearing any of their burden. See Chapter 13.

This deduction can also be considered as a way to help state and local governments finance themselves. For people who itemize on their federal tax returns, the deduction lowers the effective cost of state and local tax payments. This fact may increase the likelihood that people will support tax increases at the state and local levels.[23] Why isn't a more direct method of subsidy used? As in the case of the interest exemption for state and local bonds, political considerations are an important part of the explanation. A subsidy hidden in the tax code may be easier to maintain than an explicit subsidy.

Certain interest expenses.   The tax treatment of interest was changed dramatically in 1986. Under the old law, interest payments on business loans were deductible from taxable income. In addition, individuals could deduct interest payments on home mortgages, charge accounts, and installment contracts on personal property such as cars and televisions. The most important features of the new law are:

1. Interest paid on consumer debt such as credit card charges and car loans is *not* deductible.
2. Deductions for interest on debt incurred for investment reasons cannot exceed the amount of investment income. Suppose, for example, that your business's income was $10,000, but its interest expenses were $25,000. All you can deduct on your tax return is $10,000. The other $15,000 cannot be used to shelter other sources of income from taxation.
3. Interest on home mortgages is subject to special treatment. Mortgage interest for the purchase of up to two residences is deductible, up to a limit of $1 million. Also deductible is interest on a home equity loan—a loan for which the home serves as collateral and whose proceeds can be used to finance *any* purchase. For example, one can obtain a home equity loan and use the money to buy a car. In effect, then, the law allows homeowners to deduct interest on consumer loans, but denies this privilege to renters. However, deductible interest on home equity loans is limited to $100,000.

Do these rules make sense in terms of the Haig-Simons criterion? For a business investment, it is pretty clear that interest should be deductible. It is a cost of doing business, and hence should not be subject to income tax. There is more controversy with respect to consumer interest. Some argue that it is perfectly appropriate to deduct consumer interest payments because they represent decreases in an individual's potential consumption. Others argue that interest on consumer loans should be

---

[23] See Chapter 21 for further details.

regarded merely as a higher price one pays to obtain a commodity sooner than would otherwise be possible. Whatever view is taken, it is hard to justify a system that makes the opportunity to deduct consumer interest depend arbitrarily on one's status as a homeowner.

Note that the deductibility of interest together with the exemption of certain types of capital income from taxation can lead to lucrative opportunities for smart investors. Assume that Caesar, who has a 31 percent tax rate, can borrow all the money he wants from the bank at a rate of 15 percent. Assuming that Caesar satisfies the criteria for deductibility of interest, for every dollar of interest paid, his tax bill is reduced by 31 cents. Hence, Caesar's effective borrowing rate is only about 10.4 percent. Suppose that the going rate of return on tax-exempt state and local bonds is 11 percent. Then Caesar can borrow from the bank at about 10.4 percent and lend to states and localities at 11 percent. The tax system appears to have created a "money machine" that can be cranked to generate infinite amounts of income. The process of taking advantage of such opportunities is referred to as **tax arbitrage.**

This example overstates the potential returns to tax arbitrage, because in real-world capital markets people cannot borrow arbitrarily large sums of money.[24] Still, opportunities for gain are clearly present. The tax authorities realized this many years ago and made it illegal to deduct interest from loans whose proceeds are used to purchase tax-exempt bonds. But it is not easy to prove that someone is breaking this rule. Given that money can be used for many different purposes, how can it be proved that a given amount of borrowing was "for" municipal bond purchases rather than for some other purpose? This very simple scam illustrates some important general lessons:

1. Interest deductibility in conjunction with preferential treatment of certain capital income can create major money-making opportunities.

2. High-income individuals are more likely than their low-income counterparts to benefit from these opportunities. This is because they tend to face higher tax rates, and to have better access to borrowing.

3. The tax authorities can certainly declare various tax arbitrage schemes to be illegal, but it is hard to enforce these rules. Moreover, clever lawyers and accountants are always on the lookout for new tax arbitrage opportunities. The Internal

---

[24] Moreover, there will be a tendency for competition among those who engage in tax arbitrage to reduce the return to that activity. For example, as more and more arbitrageurs buy municipal bonds, their rate of return will go down. If everyone had a 31 percent marginal tax rate, in equilibrium we would expect the return on municipals to fall until it was exactly 69 percent of the rate on taxable bonds. At that point, there would be no net advantage to owning municipals.

Revenue Service is usually right behind them trying to plug the loopholes. In the process, many inefficient investments are made, and a lot of resources are spent on tax avoidance and tax administration. One of the main reasons for the limitations on interest deductibility passed in 1986 was to reduce the opportunities for tax arbitrage.

Charitable contributions.   Individuals can deduct the value of contributions made to religious, charitable, educational, scientific, or literary organizations. Gifts of property are deductible, but personal services are not. In most cases, total charitable deductions cannot exceed 50 percent of Adjusted Gross Income. In 1988, individuals recorded charitable deductions of $50.5 billion.

Some argue that charitable donations constitute a reduction in taxable capacity, and hence, should be excluded from taxable income. However, as long as the contributions are made voluntarily, this argument is unconvincing. If people don't receive as much utility from charity as from their own consumption, why make the donation in the first place? Probably the best way to understand the presence of the deduction is as an attempt by the government to encourage charitable giving.

Has the deduction succeeded in doing so? The deductibility provision changes an individual's "price" for a dollar's worth of charity from $1 to $(1 - t)$, where t is the taxpayer's marginal tax rate. The effectiveness of the deduction as a means for encouraging giving therefore depends on the price elasticity of demand for charitable contributions. If the price elasticity is zero, charitable giving is unaffected. The deduction is just a bonus for those who would give anyway. If the price elasticity exceeds zero, then giving is encouraged.

Several attempts have been made to estimate the elasticity of charitable giving with respect to its after-tax price. Typically, a regression is estimated in which the dependent variable is the amount of charitable donations, and the explanatory variables are: (1) the "price" of charitable donations (one minus the marginal tax rate); (2) income; and (3) personal characteristics of individuals that might influence their decisions to give, such as age and marital status. Several studies have suggested that the price elasticity of demand for donations exceeds one.[25] The implications of this result are striking. Consider an individual with a marginal tax rate of 31 percent. The deductibility of charitable donations lowers the price of giving from $1 to 69 cents, a reduction of 31 percent. If the elasticity exceeds one, the taxpayer increases charitable giving by *more* than 31 percent. Hence, charitable organizations gain more than the Treasury loses.

---

[25] Charles Clotfelter [1985] reviews these studies.

Although there is disagreement with respect to the precise value of the elasticity, the consensus is that deductibility has substantially stimulated charitable contributions. This is not to say that the deduction is uncontroversial. Whether the government should be subsidizing gifts to private charities can be questioned. Some opponents argue that allowing deduction of contributions to churches and synagogues constitutes a violation of the principle of separation of church and state. On the other hand, proponents believe that in the absence of the deduction, many institutions now funded privately would be forced to seek government support. The current decentralized system is more likely to stimulate a variety of activities, and hence promote the goal of a pluralistic society.

Deductions versus credits.   As already noted, the higher an individual's marginal tax rate, the greater the value of a deduction of a given dollar amount. In contrast, a **tax credit** is a subtraction from the tax liability (*not* taxable income), and hence, its value is independent of the individual's marginal tax rate. A tax credit of $100 reduces tax liability by $100 whether an individual's tax rate is 15 percent or 31 percent. Under current law, a credit is allowed for certain child-care expenses. There is also an earned income credit that is described later.

Some argue that deductions and exemptions should be converted into credits. For example, the deduction of mortgage interest payments would be changed to a credit for some percentage of the value of interest paid. With a 20 percent interest credit, individuals could subtract from their tax bills an amount equal to one-fifth of their interest payments. Proponents of credits argue that they are more fair than deductions. Under a regime of tax deductions, a poor person (with a low marginal tax rate) benefits less than a rich person (with a high marginal tax rate) even if they both have identical interest expenses. With a credit, the dollar benefit is the same.

The choice between deductions and credits should depend at least in part on the purpose of the exclusion. If the motivation is to correct for the fact that a given expenditure reduces ability to pay, a deduction seems appropriate. If the purpose is mainly to encourage certain behavior, it is not at all clear whether credits or deductions are superior. A credit reduces the effective price of the favored good by the *same* percentage for all individuals; a deduction decreases the price by *different* percentages for different people. If people differ with respect to their elasticities of demand, it may make sense to present them with different effective prices. For example, it is ineffective to give *any* subsidy to someone whose elasticity of demand for the favored good is zero. The subsidy is "wasted" because it encourages no new demand. In this context it is interesting to note that Charles Clotfelter and Eugene Steuerle [1981] estimated that the greater a household's income, the higher the price elasticity of demand for charitable donations. On the average, a given percentage decrease in price stimulates more charitable giving by a high- than by a low-income household.

Itemized deduction phaseout.   Under OBRA90, otherwise allowable itemized deductions are reduced by 3 percent of the amount by which AGI exceeds $100,000. However, the reduction cannot be more than 80 percent of the total of itemized deductions.[26] Consider, for example, a family with AGI of $130,000, mortgage interest of $15,000, and local property taxes of $5,000. In the absence of the phaseout, the family would be allowed to deduct $20,000. Because AGI exceeds $100,000 by $30,000, its itemized deduction must be reduced by $900 (= $30,000 × .03). Hence, only $19,100 of deductions are allowed.

The standard deduction.   Itemized deductions are listed separately on the individual's tax return, and in principle each one requires documentation (such as receipts) to prove that the expenditure has indeed been made. All this record-keeping increases the administrative cost of the system. To simplify tax returns, the standard deduction was introduced in 1944. The standard deduction currently is a fixed amount available to all taxpayers. Each household can choose between taking the standard deduction or itemizing, depending on which offers the greater advantage.

TRA86 sharply increased the standard deduction. Before the law was passed, it was $3,670 for joint filers and $2,480 for single filers. About 60 percent of all returns filed used the standard deduction. Under the new law, the standard deduction in 1991 was $5,700 for joint filers and $3,400 for singles.[27] The standard deduction is adjusted annually for inflation. About 71 percent of tax returns now use the standard deduction.

Impact on the Tax Base

To what extent does the presence of exemptions and deductions influence the size of the tax base? In 1988, AGI was about $3,097 billion. After completing all the subtractions from AGI, taxable income was only $2,081 billion, a reduction of about 33 percent. Hence, deductions and exemptions are quite large relative to the size of the potential tax base.

Tax Expenditures

Failure to include a particular item in the tax base results in a loss to the Treasury. Suppose that as a consequence of excluding item Z from the tax base, the Treasury loses a billion dollars. Compare this to a situation in which the government simply hands over $1 billion of general revenues to those who purchase item Z. In a sense, these activities are equivalent as both subsidize purchases of item Z. It just so happens that one transaction takes place on the expenditure side of the account and the other on the

---

[26] In computing the 80 percent maximum, medical expenses and investment interest are excluded. The $100,000 threshold is adjusted annually for inflation.

[27] An extra standard deduction is available for the elderly (over 65) and blind. A joint filer who is elderly or blind is entitled to a $650 deduction above the standard deduction. A single person who is elderly or blind receives an extra standard deduction of $850.

revenue side. The former is a **tax expenditure,** defined in the Congressional Budget Act of 1974 as a revenue loss "attributable to provisions of the federal tax laws which allow a special exclusion, exemption, or deduction from gross income or which provide a special credit, a preferential rate of tax, or a deferral of tax liability" [Goode, 1977, p. 26]. The list of tax expenditures for 1991 had more than 100 items. Estimates of the total revenue loss from tax expenditures exceed $325 billion [Office of Management and Budget, 1991, pp. A71–A73]. Indeed, the notion that tax expenditures had gotten out of control played an important role in the movement that led to TRA86. As already noted, the reform restored a number of previously deductible items to the tax base.

The law requires that an annual tax expenditure budget be compiled by the Congressional Budget Office. A major intent of the law was to raise public consciousness of the symmetry between a *direct* subsidy for an activity via an expenditure and an *implicit* subsidy through the tax system. However, the notion of a tax expenditure budget has been subject to several criticisms.

First, a serious technical problem arises in the way the computations are made. It is assumed that in the absence of a deduction for a given item, all the expenditures currently made on it would flow into taxable income. Given that people are quite likely to adjust their behavior in response to changes in the tax system, this is not a good assumption, so the tax expenditure estimates may be quite far off the mark.

Second, the tax expenditure budget is simply a list of items exempt from taxation. However, to characterize an item as exempt, you must first have some kind of criterion for deciding what ought to be included. As we saw, no rigorous set of principles exists for determining what belongs in income. One person's loophole may be regarded by another as an appropriate adjustment of the tax base. Hence, considerable arbitrariness is inevitably involved in deciding what to include in the tax expenditure budget.

Finally, the concept of tax expenditures has been attacked on philosophical grounds:

> The tax expenditures concept implies that all income belongs of right to the government, and that what government decides, by exemption or qualification, not to collect in taxes constitutes a subsidy. This . . . violates a widely held conviction, basic to the American polity, that government is the servant and not the master of the people; and that the income earned by the people belongs to them, not the government. They agree, through their representatives, on what portion of their income they will pay as taxes, but income not paid in taxes is definitely not a subsidy from the government. [Jones, 1978, p. 53]

Defenders of the tax expenditure concept have argued that the concept does not really carry these ideological implications. It is merely an attempt to force recognition of the fact that the tax system is a major method for subsidizing various activities. Moreover, the fact that the estimates are not exact does not mean that they are useless for assessing the implications of tax policy.

A popular argument is that when government subsidies are proper at all, they are best provided by direct government expenditure:

> Wouldn't it be more honest with the taxpayer to take [tax expenditures] out of hiding and put a price tag on them. . . . That way we know how much each social policy costs each year, and we are more inclined to curtail tax expenditures that presently go on and on, unexamined. [Safire, 1982, p. A31]

However, Feldstein [1980] has pointed out that under certain conditions, a tax expenditure may be a more effective way for the government to stimulate a given activity than is a direct payment. Assume that the government wants to stimulate the activities of charitable organizations. One possible method is a tax expenditure. When the price elasticity of demand for charitable donations exceeds 1, each dollar forgone by the Treasury generates more than a dollar in charitable giving. Now suppose that instead, the government implements a direct subsidy using funds previously forgone because of the charitable deduction. One possibility is that each government dollar spent on charity "crowds out" a private dollar—when citizens see public support for charity, they reduce their own. In this case, the government would have to spend *more* than the estimated revenue loss to provide the equivalent total expenditure on charity.

Of course, we do not expect every dollar of public spending to replace exactly a dollar of private spending. Nor can we assume that the price elasticity of demand for each preferred item exceeds unity. But this simple example illustrates the basic point: In general, whether a tax expenditure or a direct subsidy is effective depends on the amount of crowding out that takes place, and on how responsive the demand for the preferred item is with respect to its after-tax price. The issue must be examined on a case-by-case basis.

The Simplicity Issue

The income tax law has been complicated for a long time. Franklin Roosevelt did not even bother to read a major piece of his administration's tax legislation, the Revenue Act of 1942. Roosevelt observed that it "might as well have been written in a foreign language" [Samuelson, 1986]. By 1986, the set of instructions for filing the basic personal tax return (Form 1040) was 48 pages long. There were 28 possible schedules to fill out. Many people were enraged by the sheer complexity of the system. As humorist Russell Baker [1985] noted, "What is most dreadful about the tax law is that nobody understands it. It is famous for being unfathomable."

Hence, the topic of tax simplification received substantial attention during the tax reform debate. Is the current tax code simpler than its predecessor? In some respects, the answer is yes. For example, because the standard deduction is now higher, fewer families itemize their returns and have less need to keep extensive records of various transactions. And life is also simpler for the low-income families who now do not have to file at all because of the increased standard deduction and personal exemption.

On the other hand, some of the rules (such as those pertaining to the deductibility of interest) are now more complicated than they used to be. OBRA90, with its complicated system of phaseouts for exemptions and itemized deductions, has not made the system any easier to understand. People in the middle- and high-income ranges still must confront lengthy instructions and a multitude of forms when they file their returns each April. Indeed, according to a survey of tax professionals conducted by Susan Long [1989], preparation times for various individual tax forms and schedules have increased since 1986.

Rate Structure

We have now arrived at the third step in Figure 16.1, calculating the amount of tax that must be paid on a given amount of taxable income. Under U.S. law, a bracket system is used to define tax rates. The taxable income scale is divided into segments, and the law specifies the marginal tax rate that applies to income in that segment. Actually, there are four different rate schedules, one each for married couples who file together (joint returns), married people who file separately, unmarried people, and single people who are heads of households. (A head of household maintains a home that includes a dependent.)

Statutory income tax rates have grown a lot over time. When the federal income tax was introduced in 1913, the bracket rates ranged from 1 percent to 7 percent. As late as 1939, half the taxpayers faced marginal rates below 4 percent. With the advent of World War II, rates went up substantially. In 1945, the lowest bracket rate was 23 percent, and the highest 94 percent. Rates eventually came down after the war. By the mid-1980s, there were 14 brackets, with marginal tax rates ranging from 11 percent to 50 percent.

The centerpiece of TRA86 was a drastic change in the rate structure, and OBRA90 incorporated more modifications. The tax rate schedules for single and joint returns in 1991 are in Table 16.1. There are only three brackets, with rates ranging from 15 percent to 31 percent.

Unfortunately, these official statutory marginal tax rates do not necessarily correspond to the actual statutory marginal tax rates. For some people, the personal exemption phaseout and/or the itemized deduction

Table 16.1   Official statutory tax rate schedule, 1991

Single Returns		Joint Returns	
Taxable Income	*Marginal Tax Rate*	*Taxable Income*	*Marginal Tax Rate*
$0–$20,350	15%	$0–$34,000	15%
$20,350–$49,300	28	$34,000–$82,150	28
$49,300 and above	31	$82,150 and above	31

phaseout discussed earlier lead to higher marginal tax rates than those in the table. To illustrate this, we consider in turn the effects of the personal exemption phaseout and the itemized deduction phaseout.

Personal exemption phaseout.   Consider a family of four whose AGI is $150,000 and whose taxable income exceeds $82,150, so that its official marginal tax rate is 31 percent. Suppose its before-tax income increases by $5,000. What is the incremental effect on tax liability? First, with a 31 percent marginal tax rate, taxes go up by $1,550 (= .31 × $5,000). However, at the same time, because AGI now exceeds $150,000 by $5,000, the family loses 4 percent of the value of its personal exemptions, or $344 (= .04 × $8,600). Given a 31 percent marginal tax rate, the loss of $344 in exemptions costs the family $106.64 (= .31 × $344) in taxes. Thus, the $5,000 increase in income leads to an incremental tax liability of $1,656.64 (= $1550 + $106.64). The marginal tax rate is therefore 33.13 percent (= 1,656.64/5,000), which exceeds the official rate by more than 2 percentage points. Once the family has used up all of its exemptions, its actual marginal tax rate returns to the official value of 31 percent.

Note the following oddity of this system: in the phaseout range, the marginal tax rate depends on the number of people in the family. By redoing the previous example with one more exemption, you should be able to convince yourself that each exemption increases the family's marginal tax rate by about .53 percentage points.

Itemized deduction phaseout.   Consider now a family with an AGI of $110,000; and they receive another $100 in before-tax income. Assuming that the family's statutory marginal tax rate is 31 percent, the first effect is to increase the tax liability by $31. However, assuming that the family has itemized deductions, it is subject to the itemized deduction phaseout (because AGI exceeds $100,000). The $100 increase in AGI decreases itemized deductions by $3 (= .03 × 100). With a 31 percent statutory marginal tax rate, the cost of $3 less in deductions is $0.93 (= .31 × $3). Hence, the total increase in tax triggered by a $100 increase in income is $31.93, and the marginal tax rate is 31.93 percent.

Figure 16.2

Actual and official
marginal tax rate
schedules for a
family of six (1991)

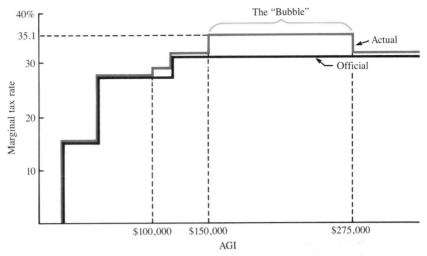

It is assumed that the family's itemized deductions are large enough that the 80 percent limitation on the phaseout does not come into play. Other provisions that can also affect marginal tax rates (earned income credit, IRA phaseout, etc.) are ignored.

SOURCE: Based on John G. Wilkins, "The Role of Tax Policy in Meeting the Competitive Challenge" (Washington, D.C.: Coopers & Lybrand, 1990), Mimeo (Figure 8).

The phaseouts together.   For families subject to both phaseouts, the effect on marginal tax rates is additive. For a family with four exemptions within the phaseout range, the marginal tax rate is 34.06 percent (= 31 percent statutory rate + 2.13 percent from exemption phaseout + 0.93 percent from deduction phaseout). In general, a family's marginal tax rate depends on the number of people in the family, and whether its AGI falls within the exemption and itemized deduction phaseout ranges. The actual and official statutory marginal tax rate schedules for a family of six are depicted in Figure 16.2.

As the figure indicates, after $275,000 of AGI, there are no more exemptions to phase out, so the actual marginal tax rate falls to its pre-phaseout value. As a consequence, at the high end of the income scale, marginal tax rates fall with income. This range between $150,000 and $275,000 is sometimes referred to as the "bubble."

Although *marginal* tax rates are higher in the bubble than beyond it, *average* tax rates are lower in the bubble than beyond. Unfortunately, the marginal-average distinction is often lost in public discussions. Some commentators claim that people in the bubble are unfairly burdened relative to richer people because they have higher marginal tax rates. As stressed in Chapter 13, however, the only sensible way to define the burden of taxation is in terms of the average rate. Hence, the existence of the bubble does not by itself provide evidence of an unfair tax structure.

To firm up your understanding of how the rate schedule works, consult the two examples in the box.

Income Taxes for Two American Families

The Bundys.   Al and Peggy Bundy live in a modest home in suburban Chicago with their two children, Kelley and Bud. Al is a shoe salesman at the local mall and earns $38,000 per year. Peggy keeps house. The Bundys' mortgage interest and property tax payments are $2,000 per year.

The Bundys are entitled to four exemptions worth $8,600 (= 4 × $2,150) altogether. They take the standard deduction of $5,700, because it exceeds their itemizable expenses of $2,000. Hence, their taxable income is $38,000 − $8,600 − $5,700, or $23,700. Applying the rate schedule in Table 16.1, tax liability is 15 percent of $23,700, or $3,555. The Bundys' average tax rate (with respect to AGI) is 9.4 percent (= 3,555/38,000); their marginal tax rate is 15 percent.

The Huxtables.   Cliff and Claire Huxtable inhabit a lovely townhouse in Brooklyn with two of their five children and a young cousin. Two of their other children are in college. Cliff is a physician who earns $175,000 per year. Claire earns $200,000 per year as a partner in a prominent law firm. Their mortgage interest, property taxes, and charitable donations sum to $56,250.

Assuming that the Huxtables claim exemptions for their two children at home and the two at college, they are entitled to six exemptions worth $12,900 (= 6 × $2,150) altogether. However, this figure must be reduced by 2 percentage points for each $2,500 by which their AGI exceeds $150,000. Since their AGI exceeds $150,000 by $225,000, this provision effectively wipes out the value of the exemptions.

With respect to deductions, it clearly makes sense for the Huxtables to itemize rather than take the standard deduction. However, the $56,250 of itemized deductions is reduced by 3 percent of the difference between AGI and $100,000, or $8,250 [= .03 × ($375,000 − $100,000)]. Net itemized deductions are thus $56,250 − $8,250, or $48,000. The Huxtables' taxable income is $327,000 (= $375,000 − $48,000). From the schedule in Table 16.1, their tax liability is $94,485.50. Their average tax rate is 25.1 percent (= 94,485.5/375,000), and their marginal tax rate is 31.93 percent (the official statutory marginal tax rate of 31 percent plus .93 percent associated with the deduction phaseout).

A natural question to ask is why we have this convoluted system of phaseouts and the bubble. The system developed as a political compromise in the negotiations surrounding OBRA90. The Democrats insisted on raising marginal tax rates at the high end of the income scale. The Republicans did not want any rate increases. The personal exemption and itemized deduction phaseouts were selected because of their ability to increase actual marginal tax rates without affecting the official values.[28]

---

[28] OBRA90 also raised the official rate at the high end of the income distribution from 28 to 31 percent.

Hence, Democrats got the higher rates that they wanted, while the Republicans were able to save face because the official rates were not raised very much. It is no accident that determining actual marginal tax rates under OBRA90 is tedious and confusing. The whole idea was to construct a system whose implications would be hard to understand.

Rates for Low-Income Individuals

Every household is allowed to subtract from income its exemptions (for 1991, roughly equal in value to the number of household members times $2,150) and a standard deduction of $5,700 for husbands and wives who file together, and $3,400 for individuals who file singly. Therefore, a family of four with an Adjusted Gross Income under $14,300 has no tax liability at all. Obviously, families with a larger number of exemptions can earn larger incomes and still be subject to a zero average tax rate.

In addition, low-income families with dependents benefit from the **earned income credit.** For a family with one dependent, a tax credit equal to 16.7 percent of all wage and salary income up to $7,140 is allowed.[29] To help guarantee that only the poor benefit from the credit, it is phased out at incomes between $11,250 and $21,245. If the credit exceeds the tax liability, the difference is refunded. Thus, some very low-income households actually have negative income tax liabilities.

The fact that the credit is phased out as earnings increase generates an implicit marginal tax on earnings in the phaseout range. The rate is about 12 percent in 1991. If the family is in the 15 percent income tax bracket, the total marginal tax rate is 27 percent. Thus, at the same time that the earned income credit augments the incomes of the poor, it can create substantial disincentives to work.[30]

The combination of exemptions, the standard deduction, and the earned income credit succeeds fairly well in sheltering the working poor with children from the personal income tax. Indeed, one reason for the political viability of TRA86 was that some legislators who had misgivings about lowering marginal tax rates for the rich were attracted to the idea of removing about 6 million poor families from the tax rolls altogether.

Rates for High-Income Individuals

As noted earlier, certain types of income such as interest on state and local bonds are treated preferentially by the tax system. It is therefore possible for some households to have rather high incomes, yet pay little or no tax. The **alternative minimum tax (AMT),** introduced in 1969 and toughened considerably by TRA86, is an attempt to ensure that people who benefit from some of these preferences pay at least some tax. The AMT is essentially a shadow tax system with its own rules for computing the tax base, and its own rate schedule. The calculation of the alternative

---

[29] The earned income tax credit does not apply to capital income. For two or more dependents, the rate is 17.3 percent. An additional 6 percent health insurance supplement is available for taxpayers paying medical insurance premiums for dependents.

[30] Note the similarity to the discussion of the negative income tax in Chapter 9.

tax base requires taking AGI and adding to it some of the income not taxed at ordinary rates. For example, the interest on some state and local bonds must be added back in.[31] Then certain deductions are permitted, but on a more limited basis than under the ordinary tax. State and local taxes, for instance, cannot be deducted. Next, an exemption is provided—$30,000 can be subtracted for individuals, and $40,000 for married couples. The exemption amount is phased out at a rate of 25 cents on the dollar for alternative taxable income above $112,500 for single taxpayers, and $150,000 for married couples. The remainder is subject to the AMT rate of 24 percent. When this amount is less than the individual's ordinary income tax, the ordinary income tax is paid. Otherwise, the AMT is paid.

Clearly, the AMT is an ad hoc method for adjusting the tax burdens of upper-income individuals. Its presence is another demonstration of the general lack of coherence in the tax system's design. Or as Senator Bill Bradley trenchantly put it, "A minimum tax is an admission of failure. It demonstrates not only that the system is broke, but also that Congress doesn't have the guts to fix it."

Effective versus Statutory Rates

At this point, recall the distinction between statutory and effective tax rates. In this section, we have been discussing the former, the legal rates established by the law. In general, these differ from effective tax rates for at least three reasons:

- Because the tax system treats certain types of income preferentially, taxable income may be considerably lower than some more comprehensive measures of income. The fact that tax rates rise rapidly with taxable income does not by itself tell us much about how taxes vary with comprehensive income.
- Even in the absence of loopholes, the link between statutory and effective tax rates is weak. As was emphasized in Chapter 13, taxes can be shifted, so there is no reason to believe that income taxes will really be borne by the people who pay the money to the government. The economic incidence of the income tax is determined by market responses when the tax is levied, and the true pattern of the burden is not known.
- The tax system imposes decreases in utility that exceed revenue collections. Excess burdens arise because taxes distort behavior away from patterns that otherwise would have occurred (see Chapter 14). Similarly, the costs of compliance with the tax code, in taxpayers' own time as well as explicit payments to accountants and lawyers, must be taken into account.

---

[31] These are "private activity bonds" issued after August 1986—bonds issued by state or local governments to finance some private sector project.

In this connection, note that contrary to the impression sometimes received in popular discussions, the existence of items such as tax-exempt bonds does not, in general, allow the rich to entirely escape the burden of taxation. Consider again Caesar, whose marginal tax rate is 31 percent, and who can buy taxable assets that pay a return of 15 percent. Suppose that the going rate on municipal bonds is 11 percent. We expect that other things being the same, Caesar will buy municipals because their 11 percent return exceeds the after-tax return of about 10.4 percent on taxable securities. To be sure, Caesar pays no tax. But the tax system nevertheless makes him worse off, because in its absence, he would have been able to make a return of 15 percent. In general, there is a tendency for the rate of return on tax-preferenced items to fall by an amount that reflects the tax advantage. Harvey Galper and Eric Toder [1982] estimate that because of this tendency, the *effective* tax rate on capital income actually increases with an individual's income, despite the availability of tax-preferred assets.

Thus, examination of statutory rates alone probably tells us little about the progressiveness of the current system. Conceivably, a statute with lower marginal tax rates but a broader base would lead to a system with incidence as progressive as that of the current system, and perhaps even more so.[32] At the same time, a system with lower marginal tax rates would reduce excess burden and perhaps lower tax evasion. Such considerations have prompted a number of proposals to restructure the income tax dramatically. One plan that has received a lot of attention is the **flat tax.** A flat tax has two attributes:

- It applies the same rate of tax to everyone and to each component of the tax base.
- It allows computation of the tax base with no deductions from total income except personal exemptions and strictly defined business expenses.[33]

Assuming that a certain amount of tax revenue must be collected, under a flat tax, the key trade-off is between the size of the personal exemption and the marginal tax rate. A higher exemption may be desirable to secure relief for those at the bottom of the income schedule and to increase progressiveness (with respect to average tax rates). But a higher exemption means that a higher marginal tax rate must be applied to maintain revenues.[34] According to one calculation, a tax rate of 19 percent

---

[32] This, of course, does not mean that the current system *should* be more progressive. For a discussion of the determinants of optimal tax progressiveness, see Chapter 15.

[33] In essence, then, a flat tax is just a linear income tax, as defined in Chapter 15.

[34] This assumes that at such tax rates, increasing marginal rates increase tax revenues, an assumption consistent with empirical evidence. See Chapter 17 under "Labor Supply."

together with a personal exemption of $6,200 for a married couple filing jointly and $3,800 for single taxpayers, would have satisfied the revenue requirements in 1982. (See Hall and Rabushka [1983].)

Proponents of the flat tax claim that lowering marginal tax rates would reduce both the excess burden of the tax system and the incentive to cheat. Moreover, the simplicity gained would cut down on administrative costs and improve taxpayer morale. And all of this could be achieved without a serious cost in equity because, as just noted, the flat tax can be made quite progressive by suitable choice of the exemption level.

Opponents of the flat tax believe that it would probably redistribute more of the tax burden from the rich to the middle classes. It is hard to evaluate this claim because of the usual difficulties involved in doing tax incidence analysis (Chapter 13). Critics also note that the whole range of conceptual and administrative problems involved in defining income will not disappear merely by declaring that business expenses are to be "strictly defined." As pointed out earlier, there will *never* be a simple income tax code.

The notion that it is desirable to keep marginal tax rates as low as possible has been influential in recent years. Prior to TRA86, the rates ranged from 11 to 50 percent. TRA86 reduced the range from 15 percent to 33 percent. However, as already noted, OBRA90 increased marginal tax rates, although not to their pre-1986 levels. In the near future, at least, any further movement in the direction of a flat tax appears unlikely.

Choice of Unit

We have discussed at length problems that arise in defining income for taxation purposes. Yet, even very careful definitions of income give little guidance with respect to choosing *who* should be taxed on the income. Should each person be taxed separately on his or her own income? Or should individuals who live together in a family unit be taxed on their joint incomes? Public debate of this question has been intense. In this section, we discuss some of the issues surrounding the controversy.[35]

Background

To begin, it is useful to consider the following three principles:

1. The income tax should embody increasing marginal tax rates.
2. Families with equal incomes should, other things being the same, pay equal taxes.
3. Two individuals' tax burdens should not change when they marry; the tax system should be **marriage neutral.**

---

[35] Much of this discussion is based on Rosen [1977].

Table 16.2   **Tax liabilities under a hypothetical tax system**

	Individual Income	*Individual Tax*	*Family Tax with Individual Filing*	*Joint Income*	*Joint Tax*
Lucy	$ 1,000	$ 100 ⎫	$12,200	$30,000	$12,600
Ricky	29,000	12,100 ⎭			
Ethel	15,000	5,100 ⎫	10,200	30,000	12,600
Fred	15,000	5,100 ⎭			

Although a certain amount of controversy surrounds the second and third principles, it is probably fair to say that they reflect a broad consensus as to desirable features of a tax system. The consensus behind the first principle is weaker, as evidenced by recent proposals for a flat tax. Nevertheless, generally increasing marginal tax rates seem to have wide political support.

Despite the appeal of these principles, a problem arises when it comes to implementing them: In general, no tax system can adhere to all three simultaneously. This point is made most easily with an arithmetic example. Assume the existence of the following simple progressive tax schedule: a taxable unit pays in tax 10 percent of all income up to $6,000, and 50 percent of all income in excess of $6,000. The first two columns of Table 16.2 show the incomes and tax liabilities of four individuals, Lucy, Ricky, Fred, and Ethel. (For example, Ricky's tax liability is $12,100 [= .10 × $6,000 + .50 × $23,000].) Now assume that romances develop— Lucy marries Ricky, and Ethel marries Fred. In the absence of joint filing, the tax liability of each individual is unchanged. However, two families with the same income ($30,000) will be paying different amounts of tax. (The Lucy-Rickys pay $12,200 while the Ethel-Freds pay only $10,200, as noted in the third column.) Suppose instead that the law views the family as the taxable unit, so that the tax schedule applies to joint income. In this case, the two families pay equal amounts of tax, but now tax burdens have been changed by marriage. Of course, the actual change in the tax burden depends on the difference between the tax schedules applied to individual and joint returns. This example has assumed for simplicity that the schedule remains unchanged. But it does make the main point: given increasing marginal tax rates, we cannot have both principles 2 and 3.

What choice has the United States made? Over time, the choice has changed. Prior to 1948, the taxable unit was the individual, and principle 2 was violated. In 1948, the family became the taxable unit, and simultaneously **income splitting** was introduced. Under income splitting, a family with an income of $50,000 is taxed as if it were two individuals with incomes of $25,000. Clearly, with increasing marginal tax rates, this can be a major advantage. Note also that under such a regime, an unmarried person with a given income finds his or her tax liability reduced substantially if he or she marries a person with little or no income. Indeed, under the 1948 law, it was possible for an individual's tax liability to fall drastically when the person married—a violation of principle 3.

The differential between a single person's tax liability and that of a married couple with the same income was so large that Congress created a new schedule for unmarried people in 1969. Under this schedule, a single person's tax liability could never be more than 20 percent higher than the tax liability of a married couple with the same taxable income. (Under the old regime, differentials of up to 40 percent were possible.)

Unfortunately, this decrease in the single/married differential was purchased at the price of a violation of principle 3 in the opposite direction: it was now possible for persons' tax liabilities to increase when they married. In effect, the personal income tax levied a tax on marriage. In 1981, Congress attempted to reduce the "marriage tax" by introducing a new deduction for two-earner married couples. Two-earner families received a deduction equal to 10 percent of the lower earning spouse's wage income, but no more than $3,000. However, the two-earner deduction was eliminated by TRA86. It was deemed to be unnecessary because lower marginal tax rates reduced the importance of the "marriage tax."

Nevertheless, a substantial penalty still exists, and it tends to be highest when both spouses have similar earnings. Under certain conditions,[36] for example, when two individuals with $25,000 AGIs marry, their joint tax liability can increase by a thousand dollars. On the other hand, when there are considerable differences in individuals' earnings, the tax code provides a bonus for marriage. If two people with $2,500 and $50,000 AGIs marry, their joint tax liability can decrease by $1,000. In cases like these, the law provides a "tax dowry."

Analysis of the Marriage Tax

The economist surveying this scene is likely to ask the usual two questions—is it equitable and is it efficient? Much of the public debate focuses on the equity issue: is it fairer to tax individuals or families? One argument favoring the family as the choice is that it allows a fairer treatment of nonlabor income (dividends, interest, profits). There are fears that with individual filing, high-earnings spouses would transfer property to their mates to lower family tax bills (*bedchamber transfers of property*). It is difficult to predict whether or not this would occur on a massive scale. The view implicit in these fears is that property rights within families are irrelevant.[37] However, given current high rates of divorce, turning prop-

---

[36] The calculations in this paragraph are for 1988. See Rosen [1987].

[37] Moreover, it is not obvious that lowering the effective rate of tax on capital income would be a bad thing. It depends on the considerations raised in Chapter 15.

erty over to a spouse just for tax purposes may be a risky strategy, and there is no strong evidence that such transfers would occur in massive amounts.

The family can also be defended as the appropriate unit of taxation on a more philosophical level:

> [T]he family is today, as it has been for many centuries, the basic economic unit in society. . . . Taxation of the individual in . . . disregard of his inevitably close financial and economic ties with the other members of the basic social unit of which he is ordinarily a member, the family, is in our view [a] striking instance of [a] lack of a comprehensive and rational pattern in . . . [a] tax system. [*Report of the Royal Commission,* 1966, pp. 122–23]

The case for the family unit is not as compelling as the quotation suggests. Boris Bittker [1975, p. 1398] argued

> If married couples are taxed on their consolidated income, for example, should the same principle extend to a child who supports an aged parent, two sisters who share an apartment, or a divorced parent who lives with an adolescent child? Should a relationship established by blood or marriage be demanded, to the exclusion, for example, of unmarried persons who live together, homosexual companions, and communes?

Clearly, beliefs concerning the choice of the fairest taxable unit are influenced by value judgments and by attitudes toward the role of the family in society. The debate continues to be lively.

When we turn to the efficiency aspects of the problem, the question is whether the marriage tax distorts individuals' behavior. As far as marriage decisions go, it is hard to construct a very strong case against the current law on efficiency grounds. Although the tax system changes the "price of marriage," there is no compelling statistical evidence that this has distorted people's decisions to marry. However, anecdotes about postponed marriage, divorce, or separation for tax reasons are becoming common. At least some couples are asking why, if corporations can merge and diverge strictly for tax benefits, couples should behave any differently.

An efficiency concern that is easier to document surrounds the impact of joint filing on labor supply decisions. Chapter 15 stated that because married women tend to have more elastic labor supply schedules than their husbands, efficient taxation requires taxing wives at a relatively lower rate. Under joint filing, both spouses face identical marginal tax rates on their last dollars of income. Hence, joint filing is inefficient.

It is hard to imagine Congress implementing separate income tax schedules for wives and husbands. This does not mean, however, that it is impossible to move family taxation in the direction of greater efficiency.

One possible reform would be simply to eliminate joint filing and have all people file as individuals. This would not only enhance efficiency, but it would produce more marriage neutrality than the current system.

Unfortunately, individual filing would lead to a violation of principle 2: equal taxation of families with equal income. This brings us back to where we started. No tax system can satisfy all three criteria, so society must decide which have the highest priority.

Taxes and Inflation

The personal exemption, the standard deduction, the minimum and maximum dollar amounts for each tax rate bracket, the earned income credit, and the thresholds for the deduction and exemption phaseouts are adjusted annually to offset the effects of inflation. The purpose of this process, referred to as **tax indexing,** is to automatically remove the influence of inflation from real tax liabilities. This section discusses motivations for tax indexing, and whether the U.S. system of indexing is an adequate response to the problems posed by inflation.

How Inflation Can Affect Taxes

Economists customarily distinguish between "anticipated" and "unanticipated" inflation. The latter is generally viewed as being much more detrimental to efficiency, because it does not allow people to adjust their behavior optimally to price level changes. However, in the presence of an unindexed income tax system, even perfectly anticipated inflation causes distortions.

The most popularly understood distortion is the phenomenon known as **bracket creep.** Suppose that an individual's earnings and the price level both increase at the same rate over time. Then that person's **real income** (the amount of actual purchasing power) is unchanged. However, an unindexed tax system is based on the individual's **nominal income**—the number of dollars received. As nominal income increases, the individual is pushed into tax brackets with higher marginal tax rates. Hence, the proportion of income that is taxed increases despite the fact that real income stays the same. Even individuals who are not pushed into a higher bracket find more of their incomes taxed at the highest rate to which they are subject. In the absence of some corrective action, then, inflation brings about an automatic increase in the real tax burden without any legislative action.

Another effect of inflation occurs because exemptions and the standard deduction are set in nominal terms. In an unindexed system, increases in the price level decrease their real value. Again, the effective tax rate increases as a consequence of inflation.

It turns out, however, that even with a simple proportional income tax without exemptions or deductions, inflation would distort tax burdens. To be sure, under such a system, general inflation would not affect the real tax burden on wage and salary incomes. If a worker's earnings during a year doubled, so would his taxes, and there would be no real effects. But inflation would change the real tax burden on *capital income.*

Suppose Calpurnia buys an asset for $5,000. Three years later, she sells it for $10,000. Suppose further that during the three years, the general price level doubled. In real terms, the change in Calpurnia's income is zero. However, capital gains liabilities are based on the difference between the *nominal* selling and buying prices. Hence, Calpurnia incurs a tax liability on $5,000 of illusory capital gains. In short, because the inflationary component of capital gains is subject to tax, the real tax burden depends on the inflation rate.

Those who receive taxable interest income are similarly affected. Suppose that the **nominal interest rate** (the rate observed in the market) is 16 percent. Suppose further that the anticipated rate of inflation is 12 percent. Then for someone who lends at the 16 percent nominal rate, the **real interest rate** is only 4 percent, because that is the percentage by which the lender's real purchasing power is increased. However, taxes are levied on nominal, not real, interest payments. Hence, tax must be paid on receipts that represent no gain in real income.

Let us consider this argument algebraically. Call the nominal interest rate i. Then the after-tax nominal return to lending for an individual with a marginal tax rate of t is $(1 - t)i$. To find the real after-tax rate of return, we must subtract the expected rate of inflation, π. Hence, the real after-tax rate of return r, is

$$r = (1 - t)i - \pi \qquad\qquad\qquad (16.1)$$

Suppose $t = .25$, $i = 16$ percent, and $\pi = 10$ percent. Then although the nominal interest rate is 16 percent, the real after-tax return is only 2 percent.

Now suppose that any increase in the expected rate of inflation increases the nominal interest rate by the same amount; if inflation increases by four points, the nominal interest rate increases by four points.[38] It might be expected that the two increases would cancel out, leaving the real after-tax rate of return unchanged at 2 percent. But Equation (16.1) contradicts this prediction. If π goes from 10 percent to 14 percent and i goes from 16 percent to 20 percent, then with t equal to 0.25, r decreases to 1 percent. Inflation, even though it is perfectly anticipated, is not "neutral." This is a direct consequence of the fact that nominal rather than real interest payments are taxed.

---

[38] There is some controversy as to whether this proposition holds exactly, but it is a useful approximation for our purposes. See Vito Tanzi [1980].

So far we have been considering the issue from the point of view of lenders. Things are just the opposite for borrowers. In the absence of the tax system, the real rate paid by borrowers is the nominal rate minus the anticipated inflation rate. However, assuming that the taxpayer satisfies certain criteria, the tax law allows deductibility of nominal interest payments from taxable income. Thus, debtors can subtract from taxable income payments that represent no decrease in their real incomes. The tax burden on borrowers is decreased by inflation.

Coping with the Tax/Inflation Problem

As inflation rates began to increase in the late 1960s, people became acutely aware of the fact that inflation leads to unlegislated increases in the real income tax burden. The initial response was to mitigate these effects by a series of ad hoc reductions in statutory rates. Such tax cuts were enacted in 1969, 1971, 1975, 1976, 1977, and 1981, and were partially successful in undoing some effects of inflation [see Aaron, 1976, p. 21].

Nevertheless, a number of legislators and academics viewed this kind of process unfavorably. Each tax cut offsets inflation only for a short time. After a while, it becomes necessary to make changes all over again. The whole business tends to increase public cynicism about the tax-setting process. Many citizens learn that the tax "reductions" about which their legislators boast are nothing of the kind when measured in *real* terms. Lenin is alleged to have said, "The way to crush the bourgeoisie is to grind them between the millstones of taxation and inflation." Although the interaction of taxes and inflation in the United States had not created quite such drastic effects, there was widespread agreement that it had produced serious distortions.

In 1981, dissatisfaction with the ad hoc approach led to the enactment of legislation requiring indexing of certain parts of the tax code. As already noted, currently the personal exemption, standard deduction, bracket widths, and earned income credit are all indexed. These provisions have effectively ended bracket creep. However, no moves have been made in the direction of indexing capital income. This is due in part to the administrative complexity such a statute would entail. For example, as suggested earlier, increases in inflation generate real gains for debtors, because the real value of the amounts they have to repay decreases. In a fully indexed system, such capital gains would have to be measured and taxed, a task that would certainly be complex.

Should indexing be maintained? Opponents of indexing argue that a system of periodic ad hoc adjustments is a good thing because it allows the legislature to examine and revise other aspects of the tax code that may need changing.[39] Proponents of indexing argue that reducing the

---

[39] We have been dealing with this debate from a microeconomic standpoint. There is also considerable disagreement about the macroeconomic consequences of indexing. Opponents argue that it would remove an important tool for conducting macroeconomic policy. For example, if more fiscal restraint is needed during an inflationary period, this is automatically generated by increases in tax revenues. In

opportunities for revising the tax code may itself be a benefit, because it is desirable to have a stable and predictable tax law. Moreover, fewer opportunities to change the law also mean fewer chances for legislative mischief. Certainly the most important argument of those who favor indexing is that it eliminates unlegislated increases in real tax rates. They believe that allowing the real tax schedule to be changed systematically by a nonlegislative process is antithetical to democratic values.

Proponents of indexing also note that its repeal would have a disproportionately large effect on the tax liabilities of low-income families. For example, high-income families lose some or all of the advantage of personal exemptions because of the exemption phaseout. Hence, if the exemption were no longer indexed, their taxes would not be affected at all but the real tax liabilities of lower-income individuals would increase. Similarly, higher-income families are more likely to itemize than take the standard deduction, so that eliminating its indexation would tend to affect mostly low-income families. In the negotiations preceding OBRA90, a threat to indexing arose in the form of a proposal by congressional Democrats to suspend income tax indexing for 1991. A political uproar ensued, and the idea was quickly dropped. At the present time, indexing seems to be safe from attack.

State Income Taxes

The role of individual income taxes in state revenue systems has been growing rapidly.[40] In 1960, 12.2 percent of state tax collections were from individual income taxes; by 1989, the figure was 39.6 percent. Presently, 40 states and the District of Columbia have an individual income tax [Tax Foundation, 1991, pp. 250–251].[41]

State income taxes tend to be similar in structure to the federal tax. The tax base is found by subtracting various deductions and exemptions from gross income, and tax liability is determined by associating a marginal tax rate with each of several income brackets. The marginal rates are much lower than those of the federal system. In 1990, for about half the states that levied an income tax, the highest bracket rate was 8 percent or below. (The maximum was 12 percent in North Dakota.)

The states differ considerably with respect to rules governing deductions and exemptions. Some rule out practically all deductions, while others follow rules similar to the federal system. As noted, state income

---

contrast, voting tax increases and/or expenditure cuts takes time. On the other hand, indexing proponents argue that the automatic rise in federal revenues may simply encourage legislators to spend more, and hence have no stabilizing effect. Indeed, they argue that a nonindexed system creates incentives for legislators to pursue inflationary policies, because these policies tend to increase the real quantity of resources available to the public sector.

[40] For local governments, income taxes are generally not of much importance in the revenue structure, although in some of the larger cities, they play a significant role.

[41] Three other states taxed only some components of income, such as dividends and interest.

taxes, like most state and local taxes, are deductible from federal tax liability. However, in only about 10 states is the federal income tax deductible. Just as the federal government does not tax interest on state and local bonds, the state governments do not tax interest on obligations issued by the federal government.

TRA86 and OBRA90: Preliminary Evaluation

TRA86 lowered statutory income tax rates and broadened the tax base. Although OBRA90 increased tax rates somewhat, the system is still very different from what it was before 1986. A natural question is whether the current system is an improvement over its pre-1986 incarnation. The answer depends on the responses to a lot of questions. For example: Will labor supply change in response to the new marginal tax rates? How will savers respond to the taxation of realized capital gains at ordinary rates? What will be the response of state government expenditures to the nondeductibility of sales taxes? As shown in the next chapter, there is much uncertainty about many of the answers. Moreover, there are severe data problems, because many of the most important provisions of TRA86 did not become fully effective until 1988, and the relevant tax data are just becoming publicly available.[42] Hence, any evaluation must begin with a humble admission of ignorance.

Still, it is possible to make a few general comments. To the extent that marginal tax rates are now lower, excess burden is likely to be lower, *ceteris paribus*. Moreover, lower marginal tax rates are likely to reduce the seriousness of several other problems associated with the income tax: evasion, non-neutrality with respect to marital status, and inflation. (Of course, as noted earlier, many taxpayers do *not* face lower marginal tax rates now than they did before 1986.) Finally, the removal of many items from tax-preferred status will probably lead to fewer tax distortions of individual behavior.

However, this discussion of efficiency issues requires an important caveat. The reduction in personal income tax rates in TRA86 was purchased in part by increasing business taxes by an estimated $120 billion over a five-year period. OBRA90 also raised taxes on businesses, by about $20 billion between 1991–95. To determine the overall consequences of these laws, one must certainly consider business as well as personal taxation. (See Chapter 19.)

Turning now to the crucial question of fairness, one's evaluation depends in part on normative judgments about the role the tax system should have in redistributing income. Those who favor use of the income tax as a redistributive mechanism generally approve of the large increases in the personal exemption and the standard deduction, which in effect lead to a zero income tax rate for many low-income families. On the other

---

[42] See the essays in Joel Slemrod [1991] for some useful preliminary results.

hand, egalitarians are likely to be less enthused by the reduction in marginal tax rates on high-income families which, even after OBRA90, are considerably lower than they used to be. However, as we have stressed repeatedly, the assumption that the statutory distribution of tax burdens is identical to the true distribution is probably incorrect. The ultimate effects of income tax changes on the distribution of income depend on the considerations raised in Chapter 13, and are hard to estimate. The changes embodied in the new law provide fertile ground for future research on the relationships among the tax system, the distribution of income, and economic efficiency.

Why Is Tax Reform So Hard?

A question that arises in any discussion of tax reform is why it is so difficult to make improvements in the tax system. One reason is that in many cases, even fairly disinterested experts disagree about what direction reform should take. For example, we noted earlier that despite a consensus among economists that differentially taxing various types of capital income is undesirable, there is disagreement about how this should be remedied. What one person views as a reform can be perceived by another as an undesirable change.

Another difficulty is that attempts to change specific provisions are likely to encounter fierce political opposition from those whom the changes will hurt. State government officials, for example, lobbied ferociously when a proposal to limit the deductibility of state income taxes was floated in 1990. In Chapter 7 we discussed some theories suggesting that in the presence of special-interest groups, the political process can lead to expenditure patterns that are suboptimal from society's point of view. The same theories might explain the difficulties involved in attempts to improve the tax system. One member of the House Ways and Means Committee, Andrew Jacobs, summed it up this way: "If you evade your taxes, you go to the penitentiary. If you want to avoid taxes, you go to the U.S. Congress—and see what they can do for you" [*Tax Policy Guide,* 1982, p. 5].

Organized lobbies are not the only impediments to reform. In many cases, once a tax provision is introduced, ordinary people modify their behavior on its basis and are likely to lose a lot if it is changed. For example, many families have purchased larger houses than they otherwise would have because of the deductibility of mortgage interest and property taxes. Presumably, if these provisions were eliminated, housing values would fall. Homeowners would not take this lying down. Indeed, some notions of horizontal equity suggest that it is unfair to change provisions that have caused people to make decisions that are costly to reverse (see Chapter 15).

Some have argued that attempts to make broad changes in the tax system are likely to be more successful than attempts to modify specific provisions on a piecemeal basis. If *everyone's* ox is being gored, people are less apt to fight for their particular loopholes. The experience with

TRA86 lends some support to this viewpoint. Part of the reason for its passage was that on certain key votes, its supporters were able to package TRA86 as an all-or-nothing proposition. Accept the whole set of changes, or no changes at all. It is noteworthy, however, that even with a very popular president and extremely powerful congressional leaders behind the bill, it nearly died several times.

What are the prospects for further improvements in the tax system? Several observers have suggested that to the extent there are future changes in the tax law, the tendency will be to reinstitute special privileges removed by TRA86. One reason for this pessimism is the higher marginal tax rates embodied in OBRA90. As stressed earlier, higher marginal tax rates increase the value to taxpayers of various exclusions from the tax base. Hence, it will be more worthwhile for special interest groups to devote resources to obtaining tax breaks for their members. More generally, political commentator Robert Samuelson [1986] has noted that "A simple, stable tax system is not in the self-interest of politicians. Granting and modifying tax breaks is a basic source of power. Tax breaks create constituencies." We conclude that one cannot be optimistic about the possibilities for improvement.

Summary

- Computation of federal individual income tax liability has three major steps: measuring total income (Adjusted Gross Income), converting total income to taxable income, and calculating taxes due.

- A traditional benchmark measure of income is the Haig-Simons definition: income during a given period is the net change in the individual's power to consume.

- Implementation of the Haig-Simons criterion is confounded by several difficulties: (1) Income must be measured net of the expenses of earning it. (2) Unrealized capital gains are not easily gauged. (3) The imputed income from durable goods is not directly observable. (4) It is difficult to measure the value of in-kind receipts.

- The Haig-Simons criterion is viewed by many public finance economists as the ideal toward which real-world tax systems should strive. However, critics note that the criterion does not necessarily guarantee either fair or efficient outcomes.

- Several sources of income are excluded from the U.S. income tax base. These include: (1) Interest on state and local bonds. (2) Employer contributions to pension and medical plans. (3) Gifts and inheritances.

- Exemptions are fixed amounts per family member. Exemptions are subtracted from Adjusted Gross Income (AGI) and phased out at high-income levels.

- Deductions are either standard or itemized. A standard deduction reduces taxable income by a fixed amount. Alternatively, taxpayers may choose to itemize their deductions from AGI. Itemized deductions are phased out at high-income levels.

- Itemized deductions are permitted for expenditures on particular goods and services. Itemized deductions change after-tax relative prices, which often affects economic behavior.

- Major itemized deductions in the U.S. tax code include: (1) Unreimbursed medical expenses in excess of 7.5 percent of AGI.

(2) State and local income and property taxes. (3) Certain interest expenses. (4) Charitable contributions.

■ Tax credits are direct reductions in tax liability instead of reductions in taxable income. In general, there is no obvious means by which to choose between deductions and credits.

■ Tax expenditures are the revenues forgone due to preferential tax treatment. In some instances, a tax expenditure may be the most effective way to stimulate a particular private activity.

■ The final step in determining tax liability is to apply a schedule of rates to taxable income. Because of various phaseouts, the actual statutory marginal tax rates exceed the official rates.

■ A flat or linear income tax has been proposed to simplify the tax code while maintaining the desired progressiveness through the choice of the personal exemption and tax rate.

■ The fundamental problem in the tax treatment of the family is that no tax system can simultaneously achieve increasing marginal tax rates, tax burdens unchanged upon marriage, and equal taxes for families with equal incomes. The U.S. tax code has been changed several times in attempts to satisfy each of these conflicting goals.

■ Under the current system, bracket widths, personal exemptions, the standard deduction, and the earned income credit are indexed against inflation. However, there are no provisions to correct for inflation's effect on the taxation of capital income.

■ Income tax systems are becoming more important as revenue raisers for the states. State income taxes have lower rates than the federal system and vary widely in their exact provisions.

Discussion Questions

1. If Rafael, a painter, donates his work to a museum, he is permitted to deduct only the value of the canvas, ink, and so on. If he sells the painting to Mellon who donates the painting, Mellon may deduct the purchase price. Does this make sense? Is it fair to the painter?

2. Before TRA86 and OBRA90, the maximum marginal tax rate was about 50 percent, and afterward it was about 34 percent. How would the heads of organizations dependent on charitable contributions feel about this change?

*3. Jones, who has a federal personal income tax rate of 28 percent, holds an oil stock which appreciates in value by 10 percent each year. He bought the stock one year ago. Jones's stockbroker now wants him to switch the oil stock for a gold stock that is equally risky. Jones has decided that if he holds on to the oil stock, he will keep it only one more year and then sell it. If he sells the oil stock now, he will invest all the (after-tax) proceeds of the sale in the gold stock and then sell the gold stock one year from now. What is the minimum rate of return that the gold stock must pay for Jones to make the switch? Relate your answer to the *lock-in effect*.

4. Consider again the situation of the Huxtables, described in the box on p. 396. Assume that Cliff's income falls to $100,000, and Claire's income falls to $125,000. What happens to their average tax rate and their marginal tax rate?

5. In 1990, a group of congressional Democrats offered a capital gains proposal that included a $1,000 annual exclusion of realized

* Difficult.

capital gains. (This exclusion would be phased out for individuals with incomes between $100,000 and $150,000.) Evaluate this proposal.

6. Suppose that a typical taxpayer has a marginal personal income tax rate of 33 percent. The nominal interest rate is 13 percent, and the expected inflation rate is 8 percent.

   a. What is the real after-tax rate of interest?

   b. Suppose that the expected inflation rate increases by 3 percentage points to 11 percent, and the nominal interest rate increases by the same amount. What happens to the real after-tax rate of return?

   *c. If the inflation rate increases as in part b, by how much would the nominal interest rate have to increase to keep the real after-tax interest rate at the same level as in part a? Can you generalize your answer using an algebraic formula?

   _____

   * Difficult.

Selected References

Auten, Gerald E., and Joseph J. Cordes. "The Current Status of Capital Gains Taxation." *Journal of Economic Perspectives,* Winter 1991.

Bradford, David F. *Untangling the Income Tax.* Cambridge, Mass.: Harvard University Press, 1986.

Pechman, Joseph A. *Federal Tax Policy,* 5th ed. Washington, D.C.: Brookings Institution, 1987.

Slemrod, Joel. *Do Taxes Matter?: The Impact of the Tax Reform Act of 1986.* Cambridge, Mass.: MIT Press, 1991.

CHAPTER 17

Personal Taxation and Behavior

If you are out to describe the truth, leave elegance to the tailor.

ALBERT EINSTEIN

The theory of taxation makes clear that ultimately the efficiency and equity of taxes depend on how they affect behavior. The impact of taxes on behavior is a matter of intense debate, both among academics and politicians. Some argue that taxes have very little effect: "disincentives, like the weather, are much talked about, but relatively few people do anything about them" [Break, 1957, p. 549]. Others suggest that high marginal tax rates lead to "worsening work attitudes, high absenteeism rates, reluctance to work overtime and to assume risks, and the lowest personal saving rate[s]" [Roberts, 1981, p. 26].

As was suggested in Chapter 16, the income tax affects incentives for myriad decisions—everything from the purchase of medical services to the amount of charitable donations. We choose to focus on four particularly important topics that have been the subject of much investigation—the effects of taxation on labor supply, saving, housing consumption, and portfolio decisions.

Labor Supply

In 1990, about 118 million Americans worked an average of almost 35 hours per week and received total compensation of roughly $3.2 trillion, approximately 73 percent of national income [*Economic Report of the President,* 1991, pp. 312, 322, 336]. How labor supply is determined and whether taxes affect it are clearly important issues. We discuss both the conceptual and practical problems that arise in investigating these issues.

Figure 17.1
Utility maximizing
choice of leisure
and income

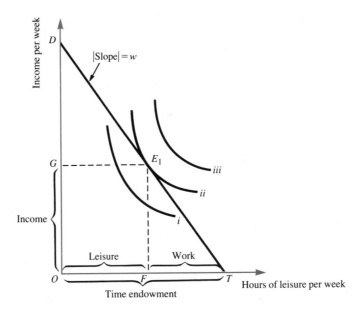

Theoretical
Considerations

Hercules is trying to decide how much of his time to devote each week to work and how much to leisure. In Chapter 9 under "Aid to Families with Dependent Children," we showed how this choice can be analyzed graphically. To review the main points in that discussion:

1. The number of hours available for market work and nonmarket uses ("leisure") is referred to as the time endowment. In Figure 17.1, it is shown by distance OT on the horizontal axis. Assuming that all time not spent on leisure is devoted to market work, any point on the horizontal axis simultaneously indicates hours of leisure and hours of work.

2. The budget constraint in a leisure-income diagram shows the combinations of leisure and income available to an individual given his or her wage rate. If Hercules has a job that allows him to bring home w per hour, then his budget constraint is a straight line whose slope in absolute value is w. In Figure 17.1, this is represented by line TD.

3. The particular point on the budget constraint that is chosen depends on the individual's tastes. Assume that preferences for leisure and income can be represented by normal, convex-to-the-origin indifference curves. Three such curves are labeled i, ii, and iii in Figure 17.1. Utility is maximized at point E_1, where Hercules devotes OF hours to leisure, works FT hours, and earns income OG.

Figure 17.2

Proportional income tax decreasing hours of labor supplied

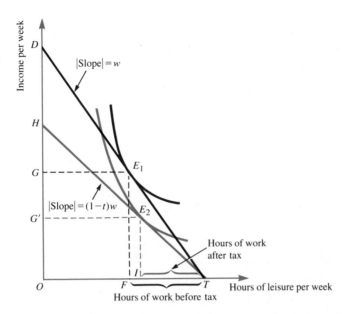

We are now in a position to analyze the effects of taxation. Suppose that the government levies a tax on earnings at rate t. The tax reduces the reward for working an hour from $\$w$ to $\$(1 - t)w$. When Hercules consumes an hour of leisure, he now gives up only $\$(1 - t)w$, not $\$w$. In effect, the tax reduces the opportunity cost of an hour of leisure. This observation is represented in Figure 17.2. The budget constraint facing Hercules is no longer TD. Rather, it is the flatter line, TH, whose slope in absolute value is $(1 - t)w$. Because of the tax, the original income-leisure choice, E_1, is no longer attainable. Hercules must choose a point somewhere along the after-tax budget constraint TH. In Figure 17.2, this is E_2, where Hercules consumes OI hours of leisure, works IT hours, and has an after-tax income of OG'. The tax has lowered Hercules' labor supply from FT hours to IT hours.

Can we therefore conclude that a "rational" individual will *always* reduce labor supply in response to a proportional tax? To answer this question, consider Theseus, who faces exactly the same before- and after-tax budget constraints as Hercules, and who chooses to work the same number of hours *(FT)* prior to imposition of the tax. As indicated in Figure 17.3, when Theseus is taxed, he *increases* his hours of work from FT to JT. There is nothing "irrational" about this. Depending on a person's tastes, it is possible to want to work more, less, or the same amount after being subjected to a tax.

The source of the ambiguity is the conflict between two effects generated by the tax, the *substitution effect* and the *income effect*. When the tax reduces the take-home wage, the opportunity cost of leisure goes

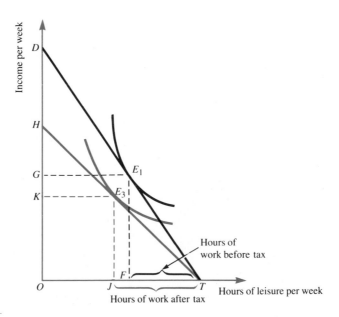

Figure 17.3

Proportional income tax increasing hours of labor supplied

down, and there is a tendency to substitute leisure for work. This is the substitution effect, and it tends to decrease labor supply. At the same time, for any number of hours worked, the tax reduces the individual's income. Assuming that leisure is a normal good, for any number of hours worked, this loss in income leads to a reduction in consumption of leisure, other things being the same. But a decrease in leisure means an increase in work. The income effect therefore tends to induce an individual to work more. Thus, the two effects work in opposite directions. It is simply impossible to know on the basis of theory alone whether the income effect or substitution effect will dominate. For Hercules, shown in Figure 17.2, the substitution effect dominates. For Theseus, shown in Figure 17.3, the income effect is more important.[1]

The analysis of a progressive tax system is very similar to that of a proportional tax. Suppose that Hercules is now confronted with increasing marginal tax rates; t_1 on his first $5,000 of earnings, t_2 on his second $5,000 of earnings, and t_3 on all income above $10,000.[2] As before, prior to the tax the budget line is TD, which is depicted in Figure 17.4. After tax, the budget constraint is the kinked line $TLMN$. Up to $5,000 of before-tax income, the opportunity cost of an hour of leisure is $(1 - t_1)w$, which is the slope (in absolute value) of segment TL. At point L, Hercules' income is $(1 - t_1) \times \$5,000$. On segment ML the absolute value of the slope is

---

[1] For a more general discussion of income and substitution effects, see the Appendix to the book.

[2] Note that this rate structure is similar to that of the U.S. income tax. However, at very high-income levels, the marginal tax rate decreases. See Chapter 16.

Figure 17.4
Leisure-income
choice under a
progressive income
tax

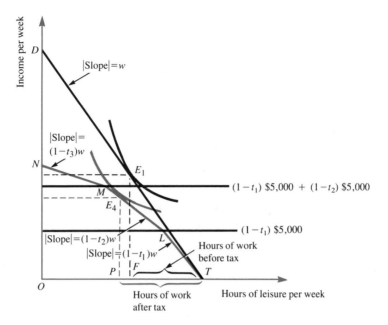

$(1 - t_2)w$. ML is flatter than TL because t_2 is greater than t_1. At point M, after-tax income is $(1 - t_1) \times \$5,000 + (1 - t_2) \times \$5,000$; this is after-tax income at point L plus the increment to income after receiving an additional \$5,000 that is taxed at rate t_2. Finally, on segment MN the slope is $(1 - t_3)w$, which is even flatter. Depending on his preferences, Hercules can end up anywhere on $TLMN$. In Figure 17.4, he maximizes utility at E_4 where he works PT hours.[3]

Empirical Findings

The theory just discussed suggests that an individual's labor supply decision depends on: (a) variables that affect the position of the budget constraint, especially the after-tax wage;[4] and (b) variables that affect the individual's indifference curves for leisure and income, such as age, sex, and marital status. Econometricians have estimated regression equations in which they seek to explain annual hours of work as a function of such variables.[5] Although considerable differences in estimates arise due to

---

[3] An issue that has received substantial attention is the effect on hours of work of replacing a proportional tax with a progressive tax that yields the same tax revenue. Richard Hemming [1980] has shown that the outcome depends on the shape of the indifference curves and exactly how progressivity is defined.

[4] Another important determinant of the budget constraint is nonlabor income: dividends, interest, transfer payments, and so forth. Nonlabor income causes a parallel shift in the budget constraint; there is a constant addition to income at every level of hours worked.

[5] See Chapter 3 for an explanation of regression analysis.

inevitable differences in samples, time periods, and statistical techniques, it would be fair to say that the following two important general tendencies have been observed:

1. For males between the ages of roughly 20 and 60, the effect of changes in the net wage on hours of work is small in absolute value and is often statistically insignificant. Most elasticity estimates fall in the range between −0.2 and zero.

2. Although estimated labor supply elasticities for women vary widely, it seems clear that the hours of work and labor force participation decisions of married women are quite sensitive to changes in the net wage. A number of investigators have found elasticities of hours worked with respect to the net wage between 0.2 and 1.0.[6]

Some Caveats

The theoretical and empirical results just described are certainly more useful than the uninformed guesses often heard in political debates. Nevertheless, we should be aware of some important qualifications.

Demand-side considerations.   The preceding analyses ignore effects that changes in the supply of labor might have on the demand side of the market. Suppose that taxes on married women were lowered in such a way that their net wages increased by 10 percent. With a labor supply elasticity of 1.0, their hours of work would increase by 10 percent. If firms could absorb all of these hours at the new net wage, that would be the end of the story. More typically, as more hours of work are offered, there is a tendency to bid down the *before*-tax wage. This mitigates the original increase in the *after*-tax wage, so that the final increase in hours of work would be less than originally guessed.

The situation becomes even more complicated when we realize that major changes in work decisions could influence consumption patterns in other markets. The resulting relative price changes might feed back on labor market decisions. For example, if married women increased their hours of work, the demand for child care would probably increase. To the extent this raised the price of child care, it might discourage some mothers of small children from working, at least in the short run. Clearly, tracing through these general equilibrium implications is a complicated business. Most investigators are willing to assume that the first-round effects are a reasonable approximation to the final result.

Individual versus group effects.   Our focus has been on how much an individual will work under alternative tax regimes. Richard Musgrave [1959] points out that it is difficult to use such results to predict how the

---

[6] See Ingemar Hansson and Charles Stuart [1985, pp. 340–41]. Note that these estimates include both substitution and income effects. That is, they are uncompensated responses.

total hours of work supplied by a *group* of workers will change. When the tax schedule is changed, incentives are changed differently for different people. For example, in a move from a proportional to a progressive tax, low-income workers may find themselves facing lower marginal tax rates while just the opposite may be true for those with high incomes. It is quite possible, then, that the labor supplies of the two groups could move in opposite directions, making the overall outcome difficult to predict.

Other dimensions of labor supply.   The number of hours worked annually is an important and interesting indicator of labor supply. But the effective amount of labor supplied by an individual depends on more than the number of hours elapsed at the workplace. A highly educated, healthy, well-motivated worker presumably is more productive than a counterpart who lacks these qualities. Some have expressed fears that taxes induce people to invest too little in the acquisition of skills. Economic theory yields surprising insights into how taxes might affect the accumulation of *human capital*—investments that people make in themselves to increase their productivity.

Consider Hera, who is contemplating entering an on-the-job training program. Suppose that over her lifetime, the program increases Hera's earnings by an amount whose present value is B. However, participation in the program reduces the amount of time currently available to Hera for income-producing activity, and hence costs her some amount, C, in forgone wages. If she is sensible, Hera makes her decision using the investment criterion described in Chapter 12, and enters the program only if the benefits exceed the costs:

$$B - C > 0 \tag{17.1}$$

Now suppose that Hera's earnings are subjected to a proportional tax at rate t. Part of the higher wages earned by virtue of participation in the training program will be taxed away. One might guess that the tax therefore lowers the likelihood that she will participate. This reasoning is misleading. To see why, assume for the moment that after the tax Hera continues to work the same number of hours as she did before.[7] The tax does indeed reduce the benefits of the training program from B to $(1 - t)B$. But at the same time, it reduces the costs. Recall that the costs of the program are the forgone wages. Because these wages would have been subject to tax, Hera gives up not C, but only $(1 - t)C$. The decision to enter the program is based on whether after-tax benefits exceed after-tax costs:

$$(1 - t)B - (1 - t)C = (1 - t)(B - C) > 0 \tag{17.2}$$

---

[7] In terms of our earlier discussion, the income and substitution effects just offset each other.

A glance at Equation (17.2) indicates that it is exactly equivalent to (17.1). Any combination of benefits and costs that was acceptable before the earnings tax is acceptable afterward. In this model, a proportional earnings tax reduces benefits and cost in the same proportion, and therefore has no effect on the human capital investment.

This unambiguous result is a consequence of the assumption that labor supply is constant after the tax is imposed. Suppose instead that as a result of the earnings tax, Hera increases her supply of labor. (The income effect predominates.) In this case, the tax leads to an increase in human capital accumulation.[8] In effect, the after-tax labor supply is the utilization rate of the human capital investment. The more hours a person works, the greater the payoff to an increase in the wage rate from a given human capital investment. Therefore, if the tax induces more work, it makes human capital investments more attractive, other things being the same. Conversely, if the substitution effect predominates so that labor supply decreases, human capital accumulation is discouraged.

Of course, the framework in which we have been discussing this problem is very simple. It ignores the important fact that the returns to a human capital investment usually cannot be known with certainty. Moreover, for some types of human capital, costs other than forgone earnings are important. College tuition is an obvious example. Finally, when the tax system is progressive, the benefits and costs of human capital investments may be taxed at different rates. However, when such factors are considered, the basic result is confirmed—from a theoretical point of view, the effect of earnings taxation on human capital accumulation is ambiguous. At this time, unfortunately, little empirical work on this important question is available.

The compensation package.   The standard theory of labor supply assumes that the hourly wage is the only reward for working. In reality, employers often offer employees a compensation *package* that includes not only wages but also health benefits, pensions, "perks" such as access to a company car, and so on. As we noted in the last chapter, most of the nonwage component of compensation is not subject to taxation. When marginal tax rates fall, the relative attractiveness of such untaxed forms of income declines, and vice versa. Hence, changes in taxes might affect the composition of the compensation package. Some evidence exists that this is the case. For example, in an econometric analysis of fringe benefits received by U.S. academics, D. Hamermesh and S. Woodbury [1990] found that a 1 percent increase in the value of fringe benefits resulting from higher tax rates induces an increase in fringe benefits of about 2 percent.[9]

---

[8] See Jonathan Eaton and Harvey Rosen [1980a].

[9] See also Frank Sloan and Killard Adamache [1986].

Figure 17.5

Tax rates, hours
of work, and
tax revenue

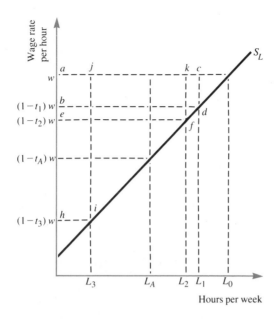

The expenditure side. The standard analysis of labor supply and taxation ignores the disposition of the tax receipts. However, at least some of the revenues are used to purchase public goods, the availability of which can affect work decisions. If the tax money is used to provide recreational facilities such as national parks, we expect the demand for leisure to increase, *ceteris paribus*. On the other hand, expenditure on child-care facilities for working parents might increase labor supply. Ideally, we should examine the labor supply consequences of the entire budget, not just the tax side. In practice, it has been difficult for empirical investigators to learn about how public expenditures affect work decisions. The difficulty stems from the fact that it is hard to determine individuals' valuations of public good consumption, a problem which we have already discussed in several different contexts.

**Labor Supply
and Tax
Revenues**

So far, our emphasis has been on finding the amount of labor supply associated with any given tax regime. We now explore the related issue of how tax collections vary with the tax rate.

Consider the supply curve of labor S_L depicted in Figure 17.5. It shows the optimal amount of work for each after-tax wage, other things being the same.[10] As it is drawn, hours of work increase with the net wage—the substitution effect dominates throughout the range of wages being considered. The following argument could be repeated using a labor supply curve for which the income effect is dominant.

---

[10] The labor supply curve (or equivalently, the leisure demand curve) can be derived from the individual's indifference map. See the Appendix at the end of the book.

Figure 17.6
Tax rates versus
tax revenue

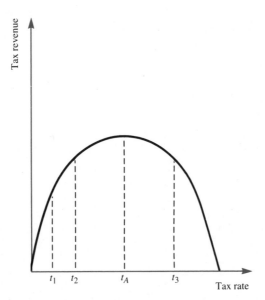

The before-tax wage, w, is associated with L_0 hours of work. Obviously, since the tax rate is zero, no revenue is collected. Now suppose a proportional tax at rate t_1 is imposed. The net wage is $(1 - t_1)w$, and labor supply is L_1 hours. Tax collections are equal to the tax per hour worked *(ab)* times the number of hours worked *(ac)*, or rectangle, *abdc*. Similar reasoning indicates that if the tax rate were raised to t_2, tax revenues would be *eakf*. Given the shape of supply curve S_L, *eakf* exceeds *abdc*—a higher tax rate leads to greater revenue collections. Does this mean that the government can always collect more revenue by increasing the tax rate? No. For example, at tax rate t_3, revenues *haji* are less than those at the lower rate t_2. Although the tax collected *per hour* is very high at t_3, the number of hours has decreased so much that the product of the tax rate and hours is fairly low. Indeed, as the tax rate approaches 100 percent, people stop working altogether and tax revenues fall to zero.

All of this is summarized compactly in Figure 17.6, which shows the tax rate on the horizontal axis and tax revenue on the vertical. At very low tax rates, revenue collections are low. As tax rates increase, revenues increase, reaching a maximum at rate t_A. For rates exceeding t_A, revenues begin to fall, eventually diminishing to zero. Note that it would be absurd for the government to choose any tax rate exceeding t_A, because tax rates could be reduced without the government suffering any revenue loss.

Hard as it may be to believe, Figure 17.6 has been the center of a major political controversy. This is largely due to the well-publicized assertion by economist Arthur B. Laffer that the United States has operated to the right of t_A [see Laffer, 1979]. Indeed, in the popular press, the tax rate–tax revenue relationship is known as the **Laffer curve.** The notion that tax rate reductions would create no revenue losses became an important tenet of the supply-side economics espoused by the Reagan administration; it continues to be a potent force in Washington policy debates.[11]

The popular debate surrounding the Laffer curve has been confused and confusing.[12] A few points are worth making:

- The shape of a Laffer curve is determined by the elasticity of labor with respect to the net wage. For any change in the tax rate, there is a corresponding percentage change in the net wage. Whether tax revenues rise or fall is determined by whether changes in hours worked offset the change in the tax rate. This is precisely the issue of the elasticity of labor supply investigated by public finance economists.[13]

- Some critics of supply-side economics argue that the very idea that tax rate reductions can lead to increased revenue is absurd. However, the discussion surrounding Figure 17.6 suggests that in principle, lower tax rates can indeed lead to higher revenue collections.

- It is therefore an empirical question whether or not the economy is actually operating to the right of t_A. A careful study of this issue suggests that given all plausible estimates of the elasticity of labor supply, the economy is *not* operating in this range [see Fullerton, 1982].[14] Tax-rate reductions are unlikely to be self-financing in the sense of unleashing so much labor supply that tax revenues do not fall.

- It does *not* follow from this observation that tax rate reduction is necessarily undesirable. As emphasized in previous chapters, determination of the optimal tax system depends on a wide array of social and economic considerations. Those who believe that the government sector is too large should presumably be quite happy to see tax revenues reduced. In this connection, we should note the unfortunate tendency of some "supply siders" to attribute important normative properties to tax rate t_A.[15] As should be clear from the theory of optimal income taxation, the

---

[11] Supply-side economics is just as concerned with the taxation of savings as of labor, and all the arguments made here apply to savings as well.

[12] For a good summary, see Don Fullerton [1982].

[13] In a general equilibrium model, the underlying labor demand curve can be shifted when a tax is imposed. This complicates the derivation of the Laffer curve. See James Malcomson [1986].

[14] See Browning [1989], however, for an analysis suggesting that t_A may not lie too far above current marginal tax rates.

[15] One influential supply sider, Jude Wanniski, argued that the peak of the curve "is the point at which the electorate desires to be taxed" [1978, p. 98]. There is absolutely no theoretical or empirical basis for this statement.

fact that revenues are maximized at rate t_A tells us *nothing* about whether it is the most desirable tax rate from either an equity or an efficiency perspective.

Overview

In the analysis of taxes and labor supply, economic theory tells us which variables to examine but provides no firm answers. Econometric work indicates that for prime age males, hours of work are not much affected by taxes. For married women, on the other hand, taxes probably reduce labor force participation rates and hours of work. An important qualification is that the effect of taxes on other dimensions of labor supply, such as educational and job-training decisions, is not well understood.

Some politicians have suggested that if tax rates were cut, such large amounts of labor supply would be unleashed that the U.S. Treasury would suffer no revenue loss. Although this is a theoretical possibility, there is no reliable empirical evidence that it would happen.

Saving

A second type of behavior that may be affected by taxation is saving. Most modern theoretical and empirical work on saving decisions is based on the **life-cycle model** that says individuals' consumption and saving decisions during a given year are the result of a planning process which considers their lifetime economic circumstances [Modigliani, 1986]. That is, the amount you save each year depends not only on your income that year but also on the income that you expect in the future and the income you have had in the past. This section uses a simple life-cycle model to explore the impact of taxes on saving decisions.

Consider Scrooge, who expects to live two periods: "now" (period 0) and the "future" (period 1). Scrooge has an income of I_0 dollars in the present period, and knows that his income will be I_1 dollars in the future period. (Think of "now" as "working years," when I_0 is labor earnings; and the "future" as retirement years, when I_1 is fixed pension income.) His problem is to decide how much to consume in each period. When Scrooge decides how much to consume, he simultaneously decides how much to save or borrow. If his consumption this period exceeds his current income, he must borrow. If his consumption is less than current income, he saves. We now show how the saving and borrowing decisions are made, and how they are affected by the introduction of a tax.

The first step is to depict the possible combinations of present and future consumption available to Scrooge—his budget constraint. In Figure 17.7, the amount of current consumption, c_0, is measured on the horizontal axis, and the amount of future consumption, c_1, is measured on the vertical axis. One option available to Scrooge is to consume all his income just as it comes in—to consume I_0 in the present and I_1 in the future. This bundle, called the **endowment point,** is denoted by A in Figure 17.7. At the endowment point, Scrooge neither saves nor borrows.

Figure 17.7

Budget constraint
for present and
future consumption

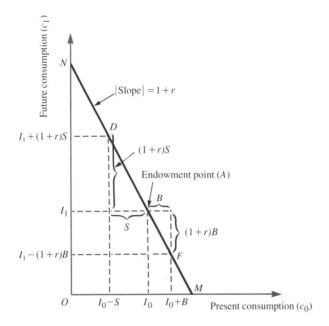

Another option is to save out of current income to be able to consume more in the future. Suppose that Scrooge decides to save S dollars this period. If he invests his savings in an asset with a rate of return of r, he can increase his future consumption by $(1 + r)S$—the principal S plus the interest rS. In other words, if Scrooge decreases present consumption by S, he can increase his future consumption by $(1 + r)S$. Graphically, this possibility is represented by moving S dollars to the left of the endowment point A, and $(1 + r)S$ dollars above it—point D in Figure 17.7.

Alternatively, Scrooge can consume more than I_0 in the present if he can borrow against his future income. Assume that Scrooge can borrow money at the same rate of interest, r, at which he can lend. If he borrows B dollars to add to his present consumption, how much does his future consumption have to be reduced? When the future arrives, Scrooge must pay back B *plus* interest of rB. Hence, Scrooge can increase present consumption by B only if he is willing to reduce future consumption by $B + rB = (1 + r)B$. Graphically, this process involves moving B dollars to the right of the endowment point, and then $(1 + r)B$ dollars below it—point F in Figure 17.7.

By repeating this process for various values of S and B, we can determine how much future consumption is feasible given any amount of current consumption. In the process of doing so, we trace out budget line MN, which passes through the endowment point A, and has a slope in absolute value of $1 + r$. As always, the slope of a budget line represents the opportunity cost of one good in terms of the other. Its slope of $1 + r$ indicates that the cost of $1 of consumption in the present is $1 + r$ dollars

Figure 17.8
Utility maximizing
choice of present
and future
consumption

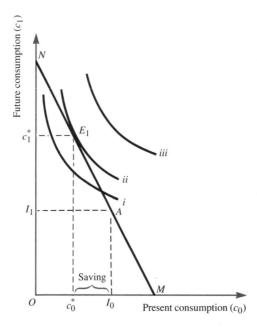

of forgone consumption in the future.[16] Because *MN* shows the trade-off between consumption across periods, it is referred to as the **intertemporal budget constraint.**

To determine which point along *MN* is actually chosen, we introduce Scrooge's preferences for future as opposed to present consumption. It is assumed that these preferences can be represented by conventionally shaped indifference curves. In Figure 17.8 we reproduce Scrooge's budget constraint, *MN*, and superimpose a few indifference curves labeled *i*, *ii*, and *iii*. Under the reasonable assumption that more consumption is preferred to less consumption, curves further to the northeast represent higher levels of utility.

Subject to budget constraint *MN*, the point at which Scrooge maximizes utility is E_1. At this point, Scrooge consumes c_0^* in the present and c_1^* in the future. With this information, it is easy to find how much Scrooge saves. Because present income, I_0, exceeds present consumption, c_0^*, then by definition the difference, $I_0 - c_0^*$, is saving.

Of course, this does not prove that it is always rational to engage in saving. If the highest feasible indifference curve had been tangent to the budget line below point *A*, present consumption would have exceeded I_0,

---

[16] Budget line *MN* has a convenient algebraic representation. The fundamental constraint facing Scrooge is that the present value of his consumption equals the present value of his income. [See Chapter 12 for an explanation of present value.] The present value of his consumption is $c_0 + c_1/(1 + r)$, while the present value of his income stream is $I_0 + I_1/(1 + r)$. Thus, his selection of c_0 and c_1 must satisfy $c_0 + c_1/(1 + r) = I_0 + I_1/(1 + r)$. The reader can verify that viewed as a function of c_0 and c_1, this is a straight line whose slope is $-(1 + r)$, and which passes through the point (I_0, I_1).

Figure 17.9

Interest taxed and
interest payments
deductible: saving
decreases

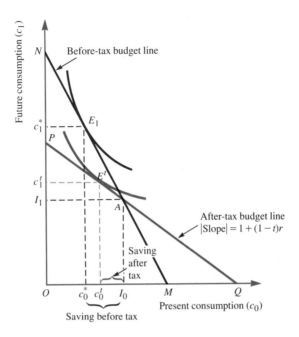

and Scrooge would have been a borrower. Although the following analysis of taxation assumes that Scrooge is a saver, the same techniques can be applied if he is a borrower.

We now consider how the amount of saving changes when a proportional tax on interest income is introduced.[17] In this context, it is important to specify whether payments of interest by borrowers are deductible from taxable income. Prior to the Tax Reform Act of 1986, interest payments generally were deductible. Under current law, however, it is not safe to assume that a particular taxpayer will be allowed to deduct interest payments. It depends, among other things, on whether he or she is a homeowner. (See the previous chapter for details.) We therefore analyze the effect on saving both with and without deductibility.

Case I: Deductible interest payments.   How does the budget line in Figure 17.8 change when interest is subject to a proportional tax at rate t, and interest payments by borrowers are deductible? Figure 17.9 reproduces the before-tax constraint MN from Figure 17.7. The first thing to note is that the after-tax budget constraint must also pass through the endowment point (I_0, I_1), because interest tax or no interest tax, Scrooge always has the option of neither borrowing nor lending.

---

[17] We could consider an *income* tax with a base of both labor and capital income, but this would complicate matters without adding any important insights.

Figure 17.10

Interest taxed and
interest payments
deductible: saving
increases

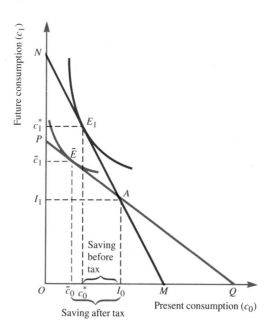

The next relevant observation is that the tax reduces the rate of interest received by savers from r to $(1 - t)r$. Therefore, the opportunity cost of consuming a dollar in the present is only $[1 + (1 - t)r]$ dollars in the future. At the same time, for each dollar of interest Scrooge pays, he can deduct one dollar from taxable income. This is worth t to him in lower taxes. Hence, the effective rate that has to be paid for borrowing is $(1 - t)r$. Therefore, the cost of increasing current consumption by one dollar, in terms of future consumption, is only $[1 + (1 - t)r]$ dollars. Together, these facts imply that the after-tax budget line has a slope (in absolute value) of $[1 + (1 - t)r]$.

The budget line that passes through (I_0, I_1) and has a slope of $[1 + (1 - t)r]$ is drawn as PQ in Figure 17.9. As long as the tax rate is positive, it is necessarily flatter than the pretax budget line MAN.

To complete the analysis, we draw in indifference curves. The new optimum is at E^t, where present consumption is c_0^t, and future consumption is c_1^t. As before, saving is the difference between present consumption and present income, distance $c_0^t I_0$. Note that $c_0^t I_0$ is less than $c_0^* I_0$, the amount that was saved before the tax was imposed. Imposition of the interest tax thus lowers saving by an amount equal to distance $c_0^* c_0^t$.

However, this outcome does not always occur. For a counterexample, consider Figure 17.10. The before- and after-tax budget lines are identical to their counterparts in Figure 17.9 as is the before-tax equilibrium at point E_1. But the tangency of an indifference curve to the after-tax budget line occurs at point $\tilde{E}$, to the left of E_1. Consumption in the present

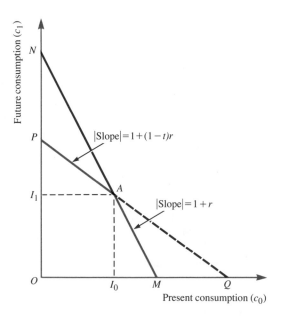

Figure 17.11
Interest taxed and interest payments nondeductible

is $\tilde{c}_0$, and in the future, $\tilde{c}_1$. In this case, a tax on interest actually increases saving, from $c_0^* I_0$ to $\tilde{c}_0 I_0$. Thus, depending on the individual's preferences, taxing interest can either increase or decrease saving.

The source of this ambiguity is the conflict between two different effects. On one hand, taxing interest reduces the opportunity cost of present consumption, which tends to increase c_0 and lower saving. This is the substitution effect, which comes about because the tax changes the price of c_0 in terms of c_1. On the other hand, the fact that interest is being taxed makes it harder to achieve any future consumption goal—it is necessary to save more to attain any given level of future consumption.[18] This is the income effect, which arises because the tax lowers real income. If present consumption is a normal good, a decrease in income lowers c_0, and hence raises saving. Just as in the case of labor supply, whether the substitution or income effect dominates cannot be known on the basis of theory alone.

Case II: Nondeductible interest payments. We now consider how the budget constraint changes when interest is taxed at rate t, but borrowers cannot deduct interest payments from taxable income. Figure 17.11 re-

---

[18] This second effect is well illustrated by the extreme case of the "target saver" described by Richard Musgrave [1959]. Suppose an individual's only goal is to have a given amount of consumption in the future—no more and no less. If the net rate of return goes down, the only way for the individual to reach the target is to increase saving. Similarly, if the net rate of return goes up, the individual's target can be met with smaller saving. Thus, for the target saver, saving and the net interest rate always move in opposite directions.

produces again the before-tax budget constraint NM from Figure 17.7. As was true for Case I, the after-tax budget constraint must include the endowment point (I_0, I_1). Now, starting at the endowment point, suppose that Scrooge decides to save \$1, that is, move \$1 to the left of point A. Because interest is taxed, this will allow him to increase his consumption next period by $[1 + (1 - t)r]$ dollars. *To the left of point A*, then, the opportunity cost of increasing present consumption by \$1 is $[1 + (1 - t)r]$ dollars of future consumption. Therefore, the absolute value of the slope of the budget constraint to the left of point A is $[1 + (1 - t)r]$. This coincides with segment PA of the after-tax budget constraint in Figure 17.9.

Now suppose that starting at the endowment point, Scrooge decides to borrow \$1, that is, move \$1 to the right of point A. Because interest is nondeductible, the tax system has no effect on the cost of borrowing. Thus, the cost to Scrooge of borrowing the \$1 now is $(1 + r)$ dollars of future consumption, just as it was prior to the interest tax. Hence, *to the right of point A* the opportunity cost of increasing present consumption by a dollar is $(1 + r)$ dollars. This coincides with segment AM of the before-tax budget constraint NM.

Putting all of this together, we see that when interest receipts are taxable but interest payments are nondeductible, the intertemporal budget constraint has a kink at the endowment point. To the left of the endowment point, the absolute value of the slope is $[1 + (1 - t)r]$; to the right, it is $(1 + r)$. What is the impact on saving? If Scrooge was a borrower before the tax was imposed, the system has no effect on him at all. That is, if Scrooge maximized utility along segment AM before the tax was imposed, it remains optimal for him to do so after. On the other hand, if Scrooge was a saver before the tax, his choice between present and future consumption must change, because points on segment NA are no longer available to him. However, just as in the discussion surrounding Figures 17.9 and 17.10, we cannot predict a priori whether Scrooge will save more or less. It depends on the relative strengths of the income and substitution effects.

Some additional considerations.   This simple two-period model ignores some important real-world complications:
■   The analysis, as usual, is couched in real terms—it is the *real* net rate of return that governs behavior. As was emphasized in Chapter 16, care must be taken to correct the *nominal* rates of return observed in the market for inflation.
■   In the model there is one vehicle for saving, and the returns to saving are taxed at a single rate. In reality, there are numerous assets, each with its own before-tax rate of return. Moreover, as observed in the last chapter, the returns to different assets are taxed at different rates. It is therefore an oversimplification to speak of how changes in the after-tax rate of return influence saving.

■   The model focuses only on private saving. For many purposes, the important variable is *social saving,* defined as the sum of government and private saving. For example, if the government were to save a sufficiently high proportion of tax receipts from an interest tax, social saving could go up even if private saving decreased.

■   Some investigators have questioned the validity of the life-cycle model itself. The life-cycle hypothesis posits that people are forward looking; critics argue that a more realistic assumption is that people are myopic. The life-cycle model also assumes that people can borrow and lend freely at the going rate of interest; critics point out that many people are not able to borrow. Of course, neither the proponents of the life-cycle view nor its detractors need be 100 percent correct. At any given time, some families' saving behavior may be explained by the model, while others' saving behavior may be myopic or constrained. In a recent study of U.S. data, Campbell and Mankiw [1990] concluded that about half of income accrues to people who behave according to the life-cycle hypothesis.

Clearly, controversies surround the life-cycle hypothesis. Nevertheless, at this time, most economists are willing to accept it as a pretty good approximation to reality. In any case, the basic result of our theoretical analysis still holds: the effect of taxation on saving cannot be predicted without empirical work.

Econometric Studies of Saving

Several econometric studies have estimated the effect of taxation on saving. In a typical study, the quantity of saving is the left-hand variable and the explanatory variables are the rate of return to saving, disposable income, and other variables that might plausibly affect saving. If the coefficient on the rate of return is positive, the conclusion is that increases in taxes (which decrease the rate of return) depress saving and vice versa.

Prior to the late 1970s, investigators typically concluded that taxes did not have much of an impact on saving.[19] However, most of these early analyses failed to correct market rates of return for inflation and/or taxes. As previously noted, theoretical considerations suggest that the after-tax, inflation-corrected rate of return governs saving decisions. Michael Boskin [1978] claimed that the rate of return, when properly measured, has an important effect on the amount of saving, finding an elasticity of saving with respect to the net real interest rate between 0.2 and 0.4. This suggests that lowering the tax rate on capital income would induce substantial amounts of saving.[20]

Boskin's results have been the subject of considerable controversy. One reason is that correcting market returns for inflation requires measuring the *expected* inflation rate. Presumably, people's expectations are

---

[19] Boskin [1978] provides a review.

[20] However, this response is not nearly large enough to imply that tax reductions on the return to saving would be self-financing. See the preceding discussion of the Laffer curve.

based on past experience plus anticipation of the future, but no one knows exactly how expectations are formed. Boskin calculated the expected inflation rate as a complicated weighted average of past inflation rates. In another study, Alan Blinder and Angus Deaton [1985] used an alternative method for computing expected inflation rates, and found that the real net rate of return does not have much of an impact on saving at all.

At this time, the difficulties involved in estimating the impact of the level of taxation on saving have defied the efforts of economists to reach a firm consensus. Taking the various pieces of research together, Jerry Hausman and James Poterba [1987] argue that a reasonable estimate of the effect on saving of changes in the after-tax rate of return is about zero. That is, for the population as a whole, the income and substitution effects more or less cancel each other out.

Individual Retirement Accounts and Saving

One feature of the income tax designed specifically to affect saving is the Individual Retirement Account (IRA). Starting in 1981, all taxpayers were eligible to save up to $2,000 each year in a tax-deductible IRA. Because amounts deposited in IRAs were excluded from the income tax, IRAs were an attractive form of saving. The principal drawback to IRAs was the lack of liquidity implied by a 15 percent penalty on any funds withdrawn before the saver reached age 59½. Tax-deductible IRAs accounted for one quarter of all personal saving from 1982 to 1986. However, tax deductibility was severely limited and the penalty for withdrawal increased in 1986; by 1987 IRAs accounted for only 14 percent of personal saving. By 1988, $393 billion had been accumulated through IRAs.

Since 1986, legislators have made numerous proposals to reinstate IRAs in their original form or with a higher deductible limit. The central question in debates over such proposals is whether IRAs actually stimulated new saving. To think about this issue, note the three sources from which IRAs could be funded. First, households could cut back on their consumption, putting the new saving into an IRA. Second, they could put into IRAs money that would otherwise have been saved in some other form; such asset transfers clearly are not new saving. The data indicate that the possibility of asset transfers has to be taken seriously: although the median household had only $3,000 in non-IRA financial assets, the median IRA-holder had $13,500 in other assets [Gale and Scholz, 1990, Table 2]. Third, part of the money used to fund an IRA could come from the tax savings generated by the IRA itself.[21]

In a careful econometric study, W. G. Gale and J. K. Scholz [1990] estimated that if the $2,000 IRA limit had been raised, only between 7 and 25 percent of the additional IRA contributions would have represented

---

[21] Note that if the government borrowed to make up for the decrease in tax revenue, then even if households saved the entire tax cut, there would be no net increase in the level of social saving.

new saving; that is, most of the new contributions would have been asset transfers. Note, however, that the Gale-Scholz result pertains to the *incremental* effect of increasing the deductible limit. The proportion of existing IRA contributions that represent new saving may have been higher. This is because those households already contributing the allowable maximum to IRAs would be the ones affected by raising the limit. These were mostly wealthy households (for whom median non-IRA wealth was $30,000) that could easily substitute IRAs for other forms of saving, or older households for whom the early withdrawal penalty was not a serious constraint. On the other hand, the overall population contributing to IRAs was younger and less affluent, and therefore less likely to see IRAs as a close substitute for other kinds of saving. It seems reasonable to assume, then, that the proportion of total IRA deposits attributable to new saving exceeds the incremental effect. Nevertheless, these results suggest that policymakers should approach the reinstatement and expansion of tax-deductible IRAs with some caution.

Taxes and the Capital Shortage

As a political issue, the taxation of capital income has been the subject of at least as much public discussion as the taxation of wages. Much of the debate has centered on the proposition that by discouraging saving, the tax system has led to a *capital shortage*—there is not enough capital around to meet our national "needs." Reduction of taxes on capital is therefore needed to end the so-called *productivity crisis*.

A major problem with this line of reasoning is that, as we have just shown, it is not at all obvious that taxation has reduced the supply of saving. Let us assume, for the sake of argument, that saving has indeed declined as a consequence of taxes. Nevertheless, as long as the capital market is competitive, a decrease in saving does not create a gap between the demand for investment funds and their supply. Instead, the interest rate will adjust to bring quantities supplied and demanded into equality.[22] However, it is true that the new equilibrium will, other things being equal, involve a lower rate of investment, possibly leading to lower productivity growth.

But to look only at these issues is unfair. Taxation of *any* factor may reduce the equilibrium quantity. Just as in any other case, the important efficiency question is whether taxation of capital income has led to large excess burdens compared to other ways of raising tax revenues. We defer to Chapter 20 a discussion of whether economic efficiency would be enhanced if taxes on capital were eliminated. In the meantime, we note that there is no reason a high rate of investment alone is a desirable objective.

---

[22] See Feldstein [1977] for a discussion of other fallacies that have arisen in discussions of the capital shortage.

In a utilitarian framework, at least, capital accumulation is a means of enhancing individual welfare, not an end in itself.

Finally, we stress that the entire argument that savings incentives can help increase the capital stock rests on the premise that investment in the economy depends on its own rate of saving: all national saving is channeled into national investment. This is true in an economy that is closed to international trade. In an open economy, however, domestic saving can be invested abroad. This means that tax policy designed to stimulate saving may not lead to more domestic investment. To the extent that saving flows freely across national boundaries to whatever investment opportunities seem most attractive, the ability of tax policy to stimulate investment through saving is greatly diminished.

How open is the American economy? Martin Feldstein and Charles Horioka [1980] find that countries with high domestic saving tend to have high domestic investment, and vice versa. While the data are open to other interpretations, this suggests that saving may not flow into and out of the economy as freely as one would expect in a completely integrated world capital market.[23] As long as saving and investment are correlated, tax policy that affects saving can generally be expected to affect investment. The size of the effect, however, is smaller than one would find in a completely closed economy.

Housing Decisions

When people talk of a capital shortage, they are usually concerned with the amount of capital available to businesses for producing goods. Such capital is only part of the nation's stock. Some capital, such as schools and roads, is government-owned infrastructure. Some capital, such as pollution abatement equipment, is used by business but not for the purpose of increasing output as conventionally measured. Other capital is in the hands of households, with owner-occupied housing being the prime example. Even a tax code that has little effect on the overall level of saving in an economy can nonetheless have significant effects on the allocation of saving across these different types of investment. As we see in this section, the tax code favors investment in housing.

The effects of the income tax on housing investment can best be illustrated with an example. Macbeth owns a house and decides to rent it out. Being a landlord entails certain annual costs. An important one is the opportunity cost (OC) of the funds invested in the house. For example, if Macbeth has invested $200,000 in the house and the going rate of interest is 12 percent, the annual opportunity cost is the $24,000 of forgone interest. If he has borrowed money to purchase the house, the interest payments on the mortgage (Mi) are also costs. In addition, expenditures for

---

[23] For example, see Frenkel and Razin [1988].

maintenance *(MA)* and property taxes *(PT)* must be incurred. Finally, some costs arise due to changes in the value of the house. If the dwelling depreciates in value during the year due to wear and tear, this is as much a cost of renting it as any of those previously listed. On the other hand, if the house increases in value, Macbeth has enjoyed a capital gain, which should be counted as a negative cost. We denote the value of capital gains by ΔV. (A negative value of ΔV, then, indicates that the house has decreased in value.)

Adding up these items, the total annual cost *(A)* is

$$A = OC + Mi + MA + PT - \Delta V \qquad (17.3)$$

For example, suppose that Macbeth's annual mortgage interest payments are \$12,000; his maintenance expenditures \$3,000; his property taxes \$2,500; and his expected appreciation on the house \$4,000 per year. Then his total annual cost (including opportunity cost) is \$37,500 (= \$24,000 + \$12,000 + \$3,000 + \$2,500 − \$4,000).

As long as the market for housing is competitive, the rental income received by the landowner will be bid down to the point at which it just equals the cost. Hence, Macbeth's yearly rental income from the house is *A*. Under a Haig-Simons income tax system, Macbeth must include *A* in his taxable income. If his marginal tax rate is 31 percent, the rental income creates a tax liability of \$11,625 (= .31 × \$37,500).[24]

Now suppose that instead of renting the house out, Macbeth and his wife choose to live in it themselves. By virtue of living in the house, they derive services from it that have a market value of *A*. Of course, they do not literally receive *A* dollars—the income is in kind. However, under a comprehensive income tax system, the form in which income is received is irrelevant, and the imputed rent from owner-occupied housing is a part of taxable income. Moreover, any increase in the value of the house is income, just like any other asset. (Decreases in house value lower income.)

Under U.S. law, the imputed rent from owner-occupied housing is *not* subject to tax, despite the fact that mortgage interest payments and property taxes are deductible. Moreover, housing capital gains are generally exempt from taxation.[25] If the Macbeths' marginal tax rate is *t* and they itemize their deductions, these tax provisions lower the effective cost of owner-occupied housing from Equation (17.3) to

$$OC + Mi + MA + PT - \Delta V - t(Mi + PT) \qquad (17.4)$$

---

[24] Of course, the landlord would be able to deduct the costs incurred in earning this income.

[25] Capital gains from the sale of a principal residence are excluded when another residence costing at least as much is purchased within two years. In addition, for taxpayers 55 years of age and older, there is a one-time housing capital gains exclusion of \$125,000.

The last term in Equation (17.4) reflects the value to the owner of being able to deduct mortgage interest and property taxes. In effect, then, the federal income tax implicitly subsidizes owner-occupied housing. Because marginal tax rates tend to increase with income, the subsidy is worth more to high-income people, other things being the same.[26] It has been estimated that the deduction of mortgage interest and property tax payments lowered tax revenues by about $52 billion in fiscal year 1992 [Executive Office of the President, 1991, p. 3-40].

The size of the implicit subsidy is affected by inflation. Higher inflation rates lead to both higher nominal interest rates (including mortgage rates) *and* to higher nominal housing capital gains. Because interest rates are a cost and capital gains are a benefit, one might guess that the two effects would cancel each other. Equation (17.4) indicates that this is not the case because mortgage interest payments are tax deductible, while the housing capital gains are untaxed. On balance, inflation *increases* the attractiveness of owner occupation, other things being the same. This is another example of how inflation affects *real* incentives in the presence of the existing tax structure (see Chapter 16). It is difficult to say just how much inflation has increased the attractiveness of housing, because the effect of inflation on nominal interest rates is an unresolved question.

Still, it is generally agreed that by lowering its effective price, the federal income tax increases the demand for owner-occupied housing. The precise size of the increase depends on the price elasticity of demand for such housing. Rosen [1979] estimated a price elasticity of about -1.0 and calculated that removal of the favorable tax provisions for housing would in the long run reduce the quantity consumed by about 14 percent.

The implicit subsidy affects not only how much housing people purchase but also whether they become owners or renters in the first place. At the end of World War II, 48 percent of U.S. households resided in owner-occupied housing; by 1987, the figure had grown to 65 percent. Over this period, increasing marginal tax rates tended to enhance the attractiveness of the implicit subsidy to owner occupation. Of course, other factors were changing that might have influenced housing patterns; for example, incomes rose considerably. However, according to an econometric study by Patric Hendershott and James Shilling [1982], about one quarter of the increase in the proportion of homeowners since World War II is attributable to tax considerations.

So far we have discussed only tax policies affecting owner-occupied housing, and ignored rental housing. Historically, however, the U.S. tax system has provided generous subsidies to the owners of rental housing. (These included accelerated depreciation, discussed in Chapter 19.) Pre-

---

[26] However, as noted in the previous chapter, marginal tax rates decrease for very high-income households.

sumably, these provisions reduced the cost of renting to individuals, although one cannot know by how much without information on the relevant supply and demand elasticities. Roger Gordon, James Hines, and Lawrence Summers [1986] argued that prior to 1986, on balance federal tax policy actually increased the attractiveness of renting relative to owning. In 1986, however, many of the tax provisions favorable to real estate were eliminated, which made renting a relatively more expensive housing option.

Proposals for Change

In Chapter 6 under "Positive Externalities," we discussed the pros and cons of providing a subsidy for owner-occupied housing. The point made there was that from an externality point of view, the subsidy does not have much merit. And since the subsidy's value increases with income, one can hardly claim that it equalizes the income distribution. In light of these facts, a number of proposals have been made to reform the federal tax treatment of housing. Probably the most radical change would be to include net imputed rent in taxable income. Such a move might create administrative problems, because the authorities would have to determine the potential market rental value of each house. Nevertheless, imputed rental income is taxed in several European countries such as Spain, Sweden, and Denmark.[27]

Moreover, taxing imputed rent does not appear politically feasible. Homeowners are more likely to perceive their houses as endless drains on their financial resources than as revenue producers. It would not be easy to convince homeowners—who comprise more than half the electorate—that taxation of imputed rental income is a good idea.

Several reform proposals have focused on reducing the value of mortgage interest and property tax deductions to upper-income individuals. One possibility would be simply to disallow these deductions. In 1984, the U.S. Treasury suggested that the property tax deduction be eliminated. The proposal created a storm and was soon abandoned. And no serious politician has even whispered about removing the mortgage interest deduction. As noted in the previous chapter, the Tax Reform Act of 1986 disallowed deductions of interest for most types of borrowing, but not the interest expense associated with indebtedness on a principal residence.

An alternative to eliminating the property tax and mortgage interest deductions would be to put upper limits on the dollar amounts that can be deducted. Another would be to convert these deductions into credits: each homeowner would be allowed to subtract the *same* proportion of interest and property tax payments from tax liability. In Equation (17.4), the marginal tax rate, t, would be replaced by some number—say 0.25—

---

[27] See Andersson [1990]. Similar problems have been dealt with by local tax authorities who levy taxes based on the value of real property. See Chapter 21.

independent of the household's tax status. In this way, those with higher marginal tax rates would not enjoy an advantage, other things being the same.

Evaluating proposals such as these is difficult because it is not clear what their objectives are and what other policy instruments are assumed to be available. For example, if a more equal income distribution is the goal, why bother with changing from deductions to credits? It would make more sense just to adjust the rate schedule appropriately.

Finally, we note that much of the debate over the tax treatment of housing implicitly assumes that full taxation of imputed rent would be the most efficient solution. Recall from the theory of optimal taxation (Chapter 15) that if lump sum taxes are excluded, the efficiency maximizing set of tax rates is generally a function of the elasticities of demand and supply for all commodities. Only in very special cases do we expect efficiency to require equal rates for all sources of income. On the other hand, it is also highly improbable that the efficient tax rate on imputed rental income is zero. Determining the appropriate rate is an important topic for further research.

Portfolio Composition

Taxes may affect not only the total amount of wealth that people accumulate but the assets in which that wealth is held as well. Some argue that taxes have discouraged people from holding risky assets. For example, the Bush administration argued that Congress could encourage risk taking if it would schedule substantial reductions in tax rates on capital gains. Superficially, this proposition seems plausible. Why take a chance on a risky investment if your gains are going to be grabbed by the tax collector? It turns out, however, that the problem is considerably more complicated than this line of argument suggests.

Most modern theoretical work on the relationship between taxes and portfolio composition is based on the path-breaking analysis of James Tobin [1958]. In Tobin's model, individuals make their decisions about whether to invest in an asset on the basis of two characteristics—the expected return on the asset, and how risky that return is. Other things being the same, investors prefer assets that are expected to yield high returns. At the same time, investors are assumed to dislike risk; other things being the same, investors prefer safer assets.

Suppose there are two assets. The first is perfectly safe but it yields a zero rate of return. (Imagine holding money in a world with no inflation.) The second is a bond that *on average* yields a positive rate of return, but it is risky—there is some chance that the price will go down, so that the investor incurs a loss.

Note that the investor can adjust the return and risk on the entire portfolio by holding different combinations of the two assets. In one extreme case he or she could hold only the safe asset—there is no return, but no risk. On the other hand, the investor could hold only the risky asset—his or her expected return rises, but so does the risk involved. The typical investor holds a combination of both the risky and safe assets to suit tastes concerning risk and return.

Now assume that a proportional tax is levied on the return to capital assets. Assume also that the tax allows for **full loss offset**—individuals can deduct all losses from taxable income. (To some extent, this reflects actual practice in the United States. See Chapter 16.) Because the safe asset has a yield of zero, the tax has no effect on its rate of return—the return is still zero. In contrast, the risky asset has a positive expected rate of return, which is lowered by the presence of the tax. It seems that the tax reduces the attractiveness of the risky asset compared to the safe asset.

However, at the same time that the tax lowers the return to the risky asset, it lowers its riskiness as well. Why? In effect, introduction of the tax turns the government into the investor's silent partner. If the investor wins (in the sense of receiving a positive return), the government shares in the gain. But because of the loss-offset provision, if the individual loses, the government also shares in the loss. Suppose, for example, that an individual loses $100 on an investment. If the tax rate is 31 percent, the ability to subtract the $100 from taxable income lowers the tax bill by $31. Even though the investment lost $100, the investor loses only $69. In short, introduction of the tax tightens the dispersion of returns—the highs are less high and the lows are less low—and hence, reduces the risk. Thus, although the tax makes the risky asset *less* attractive by reducing its expected return, it simultaneously makes it *more* attractive by decreasing its risk. If the second effect dominates, taxation can on balance make the risky asset more desirable.

An important assumption behind this discussion is the existence of a perfectly riskless asset. This is not a very realistic assumption. In a world where no one is sure exactly what the inflation rate will be, even the return on money is risky. But the basic reasoning still holds. Because taxes decrease risk as well as returns, the effect of taxes on portfolio choice is ambiguous. (See Feldstein [1969] for a demonstration.)

Resolving this ambiguity econometrically is very difficult. A major problem is that it is hard to obtain reliable information on just which assets people hold. Individuals may not accurately report their holdings to survey takers because they are not exactly sure of the true values at any point in time. Alternatively, people might purposely misrepresent their asset positions because of fears that the information will be reported to the tax authorities. In one study using a fairly reliable data set from the late 1970s, Glenn Hubbard [1985] found that other things being the same, people in higher tax brackets hold a higher proportion of their portfolios in common stock, which is quite risky, than in relatively safe assets such as money and bonds. This finding lends at least tentative support to the notion that taxation increases risk taking. But the issue is far from being resolved.

A Note on Politics and Elasticities

Despite much investigation, the effect of income taxation on several important kinds of behavior is not known for sure. Different "experts" are therefore likely to give policymakers different pieces of advice. In this situation, it is almost inevitable that policymakers will adopt those behavioral assumptions that enhance the perceived feasibility of their goals. Although it is dangerous to generalize, liberals tend to believe that behavior is not very responsive to the tax system, while conservatives take the opposite view. Liberals prefer low elasticities because they can raise large amounts of money for public sector activity without having to worry too much about charges that they are "killing the goose that laid the golden egg." In contrast, conservatives like to assume high elasticities because this limits the volume of taxes that can be collected before serious efficiency costs are imposed on the economy. Thus, when journalists, politicians, and economists make assertions about how taxes affect incentives, it is prudent to evaluate their claims in light of what their hidden agendas might be.

Summary

- The U.S. personal income tax affects myriad economic decisions, including the amount of labor supplied, the level of saving, the amount of residential housing consumed, and the choice of portfolio assets.
- For labor supply, saving, and choice of portfolio, the *direction* of the effects of taxation is theoretically ambiguous. Further, in each area, the *size* of tax-induced behavioral changes may be determined only by empirical investigation. For these reasons, the effect of taxation is among the most contentious of all areas of public policy.
- Econometric studies of labor supply indicate that prime age males vary their hours only slightly in response to tax changes, while hours of married women are quite sensitive to variations in the after-tax wage rate.
- Earnings taxes can increase, decrease, or leave unchanged the amount of human capital

investments. The outcome depends in part on how taxes affect hours of work.
- The effect of tax rates on tax revenues depends on the responsiveness of personal behavior to changes in tax rates. Theoretically, tax-rate reductions can increase tax revenues, but there is no evidence that this is currently the case for the United States.
- The effect of taxes on saving may be analyzed using the life-cycle model which assumes that people make their annual consumption and saving decisions keeping in mind their lifetime resources. Taxing interest income lowers the opportunity cost of present consumption and thereby creates incentives to lower saving. However, this substitution effect may be offset by the fact that the tax reduces total lifetime resources which tends to reduce present consumption, that is, increase saving. The net effect on saving is an empirical question.

- Econometric studies of saving behavior have foundered on both conceptual and practical difficulties. As a result, there is no firm consensus of opinion on the effects of taxation on saving.
- The personal income tax excludes the imputed rent from owner-occupied housing from taxation. *Ceteris paribus*, this increases both the percentage of those choosing to own their homes and the quantity of owner-occupied housing.
- Proposals to modify the tax treatment of housing include taxing imputed rent at the personal income tax rate, limiting the deduction for mortgage interest, or converting the deduction to a tax credit. Each proposal should be evaluated by the standards of optimal tax theory.
- The theoretical effects of taxation on portfolio composition are ambiguous. Taxes reduce the expected return on a risky asset but also lessen its riskiness. The net effect of these conflicting tendencies has not been empirically resolved.

Discussion Questions

1. Using a supply-demand diagram, illustrate the effects on hours of work of imposing a proportional wage tax under each of the following circumstances:

   a. The income effect dominates the market labor supply curve; labor demand is perfectly elastic.

   b. The substitution effect dominates the market labor supply curve; labor demand is perfectly elastic.

   c. The substitution effect dominates the market labor supply curve; labor demand is negatively related to the wage rate.

   Discuss the differences.

2. Suppose that individuals view their loss of income from income taxes as offset by the benefits of public services purchased with the revenues. How are their labor supply decisions affected? (Hint: Decompose the change in hours worked into income and substitution effects.)

3. In 1991, the Bush administration proposed the introduction of Family Savings Accounts (FSAs). Under this proposal, an individual would be permitted to deposit up to $2,500 each year in an FSA. The interest earned on FSA deposits would not be subject to income tax, provided that deposits were left in the account for at least seven years. Sketch the intertemporal budget constraint associated with an FSA. Would FSAs increase private saving? What about social saving (the sum of private and public saving)?

4. Discuss: "The capital gains tax is an example of antiproducer taxation. It is counter to the enterprise and risk taking needed in an economy where capital allocation decisions are made by individuals and not by the government."

5. The *New York Times* (October 17, 1982, p. 1) reported that:

   Time and time again, families choose one community over another simply because of the reputation of the schools. They will pay vastly more for a house that is no more desirable than another because they want their children in one school system rather than another.

   a. How does this enter into the issue of the tax deductible status of property taxes?

   b. If tax deductibility were eliminated, how would the effective cost of owner-occupied housing be changed?

   c. What impact would this have on the demand for owner-occupied housing? Why?

Selected References

Feldstein, Martin S. "The Effects of Taxation on Risk Taking." *Journal of Political Economy* 77 (1969), pp. 755–64.

Fullerton, Don. "On the Possibility of an Inverse Relationship between Tax Rates and Government Revenues." *Journal of Public Economics* 19, no. 1 (October 1982), pp. 3–22.

Hausman, Jerry A., and James M. Poterba. "Household Behavior and the Tax Reform Act of 1986." *Journal of Economic Perspectives* 1 (1987).

Poterba, James M. "Taxation and Housing Markets: Preliminary Evidence on the Effects of Recent Tax Reforms." In Joel Slemrod, *Do Taxes Matter? The Impact of the Tax Reform Act of 1986.* Cambridge, Mass.: MIT Press, 1991.

18 Deficit Finance

As a very important source of strength and security, cherish public credit.

GEORGE WASHINGTON

Having discussed the personal income tax in Chapter 16 and the Social Security payroll tax in Chapter 11, we now turn to the federal government's third-largest revenue source: borrowing. The issue of debt finance has dominated discussions of economic policy for the last decade; it is constantly debated in political campaigns and on editorial pages. As the following cartoon indicates, it is hard to avoid the subject. This chapter discusses problems in measuring the size of the debt, who bears its burden, and the circumstances under which debt is a suitable way to finance government expenditures.

The Size of the Debt

A few definitions are needed to begin our discussion. The **deficit** during a period of time is the excess of spending over revenues. That seems simple enough until we recall from Chapter 2 that the federal government does not include all of its activities in its official budget. Under current rules, for example, revenues and expenditures associated with Social Security are off-budget. Despite this legal distinction, a proper measure of the extent of government borrowing requires that all revenues and expenditures be taken into account. Hence, it is useful to consider the sum of the **on-budget deficit** (which takes into account only on-budget activity) and the **off-budget deficit** (which takes into account only off-budget activity) to arrive at the total deficit. For example, in 1990, the on-budget deficit was $277 billion, but adding in a $57 billion off-budget surplus gives a total deficit of $220 billion [Congressional Budget Office, 1991, p. xiv].

"You might ask,
'Can two people
who love each other
find happiness in an
era of skyrocketing
deficits?' I think
they can."

*Drawing by Weber; ©
1984 The New Yorker
Magazine, Inc.*

Table 18.1 shows total federal deficits (i.e., including off-budget revenues and expenditures) for selected years over the period 1962 to 1995. To put these figures in perspective, we also show their size relative to gross national product.

The table indicates a general trend for deficits to increase both in dollar value and as a proportion of GNP. Note also the ubiquity of deficit finance as a source of funds. Over the last three decades, deficit finance has been used in both Democratic and Republican administrations; only in one year during this period, 1969, was there a surplus ($3.2 billion, or 0.4 percent of GNP).

One must distinguish between the concepts of deficit and debt. The **debt** at a given time is the sum of all past budget deficits. That is, the debt is the cumulative excess of past spending over past receipts. In the jargon of economics, the debt is a "stock variable" (measured at a point in time), while the deficit is a "flow variable" (measured during a period of time). As reported in official government statistics, the federal debt at the end of 1990 was about $2.4 *trillion* [Congressional Budget Office, 1991, p. 146], a number so large that it is hard to comprehend. As humorist Russell Baker [1985] observed, "Like the light year, the trillion is an abstruse philosophical idea that can interest only persons with a morbid interest in mathematics. This explains why most people go limp with boredom when told that the national debt will soon be $2 trillion, or $20 trillion, or $200 trillion. The incomprehensible is incomprehensible, no matter how you number it."

Despite Baker's warning, let us try to put the debt in perspective, again by comparing it to GNP. The 1990 federal debt of $2.4 trillion was about 45 percent of that year's GNP—45 cents of every dollar produced would have been required to liquidate the debt. Table 18.2 reports comparable figures for other years as well. Interestingly, the debt to GNP ratio is

Table 18.1   **Federal government deficits,
1962–1995**

Fiscal Year	Total Deficit ($ billions)	Total Deficit Percent of GNP
1962	7.1	1.3%
1965	1.6	0.2
1970	2.8	0.3
1975	53.2	3.6
1980	73.8	2.9
1985	212.3	5.4
1990	220.0	4.1
1995*	128.0	1.8

* Projections.

SOURCE: Congressional Budget Office, *The Economic and Budget Outlook: Fiscal Years 1992–1996*, January 1991, pp 146–47.

Table 18.2   **Federal government debt held by the public, 1962–1995**

Fiscal Year	Debt Held by the Public ($ billions)	Debt Held by the Public as a Percent of GNP
1962	248	45.4%
1965	262	39.6
1970	285	29.4
1975	397	26.8
1980	715	27.8
1985	1,510	38.4
1990	2,410	44.6
1995*	3,405	47.0

* Projections.

SOURCE: Congressional Budget Office, *The Economic and Budget Outlook: Fiscal Years 1992–1996*, January 1991, pp. 146–47.

not too much higher now than it was in the early 1960s. However, much of the debt from that period was a legacy of the heavy borrowing to finance World War II; it was not a consequence of chronic large deficits.

Just like a private borrower, the government must pay interest to its lenders. As the federal debt has grown, so have the interest payments. In 1990 they were $265 billion, or 21 percent of federal outlays [Congressional Budget Office, 1991, pp. 82, 98]. Interest is now one of the fastest growing components of federal spending; as a proportion of GNP, net interest went up by a factor of 2.83 from 1962 to 1990, while government spending as a whole went up by a factor of only 1.21.[1]

Interpreting Deficit and Debt Numbers

For a variety of reasons, the deficit and debt figures may not be economically meaningful. In this section we describe some of their problems.

Government debt held by the Federal Reserve Bank.   In the course of conducting its monetary operations, the Federal Reserve Bank purchases U.S. government securities.[2] Its holdings in 1990 were $234 billion [*Economic Report of the President 1991*, p. 377]. Because statutorily the Federal Reserve Bank is an independent agency, its holdings are counted as debt held by the public; it would seem that the amount of debt held by nongovernmental agencies is more relevant for most purposes.

State and local government debt.   Although we often think of debt as a "problem" of the federal government, state and local governments borrow as well. In 1988, state and local debt outstanding was $755 billion [Advisory Commission on Intergovernmental Relations, 1990, p. 71]. The federal figure for that year was $2,050 billion; the sum of the two numbers is relevant if we wish to assess the pressure that government as a whole has exerted on credit markets.

Effects of inflation.   In standard calculations of the deficit, taxes are viewed as the only source of government revenue. However, when the government is a debtor and the price level changes, changes in the real value of the debt may be an important source of revenue. To see why, suppose that at the beginning of the year you owe a creditor $1,000, and the sum does not have to be repaid until the end of the year. Suppose further that over the course of the year, prices rise by 10 percent. Then the dollars you use to repay your creditor are worth 10 percent less than those you borrowed. In effect, inflation has reduced the real value of your debt by $100 (10 percent of $1,000). Alternatively, your real income has increased by $100 as a consequence of inflation. Of course, at the same time, your creditor's real income has fallen by $100.[3]

Let us apply this logic to an analysis of the federal deficit in 1990. As we noted, at the end of that year the federal government's outstanding debt was $2.4 trillion. During 1990, the rate of inflation was 6.1 percent. Hence, inflation reduced the real value of the federal debt by $146 billion

---

[1] Computed from figures in Congressional Budget Office [1991, p. 150].

[2] Some agencies of the federal government lend to the Treasury, but unlike the Federal Reserve Bank, their holdings are not included in figures on debt held by the public.

[3] If the inflation is anticipated by borrowers and lenders, one expects the interest rate charged to be increased to take inflation into account. This phenomenon was discussed in Chapter 16.

(= \$2.4 trillion $\times$ 0.061). In effect, this is as much a receipt for the government as any conventional tax. If we take this "inflation tax" into account, the conventionally measured deficit of \$220 billion is reduced to just \$74 billion, a considerably smaller figure. However, the government's accounting procedures do not allow the inclusion of gains due to inflationary erosion of the debt. This induces a tendency to overestimate the size of the real deficit.

Capital versus current accounting.   The federal government lumps together all expenditures that are legally required to be included in the budget. There is no attempt to distinguish between *current spending* and *capital spending*. Current spending refers to expenditures for services that are consumed within the year—upkeep at the Washington Monument or salaries for arms control negotiators, for example. Capital spending, in contrast, refers to expenditures for durable items that yield services over a long time, such as dams, radar stations, and aircraft carriers.

In contrast to federal government practice, the standard accounting procedure for both American corporations and many state and local governments is to keep separate budgets for current and capital expenditure. Maintaining a separate capital budget is generally believed to provide a more accurate picture of an organization's financial status. Why? Purchase of a durable does not generally represent a "loss." It is only the trade of one asset (money) for another (the durable). Hence, acquisition of the asset does not contribute to an organization's deficit. Of course, as the capital asset is used it wears out (depreciation), and this *does* constitute a loss. Thus, standard accounting procedures require that only the annual depreciation of durable assets be included in the current budget, not their entire purchase price. Robert Eisner [1986] estimates that if the federal government used capital budgeting, the conventionally measured deficit would fall by a third to a half.

The idea of the federal government adopting capital budgeting is controversial. Opponents point out that, for governments, it is particularly difficult to distinguish between current and capital expenditure. Are educational and job training programs a current expense, or an investment in human capital that will yield future returns? Is a missile an investment (because it will last a long time), or a current expenditure (because it is not reusable)? Such ambiguities could lead to political mischief, because every proponent of a new spending program could claim that it was an investment and therefore belonged in the capital budget. To the extent that the reluctance to run current deficits helps to restrain spending, this would lead to a breakdown of fiscal discipline.

In response, proponents of capital budgeting note that its absence leads to some bizarre governmental decisions. In particular, one strategy for reducing the federal deficit is to sell off government assets, such as hydroelectric projects and public housing, to the private sector. As we pointed out in Chapter 5, there may be good reasons for transferring such assets to private individuals, but such transactions have nothing to do with reducing the real budget deficit. They simply represent the government trading one asset for the other. However, under the current accounting system, the proceeds of such sales are treated as equivalent to tax revenues, and hence count toward reducing the deficit.

Tangible assets.   Suppose that a family owns tangible assets (yachts, houses, Rembrandts) altogether worth $15 million, owes the local bank $25,000 for credit card charges, and has no other assets or liabilities. It would be pretty silly to characterize the family's overall position as being $25,000 in debt. All assets and liabilities must be taken into account to assess overall financial position.

The federal government has not only massive financial liabilities (as depicted in Table 18.2), but vast tangible assets as well. These include residential and nonresidential buildings, equipment, gold, and mineral rights. However, public discussion has focused almost entirely on the government's financial liabilities, and not its tangible assets. Some have argued that the omission of tangibles leads to a highly misleading picture of the government's financial position.

One example of this phenomenon was embodied in the deficit reduction plan agreed to by President George Bush and the Congress in 1990. The negotiators projected that their plan would reduce the annual deficit by 80 percent between 1991 and 1995. However, in the early years of this period, the deficit figures include borrowing by the Resolution Trust Corporation (RTC), the governmental agency charged with the "savings and loan bail-out"—acquiring failing savings and loan associations and paying off their insured depositors. Although all of RTC borrowing adds to the measured deficit, much of it represents asset swaps (e.g., the government sells a bond and acquires a shopping center). Further, in 1995, when the RTC is expected to sell off many of these assets, the proceeds are counted as lowering the deficit. Again, however, the asset swap does not change the real financial position of the government. Thus, RTC activity artificially inflates the measured deficit in 1991, and artificially deflates it in 1995, leading to an upwardly biased estimate of the actual deficit reduction. According to Martin Feldstein [1990], more than half of the budget agreement's alleged reduction in the deficit was due to inappropriate accounting for RTC activity.

Implicit obligations.   One way to think of a bond is simply as a promise to make certain payments of money in the future. The present value of these payments is the amount by which the bond contributes to the debt. But bonds are not the only method that the federal government uses to promise money in the future. It can do so by legislation. The most important example is Social Security, which promises benefits to future retirees that must be paid out of future tax revenues.[4] The precise value is hard to estimate, but some estimates range around $7 trillion. (See Chapter 10.) In addition, legislation has been passed that promises retirement benefits to civilian and military employees. The value of these obligations is estimated to be about $1 trillion [Leonard, 1984]. Arthur Andersen & Co. [1986], a major accounting firm, estimated that if implicit obligations are taken into consideration, the national debt is almost *triple* the official figure.

Of course, legislative promises and official debt are not exactly equivalent. For one thing, their legal status is quite different; explicit forms of debt represent legal commitments, while Social Security payments can be reduced by legislative action, at least in principle. Nevertheless, political support for Social Security and other government pension programs is strong, and it would be surprising to see the government renege on these promises.

Summing Up

How big is the national debt? The answer depends on which assets and liabilities are included in the calculation, and how they are valued. As in other similar situations, the "correct" answer depends on your purposes. For example, if the goal is to obtain some sense of all the obligations that have to be met by future taxpayers, then measures including implicit obligations like Social Security might be appropriate. But if the purpose is to assess the effect of debt policy on credit markets (discussed later), then a more conventional measure including only official liabilities might be more useful. Our discussion certainly shows that considerable caution must be exercised in interpreting figures on debts and deficits.

The Burden of the Debt

Future generations either have to retire the debt, or else refinance it. (Refinancing simply means borrowing new money to pay existing creditors.) In either case, there is a transfer from future taxpayers to bondholders because even if the debt is refinanced, interest payments must be made to the new bondholders. It would appear, then, that future generations must bear the burden of the debt. But those who are familiar with the theory of incidence (Chapter 13) should be suspicious of this line of reasoning. Merely because the legal burden is on future generations does not mean that they bear a real burden. Just as in the case of tax incidence, the chain of events set in motion when borrowing occurs can make the economic incidence quite different from the statutory incidence. Just as with other incidence problems, the answer depends on the assumptions made about economic behavior.

---

[4] For further discussion along these lines, see Alan Auerbach, Jagadeesh Gokhale, and Laurence Kotlikoff [1990].

Lerner's View   Assume that the government borrows from its own citizens—the obligation is an **internal debt.** According to A. P. Lerner [1948], an internal debt creates no burden for the future generation. Members of the future generation simply owe it to each other. When the debt is paid off, there is a transfer of income from one group of citizens (those who do not hold bonds) to another (bondholders). However, the future generation as a whole is no worse off in the sense that its consumption level is the same as it would have been. As an 18th-century writer named Melon put it, the "right hand owes to the left" [Musgrave, 1985, p. 49].

The story is quite different when a country borrows from abroad to finance current expenditure. This is referred to as an **external debt.**[5] Suppose that the money borrowed from overseas is used to finance current consumption. In this case, the future generation certainly bears a burden, because its consumption level is reduced by an amount equal to the loan plus the accrued interest which must be sent to the foreign lender.[6] If, on the other hand, the loan is used to finance capital accumulation, the outcome depends on the project's productivity. If the marginal return on the investment is greater than the marginal cost of funds obtained abroad, the combination of the debt and capital expenditure actually makes the future generation better off. To the extent that the project's return is less than the marginal cost, the future generation is worse off.

The view that an internally held debt does not burden future generations dominated the economics profession in the 1940s and 1950s. There is now widespread belief that things are considerably more complicated.

An Overlapping Generations Model   In Lerner's model, a "generation" consists of everyone who is alive at a given time.[7] Perhaps a more sensible way to define a generation is everyone who was born at about the same time. Using this definition, at any given time several generations coexist simultaneously, as an **overlapping generations model** takes into account. Analysis of a simple overlapping generations model shows how the burden of a debt can be transferred across generations.

Assume that the population consists of equal numbers of young, middle-aged, and old people. Each generation lasts 20 years, and each person has a fixed income of $12,000 over the 20-year period. There is no private saving—everyone consumes their entire income. This situation is expected to continue forever. Income levels for three representative people for the period 1992 to 2012 are depicted in row 1 of Table 18.3.

---

[5] In the United States, internal debt is more important than external debt; in 1990, about 18 percent of the federal debt was held by foreign investors. However, the proportion of the debt held by foreigners has been increasing over time. See *Economic Report of the President 1991,* p. 386.

[6] If the loan is refinanced, only the interest must be paid.

[7] This argument is based on William Bowen, Richard Davis, and David Kopf [1960].

Table 18.3   **Overlapping generations model**

		The Period 1992–2012		
		Young	*Middle-Aged*	*Old*
(1)	Income	$ 12,000	$ 12,000	$12,000
(2)	Government borrowing	−6,000	−6,000	
(3)	Government-provided consumption	4,000	4,000	4,000
			The Year 2012	
		Young	*Middle-Aged*	*Old*
(4)	Government raises taxes to pay back the debt	$−4,000	$−4,000	$−4,000
(5)	Government pays back the debt		+6,000	+6,000

Now assume that the government decides to borrow $12,000 to finance public consumption. The loan is to be repaid in the year 2012. Only the young and the middle-aged are willing to lend to the government—the old are unwilling because they will not be around in 20 years to obtain repayment. Assume that half the lending is done by the young and half by the middle-aged, so that consumption of each person is reduced by $6,000 during the period 1992 to 2012. This fact is recorded in row 2 of Table 18.3. However, with the money obtained from the loan, the government provides an equal amount of consumption for all—each person receives $4,000. This is noted in line 3.

Time passes, and the year 2012 arrives. The generation that was old in 1992 has departed from the scene. The formerly middle-aged are now old, the young are now middle-aged, and a new young generation has been born. The government has to raise $12,000 to pay off the debt. It does so by levying a tax of $4,000 on each person. This is recorded in line 4. With the tax receipts in hand, the government can pay back its debt holders, the now middle-aged and old (row 5). (It is assumed for simplicity that the rate of interest is zero, so all the government has to pay back is the principal. Introducing a positive rate of interest would not change the substantive result.)[8]

---

[8] The assumption of a zero interest rate also means that there is no need to discount future consumption to find its present value.

The following results now emerge from Table 18.3:

1. As a consequence of the debt and accompanying tax policies, the generation that was old in 1992 to 2012 has a lifetime consumption level $4,000 higher than it otherwise would have had.
2. Those who were young and middle-aged in 1992 to 2012 are no better or worse off from the point of view of lifetime consumption.
3. The young generation in 2012 has a lifetime consumption stream that is $4,000 lower than it would have been in the absence of the debt and accompanying fiscal policies.

In effect, $4,000 has been transferred from the young of 2012 to the old of 1992. To be sure, the debt repayment in 2012 involves a transfer between people who are alive at the time, but the young are at the short end of the transfer because they have to contribute to repaying a debt from which they never benefited. Note also that the internal-external distinction that was key in Lerner's model is of no relevance here; even though the debt is all internal, it creates a burden for the future generation.

Of course, the model of Table 18.3 is highly restrictive—there is no private saving, no growth, and no behavioral response to government fiscal policies. However, even in more complicated models, intergenerational burden shifting remains a real possibility.

Neoclassical Model

The intergenerational models discussed so far do not allow for the fact that economic decisions can be affected by government debt policy, and changes in these decisions have consequences for who bears the burden of the debt. Instead, it has been assumed that the taxes levied to pay off the debt affect neither work nor savings behavior when they are imposed. If taxes distort these decisions, real costs are imposed on the economy. (See Chapter 14.)

More importantly, we have ignored the potentially important effect that debt finance can have on capital formation. The neoclassical model of the debt stresses that when the government initiates a project, whether financed by taxes or borrowing, resources are removed from the private sector. One usually assumes that when tax finance is used, most of the resources removed come at the expense of consumption. On the other hand, when the government borrows, it competes for funds with individuals and firms who want the money for their own investment projects. Hence, it is generally assumed that debt has most of its effect on private investment. To the extent that these assumptions are correct, debt finance leaves the future generation with a smaller capital stock, *ceteris paribus*. Its members therefore are less productive and have smaller real incomes than otherwise would have been the case. Thus, even in Lerner's model, the debt can have a burden. The mechanism through which it works is the reduction of capital formation. (Note, however, that one of the things that is held equal here is the public-sector capital stock. As suggested earlier, to the extent that the public sector undertakes productive investment with the resources it extracts from the private sector, the total capital stock increases.)

The assumption that private investment is reduced by government borrowing plays a key role in the neoclassical analysis. It is sometimes referred to as the **crowding out hypothesis**—when the public sector draws on the pool of resources available for investment, private investment is crowded out. Crowding out is induced by changes in the interest rate. When the government increases its demand for credit, the interest rate, which is just the price of credit, must go up. But if the interest rate goes up, private investment becomes more expensive and less of it is undertaken.[9]

Expressed this way, it would appear relatively straightforward to test the crowding out hypothesis. Just examine the historical relationship between the interest rate and government deficits (as a proportion of gross national product). If the correlation between the two variables is positive, this tends to support the crowding out hypothesis, and vice versa.

Unfortunately, things are complicated by the fact that other variables can also be expected to affect interest rates. For example, during a recession, investment tends to decrease, and hence the interest rate falls. At the same time, slack business conditions lead to smaller tax collections, and this tends to increase the deficit, *ceteris paribus*. Hence, the data may show an inverse relationship between interest rates and deficits, although this says nothing one way or the other about crowding out. As usual, the problem is to sort out the *independent* effect of deficits on interest rates, and as we showed in Chapter 3, this kind of problem can be quite difficult. When B. Douglas Bernheim [1989] reviewed the econometric studies of this issue, he found conflicting results.

Despite the murkiness of the econometric evidence, the theoretical case for at least some crowding out is so strong that most economists agree that large deficits cause some reduction in the capital stock.[10] However, the precise size of this reduction, and hence the reduction in welfare for future generations, is not known with any precision.

---

[9] When capital is internationally mobile, the debt-induced increase in the interest rate leads to an inflow of funds from abroad. This increases the demand for dollars, causing the dollar to appreciate, which increases the relative price of American exports. Hence, net exports are crowded out rather than domestic investment. As Janet Yellen [1989] notes, in the U.S. economy, some of both domestic investment and exports are likely to be crowded out.

[10] To the extent that higher interest rates attract foreign investment, less crowding out occurs. However, the burden on future generations is roughly unchanged because of the interest they must pay to foreigners.

Ricardian Model

Our discussion so far has ignored the potential importance of individuals' intentional transfers across generations. Robert Barro [1974] has argued that when the government borrows, members of the "old" generation realize that their heirs will be made worse off. Suppose further that the old care about the welfare of their descendants and therefore do not want their descendants' consumption levels reduced. What can the old do about this? One possibility is simply to increase their bequests by an amount sufficient to pay the extra taxes that will be due in the future. Private individuals thus can undo the intergenerational effects of government debt policy so that tax and debt finance are essentially equivalent. This view, that the form of government finance is irrelevant, is often referred to as the Ricardian model because its antecedents appeared in the work of the 19th-century British economist David Ricardo.

Barro's provocative hypothesis on the irrelevance of government fiscal policy has been the subject of much debate. Some reject the idea as being based on incredible assumptions. Information on the implications of current deficits for future tax burdens is not easy to obtain; indeed, as emphasized earlier in this chapter, it isn't even clear how big the debt is! Another criticism is that, through marriage, virtually all people end up related to one another; the model implies that the nation acts as one big happy family, busily undoing all government policy [Bernheim and Bagwell, 1988].

On the other hand, it could be argued that the ultimate test of the theory is not the plausibility of its assumptions, but whether or not it leads to predictions that are confirmed by the data. Edward Gramlich [1989] notes that in the early 1980s, there was a huge increase in federal deficits. If the Ricardian model were correct, one would have expected private saving to increase commensurately. At the same time the federal deficit increased, however, private saving (relative to net national product) actually fell. While this finding is suggestive, it is not conclusive because factors other than the deficit affect the saving rate. A number of econometric studies have analyzed the relationship between budget deficits and saving. Although the evidence is mixed, the general finding is that even after taking other variables into account, saving does not increase enough to offset increased deficits [Bernheim, 1990]. There seems to be mounting evidence that although some intergenerational altruism doubtless exists, its presence does not render debt policy irrelevant.[11]

Overview

The burden of the debt is essentially a tax incidence problem in an intergenerational setting. Like many other incidence problems, the burden of the debt is hard to pin down. First of all, it is not even obvious how burden should be defined. One possibility is to measure it in terms of the

---

[11] For a contrary view, see Barro [1989].

lifetime consumption possibilities of a group of people about the same age. Another is in terms of the consumption available to all people alive at a given point in time. Even when we settle on a definition, the existence of a burden depends on the answers to several questions: Is the debt internal or external? How are various economic decisions affected by debt policy? What kind of projects are financed by the debt? Empirical examination of some of these decisions has been attempted, but so far no consensus has emerged.

To Tax or to Borrow?

The Persian Gulf War of 1991 led to a large temporary increase in government expenditures. Immediately a public debate arose about whether the war should be financed by raising taxes or increasing borrowing. How to choose between debt and taxes is one of the most fundamental questions in the field of public finance. Armed with the results of our discussion of the burden of the debt, we are in a good position to evaluate several different views.

Benefits-Received Principle

This independent normative principle states that the beneficiaries of a particular government spending program should have to pay for it. Thus, to the extent that the program creates benefits for future generations, it is appropriate to shift the burden to future generations via loan finance. As an example, the Bush administration defended its plan to borrow to pay for the Persian Gulf War by arguing that the cost might rightfully be borne by future generations who would enjoy the war's presumed benefits.

Intergenerational Equity

Suppose that due to technological progress, our grandchildren will be richer than we are. If it makes sense to transfer income from rich to poor people within a generation, why shouldn't we transfer income from rich to poor generations? Of course, if future generations are expected to be poorer than we are (due, say, to the exhaustion of irreplaceable resources) then this logic would lead to just the opposite conclusion.

Efficiency Considerations

Here the question is whether debt or tax finance results in a higher excess burden. The key to analyzing the debt issue from this perspective is to realize that *every* increase in government spending must ultimately be financed by an increase in taxes. The choice between tax and debt finance is just a choice between the timing of the taxes. With tax finance, one large payment is made at the time the expenditure is undertaken. With debt finance, many small payments are made over time to finance the interest due on the debt. The present values of the tax collections must be the same in both cases.

   If the present values of tax collections for the two methods is the same, is there any reason to prefer one or the other on efficiency grounds? Assume for simplicity that all revenues to finance the debt are to be raised

Figure 18.1
The relationship
between tax rate
and excess burden

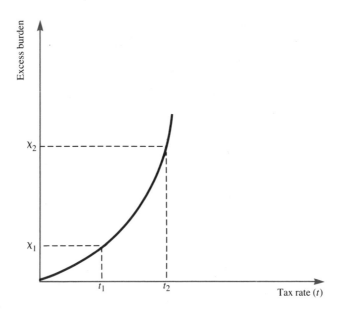

by taxes on labor income. As shown in Chapter 14 (Equation 14.4), such a tax distorts the labor supply decision, resulting in an excess burden that is approximately equal to

$$\tfrac{1}{2}\varepsilon w L t^2$$

where ε is the compensated elasticity of hours of work with respect to the wage, w is the before tax wage, L is hours worked, and t is the *ad valorem* tax rate. Note that excess burden increases with the *square* of the tax rate—when the tax rate doubles, the excess burden quadruples. Thus, from the excess burden point of view, two small taxes are not equivalent to one big tax. Two small taxes are preferred.

This point is made graphically in Figure 18.1, which depicts the quadratic relationship between excess burden and the tax rate. The excess burden associated with the low tax rate, t_1, is χ_1, and the excess burden associated with the higher rate, t_2, is χ_2. From an efficiency point of view, it is better to be taxed twice at rate t_1, than once at rate t_2. The implication is that debt finance, which results in a series of relatively small tax rates, is superior to tax finance on efficiency grounds. (For further details, see Barro [1979].)

This argument is correct as far as it goes. However, it ignores another important consideration—to the extent the increase in debt reduces the capital stock, it creates an additional excess burden.[12] Thus, while debt

---

[12] More precisely, an additional excess burden is created if the capital stock starts out below the optimal level because of, for example, capital income taxes. See Feldstein [1985, p. 234].

finance may be more efficient from the point of view of labor supply choices, it will be less efficient from the point of view of capital allocation decisions. A priori it is unclear which effect is more important, so we cannot know whether debt or tax finance is more efficient.

Thus, the "crowding out" issue, which was so important in our discussion of the intergenerational burden of the debt, is also central to the efficiency issue. Recall that according to Barro's [1974] intergenerational altruism model, there is no crowding out. Thus, only labor supply choices can be distorted, and debt finance is unambiguously superior on efficiency grounds. However, to the extent that crowding out takes place, tax finance becomes more attractive. Clearly, as long as the empirical evidence on crowding out is inconclusive, we cannot know for sure the relative efficiency merits of debt versus tax finance.

Macroeconomic Considerations

Thus far we have made our usual assumption that all resources are fully employed. This is appropriate for characterizing long-run tendencies in the economy. What do short-run macroeconomic models that explicitly allow for the possibility of unemployment say about the choice between tax and deficit finance? In the standard Keynesian model, the choice depends on the level of unemployment. When unemployment is very low, extra government spending might lead to inflation, so it is necessary to siphon off some spending power from the private sector—increase taxes. Conversely, when unemployment is high, running a deficit is a sensible way to stimulate demand. This approach is sometimes referred to as **functional finance**—use taxes and deficits to keep aggregate demand at the right level, and don't worry about balancing the budget per se.

When the Keynesian consensus collapsed in the 1970s, so did the almost universal belief in functional finance. While a thorough discussion of the relevant developments in macroeconomic theory would take us much too far afield, a couple of points are worth making:

- If Barro's intergenerational altruism model is correct, people can undo the effects of government debt policy. Government cannot stabilize the economy.[13]
- Even in the context of the Keynesian model, there is a lot of uncertainty regarding just how long it takes for changes in fiscal policy to become translated into changes in employment. But successful unemployment policy requires that the timing be right. Otherwise, one might end up stimulating the economy when it is no longer required, perhaps contributing to inflation.

---

[13] More precisely, *anticipated* changes in policy have no impact. Unanticipated changes may have an effect, because by definition, people cannot change their behavior to counteract them.

Moral and Political Considerations

Some commentators have suggested that the decision between tax and debt finance is a moral issue. Too much reliance on deficits "is not merely, or even primarily, an economic matter. It reflects moral failing, a defect in the formation of the public's character and conservatisms" [Will, 1985a]. Morality requires self-restraint; deficits are indicative of a lack of restraint; therefore, deficits are immoral. The implicit assumption that debt is immoral is a feature of many political discussions of the topic.

As emphasized throughout this text, ethical values are important considerations in the formulation of public policy, so arguments that a particular policy is immoral deserve serious consideration. One should note, however, that this *normative* view seems to rest heavily on the unproven *positive* hypothesis that the burden of the debt is shifted to future generations. Moreover, it is not clear why this particular normative view is superior to, for example, the benefits-received principle, which implies that sometimes borrowing is the morally right thing to do.

A perhaps more compelling noneconomic argument against deficit spending is a political one. As noted in Chapter 7, some have pointed out a tendency for the political process to underestimate the costs of government spending and to overestimate the benefits. The discipline of a balanced budget may produce a more careful weighing of benefits and costs, thus preventing the public sector from growing beyond its optimal size.

Overview

The national debt is an emotional and difficult subject. The analysis of this chapter brings the following perspectives to bear on the debate:

- The size of the deficit during a given year depends on one's accounting conventions. This fact underscores the arbitrariness of any number that purports to be "the" deficit or "the" debt.
- The consequences of large deficits, while potentially important, are hard to measure. And even if we knew exactly what the effects were, the implications for the conduct of debt policy would still depend on ethical views concerning the intergenerational distribution of income.

In light of all these considerations, it makes little sense to evaluate the economic operation of the public sector solely on the basis of the size of the deficit. What is more important is whether the levels of government services are optimal, particularly considering the costs of securing the resources required to provide these services. A lively debate over the spending and financing activities of government is important in a democracy. The consequences of deficit versus other forms of finance are important and worthy of public consideration. Nevertheless, the tendency of both liberals and conservatives to evaluate the state of public finance solely on the basis of the deficit has tended to obscure and confuse the debate.

Summary

- Borrowing is an important method of government finance. The deficit during a period of time is the excess of spending over revenues; the debt as of a given point in time is the accumulated value of past deficits.

- Official figures regarding the size of federal government deficits and debts must be viewed with caution for several reasons:

    They fail to take into account the facts that a substantial portion of the debt is held by the Federal Reserve Bank, and that state and local governments also have large amounts of debt outstanding.

    Inflation erodes the real value of the debt; the annual deficit does not reflect this fact.

    The federal government does not distinguish between capital and current expenditure. However, attempts to design a capital budget for the federal government could founder on both conceptual and political problems.

    Tangible assets owned by the federal government should be taken into account. While this would make the debt problem seem less severe, taking into account the government's implicit obligations would produce an estimate of the federal debt much greater than the official measure.

- There is great controversy over the extent to which the burden of debt is borne by future generations. One view is that an internal debt creates no net burden for the future generation because it is simply an intragenerational transfer. However, in an overlapping generations model, debt finance can produce a real burden for future generations.

- The burden of the debt also depends on the extent to which debt finance crowds out private investment. If it does, future generations have a smaller capital stock, and hence, lower real incomes, *ceteris paribus*. However, in a Ricardian model, voluntary transfers across generations undo the effects of debt policy, so that crowding out does not occur.

- Several factors influence whether a given government expenditure should be financed by taxes or debt. The benefits-received principle suggests that if the project will benefit future generations, then having them pay for it via loan finance is appropriate. Also, if future generations are expected to be richer than the present one, some principles of equity suggest that it is fair to burden them.

- From the point of view of efficiency, tax and debt finance must be compared on the basis of their respective excess burdens. If there is no crowding out, debt finance has less of an excess burden, because a series of small tax increases generates a smaller excess burden than one large tax increase. However, if crowding out occurs, this conclusion may be reversed.

Discussion Questions

1. How would each of the following events affect the national debt as it is currently measured?

    a. The government borrows to finance a Memorial Day parade.

    b. The Statue of Liberty is sold to a group of private entrepreneurs.

    c. A law is passed promising each veteran of the Persian Gulf War a onetime award of $10,000 at the age of 65.

    If you were designing an accounting system for the government, how would you treat each of these items?

2. Explain the logic behind this assertion: "If people care about the welfare of their descendants, then debt policy may not have any impact on capital formation."

3. Suppose that the generations are linked by bequests as suggested by the Ricardian

model, but that the optimum bequest for the current generation is negative—that is, children should make transfers to their parents. What are the implications of such a situation for your answer to question 2?

4. Suppose that the compensated elasticity of labor supply with respect to the wage is zero. On efficiency grounds, what are its consequences for the optimal choice between debt and tax finance?

Selected References

Barro, Robert J. "Are Government Bonds Net Wealth?" *Journal of Political Economy* 82 (1974), pp. 1095–117.

Eisner, Robert, and Paul J. Pieper. "A New View of the Federal Debt and Budget Deficits." *American Economic Review* 74, no. 1 (March 1984), pp. 11–29.

Feldstein, Martin. "Debt and Taxes in the Theory of Public Finance." *Journal of Public Economics* 28, no. 2 (November 1985), pp. 233–46.

Yellen, Janet L. "Symposium on the Budget Deficit." *Journal of Economic Perspectives,* Spring 1989, pp. 17–22.

CHAPTER 19

The Corporation Tax

I'll probably kick myself for having said this, but when are we going to have the courage to point out that in our tax structure, the corporation tax is very hard to justify?

RONALD W. REAGAN

In 1990, $2.95 trillion—or 54 percent of the gross domestic product—originated in nonfinancial corporations alone.[1] A **corporation** is a form of business organization created by a specific state's approval of its corporate charter. While the charter is filed by the founders of the corporation, a corporation is owned by its stockholders, with ownership usually represented by transferable stock certificates. The stockholders have limited liability for the acts of the corporation. This means that their liability to the creditors of the corporation is limited to the amount they have invested in the corporation.

Corporations are independent legal entities and as such are often referred to as artificial legal persons. A corporation may make contracts, hold property, incur debt, sue, and be sued. And just like any other person, a corporation must pay tax on its income. This chapter explains the structure of the federal corporation income tax and analyzes its effects on the allocation of resources.

The relative importance of the federal corporation tax has fallen in recent decades. In 1950, the tax accounted for 27.9 percent of all federal tax collections. By 1990, this figure was down to 9.1 percent [Congressional Budget Office, 1991, p. 148]. However, the theory of excess burden

---

[1] *Economic Report of the President, 1991*, pp. 296, 300.

suggests that a tax may create efficiency costs far out of proportion to the revenues yielded. There is some evidence that the corporation tax is an example of this important phenomenon.

Why Tax Corporations?

Before undertaking a description and analysis of the tax, we should ask whether it makes sense to have a special tax system for corporations in the first place. To be sure, from a *legal* point of view, corporations are people. But from an economic standpoint, this notion makes little sense. As we have seen in Chapter 13, only real people can pay a tax. If so, why should corporate activity be subject to a special tax? Is it not sufficient to tax the incomes of the corporation *owners* via the personal income tax?

A number of justifications for a separate corporation tax have been proposed: First, contrary to the view just stated, corporations—especially very big ones—really are distinct entities. Large corporations have thousands of stockholders, and the managers of such corporations are controlled only very loosely, if at all, by the stockholder/owners. Most economists would certainly agree that there is separation of ownership and control in large corporations, and this creates important problems for understanding just how corporations function. Nevertheless, it does not follow that the corporation should be taxed as a separate entity.

This point is related to a point raised in Chapter 13 that deserves re-emphasis. Despite the fact that a corporation is a legal entity, it cannot bear the burden of a tax—only people can. Throughout the debate preceding the Tax Reform Act of 1986, one politician after another stated that a particular reform package would leave total revenues unchanged, *and* that everybody's tax bill would go down. How was this magic to be accomplished? By pretending that no one would have to pay the associated increase in corporate income tax revenues.

A second justification for corporate taxation is that the corporation receives a number of special privileges from society, the most important of which is limited liability of the stockholders. The corporation tax can be viewed as a user fee for this benefit. However, the tax is so structured that there is no reason to believe that the revenues paid approximate the benefits received.

Finally, the corporation tax protects the integrity of the personal income tax. Suppose that Karl's share of the earnings of a corporation during a given year is $10,000. According to the standard convention for defining income, this $10,000 is income whether the money happens to be retained by the corporation or paid out to Karl. If the $10,000 is paid out, it is taxed in an amount that depends on his personal income tax rate. In the absence of a corporation tax, the $10,000 creates no tax liability if it is retained by the corporation. Hence, unless corporation income is taxed, Karl can reduce his tax liability by accumulating income within the corporation.[2]

It is certainly true that if corporate income goes untaxed, opportunities for personal tax avoidance are created. But a special tax on corporations is not the only way to include earnings accumulated in corporations. We discuss an alternative method many economists view as superior at the end of this chapter.

Structure

There is a three-bracket graduated corporate tax rate structure: 15 percent for taxable income under $50,000, 25 percent for taxable income between $50,000 and $75,000, and 34 percent for taxable income above $75,000.[3] Most corporate income is taxed at the 34 percent rate, so for our purposes, the system can safely be presented as a flat rate of 34 percent. Prior to the Tax Reform Act of 1986 the rate was a higher 46 percent.

However, this does not mean that the 1986 law lowered *effective* rates. As in the case of the personal income tax, knowledge of the rate applied to taxable income by itself gives relatively little information about the effective burden. To compute taxable income, we must know exactly which deductions from before-tax corporate income are allowed. Accordingly, we now discuss the rules for defining taxable corporate income.[4]

Wage Payments Deducted

As we saw in Chapter 16, a fundamental principle in defining personal income is that income should be measured net of the expenses incurred in earning it. The same logic applies to the measurement of corporate income. One important business expense is labor, and wages paid to workers are excluded from taxable income.

Interest, but Not Dividends, Deducted

When corporations borrow, interest payments to lenders are excluded from taxable income. Again, the justification is that business costs should be deductible. However, when firms finance their activities by issuing stock, the dividends paid to the stockholders are *not* deductible from corporate earnings. We discuss the consequences of this asymmetry in the treatment of interest and dividends later.

---

[2] Of course, the money will be taxed when it is eventually paid out, but in the meantime, the full $10,000 grows at the before-tax rate of interest. Remember from Chapter 16, taxes deferred are taxes saved.

[3] An additional 5 percent rate is imposed on corporate income between $100,000 and $335,000.

[4] The definition of corporate income occupies many hundreds of pages, and there is no attempt here to be inclusive. Note also that many of these rules apply to noncorporate businesses, as well.

Depreciation Deducted

Suppose that during a given year the XYZ Corporation makes two purchases: (1) $1,000 worth of stationery, which is used up within the year; and (2) a $1,000 drill press, which will last for 10 years.[5] Should there be any difference in the tax treatment of these expenditures?

From the accounting point of view, these are very different items. Because the stationery is entirely consumed within the year of its purchase, its entire value is deductible from that year's corporate income. But the drill press is a durable good. When the drill press is purchased, the transaction is merely an exchange of assets—cash is given up in exchange for the drill press. Thus, unlike stationery, a drill press is not entirely consumed during the year. To be sure, during its first year of use, some of the machine is used up by wear and tear, which decreases its value. This process is called **economic depreciation.** But at the end of the year, the drill press is still worth something to the firm, and in principle could be sold to some other firm at that price.

We conclude that during the first year of the life of the drill press, a consistent definition of income requires that only the economic depreciation experienced that year be subtracted from the firm's before-tax income. Similarly, the economic depreciation of the machine during its second year of use should be deductible from that year's gross income, and so on for as long as the machine is in service.

It is a lot easier to state this principle than to apply it. In practice, the tax authorities do not know exactly how much a given investment asset depreciates each year, or even what the useful life of the machine is. The tax law has rules that indicate for each type of asset what proportion of its acquisition value can be depreciated each year, and over how many years the depreciation can be done—the **tax life** of the asset. Next, we discuss these rules, which often fail to reflect true economic depreciation.

Calculating the value of depreciation allowances.   Assume that the tax life of the $1,000 drill press is 10 years, and a firm is allowed to depreciate $1/10$th the machine's value each year. How much is this stream of depreciation allowances worth to the XYZ Corporation?[6]

At the end of the first year, XYZ is permitted to subtract $1/10$th the acquisition value, or $100 from its taxable income. With a corporation income tax rate of 34 percent, this $100 deduction saves the firm $34. Note, however, that XYZ receives this benefit a year after the machine is purchased. The present value of the $34 is found by dividing it by $(1 + r)$, where r is the opportunity cost of funds to the firm.

---

[5] Understanding the impact of depreciation allowances requires the concept of present value. Readers may wish to review the relevant material in Chapter 12 under "Present Value."

[6] We assume for now that the general level of prices stays fixed over time. The impact of inflation is discussed later.

At the end of the second year, XYZ is again entitled to subtract $100 from taxable income, which generates a saving of $34 that year. Because this saving comes two years in the future, its present value is $34/(1 + r)^2$. Similarly, the present value of depreciation taken during the third year is $34/(1 + r)^3$, during the fourth year, $34/(1 + r)^4$, and so on. The present value of the entire stream of depreciation allowances is

$$\frac{\$34}{1 + r} + \frac{\$34}{(1 + r)^2} + \frac{\$34}{(1 + r)^3} + \cdots + \frac{\$34}{(1 + r)^{10}}$$

For example, if $r = 10\%$, this expression is equal to $208.95. In effect, then, the depreciation allowances lower the price of the drill press from $1,000 to $791.05 (= $1,000 − $208.95). Intuitively, the effective price is below the acquisition price because the purchase leads to a stream of tax savings in the future.

More generally, suppose that the tax law allows a firm to depreciate a given asset over T years, and the proportion of the asset that can be written off against taxable income in the nth year is $D(n)$. The $D(n)$ terms sum to one, meaning that the tax law eventually allows the entire purchase price of the asset to be written off. (In the preceding example, T was 10, and $D(n)$ was equal to $\frac{1}{10}$th every year. There are, however, several depreciation schemes for which $D(n)$ varies across years.) Consider the purchase of an investment asset which costs $1. The amount that can be depreciated at the end of the first year is $D(1)$ dollars, the value of which to the firm is $\theta \times D(1)$ dollars, where θ is the corporation tax rate. (Because the asset costs $1, $D(1)$ is a fraction.) Similarly, the value to the firm of the allowances in the second year is $\theta \times D(2)$. The present value of all the tax savings generated by the depreciation allowances from a $1 purchase, which we denote ψ, is given by

$$\psi = \frac{\theta \times D(1)}{1 + r} + \frac{\theta \times D(2)}{(1 + r)^2} + \cdots + \frac{\theta \times D(T)}{(1 + r)^T} \tag{19.1}$$

Because ψ is the tax saving for one dollar of expenditure, it follows that if the acquisition price of an asset is q, the presence of depreciation allowances lowers the effective price to $(1 - \psi)q$. For example, a value of $\psi = 0.25$ indicates that for each dollar spent on an asset, 25 cents worth of tax savings are produced. Hence, if the machine cost $1,000 ($q = \$1,000$) the effective price is only 75 percent of the purchase price, or $750.

Equation (19.1) suggests that the tax savings from depreciation depend critically on the value of T and the function $D(n)$. In particular, the tax benefits are greater: (1) the shorter the time period over which the machine is written off—the lower is T; and (2) the greater the proportion of the machine's value that is written off at the beginning of its life—the larger the value of $D(n)$ when n is small. Schemes that allow firms to write off assets faster than true economic depreciation are referred to as **accel-**

erated depreciation.[7] An extreme possibility is to allow the firm to deduct from taxable income the full cost of the asset at the time of acquisition. This is referred to as **expensing.**

Under current law, every depreciable asset is assigned one of eight possible tax lives (that is, values of T). The tax lives vary from 3 to 31½ years. Most equipment is in the 5-year class, while most nonresidential structures have a tax life of 31½ years. Generally, the tax lives are shorter than actual useful lives. This has potential consequences for corporate investment behavior, which we discuss later. With respect to the rate at which assets can be depreciated, basically three methods are currently relevant.

Straight-line method.   This is the method we have been using for our examples so far. If the tax life of the asset is T years, the firm can write off $1/T$th of the cost each year. Thus, for a $1,000 asset that may be depreciated over five years, $200 is deducted each year.

One-and-a-half method or 150-percent method.   One-and-one-half times the straight-line percentage is deductible in the first year, and in each successive year, the same percentage is applied to the amount that remains undepreciated as of that year. Consider again a $1,000 asset with a tax life of five years. One-and-one-half times the straight-line percentage is 30 percent. Thus, the firm can deduct $.30 \times \$1,000 = \$300$ during the first year. During the second year, the undepreciated balance is $700, so the allowance is $.30 \times \$700 = \$210$ and so forth. The firm can switch to straight line when the amount deductible under that method exceeds the amount from the 150-percent method. Compared to straight-line depreciation, the 150-percent method produces tax savings with a higher present value.

Double declining balance method.   Twice the straight-line percentage is deductible in the first year; and in each successive year, the same percentage is applied to the amount that remains undepreciated as of that year. For our $1,000 asset with a five-year tax life, twice the straight-line percentage is 40 percent. The firm can deduct $.40 \times \$1,000 = \$400$ during the first year; $.40 \times \$600 = \$240$ the second year, and so on. As in the case of the 150-percent method, the firm can switch to straight line whenever it becomes advantageous to do so.

The depreciation method applicable to assets with tax lives of 3, 5, 7, and 10 years is double declining balance. For property in the 15- and 20-year classes, the 150-percent method is used, while assets with greater tax lives are allowed only straight-line depreciation.

---

[7] Note also that depreciation allowances are not worth anything unless there is some income from which to deduct them. We discuss some of the consequences of this fact later.

Depreciation allowances and tax shelters.   When tax depreciation is faster than economic depreciation, tax arbitrage opportunities are created. These opportunities are most dramatic in the case of assets which are legally depreciable for tax purposes, but actually appreciate in value over time. Complicated tax shelter plans involving investments in real estate, cattle, and timber have been based on this principle. Although tax shelter opportunities were curtailed significantly in 1986, their use is still widespread.

A nice example is provided by baseball. If you buy a baseball team, part of the product you receive is the players' contracts. Normally, the amount allocated to player contracts is a large proportion of the acquisition cost of the team. These contracts are viewed as a depreciable asset. Since the tax life of contracts is relatively short, the amount allowed as a deduction in the early years generally exceeds the income generated by the team for those years. This produces an accounting loss that can be used to reduce the owners' taxable income from other sources. However, when the team is sold, if it has increased in value, the owner reaps a capital gain.[8] No wonder that an owner once claimed that you can never lose money on a baseball team!

Depreciation allowances and inflation.   Like the personal income tax, the corporation tax was designed at a time when inflation was not an important phenomenon. As a consequence, little thought was given to how the real corporate tax burden would change with inflation. It turns out that the real value of depreciation allowances is reduced by inflation.

To see why, suppose that XYZ purchases a $4,000 asset and takes straight-line depreciation over eight years—$500 per year. Suppose further that after the asset is purchased, the price level doubles. Then, the $500 that is deductible each year represents only $\frac{1}{16}$th of the real replacement cost of the asset, not the $\frac{1}{8}$th that was intended.

Now, if the real value of depreciation allowances goes down, other things being the same, the effective tax rate on corporate capital goes up. Martin Feldstein and Lawrence Summers [1979, p. 449] estimated that in the late 1970s (an era of relatively high inflation), corporate taxes were increased significantly due to inflationary erosion of the real value of depreciation allowances. They calculated that in 1977, corporate taxes were $19.1 billion higher than they would have been in the absence of inflation.[9] This figure amounts to a third of the taxes actually paid.

---

[8] Prior to TRA86, this arrangement was even more profitable because of the preferential treatment of realized capital gains.

[9] Note, however, that an acceleration in the inflation rate generates a windfall gain for firms with outstanding debts because inflation reduces the real value of the amount that must be repaid. Thus, for some firms, inflation could be beneficial.

Two methods of dealing with this problem have received considerable attention.

1. **Index Depreciation Allowances.** The value of depreciation allowances each year could be adjusted for the rise in the capital goods price index over the previous year.
2. **Shorten the Number of Years over Which the Asset Can Be Depreciated.** Allowing assets to be depreciated more rapidly tends to counteract the decline in real value of the amounts being written off.

Indexing complicates tax administration. For example, if all assets do not increase in price at the same rate, it might be necessary to design various price indexes for different types of assets. In contrast, shortening the tax lives of assets is quite simple and easy to administer. However, any particular shortening of tax lives, even if it adjusts perfectly for the *current* rate of inflation, will necessarily be inappropriate if the inflation rate changes in the future. If inflation were to decrease, the allowances based on the current rate would be too generous and vice versa. Considering the substantial variability of inflation rates that the United States has experienced, this is a serious drawback. For this reason, most economists prefer indexing. In fact, in 1984 the Treasury Department proposed that depreciation allowances be indexed. However, that proposal received little political support, and was rejected. The United States has cast its lot with shortening asset lives rather than indexing.

No Investment Tax Credit

Prior to 1986, an important aspect of the tax treatment of businesses was the **investment tax credit (ITC),** which permitted a firm to subtract some portion of the purchase price of an asset from its tax liability at the time the asset was acquired. If a drill press cost $1,000, and if the XYZ firm was allowed an investment tax credit of 10 percent, the purchase of a drill press lowered XYZ's tax bill by $100. The effective price of the drill press (before depreciation allowances) was thus $900. More generally, if the investment tax credit was k and the acquisition price was q, the effective price of the asset was $(1 - k)q$. In contrast to depreciation allowances, the value to the firm of an ITC did not depend on the corporate income tax rate. This was because the credit was subtracted from tax liability rather than taxable income. In the early 1980s, equipment with a tax life of three years was eligible for a 6 percent credit, and all equipment with a longer life was entitled to a credit of 10 percent. Most structures were not entitled to an investment tax credit.

The Tax Reform Act of 1986 eliminated the investment tax credit. Thus, k is now equal to zero. Nevertheless, the ITC remains an important concept, because debates about the future course of tax policy will certainly include arguments to reintroduce it.

"Inflation Profits" Taxed

Suppose that at the end of 1990, XYZ has an inventory of 100 widgets acquired for $1,000 each. (Widgets do not depreciate over time.) During 1991, the firm acquires 50 identical widgets at a cost of $1,500 each. Then an opportunity arises for XYZ to sell 25 of the widgets for $2,000 apiece. If XYZ takes advantage of this opportunity, what are its profits?

The answer depends on what cost is assigned to the widgets that are sold. One possibility is to value them at their 1990 cost. This is referred to as **first-in, first-out (FIFO)** accounting, because the widgets acquired first are the ones treated as having been sold first. Under FIFO, profits are $25 \times (\$2,000 - \$1,000) = \$25,000$. Alternatively, the firm can value the widgets at the cost of those obtained most recently. Now the *last* widgets acquired are viewed as the first being sold. Under **last-in, first-out (LIFO)** accounting, profits are $25 \times (\$2,000 - \$1,500) = \$12,500$.

This example illustrates that in periods of rising prices, FIFO leads to larger accounting profits than LIFO. But higher accounting profits mean higher corporate taxes. Thus, FIFO firms are taxed on profits that are due to illusory increases in inventory value. In periods of high inflation, these extra taxes can be substantial. (See Feldstein and Summers [1979, p. 449].)[10]

Treatment of Dividends versus Retained Earnings

So far we have been focusing on taxes directly payable by the corporation. For many purposes, however, the important issue is not the corporation's tax liability per se, but rather the total tax rate on income generated in the corporate sector. As noted in Chapter 16, corporate dividends received by individuals are subject to the personal income tax. Understanding how the corporate and personal tax structures interact is important.

Corporate profits may either be retained by the firm or paid out to stockholders in the form of dividends. Dividends paid are *not* deductible from corporation income and hence are subject to the corporation income tax. At the same time, stockholders who receive dividends must treat them as ordinary income and pay personal income tax in an amount that depends on their marginal tax rates. In effect, then, such payments are taxed twice—once at the corporation level, and again when distributed to the shareholder. Eliminating **double taxation** is a prime objective of many tax reformers and is discussed later.

To assess the tax consequences to the stockholder of retained earnings is a bit more complicated. Suppose that XYZ retains $1 of earnings. To the extent that the stock market accurately values firms, the fact that the firm now has one more dollar causes the value of XYZ stock to

---

[10] Why don't firms switch to LIFO? This is somewhat of a mystery. It has been conjectured that some managers prefer FIFO because it makes profits appear higher (as long as prices are increasing), and hence presents a more favorable picture of the firm to stockholders and potential creditors.

increase by $1.[11] But as we saw in Chapter 16, income generated by increases in the value of stock—capital gain—is treated preferentially for tax purposes. This is due to the fact that the gain received by a typical XYZ stockholder is not taxed at all until it is realized. The tax system thus creates incentives for firms to retain earnings rather than pay them out as dividends.

Effective Tax Rate on Corporate Capital

We began this section by noting that the statutory tax rate on capital income in the corporate sector is currently 34 percent. Clearly, it would be most surprising if this were the effective rate as well. At the corporate level, computing the effective rate requires taking into account the effects of interest deductibility, depreciation allowances, and inflation. Moreover, as just noted, corporate income in the form of dividends and realized capital gains is also taxed at the level of the personal income tax. Finally, some corporate income is subject to state corporation taxes and locally levied property taxes.

Allowing for all these considerations, the effective overall marginal tax rate on capital income has been estimated to be 28 percent. In contrast, the effective rate prior to the Tax Reform Act of 1986 was 16.6 percent [Goulder and Thalmann, 1990]. Thus, even though the statutory rate fell in 1986, factors such as the removal of the investment tax credit acted to increase the effective tax rate on income from new capital investments.

Of course, any such calculation must be based on assumptions concerning items such as the appropriate choice of discount rate [r of Equation (19.1)], the expected rate of inflation, the extent of true economic depreciation, and so forth. Moreover, as we see below, the effective burden of the corporate tax depends in part on how investments are financed—by borrowing, issuing stock, or using internal funds. It is therefore likely that investigators using other assumptions would generate a somewhat different effective tax rate. It is unlikely, however, that alternative methods would much modify the considerable difference between statutory and effective marginal tax rates.[12]

Provisions for Multinational Corporations

American firms do a substantial amount of investment abroad. In 1989, the value of the stock of assets directly invested in foreign countries was $373 billion. The tax treatment of foreign source income is a matter of

---

[11] This considerably oversimplifies the complicated relationship between share values and retained earnings. David Bradford [1981] argues that under plausible conditions, less than each dollar of retained earnings is reflected in stock values. Although this question is still in dispute, we adopt the traditional assumption that share values and retained earnings rise on a one-for-one basis.

[12] The marginal and average tax rates are expected to differ. For instance, to the extent that the new rules for depreciation are less generous than their predecessors, the marginal tax rate on new investment is higher than the average rate. This is because the average rate takes into account the lower taxes being paid on previous investments.

increasing importance. U.S. multinational corporations are subject to tax at the standard rate on their global taxable income, including income earned abroad. A credit is then allowed for foreign taxes paid. The credit cannot exceed the amount that would have been owed under U.S. tax law. In 1987, corporations' U.S. income tax liability before the foreign tax credit was $118 billion; the foreign tax credit reduced that figure by $21 billion [Internal Revenue Service, 1990, p. 25].

A number of considerations complicate the taxation of foreign-source corporate income.

Subsidiary status.   Taxation of the income from a foreign enterprise can be deferred if the operation is a **subsidiary.** (A foreign subsidiary is a company owned by a U.S. corporation but incorporated abroad, and hence, a separate corporation from a legal point of view.) Profits earned by a subsidiary are included only if returned **(repatriated)** to the parent company as dividends. Thus, for as long as the subsidiary exists, earnings retained abroad can be kept out of reach of the U.S. tax system. It is hard to say how much tax revenue is lost because of deferral. Given the credit system, the answer depends on the tax rate levied abroad. If all foreign countries have tax rates greater than that of the United States, no additional tax revenue is gained by this country. However, to the extent that a foreign country taxes corporate income less heavily than does the United States, deferral makes the country attractive to U.S. firms as a "tax haven."[13]

Income allocation.   It is often difficult to know how much of a multinational firm's total income to allocate to its operations in a given country. The procedure now used for allocating income between domestic and foreign operations is the **arm's length system.** Essentially the domestic and foreign operations are treated as separate enterprises doing business independently ("at arm's length"). The taxable profits of each entity are computed as its own sales minus its own costs.

The problem is that certain factors of production are like public goods from the firm's point of view.[14] Suppose, for example, that all research and development (R&D) is done at the firm's head office. The results of R&D are available to all the company's operations and hence serve as an "input" for all of them. But under a strict application of the arm's length system, the operation at headquarters deducts all of the R&D expenditures.

---

[13] A few countries such as the Dutch Antilles have intentionally structured their laws to allow U.S. firms to abuse the tax system. There are some provisions to limit the tax savings from these true tax havens, but they have not had much impact.

[14] Of course, all the standard problems that arise in computing domestic corporate taxable income are still present.

This procedure does not make sense, but it is not at all clear how the R&D expenditures should be allocated across operations. For practical purposes, some fairly arbitrary rules have been devised. According to Internal Revenue Service regulations issued in 1977, certain head-office charges can be allocated among operations using a formula based on the sales and assets of each operation. Essentially, the greater a given operation's share of total company assets and sales, the greater the proportion of company public goods it can deduct. This is known as the **shares allocation** approach.

A potential problem arises if different governments have different rules for allocating incomes between home and foreign operations. International tax treaties usually indicate that countries will try to coordinate their rules.

Royalties.   Multinational oil companies have presented U.S. tax makers with a special set of problems. These stem from the fact that in many countries, the host governments are essentially the owners of the oil. Formerly, these governments charged the multinationals royalty fees for exploiting their oil.

The problem from the oil companies' point of view was that unlike foreign tax payments, which are a tax *credit,* royalties are allowed only as a tax *deduction.* As we saw in Chapter 16, a deduction of a given amount is worth less to a taxpayer than a credit of the same size. At the request of the oil companies, many of the host countries simply declared that their royalty fees were now income taxes. Some of these "taxes" are levied at rates well above the U.S. level. In addition, they often exceed the host country's tax rate on other corporate activities. Operating on the premise that such tax payments are a sham, over the years Congress has developed a very complicated set of rules for the taxation of oil income. The rules substantially reduce the advantages of treating royalties as taxes.

Incidence and Excess Burden

Understanding tax rules and computing effective tax rates is only the first step in an analysis of the corporation tax. We still must determine who ultimately bears the burden of the tax and measure the costs of any inefficiencies it induces. The economic consequences of the corporation tax are among the most controversial subjects in public finance. An important reason for the controversy is disagreement with respect to just what kind of tax it is. We can identify several views.

A Tax on Corporate Capital

Recall from our discussion of the structure of the corporation tax that the firm is not allowed to deduct from taxable income the opportunity cost of capital supplied by shareholders. Since the opportunity cost of capital is included in the tax base, it appears reasonable to view the corporation tax as a tax on capital used in the corporate sector. In the classification scheme developed in Chapter 13 under "General Equilibrium Models," the corporation tax is a partial factor tax. This is the view that predominates in most writing on the subject.

In a general equilibrium model of the type developed by Arnold Harberger, the tax on corporate capital leads to a migration of capital from the corporate sector until after-tax rates of return are equal throughout the economy. In the process, the rate of return to capital in the noncorporate sector is depressed so that ultimately *all* owners of capital, not just those in the corporate sector, are affected. The reallocation of capital between the two sectors also affects the return to labor. The extent to which capital and labor bear the ultimate burden of the tax depends on the technologies used in production in each of the sectors, as well as the structure of consumers' demands for corporate and noncorporate goods. Using what he considered to be plausible values for the relevant technological and behavioral parameters, Harberger [1974c] concluded that capital bears the entire burden of the tax.

Turning now to efficiency aspects of the problem, we discussed computation of the excess burden of a partial factor tax in Chapter 14. By inducing less capital accumulation in the corporate sector than otherwise would have been the case, the corporation tax diverts capital from its most productive uses and creates an excess burden. Charles Ballard, John Shoven, and John Whalley [1982, p. 23] estimated that the increase in excess burden when one more dollar is raised via the corporation tax— the marginal excess burden—is 49 cents.

The Harberger model assumes perfect competition and profit-maximizing behavior. Without these conditions, a tax on corporate capital may have quite different incidence and efficiency implications. Moreover, the model is static—the total amount of capital to be allocated between the corporate and noncorporate sectors is fixed. Suppose that over time, the tax on corporate capital changes the total amount of capital available to the economy. If the tax lowers the total amount of capital, the marginal product of labor, and hence the wage rate, falls. Thus, labor bears a greater share of the burden than otherwise would have been the case. If the tax increases the amount of capital, just the opposite results.[15] Hence, even if we accept the view of the corporation tax as a partial factor tax, its efficiency and incidence effects are not at all clear.

A Tax on Economic Profits   An alternative view is that the corporation tax is a tax on economic profits.[16] This view is based on the observation that the tax base is determined by subtracting costs of production from gross corporate income,

---

[15] As shown in Chapter 17, whether a tax on the return to capital increases or decreases capital accumulation is logically indeterminate.

[16] Atkinson and Stiglitz [1980, p. 132] note that this view had some adherents in the 1920s.

leaving only "profits." As we explained in Chapter 13, analyzing the incidence of a tax on economic profits is straightforward. As long as a firm maximizes economic profits, a tax on them induces no adjustments in firm behavior—all decisions regarding prices and production are unchanged. Hence, there is no way to shift the tax, and it is borne by the owners of the firm at the time the tax is levied.[17] Moreover, by the very fact that the tax leaves behavior unchanged, it generates no misallocation of resources. Hence, the excess burden is zero.

Modeling the corporation tax as a simple tax on economic profits is almost certainly wrong. Recall that the base of a pure profits tax is computed by subtracting from gross earnings the value of *all* inputs *including* the opportunity cost of the inputs supplied by the owners. As noted earlier, no such deduction for the capital supplied by shareholders is allowed, so the base of the tax includes elements other than economic profits.

Nevertheless, there are circumstances under which the corporation tax is *equivalent* to an economic profits tax. Stiglitz [1973] showed that under certain conditions, as long as the corporation is allowed to deduct interest payments made to its creditors, the corporation tax amounts to a tax on economic profits.

To understand the reasoning behind Stiglitz's result, consider a firm that is contemplating the purchase of a machine costing \$1. Suppose that the before-tax value of the output produced by the machine is known with certainty to be G dollars. It is also known that the machine will experience economic depreciation equal to δ dollars. To finance the purchase, the firm borrows \$1, and must pay an interest charge of r dollars. In the absence of any taxes, the firm will buy the machine if the net return (total revenue minus depreciation minus interest) is positive. Algebraically, the firm purchases the machine if

$$G - \delta - r > 0. \tag{19.2}$$

Now assume that a corporation tax with the following features is levied: (1) net income is taxed at rate θ; and (2) in the computation of net income, the firm is allowed to subtract interest costs and economic depreciation from total revenue. How does such a tax influence the firm's decision about whether to undertake the project? Clearly, the firm must make its decision on the basis of the *after*-tax profitability of the project. In light of feature 2, the firm's taxable income is $G - \delta - r$. Given feature 1, the project therefore creates a tax liability of $\theta(G - \delta - r)$, so the after-tax profit on the project is $(1 - \theta)(G - \delta - r)$. The firm will do the project only if the after-tax profit is positive; that is, if

$$(1 - \theta)(G - \delta - r) > 0. \tag{19.3}$$

---

[17] If firms are not profit maximizing initially, the story may be quite different. See Chapter 13.

Now note that any project that passes the after-tax criterion (19.3) also satisfies the before-tax criterion (19.2). [Just divide Equation (19.3) through by $(1 - \theta)$ to get Equation (19.2).] Hence, imposition of the tax leaves the firm's investment decision completely unchanged—anything it would have done before the tax, it will do after. The owners of the firm continue to behave exactly as they did prior to the tax; they simply lose some of their profit on the investment to the government. In this sense the tax is equivalent to an economic profits tax. And like an economic profits tax, its incidence is on the owners of the firm, and it creates no excess burden.

This conclusion depends critically on the underlying assumptions, and these can easily be called into question. Stiglitz's analysis assumes that firms deduct economic depreciation. As we have seen, statutory allowances generally do not even approximate economic depreciation. In addition, the argument assumes that firms will choose to finance their additional projects by borrowing. There are several reasons why they might instead raise money by selling shares or using retained earnings. For example, firms may face constraints in the capital market and be unable to borrow all they want. Alternatively, if a firm is uncertain about what the return on the project will be, it might be reluctant to finance the project by borrowing. If things go wrong, the greater a firm's debt, the higher the probability of bankruptcy, other things being the same.

However, the fact that its assumptions are not met perfectly does not mean that Stiglitz's analysis yields no insights with respect to the impact of the corporation tax. In particular, his model highlights the important role that the source of finance plays in understanding the corporation tax. Until we learn more about such finance issues, the incidence and efficiency effects of the corporation tax will remain as much a puzzle as ever.

Effects on Behavior

The corporation tax influences a wide range of corporate decisions. In this section we discuss four important types: (1) the total amount of physical investment (equipment and structures) to make; (2) the types of physical assets to purchase; (3) the way to finance these investments; and (4) whether or not to merge with other companies.[18] In a sense, it is artificial to discuss these decisions separately because presumably the firm makes them simultaneously. However, we discuss them separately for expositional ease.

---

[18] In addition, the tax code has numerous special provisions affecting other aspects of firm behavior—everything from discouraging compliance with the Arab boycott of firms that do business with Israel to encouraging compliance with health and safety regulations.

Total Physical Investment

A firm's net investment during a given period is the increase in physical assets during that time.[19] The main policy question is whether features such as accelerated depreciation and the investment tax credit stimulate investment demand. The question is important. For example, now that the investment tax credit has been repealed, a number of people have suggested that investment is going to decline significantly. Others have argued that there will not be much effect. Who is right?

The answer depends in part on your view of how corporations make their investment decisions. Many different models have been proposed, and there is no agreement on which is the best. We discuss two investment models that have received substantial attention.

The accelerator model.   Suppose that production techniques are such that the ratio of capital to output is fixed. For example, production of every unit of output requires three units of capital. Then for each unit increase in output, the firm must increase its capital stock—invest—three units of capital. Thus, the main determinant of the amount of investment is changes in the level of output.

This theory, sometimes referred to as the accelerator model, implies that depreciation allowances and ITCs are for the most part *irrelevant* when it comes to influencing physical investment. It is only the quantity of output that influences the amount of investment, because technology dictates the ratio in which capital and output must be used. In other words, tax benefits for capital may make capital cheaper, but in the accelerator model this does not matter, because the demand for capital does not depend on its price.[20]

The neoclassical model.   A less extreme view of the investment process is that the ratio of capital to output is not technologically fixed. Rather, the firm can choose between alternative technologies. But how does it choose? According to Dale Jorgenson's [1963] neoclassical model, a key variable is the firm's **user cost of capital**—the cost that the firm incurs as a consequence of owning an asset. As we show later, the user cost of capital includes both the opportunity cost of forgoing other investments and direct costs such as depreciation and taxes. The user cost of capital indicates how high a project's rate of return has to be to be profitable. For example, if the user cost of capital on a project is 15 percent, a firm will undertake the project only if its rate of return exceeds 15 percent. The higher the user cost of capital, the fewer is the number of profitable

---

[19] Firms acquire assets both to add new plant and equipment and to replace old plant and equipment. Replacement investment is not dealt with here.

[20] These tax provisions may stimulate an increase in demand for output, and thus indirectly increase investment demand via the accelerator model.

projects, and the lower the firm's desired stock of capital. In the neoclassical model, when the cost of capital increases, firms choose less capital-intensive technologies, and vice versa. To the extent that tax policy reduces the cost of capital, it can increase the amount of capital that firms desire, and hence, increase investment.

All of this leaves open two important questions: (1) How do changes in the tax system change the user cost of capital? and (2) Just how sensitive is investment to changes in the user cost of capital? To examine these points, we must first calculate the user cost of capital.

The user cost of capital.   Consider Leona, an entrepreneur who can lend her money and receive an after-tax rate of return of 10 percent. Leona is the sole stockholder in a corporation that runs a chain of hotels. Because she can always earn 10 percent simply by lending in the capital market, she will not make any investment in the hotel that yields less than that amount. Assume that Leona is considering the acquisition of a vacuum cleaner that would experience economic depreciation of 2 percent annually. Ignoring taxes for the moment, the user cost of capital for the vacuum cleaner would be 12 percent, because the vacuum cleaner would have to earn a 12 percent return to earn Leona the 10 percent return that she could receive simply by lending her money. Algebraically, if r is the after-tax rate of return and δ is the economic rate of depreciation, the user cost of capital is $(r + \delta)$. If the vacuum cleaner cannot earn $(r + \delta)$ (or 12 percent) after taxes, there is no reason for the firm to purchase it.

Now assume that the corporate tax rate is 34 percent, that Leona's marginal tax rate is 28 percent, and that all of the corporation's earnings are paid out to Leona as dividends. Then if the corporation earns $1, a corporation tax of $0.34 (= 0.34 × $1) is due, leaving $0.66 available to distribute to Leona. When Leona receives the $0.66 as dividends, she pays individual tax at a rate of 28 percent, leading to a tax liability of $0.185 (= 0.28 × $0.66), which leaves her with $0.475. Algebraically, if θ is the corporate tax rate and t is the individual tax rate, the after-tax return from $1 of corporate profits is $(1 - \theta) \times (1 - t)$.

How does such a tax system affect the cost of capital? We have to find a before-tax return such that, after the corporate and individual income taxes, Leona receives 12 percent. Calling the user cost of capital C, then C must be the solution to the equation $(1 - .34) \times (1 - .28) \times C = 12$ percent, or $C = 25.3$ percent. Thus, Leona will be unwilling to purchase the vacuum cleaner unless its before-tax return is 25.3 percent or greater. Using our algebraic notation, the user cost of capital is the value of C that solves the equation $(1 - \theta) \times (1 - t) \times C = (r + \delta)$, or

$$C = \frac{(r + \delta)}{[(1 - \theta) \times (1 - t)]} \tag{19.4}$$

So far, we have shown how corporate and individual tax rates increase the user cost of capital. However, certain provisions in the tax code such as accelerated depreciation tend to lower the cost of capital. In Equation (19.1), we defined ψ as the present value of the depreciation allowances that flow from a \$1 investment.[21] Suppose that ψ for the vacuum cleaner is 0.25. In effect, then, depreciation allowances reduce the cost of acquiring the vacuum cleaner by one fourth, and hence lower by one fourth the before-tax return that the firm has to earn to attain any given after-tax return. In our example, instead of having to earn 25.3 percent, Leona now only has to earn 19.0 percent [$= 25.3 \times (1 - 0.25)$]. Algebraically, depreciation allowances lower the cost of capital by a factor of $(1 - \psi)$. Similarly, we showed that an investment tax credit at rate k reduces the cost of a \$1 acquisition to $(1 - k)$ dollars. In the presence of both depreciation allowances and an investment tax credit, the cost of capital is reduced by a factor of $(1 - \psi - k)$.[22] Thus, the expression for C in Equation (19.4) must be multiplied by $(1 - \psi - k)$ to adjust for the presence of accelerated depreciation and investment tax credits:

$$C = \frac{(r + \delta) \times (1 - \psi - k)}{(1 - \theta) \times (1 - t)} \qquad (19.5)$$

Equation (19.5) summarizes how the corporate tax system influences the firm's user cost of capital. By taxing corporate income, the tax makes devoting resources to capital investment more expensive, other things being the same. However, depreciation allowances and ITCs tend to lower the user cost. Any change in the corporation tax system influences some combination of θ, ψ, and k, and hence changes the user cost of capital.

Effect of user cost on investment.   Even if the impact of changes in the tax system on the user cost of capital is determined, how changes in the user cost of capital influence investment must still be ascertained. If the accelerator model is correct, even drastic reductions in the user cost have no impact on investment. On the other hand, if investment is relatively responsive to the user cost of capital, depreciation allowances and ITCs can be relatively powerful tools for influencing investment.

Jorgenson [1963] estimated a regression equation in which the right-hand side variables include (among others) the user cost of capital. Jorgenson's basic conclusion is that the amount of investment is indeed quite sensitive to tax-induced changes in the cost of capital. For example,

---

[21] Note from Equation (19.1) that ψ depends on the value of the statutory rate θ.

[22] This assumes that the basis used to compute depreciation allowances is not reduced when the firm takes the ITC. If the basis is reduced, the expression must be modified.

the parameters from one equation based on Jorgenson's model imply that without accelerated depreciation and the investment tax credit, investment in 1977 would have been about 40 percent lower than the actual level [Chirinko and Eisner, 1983].

Substantial controversy has swirled around Jorgenson's conclusion that accelerated depreciation and investment tax credits are potent inducements to investment. His analysis has been criticized on a number of grounds. One of the most important is that it takes no account of the importance of expectations. Compare scenario 1, in which firms expect the investment tax credit to be raised considerably *next* year, and scenario 2, in which investors expect it to be reduced. According to Jorgenson's model, the amount of capital that firms desire depends *only* on the user cost of capital this period. Therefore, the value of C is identical under both scenarios. This result is implausible; if firms expect the investment tax credit to go up next period, it would make sense to defer some investment until then and vice versa. The fact is that we cannot observe individuals' expectations, and as of now there is no really satisfactory way for estimating how expectations affect behavior. Given that different assumptions concerning expectations formation can have quite different implications for the effectiveness of tax policy, the validity of Jorgenson's results is thrown into question.

Other criticisms of Jorgenson's model have also been raised.[23] The key point of the critics is that when some of Jorgenson's assumptions are modified in reasonable ways, the implications for tax policy can differ substantially. Robert Chirinko and Robert Eisner [1983] used five well-known models to simulate the effects of various investment incentives. The results of the various models differed dramatically. Nevertheless, it was difficult to choose among them on the basis of standard statistical criteria. Apparently, the sheer complexity of the investment process has stymied attempts to reach a consensus with respect to how sensitive investment is to tax incentives.

Finally, we must remember that the United States is, to a large extent, an open economy. If the tax code makes investment in the United States more attractive to foreigners, saving from abroad can finance investment in this country. The consequence for tax policy toward investment is the flip side of the relationship we saw in Chapter 17 between tax policy and saving: the possibility of domestic saving flowing out of the country makes it harder to stimulate domestic investment indirectly by manipulating saving, but the possibility of attracting foreign capital makes it easier to stimulate investment through direct manipulation of the user cost of capital.

---

[23] See Chirinko [1986], who also surveys other models.

Table 19.1   **Effective marginal tax rates by asset type**

	Before TRA86	After TRA86
Equipment	12.1%	27.3%
Structures	21.3%	28.7%

SOURCE: Lawrence H. Goulder and Philippe Thalmann, "Approaches to Efficient Capital Taxation: Leveling the Playing Field vs. Living by the Golden Rule" (Cambridge, Mass.: National Bureau of Economic Research, Working Paper 3559, 1990), p. 41.

Types of Asset

So far our focus has been the total volume of investment spending without much attention to its composition. It is likely, though, that the tax system affects the types of assets purchased by firms. For example, purchases of assets that receive relatively generous depreciation allowances tend to be encouraged, other things being the same.

Lawrence Goulder and Philippe Thalmann [1990] computed the effective marginal tax rates on various assets both under TRA86 and the law that preceded it. Some of their results are reported in Table 19.1. The table indicates that both before and after the Tax Reform Act of 1986, structures were taxed more heavily than equipment. But TRA86 dramatically reduced the difference between the tax rates on these two types of assets. The system is now more nearly neutral than previously. As a consequence, one expects that there will be fewer tax-induced distortions in the pattern of investment, and hence a smaller excess burden.[24]

Table 19.1 also suggests that although different types of assets are now treated more equally, the tax burden on income generated by all assets has increased. Goulder and Thalmann argue that the efficiency gains from equalizing tax rates on different assets may have been outweighed by the efficiency losses from increasing tax rates on capital in general. In Chapter 20 we turn to the question of whether efficiency would be enhanced by lowering taxes on capital income.

As emphasized earlier, computations like those in Table 19.1 require making a number of assumptions. For example, the value of depreciation allowances depends on the discount rate used by firms [see Equation (19.1)], and different values lead to different answers. Similarly, given historic cost depreciation, assumptions about the future rate of inflation

---

[24] Using methods of excess burden calculation very similar to those introduced in Chapter 14, Patric Hendershott [1986] estimated that in 1984, the efficiency cost of tax-induced distortions in the allocation of capital was about 0.25 percent of gross national product—about $9 billion.

Note that the more "neutral" treatment of TRA86 does not *necessarily* lower excess burden. As long as some types of capital income are untaxed (e.g., imputed income on owner-occupied housing), then equal tax rates on the set of all taxable assets do not necessarily minimize excess burden. See Chapter 15 and Feldstein [1985a].

have an important impact on effective tax rates. Hence, it is possible that different investigators might find results somewhat different from those in the table. There is little doubt, however, that the qualitative picture suggested in the table is correct.

Corporate Finance

In addition to "real" decisions concerning physical investment, the owners of a firm must determine how to finance the firm's operations and whether to distribute profits or retain them. We discuss the effects of taxes on these financial decisions in this section.

Why do firms pay dividends?   Profits earned by a corporation may be either distributed to shareholders in the form of dividends or retained by the company. If it is assumed that: (1) outcomes of all investments are known in advance with certainty; and (2) there are no taxes, then the owners of a firm are indifferent in choosing between a dollar of dividends and a dollar of retained earnings. Provided that the stock market accurately reflects the firm's value, $1 of retained earnings increases the value of the firm's stock by $1. This $1 capital gain is as much income as a $1 dividend receipt. Under the previous assumptions, then, stockholders do not care whether profits are distributed.[25]

Of course, in reality, considerable uncertainty surrounds the outcomes of economic decisions, and corporate income *is* subject to a variety of taxes. As already noted, when dividends are paid out, the shareholder incurs a tax liability, while retained earnings generate no concurrent tax liability. True, the retention creates a capital gain for the stockholder, but no tax is due until the gain is realized.

On the basis of these observations, it appears that paying dividends is more or less equivalent to giving away money to the tax collector, and we would expect firms to retain virtually all of their earnings. Surprise! Between 1986 and 1990, over 60 percent of after-tax corporate profits were paid out as dividends on average [*Economic Report of the President, 1991,* p. 387]. This phenomenon continues to baffle students of corporate finance.

One possible explanation is that dividend payments serve as a signal concerning the firm's financial strength. If investors perceive firms that regularly pay dividends as in some sense "solid," then paying dividends enhances the value of the firms' shares. In the same way, a firm that reduces its dividend payments may be perceived as being in financial straits. However, although it is conceivable that the owners of a firm would be willing to pay some extra taxes to provide a positive signal to

---

[25] For a rigorous discussion of this argument, see Eugene Fama and Merton Miller [1972, pp. 80–81].

potential shareholders, it is hard to imagine that the benefits gained are worth the huge sums sacrificed. After all, there are certainly ways other than dividend policy for potential investors to obtain information about a firm's status.

Another explanation centers on the fact that not all investors have the same marginal tax rate. High-income individuals currently face rates up to about 33 percent, while untaxed institutions (such as pension funds and universities) face a rate of zero. Those with low marginal tax rates would tend to put a relatively high valuation on dividends, and it may be that some firms "specialize" in attracting these investors by paying out dividends. Martin Feldstein and Jerry Green [1983] proposed a model with two types of investors, taxable individuals and untaxed institutions. They show that if stock returns are known in advance with certainty, taxable individuals only purchase shares of firms that pay no dividends, while the untaxed institutions invest exclusively in firms that pay out all dividends. This is referred to as a **clientele effect,** because firms set their financial policies to cater to different clienteles. In the real world, of course, such dramatic segmentation of stockholders is not observed. According to Feldstein and Green, the reason for this is the uncertainty of stock returns. Even if your tax rate on dividends is high, you will not invest exclusively in low-dividend firms, because when there is uncertainty, it is bad policy to put all your eggs in one basket.

The notion that firms specialize in attracting shareholders with particular tax situations has stimulated empirical research. Studies in this area are hindered by the lack of data on just who owns shares in what firms. However, there is some indirect evidence for the existence of clientele effects. (See Elton and Gruber [1970].)

Effect of taxes on dividend policy.   Because the tax system appears to bias firms against paying dividends (although it by no means discourages them completely), the natural question is how corporate financial policy would change if the tax treatment of dividends vis-à-vis retained earnings were modified. Suppose that for whatever reasons, firms want to pay some dividends as well as retain earnings. One factor that determines the desired amount of retained earnings is the opportunity cost in terms of after-tax dividends paid to stockholders. For example, if there were no taxes, the opportunity cost of $1 of retained earnings would be $1 of dividends. On the other hand, if the stockholder faces a 31 percent marginal income tax rate, the opportunity cost of retaining a dollar in the firm is only 69 cents of dividends.[26] In effect, then, the current tax system lowers the opportunity cost of retained earnings.

---

[26] A more careful calculation would take into account the effective capital-gains tax liability that is eventually generated by the retention. This is ignored for purposes of illustration.

Over the last several decades, a number of shifts in British tax policy have generated dramatic changes in the opportunity cost of retained earnings in dividends. Data from the United Kingdom therefore provide an excellent opportunity for examining the impact of taxes on firm dividend policy. James Poterba and Lawrence Summers [1985] used British data to estimate a regression in which the dependent variable is the proportion of corporate income paid out as dividends, and the independent variables include the opportunity cost of retained earnings. They found that when the opportunity cost of retained earnings increases by 10 percent, dividend payments go up by about 18 percent.

John Brittain [1966] found qualitatively similar results for the United States. It appears, then, that the tax system has substantially increased the amount of earnings retained by corporations. Some argue that this is desirable because increasing retained earnings makes more money available for investment. Now, it is true that retained earnings represent saving. However, it may be that shareholders take corporate saving into consideration when making their personal financial decisions. Specifically, if owners of the firm perceive that the corporation is saving a dollar on their behalf, they may simply reduce their personal saving by that amount. Thus, although the composition of overall saving has changed, its total amount is just the same as before the retention. There is indeed some econometric evidence that personal and corporate saving are somewhat offsetting.[27] This analysis illustrates once again the pitfalls of viewing the corporation as a separate person with an existence apart from the stockholders.

Debt versus equity finance.   Another important financial decision for a corporation is how to raise money. The firm has basically two options. It can borrow money (issue debt). However, the firm must pay interest on its debt, and inability to meet the interest payments or repay the principal may have serious consequences. A firm can also issue shares of stock (equity) and stockholders may receive dividends on their shares.

Recall that under the U.S. tax system, corporations are permitted to deduct payments of interest from taxable income, but are not allowed to deduct dividends. The tax law therefore builds in a bias toward debt financing.[28] It is difficult to precisely estimate the impact that this bias has had on the debt-equity choice. Between 1970 and 1989, corporate debt

---

[27] See Poterba [1987].

[28] It turns out that in the absence of taxation and given complete certainty with respect to investment outcomes, firms are indifferent between debt and equity finance. This is often referred to as the Modigliani-Miller theorem after the authors who first proved it. See F. Modigliani and H. M. Miller [1958]. For a careful intuitive exposition, see Fama and Miller [1972].

increased by a factor of about 4.4, while before-tax corporate profits rose only by a factor of 3.4.[29] Many economists have argued that taxes are an important factor in explaining the growth in the use of debt finance.

Indeed, we might wonder why firms do not use debt financing exclusively. Part of the answer lies in the fact that the outcomes of a firm's decisions are not known with certainty. There is always some possibility of a very bad outcome, and therefore a fear of bankruptcy. The more a firm borrows, the higher its debt payments, and the greater the probability of bankruptcy, other things being the same. Indeed, heavy reliance on debt finance has led some major corporations to declare bankruptcy, including Southland Corporation (parent of the 7-Eleven Food Stores) and Campeau Corporation (the parent company of several major department stores). It has been argued that by encouraging the use of debt, the tax system has had the undesirable effect of increasing probabilities of bankruptcy above levels that otherwise would have prevailed.

Mergers and Acquisitions

Recent years have witnessed a wave of mergers and acquisitions. This phenomenon has a number of possible explanations. Firms may use mergers and acquisitions to increase their market power and build empires. Or mergers and acquisitions may take place because one firm is being managed inefficiently, so that it is ripe for a takeover.

One motive that receives a lot of attention in public discussions is the avoidance of federal taxes. A simple example illustrates the basic principles.[30] Suppose that the ABC firm has $10 million in income and, on the basis of prior investments, is entitled to depreciation allowances of $15 million. ABC's tax liability is zero because its depreciation allowances exceed its income. However, even after ABC reduces its taxable income to zero, it still has $5 million of depreciation allowances that are being wasted.

What can ABC do? To a limited extent, the law allows ABC to carry over this year's tax losses to the future. That is, if ABC has a larger gross income next year, the $5 million of depreciation allowances can be subtracted from its gross income then. However, if ABC's losses persist for several years, the firm will never have the opportunity to use this deduction to reduce its tax liability.

Suppose, however, that the profitable XYZ firm buys ABC (or vice versa). Then depreciation allowances from ABC's assets can be used to reduce XYZ's taxable income. The depreciation allowances are no longer "wasted." In principle, the owners of both companies can come out ahead.

---

[29] Computations based on *Economic Report of the President, 1991*, pp. 388, 392.

[30] For further discussion of the legal issues, see Auerbach and Reishus [1986].

To investigate the importance of such considerations, Alan Auerbach and David Reishus [1986] analyzed over 300 mergers between 1968 and 1986. They found that only about one fifth involved a potential gain from the transfer of unused tax losses. The average tax gain in these mergers was about 10 percent of the market value of the company that made the acquisition. On the basis of these findings, we conclude that in some circumstances, tax considerations can be an important motivating force. But one cannot attribute most mergers to the tax system.

State Corporation Taxes

Forty-six states levy their own corporation income taxes, and in 1990, corporate tax revenues accounted for about 2.5 percent of total state and local tax receipts [*Economic Report of the President, 1991,* p. 382]. As is the case with state personal income taxes, state corporate tax systems differ substantially with respect to rate structures and rules for defining taxable income.

All of the complications that arise in analyzing the incidence and efficiency effects of the federal corporation income tax also bedevil attempts to understand the state systems. Charles McLure [1981] points out that the variation in rates across state lines gives rise to a set of possibly even more intractable questions. If a given state levies a corporation tax, how much of the burden would be exported to citizens of other states? How is the portion that is not exported shared by the residents of the state?[31]

Preliminary answers to these questions may be obtained by applying the theory of tax incidence (Chapter 13).[32] Recall the general intuitive proposition that immobile factors of production are more likely to end up bearing a tax than mobile factors, other things being the same. This means, for example, that if capital is easier to move to another state than labor, there is a tendency for the incidence of a state corporation tax to fall on labor. Thus, analyzing a system of varying corporate tax rates requires that the effects of interstate mobility be added to the already formidable list of factors that come into play when studying the federal corporation tax. Research on this issue is at a formative stage.

Corporation Tax Reform

Toward the beginning of this chapter we observed that if corporation income were untaxed, individuals would be able to avoid personal income taxation by accumulating income within corporations. Evidently, this

---

[31] There are also difficult administrative questions. For example, when a corporation does business in several states, how should its income be apportioned among states for tax purposes?

[32] For additional details, see Peter Mieszkowski and George Zodrow [1985].

would lead to serious equity and efficiency problems. The government's response has been to construct a system that taxes corporate income twice: first at the corporate level, where the statutory tax rate is 34 percent, and again at the personal level, where distributions of dividends are taxed as ordinary income (currently at a maximum rate of about 33 percent).

A number of proposals have been made to integrate personal and corporate income taxes into a single system. The most radical approach is the **partnership method,** sometimes also referred to as **full integration.** Under this approach, all earnings of the corporation during a given year, whether they are distributed or not, are attributed to stockholders just as if the corporation were a partnership.[33] Each shareholder is then liable for personal income tax on his share of the earnings. Thus, if Karl owns 2 percent of the shares of IBM, each year his taxable income includes 2 percent of IBM's taxable earnings. The corporation tax as a separate entity is eliminated.

There has been considerable debate with respect to whether adopting the partnership method or some close variant would be a desirable step for the United States. The discussion has focused on several issues.

Nature of the Corporation

Those who favor full integration emphasize that a corporation is, in effect, merely a conduit for transmitting earnings to shareholders. It makes more sense to tax the people who receive the income than the institution that happens to pass it along. Those who oppose full integration argue that in large modern corporations, it is ridiculous to think of the shareholders as partners, and that the corporation is best regarded as a separate entity.

Administrative Feasibility

Opponents of full integration stress the administrative difficulties that it would create.[34] How are corporate earnings imputed to individuals who hold stock for less than a year? Would shareholders be allowed to deduct the firm's operating losses from their personal taxable income? Proponents of full integration argue that a certain number of fairly arbitrary decisions must be made to administer any complicated tax system. The administrative problems here are no worse than those that have arisen in other parts of the tax code, and can probably be dealt with satisfactorily.

Effects on Efficiency

Those who favor integration point out that the current corporate tax system imposes large excess burdens on the economy, many of which would be eliminated or at least lessened under full integration. The economy would benefit from four types of efficiency gains:

---

[33] The **dividend relief approach** is less extreme. With it, the corporation can deduct dividends paid to stockholders just as it now deducts interest payments to bondholders. Although this plan would eliminate the double taxation of dividends, it would still maintain the corporation tax as a separate entity.

[34] Administrative issues are discussed carefully by Congressional Budget Office [1985].

- The misallocation of resources between the corporate and non-corporate sectors would be eliminated.

- To the extent that integration lowered the rate of taxation on the return to capital, tax-induced distortions in savings decisions would be reduced.[35]

- Integration would remove the incentives for "excessive" retained earnings that characterize the current system. Firms with substantial amounts of retained earnings do not have to enter capital markets to finance new projects. Without the discipline that comes from having to convince investors that projects are worthwhile, such firms may invest inefficiently.

- Integration would remove the bias toward debt financing that occurs in the present system because there would be no separate corporate tax base from which to deduct payments of interest. High ratios of debt to equity increase the probability of bankruptcy. This increased risk and the actual bankruptcies that do occur lower welfare without any concomitant gain to society.

Although it is difficult to determine the value of all these efficiency gains, some estimates suggest that they are quite high. Don Fullerton et al. [1981] found that the present value of the efficiency gain from full integration could be as high as $500 billion.

Opponents of full integration point out that given all the uncertainties concerning the operation of the corporation tax, the supposed efficiency gains may not exist at all. For example, as discussed earlier, to the extent that Stiglitz's view of the tax as equivalent to a levy on pure profits is correct, the tax induces no distortion whatsoever between the corporate and noncorporate sectors. Similarly, there is no solid evidence that corporations invest internal funds less efficiently than those raised externally.

Effects on Saving

Some argue that full integration would lower the effective tax rate on capital and therefore lead to more saving. As we saw in Chapter 17, this is a nonsequitur. From a theoretical point of view, the volume of saving may increase, decrease, or stay the same when the tax rate on capital income decreases. Econometric work has not yet provided a definitive answer.

Effects on the Distribution of Income

If the efficiency arguments in favor of full integration are correct, then in principle, all taxpayers could benefit if it were instituted. Still, people in different groups would be affected differently. For example, those stockholders with relatively high personal income tax rates would tend to gain less from integration than those with low personal income tax rates. This

---

[35] As suggested in Chapter 14, lowering taxes on the return to saving could enhance efficiency even if the volume of savings stayed the same or actually fell when the tax decreased.

tendency is reflected in the estimates of Fullerton et al. of the distributional impact of adopting full integration. They found that for people in low-income groups, the increase in real income would be about 2.5 to 3.5 percent, while for high-income groups, it would be only 0.6 to 1.4 percent.[36] The usual caveat is required in interpreting these figures. They depend on the values of a number of parameters such as the elasticity of saving with respect to the tax rate. As shown in Chapter 17, there is much uncertainty about their magnitudes.

Overview

The discussion in this section makes it clear that there is considerable uncertainty surrounding the likely impact of full integration. This simply reflects our imperfect knowledge of the workings of the current system of corporate taxation. There is by no means unanimous agreement that introducing the partnership method would be a good thing. However, on the basis of the existing and admittedly imperfect evidence, many economists have concluded that both efficiency and equity would be enhanced if the personal and corporate taxes were fully integrated.

Summary

- Corporations are subject to a separate federal income tax. The tax accounts for about 9 percent of all federal revenues.

- Prior to applying the 34 percent tax rate, firms may deduct wage payments, interest payments, and depreciation allowances. These are meant to measure the cost of producing revenue. Dividends, the cost of acquiring equity funds, are not deductible.

- Because depreciation allowances are based on historic cost, their real value declines with inflation. This effect can be offset by either indexing depreciation allowances, or by shortening tax lives and increasing the proportion of value allocated to early years.

- Investment Tax Credits (ITCs) are deducted from the firm's tax bill when particular physical capital assets are purchased. The Tax Reform Act of 1986 repealed ITCs, but they are likely to be reconsidered in future policy debates.

- U.S. multilateral corporations are allowed tax credits for taxes paid to foreign governments.

- Complications arise due to tax deferral using foreign subsidiaries, allocation of net income to countries in which a multinational operates, and the correct treatment of royalties.

- The corporate tax has been viewed either as an economic profits tax or as a partial factor tax. In the former case, the tax is borne entirely by owners of firms, while in the latter the incidence depends on capital mobility between sectors, substitution of factors of production, the structure of consumer demand, and the sensitivity of capital accumulation to the net rate of return.

- The effect of the corporate tax system on physical investment depends on: (1) its effect on the user cost of holding capital goods; and (2) the sensitivity of investment to changes in the user cost. In the accelerator model, investment depends only on output, making the user cost irrelevant. The neoclassical model incorporates both effects.

---

[36] In this context, real income includes the value of leisure.

- In the neoclassical investment model, the user cost of capital is:

$$C = \frac{(r + \delta) \times (1 - \psi - k)}{(1 - \theta) \times (1 - t)}$$

where C is the user cost, r the after-tax interest rate, δ the economic depreciation rate, θ the corporation tax rate, k the ITC, and ψ the present value of depreciation allowances per dollar. Thus, corporate taxation raises the user cost, while the ITC and depreciation allowances reduce it.

- Estimates of the effect of the user cost on investment vary greatly. One reason is the critical role played by unobservable changes in expectations.

- Effective tax rates vary between equipment and structures, creating efficiency losses. The Tax Reform Act of 1986 reduced the differences among tax rates on various assets, but it raised the overall tax rate.

- Due to combined corporate and personal income taxation of dividends, it is something of a mystery why firms pay dividends. Dividends may serve as a signal of the firm's financial strength, or be used to cater to particular clienteles.

- Interest deductibility provides a strong incentive for debt finance. However, increasing the proportion of debt may lead to larger bankruptcy costs.

- The inability of some firms to take advantage of tax losses due to accelerated depreciation can create incentives for mergers. However, preliminary evidence suggests that most mergers are not motivated by tax considerations.

- Forty-six states have corporate income taxes. The possibilities for tax exporting and interstate mobility of factors of production complicate analysis of these taxes.

- One possible corporate tax reform is full integration of the corporate and personal income taxes. Owners of stock would be taxed on their share of corporate income as if they were partners. The corporation tax as a separate entity would cease to exist.

Discussion Questions

1. Suppose you were asked to calculate the economic depreciation on your new car. How might this be done? Would the task be more difficult for your new food processor?

2. Consider Equation (19.5), which shows the user cost of capital.

   a. Suppose that depreciation allowances may only be taken on that portion of the acquisition cost not covered by the ITC. What is the user cost of capital? That is, how must Equation (19.5) be modified?

   b. Suppose that Congress adopts full integration, so that dividends are taxed only once, at the shareholder level. What is the user cost of capital in these circumstances?

3. The Omnibus Reconciliation Act of 1990 contained several provisions that increased corporate taxes. The staff of the Congressional Joint Committee on Taxation (JCT) was asked to prepare an analysis of the distributional implications of all of the act's provisions, both corporate and noncorporate. The JCT staff refused to include any of the corporate tax increases in its analysis. How would you have distributed an increase in corporate taxes across households? How did the failure of the JCT to distribute the corporate provisions bias the analysis of the distributional implications, across income classes, of the act as a whole?

4. Some commentators have suggested that tax-induced distortions in the choice between debt and equity would be reduced if corporations were no longer allowed to deduct interest payments from their taxable income. What is the basis for this suggestion? Would it enhance efficiency?

Selected References

Congressional Budget Office. *Revising the Corporate Income Tax.* Washington, D.C.: U.S. Government Printing Office, May 1985.

Goulder, Lawrence H., and Philippe Thalmann. "Approaches to Efficient Capital Taxation: Leveling the Playing Field vs. Living by the Golden Rule." Cambridge, Mass.: National Bureau of Economic Research, Working Paper 3559, 1990.

Henderson, Yolanda K. "Lessons from Federal Reform of Business Taxes." *New England Economic Review.* Federal Reserve Bank of Boston, November/December 1986, pp. 9–25.

King, Mervyn A., and Don Fullerton, eds. *The Taxation of Income from Capital.* Chicago: University of Chicago Press, 1984.

20

Taxes on Consumption and Wealth

But when the impositions are laid upon those things which men consume, every man payeth equally for what he useth: nor is the common wealth defrauded by the luxurious waste of private men.

THOMAS HOBBES

Most of our attention in this part of the book has been devoted to various kinds of income taxes. As noted in Chapter 16, the base of an income tax is *potential* consumption. This chapter discusses two additional types of taxes: The first type is consumption taxes, in which the base is the value (or quantity) of commodities sold to a person for *actual* consumption. The second type is wealth taxes, where the base is accumulated saving, that is, the accumulated difference between potential and actual consumption.

Sales Taxes

In the United States today, the most important consumption taxes are retail sales taxes levied on purchases of a wide variety of commodities (see Table 20.1). A **general sales tax** imposes the same tax rate on the purchase of all commodities. In the United States, state sales taxes that cover a wide variety of goods are often given the label *general*. This is something of a misnomer, however, because even states that tax most goods exempt the sales of virtually all services from taxation.

A **selective sales tax,** also referred to as an **excise tax,** or a **differential commodity tax,** is levied at different rates on the purchase of different commodities. (Some of those rates can be zero.)[1]

---

[1] Another type of sales tax is a **use tax**—a sales tax that residents of a given state must pay on purchases made in other states. The purpose of a use tax is to prevent individuals from avoiding sales taxes by making purchases out of state. Historically, use taxes have yielded very little revenue. However, a number of states are becoming more aggressive in their collection techniques, so that use taxes may become more important in the future.

Table 20.1   **Sales tax revenues by source and level of government, 1988**
($ millions)

Source	Total	Federal	State	Local
General sales tax	$105,168	$ —	$87,010	$18,159
Motor fuel	30,649	12,876	17,196	577
Alcoholic beverages	9,311	5,830	3,188	293
Tobacco	9,523	4,523	4,801	199
Public utilities	16,202	5,701	6,179	4,321
Customs duties	16,317	16,317	—	—
Other	21,691	7,357	11,761	2,573
Percent of own-source revenue from sales taxes	16.1%	7.6%	38.5%	9.6%

SOURCE: U.S. Department of Commerce, Bureau of the Census, *Governmental Finances in 1987–88* (Washington, D.C.: U.S. Government Printing Office, 1988), p. 7.

Sales taxes generally take one of two forms: A **unit tax** is a given amount for each unit purchased. For example, most states levy a tax on motor fuel which is a certain number of cents per gallon; the median rate is 16 cents.[2] In contrast, an **ad valorem** tax is computed as a percentage of the value of the purchase. For example, the federal excise tax rate on bows and arrows is 11 percent.

Table 20.1 summarizes the role of sales taxes in the U.S. revenue structure. At the federal level, sales taxes are not very important—only 7.6 percent of total revenues. There is currently no federal general sales tax. Sales taxes play a more important role in the revenue systems of state governments. In 1989, 45 states plus the District of Columbia had general sales taxes with rates that varied from 3 to 7.5 percent. (Slightly over half the states exempt food from tax, and virtually all exempt prescription drugs.) In about half the states, municipalities and counties levy their own general sales taxes. As of 1989, the highest combined county, city, and state sales tax rate was 9.5 percent in Mobile, Alabama.

Rationalizations   **Administrative considerations.**   Perhaps the main attraction of sales taxes is ease of administration. The sales tax is collected from sellers at the retail level. Relative to an income tax, there are fewer individuals whose behavior has to be monitored by the tax authorities. This is not to say that administration of a sales tax is without complications. Many difficulties arise because it is unclear whether a given transaction creates a tax liability. In Kentucky, candy is not subject to sales tax, but cookies are. Are Twinkies and Suzy-Q's cookies or candy? In Massachusetts, athletic gear is taxed, but regular clothing is not. Are running bras ordi-

---

[2] See Advisory Commission on Intergovernmental Relations [1990] for further tax rate information.

nary or athletic clothing? The state revenue department classified them as regular clothing. "You could wear a running bra to work and nobody would know the difference," explained a spokesman [*The Wall Street Journal,* October 31, 1984, p. 1]. The point is that defining the base for a sales tax involves making arbitrary distinctions, as was true in the case of the personal and corporate income taxes. Moreover, just as is true for other taxes, tax evasion can be a real problem. For example, officials in New York State estimated that evasion of retail sales taxes costs the state about $100 million annually [Raab, 1986, p. 42].

Nevertheless, sales taxes are probably easier to administer than income taxes. Sales taxation is therefore a particularly attractive option in less-developed countries, where individual record-keeping is not widespread, and where the resources available for tax administration are quite limited.

Optimal tax considerations.   In countries with high literacy and good record-keeping, these administrative arguments do not seem very compelling. Are there any other justifications? In particular, what role is there for differential taxes on various commodities given that an income tax is already in place? A natural framework for examining this question is the theory of optimal taxation. Anthony Atkinson and Joseph Stiglitz [1980] showed that if the income tax schedule is chosen optimally, then under fairly reasonable conditions, social welfare cannot be improved by levying differential commodity taxes.[3] However, if for some reason the income tax is not optimal, differential commodity taxes can improve welfare. For example, if society has egalitarian goals, social welfare can be improved by taxing luxury goods at relatively high rates. Federal excise taxes on certain furs, jewelry, and expensive cars that were imposed in 1991 might be rationalized on such grounds.

A related question is how the rates should be set, given that it has been decided to have differential commodity taxes. Obviously, the answer depends on the government's objectives. According to optimal tax theory, if the goal is to collect a given amount of revenue as efficiently as possible, tax rates should be set so that the compensated demand for each commodity is reduced in the same proportion (see Chapter 15). When the demand for each good depends only on its own price, this is equivalent to the rule that tax rates be inversely related to compensated price elasticities of demand. Goods with inelastic demand are taxed at relatively high rates and vice versa. It seems unlikely that efficiency requires a general sales tax with the same tax rate for each commodity.

---

[3] Suppose the utility function of each individual is a function of his or her consumption of leisure and a set of other commodities. Then as long as the marginal rate of substitution between any two commodities is independent of the amount of leisure, differential commodity taxation cannot improve social welfare in the presence of an optimal earnings tax [Atkinson & Stiglitz, 1980, p. 437].

If the government cares about equity as well as efficiency, optimal tax theory requires departures from the inverse elasticity rule. As noted in Chapter 15, if price-inelastic commodities make up a high proportion of the budgets of the poor, we expect governments with egalitarian objectives to tax such goods lightly or not at all. This may help explain why so many states exempt food from sales taxation.

Within the conventional welfare economics framework, another justification for a sales tax is the presence of externalities. If consumption of a commodity generates costs not included in its price, then in general, efficiency requires a tax on the use of that good (see Chapter 7). High tax rates on tobacco—state plus federal rates now average about 40 cents a pack—are sometimes rationalized in this way. Smokers impose costs on others by polluting the atmosphere, so a tax on tobacco may enhance economic efficiency.

In some cases, sales taxes can be viewed as substitutes for user fees. With current technology, it is infeasible to charge motorists a fee for every mile driven, even though the process of driving creates costs in terms of road damage, congestion, and so on. Because the amount of road use is related to gasoline consumption, road use can be taxed indirectly by putting a tax on gasoline. Of course, the correspondence is far from perfect: some cars are more fuel efficient than others, and some do more damage than others. Still, an approximately correct user fee may be more efficient than none at all.

Other considerations.   Several rationalizations for differential commodity taxation lie outside the framework of conventional economics. Certain excises can be regarded as taxes on "sin." A particular commodity, such as tobacco or alcohol, is deemed to be bad per se, and its consumption is therefore discouraged by the state. Such commodities are just the opposite of "merit goods" (see Chapter 4), which are viewed as being good per se. In both cases, the government is essentially imposing its preferences on those of the citizenry.

Some argue that politicians are attracted to sales taxes because they are included in the final price of the commodity, and are hence relatively easy to hide. However, it is hard to determine whether citizens really are less sensitive to sales taxes than to other types of taxes.

Efficiency and Distributional Implications

From an efficiency point of view, the fundamental question is whether actual sales tax rates are set to minimize excess burden. As pointed out in Chapter 14, when a group of commodities is being taxed, the overall excess burden depends not only on the elasticities of each good but also on the degree to which the goods are complementary and substitutable. At this time, values of all the relevant elasticities are not known with any degree of certainty. Therefore, no definitive judgment as to the efficiency of the existing pattern of sales taxes is available.

As noted earlier, setting all rates equal is almost certainly not efficient. On the other hand, given that the information required to determine
fully efficient taxes is not presently available (and perhaps never will be),
uniform tax rates may not be a bad approach. This is particularly likely if
departures from uniformity open the door to tax rate differentiation based
on political rather than equity or efficiency considerations.[4]

The conventional view of the distributional effects of general sales
taxes is that they are regressive. As the Washington organization Citizens
for Tax Justice put it, "Wealthy people are taxed at a far lower rate than
middle-income families. Why? Because higher-income people spend a
smaller proportion of their income."[5]

There are two problems with this line of reasoning: First, it looks at
the tax as a proportion of *annual* income. In the absence of severe credit
market restrictions, *lifetime* income is more relevant, and there is reasonably strong evidence that the proportion of lifetime income devoted to
consumption is about the same at all levels.[6] Second, and perhaps more
fundamentally, the conventional view totally ignores the theory of tax
incidence. Implicitly, it is assumed that the taxes on a good are borne
entirely by the consumers of that good. As emphasized in Chapter 13,
however, a commodity tax generally is shifted in a complicated fashion
that depends on the supply and demand responses when the tax is imposed. The effect of sales taxes on the distribution of income is still an
open question.[7]

The incidence of selective sales tax systems depends crucially on
which goods are taxed at low rates or exempted altogether. By exempting
those goods consumed intensively by the poor, the after-tax income distribution can be made more equal, other things being the same. But problems can arise with attempts to achieve equality in this way. Even if it is
true that food expenditures on average play an especially important role
in the budgets of the poor, there are still many upper-income families
whose food consumption is proportionately very high. Moreover, exempting certain commodities creates administrative complexities, because it is not always clear whether certain goods belong in the favored
category. Are soft drinks "food"? If so, how much syrup has to be added
to carbonated water before it becomes a soft drink? In New York State, at

---

[4] In New York, Broadway theater tickets are exempt from tax, but baseball tickets are not. Purchase of a flag is subject to tax—unless it is a New York State flag. It is hard to believe that the legislators
who approved these rules were much concerned with optimal taxation.

[5] Citizens for Tax Justice, "The Loophole Lobbyists vs. The People," Washington, D.C., undated.

[6] See, e.g., Milton Friedman [1957] and James Poterba [1991].

[7] In the United States, analyzing the incidence of sales taxes is further complicated by the fact that
the rate on a given good varies from jurisdiction to jurisdiction. This may induce citizens from one
jurisdiction to make purchases in another, so it is hard to tell just who is paying the tax. In New York,
clothing is taxed; in New Jersey, it is not. Not surprisingly, many New Yorkers who live near New Jersey
do their clothes shopping in the latter. Similarly, it is not unknown for Massachusetts citizens to buy their
alcohol in New Hampshire, where the tax rate on liquor is relatively low.

one time *hot* nuts were deemed to be food, and not subject to tax, but *cold* nuts were not exempted. In several states, if you buy a sandwich and eat it in the store, it is subject to an excise tax on restaurant meals. If you buy the same sandwich in the same store but take it out, the sandwich is food, and therefore exempt from tax.

We conclude that the use of selective sales taxation is a fairly clumsy way to achieve egalitarian goals, particularly if a progressive income tax system is already in place.

Two proposals for substantially expanding the role of consumption-based taxes in the U.S. revenue system have been receiving increased attention. Both involve fairly novel tax bases, at least in the context of U.S. fiscal experience. The first is a value-added tax (VAT), and the second is a personal consumption tax. We now discuss each in turn.

Value-Added Tax

Typically, goods are produced in several stages. Consider a simple model of bread production.[8] The farmer grows wheat and sells it to a miller who turns it into flour. The miller sells the flour to a baker who transforms it into bread. The bread is purchased by a grocer who sells it to consumers. A hypothetical numerical example is provided in Table 20.2. Column 1 shows the purchases made by the producer at each stage of production, and column 2 shows the sales value at each stage. For example, the miller pays $400 to the farmer for wheat, and sells the processed wheat to the baker for $700. The **value added** at each stage of production is the difference between the firm's sales and the purchased material inputs used in production. The baker paid $700 for the wheat and sold the bread for $950, so his value added is $250. The value added at each stage of production is computed by subtracting purchases from sales, shown in column 3.[9]

A **value-added tax (VAT)** is a percentage tax on value added applied at each stage of production. For example, if the rate of the VAT is 20 percent, the grocer would pay $10, which is 20 percent of $50. Column 4 shows the amount of VAT liability at each stage of production. The total revenue created by the VAT is found by summing the amounts paid at each stage, and equals $200.

The identical result could have been generated by levying a 20 percent tax at the retail level, that is, by a tax of 20 percent on the value of sales made to consumers by the grocer. In essence, then, a VAT is just an alternative method for collecting a sales tax.[10]

---

[8] For an excellent description of how value-added taxes work, see U.S. Department of the Treasury [1984, vol. 3].

[9] By definition, value added must equal the sum of factor payments made by the producer: wages, interest, rent, and economic profits.

[10] Note that in this example, net income is $1,000, the same as value added. Hence, the VAT is equivalent to a proportional income tax. As we see later, this is not always true.

Table 20.2   **Implementation of a value-added tax (VAT)**

Producer	Purchases	Sales	Value Added	VAT at 20 Percent Rate
Farmer	$ 0	$ 400	$ 400	$ 80
Miller	400	700	300	60
Baker	700	950	250	50
Grocer	950	1,000	50	10
Total	$2,050	$3,050	$1,000	$200

Implementation Issues

Although the United States has never had a national VAT, this method of raising revenue is quite popular in Europe. The European experience indicates that certain administrative decisions have a major impact on a VAT's ultimate economic effects.

First, it must be decided how purchases of investment assets by firms will be treated in the computation of value added. There are three possibilities:

1. The purchase of an investment good is treated like any other material input. Its full value is subtracted from sales in the computation, despite the fact that it is durable. This is referred to as a **consumption-type VAT** because the tax base excludes investment and involves only consumption.
2. Each period, firms may deduct only the amount by which investment goods depreciate. The tax base is thus total income net of depreciation, which is why this is characterized as a **net income–type VAT.**
3. Firms are allowed no deductions at all for investment and depreciation. This is called a **gross income–type VAT.**

Thus, by making different provisions with respect to the treatment of investment goods, a VAT can be transformed into three distinct taxes, each of which presumably has different efficiency and distributional effects. A VAT does not necessarily have to be a tax on consumption. In fact, however, most European VATs are of the consumption type [Tait, 1988].

Second, a procedure for collection must be devised. European countries use the **invoice method,** which can be illustrated in the hypothetical example in Table 20.2. Each firm is liable for tax on the basis of its total sales, but it can claim the taxes already paid by its suppliers as a credit against this liability. For example, the baker is liable for taxes on his $950 in sales, giving him a tax obligation of $190 (= .20 × $950). However, he can claim a credit of $140 (the sum of taxes paid by the farmer and the miller), leaving him a net obligation of $50. The catch is that the credit is allowed only if supported by invoices provided by the baker and the miller. This system provides an incentive for the producers to police themselves against tax evasion, for example, whatever taxes the farmer and miller evade must be paid by the baker. The invoice method cannot eliminate evasion completely. For example, producers can collude to falsify invoices. Nevertheless, there appears to be some evidence that multistage collection has cut down on fraud.

Finally, a rate structure must be established. In our simple example, all commodities are taxed at the same rate. In Europe, commodities are taxed differentially. Food and health-care products are taxed at low rates, presumably because of equity considerations. For reasons of administrative feasibility, very small firms are exempted altogether in some countries. Similarly, banking and finance institutions escape taxation because they tend to provide services in kind; therefore, it is difficult to compute value added. The consumption of services generated by owner-occupied housing is exempt from tax for the same reasons that it is usually exempted from income taxation (see Chapter 17).

Nonuniform taxation increases administrative complexity, especially when firms produce multiple outputs, some of which are taxable and some of which are not. But the system can work, as evidenced by the European experience. For the United States, then, the question is not whether a national VAT is feasible, but whether its introduction would be an improvement over the status quo.

A VAT for the United States?

The VATs suggested for the United States are usually of the European consumption type, and hence essentially general sales taxes. Therefore, the arguments regarding the efficiency and equity of sales taxes made earlier in this chapter are applicable, and there is no need to repeat them. The fundamental problem is the same: Attempts to obtain additional equity by exempting various goods may increase the excess burden of the tax system as a whole and certainly lead to greater administrative complexity.

More generally, the desirability of a national VAT can be determined only if we know what tax (or taxes) it would replace, how the revenues would be spent, and so forth. For example, many public finance economists believe that the corporation income tax is undesirable in practically all respects and would be happy to see a VAT replace it, other things being the same. However, they would probably not be as well disposed toward replacing the personal income tax with a VAT.[11] Charles Ballard, J. K. Scholz, and John Shoven [1986] studied the efficiency consequences of introducing a European-type VAT in the United States, under the

---

[11] The only serious attempt to introduce a VAT in the United States was the unsuccessful Tax Restructuring Act of 1979. According to this bill, revenues from the VAT would have reduced the Social Security and income taxes, liberalized depreciation allowances for business firms, and increased certain welfare payments, among other things. (See McLure [1980] for details.) It is hard to predict the effects of such a hodgepodge.

assumption that the VAT revenues would be used to scale down the personal income tax. They estimated that in present value terms, a VAT would reduce excess burden by about $625 billion.[12] This result, however, depends importantly on assumptions about the responsiveness of saving to changes in the income tax. As noted in Chapter 17, this is a controversial issue. Hence, this particular figure must be regarded with some caution.

In the context of the efficiency consequences of a VAT, it is useful to note that in a number of European countries, the VAT replaced a **turnover tax,** which has as its base the *total* value of sales at each level of production. In Table 20.2, under a 20 percent turnover tax, the farmer's liability is $80, the miller's $140, the baker's $190, and the grocer's $200. The total yield is $610. Now suppose that the farmer, miller, baker, and grocer merge into one firm. Then there is only one stage of production, which has sales of $1,000, and hence a liability of only $200. Thus, the yield of the turnover tax depends arbitrarily on the number of stages of production. Virtually all notions of efficient and equitable taxation suggest that such a system is inferior, and a VAT is certainly an improvement.

Introduction of a national VAT to the United States would create transitional problems, the precise nature of which would depend on the exact form of the VAT, and what it was replacing. For example, if a consumption-type VAT were to replace the personal income tax, members of the older generations would suffer during the transition period. During their working years, they accumulated wealth to consume during retirement. The interest, dividends, and realized capital gains that they received along the way were subject to the personal income tax. A reasonable expectation for such people is that when they reach retirement, their consumption would not be subject to new taxes. If a consumption-type VAT were suddenly introduced, however, these expectations would be disappointed. Clearly, equity—not to mention political feasibility—requires some method for compensating the elderly during the transition.

In addition, we must consider the political implications of introducing a VAT. Once it is in place, each percentage point increase in the VAT would yield roughly $27 billion in tax revenues, measured in 1993 dollars.[13] In a world where political institutions accurately reflect the wishes of the citizenry, this observation may not be of much significance. But for those who believe that at least to some extent the interests of the government differ from those of the public (see Chapter 7), the revenue potential of a VAT is frightening. Some fear that the VAT might be used to sneak by an increase in the size of the government sector:

---

[12] This figure is determined by adjusting Ballard, Scholz, and Shoven's estimate for changes in the price level between 1973 and 1985.

[13] This is a projection by the Congressional Budget Office [1990, p. 417].

> Because it would be collected by business enterprises, VAT would be
> concealed in the total price the consumer paid and hence not perceived as
> a direct tax burden. That is its advantage to legislators—and its major
> defect to the taxpayers. [Friedman, 1980, p. 90]

Indeed, in virtually all countries with a VAT, the rate has increased
over time, as has the share of gross domestic product devoted to taxes.
For example, when Denmark introduced a VAT of 10 percent in 1967,
total tax revenues as a percent of gross domestic product were 36.1 percent. By 1978, the VAT rate was 22 percent, and the ratio of taxes to gross
domestic product was 43.6 percent [Aaron, 1981, p. 14]. Of course, this
does not prove that the VAT was responsible for a larger government
sector. (See Stockfisch [1985].) On the other hand, one would not expect
to be successful in assuaging the fears just expressed by appealing to the
European experience.

Finally, it is important to consider the international implications of a
VAT, because some VAT proponents have argued that the tax would
enhance America's trade position vis-à-vis its competitors. This notion
rests on the fact that according to the General Agreement on Tariffs and
Trade (GATT), which regulates international trade practices, a VAT can
be rebated on a country's exports and levied on imports. In contrast,
personal and corporate income taxes cannot be rebated. Since a VAT can
be rebated while income taxes cannot, some have argued that U.S. international competitiveness would be enhanced if the U.S. adopted a VAT
and simultaneously reduced the role of income taxation. For example,
Senator William Roth [1986] argued that such a scheme would "help our
domestic industries compete with imports."

To analyze this plan, consider each part separately: introduction of a
VAT, and then reduction in personal and corporate income taxes. Imposing a VAT would tend to increase the relative prices of the taxed goods by
an amount determined by the relevant supply and demand elasticities.
As Aaron [1986] points out, rebating the VAT "at the border simply
undoes this effect for exported goods. There is no reason why loading
weight on a horse's back and then taking it off should help the horse run
faster."

Turning now to the second part of the plan, would reducing corporate
and personal income taxes reduce the relative prices of American exports? Again, the answer depends on the incidence of these taxes, and it is
not at all obvious. For example, if the market for labor is competitive and
its supply is perfectly inelastic, producers' wage costs are unchanged
when income taxes are reduced. The entire benefit of the tax reduction
goes to workers. (See Chapter 13.) In this case, prices may not change at
all. More generally, of course, prices might fall, but no evidence suggests
that the reduction would be very large.

In short, there is no reason to believe that adoption of a VAT would dramatically improve the U.S. trade position. Of course, this fact by itself does not mean that a VAT would be a bad thing. As noted above, VATs have both advantages and disadvantages. But they are not a panacea for U.S. trade problems.

Personal Consumption Tax

A major objection to both sales taxes and VATs is that they do not allow personal circumstances to be taken into account when determining tax liabilities. In particular, differentiating among people on the basis of ability to pay is difficult.

In contrast, a personal tax based on total consumption expenditures during a given period allows the tax authorities to take individual characteristics into account in determining tax liability. Under a **personal consumption tax** (also referred to as an **expenditure tax**), each household files a return reporting its consumption expenditures during the year. Unlike an income tax, the base of a consumption tax excludes unconsumed additions to wealth—saving. However, just as under the personal income tax, various exemptions and deductions can be taken to allow for special circumstances such as extraordinary medical expenses. Each individual's tax bill is then determined by applying a rate schedule to the adjusted amount of consumption. The rate schedule can be as progressive as policymakers desire.

Some argue that if the income tax were replaced by a consumption tax, efficiency, equity, and administrative simplicity would be enhanced. The defenders of the income tax have argued that the case for expenditure taxation is seriously flawed. We now discuss the controversy.[14]

Efficiency Issues

The efficiency implications of personal consumption versus income taxation can be examined using the life-cycle model of consumption and saving introduced in Chapter 17. In that model, the individual's labor supply each period is fixed. The two commodities she purchases are present consumption, c_0, and future consumption, c_1. If r is the interest rate, every additional dollar of consumption today means that the individual's future consumption is reduced by $(1 + r)$. Hence, the relative price of c_0—its opportunity cost—is $(1 + r)$.

Consider now the case of Juliet, on whom a 31 percent income tax is levied. Assuming that the tax allows for the deductibility of interest payments, how does this affect the relative price of c_0?[15] If Juliet saves a

---

[14] For a good discussion of the pros and cons, see Joseph Pechman [1980].

[15] As stressed in Chapters 16 and 17, not all taxpayers can deduct payments of interest. As an exercise, discuss how the following analysis is modified when interest is not deductible.

dollar and it earns a return of r, the government taxes away 31 percent of the return, leaving her only $.69 \times r$. If she borrows a dollar, the interest payments are deductible, so the cost of borrowing is reduced to $.69 \times r$. In short, as a consequence of the income tax, the relative price of present consumption falls from $(1 + r)$ to $(1 + .69r)$. A wedge is inserted between the amount that a borrower pays and a lender receives. However, we showed in Chapter 14 that the presence of such a tax wedge creates an excess burden. We conclude that an income tax generates an excess burden.

Now consider a consumption tax that raises the same amount of revenue as the income tax. The key thing to note in this context is that the consumption tax leaves unchanged the market rate of return available to Juliet. This is because the receipt of interest income by itself does not create a tax liability—only consuming it does. Hence, after the consumption tax, the relative price of c_0 is still $(1 + r)$. Unlike the income tax, there seems to be no tax wedge, and hence no excess burden. Apparently, consumption taxation is superior to income taxation on efficiency grounds.

Is this result general, or is it a consequence of some special assumptions? Recall that in Chapter 14 a similar argument was used to "prove" that taxes at equal rates on all commodities are always more efficient than differential rates on different commodities. We showed there the fallacy in that argument. Once it is recognized that even an equiproportional tax distorts the choice between leisure and each of the taxed commodities, it is no longer clear that taxing all commodities at the same rate is efficient. The same consideration applies here. The argument in the preceding paragraphs was built on the *assumption* that the supply of labor is fixed. Once the possibility that labor-supply decisions are choices is raised, it is no longer true that the consumption tax is *necessarily* more efficient than an income tax.

True, unlike the income tax, the consumption tax leaves unchanged the rate at which Juliet can trade off consumption between the two periods. However, in general, the consumption tax *does* distort the rate at which she can trade off leisure against consumption. Suppose that Juliet's wage rate is w. Prior to the consumption tax, she can trade off one hour of leisure for w dollars worth of consumption. If consumption is taxed at rate t_c, however, surrendering one hour of leisure allows her only $w/(1 + t_c)$ dollars worth of consumption. Thus, the consumption tax distorts the decision between leisure and consumption.

In short, as long as labor supply is a matter of choice, both income and consumption taxes distort some decisions. Therefore, both systems induce an efficiency cost, and only empirical work can determine which tax's cost is smaller.

Several studies have suggested that given what is known about labor supply and saving behavior, a consumption tax creates a smaller excess burden than an income tax, even when labor supply distortions created by both taxes are taken into account. For example, Don Fullerton, John Shoven, and John Whalley [1982, p. 28] estimate that the efficiency gain from moving to a consumption tax would be about 2 to 3 percent of national income each year. However, such results are quite sensitive to assumptions about the responsiveness of consumption to changes in the interest rate. As we saw in Chapter 17, this is notoriously hard to measure. As research on saving behavior progresses, our understanding of the efficiency aspects of income versus consumption taxation will improve.

Equity Issues

Progressiveness.   Earlier we noted the widespread assumption that sales taxes are regressive. Whatever the merits of this view, there is an unfortunate tendency to assume that it applies to any tax with consumption as a base. This is simply wrong. Given that the base of the tax being considered here is *personal* consumption expenditures, the structure can be made as progressive as desired. For example, Henry Aaron and Harvey Galper [1985, p. 70] estimated that the following schedule of marginal consumption tax rates would have approximately reproduced the distribution of statutory personal income tax burdens in 1986: 5 percent up to $11,000 of consumption; 20 percent on consumption between $11,000 and $43,750; and 32 percent on consumption in excess of $43,750.[16]

Ability to pay.   Those who favor the income base argue that *actual* consumption is merely one component of *potential* consumption. It is the power to consume, not necessarily its exercise, that is relevant. They point out that under a consumption tax, it would be possible for a miserly millionaire to have a smaller tax liability than a much poorer person. A possible response is that it is fairer to tax an individual according to what he or she "takes out" of the economic system, in the form of consumption, than what he or she "contributes" to society, as measured by income. As Thomas Hobbes said in the 17th century:

> For what reason is there, that he which laboureth much, and sparing the
> fruit of his labour, consumeth little, should be more charged, than he that
> liveth idly, getteth little, and spendeth all he gets; seeing the one hath
> no more protection from the commonwealth than the other. [1651/1963,
> p. 303]

---

[16] These figures are for joint returns. The consumption amounts are in excess of personal exemptions.

From this point of view, if the miserly millionaire chooses not to consume very much, that is all to the good, because the resources he or she saves become available to society for capital accumulation.

A related question is whether or not an income tax results in double taxation of interest income. Some argue that an income tax is unfair because it taxes capital income twice: once when the original income is earned, and again when the investment produces a return.[17] As Richard Goode [1980, p. 54] notes, the logic of income taxation impels that the return to saving be taxed. Whether or not this is fair depends, as usual, on value judgments. The debate is likely to continue.

Annual versus lifetime equity.   It is widely agreed that events influencing a person's economic position for only a very short time do not provide an adequate basis for determining ability to pay. Indeed, some have argued that ideally tax liabilities should be related to lifetime income. Proponents of consumption taxation point out that an annual income tax leads to tax burdens that can differ quite substantially even for people who have the same lifetime wealth.

To see why, consider Mr. Grasshopper and Ms. Ant, both of whom live for two periods. In the present, they have identical fixed labor incomes of I_0, and in the future, they both have labor incomes of zero. (The assumption of zero second-period income is made solely for convenience.) Grasshopper chooses to consume heavily early in life because he is not very concerned about his retirement years. Ant chooses to consume most of her wealth later in life, because she wants a lavish retirement.

Define Ant's present consumption in the presence of a proportional income tax as c_0^A, and Grasshopper's as c_0^G. By assumption, $c_0^G > c_0^A$. Ant's future income before tax is the interest she earns on her savings: $r(I_0 - c_0^A)$. Similarly, Grasshopper's future income before tax is: $r(I_0 - c_0^G)$.

Now, if the proportional income tax rate is t, in the present Ant and Grasshopper have identical tax liabilities of tI_0. However, in the future, Ant's tax liability is $tr(I_0 - c_0^A)$, while Grasshopper's is $tr(I_0 - c_0^G)$. Because $c_0^G > c_0^A$, Ant's future tax liability is higher. Solely because Ant has a greater taste for saving than Grasshopper, her lifetime tax burden (the discounted sum of her tax burdens in the two periods) is greater than Grasshopper's.

In contrast, under a proportional consumption tax, lifetime tax burdens are *independent* of tastes for saving, other things being the same.[18] To prove this, all we need to do is write down the equation for each

---

[17] "The fundamental bias against capital formation in our tax system results from the multiple taxation of income which is saved and invested" [Meiselman, 1977, p. 30].

[18] However, when marginal tax rates depend on the level of consumption, this may not be the case.

taxpayer's budget constraint. Because all of Ant's noncapital income (I_0) comes in the present, its present value is simply I_0. Now, the present value of lifetime consumption must equal the present value of lifetime income. Hence, Ant's consumption pattern must satisfy the relation

$$I_0 = c_0^A + \frac{c_1^A}{1 + r} \tag{20.1}$$

Similarly, Grasshopper is constrained by

$$I_0 = c_0^G + \frac{c_1^G}{1 + r} \tag{20.2}$$

Equations (20.1) and (20.2) say simply that the lifetime value of income must equal the lifetime value of consumption.

If the proportional consumption tax rate is t_c, Ant's tax liability in the first period is $t_c c_0^A$; her tax liability in the second period is $t_c c_1^A$; and the present value of her lifetime consumption tax liability, R_c^A is

$$R_c^A = t_c c_0^A + \frac{t_c c_1^A}{1 + r} \tag{20.3}$$

Similarly, Grasshopper's lifetime tax liability is

$$R_c^G = t_c c_0^G + \frac{t_c c_1^G}{1 + r} \tag{20.4}$$

By comparing Equations (20.3) and (20.1), we see that Ant's lifetime tax liability is equal to $t_c I_0$. [Just multiply Equation (20.1) through by t_c.] Similar comparison of Equations (20.2) and (20.4) indicates that Grasshopper's lifetime tax liability is also $t_c I_0$. We conclude that under a proportional consumption tax, two people with identical lifetime incomes always pay identical lifetime taxes (where lifetime is interpreted in the present value sense). This stands in stark contrast to a proportional income tax, where the pattern of lifetime consumption influences lifetime tax burdens.

A related argument in favor of the consumption tax centers on the fact that income tends to fluctuate more than consumption. In years when income is unusually low, individuals may draw on their savings or borrow to smooth out fluctuations in their consumption levels. The point is that annual consumption is likely to be a better reflection of lifetime circumstances than is annual income.

Opponents of consumption taxation would question whether a lifetime point of view is really appropriate. There is too much uncertainty in both the political and economic environments for a lifetime perspective to be very realistic. Moreover, the consumption smoothing required for the lifetime arguments requires that individuals be able to save and borrow freely at the going rate of interest. Given that capital markets are imperfect—individuals often face constraints on the amounts they can borrow—it is not clear how relevant the lifetime arguments are. Although a considerable body of empirical work suggests that the life-cycle model is a good representation for most households (see King [1983]), this argument still deserves some consideration.

Administrative Issues

In discussions of personal consumption taxation, administrative issues are of more than usual interest. This is because such a tax system has never been implemented successfully.[19] Indeed, for many years a consumption tax has been viewed mostly as an intellectual curiosity rather than a realistic policy option. But recently, growing numbers of economists and lawyers have suggested that a consumption tax is quite feasible and not as different from the current income tax system as one might think.

If the only way to compute annual consumption were to add up all expenditures made over the course of a year, taxpayers would have to keep records and receipts for every purchase. This would be administratively infeasible. All taxpayers cannot be expected to maintain complete balance sheets.

William Andrews [1974] and others have suggested that consumption be measured on a **cash-flow basis,** meaning that it would be calculated simply as the difference between all cash receipts and savings. To keep track of saving, qualified accounts would be established at savings banks, savings and loan associations, security brokerage houses, and other types of financial institutions. Funds that were certified by these institutions as having been deposited in qualified accounts would be exempt from tax.[20] Most of the record-keeping responsibility would be met by these institutions and would not involve more paperwork than exists already. As long as capital gains and interest from such accounts were retained, they would not be taxed. For some taxpayers, such qualified accounts already exist in the forms of Keogh plans and Individual Retirement Accounts (see Chapter 16). One way to look at a consumption tax is simply as an expansion of the opportunities to invest in such accounts.

A potentially important administrative problem concerns the valuation of the consumption benefits produced by durable goods. The purchase of a durable is an act of saving and hence would be deductible under a consumption tax. Over time, the durable generates consumption benefits subject to tax. But here the usual problems of imputing consumption streams arise. How do we measure the annual flow of benefits produced by a house or a car?

---

[19] India and Sri Lanka were the only two countries to adopt a consumption tax, and both nations soon abandoned it.

[20] For further details, see Aaron and Galper [1985].

Proponents of a consumption tax argue that this problem is avoidable if a **tax prepayment approach** for durables is used. When the original durable investment is made, it is taxed as if it were consumption. There is no attempt later to tax the returns generated by the investment. Thus, imputation problems are avoided. But does prepayment yield the appropriate amount of tax? In present value terms, tax prepayment does indeed yield the same amount as would have been collected if the consumption were taxed when it actually occurred, as long as the tax rate is fixed. To see why, suppose that the durable lasts for T years, and produces expected consumption benefits of c_1 in year 1, c_2 in year 2, and so forth. In equilibrium, the price of the durable, V, just equals the present value of the stream of consumption the durable generates:

$$V = \frac{c_1}{1 + r} + \frac{c_2}{(1 + r)^2} + \cdot \cdot \cdot + \frac{c_T}{(1 + r)^T} \tag{20.5}$$

where r is the interest rate. Now, if consumption is taxed at rate t_c, revenue collections under the tax prepayment approach are $t_c V$. On the other hand, if consumption is taxed when it occurs, the present value of the tax proceeds (R_c) is

$$R_c = \frac{t_c c_1}{1 + r} + \frac{t_c c_2}{(1 + r)^2} + \cdot \cdot \cdot + \frac{t_c c_T}{(1 + r)^T} \tag{20.6}$$

Examining Equations (20.5) and (20.6) together, we note that R_c is exactly equal to $t_c V$. Hence, the same amount of tax is collected in present value terms.

Advantages of a consumption tax.   Although many people have become convinced that consumption taxation is practical, many others believe it would be an administrative nightmare. We now catalog some advantages and disadvantages of consumption taxation relative to income taxation, and also note a few problems that are common to both.

No need to measure capital gains and depreciation.   Some of the most vexing problems in administering an income tax arise from difficulties in measuring additions to wealth. For example, it requires calculation of capital gains and losses even on those assets not sold during the year, a task so difficult that it is not even attempted under the current system. Similarly, for those who have income produced by capital equipment, additions to wealth must be lowered by the amount the equipment depreciates during the year. As noted in Chapter 19, we know very little about actual depreciation patterns. Andrews [1983] views the inability of real-world income tax systems to measure and tax additions to wealth as their fatal flaw: "A comprehensive income tax ideal with an immediate concession that taxation is not to be based on actual value is like a blueprint for constructing a building in which part of the foundation is required to be located in quicksand. If the terrain cannot be changed, the blueprint had better be amended [p. 282].'' Under a consumption tax, all such problems disappear because additions to wealth are no longer part of the tax base.

Fewer problems with inflation.   In the presence of a nonindexed income tax, inflation creates important distortions. Some of these are a consequence of a progressive rate structure, but some would occur even if the tax were proportional. These distortions occur because computing capital income requires the use of figures from years which have different price levels. For example, if an asset is sold, calculation of the capital gain or loss requires subtracting the value in the year of purchase from its value in the current year. In general, part of the change in value is due to inflation, so that individuals are taxed on gains that do not reflect increases in real income.[21] As noted in Chapter 16, setting up an appropriate scheme for indexing income generated by investments is very complicated, and has not been attempted in the United States.

In contrast, under a consumption tax, calculation of the tax base involves only current-year transactions. Therefore, any distortions associated with inflation are likely to be much less of a problem.

No need for separate corporation tax.   Some argue that implementation of a consumption tax would allow removal of the corporation income tax, at least in theory. Recall from Chapter 19 that one of the main justifications of the corporation tax is to get at income that people accumulate in corporations. If accumulation per se were no longer part of the personal income tax base, this would not be necessary. Elimination of the corporation tax would probably enhance efficiency.

Advocates of the consumption tax often point out that adoption would not be as radical a move as first appearances might suggest. In some respects, the present system *already* looks very much like a consumption tax:

1. For some taxpayers, income is exempt from taxation when it is saved in certain forms such as Keogh plans, IRAs, and pensions.
2. Unrealized capital gains on financial assets are untaxed, as are virtually all capital gains on housing.
3. Realized capital gains are free of all taxation at the death of the owner.
4. Accelerated depreciation reduces the amount of investment purchases included in the tax base.

---

[21] Suppose, for example, that Smith buys an asset for $100. After a year, the asset is worth $200, but the price level has also doubled. In real terms, there has been no increase in income, yet Smith nevertheless has incurred a tax liability.

In light of these considerations, characterizing the status quo as an income tax is a serious misnomer; it is more a hybrid between income and consumption taxation.

Disadvantages of a consumption tax.   Critics of personal consumption taxation have noted a number of disadvantages:

Administrative problems.   An important consideration raised by opponents of consumption taxation is that monitoring and accounting costs would be larger than at present. They argue that even if the cash-flow method were adopted, people would have to keep more records with respect to their asset positions.[22] The tax prepayment approach, which is central to the taxation of durables under a consumption tax, has also been criticized. Equation (20.5) indicates the relation between the *expected* benefits of an investment and its cost. But these returns cannot be known with certainty. If the stream of c's turns out to be higher than expected, the tax prepayment plan would result in a tax liability that is lower than it would be otherwise. Similarly, if the c's are lower, tax prepayment results in higher liabilities. Critics argue that taxes should be based on outcomes, not expectations, so that the tax prepayment approach is fundamentally unfair.

Transitional problems.   Critics have also argued that despite already existing elements of consumption taxation in the present system, the switch to a consumption tax would be a major one, and would be accompanied by enormous transitional problems. During the transition, people would have incentives to conceal their assets, and to liquidate them later without reporting the proceeds. Moreover, during the transition, the elderly generation would be hurt by moving to a consumption tax. In a sense, they would be subject to double jeopardy—in their working years, when they were accumulating wealth for retirement, their capital income was subject to tax. Then, when they reach retirement, they have to pay tax on the consumption itself. This problem arises in any major tax reform—people who have made commitments on the basis of the existing system are likely to be hurt when it changes. Fairness would seem to require that the elderly be compensated for the losses they would incur during the transition. Those advocating the consumption tax have proposed a number of rules for alleviating transitional problems [see Aaron and Galper, 1985].

Gifts and bequests.   The discussion surrounding Equations (20.1) through (20.4) demonstrated that in a simple life-cycle model, a proportional consumption tax is equivalent to a tax on lifetime income. Contrary

---

[22] Other problems that might occur under a consumption tax are discussed by Michael Graetz [1980].

to the assumptions of the life-cycle model, some people set aside part of their lifetime income for gifts and bequests. How should such transfers be treated under a consumption tax? One view is that there is no need to tax gifts and bequests until they are consumed by their recipients. On the other hand, others argue that gifts and bequests should be treated as consumption on the part of the donor. Hence, gifts and bequests should be taxed at the time the transfer is made. Proponents of this view point out that it would not be politically viable to institute a tax system that allowed substantial amounts of wealth to accumulate free of tax, and then failed to tax it on transfer. However, as explained later, there are major conceptual and practical problems involved in taxing transfers of wealth.

Problems with both systems.   Even the most enthusiastic proponents of the consumption tax recognize that its adoption would not usher in an era of tax nirvana. Several of the most intractable problems inherent in the income tax system would also plague any consumption tax. These include, but are not limited to:

1. Distinguishing consumption commodities from commodities used in production. (Should a desk purchased for use at home be considered consumption or a business expense?)
2. Defining consumption itself. (Are health-care expenditures part of consumption, or should they be deductible?)
3. Choosing the unit of taxation and determining an appropriate rate structure.
4. Valuing fringe benefits of various occupations. (If a job gives a person access to the company swimming pool, should the consumption benefits be taxed? If so, how can they be valued?)
5. Determining a method for averaging across time if the schedule has increasing marginal tax rates.
6. Taxing production that occurs in the home.
7. Discouraging incentives to avoid taxes altogether by participating in the underground economy.

Finally, we emphasize that it is not quite fair to compare an *ideal* consumption tax to the *actual* income tax. Historically, special interests have effectively persuaded politicians to tax certain types of income preferentially. Adoption of a consumption tax could hardly be expected to eliminate political corruption of the tax structure. Indeed, one pessimistic observer has suggested, "I find the choice between the consumption base and the income base an almost sterile debate; we do not tax all income now, and were we to adopt a consumption tax system, we would end up exempting as much consumption from the tax base as we do income now.''[23] It is hard to predict whether a real-world consumption tax would be better than the current system.

Wealth Taxes

The taxes we have discussed so far are levied on items such as income, consumption, and sales. In the jargon of economics, these are known as **flow variables** because they are associated with a time dimension. For instance, income is a flow, because the concept is meaningful only when put in the context of some time interval. If you say "My income is $10,000," it means nothing unless one knows whether it is over a week, month, or year. A **stock variable,** on the other hand, has no time dimension. It is a quantity at a point in time, not a rate per unit of time. Wealth is a stock, because it refers to the value of the assets an individual has accumulated as of a given time. This section discusses some taxes that are levied on the stock of wealth.

Why Tax Wealth?

Before turning to the specifics of each tax, we might ask what justifications there are for using wealth as a tax base. Several answers have been proposed. First, wealth taxes help to correct certain (inevitable) problems that arise in the administration of a comprehensive income tax. Recall that *all* capital gains, realized or not, belong in the tax base of a comprehensive income tax. In practice, for many assets it is impossible to tax unrealized capital gains. By taxing the wealth of which these gains become a part, perhaps this situation can be remedied. Now, it is true that wealth at a given point in time includes the sum of capital gains and losses from all earlier years. However, there is no reason to believe that the yield from an annual wealth tax approximates the revenues that would have been generated by full annual taxation of unrealized capital gains.

Second, the higher an individual's wealth, the greater his or her ability to pay, other things—including income—being the same. Therefore, wealthy individuals should have a higher tax liability. Suppose that a miser has accumulated a huge hoard of gold that yields no income. Should she be taxed on the value of the hoard? Some believe that as long as the miser was subject to the income tax while the hoard was accumulating, it should not be taxed again. Others would argue that the gold per se generates utility and should be subject to tax. In any case, note that the logic of the ability to pay argument requires that if wealth is to be taxed, it must be net wealth—assets minus debts. If Cain and Abel both own $100,000

---

[23] Emil Sunley quoted in John Makin [1985, p. 20].

houses, but Cain has a $75,000 mortgage while Abel owns his house outright, it is absurd to treat them as having identical amounts of wealth. As we see in the next chapter, property taxes in the United States do not allow deductions for liabilities.

Third, wealth taxation reduces the concentration of wealth, which is desirable socially and politically. As we saw in Chapter 8, although it is difficult to measure income precisely, the best estimates suggest that the distribution of income in the United States is quite unequal. The quality of data on wealth is even less precise. What information there is suggests that the distribution of wealth is very unequal. One study using data from 1984 indicated that the bottom 26 percent of the income distribution owned 10 percent of total net worth, while the top 12 percent of the income distribution owned 38 percent of total net worth [U.S. Bureau of the Census, 1986b, p. 2]. The desirability of such inequality turns on a complicated set of ethical issues quite similar to those discussed in Chapter 8 in connection with the distribution of income. A related issue is whether a highly concentrated distribution of wealth is likely to lead to corruption of democratic political processes. While this is a vitally important question, it is beyond our scope. Note that this whole line of argument *assumes* that wealth taxation does indeed lead to a more equal distribution of wealth. Later we show that this is not necessarily the case.

Finally, wealth taxes are payments for benefits that wealth holders receive from government. One might argue, for example, that a major goal of defense spending is to protect (from foreign enemies) our existing wealth. If so, perhaps a wealth tax is a just method for financing defense. In addition, government makes certain expenditures that are likely to benefit wealth holders especially. If the state builds and maintains a road that goes by my store, then it confers a benefit on me for which I should pay. Although the notion of basing taxes on benefits has some appeal, it is not clear that any feasible wealth tax can achieve this goal. A lawyer arguing the case for the property tax asked rhetorically, "[I]sn't it true that one with twice as much house receives twice as much benefit from . . . police and fire services rendered to property?" [Hagman, 1978, p. 42]. Contrary to what he apparently believed, the answer is "probably not." The value to a given household of most services provided by local government depends on factors other than house size. For example, the value of education depends on the number of children. Even the value of fire and police services depends on how much furniture is in the house and how much insurance protection has been purchased. If benefit taxation is the goal, a system of user fees for public services would be more appropriate than a wealth tax.

To summarize, wealth taxes have been rationalized on both ability-to-pay and benefit grounds. Both sets of arguments are very controversial.

By far the most important wealth tax in the United States is the property tax. This tax base has been reserved for state and local governments and is particularly crucial to the operations of local governments. Accordingly, we postpone our discussion of the property tax until the next chapter, in which we discuss subnational units of government.

Estate and Gift Taxes

The federal government levies wealth taxes against estates and gifts. Estate and gift taxes are levied at irregular intervals on the occurrence of certain events—the estate tax on the death of the wealth holder **(decedent),** and the gift tax when property is transferred between the living *(inter vivos)*. Both federal and some state governments levy taxes on gifts and estates. At neither level are the taxes very important as revenue raisers. Estate and gift taxes account for less than 1 percent of the tax revenues raised by both federal and state governments from their own sources [*Facts and Figures on Government Finance*, 1990, p. 13]. The federal tax does not touch the lives of most citizens. In 1988, there were over 2 million deaths in the United States, but only about 44,000 decedents were subject to filing an estate tax return [Internal Revenue Service, 1990, p. 27]. Some have suggested that the role of estate and gift taxes should be expanded. The arguments for and against doing so are explored in this section.

We begin by describing the rationales for estate and gift taxation, and then discuss briefly the system as it operates in the United States. At the end, we present several suggestions for change.

Rationalizations

Estate taxes have been around a long time, but they are very controversial. The following issues have been raised in the debate over their desirability:[24]

Payment for services.   First, it is argued that the government protects property rights and oversees the transfer of property from the decedent to his or her heirs. As compensation for providing these services, the state is entitled to a share of the estate. Those who oppose the estate tax argue that provision of such services is a fundamental right that does not have to be paid for. Moreover, it seems arbitrary to pick out property transfers as special objects of taxation. If Moe spends $10,000 on a trip to Europe, Curly spends $10,000 on his daughter's college education, and Larry leaves $10,000 to his son, why should Larry face a special tax?

---

[24] This discussion ignores gift taxes for the most part. They are discussed subsequently.

Reversion of property to society.   In addition, some claim that ultimately, all property belongs to society as a whole. During an individual's lifetime, society permits her to dispose of the property she has managed to accumulate as she wishes. But at death, the property reverts to society, which can dispose of it at will. In this view, although people may be entitled to what they earn, it is not at all clear that their descendants hold any compelling ethical claim to it. Recall from Chapter 8 that many controversial value judgments lie behind such assertions. Some suggest it is fundamentally wrong to argue that a person holds wealth only at the pleasure of "society," or that "society" ever has any valid claim on personal wealth.

Incentives.   Some suggest that estate taxes are good for incentives. Perhaps the most famous statement of this theme is attributed to Andrew Carnegie: "The parent who leaves his son enormous wealth generally deadens the talents and energies of the son, and tempts him to lead a less useful and less worthy life than he otherwise would" [Pechman, 1977a, p. 221]. By taxing away estates, the government can prevent this from happening.

The incentive problem is much more complicated than suggested by Carnegie, because we must take into account the behavior of the donor as well as the recipient. Consider Lear, an individual who is motivated to work hard during his lifetime to leave a big estate to his daughters. The presence of an estate tax might discourage Lear's work effort. ("Why should I work hard if my wealth is going to the tax collector instead of my daughters?") On the other hand, in the presence of an estate tax, a greater amount of wealth has to be accumulated to leave a given after-tax bequest. Thus, the presence of an estate tax might induce Lear to work harder to maintain the net value of his estate. Consequently, whether or not an estate tax induces a donor to work more or less is logically indeterminate.[25] Even if Carnegie were right and estate taxation induces potential heirs to work more, it might also generate incentives for donors to work less. On balance, we cannot know on the basis of theory alone which tendency dominates.

Similarly, we cannot predict how an estate tax affects the donor's saving behavior. It is easy to describe scenarios in which he saves less and in which he saves more.

In this context, observe that the presence of an estate tax can affect not only the amount of wealth transferred across generations but also the form in which the transfers take place. A tax on bequests of physical capital creates incentives to transmit wealth in the form of human capital.

---

[25] Recognize that the ambiguity arises because of the familiar conflict between substitution and income effects. See Chapter 17.

Thus, instead of giving each daughter $40,000 worth of stocks and bonds, Lear might spend $40,000 on each of their college educations. An estate tax could thus lead to overinvestment in human capital.

Unfortunately, there is very little in the way of empirical evidence to settle any of these incentive issues. A thorough study requires lifetime data on the labor supply and saving behavior of a group of individuals and their heirs. Economists have had to settle for rather more fragmentary sources of data, and no definitive results exist.

Relation to personal income tax.   Estate and gift taxation is necessary, it can be argued, because receipts of gifts and inheritances are excluded from the recipient's personal income tax base. A natural response to this observation is to ask why gifts and estates are not included in Adjusted Gross Income in the first place. After all, they constitute additions to potential consumption, and by the conventional definition are therefore income to the recipient. However, there has always been a strong aversion to including inheritances and gifts in the income tax base.[26] Such receipts simply are not perceived as being in the same class as those from wages and interest. It is not necessarily the case, though, that a tax on gifts and estates is the best remedy for this omission. We discuss a possible alternative later.

Income distribution.   An estate tax is a valuable tool for creating a more equal distribution of income. Let us leave aside the normative question of whether or not the government ought to pursue a more equal income distribution and consider the positive issue of whether or not an effective system of estate taxation is likely to achieve this goal. Certainly the prevailing assumption is that it would; "the one aim of a death tax that stands scrutiny is its redistributive or anticoncentration aim" [Jantscher, 1977, p. 51]. However, Stiglitz [1978] has suggested several reasons that taxing bequests might backfire and create a less equal distribution of income.

  - If the estate tax reduces saving, there will be less capital. This leads to a lower real wage for labor, and under certain conditions, a smaller share of income going to labor.[27] To the extent that capital income is more unequally distributed than labor income, the effect is to increase inequality.

---

[26] One possible explanation is that taxing estates and gifts under a progressive tax system would be unfair because these forms of income tend to come in large lumps. However, it would surely be possible to develop an appropriate averaging scheme to mitigate such effects.

[27] When the wage rate decreases, the quantity of labor demanded increases. Thus, what happens to labor income—the product of the wage and the quantity demanded—depends on the elasticity of demand for labor. This in turn depends on the ease with which capital may be substituted for labor (the elasticity of substitution of capital for labor) [see Henderson and Quandt, 1980, pp. 111–14].

- *Within* a generation, it is likely that most individuals transfer wealth only to others who are worse off than they are. Such transfers clearly tend to enhance equality. Reducing such voluntary transfers could well lead to more inequality than otherwise would have been the case.

- Suppose that parents whose earnings capacities are much higher than average produce children whose earnings capacities are closer to the average level. (This phenomenon is known as *regression toward the mean*.) Well-off parents, who wish to compensate their children for their lesser earnings capacity by making bequests, tend to decrease inequality *across* generations. Conversely, reducing such transfers increases intergenerational inequality.

From a theoretical point of view, the effect of estate taxation on inequality is ambiguous. Ultimately, of course, the important question is whether the equality-increasing or equality-decreasing effect dominates empirically. While Stiglitz's observations may be correct theoretically, from an empirical point of view they may not be very important. In any case, they remind us that there are many facets to the problem.

Provisions

Note at the outset that gift taxation and estate taxation are inextricably bound. Suppose that estates are taxed and gifts are not. If Lear desires to pass his wealth on to his daughters and knows that it will be taxed at his death, then he can avoid tax by making the transfer as a gift *inter vivos*. Similar opportunities would arise if there were a gift tax but no estate tax. Since 1976, the gift and estate taxes in the United States have been integrated and are officially referred to as the **unified transfer tax.**

The unified transfer tax is similar in basic structure to the personal income tax. After the gross estate is calculated, various deductions and exemptions are subtracted, leaving the taxable estate. The tax liability is determined by applying a progressive rate schedule to the taxable estate.

Computing the taxable base.   The **gross estate** consists of all property owned by the decedent at the time of death. This includes real property, stocks, bonds, and insurance policies. It also includes gifts made during the decedent's lifetime. To find the **taxable estate,** deductions are allowed for funeral expenses, costs of settling the estate (lawyers' fees), and any outstanding debts of the estate. Gifts to charity are deductible without limit.

The following deductions are available under legislation passed in 1981.[28]

---

[28] For further details, see *Economic Recovery Tax Act of 1981* [1981].

1. Each estate is allowed a lifetime exemption of $600,000. No federal estate tax is levied on estates that are less than the lifetime exemption.

2. All qualified transfers to spouses—by gift or bequest—are deductible in arriving at the taxable base.[29] Thus, the estate of a multimillionairess who leaves $600,000 to her children and the rest to her husband bears no tax liability.

3. Each individual is qualified for an annual gift exclusion of $10,000 per recipient. (The recipient need not be a relative.) Consider a family with three children. Each year Mom can give $10,000 to each child, as can Dad. Together, then, the couple can give their three children annually $60,000 tax-free. Interestingly, there is some evidence that wealthy people do not fully exploit the tax advantages of distributing wealth before death. [See Pechman, 1977a, p. 231.] Why? There is a story about a rich man who gave each of his children $1 million when they reached the age of 21. When asked why he did so, the millionaire explained that he wanted his children to be able to tell him to "go to hell"—to have total financial independence. It appears that most people would just as soon *not* have their children be able to tell them to go to hell. These people therefore keep control of their wealth as long as possible, even at the cost of a larger-than-necessary tax liability.

Rate structure. The taxable base is subject to marginal rates ranging from 18 percent (on the first $10,000) to 55 percent (for amounts over $3 million). Whether or not these rates are efficient in the sense of optimal tax theory is hard to say. As usual, the answer depends on the responsiveness of behavior to changes in the tax rate. But as indicated earlier, little is known about how economic decisions are affected by estate and gift taxes.

Special problems. A number of difficulties arise in the administration of an estate and gift tax.

Jointly held property. Suppose a husband and wife own property together. For purposes of estate taxation, should this be considered one estate or two? We discussed the philosophical problems concerning whether the family or the individual should be the unit of taxation in Chapter 16 under "Choice of Unit," and there is no need to do so again

---

[29] Special rules apply to **terminable interests,** which are transfers that can be revoked under specified conditions. For example, a woman might leave her husband certain property on the condition that he not remarry.

here. Under current federal law, one half of the value of jointly held property is now included in the gross estate of the first spouse to die, regardless of the relative extent to which the spouses contributed to the accumulation of the property.[30]

Closely held businesses.   Suppose Lear wants to bequeath his business, which is the only asset he owns, to his daughters. Because there is no cash in Lear's estate, it may happen that the daughters have to sell the business to pay the estate tax due. To reduce the likelihood of such an event, the law allows the estate taxes on closely held businesses to be paid off over as long as 15 years, at favorable rates of interest. Moreover, in computing the gross estate, the fair market value of family farms can be reduced by $750,000. Such provisions reflect a value judgment that there is something socially desirable per se in having the same family control a given business for several generations.

Avoidance strategies.   An implicit goal of the estate tax is to tax wealth at least once a generation. In the past, it was relatively straightforward for an individual to arrange his estate so that one or more generations of his descendants would avoid the tax. The vehicle for such **generation skipping** was a **trust.** This is an arrangement whereby a person or institution known as a **trustee** holds legal title to assets with the obligation to use them for the benefit of another party. The trustee can be a relative, friend, attorney, or bank.

Consider the following simple version of how trusts might be used to avoid estate tax. Lear puts his estate into trust, at which time an estate tax is paid. He assigns his daughters the income from the trust for as long as they live. Although the daughters receive income from the trust, legally they do not own the assets. When the trust terminates, the property is legally transferred to some other parties, say Lear's grandchildren.[31] Tax is not due until the grandchildren transfer the property. Because the property was never legally transferred to the daughters, they never incurred an estate tax liability. Hence, their generation was skipped.

In 1976, the laws on the tax treatment of trusts were tightened to make generation skipping more difficult. Nevertheless, generation skipping is still possible, as are other legal maneuvers for avoiding estate taxation. One relatively simple and popular technique described by George Cooper [1979] involves granting one's heirs shares of stock in a closely held corporation. Specifically, suppose that Mickey incorporates his business, and owns all the stock. During his lifetime, Mickey makes

---

[30] More precisely, this rule holds for joint property owned with **right of survivorship,** meaning that on the death of one owner, the property automatically passes to the other owner.

[31] It might be asked why the property would not be kept in trust forever. There are laws that prohibit this and make the effective life of most trusts less than 100 years.

gifts of a substantial portion of the stock—but less than half—to his heirs, Morty and Ferdy. If the transfers take place relatively early in the life of the business, the shares are not worth very much, so that little if any gift tax liability is incurred. Because Mickey owns the majority of the firm's stock, he stays in charge of the company, and effectively controls the value of the transferred shares.[32] If Mickey's firm prospers, by the time he dies, Morty and Ferdy's shares may be extremely valuable. Mickey has thus managed to transfer substantial wealth to his heirs, and keep the transfer outside the purview of the gift and estate tax. What about the shares that Mickey still owns at death? Other more complicated techniques are available to shelter them; see Cooper [1979] for details.

In short, a variety of methods are available for making intergenerational transfers of wealth without bearing any taxes and without losing effective control of the property during your life. We must add, of course, that even in cases where the tax generates no revenues, it may create excess burdens and/or compliance costs for people who modify their behavior to avoid it.

State taxes.   In addition to the federal estate and gift tax, wealth transfers at death are also taxed by most states. Many states levy **inheritance taxes.** While estate taxes are imposed on the wealth itself, inheritance taxes are levied on the individual receiving the wealth. The inheritance tax schedule faced by a recipient depends on his or her relationship to the decedent. In general (but not in all states), a spouse, child, or parent faces lower rates than a brother or sister, who, in turn, has a lower rate than a nonrelative. Complications in estate taxation arise when a decedent's wealth is held in more than one state. In some states, the estates of nonresidents are taxed according to the amount of their property located in the state.

Given that the rates tend to vary considerably across states, a natural question is whether elderly citizens make their residential decisions in such a way as to lower the tax burden on their bequests. It is sometimes suggested that the choice of Florida as a retirement place for those from the Northeast is influenced by such considerations. Obviously, many factors determine locational decisions, and the relative importance of differential estate taxation is not known.

Reforming Estate and Gift Taxes

For those who wish to expand the role of estate and gift taxes, the most straightforward approach would be to lower the lifetime exemption. However, if the estate tax is ever to play an important part in the revenue system, methods for dealing with avoidance via trusts and other such instruments must be devised.

---

[32] One might want to maintain control of the property to manipulate the behavior of one's heirs. See Douglas Bernheim, Andrei Shleifer, and Lawrence Summers [1985].

A popular reform among many tax theorists is integrating the estate- and gift-tax system into the personal income tax. Gifts and inheritances would be taxed as income to the recipients. As noted earlier, such receipts are income, and according to conventional notions, should therefore be included in Adjusted Gross Income. To account for the fact that income in this form tends to be "lumpy," some form of averaging would have to be devised.

There is, however, popular resistance to taxing gifts and inheritances as ordinary income. A somewhat different method of changing the focus of estate and gift taxation from the donor to the recipient has been suggested. Specifically, under an **accessions tax,** each individual would be taxed on total lifetime acquisitions from inheritances and gifts. The rate schedule could be made progressive and include an exemption, if so desired. The attraction of such a scheme is that it relates tax liabilities to the recipient's ability to pay rather than to the estate. Administrative difficulties would arise from the need for taxpayers to keep records of all sizable gifts and estates. But if it is ever decided to put more of an emphasis on taxing wealth transfers, an accessions tax deserves serious consideration.

Summary

- Sales taxes may be levied per unit or as a percentage of purchase value (ad valorem), on all (general sales tax) or specific (excise tax) purchases. General sales and excise taxes are important revenue sources at the state and local levels.

- A major attraction of sales taxes is that they are relatively easy to administer. Some sales taxes can be justified as correctives for externalities or as substitutes for user fees.

- Sales taxes are typically viewed as regressive. However, this is based on calculations involving annual rather than lifetime income. This view also assumes that the incidence of the tax lies with the purchaser.

- The value-added tax (VAT) is quite popular in Europe, but is not used in the United States. The VAT is levied on the difference between sales revenue and cost of purchased commodity inputs. Different treatments of input costs lead to a consumption-type, net income-type, or gross income-type VAT.

- The base of a personal consumption tax is found by subtracting additions to wealth from income.

- Proponents of the personal consumption tax argue that it eliminates double taxation of interest income, promotes lifetime equity, taxes individuals on the basis of the amount of economic resources they use up, may be adjusted to achieve any desired level of progressiveness, and is administratively superior to an income tax.

- Opponents of the personal consumption tax point out difficult transition problems, argue that income better measures ability to pay, feel that it is administratively burdensome, and argue that in the absence of appropriate taxes on gifts and bequests, it would lead to excessive concentration of wealth.

- Wealth taxes are assessed on a tax base that is a stock of assets instead of a flow such as income or sales.

- Wealth taxes have been rationalized as a way to correct the income tax for unrealized capital gains, as a way to reduce the concentration of wealth, and as compensation for benefits received by wealth holders. Some also argue that wealth by itself is a good index of ability to pay and should, therefore, be subject to tax.

- Estate and gift taxes are levied on the value of wealth transfers, either from a decedent or from another living individual. Neither is a major revenue source at any level. There is little empirical evidence on the incentive effects or incidence of estate and gift taxes.

- Major proposals for reform of estate and gift taxes are either to incorporate these transfers in the personal income tax system or to institute an accessions tax (a tax based on total lifetime gifts and bequests received).

Discussion Questions

1. "Because the tax base includes the purchase of necessities, both general sales taxes and personal consumption taxes are regressive." Discuss.

2. "Movement from income to consumption taxation would increase personal saving, and hence promote economic efficiency." Comment.

3. "When Batman makes a gift to Robin, the gift is not included in Robin's taxable income. However, this is not a flaw in the income tax system because the gift is not deductible from Batman's income." Comment. Your answer should include a discussion of whether gift giving reduces the donor's "ability to pay."

4. "People have a right to leave bequests, but almost no one has a right to receive them. Unless children worked in a family business, bequests seem to be the ultimate in unearned income. Thus, there is an ethical dilemma." Do you agree? What are the implications for estate taxation?

Selected References

Aaron, Henry J., and Harvey Galper. *Assessing Tax Reform*. Washington, D.C.: Brookings Institution, 1985, Chap. 4 (The Cash Flow Income Tax) and Chap. 5 (Sales Taxes).

Cooper, George. *A Voluntary Tax? New Perspectives on Sophisticated Estate Tax Avoidance*. Washington, D.C.: Brookings Institution, 1979.

Poterba, James M. "Is the Gasoline Tax Regressive?" Cambridge, Mass.: National Bureau of Economic Research, Working Paper 3578, 1991.

Tait, Alan A. *Value Added Tax—International Practice and Problems*. Washington, D.C.: International Monetary Fund, 1988.

Multigovernment Public Finance

For many purposes it is useful to think of public finance decisions as being made by a single government. In the United States, however, an astounding number of entities have the power to tax and spend. As of the late 1980s, there were more than 83,000 governmental jurisdictions: 1 federal, 50 state, 3,042 county, 19,205 municipality, 16,691 township, 14,741 school district, and 29,487 special district.[1] The interaction of state, local, and federal governments plays a crucial role in the U.S. fiscal system. Thus, in Chapter 21 we examine the public finance issues that arise in federal systems.

---

[1] From *Facts and Figures on Government Finance* [1990, p. 4]. Special districts generally perform a single function or oversee some specific area of responsibility.

CHAPTER 21

Public Finance in a Federal System

A community of a higher order should not interfere in the internal life of a community of a lower order, . . . but rather should support it in case of need and help to coordinate its activity with the activities of the rest of society, always with a view to the common good.

JOHN PAUL II

In the summer of 1982, the city of Glen Cove, Long Island, banned Soviet diplomats who lived there from using its tennis courts and other recreational facilities. The stated reason for the ban was the fact that the property inhabited by the Soviets was exempt from local property taxes.[1] Glen Cove's action caused an international furor, and the State Department requested that the city desist from meddling in foreign affairs. But the mayor responded, ''Unless the State Department wants to pay up all the property taxes the Soviets have never had to pay like other Glen Cove residents, then the Russians will have to stay off the tennis courts.''

This incident highlights three areas that surround the operation of the U.S. system of public finance.

- Subfederal units of government function with considerable autonomy. Attempts from the outside to change their behavior are likely to be met with active or passive resistance. Is decentralized decision making desirable?

[1] Note, however, that the ban originated after federal officials said that the Soviets had installed eavesdropping equipment in their mansion. The controversy was finally settled in 1984, when the Soviets agreed to make some payment for city services.

- Different types of public services are customarily provided by various levels of government. The reason that the Glen Cove incident received so much attention—and created such amusement (diplomats excepted)—was the incongruity of a local level of government in effect making foreign policy. International relations "belong" to the central government. On the other hand, decisions on the quantity and type of recreational facilities "belong" to localities. How should different functions be allocated to various levels of government?
- The story illustrates the crucial role of property taxes in the finance of U.S. local governments: no property taxes, no tennis. Are locally raised taxes a good way for the services provided by municipalities to be financed? Or should the money come from the state and federal governments?

These are important issues in the United States where, as noted earlier, there are a multitude of governmental jurisdictions. The appropriate division of power among them has been a matter of controversy since the founding of the nation. This chapter examines the normative and positive aspects of public finance in a federal system. We devote special attention to the fiscal issues that currently confront localities.

| **Background** | Wallace Oates [1972, p. 17] provides a useful economic definition of **federal government:** |

> A public sector with both centralized and decentralized levels of decision making in which choices made at each level concerning the provision of public services are determined largely by the demands for those services of the residents of (and perhaps others who carry on activities in) the respective jurisdictions.

We can imagine situations in which a single government controls all aspects of economic activity, or the opposite extreme in which each community operates with total autonomy. It is best, however, to think of the extent of federalism as a continuum rather than an either-or proposition. Between the polar cases, one system is characterized as being more centralized than another when more of its decision-making powers are in the hands of authorities with a larger jurisdiction.

When is one system more centralized than another? The most common measure is the **centralization ratio,** the proportion of total direct government expenditures made by the central government. ("Direct" government expenditure comprises all expenditure except transfers made to other governmental units.) The centralization ratio is by no means a foolproof indicator. Suppose that states make expenditures for highways, but the money comes in the form of grants from the federal government.

Table 21.1   **Distribution of all U.S. government expenditure by level of government, 1900–1988**

	Federal	State	Local
1900	34.1%	8.2%	57.7%
1910	30.1	9.0	60.9
1920	39.7	9.8	50.5
1930	32.5	16.3	51.2
1938	45.5	16.2	38.3
1950	59.3	15.2	26.5
1960	57.6	13.8	28.6
1971	48.4	18.6	33.0
1980	54.9	18.1	27.0
1988	57.1	17.4	25.6

SOURCE: Werner Pommerehne, "Quantitative Aspects of Federalism: A Study of Six Countries," in *The Political Economy of Fiscal Federalism,* ed. W. Oates (Lexington, Mass.: D.C. Heath, 1977), p. 311, except for 1980 figures, which are computed from U.S. Bureau of the Census, *Statistical Abstract of the United States: 1982–83* (Washington, D.C.: U.S. Government Printing Office, 1982), p. 274, and 1988 figures, from Advisory Commission on Intergovernmental Relations, *Significant Features of Fiscal Federalism* 2, August 1990, p. 67.

Congress decides that no state will receive highway grants unless it mandates a 55-mile-per-hour speed limit. Virtually every state complies.[2] Who is really in charge? The point is that if local and state government spending behavior is constrained by the central government, the centralization ratio underestimates the true extent of centralization in the system. Conversely, if states and localities effectively lobby the federal government to achieve their own ends, the centralization ratio may overestimate the degree of decentralized economic power. In any case, centralization ratios vary widely across nations. In France it is 71 percent, in Canada 40 percent, and in the United States 57 percent.[3]

Table 21.1 shows how the distribution of United States government expenditure by level of government has been changing over time. The long-run trend has been for the centralization ratio to increase, although the movement upward has not been steady.

Figure 21.1 shows the division of public spending by level of government for various government functions. The figures indicate that a number of activities having an important impact on the quality of life are in the hands of state and local governments. In the context of the current debate

---

[2] In 1986 the Department of Transportation moved against Arizona and Vermont for not enforcing the speed limit. In 1987, the Congress gave states the option of increasing speed limits on some roads up to 65 miles per hour.

[3] Computed from Organization for Economic Cooperation and Development [1990]; except see Table 21.1 for the United States.

Figure 21.1
Percentage of
expenditures by
selected functions
and levels of
government (fiscal
year 1988)

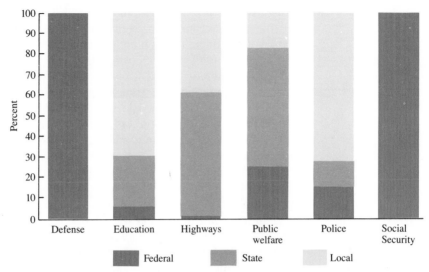

SOURCE: Computed from U.S. Department of Commerce, Bureau of the Census, *Government Finances in 1987–88* (Washington, D.C.: U.S. Government Printing Office, 1990), pp. 2, 14.

over who should pay for welfare, it is noteworthy that more than 75 percent of public welfare expenditures are made by state and local governments. This figure gives a somewhat exaggerated view of the importance of decentralized redistribution for two reasons: (1) most of the financing (about three quarters) of these expenditures is done by the federal government; and (2) much of the spending is subject to federal standards on eligibility and benefit levels.[4] Aid to Families with Dependent Children is an example of a program with extensive federal guidelines, despite the fact that states have some autonomy in setting benefit levels and standards.

Be this as it may, we are left with a critical question: Is the division of powers reflected in Figure 21.1 sensible? Before we can answer this, we need to understand the special features associated with local government.

**Community
Formation**

To understand the appropriate fiscal roles for local jurisdictions, we consider why communities are formed in the first place. In this context, it is useful to think of a community as a **club**—a voluntary association of people who band together to share some kind of benefit. This section develops a theory of clubs and uses that theory to explain how the size of a community and its provision of public goods are determined.[5]

---

[4] See Helen Ladd and Fred Doolittle [1982] for further details.

[5] Most club models are based on the work of James Buchanan [1965]. For a survey of this area, see Todd Sandler and John Tschirhart [1980].

Consider a group of people who wish to band together to purchase land for a public park. For simplicity, assume that all members of the group have identical utility functions and that they intend to share equally the use of the park and its costs. The "community" can costlessly exclude all nonmembers, and it operates with no transaction costs. Given the assumption of identical tastes, we need consider only the desires of a representative member. Two decisions must be made: how large a park to acquire and how many members to have in the community.

Assuming that it wants to maximize the welfare of its citizens, how does the community make these decisions? Consider first the relationship between the total cost per member and the number of members, *given* that a certain size park is selected. Clearly, the larger the community, the more people there are to shoulder the expense of the park, and the smaller the required contribution per member. But if the per capita cost continually decreases with membership size, why not simply invite an infinite number of people to join? The problem is that as more people join the community, the public park becomes congested. The marginal congestion cost measures the dollar cost of the incremental congestion created by each new member. We assume that marginal congestion cost increases with the number of members. *The community should expand its membership until the marginal decrease in the membership fee just equals the per-person marginal increase in congestion costs.*

Now turn to the flip side of the problem: for any given number of members in the community, how big should the park be? A bigger park yields greater benefits, although like most goods, we assume it is subject to diminishing marginal utility. The per-member marginal cost of increased park acreage is just the price of the extra land divided by the number of members sharing its cost. *Acreage should be increased to the point where each member's marginal benefit just equals the per-member marginal cost.*

We can now put together these two pieces of the picture to describe an optimal community or club. The optimal community is one in which the number of members and the level of services simultaneously satisfy the condition that the marginal cost equal the corresponding marginal benefit. Although this club model is very simple, it highlights the crucial aspects of the community-formation process. Specifically, it suggests how community size depends on the type of public goods the people want to consume, the extent to which these goods are subject to crowding, and the costs of obtaining them, among other things. However, viewing communities as clubs leaves unanswered several important questions that are relevant for understanding local public finance:

1. How are the public services to be financed? A country club can charge a membership fee, but a community normally levies taxes to pay for public goods.

2. A club can exclude nonmembers and so eliminate the free rider problem. How can communities achieve this end?

3. When people throughout the country organize themselves into many different clubs (communities), will the overall allocation of public goods prove to be equitable and efficient?

These questions are taken up in the next section.

The Tiebout Model

"Love it or leave it." When people who oppose U.S. federal government policy are given this advice, it is generally about as constructive as telling them to "drop dead." Only in extreme cases do we expect people to leave their country because of government policy.[6] Because of the large pecuniary and psychic costs of emigrating, a more realistic option is to stay home and try to change the policy. On the other hand, most citizens are not as strongly attached to their local communities. If you dislike the policies being followed in Skokie, Illinois, the easiest thing to do may be to move a few miles away to Evanston. This section discusses the relationship between intercommunity mobility, voluntary community formation, and the efficient provision of public goods.

Chapter 5 examined the idea that markets generally fail to provide public goods efficiently. The root of the problem is that the market does not force individuals to reveal their true preferences for public goods. Everyone has an incentive to be a free rider. The usual conclusion is that some kind of government intervention is required.

In an important article, Charles Tiebout [1956] (rhymes with "me too") argued that the ability of individuals to move among jurisdictions produces a market-like solution to the local public goods problem. As suggested in the cartoon, individuals vote with their feet and locate in the community that offers the bundle of public services and taxes they like best. Much as Jones satisfies her desire for private goods by purchasing them on the market, she satisfies her desire for public goods by the appropriate selection of a community in which to live, and pays taxes for the services. In equilibrium, people distribute themselves across communities on the basis of their demands for public services. Each individual receives his or her desired level of public services and cannot be made better off by moving (or else the individual would). Hence, the equilibrium is Pareto efficient, and there is no market failure. Government action is not required to achieve efficiency.

---

[6] For example, in the 1960s a number of young men left the country to evade military service in Vietnam.

Drawing by Lorenz; ©
1985 The New Yorker
Magazine, Inc.

More Rigorous Statement

Tiebout's provocative assertion that a quasi-market process can solve the public goods problem has stimulated a large amount of research.[7] Much of that research has been directed toward finding a precise set of sufficient conditions under which the ability of citizens to vote with their feet leads to efficient public goods provision. Some of the conditions are as follows:[8]

1. No externalities arise from local government behavior. As noted later, to the extent there are spillover effects between communities, the allocation of resources is inefficient.
2. Individuals are completely mobile. Each person can travel cost-lessly to a jurisdiction with a bundle of public services that is best for him. The location of an individual's place of employment puts no restriction on where he resides and does not affect his income.
3. People have perfect information with respect to the public services they receive in each community and the taxes they have to pay.
4. There are enough different communities so that each individual can find one with public services meeting her demands.
5. The cost per unit of public services is constant, which implies that if the quantity of public services doubles, the total cost also doubles. In addition, the technology of public service provision

---

[7] See Peter Mieszkowski and George Zodrow [1989].

[8] Bruce Hamilton [1975a] and Truman Bewley [1981] provide more detail. Not all of these conditions were included in Tiebout's original article.

is such that if the number of residents is doubled, the quantity of the public service provided must be doubled. To see why these conditions are required for a Tiebout equilibrium to be efficient, imagine instead that the cost per unit of public services fell as the scale of provision increased. In that case, there would be scale economies of which independently operating communities might fail to take advantage.

This assumption makes the public service essentially a publicly provided private good. "Pure" public goods (such as national defense) do not satisfy this assumption. However, many local public services such as education and garbage collection appear to fit this description to a reasonable extent.

6. Public services are financed by a proportional property tax. The tax rate can vary across communities.[9]

7. Communities can enact **exclusionary zoning laws**—statutes that prohibit certain uses of land. Specifically, they can require that all houses be of some minimum size. To see why this assumption is crucial, recall that in Tiebout equilibrium, communities are segregated on the basis of their members' demands for public goods. To the extent that income is positively correlated with the demand for public services, community segregation by income results. In high-income communities, the *level* of property values tends to be high, and, hence, the community can finance a given amount of public spending with a relatively low property tax *rate*. In the absence of exclusionary zoning, low-income families have an incentive to move into rich communities and build relatively small houses. Because of the low tax rate, low-income families have relatively small tax liabilities, but nevertheless enjoy the high level of public service provision. As more low-income families get the idea and move in, the tax base per family in the community falls perceptibly. Tax rates must be increased to finance the expanded level of public services required to serve the increased population.

Since we assume perfect mobility, there is no reason for the rich to put up with this. They can just move to another community. But what stops the poor from following them? In the absence of constraints on mobility, nothing. Clearly, it is possible for a game of musical suburbs to develop in a Tiebout model. Exclusionary zoning is a way of preventing this phenomenon and thus maintaining a stable Pareto efficient equilibrium.

---

[9] Tiebout [1956] assumed finance by head taxes. The more realistic assumption of property taxation is from Hamilton [1975b].

Tiebout and the Real World

Exactly meeting the list of conditions required for the Tiebout model is unlikely. People are not perfectly mobile; there are probably not enough communities so that each family can find one with a bundle of services that suits it perfectly, and so on. Moreover, contrary to the model's implication, we observe many communities within which there are massive income differences and, hence, presumably different desired levels of public service provision. Just consider any major city.

However, we should not dismiss the Tiebout mechanism too hastily. There is a lot of mobility in the American economy. A persistent pattern is that in any given year, about 17 percent of Americans have different residences than they had the year before [U.S. Bureau of the Census, 1985, p. 15]. Moreover, within most metropolitan areas, there is a wide range of choice with respect to type of community. As Michelle White [1975, p. 52] notes, "The salient fact about location choice in a large American metropolis is that households have a wide choice of places to live. Within a 20-mile radius they generally have a choice of one or more central cities and up to several hundred suburbs." Certainly, casual observation suggests that across suburbs there is considerable residential segregation by income, and that exclusionary zoning is practiced widely. In addition, it is not hard to find anecdotal evidence of classic Tiebout behavior:

> Police departments in California are in a bind: Crime is increasing, but after Proposition 13 took its toll of local property taxes, they are running out of money.[10] So some communities are turning to the 'police tax.'
>
> State law allows two-thirds of the voters of any community to override the limits of Proposition 13 and pass a supplemental assessment for police services. In affluent suburban communities, this works well. "We all gained huge savings as homeowners from Proposition 13," explains a member of the Atherton City Council. So paying up to $200 a year to help the police protect expensive homes from increasingly active burglars seems a good investment.
>
> But in larger, poorer cities, the idea did not fare well. Los Angeles and Oakland voters turned down police taxes. With lower property values, they have gained less from Proposition 13, and didn't consider a new tax so affordable. They also have less faith in police, and don't see how extra money would help.
>
> Despite the attention that it receives from politicians and the media, the fear of crime is evidently not absolute; it's just another part of life, factored in with all the others. ["Relative Crime," *New York Times,* June 22, 1981]

It appears that communities' decisions with respect to public good provision sometimes can be explained on the basis of the tastes and incomes of their members.

---

[10] Proposition 13 is discussed later.

There have been several formal empirical tests of the Tiebout hypothesis. One type of study looks at whether the values of local public services and taxes are capitalized into local property values. The idea is that if people move in response to local packages of taxes and public services, differences in these packages should be reflected in property values.[11] A community with better public services should have higher property values, other things (including taxes) being the same. These capitalization studies are discussed later in this chapter in the context of property taxation. As noted there, capitalization does appear to be a widespread phenomenon.

Another interesting test was done by Edward Gramlich and Daniel Rubinfeld [1982]. They analyzed responses to survey questions in which individuals were asked about their desired levels of local public expenditures. If the Tiebout mechanism is operative, we would expect to find substantial homogeneity of demands within suburbs located near many other communities, because, in such a setting, the model suggests that those who are dissatisfied with current spending levels simply move elsewhere. On the other hand, in areas where there are not a lot of other communities nearby, it is less easy to exit if you are not happy. In such areas, people with very different demands for public goods may be lumped together in a single community. Gramlich and Rubinfeld found that compared to areas where there is not much scope for choice, there are indeed relatively small differences in tastes for public goods within communities located in large metropolitan areas.

Gramlich and Rubinfeld's results must be regarded with caution because they are based on survey questions concerning the demand for public services. What people *say* they want is not necessarily what they really want. Nevertheless, the study suggests that, at least in some settings, the Tiebout model is a good depiction of reality.

Now that we have an idea of how to characterize local governments, we return to our earlier question. What is the optimal allocation of economic responsibilities among levels of government in a federal system?

Optimal Federalism

The goal of the theory of optimal federalism is to determine the proper division of activities among the levels of government. Let us briefly consider macroeconomic functions. There is virtually universal agreement that spending and taxing decisions intended to affect the levels of unemployment and inflation should be made by the central government. No state or local government is large enough to affect the overall level of economic activity. It would not make sense, for example, for each locality

---

[11] Actually, there are some circumstances under which the Tiebout hypothesis does not imply that capitalization necessarily will occur. See Rubinfeld [1987].

to issue its own money supply and pursue an independent monetary policy.[12] Now, some macroeconomists have suggested that it may not be possible for even a central government to pursue effective policies to counter the business cycle. This issue is beyond the scope of this text. (See Gregory Mankiw [1990] for a discussion.) We merely note that to the extent a stabilization policy is feasible and desirable, it should be done at the national level.

With respect to the microeconomic activities of enhancing economic efficiency and modifying the income distribution, there is considerably more controversy. Posed within the framework of welfare economics, the question is whether a centralized or decentralized system is more likely to maximize social welfare. For simplicity, most of our discussion assumes just two levels of government, "central" and "local." No important insights are lost with this assumption.

Disadvantages of a Decentralized System

Consider a country composed of a group of small communities. Each community government makes decisions to maximize a social welfare function depending only on the utilities of its members—outsiders do not count.[13] How do the results compare to those that would emerge if a national social welfare function that took into account all citizens' utilities were maximized? We consider efficiency and then equity issues.

Efficiency issues.   There are several reasons why a system of centralized governments might lead to an inefficient allocation of resources.

Externalities.   We define a public good with benefits that accrue only to members of a particular community as a **local public good.** For example, the public library in Idaho Falls has little effect on the welfare of people in Baton Rouge. However, in many situations, local public goods (or publicly provided private goods) purchased by one community may affect the utility levels of people in other communities. If one town provides good public education for its young people and some of them eventually emigrate, then members of other communities may benefit from having a better-educated work force. Or if one town's sewage-treatment plant pollutes a river that passes by other communities downstream, people in the downstream communities are made worse off. In short, communities impose externalities (both positive and negative) on each other. If each community cares only about its own members, these externalities are overlooked. Hence, according to the standard argument (see Chapter 6), an inefficient allocation of resources results.

---

[12] Under the Articles of the Confederation, states did issue their own monies.

[13] We ignore for now the questions of how the social welfare function is determined and whether the people who run the government actually try to maximize it. (See Chapters 4 and 7.)

Scale economies in provision of public goods.   For certain public services, the cost per person may fall as the number of users increases. If several communities coordinated their use of such services, the members of all participating communities could be made better off because each person would need to pay less for the service. Thus, for example, it might make sense for neighboring communities to run their police departments jointly and so avoid the costs of acquiring duplicates of certain equipment. Communities that operate with complete independence lose such opportunities for cost savings.

Of course, various activities are subject to different scale economies. The optimal scale for the provision of library services might differ from that for fire protection. And both surely differ from the optimal scale for national defense. This observation, incidentally, helps rationalize a system of overlapping jurisdictions—each jurisdiction can handle those services with scale economies that are appropriate for the jurisdiction's size.

On the other hand, there are ways other than consolidation that a community could take advantage of scale economies. It might contract out to other governments or to the private sector for the provision of certain public goods and services. Such practices are quite common, for example, in parts of California. These arrangements weaken the link between the jurisdiction's decisions of how much of the good to consume and how much to produce.

Inefficient tax systems.   Roughly speaking, efficient taxation requires that inelastically demanded or supplied goods be taxed at relatively high rates and vice versa.[14] Suppose that the supply of capital to the entire country is fixed, but capital is highly mobile between communities. Each community realizes that if it levies a substantial tax on capital, the capital will simply move elsewhere, thus making the community worse off. In such a situation, a rational community taxes capital very lightly, if at all. In contrast, from a national point of view, efficiency requires a very high tax on capital, because it is inelastic in total supply.

In reality, of course, the total capital stock is not fixed in supply. Nor is it known just how responsive firms' locational decisions are to differences in local tax rates. (See White [1986].) However, the basic point remains: taxes levied by decentralized communities are unlikely to be efficient from a national point of view. Instead, communities are likely to select taxes on the basis of whether they can be exported to outsiders. For example, if a community has the only coal mine in the country, there is a reasonable chance that the incidence of a locally imposed tax on coal will fall largely on coal users outside the community.[15] A coal tax would be a

---

[14] See Chapter 15.

[15] As usual, a precise answer to the incidence question requires information on market structure, elasticity of demand, and the structure of costs. See Chapter 13.

good idea from the community's point of view, but not necessarily from the viewpoint of the nation.[16] Donald Phares [1980] estimated that about 17 percent of state taxes are exported to residents of other states, a substantial proportion.

An important implication of tax shifting is that communities may purchase local public goods in inefficiently large amounts. Efficiency requires that local public goods be purchased up to the point where their marginal social benefit equals marginal social cost. If communities can shift some of the burden to other jurisdictions, the community's perceived marginal cost is less than marginal social cost. This induces them to purchase local public goods with marginal social benefit equal to the perceived marginal cost, but less than marginal social cost. The result is an inefficiently large amount of local public goods.

Scale economies in tax collection.   Individual communities may not be able to take advantage of scale economies in the collection of taxes. Each community has to devote resources to tax administration, and savings may be obtained by having a joint taxing authority. Why not split the costs of a single computer to keep track of tax returns, rather than have each community purchase its own? Of course, some of these economies might be achieved just by cooperation between the jurisdictions, without actual consolidation taking place. In some states, for example, taxes levied by cities are collected by state revenue departments.

Equity issues.   In a utilitarian philosophical framework, the maximization of social welfare may require income transfers to the poor. Suppose that a particular community adopts an expenditure-tax pattern favorable to its low-income members. If there are no barriers to movement between communities, we expect an in-migration of the poor from the rest of the country. As the poor population increases, so does the cost of the redistributive fiscal policy. At the same time, the town's upper-income people may decide to exit. Why should they pay high taxes for the poor when they can move to another community where the expenditure pattern is to their own benefit? Thus, the demands on the community's tax base increase while its size decreases. Eventually the redistributive program has to be abandoned.

This argument relies heavily on the notion that people's decisions to locate in a given community are influenced by the available tax-welfare package. There is some anecdotal support for this proposition. In 1985, for example, so many unemployed people traveled to Hennepin County, Minnesota, to take advantage of its generous welfare programs that

---

[16] Coal-producing states such as Montana have indeed tried to export their tax burdens to the rest of the country.

county officials instituted a policy of giving recent arrivals one-way bus tickets back home.[17] Unfortunately, econometric evidence on the location decisions of the poor is scanty [Blank, 1985]. Nevertheless, on the basis of casual observation, most economists would argue that substantial income redistribution cannot be carried out by decentralized communities.

Advantages of a Decentralized System

Tailoring outputs to local tastes.   Some people want expensive computers used in the education of their children; others believe that this is unnecessary. Some people enjoy parks; others do not. A centralized government tends to provide the same level of public services throughout the country, regardless of the fact that people's tastes differ. As de Tocqueville observed, "In great centralized nations the legislator is obliged to give a character of uniformity to the laws, which does not always suit the diversity of customs and of districts" [Oates, 1972, p. 31]. Clearly it is inefficient to provide individuals with more or less of a public good than they desire if the quantity they receive can be more closely tailored to their preferences. It is often argued that under a decentralized system, individuals with similar tastes for public goods group together, so that communities provide the types and quantities of public goods desired by their inhabitants. (Remember the "club" view of communities.)

A closely related notion is that local government's greater proximity to the people makes it more responsive to citizens' preferences than central government.[18] This is especially likely to be the case in a large country where the costs of obtaining and processing information on everybody's tastes are substantial. As a political stance, this view has always been influential in the United States. (Just think about the issue of states' rights.) We examine it from an economic perspective more carefully later.

In the same way, economic regulations enacted at the national level may not make sense in every community. Consider the Fair Labor Standards Act, which sets national rules for wages, hours, and working conditions. Certain provisions of the act prohibit *industrial homework*—doing factory work in the home. The idea is to eliminate sweatshop conditions that were once common in big cities and that might become a problem again in industrial areas. But in 1983, a federal judge ruled that the act also applied to Vermont farmers who knit ski caps at home to supplement their incomes. The ruling created a furor: "Tell them to do their work down in Washington and leave us alone, and let us do our work up here," said one 63-year-old Vermonter [Clendinen, 1983, p. 8]. The story shows how a

---

[17] Legal challenges eventually stopped the program.

[18] However, if one believes that the preferences of members of some communities are wrong, this advantage turns into a disadvantage. For example, a community might decide to legalize slavery. Under what circumstances should the central government be able to overrule state and local governments? This is a fundamental issue beyond our scope.

regulation that is sensible in some areas might not be in others. Similarly, the laws desired by California to govern private sexual behavior need not suit Georgians. Why not let each state decide for itself, rather than impose uniformity? Indeed, it may not even be optimal to provide a uniform level of a publicly provided good to each *neighborhood* within the same *city*. For example, several years ago some residents of the crime-ridden South Central area of Los Angeles asked for a special vote to raise their own property taxes to finance more police protection for their neighborhoods.

Fostering intergovernment competition.   Many theories of government behavior focus on the fact that those who run the governments may lack incentives to produce at minimum feasible cost (see Chapter 7). Managers of private firms who fail to minimize costs are eventually driven out of business. In contrast, government managers can continue to muddle along. However, if citizens can choose among communities, then substantial mismanagement may cause citizens simply to choose to live elsewhere. This threat may create incentives for government managers to produce more efficiently and be more responsive to the desires of citizens.

Experimentation and innovation in locally provided goods and services.
For many policy questions, no one is certain what the right answer is, or even whether there is a single solution that is best in all situations. One way to find out is to let each community choose its own way, and then compare the results. A system of diverse governments enhances the chances that new solutions to problems will be sought. As Supreme Court Justice Louis Brandeis once observed, "It is one of the happy incidents of the Federal system that a single courageous state may, if its citizens choose, serve as a laboratory, and try moral, social, and economic experiments without risk to the rest of the country."
From all appearances, Brandeis' laboratories are busily at work:

- Item: Sunnyvale, California has adopted performance-based budgeting, under which budget laws contain clear and precise goals for various programs. For example, in return for its appropriation, the city parks department is obligated to repair all reported vandalism within three working days 90 percent of the time. Other towns are watching to see if the system leads to better performance.
- Item: Maryland offers incentive bonuses to teenage parent recipients of Aid to Families with Dependent Children who stay in school. State officials hope that, if the teenagers remain in school, their long-term prospects of getting off welfare will improve.

■ Item: Bronx Regional, a high school in New York City, is building a dormitory to house 20 students who come from dysfunctional homes. School officials expect that with a more stable home environment, these students will be able to learn more effectively.

Interestingly, in the past, some programs that began as experiments at the state level eventually became federal policy. During the Great Depression, for example, the designers of Social Security took advantage of the experience of several states that had earlier instituted social insurance programs.

Implications

The foregoing discussion makes it clear that a purely decentralized system cannot be expected to maximize social welfare. Efficiency requires that those commodities with spillovers that affect the entire country—national public goods—be provided at the national level. Defense is a classic example. On the other hand, it seems perfectly appropriate for local public goods to be provided locally.[19]

This leaves us with the in-between case of community activities that create spillover effects that are not national in scope. One possible solution would be to put all the communities that affect each other under a single regional government. In theory, this government would take into account the welfare of all its citizens, and hence internalize the externalities. However, a larger governmental jurisdiction carries the cost of less responsiveness to local differences in tastes. Moreover, there is some evidence that attempts to correct externalities through regional government have not worked very well.[20]

An alternative method for dealing with externalities would be a system of Pigouvian taxes and subsidies. Chapter 6 shows that efficiency can be enhanced when the government taxes activities that create negative externalities and subsidizes activities that create positive externalities. We can imagine the central government using similar devices to influence the decisions of local governments. For example, if primary and secondary education create benefits that go beyond the boundaries of a jurisdiction, the central government can provide communities with educational subsidies. Local autonomy is maintained, yet the externality corrected. We see later that some federal grants to communities follow this model.

---

[19] This is subject to the usual proviso that the various levels of government are actually capable of providing goods in Pareto efficient quantities (see Chapter 5).

[20] See Bruce Ackerman, Susan Rose-Ackerman, James Sawyer, and Dale Henderson [1974] for a discussion of the Delaware River Basin Commission, which was established to deal with environmental problems faced in common by Delaware, New Jersey, New York, and Pennsylvania.

Our theory suggests a fairly clean division of responsibility for public good provision—local public goods by localities, and national public goods by the central government. In practice, there is considerable interplay between levels of government. For example, although localities have primary responsibility for education and public transportation, they must obey numerous federal regulations. Given that localities might act inappropriately in the absence of such regulations, the presence of regulations may improve welfare. However, some believe that the system of federal regulation over subfederal governmental units has become so complicated that it may be difficult to determine which level of government has responsibility for what. Recently, proposals have been made to reform the U.S. federal system to clarify the division of responsibilities. These proposals are discussed later.

If a division of responsibilities is appropriate from an efficiency point of view, does the same hold for income distribution? Most economists believe that the mobility considerations just discussed rule out relying heavily on local governments to achieve distributional aims. An individual jurisdiction that attempts to do so is likely to find itself in financial trouble. This is probably one of the reasons New York City nearly went bankrupt in the late 1970s. (See Gramlich [1976].)

Public Education in a Federal System

A useful way to apply the theory of optimal federalism is to employ it to analyze education, one of the most important items in the budgets of state and local governments. Their combined spending on education in 1988 was $236 billion. The federal government, in contrast, spent only $20 billion on education. As shown in Figure 21.1, local governments are responsible for 70 percent of education expenditures, with state governments contributing 25 percent. Education accounts for one fifth of direct expenditures at the state level and more than one third of local spending [The Tax Foundation, 1990, p. 8]. Nine out of 10 American children are educated in public schools.

Before asking whether local government is the proper level for providing education, we must investigate a more fundamental question: Why does the government involve itself so extensively in education, rather than leave its provision to the market? As we saw in Chapter 5, markets do not provide goods efficiently when those goods are public goods, they give rise to externalities, or they are provided monopolistically. Education is primarily a private good, improving students' welfare by enhancing their ability "to perform in and cope with society" [Hanushek, 1986, p. 1151]. Where transportation costs are high, local schools do have an element of monopoly power, but this argument is not very persuasive, except perhaps in rural areas.

Others point to public goods characteristics of education. Schools can be a powerful force for socialization. As the Roman historian Plutarch wrote in his *Morals,* "The very spring and root of honesty and virtue lie in good education." It has also been argued that education provides an avenue for political indoctrination that makes citizens more accepting of their governments, thus contributing to political stability. And in democratic governments, education gives voters background and perspective on which to base their political choices. In his Farewell Address, George Washington wrote, "In proportion as the structure of a government gives force to public opinion, it is essential that public opinion should be enlightened."

These arguments in support of intervention in the market for education are concerned with economic efficiency. Welfare economics suggests that equity must also be taken into account, and here, too, arguments can be made for public education. Recall from Chapter 8 the notion of commodity egalitarianism. Because access to education is arguably an important source of social mobility, it is an important good to be made available to all citizens.

If education does give rise to positive externalities or public goods, it follows that government may wish to subsidize it. We go beyond subsidization, however, when we make public elementary and secondary education both compulsory and free; this system cannot be rationalized on efficiency grounds alone. Furthermore, we noted in Chapter 5 the distinction between government provision (i.e., financing) of a good and government production of that good. What is so special about education that leads the government not only to fund it but to produce it as well? One theory is that public education produces human capital while simultaneously inculcating belief in the existing political system. Because individuals care about their human capital but receive no private gains from belief in the political system, private schools in competition for students would devote all their resources to producing human capital. According to this view, the development of a common commitment to established democratic processes is more easily carried out in a system of public schools protected from competition [Lott, 1990, p. 201].

Whatever the rationale for providing free public schools, a surprising result of economic theory is that such a system does not necessarily induce everyone to consume more schooling than they would have in a private market. Consider the case of Gepetto, who is deciding how much education his son Pinocchio should consume. In Figure 21.2, the amount of education is measured on the horizontal axis, and the quantity of all other goods consumed by the family on the vertical. (For simplicity, think of the amount of education as hours spent in the classroom. A more complicated model would also include aspects of the education that enhance its quality.) In the absence of a public school system, Gepetto can purchase as much education in the private market as he chooses at the going price, and his options are summarized by budget constraint AB. Subject to this constraint, he purchases e_o hours of education for Pinocchio; c_o is left over for expenditure on other goods.

Figure 21.2
Free public
schooling and the
amount of education
consumed

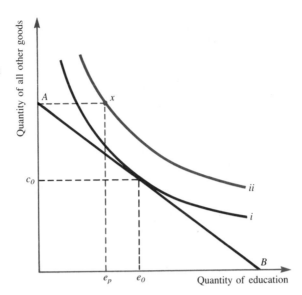

Now suppose that a public school opens. Gepetto can send Pinocchio to the public school for e_p hours per week at no cost to himself.[21] This option is represented not by a line, but by the single point x, where education consumption is e_p and Gepetto can spend his entire income on all other goods. Because indifference curve *ii*, which passes through x, is higher than indifference curve *i*, Gepetto takes Pinocchio out of private school and enrolls him in the public system. Importantly, e_p is less than e_o. Pinocchio's consumption of education falls. Intuitively, the existence of public education leads to a large increase in the opportunity cost of private education, inducing Gepetto to opt out of the private system, reducing Pinocchio's consumption of education as he does so.

Of course, for a different set of indifference curves, public education could have induced Gepetto to increase his household's consumption of education. Moreover, Figure 21.2 views public schooling as a "take it or leave it" option. To the extent that the amount of education offered through public schools can be supplemented by private lessons, it is less likely that public schooling would lead to reductions in the quantity of education consumed. Nevertheless, this analysis shows that one cannot take for granted that the government provision of free education (or any other commodity, for that matter) leads to an increase in its consumption.

Education and optimal federalism. With this general background on the rationales for government provision of education, we can now ask whether the pattern of spending on education by the different levels of

---

[21] We assume that Gepetto's tax payments are independent of whether he has children enrolled in public school.

government conforms to our views of optimal federalism. One argument for the decentralized provision of a good is that it can be tailored to local tastes. Because many parents hold strong views about the education of their children and these views differ across communities, this is an important argument for the leading role played by local governments in providing education. One could, of course, allow local discretion over school policy while having funding come from state or federal levels of government. Politically, however, it may be difficult to maintain control of the schools if the financing comes from some other level of government—he who pays the piper, calls the tune.

Local governments raise money for education primarily through property taxation; there are wide variations in the amount of property wealth available to school districts. Variations in the property tax base can be associated with huge differences in funding for school districts; in 1990, for example, the poorest district in Illinois spent $2,100 annually per pupil while the richest district spent more than $12,000 [Secter, 1991, p. A1]. An egalitarian view of education would call for funding from a level of government that could redistribute resources across local boundaries, regardless of its possible effects on local autonomy. As we see later in this chapter, intergovernmental grants are indeed an important part of education finance.

Federal funding for education is centered in two areas: At the elementary and secondary levels, Department of Education funding goes primarily to programs serving educationally disadvantaged ($4.6 billion in 1989) and handicapped ($3.2 billion in 1989) populations [Hanushek, 1989, p. 47]. This is consistent with the observation that redistribution is hard to carry out at the local level. In higher education, a great deal of federal spending is directed toward research. The information forthcoming from research is a public good, and we have seen that centralized provision or subsidization of public goods can avoid the free-rider problem that might arise at the local level. The system of American educational finance, then, seems broadly consistent with the basic tenets of optimal federalism.

Relation of Federalism to the Urban Crisis

Many American cities are experiencing major social and economic difficulties. The urban problem has many dimensions: loss of population, physically decaying neighborhoods, inability to pay for public services, and a high proportion of residents on public assistance, among others. There is no dearth of theories to explain the cities' difficulties. One survey listed about 40 possible explanations![22] Our purpose is to discuss how the U.S. system of local public finance may have contributed to the urban crisis.

---

[22] See Katharine Bradbury, Anthony Downs, and Kenneth Small [1982], who also provide an excellent treatment of the methodological problems involved in attempts to measure and explain urban decline.

Imagine a situation where low-income households in a city gain political power and use this power to establish a pro-poor pattern of expenditures and taxes. Provided that they are sufficiently mobile, those high-income individuals who do not wish to support such a fiscal pattern can leave for the suburbs. The poor are unable to follow them, either because their personal circumstances make them less mobile, or because of exclusionary zoning in the suburbs. As a consequence, the proportion of low-income families in the city increases. At the same time, the city's income- and property-tax bases fall because of the exit of the middle and upper classes.

In this extremely simple model of urban decline, the villain is the fragmented system of local public finance. If an entire metropolitan area had a unified government, fiscal decisions would apply uniformly to the entire jurisdiction. As a consequence, there would be less incentive for those with relatively high incomes to leave the central city behind.

David Bradford and Wallace Oates [1974] used data on a group of New Jersey cities and suburban communities to estimate the potential effects of moving to a metropolitan-wide system of local public finance. As expected, they found that in the long run, the central cities would have a greater proportion of high-income families under the unified system than under the status quo. However, it is hard to say what the distributional consequences of moving to a unified system would be. Changes in both the patterns of taxation and expenditure must be considered.

Imposing uniform property tax rates throughout the metropolitan area would create substantial capital losses for those property owners whose tax rates were formerly lower than average and vice versa (other things being the same). Would these changes tend to make the distribution of wealth more or less equal? To answer this question, we need information on the initial wealth positions of city landlords, among other things. If the move to a unified system ended up lowering tax rates in the city, and urban landlords were wealthy to begin with, there would be a tendency for the distribution of wealth to become more unequal. If it turned out that urban landlords were less wealthy then their suburban counterparts, just the opposite conclusion would emerge. Unfortunately, little information on the wealth of inner-city landlords is available. Therefore, it is hard to guess what the redistributive impact of the changing tax rates would be.

On the expenditure side of the account, Bradford and Oates found that guaranteeing equal school expenditures for each pupil in the metropolitan area would tend to redistribute real income from high- to low-income people. This is because under the current system, communities with more income tend to spend greater amounts on education than do those communities with less. Interestingly, if expenditures on all public services were equalized throughout the metropolitan area, it might work to the disadvantage of poorer central city residents, because smaller suburban communities often provide fewer public sector services than the cities provide. A small suburb, for example, may have a volunteer fire department and leave garbage collection to private firms. Requiring equal expenditure everywhere would benefit such communities, other things being the same.

A major problem with a unified system is that community autonomy would be severely limited. As noted earlier, the ability of communities to make their own decisions has certain efficiency advantages. After considering both distributive and efficiency issues, Bradford and Oates concluded that there is simply not enough information to say which system is superior. In any case, metropolitan consolidation has received very little political support in the United States. In practice, the main method for dealing with urban fiscal problems has been to use grants-in-aid from federal and state governments to supplement local property-tax revenues. These two major revenue sources for local governments, property taxes and intergovernmental grants, are examined next.

Local Government Revenues

In the late 1980s, local governments received a third of their revenue from intergovernmental grants and a quarter from property taxes [The Tax Foundation, 1990, p. 13]. We now discuss each of these local revenue sources in turn.

Property Tax

At the turn of the 20th century, the property tax accounted for 42 percent of tax revenues raised by all levels of government [U.S. Bureau of the Census, 1975, p. 1119]. By 1988, this figure was down to 13.2 percent. Of the $132.2 billion raised by property taxes that year, $5 billion was collected by the states (2 percent of their tax revenues) and $127.2 billion by localities (74 percent of their tax revenues) [Tax Foundation, 1990, p. 244]. There is no federal property tax. Although it is not as important as many other taxes when viewed from a national perspective, the property tax clearly plays a key role in local public finance.

How is the tax liability on a given piece of property determined? An individual's property tax liability is the product of the tax rate and the property's **assessed value**—the value the jurisdiction assigns to the property. In most cases, jurisdictions attempt to make assessed values correspond to market values.[23] However, if a piece of property has not been sold recently, the tax collector does not know its market value and must therefore make an estimate. This estimate is based in part on the market values of comparable properties that have been sold recently.

Market and assessed values diverge to an extent that depends on the accuracy of the jurisdiction's estimating procedure. The ratio of the assessed value to market value is called the **assessment ratio.** If all proper-

---

[23] However, sometimes certain types of property are systematically assessed at lower rates than others. For example, many states have special assessment rates for farm property.

Table 21.2   **Residential property tax rates in
                 selected cities, 1988**

City	Effective Tax Rate
Detroit	4.10%
Chicago	1.55
Atlanta	1.50
New Orleans	1.39
Charlotte	1.25
Boston	1.08
Phoenix	0.68
Los Angeles	0.64

SOURCE: U.S. Department of Commerce, Bureau of the Census,
Statistical Abstract of the United States: 1989 (Washington,
D.C.: U.S. Government Printing Office, 1990).

ties have the same statutory rate and the same assessment ratio, their effective tax rates are the same. Suppose, however, that assessment ratios differ across properties. Ophelia and Hamlet both own properties worth $100,000. Ophelia's property is assessed at $100,000 and Hamlet's at $80,000. Clearly, even if they face the same statutory rate (say 2 percent), Ophelia's effective rate of 2 percent (= $2,000/100,000) is higher than Hamlet's 1.6 percent (= $1,600/$100,000). In fact, in many communities, tax authorities have done a very poor job of assessing property values so that properties with the same statutory rate differ drastically with respect to effective rates.

To understand how the actual system of property taxes works, consider a hypothetical system in which all forms of wealth are taxed at a uniform rate. The base of such a tax would include the value of homes, automobiles, land, and property used for business purposes. In contrast, in the United States, literally thousands of jurisdictions operate their property tax systems more or less independently.[24] No jurisdiction includes a comprehensive measure of wealth in its tax base, but there are major differences with respect to just what types of property are excludable and what rates are applied. Religious and nonprofit institutions make "voluntary" contributions in lieu of taxes for property owned. Some communities tax new business plants preferentially, presumably to attract more commercial activity. Few areas tax personal wealth other than homes so that items such as cars, jewels, and stocks and bonds are usually exempt. Typically, structures and the land upon which they are built are subject to tax. But, as Table 21.2 demonstrates, the effective rates differ substantially across jurisdictions.

---

[24] Including counties, municipalities, townships and towns, school districts, and special districts, there are over 83,000 local governments. About 80 percent of them have the power to levy property taxes. See *Facts and Figures on Government Finance*, 1991, p. 4.

Figure 21.3
Incidence of a tax
on land

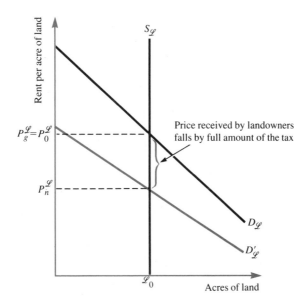

Thus, although we continue to describe the subject matter of this section as "the" property tax, it should now be clear that there is no such thing. The fact that there are many different property taxes is crucial to assessing the economic effects of the system as a whole.

Incidence and Efficiency Effects

There is considerable controversy as to who ultimately bears the burden of the property tax. We discuss three different views and then try to reconcile them.

Traditional view: property tax as an excise tax. The traditional view is that the property tax is an excise tax that falls on land and structures. Incidence of the tax is determined by the shapes of the relevant supply and demand schedules in precisely the manner explained in Chapter 13. The shapes of the schedules are different for land and structures.

Land. As long as the amount of land cannot be varied, by definition its supply curve is perfectly vertical. A factor with such a supply curve bears the entire burden of a tax levied on it. Intuitively, because its quantity is fixed, land cannot "escape" the tax. This is illustrated in Figure 21.3. $S_{\mathscr{L}}$ is the supply of land. Prior to the tax, the demand curve is $D_{\mathscr{L}}$, and the equilibrium rental value of land is $P_0^{\mathscr{L}}$. The imposition of an ad valorem tax on land pivots the demand curve. The after-tax demand curve is $D'_{\mathscr{L}}$. The rent received by suppliers of land (landowners) is found at the intersection of the supply curve with $D'_{\mathscr{L}}$, and is given by $P_n^{\mathscr{L}}$. The rent paid by the users of land is found by adding the tax per acre of land to $P_n^{\mathscr{L}}$, giving

$P_g^{\mathcal{L}}$. As expected, the rent paid by the users of the land is unchanged ($P_0^{\mathcal{L}} = P_g^{\mathcal{L}}$); the rent received by landowners falls by the full amount of the tax. Landowners bear the entire burden of the tax.

As discussed in Chapter 13, under certain circumstances the tax is capitalized into the value of the land. Prospective purchasers of the land take into account the fact that if they buy the land, they also buy a future stream of tax liabilities. This lowers the amount they are willing to pay for the land. Therefore, the person who bears the full burden of the tax is the landlord at the time the tax is levied. To be sure, future landlords make payments to the tax authorities, but such payments are not really a burden because they just balance the lower price paid at purchase. Capitalization complicates attempts to assess the incidence of the land tax. Knowing the identities of current owners is not sufficient; we must know who the landlords *were* at the time the tax was imposed.

To the extent that land is *not* fixed in supply, the preceding analysis requires modification. For example, the supply of urban land can be extended at the fringes of urban areas that are adjacent to farmland. Similarly, the amount of land can be increased if landfills or reclamation of wasteland is feasible. In such cases, the tax on land is borne both by landlords and the users of land, in proportions that depend on the elasticities of demand and supply. But it is usually assumed that a vertical supply curve for land is a good approximation of reality.

Structures.   To understand the traditional view of the tax on structures, we begin by considering the national market for capital. Capital can be used for many purposes: construction of structures, equipment for manufacturing, public sector projects like dams, and so forth. At any given time, capital has some price which rations the capital among alternative uses. According to the traditional view, in the long run, the construction industry can obtain all the capital it demands at the market price. Thus, the supply curve of structures is perfectly horizontal—a higher price is not required to obtain more of them.

The market for structures under these conditions is depicted in Figure 21.4. Prior to the tax, the demand for structures by tenants is D_B, and the supply curve, S_B, is horizontal at the going price, P_0^B. At price P_0^B the quantity exchanged is B_0. On imposition of the tax, the demand curve pivots to D_B', just as the demand for land pivoted in Figure 21.3. But the outcome is totally different. The price received by the suppliers of structures, P_n^B, is the same as the price before the tax was imposed ($P_n^B = P_0^B$). Demanders of structures pay a price, P_g^B, which exceeds the original price, P_0^B, by precisely the amount of the tax. Hence, the burden is shifted entirely to tenants. This result, of course, is a consequence of the assumption that the supply curve is horizontal. Intuitively, the horizontal supply curve means that capital will not stay in the housing sector if it does not receive a return of at least P_0^B. But if the price received by the suppliers of capital cannot be lowered, the tax must be borne entirely by tenants.

Figure 21.4

Incidence of a tax on structures

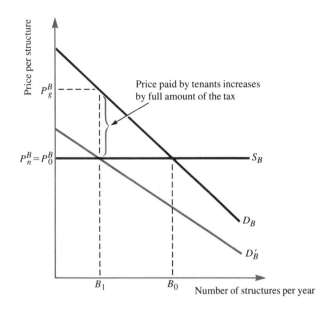

Summary of the traditional view.   The part of the tax on land is borne by landowners (or, at least the landowners at the time the tax is levied); the tax on structures is passed on to tenants. Therefore, the land part of the property tax is borne by people in proportion to the amount of rental income they receive, and the structures part of the tax is borne by people in proportion to the amount of housing they consume.

Implications for progressiveness.   With these observations in mind, we can assess the distributional implications of the traditional view of the property tax. The effect of the land part of the tax on progressiveness hinges on whether or not the share of income from land ownership tends to rise with income. There is fairly widespread agreement that it does, so this part of the tax is progressive.

Similarly, the progressiveness of the tax on structures depends critically on whether the proportion of income devoted to housing rises or falls as income increases. If it falls, then the structures part of the tax tends to be regressive and vice versa.

An enormous amount of econometric work has been done to estimate how housing expenditures actually do respond to changes in income. The ability to reach a consensus has been impeded by disagreement over which concept of income to use. Some investigators use *yearly* income. They tend to find that the proportion of income devoted to housing falls as income increases, suggesting that the tax is regressive. Other investigators believe that some measure of *normal* or *permanent* income is more relevant to understanding housing decisions. According to this view, the fact that a family's annual income in a given year happens to be higher or lower than its normal income should not have much of an impact on that year's housing consumption. Housing decisions are made in the context of the family's long-run prospects, not yearly variations.

Of course, those who believe that permanent income is the appropriate variable must find some way to estimate it. One approach is to define permanent income as the average of several years' annual incomes.[25] Housing expenditures turn out to be more responsive to changes in permanent income than to changes in annual income. Indeed, although the evidence is mixed, it appears reasonable to say that housing consumption is roughly proportional to permanent income. Hence, the structures part of the tax is probably neither regressive nor progressive. Unfortunately, housing demand estimates based on annual income, which suggest the tax is regressive, have tended to have the greater influence on public discussion of the tax.

The new view: property tax as a capital tax.   The traditional view uses a standard partial equilibrium framework. As we noted in Chapter 13, although partial equilibrium analysis is often useful, it may produce misleading results for taxes that are large relative to the economy. The new view of the property tax proposed by Peter Mieszkowski [1972] involves a general equilibrium perspective and generates some surprising conclusions.

According to the new view, it is best to think of the property tax as a general wealth tax with some assets taxed below the average rate, and some taxed above. Both the average level of the tax and the deviations from that average have to be analyzed.

General tax effect.   Assume for the moment that the property tax can be approximated as a uniform tax on all capital. Then the property tax is just a general factor tax on capital. Now assume further that the supply of capital to the economy is fixed. As shown in Chapter 13, when a factor is fixed in supply, it bears the full burden of a general tax levied on it. Hence, the property tax falls entirely on owners of capital. And since the proportion of income from capital tends to rise with income, a tax on capital tends to be progressive. Thus, the property tax is progressive, a conclusion that turns the traditional view exactly on its head!

Excise tax effects.   As noted earlier, the property tax is emphatically not a uniform tax. Rates vary according to the type of property and the jurisdiction in which the property is located. Some rates are higher than average, and some are lower. Hence, the property tax is a set of excise taxes on capital. According to the new view, there is a tendency for capital to migrate from areas where it faces a high tax rate to those where

---

[25] See, for example, Geoffrey Carliner [1973].

the rate is low.[26] In a process reminiscent of the Harberger model presented in Chapter 13, as capital migrates into low-tax-rate areas, its before-tax rate of return there is bid down. At the same time, the before-tax rate of return in high-tax areas increases as capital leaves. The process continues until after-tax rates of return are equal throughout the economy. In general, as capital moves, returns to other factors of production also change. The impact on the other factors depends in part on their mobility. Land, which is perfectly immobile, cannot shift the tax. (In this conclusion, at least, the new and old views agree.) Similarly, the least-mobile types of capital are most likely to bear the tax.

As is usually the case in general equilibrium models, the ultimate incidence depends on how production is organized, the structure of consumer demand, and the extent to which various factors are mobile.

Long-run effects.   In our discussion of the general tax effect of the property tax, we assumed that the amount of capital available to the economy is fixed. However, in the long run, the supply of capital may depend on the tax rate. If the property tax decreases the supply of capital, the productivity of labor, and hence the real wage, falls. If the tax increases capital accumulation, just the opposite occurs.

Summary of the new view.   The property tax is a general tax on capital with some types of capital taxed at rates above the average, others below. The general effect of the tax is to lower the return to capital, which tends to be progressive in its impact on the income distribution. The differentials in tax rates create excise effects, which tend to hurt immobile factors in highly taxed jurisdictions. The adjustment process set in motion by these excise effects is very complicated, and not much is known about their effects on progressiveness. Neither can much be said concerning the importance of long-term effects created by changes in the size of the capital stock. If the excise and long-run effects do not counter the general effect too strongly, the overall impact of the property tax is progressive.

Property tax as a user fee.   The discussion so far has ignored the fact that property taxes are often used by communities to purchase public services such as education and police protection. In the Tiebout model, the property tax is just the cost of purchasing public services, and each individual buys exactly the amount he or she desires. Thus, the property tax is really not a tax at all; it is more like a user fee for public services. This view has three important implications:

1. The notion of the *incidence of the property tax* is meaningless because the levy is not a tax in the normal sense of the word.

---

[26] There have been some attempts to estimate how responsive business location decisions are to local property tax rates, but the evidence is mixed. See White [1986] for a survey.

2. The property tax creates no excess burden. As Bruce Hamilton [1975a, p. 13] points out, "If consumers treat the local property tax as a price for public services, then this price should not distort the housing market any more than the price of eggs should distort the housing market."

3. By allowing the deduction of property tax payments, the federal income tax in effect subsidizes the consumption of local public services for individuals who itemize on their tax returns. As long as the demand for local public services slopes downward, the deduction increases the size of the local public sector desired by itemizers, other things being the same.

As noted earlier, the link between property taxes and services received is often tenuous, so we should not take the notion of the property tax as a user fee too literally. Nevertheless, this line of reasoning has some interesting implications. For example, if people care about the public services they receive, we expect that the depressing effects of high property taxes on housing values may be counteracted by the public services financed by these taxes. In an important paper, Oates [1969] constructed an econometric model of property value determination. In his model, the value of homes in a community depends positively on the quality of public services in the community and negatively on the tax rate, other things being the same. Of course, across communities, factors that influence house prices do differ. These include physical characteristics of the houses, such as number of rooms, and characteristics of the communities themselves, such as distance from an urban center. These factors must be taken into account when trying to sort out the effects of property taxes and local public goods on property values. Oates used multiple regression analysis to do so.

Oates's regression results suggest that increases in the property tax rate decrease housing values, while increases in per-pupil expenditures increase housing values. Moreover, the parameter values implied that the increase in property values created by expanding school expenditures approximately offset the decrease generated by the property taxes raised to finance them. These results need to be interpreted with caution. For one thing, expenditure per pupil may not be an adequate measure of local public services. Localities provide many public services other than education, such as police protection, parks, and libraries. Furthermore, as noted below, even if education were the only local public good, expenditure per pupil might not be a good measure of educational quality. It is possible, for example, that expenditures in a given community are high because the community has to pay a lot for its teachers, its schools are not administered efficiently, or its students are particularly difficult to educate.

Subsequent to Oates's study, a number of other investigators have examined the relationships among property values, property taxes, and local public goods using data from different geographical areas and employing different sets of explanatory variables. Although the results are a bit mixed, Oates's general conclusion seems to be valid—property taxes and the value of local public services are capitalized into housing prices.[27] Thus, if two communities have the same level of public services, but the first has higher taxes than the second (perhaps because its cost of providing the services is greater), we expect the first to have lower property values, other things being the same. More generally, these results imply that to understand how well off members of a community are, we cannot look at property tax rates in isolation. Government services and property values must also be considered.

Reconciling the three views. It is a mistake to regard the three views of the property tax as mutually exclusive alternatives. As Henry Aaron [1975] emphasizes, which one is valid depends on what question is being asked. If, for example, we want to find the consequences of eliminating all property taxes and replacing them with a national sales tax, the "new view" is appropriate because a change that affects all communities requires a general equilibrium framework. On the other hand, if a given community is considering lowering its property tax rate and making up the revenue loss from a local sales tax, the "traditional" view offers the most insight. This is because a single community is so small relative to the economy that its supply of capital is essentially perfectly horizontal, and Figure 21.4 applies. Finally, when taxes and benefits are jointly changed and there is sufficient mobility for people to pick and choose communities, the "user fee view" is useful.[28]

Why Do People Hate the Property Tax So Much?

On June 7, 1978, the voters of California approved a statewide property tax limitation initiative known as Proposition 13. Its key provisions were (1) to put a 1 percent ceiling on the property tax rate that any locality could impose, (2) to limit the assessed value of property to its 1975 value,[29] and (3) to forbid state and local governments to impose any additional property taxes without approval by a two thirds majority local vote. Proposition 13 was the most famous of a number of tax limitation statutes, and is typical in its focus on property tax finance.

---

[27] For further discussion, see Mieszkowski and Zodrow [1989].

[28] A more precise characterization of the conditions under which the user fee approach is appropriate is given in the earlier section on the Tiebout model.

[29] For property transferred after 1975, the assessed value was defined as the market value at which the transaction took place.

Why is the property tax so unpopular? Several explanations have been advanced:

1. Aaron [1975, p. 12] emphasizes that more than any other major tax, "The impact of the property tax depends on the vagaries of administration." Because housing market transactions typically occur infrequently, the tax must be levied on an estimated value. To the extent that this valuation is done incompetently (or corruptly), the tax is perceived as unfair.

2. The property tax is highly visible. Under the federal income and payroll taxes, payments are withheld from each of the worker's paychecks, and the employer sends the proceeds to the government. In contrast, the property tax is often paid directly by the taxpayer. Moreover, the payments are often made on a quarterly or an annual basis, so each payment comes as a large shock. It is hard to know how seriously to take this argument. Even those citizens who are somehow oblivious to the fact that federal income and payroll taxes are withheld during the year receive a pointed reminder of how much they have paid every April. There may be enough rage in that one month to last a whole year.

3. The property tax is perceived as being regressive. This perception is partly a consequence of the fact that the "traditional view" of the property tax continues to dominate public debate. It is reinforced by the fact that some property owners, particularly the elderly, do not have enough cash to make property tax payments, and may therefore be forced into selling their homes. Some states have responded to this phenomenon by introducing **circuit breakers** that provide benefits to taxpayers (usually in the form of a refund on state income taxes) that depend on the excess of residential property tax payments over some specified proportion of income. A more appropriate solution would be to defer tax payments until the time when the property is transferred.

4. Taxpayers may dislike other taxes as much as the property tax, but they feel powerless to do anything about the others. It is relatively easy to take aim at the property tax, which is levied locally. In contrast, mounting a drive against, say, the federal income tax would be very difficult, if for no other reason than a national campaign would be necessary and hence involve large coordination costs.

In light of the widespread hostility toward the tax, it is natural to ask whether there are any ways to improve it. A very modest proposal is to improve assessment procedures. The use of computers and modern valuation techniques can make assessments more uniform.[30] Compared to the current system of differing effective tax rates within a jurisdiction, uniform tax rates would probably enhance efficiency. The equity issues are more complicated. On one hand, it seems a violation of horizontal equity for two people with identical properties to pay different taxes on them. However, the phenomenon of capitalization requires that we distinguish carefully between the owners at the time the tax is levied and the current owners. A property with an unduly high tax rate can be expected to sell for a lower price, other things being the same. Thus, an individual who buys the property *after* the tax is imposed is not necessarily worse off due to the high tax rate. Indeed, equalizing assessment ratios could generate a whole new set of horizontal inequities.

A more ambitious reform of the property tax would be to convert it into a **personal net worth tax.** The base of such a tax is the difference between the market value of all the taxpayer's assets and liabilities.[31] An advantage of such a system over a property tax is that by allowing for deduction of liabilities, it provides a better index of ability to pay. Moreover, because it is a personal tax, exemptions can be built into the system and the rates can be varied to attain the desired degree of progressivity.

The administrative problems associated with a net worth tax are formidable. We indicated earlier the difficulties that arise in valuing housing for property tax purposes. These pale in comparison to valuing many other types of assets. (Think of trying to value paintings, antiques, or Persian rugs.) Moreover, while a house is difficult to conceal, other types of assets are relatively easy to hide from the tax collector. Note also that because individuals can have assets and liabilities in different jurisdictions, a net worth tax would undoubtedly have to be administered by the federal government.

This brings us to what many people consider to be the main justification for the current system of property taxation. Whatever its flaws, the property tax can be administered locally without any help from the federal or state governments. Hence, it provides local government with considerable fiscal autonomy. As one observer put it, "Property taxation offers people in different localities an instrument by which they can make local choices significant" [Harris, 1978, p. 38]. According to this view, elimination of the property tax would ultimately destroy the economic independence of local units of government. California's experience after Proposition 13 is consistent with this view. Because Proposition 13 limited the ability of communities to raise money via property taxes, that measure

---

[30] Aaron [1975] cites evidence that assessment procedures have generally been getting better over time, but suggests that there is still a lot of room for improvement.

[31] Some version of a net worth tax is used in several European countries. See Aaron [1975, pp. 90–91].

"concentrated power to raise revenue in the State Legislature, and with it the right to determine policies and priorities once set locally" [Lindsey, 1986]. Thus, despite the fact that localities do have access to other tax bases, the political role of the property tax needs to be taken seriously in any discussion of its reform.

Intergovern-mental Grants

As already noted, federal grants are a very important source of revenue to states and localities. Grants from one level of government to another are the main method for changing fiscal resources within a federal system. Table 21.3 indicates that between 1950 and 1990, grants from the federal government increased both in real terms and as a proportion of total federal outlays. In recent years, however, there has been some reversal of these trends. Grants as a percentage of state and local expenditures exhibit the same pattern. The importance of grants as an element in local public finance is particularly striking. Table 21.4 indicates that grants from federal and state government are now more than one third of total local revenues.

Grants are used to finance activities that run practically the entire gamut of government functions. More than half of federal grant outlays go for programs relating to income security and health [*Facts and Figures on Government Finance,* 1990, p. 103]. Grants are also used for education, development of infrastructure, transportation, general fiscal assistance, and other purposes.

Why have intergovernmental transfers grown so much over the long run? This question is closely related to why government spending in general has increased. As we saw in Chapter 7, the answer is far from clear. One explanation for the growth of grants emphasizes that over the last several decades, the demand for the types of services traditionally provided by the state and local sector—education, transportation, and police protection—has been growing rapidly. However, the state and local revenue structures, which are based mainly on sales and property taxes, have not provided the means to keep pace with the growth of desired expenditures. In contrast, federal tax revenues have tended to grow automatically over time, largely due to the progressive nature of the federal personal income tax and, until the advent of indexing in the mid-1980s, inflation. Hence, there is a "mismatch" between where tax money is collected and where it is demanded. Grants from the central government to states and localities provide a way of correcting this mismatch.

A major problem with the mismatch theory is that it fails to explain why states and localities cannot raise their tax *rates* to keep up with increases in the demand for local public goods and services. Robert Inman [1985] proposes a politically oriented alternative explanation for the growth of grants. During 1945 to 1960, new coalitions emerged that had a common interest in larger state and local governments. These coalitions

Table 21.3 **Relation of federal grants-in-aid to federal, state, and local expenditures** (*selected fiscal years*)

Fiscal Year	Total Grants (billions of 1990 dollars)*	Grants as a Percent of Total Federal Outlays	Grants as a Percent of State and Local Expenditures
1950	$ 12.7	5.3%	10.4%
1960	30.0	7.7	14.7
1970	75.7	12.3	19.2
1980	141.5	15.9	26.2
1985	125.6	11.2	21.0
1990	137.0	10.9	17.9

* Amounts are converted to 1990 dollars using the GNP deflator as reported in *Economic Report of the President 1991*, p. 290.

SOURCE: Office of Management and Budget, *Budget of the United States Government, Fiscal Year 1992* (Washington, D.C.: U.S. Government Printing Office, 1991), pp. 7–132.

Table 21.4. **Federal and state grants to local government** (*selected fiscal years*)

Fiscal Year	State and Federal Aid	
	Amount (billions of 1990 dollars)*	Percent of Total Local General Revenue
1950	$ 24.5	31.6%
1960	43.3	30.6
1965	59.3	31.9
1970	93.0	36.5
1975	138.1	42.3
1980	158.1	44.1
1985	163.6	39.0
1988	176.4	37.5

* Amounts are converted to 1990 dollars using the GNP deflator as reported in *Economic Report of the President 1991*, p. 290.

SOURCE: Computed from Advisory Commission on Intergovernmental Relations, *Significant Features of Fiscal Federalism* 2, August 1990, pp. 94–95.

included public employee unions, suburban developers (who wanted increased infrastructure spending), and welfare rights organizations. Because of the mobility of their tax bases, local politicians were unable to transfer much income to these coalitions. Therefore, they organized as the intergovernmental lobby, and went to Washington looking for money. The federal government responded with increased grants.

As we noted in Chapter 7, it is hard to construct careful econometric tests of theories based on interest group formation. It does seem plausible, however, that such considerations played a role in the growth of the grant system.

Types of Grants

A grant's structure can influence its economic impact. There are basically two types, conditional and unconditional, which we discuss in turn.

Conditional grants.   These are sometimes called **categorical grants.** The donor specifies, to some extent, the purposes for which the recipient can use the funds. More than 90 percent of federal grants are earmarked for specific purposes.[32] The ways in which conditional grant money must be spent are often spelled out in minute detail. In 1982, the U.S. House of Representatives decided to try to discourage drunken driving and voted to give money to states that established anti-drunk driving programs. The House specified everything from the percent of blood-alcohol concentration that would be the criterion for intoxication to the length of time the driver's license would be suspended for a first offense. This is not atypical. According to one count, the federal government imposes more than a thousand spending mandates on states and localities.[33] There are several types of conditional grants.

Matching grants.   For every dollar given by the donor to support a particular activity, a certain sum must be expended by the recipient. For example, a grant might indicate that whenever a community spends a dollar on education, the federal government will contribute a dollar as well.

The standard theory of rational choice can help us understand the effects of a matching grant. In Figure 21.5, the horizontal axis measures the quantity of local government output, G, consumed by the residents of the town of Smallville. The vertical axis measures Smallville's total consumption, c. Assume for simplicity that units of G and c are defined so that the price of one unit of each is $1. Hence, assuming no saving, c is equal to after-tax income. With these assumptions, Smallville's budget constraint between c and G is a straight line whose slope in absolute value is one.[34] The unitary slope indicates that for each dollar Smallville is willing to spend, it can obtain one unit of public good. The budget constraint is denoted AB in Figure 21.5.

---

[32] Executive Office of the President [1991].

[33] Claude Barfield, quoted in Norman Ornstein [1982, p. 12].

[34] Details on the construction of budget constraints are provided in the Appendix at the end of the book. This model ignores the deduction of state and local property taxes in the federal income tax system. If taxpayers itemize deductions and the marginal federal income tax rate is t, the absolute value of the slope of AB is $(1 - t)$.

Figure 21.5
Analysis of a
matching grant

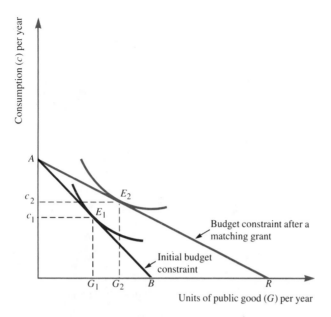

Suppose that Smallville's preferences for G and c can be represented by a set of conventionally shaped indifference curves.[35] Then if the town seeks to maximize its utility subject to the budget constraint, it will choose point E_1, where public good consumption is G_1 and community after-tax income is c_1.

Now suppose that a matching grant regime of the sort just described is instituted. The federal government matches every dollar that Smallville spends. When Smallville gives up \$1 of income, it can obtain *\$2* worth of G—one of its own dollars, and one from the federal government. The slope (in absolute value) of Smallville's budget line therefore becomes one half. In effect, the matching grant halves the price of G. It is an ad valorem subsidy on consumption of the public good. The new budget line is drawn in Figure 21.5 as AR.

At the new equilibrium, Smallville consumes G_2 public goods and has c_2 available for private consumption. Note that not only is G_2 greater than G_1 but c_2 is also greater than c_1. Smallville uses part of the grant to buy more of the public good and part to reduce its tax burden. It would be possible, of course, to draw the indifference curves so that c_2 equals c_1, or even so that c_2 is less than c_1. Nevertheless, there is a distinct possibility that part of the grant meant to stimulate public consumption will be used not to buy more G, but to obtain tax relief. In an extreme case, the community's indifference curves might be such that $G_2 = G_1$—the com-

---

[35] Of course, this supposition ignores all the problems—and perhaps the impossibility—of preference aggregation raised in Chapter 7. We return to this issue later.

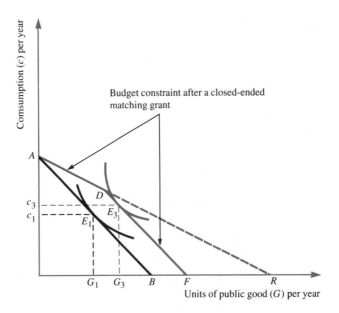

munity consumes the same amount of the public good and uses the entire
grant to reduce taxes. Thus, theory alone cannot indicate how a matching
grant affects a community's expenditure on a public good. It depends on
the responsiveness of demand to changes in price.

A matching grant is a sensible way to correct for the presence of a
positive externality. As explained in Chapter 6, when an individual or a
firm generates a positive externality at the margin, an appropriate subsidy
can enhance efficiency. The same logic applies to a community. Of
course, all the problems that arise in implementing the subsidy scheme
are still present. In particular, the central government has to be able to
measure the actual size of the externality.

Matching closed-ended grant.   With a matching grant, the cost to the
donor ultimately depends on the recipient's behavior. If Smallville's consumption of G is very stimulated by the program, the central government's contributions will be quite large and vice versa. To put a ceiling on
the cost, the donor may specify some maximum amount that it will contribute. Such a closed-ended matching grant is illustrated in Figure 21.6.
As before, prior to the grant, Smallville's budget line is AB, and the
equilibrium is at point E_1. With the closed-ended matching grant, the
budget constraint is the kinked line segment ADF. Segment AD has a
slope of minus one half, reflecting the one-for-one matching provision.
But after some point D, the donor no longer matches dollar for dollar.
Smallville's opportunity cost of a unit of government spending again becomes $1, which is reflected in the slope of segment DF.

Figure 21.7
Analysis of a
nonmatching grant

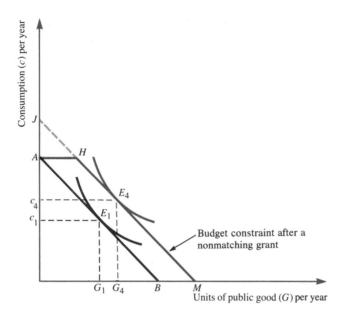

The new equilibrium at E_3 involves more consumption of G than under the status quo, but less than under the open-ended matching grant. The fact that the grant runs out limits its ability to stimulate expenditure on the public good. Note, however, that in some cases the closed-endedness can be irrelevant. If desired community consumption of G involves an expenditure below the ceiling, the presence of the ceiling simply does not matter. In graphical terms, if the new tangency had been along segment AD of Figure 21.6, it would be irrelevant that points along DR were not available.

Nonmatching grant.   Here the donor gives a fixed sum of money with the stipulation that it be spent on the public good. Figure 21.7 depicts a nonmatching grant to buy AH units of G. At each level of community income, Smallville can now buy AH more units of the public good than it did before. Thus, the new budget constraint is found by adding a horizontal distance AH to the original budget constraint AB. The result is the kinked line AHM.

Smallville maximizes utility at point E_4. Note that although public good consumption goes up from G_1 to G_4, the difference between the two is less than the amount of the grant, AH. Smallville has followed the stipulation that it spend the entire grant on G, *but* at the same time, it has reduced its own expenditures for the public good. If the donor expected expenditures to be increased by exactly AH, then Smallville's reaction has frustrated these hopes. It turns out that the situation depicted in

Figure 21.7 is a good description of reality. Communities often use some portion of nonmatching conditional grant money to reduce their own taxes [see Craig and Inman, 1986].

Unconditional grants.   Observe from Figure 21.7 that budget line *AHM* looks almost as if it were created by giving the community an unrestricted lump sum grant of *AH* dollars. Such unconditional grants are sometimes referred to as **revenue sharing.** An unconditional grant would have led to a budget line *JM*, which is just segment *MH* extended to the vertical axis. Smallville happens to behave exactly the same way facing constraint *AHM* as it would have if it had faced *JM*. In this particular case, then, *the conditional grant could just as well have been an unrestricted lump sum grant.* Intuitively, as long as the community wants to consume at least an amount of the public good equal to the grant, the fact that the grant is conditional is irrelevant. In contrast, if the community wanted to consume less of the public good than *AH* (if the indifference curves were such that the optimum along *JM* is to the left of *H*), then the conditional nature of the grant actually affects behavior.[36]

Why should the central government be in the business of giving unconditional grants to states and localities? The usual response is that such grants can equalize the income distribution. It is not clear that this argument stands up under close scrutiny. Even if a goal of public policy is to help poor people, it does not follow that the best way to do so is to help poor communities. After all, the chances are that a community with a low average income will probably have some relatively rich members and vice versa. If the goal is to help the poor, why not give them the money directly?

One possible explanation is that the central government is particularly concerned that the poor consume a greater quantity of the publicly provided good. An important example is education. This is a kind of commodity egalitarianism (Chapter 8) applied to the output of the public sector. However, as we just demonstrated, with unconditional grants we cannot know for sure that all the money will ultimately be spent on the favored good. (Indeed, the same is generally true for conditional grants as well.)

Measuring need.   In any case, an unconditional grant program requires that the donor determine which communities "need" money and in what amounts.[37] Federal allocations are based on complicated formulas established by Congress. The amount of grant money received by a state depends on such factors as per capita income, the size of its urban popula-

---

[36] Note the similarity to analysis of in-kind transfer programs discussed in Chapter 8.

[37] In some cases, eligibility for conditional grants is also based on need.

tion, and the amount of its state income tax collections. The allocations to localities are not only functions of such conventional economic factors but can also depend on items like the ethnicity of the population.

An important factor in determining how much a community receives from the federal government is its **tax effort,** normally defined as the ratio of tax collections to tax capacity. The idea is that communities that try hard to raise taxes but still cannot finance a very high level of public services are worthy of receiving a grant. Unfortunately, it is quite possible that this and related measures yield little or no information about a community's true effort. Suppose that Smallville is in a position to export its tax burden in the sense that the incidence of any taxes it levies falls on outsiders. Then a high tax rate tells us nothing about how much the members of the community are sacrificing.[38]

More fundamentally, the tax effort approach may be rendered totally meaningless because of the phenomenon of capitalization. Consider two towns, Sodom and Gomorrah. They are identical except for the fact that Sodom has a brook providing water at essentially zero cost. In Gomorrah, on the other hand, it is necessary to dig a well and pump out the water.

Gomorrah levies a property tax to finance the water pump. If there is a tax in Gomorrah and none in Sodom, and the communities are otherwise identical, why should anyone live in Gomorrah? As people migrate to Sodom, property values increase there (and decrease in Gomorrah) until there is no net advantage to living in either community. In short, property values are higher in Sodom to reflect the presence of the brook.

For reasons discussed previously, we do not expect the advantage to be necessarily 100 percent capitalized into Sodom's property values. Nevertheless, capitalization compensates at least partially for the differences between the towns. Just because Gomorrah levies a tax does *not* mean that it is "trying harder" than Sodom, because the Sodomites have already paid for their water in a higher price for living there. We conclude that conventional measures of tax effort may not be very meaningful.

Grants and Spending Behavior

The community indifference curve analysis just given begs a fundamental question: *whose* indifference curves are they? According to median voter theory (Chapter 7), the answer is that the preferences are those of the community's median voter. Bureaucrats and elected officials play a passive role in implementing the median voter's wishes.

A straightforward implication of the median voter rule is that a $1 increase in community income has exactly the same impact on public spending as receipt of a $1 unconditional grant. In terms of Figure 21.7,

---

[38] Recall from our earlier discussion that the property tax plays a key role in local public finance, but the incidence of that tax is a matter of some controversy.

both events generate identical parallel outward shifts of the initial budget line. If the budget line changes are identical, the changes in public spending levels must also be identical.

A considerable amount of econometric work has been done on the determinants of local public spending. (Many of these studies are summarized in Rubinfeld [1987].) Contrary to what one might expect, a conclusion common to virtually all studies is that a dollar received by the community in the form of a grant results in *greater* public spending than a dollar increase in community income. Roughly speaking, the estimates suggest that a dollar received as a grant generates 40 cents of public spending, while an additional dollar of private income increases public spending by only 10 cents. This phenomenon has been dubbed the **flypaper effect,** because the money seems to stick in the sector where it initially hits.

Some explanations of the flypaper effect focus on the role of bureaucrats. In the model of R. Filimon, T. Romer, and H. Rosenthal [1982], bureaucrats seek to maximize the sizes of their budgets. As budget maximizers, the bureaucrats have no incentive to inform citizens about the true level of grant funding being received by the community. By concealing this information, the bureaucrats may trick citizens into voting for a higher level of funding than would otherwise have been the case. According to this view, the flypaper effect is a consequence of the fact that citizens are unaware of the true budget constraint. To support their theory, Filimon, Romer, and Rosenthal noted that in states that have direct referenda on spending questions, ballots often contain information about the tax base but rarely have data on grants.

Intergovernmental Grants for Education

In 1971, the court case of *Serrano* vs. *Priest* ushered in a new era in education finance. The California Supreme Court ruled that disparities in property wealth across school districts led to unconstitutionally disparate school quality when local property taxation was exclusively relied on for school finance. Since then, courts have struck down similar financing schemes in 12 other states [Secter, 1991, p. A20]. In response, states have assumed an increasingly large role in financing elementary and secondary education. States use two basic kinds of grants to support local schools: **Foundation aid** seeks to assure a minimum level of expenditure per pupil, regardless of local property wealth. **District Power Equalization (DPE)** grants assure that the revenue raised by the local property tax rate corresponds to what would be raised if the district's property wealth per pupil did not fall below a guaranteed level.[39]

---

[39] For greater detail, see Fisher [1989].

Foundation aid.   Foundation aid grants are basically conditional (that is, they must be spent on education) nonmatching grants. The amount of grant per pupil depends on local property wealth. The wealthier a district, the smaller the grant received from the state. Neither the district's own spending on education nor its property-tax rate affects the amount of the transfer received from the state. Such grants are expected to have income effects but no substitution effects on local spending.

District power equalization.   Sometimes called *guaranteed tax base grants,* these are conditional matching grants. Such grants allow poor districts to imagine that their property wealth per student achieves a guaranteed level. When a district sets its tax rate, the locally raised revenue is supplemented so that the total revenue equals the local tax rate multiplied by the guaranteed tax base. This type of grant rewards tax effort, as described earlier in this chapter; when a district raises its tax rate, it increases the size of the grant it receives.

What do grants for education accomplish?   State grants to local school districts transfer resources into poorer districts. But do they affect educational outcomes? There are two questions here. The first is, do grants lead to higher expenditures on education? This is an important question to ask in light of our discussion surrounding Figures 21.5 and 21.7, which suggested that *net* spending on education may not increase if the community chooses to substitute grant money for money raised from its own sources. However, empirical studies generally suggest that state and local education spending does increase in response to grants. One recent econometric study, for example, indicated that for each dollar of grants received, spending on education increased by 32 cents [Case, Hines, and Rosen, 1989].

Given that grants increase school expenditures, we must confront the second question: Do higher expenditures lead to better education? After all, we are ultimately concerned with educational outcomes for students, not educational expenditures per se. If we knew the production function for education, we would know the relationship between inputs purchased and the amount of education produced. Attempts to measure the relationship between usage levels of various inputs to education, such as teachers' years of experience and the number of teachers available per student, have faced major difficulties. Part of the difficulty comes in defining, let alone measuring, the output "education." Some measures that have been used to capture the increased human capital imparted through education are test scores, attendance records, drop-out rates or continuation rates to higher levels of schooling, and labor market outcomes such as unemployment rates and earnings [Hanushek, 1986, pp. 1150–52]. Hanushek surveys 147 statistical estimates of the relationship between input usage and various measures of educational attainment. The inputs considered are the teacher/pupil ratio, teacher education, teacher experience, teacher salary, and expenditures per pupil. He reaches the startling conclusion that the data support virtually no correspondence between input usage per student and the quality of the educational experience [Hanushek, 1986, pp. 1160–62].

What are we to make of these results? We do *not* conclude that schooling is unimportant; there are clearly effective and ineffective schools. However, the research indicates that we cannot predict which schools will be effective simply by looking at data on their purchased inputs. The same is true of teachers; although principals can identify "good" teachers (those whose classes show educational gains), data on degrees held or years of teaching experience do not usefully discriminate between effective and ineffective teachers [Hanushek, 1986, pp. 1164–65].

One particularly notable result emerges from the research on class size. It appears that, over a wide range, class size does not matter. Given the conventional methods of measuring education, teaching to a class of 20 appears no more effective than teaching to a class of 30 [Hanushek, 1986, p. 1161]. This research has tremendous policy implications for a state such as California, where class size currently averages more than 30 and the annual cost of a statewide reduction of class size by one student approaches $250,000,000 [Odden, p. 213]. In cost-benefit terms, one cannot support the position that class sizes should be reduced. This does not mean that all expenditures are futile. For example, there is some evidence that, while classes of 20 are not measurably better than classes of 30, classes of three or fewer students are, especially if the students are in the early grades and are performing at below-average levels. Well-targeted class size reductions below the levels considered in the studies reviewed by Hanushek, such as tutoring sessions, might have significant payoffs.

New directions for public education.   The American public school system has been accused of producing a rising tide of mediocrity that puts our nation at economic and social risk [The National Commission on Excellence in Education, 1983]. Measures of achievement such as SAT scores suggest that students in the 1960s were better educated than students today. In such an environment, school reform is a widely debated issue.

If simply spending more on education won't improve the situation, what will? Economists are often quick to consider whether any market in trouble might not benefit from an infusion of competition. This is true in the debate over what to do about the nation's schools. Some economists are convinced that the schools would improve if they were forced to compete with one another to attract students. The essence of competition is that consumers can choose among suppliers. In contrast, the elementary and secondary public school system has generally operated on a take-it-or-leave-it basis: the only public school available to a student is the one assigned to the student's neighborhood. Important exceptions are magnet schools offering special resources to attract students from beyond the school's local neighborhood. The option of sending children to magnet schools is one bit of choice that some parents have within the public school system.

Recently, a great deal of attention has been paid to plans to improve public school quality by increasing dramatically the scope of choice. The basic approach is to provide financial support to students rather than directly to schools. Each student could be given a tuition voucher, for example, that could be redeemed at whatever qualified school the student's family liked best. The theory is that the effects of competition would be as salutary in the education market as they are in other markets. Terrible schools would have few enrollees and would be forced to close. The availability of tuition monies would prompt entrepreneurs to establish new schools in areas where the existing schools were poor.

There are, of course, many issues involved in designing such a system. How much latitude can schools have in designing their curricula? Can schools hire teachers who are not credentialed? What criteria can oversubscribed schools use to choose which students will be enrolled? Can church-run schools be included in the program? Can parents donate extra resources to the schools of their choice, or would this violate standards of equal education? How will students' families be informed about the different schooling choices available to them?

Critics of market-oriented schemes offer a number of objections. Principal among them is that consumers in the education market are not well informed and, as in medical markets, the competitive outcome would be far from satisfactory. Supporters of this view point to the proliferation of vocational schools of dubious value that prey on students eligible for federal student loans and grants. Further, they argue that if bad public schools in urban ghettos were replaced by what turned out to be even worse private schools, it would be hard to get middle-class taxpayers to vote for the additional funds necessary to re-establish the system we now have [Lemann, 1991, p. 105].

In response, supporters of choice note that the quality of public schools appears to be declining despite massive increases in spending over time. They argue that just because people are poor doesn't mean that they are unwilling or unable to seek out the best opportunities available for their children.[40] A number of communities have recently begun experi-

---

[40] See John Chubb and Terry Moe [1990] for further arguments along these lines.

menting with choice-based public schooling. In Milwaukee, for example, about 1,000 low-income students have begun attending private schools using $2,500 state-aid vouchers. The results of these experiments should help inform future debates over competition in the market for education.

Tax Expenditures as Intergovernmental Grants

In Chapter 16 under "Exemptions and Deductions," we introduced the notion of tax expenditures—special tax provisions that deliver aid through the revenue side of the federal budget. By excluding expenditures for an item from the income tax, the federal government in effect subsidizes the purchase of that item. Currently, two tax expenditures are of crucial importance to state and local public finance—the exemption of interest on state and local bonds, and the deductibility of some state and local taxes. These tax expenditures can be viewed as intergovernmental aid because of the activities they subsidize. State and local bonds finance capital spending, while tax deductibility finances general purpose spending. Moreover, they are open-ended grants in the sense that their cost to the federal government depends on state and local decisions.

In 1991, tax expenditures for the interest exclusion were $55 billion; for tax deductibility, $30 billion.[41] The total, $85 billion, was more than half of total explicit grants-in-aid.[42] In addition, while explicit federal grants-in-aid in real dollars have been declining in recent years, real tax expenditures have been increasing.

From a political point of view, the exemption of state and local bond interest is not terribly controversial. To be sure, there has been some debate over precisely what activities can be financed by tax-free bonds (see Ladd [1984]); but no serious proposals have been made to eliminate the exemption altogether. Because the issues surrounding tax-exempt bonds were covered in Chapter 16, we do not discuss them further here.

In contrast, the deductibility of state and local taxes has been a hot policy issue. For most of the life of the federal income tax, state and local income, general sales, and property taxes have been deductible by itemizers. In the Tax Reform Act of 1986, the deduction for general sales taxes was eliminated, but deductibility for income and property taxes was left in place. In the debate preceding the Omnibus Budget Reconciliation Act of 1990, serious attention was given to putting an upper limit on the deductibility of state taxes, but ultimately this idea was rejected. It seems likely that the possibility of at least partially disallowing deductions for state and local income and property taxes will continue to arise in future discussions of tax reform.

---

[41] However, recall from Chapter 16 the conceptual and practical problems in measuring tax expenditures.

[42] These figures are estimates from Executive Office of the President, 1991, pp. 3–37 and 7–132.

What would happen to state and local public finance if these tax expenditure "grants" were totally eliminated? It depends on the role of itemizers in the collective choice process, and the other revenue raising tools available to jurisdictions. To begin thinking about the problem, we make two assumptions: (1) a community is comprised entirely of identical itemizers, each of whom has a marginal tax rate of 28 percent; (2) the property tax is the only source of revenue.

Now, for itemizers, the *effective price of one dollar of public spending* financed by property taxes is just one minus their federal marginal income tax rate. In this particular case, elimination of deductibility raises the effective price of $1 of public spending from 72 cents to $1, an increase of about 39 percent. Assuming for illustrative purposes a price elasticity of demand for local public goods of −0.3, when deductibility is eliminated, each voter's desired amount of local public goods falls by 11.7 percent (= 0.3 × 39). If the community's decisions are guided by the median voter rule, expenditures fall by that amount.

The analysis increases in complexity when we make the more realistic assumption that not all voters itemize. Indeed, in 1988, only about 29 percent of all tax returns were itemized [Internal Revenue Service, 1990, p. 105]. Of course, the elimination of deductibility has no effect on the effective price for public spending facing a nonitemizer—it is $1 with or without deductibility. Thus, if community decisions are governed by the median voter model and the median voter is a nonitemizer, the elimination of deductibility has no impact on public spending at all.

How likely is the median voter to be an itemizer? The likelihood of voting increases with income, but as income increases, so does the propensity to itemize. Hence, we expect itemizers to vote in disproportionately large numbers, a conjecture that is borne out by voter surveys [Ladd, 1984]. On this basis, a number of investigators have argued that it is safe to assume that the median voter is an itemizer, and local expenditure would fall if deductibility were eliminated. However, the answer clearly differs across communities.

The discussion so far has assumed that the only sources of state and local revenues are deductible taxes paid by individuals. In fact, governments have access to other sources, such as business taxes. Perhaps the removal of deductibility would merely induce state and local governments to shift more of the tax burden from individuals to firms. Martin Feldstein and Gilbert Metcalf [1986] estimated a regression in which each state's use of nondeductible taxes depended on its average effective price of public spending financed by deductible taxes, among other variables. They found that states with higher effective prices do indeed rely more heavily on nondeductible taxes. According to their estimates, if deductibility were eliminated, the increased taxes on businesses would just about balance the decreased taxes from individuals, leaving state and local spending unchanged.

An interesting implication of Feldstein and Metcalf's calculations is that the federal Treasury might not gain much revenue if deductibility were eliminated. Recall that businesses would still be allowed to subtract state and local taxes in the computation of their federal taxable income. If businesses have to pay higher taxes to state and local governments, their net income drops, and their federal tax liability goes down. Thus, while federal personal income tax collections increase, collections from businesses decline. The net effect is hard to predict.

Another implication of the Feldstein-Metcalf analysis is that after the Tax Reform Act of 1986, states and localities should have increased their reliance on income and property taxes (which remained deductible) and reduced reliance on sales taxes (whose deductibility was eliminated). To the contrary, between 1987 and 1989 states tended to increase their sales taxes and decrease their income taxes. While several hypotheses to explain this phenomenon have been proposed (see Courant and Gramlich [1991]), none is totally satisfactory. This puzzle is indicative of the complexities involved in correctly sorting out the effects of the federal tax structure on state and local public finance.

Overview

At the beginning of this chapter we posed some questions concerning federal systems: Is decentralized decision making desirable? How should responsibilities be allocated? How should local governments finance themselves? We have seen that economic reasoning suggests federalism is a sensible system. Allowing local communities to make their own decisions very likely enhances efficiency in the provision of local public goods. However, efficiency and equity are also likely to require a significant economic role for a central government. In particular, a system in which only local resources are used to finance local public goods is viewed by many as inequitable.

While our focus has naturally been on economic issues, questions of power and politics are never far beneath the surface in discussions of federalism. The dispersion of economic power is generally associated with the dispersion of political power. How should power be allocated? Is your image of subfederal government a racist governor keeping black students out of the state university, or a town hall meeting in which citizens democratically make collective decisions? When you think of the central government, do you picture an uncaring and remote bureaucrat imposing bothersome regulations, or a justice department lawyer seeing to it that the civil rights of all citizens are maintained? The different images coexist in most of our minds, creating conflicting feelings about the proper distribution of governmental power.

Summary

- In a federal system, different governments provide different services to overlapping jurisdictions. The U.S. federal system includes the federal government, states, counties, townships, cities, school districts, and special districts.

- In a federal system, local responsibility for education can be justified on the basis of different tastes across communities. However, to the extent that education is viewed as an example of commodity egalitarianism, some federal involvement in the distribution of resources available for education may be appropriate.

- The issue of why communities form may be analyzed using the club model. The club model indicates that community size and quantity of public goods depend on tastes for public goods, costs of providing public services, and the costs of crowding.

- The Tiebout model emphasizes the key roles of mobility, property tax finance, and zoning rules in local public finance. Under certain conditions, "voting with the feet"—moving to one's preferred community—results in a Pareto efficient allocation of public goods.

- Disadvantages of decentralization are intercommunity externalities, forgone scale economies in the provision of local public goods, inefficient taxation, and loss of scale economies in tax collection.

- Advantages of decentralization are the ability to alter the mix of public services to suit local tastes, the beneficial effects of competition between local governments, and the potential for low-cost experimentation at the subfederal level.

- Property taxes in the United States are levied by state and local governments. The incidence and efficiency effects of the property tax are generally viewed in one of three, not mutually exclusive, ways. The "traditional view" is that the property tax is an excise tax on land and structures. The "new view" is that the

property tax is a general tax on all capital with rates that vary across jurisdictions and different types of capital. The "user-fee view" regards property taxes as payment for local public services. An implication is that the tax has no excess burden.

- The property tax is one of the most unpopular taxes. One reform proposal is to institute a personal net worth tax in which the tax base is the difference between the market value of assets and liabilities. However, this is administratively complex and may undermine the most appealing aspect of the property tax in the context of a federal system—local administration.

- Grants may be either conditional (categorical) or unconditional (lump sum). Each type of grant embodies different incentives for local governments. The final mix of increased expenditure versus lower local taxes depends on the preferences dictating local choices.

- Empirical studies of intergovernmental grants indicate a *flypaper effect*—an increase in grant money induces greater spending on public goods than does an equivalent increase in local income. Models that emphasize the importance of bureaucrats' preferences explain this phenomenon as the result of incomplete citizen information about the budget constraints.

- One goal of grants policies is to increase educational spending levels. However, statistical research suggests that there may not be a link between spending and educational outcomes. Some economists argue that the entire educational system needs to be infused with competition.

- The federal tax deductibility of some state and local taxes can be viewed as a kind of intergovernmental grant. The impact of removing deductibility would depend on the role of itemizers in collective choice decisions and on the availability of other revenue sources to state and local governments.

Discussion Questions

1. For each of the following, decide whether the activity should be under the control of the federal, state, or local government, and explain why.

   a. Auto air-pollution control regulations.

   b. Fishing licenses for the Colorado River.

   c. Provision of weather satellites.

   d. Public refuse collection.

2. David and Jonathan own identical homes. David has owned his home for many years and paid $100,000 for it. Jonathan purchased his home after a recent property tax increase and paid $80,000. Should the local assessor change the assessed value of Jonathan's home to maintain horizontal equity? (Assume that there has been no inflation in housing prices since David purchased his home and that David and Jonathan value equally all public services provided in the local community.) In your answer, carefully define all key concepts.

3. Illustrate the following circumstances using community indifference curves and the local government budget constraint:

   a. An unconditional grant increases both the quantity of public goods purchased and local taxes.

   b. A matching grant leaves provision of the public good unchanged.

   c. A closed-ended matching grant has the same impact as a conditional nonmatching grant.

   d. A closed-ended matching grant leaves local taxes unchanged.

4. President Bush's budget for fiscal year 1992 proposed scrapping $15 billion a year in categorical grants. Instead, each state would get its money in one lump sum. If Bush's New Federalism program were implemented, how might it affect:

   a. The level of spending by state and local governments.

   b. The composition of spending by state and local governments.

   c. The quality of public education.

5. In 1985, Governor Mario Cuomo of New York argued that removing deductibility of state and local taxes "would have pulverized the middle class." How would you go about finding out whether this statement is true?

Selected References

Buchanan, James N. "An Economic Theory of Clubs." *Economica* 32 (February 1965), pp. 1–14.

Chubb, John E., and Terry M. Moe. *Politics, Markets, and America's Schools.* Washington, D.C.: Brookings Institution, 1990.

Courant, Paul N., and Edward M. Gramlich. "The Impact of TRA on State and Local Fiscal Behavior." In J. Slemrod, *Do Taxes Matter? The Impact of the Tax Reform Act of 1986.* Cambridge, Mass.: MIT Press, 1991.

Rubinfeld, Daniel. "The Economics of the Local Public Sector." In *Handbook of Public Economics, vol. 2,* ed. Alan J. Auerbach and Martin Feldstein. Amsterdam: North-Holland, 1987, Chapter 11.

Tiebout, Charles. "A Pure Theory of Local Expenditures." *Journal of Political Economy* 64 (1956), pp. 416–24.

Some Basic Microeconomics

A P P E N D I X

He who has choice also has pain.

GERMAN PROVERB

Certain tools of microeconomic theory are used throughout the text. They are briefly reviewed in this Appendix. Readers who have had an introductory course in microeconomics will likely find this review sufficient to refresh their memories. Those confronting the material for the first time may want to consult one of the standard introductory texts.[1] The subjects covered are demand and supply, consumer choice, and marginal analysis.

Demand and Supply

The demand and supply model shows how the price and output of a commodity are determined in a competitive market. We discuss in turn the determinants of demand, supply, and their interaction.

Demand

Which factors influence people's decisions to consume certain goods? To make the problem concrete, let us consider the specific case of coffee. A bit of introspection suggests that the following factors affect the amount of coffee that people want to consume during a given period of time:

1. **Price.** We expect that as the price goes up, the quantity demanded goes down.
2. **Income.** Changes in income modify people's consumption opportunities. It is hard to say a priori, however, what effect such changes have on consumption of a given good. One possibility

---

[1] See, for example, Paul Samuelson and William Nordhaus [1989].

is that as incomes go up, people use some of their additional income to purchase more coffee. On the other hand, it may be that as incomes increase, people consume less coffee, perhaps spending their money on cognac instead. We expect that changes in income affect demand one way or the other, but in some cases it is hard to predict the direction of the change. If an increase in income increases the demand (other things being the same), the good is called a **normal** good. If an increase in income decreases demand (other things being the same), the good is called an **inferior** good.

3. **Prices of Related Goods.** Suppose the price of tea goes up. If people can substitute coffee for tea, this increase in the price of tea increases the amount of coffee people wish to consume. Now suppose the price of cream goes up. If people consume coffee and cream together, this would tend to decrease the amount of coffee consumed. Goods like tea and coffee are called **substitutes;** goods like coffee and cream are called **complements.**

4. **Tastes.** The extent to which people "like" a good will affect the amount they demand. Presumably, less coffee is demanded in Mormon communities because that religion prohibits its consumption. Often, it is realistic to assume that consumers' tastes stay the same over time, but this is not always the case. For example, the announcement made by some scientists that coffee might cause birth defects presumably changed the tastes of pregnant women for coffee.[2]

We see, then, that a wide variety of things can affect demand. However, it is often useful to focus on the relationship between the quantity of a commodity demanded and the price. Suppose that we fix income, the prices of related goods, and tastes. We can imagine varying the price of coffee and seeing how the quantity demanded changes under the assumption that the other relevant variables stay at their fixed values. A **demand schedule** (or **demand curve**) is the relation between the market price of a good and the quantity demanded of that good during a given time period, other things being the same. (Economists often use the Latin for "other things being the same," *ceteris paribus.*)

A hypothetical demand schedule for coffee is represented graphically by curve D_c in Figure A.1. The horizontal axis measures pounds of coffee per year in a particular market, and the price per pound is measured on the vertical. Thus, for example, if the price is $2.29 per pound, people are willing to consume 750 pounds; when the price is only $1.38, they are

---

[2] Depending on the good under consideration, other items could be added to the list.

Figure A.1
Hypothetical
demand curve for
coffee

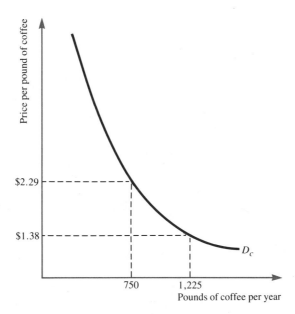

willing to consume 1,225 pounds. The downward slope of the demand
schedule reflects the reasonable assumption that when the price goes up,
the quantity demanded goes down.

The demand curve can also be interpreted as an approximate schedule of "willingness to pay," because it shows the maximum price that
people would pay for a given quantity. For example, when people purchase 750 pounds per year, they value it at $2.29 per pound. At any price
more than $2.29, they would not willingly consume 750 pounds per year.
If for some reason people were able to obtain 750 pounds at a price less
than $2.29, this would in some sense be a "bargain."

As already stressed, the demand curve is drawn on the assumption
that all other variables that might affect quantity demanded do not
change. What happens if one of them does? Suppose, for example, that
the price of tea increases, and as a consequence, people want to buy more
coffee. In Figure A.2, schedule D_c from Figure A.1 (before the increase) is
reproduced. As a consequence of the increase in the price of tea, at *each
price* of coffee people are willing to purchase more coffee than they did
previously. In effect, then, an increase in the price of tea shifts each point
on D_c to the right. The collection of new points is D_c'. Because D_c' shows
how much people are willing to consume at each price *(ceteris paribus)*, it
is by definition the demand curve.

More generally, a change in any variable that influences the demand
for a good—except its own price—shifts the demand curve.[3] (A change in
a good's own price induces a movement *along* the demand curve.)

---

[3] There is no need, incidentally, for D_c' to be parallel to D_c. In general, this will not be the case.

Figure A.2
Effect of an
increase in the price
of tea on the
demand for coffee

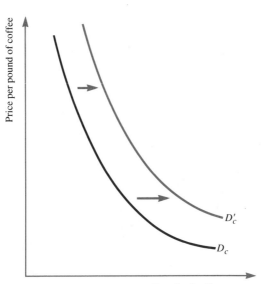

Pounds of coffee per year

Supply

Now consider the factors that determine the quantity of a commodity that firms supply to the market. We will continue using coffee as our example.

1. **Price.** In many cases, it is reasonable to assume that the higher the price per pound of coffee, the greater the quantity that profit-maximizing firms are willing to supply.

2. **Price of Inputs.** Coffee producers employ inputs to produce coffee—labor, land, and fertilizer. If their input costs go up, the amount of coffee that they can profitably supply at any given price goes down.

3. **Conditions of Production.** The most important factor here is the state of technology. If there is a technological improvement in coffee production, the supply increases. Other variables also affect production conditions. For agricultural goods, weather is important. Several years ago, for example, flooding in Latin America seriously reduced the coffee crop.

As with the demand curve, it is useful to focus attention on the relationship between the quantity of a commodity supplied and the price, holding the other variables at fixed levels. The **supply schedule** is the relation between market prices and the amount of a good that producers are willing to supply during a given period of time, *ceteris paribus*.

A supply schedule for coffee is depicted as S_c in Figure A.3. Its upward slope reflects the assumption that the higher the price, the greater the quantity supplied, *ceteris paribus*.

When any variable that influences supply (other than the commodity's own price) changes, the supply schedule shifts. Suppose, for example, that the wage rate for coffee-bean pickers increases. This increase

Figure A.3
Hypothetical supply
curve for coffee

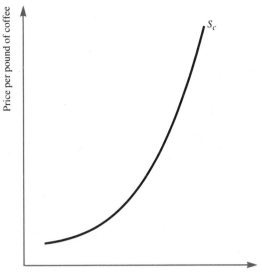

Figure A.4
Effect of an
increase in the
wages of coffee
pickers on the
supply of coffee

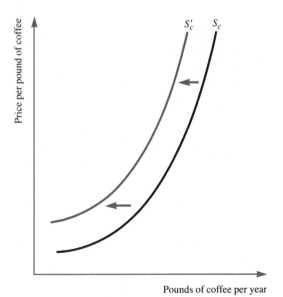

reduces the amount of coffee that firms are willing to supply at any given price. The supply curve therefore shifts to the left. As depicted in Figure A.4, the new supply curve is S_c'. More generally, when any variable other than the commodity's own price changes, the supply curve shifts. (A change in the commodity price induces a movement along the supply curve.)

Figure A.5

Equilibrium in the coffee market

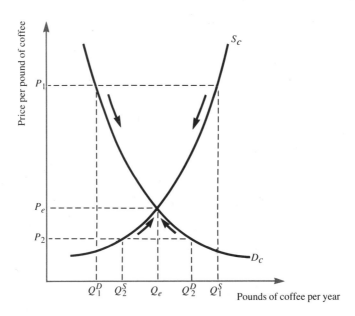

Equilibrium

The demand and supply curves provide answers to a set of hypothetical questions: *If* the price of coffee is $2 per pound, how much are consumers willing to purchase? *If* the price is $1.75 per pound, how much are firms willing to supply? Neither schedule by itself tells us what will be the actual price and quantity. But taken together, the schedules determine price and quantity.

In Figure A.5 we superimpose demand schedule D_c from Figure A.1 on supply schedule S_c from Figure A.3. We want to find the price and output at which there is an **equilibrium**—a situation which tends to be maintained unless there is an underlying change in the system. Suppose the price is P_1 dollars per pound. At this price, the quantity demanded is Q_1^D and the quantity supplied is Q_1^S. Price P_1 cannot be maintained, because firms want to supply more coffee than consumers are willing to purchase. This excess supply tends to push the price down, as suggested by the arrows.

Now consider price P_2. At this price, the quantity of coffee demanded, Q_2^D, exceeds the quantity supplied, Q_2^S. Because there is excess demand for coffee, we expect the price to rise.

Similar reasoning suggests that any price at which the quantity supplied and quantity demanded are unequal cannot be an equilibrium. In Figure A.5, quantity demanded equals quantity supplied at price P_e. The associated output level is Q_e pounds per year. Unless something else in the system changes, this price and output combination continues year after year. It is an equilibrium.

Suppose now that something else does change. For example, the weather turns bad, ruining a considerable portion of the coffee crop. In Figure A.6, D_c and S_c are reproduced from Figure A.5, and as before, the

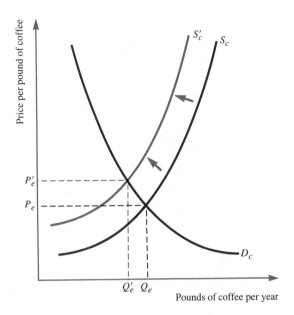

Figure A.6
Effect of bad
weather on the
coffee market

equilibrium price and output are P_e and Q_e, respectively. As a consequence of the weather change, the supply curve shifts to the left, say to S'_c. Given the new supply curve, P_e is no longer the equilibrium price. Rather, equilibrium is found at the intersection of D_c and S'_c, at price P'_e and output Q'_e. Note that, as one might expect, the crop disaster leads to a higher price and smaller output. (That is, $P'_e > P_e$ and $Q'_e < Q_e$.) More generally, a change in any variable that affects supply or demand creates a new equilibrium combination of price and quantity.

Supply and Demand for Inputs

Supply and demand can be used not only to investigate the markets for consumption goods but also the markets for **inputs** into the production process. (Inputs are sometimes referred to as **factors of production.**) For example, we could label the horizontal axis in Figure A.5 "number of hours worked per year" and the vertical axis "wage rate per hour." Then the schedules would represent the supply and demand for labor, and the market would determine wages and employment. Similarly, supply and demand analysis can be applied to the markets for capital and for land.

Measuring the Shapes of Supply and Demand Curves

Clearly, the market price and output for a given item depend substantially on the shape of its demand and supply curves. Conventionally, the shape of the demand curve is measured by the **price elasticity of demand:** the absolute value of the percentage change in quantity demanded divided by the percentage change in price.[4] If a 10 percent increase in price leads to a 2 percent decrease in quantity demanded, the price elasticity of demand is

---

[4] The elasticity need not be constant all along the demand curve.

"It's true that more is not necessarily better, Edward, but it frequently is."

Drawing by Saxon; © 1985 The New Yorker Magazine, Inc.

0.2. An important special case is when the quantity demanded does not change at all with a price increase. Then the demand curve is vertical and elasticity is zero. At the other extreme, when the demand curve is horizontal, then even a small change in price leads to a huge change in quantity demanded. By convention, this is referred to as an infinitely elastic demand curve. Similarly, the **price elasticity of supply** is defined as the percentage change in quantity supplied divided by the percentage change in price.

Theory of Choice

The fundamental problem of economics is that resources available to people are limited relative to people's wants. The theory of choice shows how people can make sensible decisions in the presence of such scarcity. In this section we develop a graphical representation of consumer tastes and show how these tastes can best be gratified in the presence of a limited budget.

Tastes

We assume that an individual derives satisfaction from the consumption of commodities.[5] Economists use the slightly archaic word **utility** as a synonym for satisfaction. Consider Oscar who consumes only two com-

---

[5] In this context, the notion of *commodities* should be interpreted very broadly. It includes not only items such as food, cars, and stereos, but also less tangible things like leisure time, clean air, and so forth.

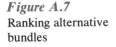

Figure A.7
Ranking alternative
bundles

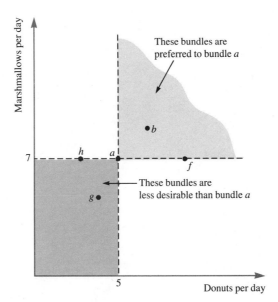

modities, marshmallows and donuts. (Using mathematical methods, all
the results for the two-good case can be shown to apply to situations in
which there are many commodities.) Assume further that for all feasible
quantities of marshmallows and donuts, Oscar is never satiated—more
consumption of either commodity always produces some increase in his
utility. Like the father in the cartoon on page 580, economists believe that
under most circumstances, this assumption is pretty realistic.

In Figure A.7, the horizontal axis measures the number of donuts
consumed each day, and the vertical axis shows daily marshmallow consumption. Thus, each point in the quadrant represents some bundle of
marshmallows and donuts. For example, point *a* represents a bundle with
seven marshmallows and five donuts.

Because Oscar's utility depends only on his consumption of marshmallows and donuts, we can also associate with each point in the quadrant
a certain level of utility. For example, if seven marshmallows and five
donuts create 100 "utils" of happiness, then point *a* is associated with 100
"utils."

Some commodity bundles create more utility than point *a*, and others
less. Consider point *b* in Figure A.7, which has both more marshmallows
and donuts than point *a*. Since satiation is ruled out, *b* must yield higher
utility than *a*. Bundle *f* has more donuts than *a* and no fewer marshmallows, and is also preferred to *a*. Indeed, any point to the northeast of *a* is
preferred to *a*.

The same reasoning suggests that bundle *a* is preferred to bundle *g*,
because the latter has fewer marshmallows and donuts than the former.

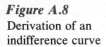

Figure A.8
Derivation of an
indifference curve

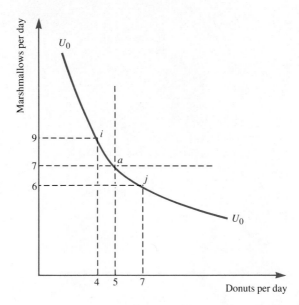

Point h is also less desirable than a, because although it has the same number of marshmallows as a, it has fewer donuts. Point a is preferred to any point southwest of it.

We have identified some bundles that yield more utility than a, and some that yield less. Can we find some bundles that produce just the same amount of utility as point a? Presumably there are such bundles but we need more information about the individual to find out which they are. Consider Figure A.8, where point a from Figure A.7 is reproduced. Imagine that we pose the following question to Oscar: "You are now consuming seven marshmallows and five donuts. If I take away one of your donuts, how many marshmallows do I need to give you to make you just as satisfied as you were initially?" Suppose that after thinking a while, Oscar (honestly) answers that he would require two more marshmallows. Then by definition, the bundle consisting of four donuts and nine marshmallows yields the same amount of utility as a. This bundle is denoted i in Figure A.8.

We could find another bundle of equal utility by asking: "Starting again at point a, suppose I take away one marshmallow. How many more donuts must I give you to keep you as well off as you originally were?" Assume that the answer is two donuts. Then the bundle with six marshmallows and seven donuts, denoted j in Figure A.8, must also yield the same amount of utility as bundle a.

We could go on like this indefinitely—start at point a, take away various amounts of one commodity, find out the amount of the other commodity required for compensation, and record the results on Figure

Figure A.9
An indifference
curve with a
diminishing marginal
rate of substitution

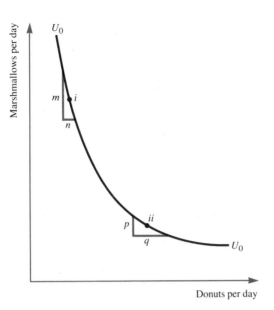

A.8. The outcome is curve $U_0 U_0$, which shows all points that yield the same amount of utility. $U_0 U_0$ is referred to as an **indifference curve,** because it shows all consumption bundles among which the individual is indifferent.

By definition, the **slope** of a curve is the change in the value of the variable measured on the vertical axis divided by the change in the variable measured on the horizontal—the "rise over the run." The slope of an indifference curve has an important economic interpretation. It shows the rate at which the individual is willing to trade one good for another. For example, in Figure A.9, around point i, the slope of the indifference curve is m/n. But by definition of an indifference curve, n is just the amount of donuts that Oscar is willing to substitute for sacrificing m marshmallows. For this reason, the absolute value of the slope of the indifference curve is often referred to as the **marginal rate of substitution** of donuts for marshmallows.[6] This is abbreviated MRS_{dm}.

As drawn in Figure A.9, the marginal rate of substitution declines as we move down along the indifference curve. For example, around point ii, MRS_{dm} is given by p/q, which is clearly smaller than m/n. Introspection leads one to conclude that this makes sense. Around point i, Oscar has a lot of marshmallows relative to donuts, and is therefore willing to give up quite a few marshmallows in return for an additional donut—hence a high

---

[6] As noted later, *marginal* means *additional* or *incremental*. The indifference curve's slope shows the *marginal* rate of substitution because it indicates the rate at which the individual would be willing to substitute marshmallows for an *additional* donut.

Figure A.10
An indifference map

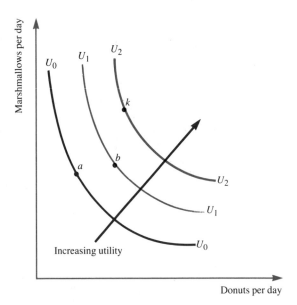

MRS_{dm}. On the other hand, around point *ii*, Oscar has a lot of donuts relative to marshmallows, so he is not willing to sacrifice a lot of marsh-mallows in return for yet another donut. The decline of MRS_{dm} as we move down along the indifference curve is called a **diminishing marginal rate of substitution.**

Recall that our construction of indifference curve $U_0 U_0$ was based on bundle *a* as a starting point. But point *a* was chosen arbitrarily, and we could just as well have started at any other point in the quadrant. In Figure A.10, if we start with point *b* and proceed in the same way, we can generate indifference curve $U_1 U_1$. Or starting at point *k*, we can generate indifference curve $U_2 U_2$. Note that any point on $U_2 U_2$ represents a higher level of utility than any point on $U_1 U_1$, which in turn, is preferred to any point on $U_0 U_0$. If Oscar is interested in maximizing his utility, he will try to reach the highest indifference curve that he can.

The entire collection of indifference curves is referred to as the **indifference map.** Once we have the indifference map, we know everything there is to know about the individual's preferences.

Budget Constraint

Basic setup. Suppose that marshmallows *(M)* cost 3 cents apiece, do-nuts *(D)* cost 6 cents, and Oscar's weekly income is 60 cents. What options does Oscar have? Whatever amounts he purchases must satisfy the equation

$$3 \times M + 6 \times D = 60 \tag{A.1}$$

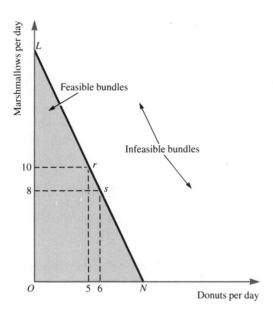

Figure A.11
Budget constraint

In words, expenditures on marshmallows ($3 \times M$) plus expenditures on donuts ($6 \times D$) must equal income (60).[7] Thus, for example, if $M = 10$, then to satisfy Equation (A.1), D must equal 5 ($3 \times 10 + 6 \times 5 = 60$). Alternatively, if $M = 8$, then D must equal 6 ($3 \times 8 + 6 \times 6 = 60$).

Let us represent Equation (A.1) graphically. The usual way is to graph a number of points that satisfy the equation. This is straightforward once we recall from basic algebra that (A.1) is just the equation of a straight line. Given two points on the line, the rest of the line is determined by connecting them. In Figure A.11, point r represents 10 marshmallows and 5 donuts, and point s represents 8 marshmallows and 6 donuts. Therefore, the line associated with Equation (A.1) is LN which passes through these points. By construction, *any* combination of marshmallows and donuts that lies along LN satisfies Equation (A.1). Line LN is known as the **budget constraint** or the **budget line.** Any point on or below LN (the shaded area) is feasible because it involves an expenditure less than or equal to income. Any point above LN is impossible because it involves an expenditure greater than income.

Two aspects of line LN are worth noting. First, the horizontal and vertical intercepts of the line have economic interpretations. By definition, the vertical intercept is the point associated with $D = 0$. At this

---

[7] If Oscar is a utility maximizer, we can assume that he will not throw away any of this income. It is also assumed that 60 cents is net of any saving he desires to make.

point, Oscar spends all his 60 cents on marshmallows, buying 20 of them (60/3). Hence, distance *OL* is 20. Similarly, at point *N*, Oscar consumes zero marshmallows, but can afford a binge consisting of 10 donuts (60/6). Distance *ON* is therefore 10. In short, the vertical and horizontal intercepts represent bundles in which only one of the commodities is consumed.

The slope also has an economic interpretation. To calculate the slope, recall that the "rise" *(OL)* is 20 and the "run" *(ON)* is 10, so the slope (in absolute value) is 2. Note that 2 is the ratio of the price of donuts (6 cents) to the price of marshmallows (3 cents). This is no accident. The absolute value of the slope of the budget line indicates the rate at which the market permits an individual to substitute marshmallows for donuts. Because the price of donuts is twice the price of marshmallows, Oscar can trade two marshmallows for each donut.

To generalize this discussion, suppose that the price per marshmallow is P_m, the price per donut is P_d, and income is I. Then in analogy to Equation (A.1), the budget constraint is

$$P_m M + P_d D = I \tag{A.2}$$

If M is measured on the vertical axis and D on the horizontal, the vertical intercept is I/P_m and the horizontal intercept is I/P_d. The slope of the budget constraint, in absolute value, is P_d/P_m. A common mistake is to assume that because M is measured on the vertical axis, the absolute value of the slope of the budget constraint is P_m/P_d. To see that this is wrong just divide the rise (I/P_m) by the run (I/P_d): $(I/P_m) \div (I/P_d) = P_d/P_m$. Intuitively, P_d must be in the numerator because its ratio to P_m shows the rate at which the market permits one to trade M for D.

Changes in prices and income.   The budget line shows Oscar's consumption opportunities given his current income and the prevailing prices. What if any of these change? Return to the case where $P_m = 3$, $P_d = 6$ and $I = 60$. The associated budget line, $3M + 6D = 60$, is drawn as *LN* in Figure A.12. Now suppose that Oscar's income falls to 30. Substituting into Equation (A.2), the new budget line is described by $3M + 6D = 30$. To graph this equation, note that the vertical intercept is 10 and the horizontal intercept is 5. Denoting these two points in Figure A.12 as *R* and *S*, respectively; and recalling that two points determine a line, we find that the new budget constraint is *RS*. The slope of *RS* in absolute value is 2, just like that of *LN*. This is because the relative prices of donuts and marshmallows have not changed. When income changes but relative prices do not, a parallel shift in the budget line is induced. If income decreases, the constraint shifts in; if income increases, it shifts out.

Figure A.12
Effect on the budget
constraint of a
decrease in income

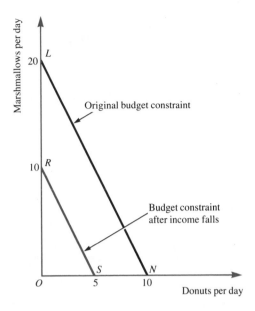

Figure A.13
Effect on the budget
constraint of a
change in relative
prices

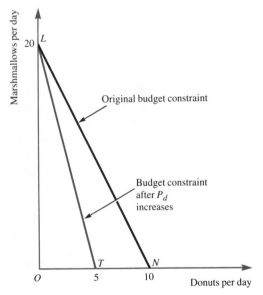

Return again to the original constraint, $3M + 6D = 60$, which is reproduced in Figure A.13 as LN. Suppose that the price of D increases to 12, but everything else stays the same. Then by Equation (A.2), the relevant budget constraint is $3M + 12D = 60$. To graph this new constraint, we begin by noting that it has a vertical intercept of 20, which is the same as that of LN. Because the price of M has stayed the same, if

Figure A.14
Utility maximization
subject to a budget
constraint

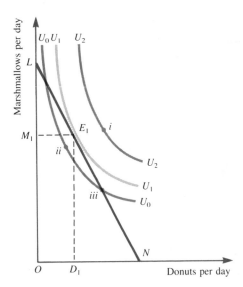

Oscar spends all his money only on M, then he can buy just as much as he did before. The horizontal intercept, however, is changed. It is now at five donuts (60/12), a point denoted T in Figure A.13. The new budget constraint is then LT. The slope of LT in absolute value is 4 (20/5), reflecting the fact that the market now allows each individual to trade four marshmallows per donut.

More generally, when the price of one commodity changes and other things stay the same, the budget line pivots along the axis of the good whose price changes. If the price goes up, the line pivots in; if the price goes down, the line pivots out.

Equilibrium

The indifference map shows what Oscar *wants* to do; the budget constraint shows what he *can* do. To find out what Oscar *actually* does, they must be put together.

In Figure A.14, we superimpose the indifference map from Figure A.10 onto budget line LN from Figure A.11. The problem is to find the combination of M and D that maximizes Oscar's utility subject to the constraint that he cannot spend more than his income.

Consider first the bundle represented by point i on $U_2 U_2$. This point is ruled out, because it is above LN. Oscar might like to be on indifference curve $U_2 U_2$, but he simply cannot afford it. Next consider point ii, which is certainly feasible, because it lies below the budget constraint. But it cannot be optimal, because Oscar is not spending his whole income. In effect, at bundle ii, he is just throwing away money that could have been spent on more marshmallows and/or donuts.

What about point iii? It is feasible, and Oscar is not throwing away any income. Yet he can still do better in the sense of putting himself on a higher indifference curve. Consider point E_1, where Oscar consumes D_1

donuts and M_1 marshmallows. Because it lies on LN, it is feasible. More-over, it is more desirable than bundle *iii*, because E_1 lies on U_1U_1, which is above U_0U_0. Indeed, no point on LN touches an indifference curve that is higher than U_1U_1. Therefore, the bundle consisting of M_1 and D_1 maxi-mizes Oscar's utility subject to budget constraint LN. E_1 is an equilibrium because unless something else in the system changes, Oscar will continue to consume M_1 marshmallows and D_1 donuts day after day.

Note that at the equilibrium, indifference curve U_1U_1 just barely touches the budget line. Intuitively, this is because Oscar is trying to achieve the very highest indifference curve he can while still keeping on LN. In more technical language, line LN is *tangent* to curve U_1U_1 at point E_1. This means that at point E_1 the slope of U_1U_1 is equal to the slope of LN.

This observation suggests an equation to characterize the point of utility maximization. Recall that by definition, the slope of the indiffer-ence curve (in absolute value) is the marginal rate of substitution of do-nuts for marshmallows, MRS_{dm}. The slope of the budget line (in absolute value) is P_d/P_m. But we just showed that at equilibrium, the two slopes are equal, or

$$MRS_{dm} = P_d/P_m \qquad\qquad (A.3)$$

Equation (A.3) is a necessary condition for a utility maximization.[8] That is, if the bundle being consumed is not consistent with Equation (A.3), then Oscar could do better by reallocating his income between the two commodities. Intuitively, MRS_{dm} is the rate at which Oscar is willing to trade M for D. On the other hand, P_d/P_m is the rate at which the market allows Oscar to trade M for D. At equilibrium, these two rates must be equal.

Now let us suppose that the price of marshmallows falls by some amount. Figure A.15 reproduces the equilibrium point E_1 from Figure A.14. As we showed earlier, when a price changes *(ceteris paribus)* the budget line pivots along the axis of the good whose price has changed. Because P_m falls, the budget line LN pivots around N to a point that is higher on the vertical axis. The new budget line is VN. Given that Oscar now faces budget line VN, E_1 is no longer an equilibrium. The fall in P_m has created new opportunities for Oscar, and utility maximization re-quires that he take advantage of them. Specifically, subject to budget line VN, Oscar maximizes utility at point E_2, where he consumes M_2 marsh-mallows and D_2 donuts.

At the new equilibrium, the amounts of both D and M have increased relative to the amounts consumed at the old equilibrium. ($D_2 > D_1$ and $M_2 > M_1$.) In effect, the price decrease in marshmallows allows Oscar to

---

[8] The equation holds only if some of each commodity is consumed. If the consumption of some commodity is zero, then Equation (A.3) need not be satisfied.

Figure A.15
Effect on
equilibrium of a
change in relative
prices

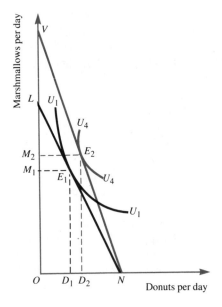

Figure A.16
Change in relative
prices with no effect
on donut
consumption

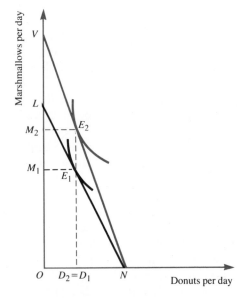

purchase more marshmallows and still have money left over to purchase
more donuts. While this is common, it need not always be the case. The
change depends on the tastes of the particular individual. Suppose that
Bert faces exactly the same prices as Oscar, and also has the same income. Bert's indifference map and budget constraints are depicted in
Figure A.16. For Bert, donut consumption is totally unchanged by the

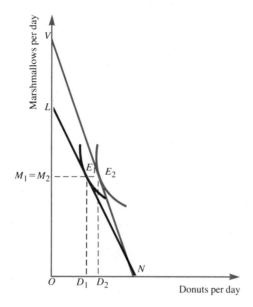

Figure A.17
Change in relative
prices with no effect
on marshmallow
consumption

decrease in the price of marshmallows. On the other hand, Ernie's preferences, depicted in Figure A.17, are such that a fall in P_m leaves the
amount of marshmallows the same, and only the amount of donuts increases. Thus, unless we have information about the individual's indifference map, we cannot predict just how he or she will respond to a change
in relative prices.

More generally, a change in prices and/or income changes the position of the budget constraint. The individual then *reoptimizes*—finds the
point that maximizes utility subject to the new budget constraint. This will
usually involve the selection of a new commodity bundle, but without
information on the individual's tastes, one cannot know for sure exactly
what the new bundle will look like. We do know, however, that as long as
the individual is a utility maximizer, the new bundle will satisfy the condition that the price ratio equal the marginal rate of substitution.

**Derivation of
Demand Curves**

There is a simple connection between the theory of consumer choice and
individual demand curves. Recall from Figure A.15, that at the original
price of marshmallows—call it P_m^1—Oscar consumed M_1 marshmallows.
When the price fell to P_m^2, Oscar increased his marshmallow consumption
to M_2. This pair of points may be plotted as in Figure A.18.

Repeating this experiment for various prices of marshmallows, we
find the quantity of marshmallows demanded at each price, holding fixed
money income, the price of donuts, and tastes. By definition, this is the
demand curve for marshmallows, shown as D_m in Figure A.18. Thus, we
see how the demand curve is derived from the underlying indifference map.

Figure A.18
Demand curve for
marshmallows
derived from an
indifference map

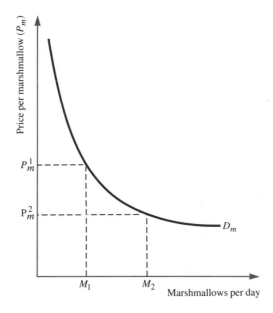

Figure A.19
Substitution and
income effects of a
price change

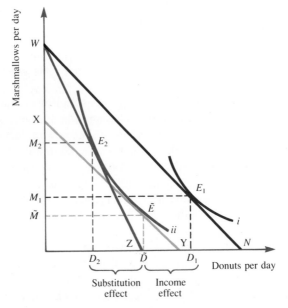

**Substitution and
Income Effects**

Figure A.19 depicts the situation of Grover, who initially faces budget
constraint WN, and maximizes utility at point E_1 on indifference curve i,
where he consumes D_1 donuts. Suppose now that the price of donuts
increases. Grover's budget constraint pivots from WN to WZ, and at the
new equilibrium, point E_2 on indifference curve ii, he consumes D_2 marshmallows.

Just for hypothetical purposes, suppose that at the new equilibrium E_2, the price of donuts falls back to its initial level, but that *simultaneously,* Grover's income is adjusted so that he is kept on indifference curve *ii*. If this hypothetical adjustment were made, what budget constraint would Grover face? Suppose we call this budget constraint XY. We know that XY must satisfy two conditions:

- Because Grover is kept on indifference curve *ii*, XY must be tangent to indifference curve *ii*.
- The slope (in absolute value) must be equal to the ratio of the original price of donuts to the price of marshmallows. This is because of the stipulation that the price of donuts is at its original value. Recall, however, that the slope of WN is the ratio of the original price of donuts to the price of marshmallows. Hence, XY must have the same slope as WN; that is, it must be parallel to WN.

In Figure A.19, XY is drawn so that these two conditions are satisfied—the line is parallel to WN and is tangent to indifference curve *ii*. If Grover were confronted with constraint XY, he would maximize utility at a point like $\bar{E}$, where his consumption of donuts is $\bar{D}$.

Why should this hypothetical budget line be of any interest? Because drawing line XY helps us break down the effect of the change in the price of donuts into two components, the first from E_1 to $\bar{E}$, and the second from $\bar{E}$ to E_2.

1. The movement from E_1 to $\bar{E}$ is generated by the parallel shift of WN down to XY. But recall from Figure A.12 that such parallel movements are associated with changes in income, holding relative prices constant. Hence, the movement from E_1 to $\bar{E}$ is in effect due to a change in income, and is called the **income effect** of the price change.

2. The movement from $\bar{E}$ to E_2 is a consequence purely of the change in the relative price of donuts to marshmallows. This movement shows that Grover substitutes marshmallows for donuts when donuts become more expensive. Hence, the movement from $\bar{E}$ to E_2 is called the **substitution effect.** Since the movement from $\bar{E}$ to E_2 involves compensating income (in the sense of changing income to stay on the same indifference curve), the movement from $\bar{E}$ to E_2 is sometimes called the **compensated response** to a change in price. If we wish to keep utility at the level represented by indifference curve *ii*, we measure the substitution effect by moving along *ii*. If, alternatively, we had wanted to keep utility at the level enjoyed along indifference curve *i*, we could have measured the substitution effect along indifference curve *i* instead. In any case, the compensated

response to a price change shows how the price change affects quantity demanded when income is simultaneously altered so that the level of utility is unchanged.

Intuitively, when the price of donuts increases two things happen:

- The increase in price reduces the individual's real income—his or her ability to afford commodities. When income goes down, the quantity purchased generally changes, even without any change in relative prices.[9] This is the income effect.
- The increase in the price of donuts makes donuts less attractive relative to marshmallows, inducing the substitution effect.

Any change in prices can be broken down into an income effect and a substitution effect.

We could repeat the exercise depicted in Figure A.19 for any change in the price of marshmallows. Suppose that for each price, we find the compensated quantity of donuts demanded, and make a plot with price on the vertical axis, and donuts on the horizontal. This plot is called the **compensated demand curve** for donuts. Note that the ordinary demand curve discussed at the beginning of this Appendix shows how quantity demanded varies with price, holding I fixed, where I is income measured in dollars. In contrast, the compensated demand curve shows how quantity demanded varies with price, holding the level of utility fixed.

Marginal Analysis in Economics

In economics, the word **marginal** usually means *additional* or *incremental*. Suppose, for example, that the annual total benefit per citizen of a 50-mile road is $42, and the annual total benefit of a 51-mile road is $43.50. Then the marginal benefit of the 51st mile is $1.50 ($43.50 − $42.00). Similarly, if the annual total cost per person of maintaining a 50-mile road is $38, and the total cost of a 51-mile road is $40, then the marginal cost of the 51st mile is $2.

Economists focus a lot of attention on marginal quantities because they usually convey the information required for rational decision making. Suppose that the government is trying to decide whether to construct the 51st mile. The key question is whether the *marginal* benefit is at least as great as the *marginal* cost. In our example, the marginal cost is $2 while the marginal benefit is only $1.50. Does it make sense to spend $2 to create $1.50 worth of benefits? The answer is no, and the extra mile should not be built. Note that basing the decision on total benefits and

---

[9] If the good is normal, the income effect of a price decrease increases the quantity demanded, and vice versa if it is inferior. In Figure A.19, donuts are a normal good because D_1 exceeds $\tilde{D}$.

Table A.1   **Total profit**

Tons of Fertilizer	Wheat	Corn
0	$ 0	$ 0
1	100	325
2	150	385
3	170	415
4	175	435
5	177	441
6	178	444

Table A.2   **Marginal profit**

Tons of Fertilizer	Wheat	Corn
1	$100	$325
2	50	60
3	20	30
4	5	20
5	2	6
6	1	3

costs would have led to the wrong answer. The total cost per person of the 51-mile road ($40) is less than the total benefit ($43.50). Still, it is not sensible to build the 51st mile. An activity should be pursued only if its marginal benefit is at least as large as its marginal cost.[10]

Another example of marginal analysis: Farmer McGregor has two fields. The first is planted in wheat and the second in corn. McGregor has seven tons of fertilizer to distribute between the two fields, and wants to allocate the fertilizer so that his total profits are as high as possible. The relationship between the amount of fertilizer and *total* profitability for each crop is depicted in Table A.1. Thus, for example, if six tons of fertilizer were devoted to wheat, and one ton to corn, total profits would be $503 (=$178 + $325).

To find the optimal allocation of fertilizer between the fields, it is useful to compute the marginal contribution to profits made by each ton of fertilizer. The first ton in the wheat field increases profits from $0 to $100, so the marginal contribution is $100. The second ton increases profits from $100 to $150, so its marginal contribution is $50. The complete set of computations for both crops is recorded in Table A.2.

---

[10] If the marginal cost of an action just equals its marginal benefit, one is indifferent between taking the action and not taking it.

Suppose that McGregor puts two tons of fertilizer on the wheat field and five tons on the corn field. Is this a profit maximizing allocation? To answer this question, we must determine whether any other allocation would lead to higher total profits. Suppose that one ton of fertilizer were removed from the corn field and devoted instead to wheat. As a consequence of removing the fertilizer from the corn field, profits from corn would go down by $6. But at the same time, profits from the wheat field would increase by $20 (the marginal profit associated with the third ton of fertilizer in the wheat field). Farmer McGregor would therefore be $14 richer on balance. Clearly, it is not sensible for McGregor to put two tons of fertilizer on the wheat field and five tons on the corn, because he can do better (by $14) with three tons devoted to wheat and four to corn.

Is this latter allocation optimal? To answer, note that at this allocation, the marginal profit of fertilizer in each field is equal to $20. When the marginal profitability of fertilizer is the same in each field, there is *no way* that fertilizer can be reallocated between fields to increase total profit. In other words, total profits are maximized when the marginal profit in each field is the same. Readers who are skeptical of this result should try to find an allocation of the seven tons of fertilizer such that the total profit is higher than the $605 ($170 + $435) associated with the allocation at which the marginal profits are equal.

In general, if resources are being distributed across several activities, maximization of *total* returns requires that *marginal* returns in each activity be equal.[11]

---

[11] More precisely, this result also requires that the marginal returns be diminishing, as they are in Table A.2. In most applications, this is a reasonable assumption.

Glossary

Absolute Tax Incidence
The effect of a tax on the distribution of income when there is no change in either other taxes or government spending.

Accelerated Depreciation
Allowing firms to write off depreciation faster than true economic depreciation.

Accessions Tax
A tax levied on an individual's total lifetime acquisitions from inheritances and gifts.

Ad Valorem Tax
A tax computed as a percentage of the value of the purchase.

Additive Social Welfare Function
An equation defining social welfare as the sum of individuals' utilities.

Adjusted Gross Income (AGI)
Total income from all taxable sources less certain expenses incurred in earning that income.

Adverse Selection
The situation that occurs when the people who are most likely to receive benefits from a certain type of insurance are the

ones who are most likely to purchase it.

Agenda Manipulation
The process of organizing the order in which votes are taken to assure a favorable outcome.

Alternative Minimum Tax
The tax liability calculated by an alternative set of rules designed to force individuals with high levels of preference income to incur at least some tax liability.

Arm's Length System
A method of calculating taxes for multinational corporations by treating transactions between domestic and foreign operations as if they were separate enterprises.

Arrow's Impossibility Theorem
It is impossible to translate individual preferences into collective preferences without violating at least one of a brief, specified list of ethically reasonable conditions.

Assessed Value
The value a jurisdiction assigns to a property for tax purposes.

Assessment Ratio
The ratio of a property's assessed value to its market value.

Average Indexed Monthly Earnings (AIME)
The average wages in covered employment over the length of an individual's working life. The AIME is used in the computation of an individual's Social Security benefit.

Balanced Budget Incidence
The combined distributional effect of levying taxes and the government spending financed by those taxes.

Benefit-Cost Ratio
The ratio of the present value of a stream of benefits to the present value of a stream of costs for a project.

Benefits-Received Principle
Consumers of a publicly provided service should be the ones who pay for it.

Bequest Effect
Individuals save more to counteract the redistribution of income from children to parents implicit in the Social Security

system. The increased saving is used to finance a larger bequest to children.

Bracket Creep
The situation in which an increase in an individual's nominal income pushes her into a higher tax bracket despite the fact that her real income is unchanged. See also **tax indexing.**

Brain Drain
The emigration of highly skilled citizens of less developed countries to more developed countries.

Budget Constraint
The representation of the bundles among which a consumer may choose, given his income and the prices he faces.

Budget Line
See **budget constraint.**

Capital Gain (Loss)
An increase (decrease) in the value of an asset.

Capital Intensive
An industry in which the ratio of capital to labor inputs is relatively high.

Capitalization
The process by which a stream of tax liabilities becomes incorporated into the price of an asset.

Capitation Fee
A system under which medical care is provided for a particular individual or set of individuals for a fixed monthly fee.

Catastrophic Cap
An upper limit to the amount of an individual's out-of-pocket costs for an illness.

Categorical Grants
Grants for which the donor may specify to an extent how the funds can be used.

Centralization Ratio
The proportion of total direct government expenditures made by the central government.

Certainty Equivalent
The value of an uncertain project measured in terms of how much certain income an individual would be willing to give up for the set of uncertain outcomes generated by the project.

Ceteris Paribus
Other things being the same.

Circuit Breakers
Tax benefits to individuals based on the excess of residential property tax payments over some specified portion of income.

Clientele Effect
Firms structure their financial policies to meet different clienteles' needs. Those with low dividend payments attract shareholders with high marginal tax rates, and vice versa.

Club
A voluntary association of people who band together to finance and share some kind of benefit.

Coase Theorem
Provided that transactions costs are negligible, an efficient solution to an externality problem will be achieved as long as someone is assigned property rights, independent of who is assigned those rights.

Coinsurance Rate
The proportion of costs above the deductible for which an insured individual is liable.

Commodity Egalitarianism
The idea that some commodities ought to be made available to everybody.

Compensated Demand Curve
A demand curve that shows how quantity demanded varies with price, holding utility constant.

Compensated Response
How a price change affects quantity demanded when income is simultaneously altered so that the level of utility is unchanged.

Complements
Two goods are complements if an increase in the price of one good leads to decreased consumption of the other good.

Conditional Grants
See **categorical grants.**

Consumer Surplus
The amount by which consumers' willingness to pay for a commodity exceeds the sum they actually have to pay.

Consumption-Type VAT
The full value of capital investments is subtracted from sales in the computation of the value added.

Contract Curve
The locus of all Pareto-efficient points.

Corlett-Hague Rule
Efficient taxation requires taxing commodities that are complementary to leisure at relatively high rates.

Corporation
A state-chartered form of business organization usually with limited liability for shareholders (owners) and an independent legal status.

Cost-Plus Contract
A contract specifying that a firm is paid a certain fee plus all costs it incurs in completing a project.

Cost-Based Reimbursements
A system under which health-care providers report their costs to the government and receive payment in that amount.

Cost-Benefit Analysis
A set of practical procedures based on welfare economics for guiding public expenditure decisions.

Cost-Effectiveness Analysis
A systematic study of the costs of the various alternatives that attain similar benefits in order to determine which one is the cheapest.

Credit Budget
An annual statement that estimates the volume of new direct loans and loan guarantees made by the federal government for the fiscal year.

Crowding Out Hypothesis
Government borrowing decreases private investment by raising the market interest rate.

Cycling
When paired majority voting on more than two possibilities goes on indefinitely without a conclusion ever being reached.

Debt
The total amount owed at a given point in time; the sum of all past deficits.

Decedent
A deceased person.

Deductible
The amount of expenses that an individual must pay out of his or her pocket before an insurance policy makes any contribution.

Deductions
Certain expenses that may be subtracted from Adjusted Gross Income in the computation of taxable income.

Deficit
The excess of expenditures over revenues during a period of time.

Demand Curve
A graph of the demand schedule.

Demand Schedule
The relation between the price of a good and the quantity demanded, *ceteris paribus*.

Diagnostic Related Groups (DRGs)
Categories of illnesses and treatment types defined by the Medicare system; they determine how much a hospital will be paid for an individual's treatment under a prospective reimbursement system.

Differential Commodity Tax
See **excise tax.**

Differential Tax Incidence
The effect on the income distribution of a change in taxes, with government expenditures held constant.

Diminishing Marginal Rate of Substitution
The marginal rate of substitution falls as we move down along an indifference curve.

Direct Loans
Loans from the federal government made directly to individuals, businesses, nonprofit institutions, and local governments.

Director's Law
Government expenditures tend to benefit the middle class, while taxes are borne also by the rich and the poor.

Discount Factor
The number by which an amount of future income must be divided to compute its present value. If the interest rate is r and the income is receivable T periods in the future, the discount factor is $(1 + r)^T$.

Discount Rate
The rate of interest used to compute present value.

District Power Equalization Grant
Grant to local government to raise local revenue to a level that would be achieved if the local property tax base were at a certain hypothetical level.

Dividend Relief Approach
A method for relieving double taxation under which the corporation deducts dividends paid to the stockholders.

Double-Peaked Preferences
If, as a voter moves away from his or her most preferred out-

come, utility goes down, but then goes back up again.

Double Taxation
Taxing income generated in a corporation first at the corporate level, and again when it is distributed to shareholders.

Earned Income Tax Credit
A tax credit for low income individuals with dependents.

Earnings Test
A test based on earnings to determine whether an individual can receive full Social Security benefits. An individual whose earnings exceed a certain ceiling faces a reduction in concurrent Social Security benefits.

Econometrics
The statistical tools for analyzing economic data.

Economic Depreciation
The extent to which a durable asset decreases in value over a period of time.

Economic Incidence
The change in the distribution of real income brought about by a tax.

Economic Profit
The return to owners of a firm in excess of the opportunity costs of all the factors used in production. Also called supranormal or excess profit.

Edgeworth Box
A device used to depict the distribution of goods in a two good–two person world. The box is formed by drawing a separate set of axes for each person with one good on each axis.

Efficient
See **Pareto efficient.**

Elasticity of Substitution
A measure of the ease with which one factor of production can be substituted for another.

Empirical Work
Analysis based on observation and experience as opposed to theory.

Endowment Point
The consumption bundle that is available if there are no exchanges with the market. In the intertemporal consumption model, this is the bundle at which there is no saving or borrowing.

Entitlement Programs
Programs whose expenditures are determined by the number of people who qualify, rather than preset budget allocations.

Equilibrium
A situation that tends to be maintained unless there is an underlying change in the system.

Equivalent Variation
A change in income that is equivalent in its effect on utility to a change in the price of a commodity.

Excess Burden
A loss of welfare above and beyond taxes collected. Also called welfare cost or deadweight loss.

Excise Tax
A tax levied on the purchase of a particular commodity.

Exclusionary Zoning Laws
Statutes that prohibit certain uses of land.

Exemption
When calculating taxable income, an amount per family member that can be subtracted from Adjusted Gross Income.

Expenditure Incidence
The impact of government expenditures on the distribution of real income.

Expenditure Tax
See **personal consumption tax.**

Expensing
Deducting the entire value of an asset in the computation of taxable income.

Experience Rated
A method of determining what unemployment insurance tax rate a firm should pay based on the firm's past layoff experience.

External Debt
The amount that a government owes to foreigners.

Externality
An activity of one entity affects the welfare of another entity in a way that is outside the market.

Factors of Production
See **inputs.**

Federal Government
A public sector with both centralized and decentralized levels of decision making.

First-In, First-Out (FIFO)
The method of inventory valuation in which units of inventory purchased first are assumed to be sold first.

Fixed-Price Contract
A contract stipulating that the firm will complete a project in

return for a price independent of its costs.

Flat Tax
A tax schedule for which the marginal tax rate is constant throughout the entire range of incomes.

Flow Variable
A variable that is measured over a period of time. See also **stock variable.**

Flypaper Effect
A dollar received by the community in the form of a grant to its government results in greater public spending than a dollar increase in community income.

Foreign Subsidiary
A company incorporated abroad, but owned by a U.S. corporation.

Foundation Aid
Grant designed to assure a minimum level of expenditure.

401(k) Plan
A savings plan under which an employee can earmark a portion of his or her salary each year, with no income tax liability incurred on that portion.

Free Rider Problem
The incentive to let other people pay for a public good while you enjoy the benefits.

Full Loss Offset
Allowing individuals to deduct from taxable income all losses on capital assets.

Functional Distribution of Income
The way that income is distributed among people when they are classified according to the inputs they supply to the pro-

duction process (for example, landlords, capitalists, laborers).

Functional Finance
Using fiscal policy to keep aggregate demand at the desired level, regardless of the impact on deficits.

General Agreement on Tariffs and Trades (GATT)
A multinational pact that regulates international trade practices. Under this agreement, a country can grant an export rebate on certain taxes.

General Equilibrium Analysis
The study of how various markets are interrelated.

General Sales Tax
A tax levied at the same rate on the purchase of all commodities.

Generation Skipping
Arranging an estate in such a way that one or more generations avoid paying taxes on it.

Global System
A system under which an individual is taxed on income whether it is earned in the home country or abroad.

Government-Sponsored Enterprises
Privately owned institutions established by the federal government.

Gramm-Rudman-Hollings Act (GRH)
A law designed to reduce the national deficit. An important feature of this law is that if Congress fails to achieve certain designated deficit targets during the fiscal year, the excess deficit is reduced through automatic spending cuts.

Gross Estate
All property owned by the decedent at the time of death.

Gross Income-Type VAT
No deductions are allowed for capital investments when calculating value added.

Gross Replacement Rate
The proportion of pretax earnings replaced by unemployment insurance.

Haig-Simons (H-S) Definition of Income
Money value of the net increase to an individual's power to consume during a period.

Hicks-Kaldor Criterion
A project should be undertaken if it has a positive net present value, regardless of the distributional consequences.

Horizontal Equity
People in equal positions should be treated equally.

Horizontal Summation
The process of creating a market demand curve by summing the quantities demanded by each individual at every price.

Hospital Insurance (HI)
A provision of Medicare that covers specified amounts of inpatient medical care and care in a nursing facility.

Impure Public Good
A good that is rival to some extent. See **public good.**

Imputed Rent
The net monetary value of the services that a homeowner receives from a dwelling.

Incentive Contract
A contract specifying that the contracting firm receives a fixed fee plus some fraction of the costs of the project.

Income Effect
The effect of a price change on the quantity demanded due exclusively to the fact that the consumer's real income has changed.

Income Splitting
Using the arithmetic average of family income to determine each family member's taxable income, regardless of who actually earned the money.

Independence of Irrelevant Alternatives
A society's ranking of two different projects depends only on individuals' rankings of the two projects, not on how individuals rank the two projects relative to other alternatives.

Indifference Curve
A graph of all different consumption bundles that yield the same total utility.

Indifference Map
The collection of all indifference curves.

Individual Retirement Account (IRA)
For qualified individuals, a savings account in which the contributions are tax deductible and the interest accrues tax free, provided the funds are held until retirement. Upon withdrawal, both contributions and accrued interest are subject to tax.

Inferior Good
A good whose demand decreases as income increases.

Inheritance Tax
Taxes levied on an individual receiving an inheritance.

In-Kind Transfers
Payments from the government to individuals in the form of commodities or services rather than cash.

Inputs
Factors that are used in the production process.

Inter Vivos Transfers
Transfers of wealth between living people.

Internal Debt
The amount that a government owes to its own citizens.

Internal Rate of Return
The discount rate that would make a project's net present value zero.

Intertemporal Budget Constraint
The schedule showing all feasible consumption patterns over more than one time period.

Inverse Elasticity Rule
As long as goods are unrelated in consumption, tax rates should be inversely proportional to elasticities in order to achieve efficiency.

Investment Tax Credit (ITC)
A provision of the tax code that permitted a firm to subtract some portion of the purchase price of an asset from its tax liability. The Tax Reform Act of 1986 eliminated **ITCs** in the United States.

Invoice Method
The method for administering a VAT under which each firm is liable for taxes on total sales, but can claim the taxes already paid by suppliers as a credit against this liability, provided

this tax payment is verified by invoices from suppliers.

Iron Triangle
The cooperation of three major groups—the legislators who authorize a program, the bureaucrats who administer it, and the special interest groups that benefit from it—to obtain mutually beneficial outcomes.

Itemized Deduction
A specific type of expenditure that can be subtracted from adjusted gross income in the computation of taxable income.

Keogh Plan
A savings plan under which self-employed individuals can exclude some percentage of their net business income from taxation if the money is deposited into a qualified account.

Labor Intensive
An industry in which the ratio of capital to labor inputs is relatively low.

Laffer Curve
A graph of the tax rate–tax revenue relationship.

Last In, First Out (LIFO)
The method of inventory valuation in which the most recently purchased units of inventory are assumed to be sold first.

Life-Cycle Model
Individuals' consumption and saving behavior during a given year is the result of a planning process that considers their lifetime economic circumstances.

Lindahl Prices
The tax share an individual must pay per unit of public good.

Linear Income Tax Schedule
See flat tax.

Loan Guarantee
Promises to repay principal and interest on a loan in case the borrower defaults.

Local Public Good
A public good that benefits only the members of a particular community.

Lock-In Effect
The disincentive to change portfolios that arises because an individual incurs a tax on realized capital gains.

Logrolling
The trading of votes to obtain passage of a package of legislative proposals.

Lump Sum Tax
A tax for which the individual's liability does not depend on his or her behavior.

Majority Voting Rule
One more than half of the voters must favor a measure for it to be approved.

Marginal
Incremental, additional.

Marginal Cost
The incremental cost of producing one more unit of output.

Marginal Rate of Substitution
The rate at which an individual is willing to trade one good for another; it is the slope of an indifference curve.

Marginal Rate of Transformation
The rate at which the economy can transform one good into

another good; it is the slope of the production possibilities frontier.

Marginal Tax Rate
The proportion of the last dollar of income taxed by the government.

Marriage Neutral
A system under which two individuals' tax liabilities do not change when they marry.

Maximin Criterion
The notion that social welfare depends on the utility of the individual who has the minimum utility in the society.

Means-Tested
A spending program whose benefits flow only to those whose financial resources fall below a certain level.

Mechanistic View of Government
The political philosophy based on the assumption that individuals are the fundamental unit of society. According to this philosophy, government is a creation of individuals to better achieve their individual goals.

Median Voter
The voter whose preferences lie in the middle of the set of all voters' preferences; half the voters want more of the item selected, and half want less.

Median Voter Theorem
As long as all preferences are single-peaked and several other conditions are satisfied, the outcome of majority voting reflects the preferences of the median voter.

Merit Good
A commodity that ought to be provided even if the members of society do not demand it.

Monopoly
A market in which there is only one seller of a good.

Moral Hazard
The situation that occurs when an individual's behavior is affected by the fact that he or she is insured.

Multiple Regression Analysis
An econometric technique for estimating the parameters of a theoretical equation involving a dependent variable and more than one explanatory variable.

Natural Monopoly
A situation in which cost factors inherent in the production process lead to a single firm supplying the entire industry's output.

Neoclassical Model
A model of investment behavior in which the cost of capital is the primary determinant of the amount invested.

Net Income-Type VAT
The tax base for the VAT is based on net income so that depreciation is excluded from the base.

Net Replacement Rate
The proportion of after-tax income replaced by unemployment insurance.

Net Wage
The wage after taxes.

Neutral Taxation
Taxing every good at the same rate.

Nominal Amounts
Amounts of money that are valued according to the price

levels that exist in the year that the amount is received.

Nominal Income
Income measured in terms of current prices.

Nominal Interest Rate
The interest rate observed in the market.

Noncategorical Welfare Program
A program in which an individual's benefit depends only on income, not on whether he or she has a particular personal characteristic (such as being a single parent).

Normal Good
A good whose demand increases as income increases.

Normative Economics
The study of whether or not the economy is producing socially desirable results.

Off-Budget Deficit
The deficit resulting from off-budget expenditures and revenues.

Off-Budget Federal Agencies
Federally owned and controlled agencies whose fiscal activities are excluded by law from budget totals.

On-Budget Deficit
The deficit resulting from on-budget expenditures and revenues.

Organic View of Government
The political philosophy that views society as a natural organism with the government as its heart. Individuals are viewed as merely parts of the organism, having significance only as part of the community.

Original Position
An imaginary situation in which people have no knowledge of what their economic place in society will be, whether they will be relatively rich or relatively poor.

Overlapping Generations Model
A model that takes into account the fact that several different generations may coexist simultaneously.

Parameters
In econometrics, the coefficients of the explanatory variables (on the right-hand side of the equation) that define the statistical relationship between a change in an explanatory variable and a change in the dependent variable.

Pareto Efficient
An allocation of resources such that no person can be made better off without making another person worse off.

Pareto Improvement
A reallocation of resources such that at least one person is made better off without making anyone else worse off.

Partial Equilibrium Models
Models that study only one market and ignore possible spillover effects in other markets.

Partial Factor Tax
Tax levied on an input in only some of its uses.

Partnership Method
All earnings of the corporation during a given year, distributed or not, are attributed to stockholders. Each stockholder incurs a tax liability on her share of the earnings at her personal income tax rate.

Pay-As-You-Go
A Social Security system under which benefits paid to current retirees come from payments made by those who are presently working.

Peak
A point on the graph of an individual's preferences at which all the neighboring points have lower utility.

Pecuniary Externality
Effects on welfare that are transmitted via the price system.

Perfect Price Discrimination
When a producer charges each person the maximum he is willing to pay for the good.

Personal Consumption Tax
A system under which each household's tax base is its expenditures on consumption.

Personal Net Worth Tax
A tax based on the difference between the market value of all the taxpayer's assets and liabilities.

Pigouvian Tax
A tax levied on each unit of a polluter's output in an amount just equal to the marginal damage that it inflicts at the efficient level of pollution.

Positive Economics
The study of how the economy actually functions (as opposed to how it ought to function).

Poverty Gap
The amount of money that would be required to raise the

incomes of all poor households to the poverty line, assuming that the transfers would induce no changes in behavior.

Poverty Line
A fixed level of real income considered enough to provide a minimally adequate standard of living.

Present Value
The maximum amount that an individual would be willing to pay now for the right to a future benefit.

Present Value Criteria
Rules for evaluating projects stating that (1) a project should be carried out only if it has a positive net present value; and (2) of two mutually exclusive projects, the preferred project is the one with the higher net present value.

Price Elasticity of Demand
The absolute value of the percentage change in quantity demanded divided by the percentage change in price.

Price Elasticity of Supply
The absolute value of the percentage change in quantity supplied divided by the percentage change in price.

Price Taker
An agent unable to affect the market price of a good.

Primary Insurance Amount (PIA)
The basic Social Security benefit payable to a worker who retires at age 65 or who becomes disabled.

Principal-Agent Problem
In a situation where one person (the principal) wants another

person (the agent) to perform a task, the principal may find it difficult to monitor the agent's behavior. The principal-agent problem is to design the agent's incentives so that the principal's expected gain is as high as possible.

Privatization
The process of changing ownership or control of an enterprise from the public to the private sector.

Production Possibilities Frontier
The set of all the feasible combinations of goods that can be produced with a given quantity of inputs which are all used efficiently.

Progressive
A tax system under which an individual's average tax rate increases with income.

Proportional
A tax system under which an individual's average tax rate is the same at each level of income.

Public Economics
See **public finance.**

Public Finance
The field of economics that analyzes government taxation and spending policies.

Public Good
A good which is not rival in consumption; the fact that one person benefits from this good does not prevent another person from doing the same simultaneously.

Public Sector Economics
See **public finance.**

Pure Public Good
See **public good.**

Ramsey Rule
To minimize total excess burden, tax rates should be set so that the percentage reduction in the quantity demanded of each commodity induced by the taxes is the same.

Random Error
The term of a regression equation that represents the unexplained difference between the dependent variable and its value as predicted by the model.

Rate Schedule
A list of the tax liabilities associated with each level of taxable income.

Real Amounts
Amounts of money adjusted for changes in the general price level.

Real Income
A measure of income taking into account changes in the general price level.

Real Interest Rate
The nominal interest rate corrected for changes in the level of prices by subtracting the expected inflation rate.

Realized Capital Gain
A capital gain resulting from the sale of an asset.

Regression Coefficient
See **parameter.**

Regression Line
The line that provides the best fit through a group of points, usually determined by minimizing the squares of the vertical distances between the points and the line.

Regressive
A tax system under which an individual's average tax rate decreases with income.

Regulatory Budget
An annual statement of the costs imposed on the economy by government regulations. Although a federal regulatory budget has been proposed, currently none exists.

Repatriate
To return the earnings of a subsidiary to its parent company.

Retirement Effect
Social Security may induce an individual to retire earlier, which means that, *ceteris paribus,* he or she has to save more to finance a longer retirement period.

Revenue Sharing
A grant from the federal government to a state or a local government that places no restrictions on the use of funds.

Right of Survivorship
For jointly owned property, on the death of one owner, the property is automatically passed on to the other owner.

Rivalness of Consumption
When one person benefiting from consumption of a specific good prevents another person from doing so simultaneously.

Selective Sales Tax
See **excise tax.**

Shadow Price
The underlying social cost of an input. This cost may not be fully reflected in its market price.

Shares Allocation Approach
For purposes of determining the tax liabilities of an enterprise that does business in several jurisdictions, the practice of allocating central costs among jurisdictions according to the proportion of total company assets and sales located in each jurisdiction.

Single-Peaked Preferences
Utility consistently falls as a voter moves away from his most preferred outcome.

Size Distribution of Income
The way that total income is distributed across income classes.

Slope
The change in the variable measured on the vertical axis divided by the change in the variable measured on the horizontal axis.

Social Insurance
Government programs that replace income losses which are, at least in part, outside personal control.

Social Rate of Discount
A discount rate that measures the rate at which society is willing to trade off present consumption for future consumption.

Social Security Trust Fund
A fund in which Social Security payroll taxes are accumulated for the purpose of paying out benefits in the future.

Social Security Wealth
The present value of expected future Social Security benefits.

Social Welfare Function
A function reflecting society's views on how the utilities of its members affect the well being of society as a whole.

Standard Deduction
Subtraction of a fixed amount from adjusted gross income that does not require documentation.

Standard Error
A statistical measure of how much an estimated parameter can vary from its true value.

Statistically Significant
When the standard error of a regression coefficient is low in relation to the size of the estimated parameter.

Statutory Incidence
Indicates who is legally responsible for a tax.

Stock Variable
Variable that is measured as of a given point in time. See also **flow variable.**

Subsidiary
A company owned by one corporation but chartered separately from the parent corporation.

Substitutes
Two goods are substitutes if an increase in the price of one good leads to increased consumption of the other good.

Substitution Effect
The tendency of an individual to consume more of one good and less of another because of a change in the two goods' relative prices.

Supplementary Medical Insurance (SMI)
The portion of Medicare that pays for physicians, supplies ordered by physicians, and medical services rendered outside a hospital.

Supplementary Security Income (SSI)
A welfare program that provides a minimum income guarantee for the aged and disabled.

Supply Schedule
The relation between market price of a good and the quantity that producers are willing to supply, *ceteris paribus*.

Tax Amnesty
Allowing delinquent taxes to be paid without prosecution.

Tax Arbitrage
Producing a risk-free profit by exploiting inconsistencies in the tax code.

Tax Avoidance
Altering behavior in such a way to reduce your legal tax liability.

Tax Credit
A subtraction from tax liability (as opposed to a subtraction from taxable income).

Tax Effort
The ratio of tax collections to tax capacity.

Tax Evasion
Not paying taxes legally due.

Tax Expenditure
A loss of tax revenue because some item is excluded from the tax base.

Tax Indexing
Automatically adjusting the tax schedule to compensate for changes in inflation so that an individual's real tax burden is independent of inflation.

Tax Life
The number of years an asset can be depreciated.

Tax Prepayment Approach
Under a personal consumption tax, durables are taxed when they are purchased, and future consumption benefits generated by the durable are not taxed.

Tax Shifting
The difference between statutory incidence and economic incidence.

Tax Wedge
The tax-induced difference between the price paid by consumers and the price received by producers.

Taxable Estate
The gross estate less deductions for costs of settling the estate, outstanding debts of the estate, and charitable contributions.

Taxable Income
The amount of income subject to tax.

Territorial System
A system under which an individual earning income in a foreign country only needs to pay taxes to the host government.

Theory of the Second Best
In the presence of existing distortions, policies that in isolation would increase efficiency can decrease it, and vice versa.

Third Party Payment
Payment for services by someone other than the provider or the consumer.

Time Endowment
The maximum number of hours per year that an individual can work.

Trust
An arrangement whereby a trustee holds legal title to assets with the obligation to use them for the benefit of another party.

Turnover Tax
A tax whose base is the total value of sales at each level of production.

Two-Part Tariff
A system under which a consumer first pays a lump sum for the right to purchase a good and then pays a price for each unit of the good actually purchased.

Underground Economy
Those economic activities that are either illegal, or legal but structured so that they are hidden from tax authorities.

Unearned Income
Income, such as dividends or interest income, that is not directly gained through supplying labor.

Unified Budget
A document in which the federal government itemizes all its expenditures and revenues.

Unified Transfer Tax
A tax in which amounts transferred as gifts and bequests are jointly taken into account.

Unit Tax
A tax levied as a fixed amount per unit of commodity purchased.

Unrealized Capital Gain
A capital gain on an asset not yet sold.

Use Tax
A sales tax that residents of a given state must pay to that state even if the commodity was purchased in another state.

User Cost of Capital
The opportunity cost to a firm of owning a piece of capital.

User Fee
A price paid by users of a good or service provided by the government.

Utilitarian Social Welfare Function
An equation stating that social welfare is some function of individuals' utilities.

Utility
The amount of satisfaction a person derives from consuming a particular bundle of commodities.

Utility Definition of Horizontal Equity
A method of classifying people of "equal positions" in terms of their utility levels. This definition states: (1) that if two individuals would have the same utility level without taxes, they should have the same utility level after taxes; and (2) that taxes should not alter the order of individual utilities.

Utility Possibilities Curve
A graph showing the maximum amount of one person's utility given each level of utility attained by the other person.

Value Added
The difference between sales and the cost of purchased material inputs at each stage of production.

Value-Added Tax (VAT)
A percentage tax on value added at each stage of production.

Vertical Equity
Distributing tax burdens fairly across people with different abilities to pay.

Vertical Summation
The process of creating an aggregate demand curve for a public good by adding the prices each individual is willing to pay for a given quantity of the good.

Voting Paradox
With majority voting, community preferences can be inconsistent even though each individual's preferences are consistent.

Vouchers
Grants earmarked for particular commodities, such as medical care or education, given to individuals.

Wagner's Law
Government expenditures rise faster than incomes.

Wealth Substitution Effect
Under a pay-as-you-go system of Social Security finance, a reduction in total capital accumulation that arises because individuals save less in anticipation of the fact that they will receive Social Security benefits after retirement.

Welfare Economics
The branch of economic theory concerned with the social desirability of alternative economic states.

Workfare
Able-bodied individuals who qualify for income support receive transfer payments only if they agree to participate in a work-related activity.

References

Aaron, Henry J. *Shelters and Subsidies.* Washington, D.C.: Brookings Institution, 1972.

Aaron, Henry J. *Who Pays the Property Tax? A New View.* Washington, D.C.: Brookings Institution, 1975.

Aaron, Henry J. "Inflation and the Income Tax: An Introduction." In *Inflation and the Income Tax,* ed. Henry J. Aaron. Washington, D.C.: Brookings Institution, 1976, pp. 1–31.

Aaron, Henry J. *Politics and the Professors—The Great Society in Perspective.* Washington, D.C.: Brookings Institution, 1978.

Aaron, Henry J. "Introduction and Summary." In *The Value-Added Tax—Lessons from Europe,* ed. Henry J. Aaron. Washington, D.C.: Brookings Institution, 1981, pp. 1–18.

Aaron, Henry J. "Six Welfare Questions Still Searching for Answers." *Brookings Review* 3, no. 1 (Fall 1984), pp. 12–17.

Aaron, Henry J. "How a V.A.T. Would Hurt Our Exports." *New York Times,* March 23, 1986, p. 2F.

Aaron, Henry J. *Can America Afford to Grow Old? Financing Social Security.* Washington, D.C.: Brookings Institution, 1989.

Aaron, Henry J., and Harvey Galper. *Assessing Tax Reform.* Washington, D.C.: Brookings Institution, 1985.

Ackerman, Bruce A.; Susan Rose-Ackerman; James W. Sawyer, Jr.; and Dale W. Henderson. *The Uncertain Search for Environmental Quality.* New York: Free Press, 1974.

Adams, Roy B., and Ken Mc-Cormick. "Private Goods, Club Goods and Public Goods as a Continuum." Iowa State University, Mimeo.

Advisory Commission on Intergovernmental Relations. *Significant Features of Fiscal Federalism* 2, August 1990.

Allen, Garland E.; Jerry J. Pitts; and Evelyn S. Glatt. "The Experimental Housing Allowance Program." In *Do Housing Allowances Work?,* ed. Katharine J. Bradbury and Anthony Downs. Washington, D.C.:

Brookings Institution, 1981, pp. 1–32.

Andersson, Krister. "Investment in Housing in the United States: A Portfolio Approach." International Monetary Fund, Working paper, Washington, D.C., 1990.

Andrews, William D. "A Consumption-Type or Cash Flow Personal Income Tax." *Harvard Law Review* 87 (April 1974), pp. 1113–88.

Andrews, William D. "The Achilles' Heel of the Comprehensive Income Tax." In *New Directions in Federal Tax Policy for the 1980s,* ed. Charles E. Walker and Mark A. Bloomfield. Cambridge, Mass.: Ballinger, 1983, pp. 278–84.

Armitage-Smith, George. *Principles and Methods of Taxation.* London: John Murray, 1907.

Arrow, Kenneth J. *Social Choice and Individual Values.* New York: John Wiley & Sons, 1951.

Arrow, Kenneth J. "The Economic Implications of Learning by Doing." *Review of Eco-*

nomic Studies 29 (1962), pp. 155–73.

Arrow, Kenneth J. The Limits of Organization. New York: W. W. Norton, 1974.

Arrow, K. J., and R. C. Lind. "Uncertainty and the Evaluation of Public Investment Decisions." American Economic Review 60 (1970), pp. 364–78.

Arthur Andersen and Company. Sound Financial Reporting in the U.S. Government. New York, 1986.

Atkinson, Anthony B. The Economics of Inequality. Oxford: Oxford University Press, 1983.

Atkinson, Anthony B., and Nicholas H. Stern. "Pigou, Taxation and Public Goods." Review of Economic Studies 41 (1974), pp. 119–28.

Atkinson, Anthony B., and Joseph E. Stiglitz. Lectures on Public Economics. New York: McGraw-Hill, 1980.

Auerbach, Alan J. "The Theory of Excess Burden and Optimal Taxation." In Handbook of Public Economics, Vol. 1, ed. Alan J. Auerbach and Martin Feldstein. Amsterdam: North-Holland, 1985, pp. 61–128.

Auerbach, Alan J., and David Reishus. "Taxes and the Merger Decision." National Bureau of Economic Research, Working Paper 1855, March 1986.

Auerbach, Alan J., and Harvey S. Rosen. Will the Real Excess Burden Please Stand Up? (or, Seven Measures in Search of a Concept). Cambridge, Mass.: National Bureau of Economic

Research, Working Paper 495, 1980.

Auerbach, Alan J.; Jagadeesh Gokhale; and Laurence J. Kotlikoff. "Generational Accounts— A Meaningful Alternative to Deficit Accounting." In Tax Policy and the Economy, ed. David Bradford. Cambridge, Mass.: National Bureau of Economic Research, 1990.

Auten, Gerald E., and Joseph J. Cordes. "Policy Watch: Cutting Capital Gains Taxes." Journal of Economic Perspectives, Winter 1991, pp. 181–92.

Baker, Russell. "Stand by for Looting." New York Times, May 19, 1985a, p. A23.

Baker, Russell. "Reagan Revises Dirksen." New York Times, October 2, 1985b, p. A27.

Ballard, Charles L. "The Marginal Efficiency Cost of Redistribution." Michigan State University, November 1985, Mimeo.

Ballard, Charles L.; John B. Shoven; and John Whalley. The Welfare Costs of Distortions in the United States Tax System: A General Equilibrium Approach. Cambridge, Mass.: National Bureau of Economic Research, Working Paper 1043, 1982.

Ballard, Charles L.; John B. Shoven; and John Whalley. "General Equilibrium Computations of the Marginal Welfare Costs of Taxes in the United States." American Economic Review 75, no. 1 (March 1985a), pp. 128–38.

Ballard, Charles L.; John B. Shoven; and John Whalley. "The Total Welfare Cost of the United States Tax System: A General Equilibrium Approach." National Tax Journal 38, no. 2 (June 1985b), pp. 125–40.

Ballard, Charles L.; John Karl Scholz; and John B. Shoven. "The Value-Added Tax: A General Equilibrium Look at its Efficiency and Incidence." Stanford University, 1986, Mimeo.

Bane, Mary Jo, and David T. Ellwood. "Slipping into and out of Poverty: The Dynamics of Spells." Journal of Human Resources, 1986.

Barlow, Robin; Harvey E. Brazer; and James N. Morgan. Economic Behavior of the Affluent. Washington, D.C.: Brookings Institution, 1966.

Barro, Robert J. "Are Government Bonds Net Wealth?" Journal of Political Economy 82 (1974), pp. 1095–117.

Barro, Robert J. "On the Determination of the Public Debt." Journal of Political Economy 87, no. 5, part 1 (October 1979), pp. 940–71.

Barro, Robert J. "The Ricardian Approach to Budget Deficits." Journal of Economic Perspectives, Spring 1989, pp. 37–54.

Bassi, Laurie, J., and Orley Ashenfelter. "The Effect of Direct Job Creation and Training Programs on Low-Skilled Workers." In Fighting Poverty: What Works and What Doesn't, ed. Sheldon H. Danziger and Daniel H. Weinberg. Cambridge, Mass.: Harvard University Press, 1986, pp. 133–51.

Bator, F. M. "The Simple Analytics of Welfare Maximization." *American Economic Review* 47 (March 1957), pp. 22–59.

Bator, F. M. "The Anatomy of Market Failure." *Quarterly Journal of Economics* 72 (August 1958), pp. 351–79.

Bator, Paul M. "The Constitution and the Art of Practical Government." *The Law School Record* 32 (Spring 1986), pp. 8–12.

Baumol, William J. "Book Reviews—Economics and Clean Water." *The Yale Law Journal* 85, no. 3 (January 1976), pp. 441–46.

Baumol, William J. *Economic Theory and Operations Analysis*. 4th ed. Englewood Cliffs, N.J.: Prentice-Hall, 1977, Chapter 21.

Baumol, William J., and Hilda Baumol. "Book Review." *Journal of Political Economy* 89, no. 2 (April 1981), pp. 425–28.

Baumol, William J., and Alan S. Blinder. *Economics Principles and Policy*. 2d ed. New York: Harcourt Brace Jovanovich, 1982.

Baumol, William J., and Wallace E. Oates. *Economics, Environmental Policy, and the Quality of Life*. Englewood Cliffs, N.J.: Prentice Hall, 1979.

Becker, Gary S. "Irrational Behavior and Economic Theory." *Journal of Political Economy* 70 (February 1962), pp. 1–13.

Becker, Gary S. "Crime and Punishment: An Economic

Approach." *Journal of Political Economy* 76 (March–April 1968), pp. 169–217.

Becker, Gary S. "Altruism, Egoism, and Genetic Fitness: Economics and Sociobiology." *Journal of Economic Literature* 14, no. 3 (September 1976), pp. 817–26.

Becker, Gary S., and H. Gregg Lewis. "On the Interaction between the Quantity and Quality of Children." *Journal of Political Economy* 81 (March–April 1973), pp. S279–88.

Bernheim, B. Douglas. "A Neoclassical Perspective on Budget Deficits." *Journal of Economic Perspectives*, Spring 1989, pp. 55–72.

Bernheim, B. D., and K. Bagwell. "Is Everything Neutral?" *Journal of Political Economy*, April 1988, pp. 308–38.

Bernheim, B. Douglas; Andrei Shleifer; and Lawrence H. Summers. "The Strategic Bequest Motive." *Journal of Political Economy* 93, no. 6 (December 1985), pp. 1045–76.

Beron, K. J.; H. V. Tauchen; and A. D. Witte. "The Effect of Audits and Socioeconomic Variables on Compliance." Wellesley College, 1990, Mimeo.

Bewley, Truman F. "A Critique of Teibout's Theory of Local Public Expenditures." *Econometrica* 49 (1981), pp. 713–39.

Bhagwati, Jagdish N. "Introduction." *Journal of Public Economics* 18, no. 3 (August 1982), pp. 285–90.

Bhagwati, Jagdish N., and Koichi Hamada. "Tax Policy in the Presence of Emigration."

Journal of Public Economics 18, no. 3 (August 1982), pp. 291–318.

Bishop, Robert L. "The Effects of Specific and Ad Valorem Taxes." *Quarterly Journal of Economics,* May 1968, pp. 198–218.

Bittker, Boris. "Federal Income Taxation and the Family." *Stanford Law Review* 27 (July 1975), 1392–1463.

Black, D. "On the Rationale of Group Decision Making." *Journal of Political Economy* 56 (February 1948), pp. 23–34.

Blair, Douglas H., and Robert A. Pollak. "Rational Collective Choice." *Scientific American* 249, no. 2 (August 1983), pp. 88–95.

Blanchard, Lois; J. S. Butler; T. Doyle; R. Jackson; J. Ohls; and Barbara Posner. *Final Report, Food Stamp SSI/Elderly Cashout Demonstration Evaluation*. Princeton, N.J.: Mathematica Policy Research, 1982.

Blank, Rebecca M. "The Impact of State Economic Differentials on Household Welfare and Labor Force Behavior." *Journal of Public Economics* 28, no. 1 (October 1985), pp. 25–58.

Blinder, Alan S. "The Level and Distribution of Economic Well-Being." In *The American Economy in Transition*, ed. Martin Feldstein. Chicago: University of Chicago Press, 1980.

Blinder, Alan S., and Angus Deaton. "The Time Series Consumption Function Revisited." *Brookings Papers on*

Economic Activity 2 (1985), pp. 465–511.

Blinder, Alan S.; Roger H. Gordon; and Donald E. Wise. "Reconsidering the Work Disincentive Effects of Social Security." *National Tax Journal* 33, no. 4 (December 1980), pp. 431–42.

Bloom, Alan. *The Closing of the American Mind.* New York: Simon and Schuster, 1987.

Borcherding, Thomas E. "The Causes of Government Expenditure Growth: A Survey of the U.S. Evidence." *Journal of Public Economics* 28, no. 3 (December 1985), pp. 359–82.

Boskin, Michael J. "Efficiency Aspects of the Differential Tax Treatment of Market and Household Economic Activities." *Journal of Public Economics* 4 (1975), pp. 1–25.

Boskin, Michael J. "Taxation, Saving, and the Rate of Interest." *Journal of Political Economy* 86, no. 2 (April 1978), pp. S3–S28.

Boskin, Michael J.; Laurence J. Kotlikoff; Douglas J. Puffert; and John B. Shoven. "Social Security: A Financial Appraisal across and within Generations." Cambridge, Mass.: National Bureau of Economic Research, Working Paper 1891, April 1986.

Boskin, Michael J., and Eytan Sheshinski. "Optimal Income Redistribution when Individual Welfare Depends on Relative Income." *Quarterly Journal of Economics* 92 (1978), pp. 589–602.

Boskin, Michael J., and Eytan Sheshinski. *Optimal Tax Treatment of the Family: Married Couples.* Cambridge, Mass.: National Bureau of Economic Research, Working Paper 368, 1979.

Boskin, Michael J., and John B. Shoven. "Poverty Among the Elderly: Where Are the Holes in the Safety Net?" Cambridge, Mass.: National Bureau of Economic Research, Working Paper 1923, May 1986.

Bowen, William G. *Economic Aspects of Education.* Princeton, N.J.: Industrial Relations Section, Princeton University, 1964.

Bowen, William G.; Richard Davis; and David Kopf. "The Public Debt: A Burden on Future Generations?" *American Economic Review* 50, no. 4 (September 1960), pp. 701–6.

Bradbury, Katharine L., and Anthony Downs, eds. *Do Housing Allowances Work?* Washington, D.C.: Brookings Institution, 1981.

Bradbury, Katharine L.; Anthony Downs; and Kenneth A. Small. *Urban Decline and the Future of American Cities.* Washington, D.C.: Brookings Institution, 1982.

Bradford, David F. "The Incidence and Allocation Effects of a Tax on Corporate Distributions." *Journal of Public Economics* 15, no. 1 (February 1981), pp. 1–22.

Bradford, David F. *Untangling the Income Tax.* Cambridge, Mass.: Harvard University Press, 1986.

Bradford, David, and Wallace Oates. "Suburban Exploitation of Central Cities and Government Structure." In *Redistribution Through Public Choice,* ed. Harold Hochman and George Peterson. New York: Columbia University Press, 1974.

Break, George F. "Income Taxes and Incentives to Work." *American Economic Review* 47 (1957), pp. 529–49.

Brennan, Geoffrey, and James M. Buchanan. "Towards a Tax Constitution for Leviathan." *Journal of Public Economics* 8, no. 3 (December 1977), pp. 255–74.

Brittain, John A. *Corporate Dividend Policy.* Washington, D.C.: Brookings Institution, 1966.

Broome, J. "Trying to Value a Life." *Journal of Public Economics,* February 1978, pp. 91–100.

Browning, Edgar K. "A Critical Appraisal of Hausman's Welfare Cost Estimates." *Journal of Political Economy* 93, no. 5 (October 1985), pp. 1025–34.

Browning, Edgar K. "Elasticities, Tax Rates, and Tax Revenue." *National Tax Journal,* March 1989, pp. 45–58.

Browning, Edgar K., and William R. Johnson. "The Tradeoff between Equality and Efficiency." *Journal of Political Economy,* April 1984, pp. 175–203.

Buchanan, James M. "Social Choice, Democracy, and Free Markets." In *Fiscal Theory and Political Economy—Selected Essays,* ed. James M. Buchanan. Chapel Hill: University of North Carolina Press, 1960, pp. 75–89.

Buchanan, James M. "An Economic Theory of Clubs." *Economica* 32 (February 1965), pp. 1–14.

Buchanan, James M., and Gordon Tullock. *The Calculus of Consent.* Ann Arbor: University of Michigan Press, 1962.

Burtless, Gary. "Public Spending for the Poor: Trends, Prospects, and Economic Limits." In *Fighting Poverty: What Works and What Doesn't,* Sheldon H. Danziger and Daniel H. Weinberg. Cambridge, Mass.: Harvard University Press, 1986.

Burtless, Gary, and Larry L. Orr. "Are Classical Experiments Needed for Manpower Policy?" *Journal of Human Resources,* Fall 1986, pp. 605–39.

Campbell, John Y., and N. Gregory Mankiw. "Consumption, Income, and Interest Rates: Reinterpreting the Time-Series Evidence." National Bureau of Economic Research reprint 1404, May 1990.

"The Candidates' Finances." *New York Times,* October 12, 1984, p. B5.

Card, David, and Alan Krueger. "Does School Quality Matter? Returns to Education and the Characteristics of Public Schools in the United States." Cambridge, Mass.: National Bureau of Economic Research, Working Paper 3358, May 1990.

Carliner, Geoffrey. "Income Elasticity of Housing Demand." *Review of Economics and Statistics* 55 (1973), pp. 528–32.

Case, Anne C.; James R. Hines; and Harvey S. Rosen. "Copycatting: Fiscal Policies of States and Their Neighbors." Cambridge, Mass.: National Bureau of Economic Research, Working Paper 3032, 1989.

Caves, Douglas W., and Laurits R. Christensen. "The Relative Efficiency of Public and Private Firms in a Competitive Environment: The Case of Canadian Railroads." *Journal of Political Economy* 88, no. 5 (October 1980), pp. 958–76.

Center on Budget and Policy Priorities, "Rich-Poor Income Gap Hits 40-Year High as Poverty Rate Stalls." July 23, 1990.

Chambers, Marcia. "California's Private Trial System Seems Settled In." *New York Times,* February 24, 1986, p. B7.

"Changes in Tax Bill Expected." *New York Times,* May 26, 1986, p. 31.

Chirinko, Robert S. "Business Investment and Tax Policy: A Perspective on Existing Models and Empirical Results." *National Tax Journal* 39, no. 2 (June 1986), pp. 137–56.

Chirinko, Robert S., and Robert Eisner. "Tax Policy and Investment in Major U.S. Macroeconomic Econometric Models." *Journal of Public Economics* 20, no. 2 (March 1983), pp. 139–66.

"Chrysler's Stock Plea Angers Congressmen." *New York Times,* May 10, 1983, p. D6.

Chubb, John E., and Terry M. Moe. *Politics, Markets, and America's Schools.* Washington, D.C.: Brookings Institution, 1990.

Citizens for Tax Justice. "The Loophole Lobbyists vs. The People." Washington, D.C., undated.

City of Clinton v. *Cedar Rapids and Missouri River RR. Co.,* 24 Iowa 475 (1868).

Clendinen, Dudley. "Court Ban on Work at Home Brings Gloom to Knitters in Rural Vermont." *New York Times,* December 3, 1983, p. 8.

Clotfelter, Charles T. "Public Services, Private Substitutes, and the Demand for Protection Against Crime." *American Economic Review* 67, no. 5 (December 1977), pp. 867–77.

Clotfelter, Charles T. "Tax Evasion and Tax Rates: An Analysis of Individual Returns." *Review of Economics and Statistics* 65, no. 3 (August 1983), pp. 363–73.

Clotfelter, Charles T. *Federal Tax Policy and Charitable Giving.* Chicago: University of Chicago Press, 1985.

Clotfelter, Charles T., and C. Eugene Steuerle. "Charitable Contributions." In *How Taxes Affect Economic Behavior,* ed. Henry J. Aaron and Joseph A. Pechman. Washington, D.C.: Brookings Institution, 1981.

Coase, Ronald H. "The Problem of Social Cost." *Journal of Law and Economics,* October 1960.

Coase, Ronald H. "The Lighthouse in Economics." *Journal of Law and Economics,* October 1974.

Commissioner of Internal Revenue and the Chief Counsel for the Internal Revenue Service. *Annual Report 1989.* Washington, D.C.: U.S. Government Printing Office, 1990.

Committee on Ways and Means. *Overview of Entitlement Programs: 1990 Green Book.* Washington, D.C.: U.S. Government Printing Office, 1990.

Congressional Budget Office. *Balancing the Federal Budget and Limiting Federal Spending: Constitutional and Statutory Approaches.* Washington, D.C.: U.S. Government Printing Office, 1982b.

Congressional Budget Office. *Financing Social Security: Issues and Options in the Long Run.* Washington, D.C.: U.S. Government Printing Office, 1982c.

Congressional Budget Office. *Tax Expenditures: Budget Control Options and Five-Year Budget Projections for the Fiscal Years 1983–1987.* Washington, D.C.: U.S. Government Printing Office, 1982d.

Congressional Budget Office. *Promoting Employment and Maintaining Incomes with Unemployment Insurance.* Washington, D.C.: U.S. Government Printing Office, March 1985b.

Congressional Budget Office. *Revising the Corporate Income Tax.* Washington, D.C.: U.S. Government Printing Office, May 1985c.

Congressional Budget Office. *Earnings Sharing Options for the Social Security System.* Washington, D.C.: U.S. Government Printing Office, January 1986.

Congressional Budget Office. *Reducing the Deficit: Spending and Revenue Options.* Washington, D.C.: U.S. Government Printing Office, 1990.

Congressional Budget Office. *The Economic and Budget Outlook: Fiscal Years 1992–1996.* Washington, D.C.: U.S. Government Printing Office, 1991.

Congressional Budget Office. *Student Aid and the Cost of Postsecondary Education.* Washington, D.C.: U.S. Government Printing Office, 1991.

Congressional Research Service, The Library of Congress. *Cash and Noncash Benefits for Persons with Limited Incomes: Eligibility Rules, Recipient and Expenditure Data, FY 1986–88.* Washington, D.C., October 24, 1989.

Cooper, George. *A Voluntary Tax? New Perspectives on Sophisticated Estate Tax Avoidance.* Washington, D.C.: Brookings Institution, 1979.

Corlett, W. J., and D. C. Hague. "Complementarity and the Excess Burden of Taxation." *Review of Economic Studies* 21 (1953), pp. 21–30.

"The Cuts in Federal Aid." *Newsweek,* June 29, 1981, pp. 66–67.

Courant, Paul N., and Edward M. Gramlich. "The Impact of TRA on State and Local Fiscal Behavior." In J. Slemrod, *Do Taxes Matter? The Impact of the Tax Reform Act of 1986.* Cambridge, Mass.: MIT Press, 1991.

Cowell, Frank A. "The Economics of Tax Evasion: A Survey." Economic and Social Research Council Program, no.

80, London School of Economics, July 1985.

Danziger, Sheldon H.; Robert H. Haveman; and Robert D. Plotnick. "Anti-Poverty Policy: Effects on the Poor and the Non-Poor." In *Fighting Poverty: What Works and What Doesn't,* ed. Sheldon H. Danziger and Daniel H. Weinberg. Cambridge, Mass.: Harvard University Press, 1986.

Darman, Richard. "Introductory Statement: The Problem of Rising Health Costs." Washington, D.C.: Office of Management and Budget, April 16, 1991.

Davies, J.; F. St-Hilaire; and J. Whalley. "Some Calculations of Lifetime Tax Incidence." *American Economic Review,* 1984, pp. 633–49.

Davis, James W., "Bring Back the Draft." *New York Times,* February 5, 1987, p. A27.

Devarajan, S.; D. Fullerton; and R. Musgrave. "Estimating the Distribution of Tax Burdens: A Comparison of Alternative Approaches." *Journal of Public Economics* 13 (1980), pp. 155–82.

Diamond, Peter A. "A Many-Person Ramsey Tax Rule." *Journal of Public Economics* 4 (1975), pp. 335–42.

Diamond, Peter A. "A Framework for Social Security Analysis." *Journal of Public Economics* 8, no. 3 (December 1977), pp. 275–98.

Diamond, Peter A., and Daniel L. McFadden. "Some Uses of the Expenditure Function in Public Finance." *Journal of*

Public Economics 3 (1974), pp. 3–21.

Downs, Anthony. *An Economic Theory of Democracy.* New York: Harper & Row, 1957.

Doyle, Michael W. "Stalemate in the North-South Debate: Strategies and the New International Economic Order." *World Politics* 35, no. 3 (April 1983), pp. 426–64.

Dreze, J., and M. Stern. "The Theory of Cost-Benefit Analysis." London School of Economics, July 1985, Mimeo.

Drinan, Robert F. "Education: To Cherish." *New York Times,* February 27, 1983, p. E17.

Eaton, Jonathan, and Harvey S. Rosen. "Taxation, Human Capital, and Uncertainty." *American Economic Review* 70, no. 4 (September 1980a), pp. 705–15.

Eaton, Jonathan, and Harvey S. Rosen. "Labor Supply, Uncertainty, and Efficient Taxation." *Journal of Public Economics* 14, no. 3 (December 1980b), pp. 365–74.

Economic Recovery Tax Act of 1981. Chicago: Commerce Clearing House, 1981.

Economic Report of the President, 1985. Washington, D.C.: U.S. Government Printing Office, 1985, Chapter 5.

Economic Report of the President, 1986. Washington, D.C.: U.S. Government Printing Office, 1986.

Edgeworth, F. Y. "The Pure Theory of Taxation." [1897] Reprinted in *Readings in the Economics of Taxation,* ed. Richard A. Musgrave and Carl S. Shoup. Homewood, Ill.: Richard D. Irwin, 1959, pp. 258–96.

Eisner, Robert. "Piercing the Myths of the Budget Deficit." *New York Times,* May 4, 1986, p. F3.

Eisner, Robert, and Paul J. Pieper. "A New View of the Federal Debt and Budget Deficits." *American Economic Review* 74, no. 1 (March 1984), pp. 11–29.

Ellwood, David T., *Poor Support: Poverty and the American Family.* New York: Basic Books, 1988.

Ellwood, David T., and Jonathan Crane, "Family Change among Black Americans: What Do We Know?" *Journal of Economic Perspectives* 4, no. 4 (Fall 1990), pp. 47–64.

Ellwood, David T., and Lawrence H. Summers. "Poverty in America: Is Welfare the Answer or the Problem?" In *Fighting Poverty: What Works and What Doesn't,* ed. Sheldon H. Danziger and Daniel H. Weinberg. Cambridge, Mass.: Harvard University Press, 1986.

Elton, Edwin J., and Martin J. Gruber. "Marginal Stockholder Tax Rates and the Clientele Effect." *Review of Economics and Statistics* 53, no. 1 (February 1970), pp. 68–74.

Executive Office of the President, Office of Management and Budget. *Budget of the United States Government, Fiscal Year 1991.* Washington, D.C.: U.S. Government Printing Office, 1990.

Executive Office of the President, Office of Management and Budget. *Budget of the United States Government, Fiscal Year 1992.* Washington, D.C.: U.S. Government Printing Office, 1991.

Facts and Figures on Government Finance, 1990 Edition. Washington, D.C.: Tax Foundation, 1990.

Facts and Figures on Government Finance, 1991 Edition. Washington, D.C.: Tax Foundation, 1991.

Fair, Ray C. "The Optimal Distribution of Income." *Quarterly Journal of Economics* 85 (1971), pp. 551–79.

Fair, Ray C. "The Effects of Economic Events on Votes for President." *Review of Economics and Statistics* 70 (May 1978), pp. 159–73.

Fair, Ray C. "The Effect of Economic Events on Votes for President: 1980 Results." *Review of Economics and Statistics* 44, no. 2 (May 1982), pp. 322–24.

Fama, Eugene F., and Merton H. Miller. *The Theory of Finance.* New York: Holt, Rinehart and Winston, 1972.

Feldstein, Martin S. "The Effects of Taxation on Risk-Taking." *Journal of Political Economy* 77 (1969), pp. 755–64.

Feldstein, Martin S. "Equity and Efficiency in Public Sector Pricing: The Optimal Two-Part Tariff." *Quarterly Journal of Economics* 86 (1972), pp. 175–87.

Feldstein, Martin S. "Social Security, Induced Retirement, and Aggregate Capital Accumulation." *Journal of Political Economy* 82, no. 5 (September–October 1974), pp. 905–26.

Feldstein, Martin, S. "On the Theory of Tax Reform." *Journal of Public Economics* 6 (1976a), pp. 77–104.

Feldstein, Martin S. *Social Insurance.* Cambridge, Mass.: Harvard Institute of Economic Research, Discussion Paper 477, 1976b.

Feldstein, Martin S. "Does the United States Save Too Little?" *American Economic Review Papers and Proceedings,* February 1977, pp. 116–21.

Feldstein, Martin S. "A Contribution to the Theory of Tax Expenditures: The Case of Charitable Giving." In *The Economics of Taxation,* ed. Henry J. Aaron and Michael J. Boskin. Washington, D.C.: Brookings Institution, 1980, pp. 99–122.

Feldstein, Martin S. "Social Security and Private Saving: Reply." *Journal of Political Economy* 90, no. 3 (June 1982a), pp. 630–42.

Feldstein, Martin S. "Inflation, Tax Rules, and Investment: Some Econometric Evidence." *Econometrica* 50, no. 4 (July 1982b), pp. 825–62.

Feldstein, Martin S. "Capital Taxation." Cambridge, Mass.: National Bureau of Economic Research, Working Paper 877, 1982c.

Feldstein, Martin S. "Debt and Taxes in the Theory of Public Finance." *Journal of Public Economics* 28, no. 2 (November 1985a), pp. 233–46.

Feldstein, Martin S. "The Second Best Theory of Differential Capital Taxation." Cambridge, Mass.: National Bureau of Economic Research, Working Paper 1781, December 1985b.

Feldstein, Martin. "Bush's Budget Deal Made the Deficit Bigger." *Wall Street Journal,* November 29, 1990, p. A13.

Feldstein, Martin S.; Louis Dicks-Mireaux; and James Poterba. "The Effective Tax Rate and the Pretax Rate of Return." *Journal of Public Economics* 21, no. 2 (July 1983), pp. 129–58.

Feldstein, Martin S., and Jerry Green. "Why Do Companies Pay Dividends?" *American Economic Review* 73, no. 1 (March 1983), pp. 17–30.

Feldstein, Martin S., and David Hartman. "The Optimal Taxation of Foreign Source Investment Income." Cambridge: Mass.: Harvard Institute of Economic Research, Discussion Paper 563, 1977.

Feldstein, M., and C. Horioka. "Domestic Saving and International Capital Flows." *Economic Journal,* June 1980, pp. 314–29.

Feldstein, Martin S., and Gilbert Metcalf. "The Effect of Federal Tax Deductibility on State and Local Taxes and Spending." Cambridge, Mass.: National Bureau of Economic Research, Working Paper 1791, January 1986.

Feldstein, Martin S., and Lawrence Summers. "Inflation and the Taxation of Capital Income in the Corporate Sector." *National Tax Journal* 32, no. 4 (December 1979), pp. 445–70.

Filimon, R.; T. Romer; and H. Rosenthal. "Asymmetric Information and Agenda Control: The Bases of Monopoly Power and Public Spending." *Journal of Public Economics* 17 (1982), pp. 51–70.

Finley, Murray. "Brown Lungs." *New York Times,* May 4, 1981, p. A23.

Fisher, Ronald. *State and Local Public Finance.* New York: Scott, Foresman, 1988.

Formby, John P.; W. James Smith; and David Sykes. "Intersecting Tax Concentration Curves and the Measurement of Tax Progressivity: A Comment." *National Tax Journal* 39, no. 1 (March 1986), pp. 115–18.

Fortin, Bernard; Thomas Lemieux; and Pierre Frechette. "An Empirical Model of Labor Supply in the Underground Economy." National Bureau of Economic Research, Working Paper 3392, June 1990.

Fraker, Thomas; Barbara Devaney; and Edward Cavin. "An Evaluation of the Effect of Cashing Out Food Stamps on Food Expenditures." *American Economic Review, Papers and Proceedings* 76, no. 2 (May 1986), pp. 230–34.

Frant, Howard L., and Herman B. Leonard. "State and Local Government Pension Plans: Labor Economics or Political Economy?" JFK School, Harvard University, 1984, Mimeo.

Freeman, Richard B. "How Do Public Sector Wages and Employment Respond to Economic Conditions?" Cambridge, Mass.: National Bureau of Economic Research, Working Paper 1653, June 1985.

Friedlander, Daniel; Barbara Goldman; Judith Gueron; and David Wong. "Initial Findings from the Demonstration of State Work/Welfare Initiatives." *American Economic Review, Papers and Proceedings* 76, no. 2 (May 1986), pp. 224–29.

Friedman, Milton. *A Theory of the Consumption Function.* Princeton, N.J.: Princeton University Press, 1957.

Friedman, Milton. "Our New Hidden Taxes." *Newsweek,* April 14, 1980, p. 90.

Fuchs, Victor R. " 'Though Much Is Taken'; Reflections on Aging, Health, and Medical Care." *Milbank Memorial Fund Quarterly* 62, no. 2 (Spring 1984), pp. 143–66.

Fullerton, Don. "On the Possibility of an Inverse Relationship between Tax Rates and Government Revenues." *Journal of Public Economics* 19, no. 1 (October 1982), pp. 3–22.

Fullerton, Don; Yolanda K. Henderson; and John B. Shoven. "A Comparison of Methodologies in Empirical General Equilibrium Models of Taxation." Cambridge, Mass.: National Bureau of Economic Research, Working Paper 911, 1982.

Fullerton, Don; A. Thomas King; John B. Shoven; and John Whalley. "Corporate Tax Integration in the United States: A General Equilibrium Approach." *American Economic Review* 71, no. 4 (September 1981), pp. 677–91.

Fullerton, Don; John B. Shoven; and John Whalley. "Replacing the U.S. Income Tax with a Progressive Consumption Tax: A Sequenced General Equilibrium Approach." Cambridge, Mass.: National Bureau of Economic Research, Working Paper 892, 1982.

Funkhauser, Richard. "Ask about Acid Rain." *New York Times,* August 18, 1983, p. A27.

Gale, W. G., and J. K. Scholz. "IRAs and Household Saving." University of Wisconsin, 1990, Mimeo.

Galper, Harvey, and Eric Toder. "Measuring the Incidence of Taxation of Income from Capital." In *1982 Proceedings of the Seventy-Fifth Annual Conference on Taxation,* ed. Stanley J. Bowers. Cincinnati: October 1982.

Garen, J. "Compensating Wage Differentials and the Endogeneity of Job Riskiness." *Review of Economics and Statistics* 70, no. 1 (February 1988).

"Gas Tax Rise Likely to Show Up at Pump." *New York Times,* April 1, 1983, p. D1.

George, Henry. *Progress and Poverty.* New York: Doubleday Publishing, 1914, Book VII.

Gillis, Malcolm, and Charles E. McLure. "Excess Profits Taxation: Post-Mortem on the Mexican Experience." *National Tax Journal* 32, no. 4 (December 1979), pp. 501–11.

Goode, Richard. "The Economic Definition of Income." In *Comprehensive Income Taxation,* ed. Joseph A. Pechman. Washington, D.C.: Brookings Institution, 1977, pp. 1–37.

Gordon, Roger H.; James R. Hines, Jr.; and Lawrence H. Summers. "Notes on the Tax Treatment of Structures." Cambridge, Mass.: National Bureau of Economic Research, Working Paper 1896, April 1986.

Gornick, Marian; J. N. Greenberg; Paul W. Eggers; and Allen Dobson. "Twenty Years of Medicare and Medicaid: Covered Populations, Use of Benefits, and Program Expenditures." *Health Care Financing Review, 1985 Annual Supplement.* Washington, D.C.: U.S. Department of Health and Human Services, December 1985.

Goulder, Lawrence H., and Philippe Thalmann. "Approaches to Efficient Capital Taxation: Leveling the Playing Field vs. Living by the Golden Rule." Cambridge, Mass.: National Bureau of Economic Reserch, Working Paper 3559, 1990.

Graetz, Michael J. "Expenditure Tax Design." In *What Should Be Taxed: Income or Expenditure?* ed. Joseph A. Pechman. Washington, D.C.: Brookings Institution, 1980, pp. 161–298.

Graetz, Michael J. *Federal Income Taxation.* Westbury, N.Y.: Foundation Press, 1988.

Graetz, Michael J. Statement before the Subcommittee on Commerce, Consumer and Monetary Affairs, Committee on Government Operations, U.S. House of Representatives. July 25, 1990.

Gramlich, Edward M. "The New York City Fiscal Crisis: What Happened and What Is to Be Done?" *American Economic Review, Papers and Proceedings* 66, no. 2 (May 1976), pp. 415–29.

Gramlich, Edward M. *Benefit-Cost Analysis of Government Programs*. Englewood Cliffs, N.J.: Prentice-Hall, 1981.

Gramlich, Edward M. "Budget Deficits and National Savings: Are Politicians Exogenous?" *Journal of Economic Perspectives,* Spring 1989, pp. 23–36.

Gramlich, Edward M., and Daniel L. Rubinfeld. "Microestimates of Public Spending Demand Functions and Test of the Tiebout and Median-Voter Hypotheses." *Journal of Political Economy* 90 (June 1982), pp. 536–60.

Greer, William R. "Value of One Life? From $8.37 to $10 Million." *New York Times,* June 26, 1985, p. A1.

Greider, William. "The Education of David Stockman." *Atlantic Monthly,* December 1981, pp. 27–54.

Groves, T., and J. Ledyard. "Optimal Allocation of Public Goods: A Solution to the 'Free Rider' Problem." *Econometrica* 45 (1977), pp. 783–809.

Groves, Theodore, and Martin Loeb. "Incentives and Public Inputs." *Journal of Public Economics* 4, no. 3 (August 1975), pp. 211–26.

Gujarati, D. *Basic Econometrics*. New York: McGraw-Hill, 1978.

Hagman, Donald C. "Proposition 13: A Prostitution of Conservative Principles." *Tax Review* 39, no. 9 (September 1978), pp. 39–42.

Hall, Robert E., and Alvin Rabushka. *Low Tax, Simple Tax, Flat Tax*. New York: McGraw-Hill, 1983.

Hamermesh, D., and S. Woodbury. "Taxes, Fringe Benefits, and Faculty." Cambridge, Mass.: National Bureau of Economic Research, Working Paper 3455, 1990.

Hamilton, Bruce. "Property Taxes and the Tiebout Hypothesis: Some Empirical Evidence." In *Fiscal Zoning and Land Use Controls, The Economic Issues,* ed. Edwin S. Mills and Wallace E. Oates. Lexington, Mass.: Lexington Books, 1975a, pp. 13–30.

Hamilton, Bruce. "Zoning and Property Taxation in a System of Local Governments." *Urban Studies* 12 (June 1975b), pp. 205–11.

Hansson, Ingemar, and Charles Stuart. "Tax Revenue and the Marginal Cost of Public Funds in Sweden." *Journal of Public Economics* 27, no. 3 (August 1985), pp. 331–54.

Hanushek, Eric A. "The Economics of Schooling: Production and Efficiency in the Public Schools," *Journal of Economic Literature,* September 1986, pp. 1141–77.

Hanushek, Eric A. "Expenditures, Efficiency, and Equity in Education: The Federal Government's Role." *American Economic Review,* May 1989, pp. 46–51.

Hanushek, Eric A., and John M. Quigley. "Consumption Aspects." In *Do Housing Allowances Work?* ed. Katharine L. Bradbury and Anthony Downs. Washington, D.C.: Brookings Institution, 1981, pp. 185–240.

Harberger, A. C. *Project Evaluation: Collected Papers*. Chicago: Markham Publishing, 1974.

Harberger, Arnold C. "Taxation, Resource Allocation, and Welfare." In *Taxation and Welfare,* ed. Arnold C. Harberger. Boston: Little, Brown, 1974a, pp. 25–62.

Harberger, Arnold C. "Efficiency Effects of Taxes on Income from Capital." In *Taxation and Welfare,* ed. Arnold C. Harberger. Boston: Little, Brown, 1974b, pp. 163–70.

Harberger, Arnold C. "The Incidence of the Corporation Income Tax." In *Taxation and Welfare,* ed. Arnold C. Harberger. Boston: Little, Brown, 1974c, pp. 135–62.

Harris, C. Lowell. "Property Taxation after the California Vote." *Tax Review* 39, no. 8 (August 1978), pp. 35–38.

Harrison, David, Jr., and Daniel L. Rubinfeld. "Hedonic Housing Prices and the Demand for Clean Air." *Journal of Environmental Economics and Management* 5 (March 1978), pp. 81–102.

Hartman, David G. "Tax Policy and Foreign Direct Investment

in the United States." Cambridge, Mass.: National Bureau of Economic Research, Working Paper 967, 1982.

Hausman, Jerry A., and James M. Poterba. "Household Behavior and the Tax Reform Act of 1986." *Journal of Economic Perspectives* 1 (1987).

Hemming, Richard. "Income Tax Progressivity and Labour Supply." *Journal of Public Economics* 14, no. 1 (August 1980), pp. 95–100.

Hendershott, Patric H. "Tax Changes and Capital Allocation in the 1980s." Cambridge, Mass.: National Bureau of Economic Research, Working Paper 1911, April 1986.

Hendershott, Patric H., and James D. Shilling. "The Economics of Tenure Choice, 1955–79." In *Research in Real Estate,* ed. C. Sirmans. Greenwich, Conn.: Jai Press, 1982, pp. 105–33.

Henderson, James M., and Richard E. Quandt. *Microeconomic Theory: A Mathematical Approach.* 3d ed. New York: McGraw-Hill, 1980.

Henderson, Yolanda K. "Lessons from Federal Reform of Business Taxes." *New England Economic Review,* Federal Reserve Bank of Boston, November/December 1986, pp. 9–25.

Hettich, Walter, and Stanley Winer. "Blueprints and Pathways: The Shifting Foundations of Tax Reform." *National Tax Journal* 38, no. 4 (December 1985), pp. 423–46.

Hicks, J. R. "The Valuation of the Social Income." *Economica,* May 1940, pp. 105–24.

"A High Court Win for OSHA." *Newsweek,* June 29, 1981, p. 59.

Hitler, Adolf. *Mein Kampf.* Trans. by Ralph Manheim. Boston: Houghton Mifflin, 1971 (1925).

Hobbes, Thomas. *Leviathan.* New York: Meridian Books, 1963 (1651).

Hochman, H. M., and J. D. Rodgers. "Pareto Optimal Redistribution." *American Economic Review* 59 (1969), pp. 542–57.

Holtz-Eakin, Douglas. "Unobserved Tastes and the Determination of Municipal Services." *National Tax Journal,* December 1986, pp. 527–32.

"How Congress Slices the Pork." *Newsweek,* August 2, 1982, p. 18.

Hubbard, R. Glenn. "Personal Taxation, Pension Wealth, and Portfolio Composition." *Review of Economics and Statistics* 67, no. 1 (February 1985), pp. 53–60.

Ingram, Gregory K. "Comment." In *Social Experimentation,* ed. Jerry A. Hausman and David A. Wise. Chicago: University of Chicago Press, 1985, pp. 87–94.

Inman, Robert P. "The Fiscal Performance of Local Governments: An Interpretative Review." In *Current Issues in Urban Economics,* ed. Peter

Mieszkowski and Mahlon Straszheim. Baltimore: Johns Hopkins University Press, 1979, pp. 270–321.

Inman, Robert P. "Fiscal Allocations in a Federalist Economy: Understanding the 'New' Federalism." In *American Domestic Priorities—An Economic Appraisal,* ed. John M. Quigley and Daniel L. Rubenfeld. Berkeley: University of California Press, 1985, pp. 3–33.

Internal Revenue Service. *Statistics of Income—1987 Corporation Income Tax Returns.* Washington, D.C.: U.S. Government Printing Office, 1990.

Internal Revenue Service. *Statistics of Income Bulletin.* Spring 1990. Washington, D.C.: U.S. Government Printing Office, 1990.

Internal Revenue Service. *Statistics of Income Bulletin.* Fall 1990. Washington, D.C.: U.S. Government Printing Office, 1990.

Isaac, R. Mark; Kenneth F. McHugh; and Charles R. Plott. "Public Goods Provision in an Experimental Environment." *Journal of Public Economics* 26, no. 1 (February 1985), pp. 51–74.

Jantscher, Gerald R. "The Aims of Death Taxation." In *Death, Taxes and Family Property: Essays and American Assembly Report,* ed. Edward C. Halbach, Jr. New York: West Publishing Company, 1977, pp. 40–55.

Jencks, Christopher. "Comment." In *Fighting Poverty:*

What Works and What Doesn't, ed. Sheldon H. Danziger and Daniel H. Weinberg. Cambridge, Mass.: Harvard University Press, 1986, pp. 173–79.

Johansen, Leif. "The Theory of Public Goods: Misplaced Emphasis?" *Journal of Public Economics* 7, no. 1 (February 1977), pp. 147–52.

Johnson, Paul. *Modern Times.* New York: Harper & Row, 1983.

Jones, Reginald H. "Sunset-Legislation." *Tax Review,* December 1978, p. 53.

Jorgenson, Dale W. "Capital Theory and Investment Behavior." *American Economic Review* 53, no. 2 (May 1963), pp. 247–59.

Jorgenson, D. W., and K. Yun. "The Excess Burden of Taxation in the U.S." Harvard Institute of Economic Research, Discussion Paper 1528, 1990.

Kaldor, N. "Welfare Propositions of Economists and Interpersonal Comparisons of Utility." *Economic Journal,* September 1939, pp. 549–52.

Kemper, Peter, and John M. Quigley. *The Economics of Refuse Collection.* Cambridge, Mass.: Ballinger, 1976.

Kenan, Amos. "Smothering Israel." *New York Times,* October 26, 1982.

Kenworthy, Tom. "Trick-Laden Deficit-Cut Bill Passed." *Washington Post,* October 6, 1989, p. 14A.

Keynes, John Maynard. *The General Theory of Employment, Interest, and Money.* New York, Harcourt Brace and World, 1965 (1936).

Kilborn, Peter T. "The Temptations of the Social Security Surplus." *New York Times,* November 27, 1988, p. 1.

King, Mervyn A., and Don Fullerton, eds. *The Taxation of Income from Capital: A Comparative Study of the United States, the United Kingdom, Sweden, and West Germany.* Chicago: University of Chicago Press, 1984.

King, Wayne. "Alternatives to Social Security Urged." *New York Times,* November 24, 1987, p. A18.

Klarman, Herbert E. "Syphilis Control Programs." In *Measuring Benefits of Government Investments,* ed. Robert Dorfman. Washington, D.C.: Brookings Institution, 1965, pp. 367–409.

Kotlikoff, Laurence J. "Taxation and Savings: A Neoclassical Perspective." *Journal of Economic Literature* 22, no. 4 (December 1984), pp. 1576–1675.

Kotlikoff, Laurence J., and Lawrence Summers. "The Role of Intergenerational Transfers in Aggregate Capital Accumulation." *Journal of Political Economy* 89, no. 4 (August 1981), pp. 706–32.

Kotlikoff, Laurence, and Lawrence Summers. "Tax Incidence." In *Handbook of Public Economics.* Vol. II, ed. Alan J. Auerbach and Martin S. Feldstein. Amsterdam: North-Holland, 1987, Chapter 16.

Kovenock, Daniel J., and Michael Rothschild. "Notes on the Effect of Capital Gains Taxation on Non-Austrian Assets." Cambridge, Mass.: National Bureau of Economic Research, Working Paper 1568, February 1985.

Kristol, Irving. "Some Personal Reflections on Economic Well-Being and Income Distribution." In *The American Economy in Transition,* ed. Martin Feldstein. Chicago: University of Chicago Press, 1980, pp. 479–86.

Krutilla, John V., and Anthony C. Fisher. *The Economics of Natural Environments: Studies in the Valuation of Commodity and Amenity Resources.* Baltimore: Johns Hopkins Press, 1975.

Ladd, Helen F. "An Economic Evaluation of State Limitations on Local Taxing and Spending Powers." *National Tax Journal* 3, no. 1 (March 1978), pp. 1–18.

Ladd, Helen F. "Federal Aid to State and Local Governments." In *Federal Budget Policy in the 1980s,* ed. Gregory V. Mills and John L. Palmer. Washington, D.C.: Urban Institute Press, 1984, pp. 165–202.

Ladd, Helen F., and Fred C. Doolittle. "Which Level of Government Should Assist the Poor?" *National Tax Journal* 35, no. 3 (September 1982), pp. 323–36.

Laffer, Arthur B. "Statement Prepared for the Joint Economic Committee, May 20." Reprinted in *The Economics of the Tax Revolt: A Reader,* ed. Arthur B. Laffer and Jan P. Seymour. New York: Harcourt

Brace Jovanovich, 1979, pp. 75–79.

Laidler, David. "Income Tax Incentives for Owner-Occupied Housing." In *The Taxation of Income from Capital,* ed. Arnold C. Harberger and Martin J. Baily. Washington, D.C.: Brookings Institution, 1969, pp. 50–76.

Lave, Lester B., and Gilbert S. Omenn. *Clearing the Air: Reforming the Clean Air Act.* Washington, D.C.: Brookings Institution, 1981.

Layard, Richard, ed. *Cost-Benefit Analysis.* New York: Penguin Books, 1977, pp. 1–70.

Leimer, Dean R., and Selig D. Lesnoy. "Social Security and Private Saving, New Time-Series Evidence." *Journal of Political Economy* 90, no. 3 (June 1982), pp. 606–29.

Lemann, Nicholas, "A False Panacea." *The Atlantic,* January 1991, pp. 101–105.

Lenin, Nikolai. "The Marxist Theory of the State and the Tasks of the Proletariat in the Revolution." In *Lenin on Politics and Revolution,* ed. James E. Connor. Indianapolis, Ind.: Bobbs-Merrill, 1968 (1917), pp. 184–232.

Leonard, Herman B. "The Federal Civil Service Retirement System: An Analysis of Its Financial Condition and Current Reform Proposals." Cambridge, Mass.: National Bureau of Economic Research, Working Paper 1258, 1984.

Lerman, Allen H. "Tax Amnesty: The Federal Perspective." *National Tax Journal,* 1986, pp. 325–32.

Lerman, Allen H. "Average and Marginal Income Tax and Social Security (FICA) Tax Rates for Four-Person Families at the Same Relative Positions in the Income Distribution, 1955–1988." Office of Tax Analysis, U.S. Department of the Treasury, mimeo, 1988.

Lerman, Robert I., and Shlomo Yitzhaki. "Income Inequality Effects by Income Source: A New Approach and Applications to the United States." *Review of Economics and Statistics* 67, no. 1 (February 1985), pp. 151–56.

Lerner, A. P. "The Burden of the National Debt." In *Income, Employment and Public Policy: Essays in Honor of Alvin H. Hansen,* ed. L. A. Metzler et al. New York: W. W. Norton, 1948.

Levitan, Sar. *Programs in Aid of the Poor.* 5th ed. Baltimore: Johns Hopkins University Press, 1985.

Lichtenberg, Frank R. "How Elastic Is the Government's Demand for Weapons?" *Journal of Public Economics* 40 (1989), pp. 57–78.

Lind, R. C. "A Primer on the Major Issues Relating to the Discount Rate for Evaluating National Energy Options." In *Discounting for Time and Risk in Energy Policy,* ed. R. C. Lind et al. Washington, D.C.: Resources for the Future, 1982, pp. 21–114.

Lindahl, E. "Just Taxation—A Positive Solution." In *Classics in the Theory of Public Finance,* ed. R. A. Musgrave and

A. T. Peacock. New York: St. Martin's Press, 1958.

Lindbeck, Assar. *Tax Effects versus Budget Effects on Labor Supply.* Institute for International Economic Studies, Seminar Paper 148, Stockholm, 1980a.

Lindbeck, Assar. *Work Disincentives in the Welfare State.* Institute for International Economic Studies, Seminar Paper 164, Stockholm, 1980b.

Lindsey, Lawrence B. "Taxpayer Behavior and the Distribution of the 1982 Tax Cut." Cambridge, Mass.: National Bureau of Economic Research, Working Paper 1760, October 1985.

Lindsey, Robert. "California Agencies Begin to Feel Tax Revolt." *New York Times,* April 21, 1986, p. A13.

Lipton, James. *An Exaltation of Larks.* New York: Penguin Books, 1977.

Lohr, Kathleen M., and M. Susan Marquis. *Medicare and Medicaid: Past, Present, and Future.* Santa Monica, Calif.: Rand Corporation, 1984.

Lohr, Steve. "How Tax Evasion Has Grown." *New York Times,* March 15, 1981, Section 3, p. 1.

Long, Susan B. "The Impact of the Tax Reform Act of 1986 on Compliance Burdens: Preliminary National Survey Results." Syracuse University, 1989, Mimeo.

Lowi, Theodore, J. *The End of Liberalism.* New York: W. W. Norton, 1979.

Lubar, Robert. "Making Democracy Less Inflation-Prone."

Fortune, September 22, 1980, pp. 78–86.

Luft, Harold S. "On the Use of Vouchers for Medicare." *Milbank Memorial Fund Quarterly* 62, no. 2 (Spring 1984), pp. 237–50.

MacAvoy, Paul W. "The Nondecision Cotton Dust Decision." *New York Times,* July 5, 1981.

MacAvoy, Paul W. "The Record of the Environmental Protection Agency in Controlling Industrial Air Pollution." University of Rochester, March 1984, Mimeo.

Makin, John H., ed. *Real Tax Reform-Replacing the Income Tax.* Washington, D.C.: American Enterprise Institute for Public Policy Research, 1985.

Malcomson, James M. "Some Analytics of the Laffer Curve." *Journal of Public Economics* 29, no. 3 (April 1986), pp. 263–80.

Mankiw, N. Gregory. "A Quick Refresher Course in Macroeconomics." *Journal of Economic Literature,* December 1990, pp. 1645–60.

Marwell, Gerald, and Ruth E. Ames. "Economists Free Ride, Does Anyone Else? Experiments on the Provision of Public Goods, IV." *Journal of Public Economics* 15, no. 3 (June 1981), pp. 295–310.

Massie, Robert K. *Peter the Great—His Life and World.* New York: Random House, 1980.

McKean, R. N. "The Use of Shadow Prices." In *Cost-Bene-fit Analysis,* ed. Richard Layard. New York: Penguin Books, 1977, pp. 119–39.

McLure, Charles E., Jr. "The Theory of Tax Incidence with Imperfect Factor Mobility." *Finanzarchiv* 30 (1971), pp. 27–48.

McLure, Charles E., Jr. "Tax Restructuring Act of 1979: Time for an American Value-Added Tax?" *Public Policy* 28, no. 3 (Summer 1980), pp. 301–22.

McLure, Charles E., Jr. "The Elusive Incidence of Corporate Income Tax: The State Case." *Public Finance Quarterly* 9, no. 4 (October 1981), pp. 395–413.

McNaugher, Thomas L. "Buying Weapons: Bleak Prospects for Real Reform." *Brookings Review* 4, no. 3 (Summer 1986), pp. 11–16.

Meiselman, David I. "Breaking the Tax Barriers to Economic Growth." *Tax Review* 38, no. 8 (August 1977), pp. 29–32.

Meiselman, David I. "The Oil Excise Tax: Another Government Windfall." *Tax Review* (October 1979), pp. 33–37.

Melton, Carroll R. *Housing, Finance and Homeownership: Public Policy Initiatives in Selected Countries.* Chicago: International Union of Building Societies and Savings Associations, 1979.

Meltzer, Allan H., and Scott F. Richard. "A Rational Theory of the Size of Government." *Journal of Political Economy* 89, no. 5 (October 1981), pp. 914–27.

Mermelstein, David, ed. *Economics: Mainstream Readings and Radical Critiques.* New York: Random House, 1973.

Meyer, Bruce. "Unemployment Insurance and Unemployment Spells." Cambridge, Mass.: National Bureau of Economic Research, Working Paper 2546, 1990.

Mieszkowski, Peter M. "Tax Incidence Theory: The Effects of Taxes on the Distribution of Income." *Journal of Economic Literature* 7 (1969), pp. 1103–24.

Mieszkowski, Peter M. "The Property Tax: An Excise Tax or a Profits Tax?" *Journal of Public Economics* 1 (1972), pp. 73–96.

Mieszkowski, Peter, and George R. Zodrow. "The Incidence of a Partial State Corporate Income Tax." *National Tax Journal* 38, no. 4 (December 1985), pp. 489–96.

Mieszkowski, Peter, and George R. Zodrow. "Taxation and the Tiebout Model." *Journal of Economic Literature,* September 1989, pp. 1098–146.

Mills, Edwin S. *The Burden of Government.* Stanford, Calif.: Hoover Institution Press, Stanford University, 1986.

Mishan, E. J. "The Post-War Literature on Externalities: An Interpretative Essay." *Journal of Economic Literature* 9 (1971a), pp. 1–28.

Mishan, E. J. "Evaluation of Life and Limb: A Theoretical Approach." *Journal of Political Economy* 79, no. 4 (1971b), pp. 687–705.

Modigliani, Franco. "Life Cycle, Individual Thrift, and the Wealth of Nations." *American Economic Review* 76, no. 3 (June 1986), pp. 297–313.

Modigliani, F., and H. M. Miller. "The Cost of Capital, Corporation Finance, and the Theory of Investment." *American Economic Review* 48 (1958), pp. 261–97.

Moffitt, Robert. "An Economic Model of Welfare Stigma." *American Economic Review* 73, no. 5 (December 1983), pp. 1023–35.

Mueller, Dennis C. "Public Choice: A Survey." *Journal of Economic Literature* 14, no. 2 (June 1976), pp. 395–433.

Munnell, Alicia H. *The Future of Social Security.* Washington, D.C.: Brookings Institution, 1977.

Munnell, Alicia H. "The Couple versus the Individual under the Federal Income Tax." In *The Economics of Taxation,* ed. Henry J. Aaron and Michael J. Boskin. Washington, D.C.: Brookings Institution, 1980, pp. 247–80.

Murray, Charles A. *Losing Ground: American Social Policy, 1950–1980.* New York: Basic Books, 1984.

Musgrave, Richard A. *The Theory of Public Finance.* New York: McGraw-Hill, 1959.

Musgrave, Richard A. "Theories of Fiscal Crises: An Essay in Fiscal Sociology." In *The Economics of Taxation,* ed. Henry J. Aaron and Michael J. Boskin. Washington, D.C.: Brookings Institution, 1980.

Musgrave, Richard A. "A Brief History of Fiscal Doctrine." In *Handbook of Public Economics.* Vol. 1, ed. Alan Auerbach and Martin S. Feldstein. Amsterdam: North-Holland, 1985.

Musgrave, Richard A. "An Overall Assessment: Is It Worth It?" In Federal Reserve Bank of Boston, *Economic Consequences of Tax Simplification.* Boston, 1986, pp. 259–84.

Musgrave, R. A.; K. E. Case; and H. Leonard. "Distribution of Fiscal Burdens and Benefits." *Public Finance Quarterly* 2 (1974), pp. 259–311.

Newhouse, Joseph E. *Economics of Medical Care: A Policy Perspective.* Reading, Mass.: Addison-Wesley, 1978.

Nichols, Albert L., and Richard J. Zeckhauser. "Targeting Transfers through Restrictions on Recipients." *American Economic Review Papers and Proceedings* 72 (May 1982), pp. 372–77.

Niskanen, William A., Jr. *Bureaucracy and Representative Government.* Chicago: Aldine, 1971.

"No End in Sight." *Time,* August 13, 1990, p. 50.

"No Pap from NAPAP." Review and Outlook, *The Wall Street Journal,* January 26, 1990, p. A14.

Nozick, Robert. *Anarchy, State and Utopia.* Oxford: Basil Blackwell, 1974.

Oates, Wallace. "The Effects of Property Taxes and Local Spending on Property Values: An Empirical Study of Tax Capitalization and the Tiebout Hypothesis." *Journal of Political Economy* 77 (1969), pp. 957–71.

Oates, Wallace E. *Fiscal Federalism.* New York: Harcourt Brace, 1972.

Oates, Wallace E. "The Environment and the Economy: Environmental Policy at the Crossroads." In *American Domestic Priority—An Economic Appraisal,* ed. John M. Quigley and Daniel L. Rubinfeld. Berkeley: University of California Press, 1985, pp. 311–45.

O'Connor, Colleen. "Folly, Fraud and Restraint." *Newsweek,* October 27, 1986, p. 35.

Odden, Allan. "Class Size and Student Achievement: Research-Based Policy Alternatives." *Educational Evaluation and Policy Analysis,* Summer 1990, pp. 213–27.

OECD, Department of Economics and Statistics. *National Accounts of OECD Countries 1964–1981, Vol. II.* Paris, 1983.

OECD, Department of Economics and Statistics. *National Accounts of OECD Countries 1975–1987, Vol. II.* Paris, 1990.

Office of Management and Budget. *Midsession Review of the Budget.* Washington, D.C.: U.S. Government Printing Office, 1990.

Olson, Mancur. *The Rise and Decline of Nations: Economic Growth, Stagflation, and Social Rigidities.* New Haven: Yale University Press, 1982.

Olvey, Lee D.; James R. Golden; and Robert C. Kelly. *Economics of National Security.* Wayne, N.J.: Avery Publishing Group, 1984.

Ornstein, Norman J. "Chipping Away at the Old Blocks."

Brookings Bulletin 18, nos. 3 and 4 (1982), pp. 11–15.

Passell, Peter. "Lend to Any Student." *New York Times,* April 1, 1985, p. A20.

Pauly, Mark V. "Taxation, Health Insurance, and Market Failure in the Medical Economy." *Journal of Economic Literature* 24, no. 2 (June 1986), pp. 629–75.

Peacock, A. T., and J. Wiseman. *The Growth of Public Expenditure in the United Kingdom.* 2d ed. London: Allen & Unwin, 1967.

Pear, Robert. "States Are Found More Responsive on Social Issues." *New York Times.* May 19, 1985, p. A1.

Pear, Robert. "Chipping Away at the Idea of 'Entitlement' . . ." *New York Times,* February 9, 1986, p. 4E.

Pear, Robert. "Behind the Dealing on Deficit Reduction, Deals That Could Swell the Deficit." *New York Times,* October 22, 1990, p. A16.

Pechman, Joseph A., ed. *Comprehensive Income Taxation.* Washington, D.C.: Brookings Institution, 1977.

Pechman, Joseph A., ed. *What Should Be Taxed: Income or Expenditure?* Washington, D.C.: Brookings Institution, 1980.

Pechman, Joseph A. *Who Paid the Taxes, 1966–1985.* Washington, D.C.: Brookings Institution, 1985.

Pechman, Joseph A. *Federal Tax Policy.* 5th ed. Washington, D.C.: Brookings Institution, 1987.

Penner, Rudolph G. "The Nonsense Amendment." *New York Times.* March 28, 1982.

Perlez, Jane. "City and State Lobbyists Vie for Dwindling Federal Aid." *New York Times,* October 24, 1983, p. B1.

Perlez, Jane. "A Factory Town, Worried about Jobs, Supports Companies in E.P.A. Dispute." *New York Times,* November 23, 1985, p. 29.

Phares, Donald. *Who Pays State and Local Taxes?* Cambridge, Mass.: Oelgeschlager, Gunn and Hain, 1980.

Pigou, A. C. *The Economics of Welfare.* New York: Macmillan, 1932.

Pommerehne, Werner. "Quantitative Aspects of Federalism: A Study of Six Countries." In *The Political Economy of Fiscal Federalism,* ed. Wallace Oates. Lexington, Mass.: D.C. Heath, 1977, pp. 275–355.

Portney, Paul R. "Policy Watch: Economics and the Clean Air Act." *Journal of Economic Perspectives,* Fall 1990, pp. 178–82.

Poterba, James M. "Tax Policy and Corporate Saving." *Brookings Papers on Economic Activity* 2 (1987), pp. 455–515.

Poterba, James M. "Is the Gasoline Tax Regressive?" Cambridge, Mass.: National Bureau of Economic Research, Working Paper 3578, 1991.

Poterba, James M., and Lawrence H. Summers. "The Economic Effects of Dividend Taxation." In *Recent Advances in Corporate Finance,* ed. Edward I. Altman and Marti G. Subrahmanyam. Homewood, Ill.: Richard D. Irwin, 1985, pp. 227–84.

Quandt, Richard E., and Harvey S. Rosen. "Unemployment, Disequilibrium and the Short-Run Phillips Curve: An Econometric Approach." *Journal of Applied Econometrics* 1, no. 3 (July 1986), pp. 235–53.

Quandt, Richard E., and Harvey S. Rosen. *The Conflict between Equilibrium and Disequilibrium Theories: The Case of the U.S. Labor Market.* Kalamazoo, Mich.: Upjohn Institute, 1987.

Raab, Selwyn. "12% of Stores Inspected Evaded Tax, Study Says." *New York Times,* November 2, 1986, p. 42.

Ramsey, Frank P. "A Contribution to the Theory of Taxation." *Economic Journal* 37 (1927), pp. 47–61.

Rawls, John. *A Theory of Justice.* Cambridge, Mass.: Harvard University Press, 1971.

Roberts, Paul C. "The Keynesian Attack on Mr. Reagan's Plan." *Wall Street Journal,* March 19, 1981, p. 26.

Roberts, Stephen B. "'Funny Kind of Coalition' on Textiles." *New York Times,* September 25, 1985, p. A14.

Robison, H. David. "Who Pays for Industrial Pollution Abatement?" *Review of Economics and Statistics* 67, no. 4 (November 1985), pp. 702–6.

Rosen, Harvey S. "Is It Time to Abandon Joint Filing?" *National Tax Journal* 30 (December 1977), pp. 423–28.

Rosen, Harvey S. "Housing Decisions and the U.S. Income Tax: An Econometric Analysis." *Journal of Public Economics* 11 (February 1979), pp. 1–23.

Rosen, Harvey S. "The Marriage Tax Is Down but Not Out." *National Tax Journal,* December 1987.

Rosen, Kenneth T. "The Impact of Proposition 13 on House Prices in Northern California: A Test of the Interjurisdictional Capitalization Hypothesis." *Journal of Political Economy* 90, no. 1 (February 1982), pp. 191–200.

Roth, William V. "Why We Need to Tax Consumption." *New York Times,* March 23, 1986, p. 2F.

Royal Commission on Taxation. *Report of the Royal Commission on Taxation.* Vol. 3. *Taxation of Income.* Ottawa, Canada, 1966.

Rubinfeld, Daniel. "The Economics of the Local Public Sector." In *Handbook of Public Economics.* Vol. II, ed. Alan J. Auerbach and Martin Feldstein. Amsterdam: North-Holland, 1987, Chapter 11.

Russell, Louise. *Medicare's New Hospital Payment System: Is It Working?* Washington, D.C.: Brookings Institution, 1989.

Safire, William. "The Flat Tax." *New York Times,* April 30, 1982, p. A31.

Samuelson, Paul A. "The Pure Theory of Public Expenditure." *Review of Economics and Statistics* 36 (1954), pp. 387–89.

Samuelson, Paul A. "Diagrammatic Exposition of a Theory of Public Expenditure." *Review of Economics and Statistics* 37 (1955), pp. 350–56.

Samuelson, Paul A., and William D. Nordhaus. *Economics.* 13th ed. New York: McGraw-Hill, 1989.

Samuelson, Robert J. "The True Tax Burden." *Newsweek,* April 21, 1986, p. 68.

Sandler, Todd, and John T. Tschirhart. "The Economic Theory of Clubs: An Evaluative Survey." *Journal of Economic Literature* 18, no. 4 (December 1980), pp. 1481–1521.

Sandmo, Agnar. "Optimal Taxation—An Introduction to the Literature." *Journal of Public Economics* 6 (1976), pp. 37–54.

Sandmo, Agnar. "Income Tax Evasion, Labour Supply, and the Equity-Efficiency Trade-off." *Journal of Public Economics* 16, no. 3 (December 1981), pp. 265–88.

Sawhill, Isabel. "Poverty in the U.S.: Why Is It So Persistent?" *Journal of Economic Literature* 56 (1988), pp. 1073–119.

Scherer, F. M. *Weapons Acquisition Process: Economic Incentives.* Cambridge, Mass.: Harvard University Press, 1964.

Schmedel, Scott R. "Tax Report." *Wall Street Journal,* January 9, 1991, p. A1.

Schneider, Keith. "Cost of Farm Law Might Be Double Original Estimate." *New York Times,* July 22, 1986, pp. A1, A15.

Schorske, Carl E. *Fin-de-Siècle Vienna—Politics and Culture.* New York: Vintage Books, 1981.

Schwarzschild, Maimon. "Liberty and Autonomy for All." *New York Times Book Review,* June 15, 1986, p. 27.

Seade, J. K. "The Shape of Optimal Tax Schedules." *Journal of Public Economics* 7, 1977, pp. 203–36.

Secter, Bob. "Gaps between Rich, Poor Schools Ignite Legal Fights." *Los Angeles Times,* November 26, 1990, pp. A1, A20.

Seligmann, Jean, and Roxie Hammill. "Can a Judge Raise Taxes?" *Newsweek,* October 12, 1987, p. 98.

Shabecoff, Philip. "Toward a Neutral Role for OSHA." *New York Times,* March 19, 1981, p. E9.

Shabecoff, Philip. "Tacoma Gets Choice: Cancer Risk or Lost Jobs." *New York Times,* July 13, 1983, p. 1.

Shipler, David K. "Shcharansky Urges Public Pressure on Soviet." *New York Times,* May 10, 1986, p. 28.

Short, Pamela F. "Estimates of the Uninsured Population, Calendar Year 1987." DHHS Pub. no. (PHS) 90-3469. National Medical Expenditure Survey Data Summary 2, Agency for Health Care Policy and Research. Rockville, MD: Public Health Service, 1990.

Shoven, John B. "The Incidence and Efficiency Effects of Taxes on Income from Capital." *Journal of Political Economy* 84 (1976), pp. 1261–84.

Shoven, John B., and John Whalley. "Applied General-Equilibrium Models of Taxation and International Trade." *Journal of Economic Literature* 22, no. 3 (September 1984), pp. 1007–51.

Simon, Carl P., and Ann D. Witte. "The Underground Economy: Estimates of Size, Structure and Trends." In *Special Study on Economic Change*, Vol. 5: *Government Regulation: Achieving Social and Economic Balance*. Washington, D.C.: U.S. Government Printing Office, 1980, pp. 70–120.

Slemrod, Joel. "Do We Know How Progressive the Income Tax System Should Be?" *National Tax Journal* 36, no. 3 (September 1983), pp. 361–70.

Slemrod, Joel. *Do Taxes Matter? The Impact of the Tax Reform Act of 1986*. Cambridge, Mass.: MIT Press, 1991.

Slemrod, Joel, and Nikki Sorum. "The Compliance Cost of the U.S. Individual Income Tax System." Minneapolis: University of Minnesota, 1983, Mimeo.

Sloan, Frank A., and Killard W. Adamache. "Taxation and the Growth of Non-Wage Compensation." *Public Finance Quarterly* 14, no. 2 (April 1986), pp. 115–38.

Small, Kenneth A. "Bus Priority and Congestion Pricing on Urban Expressways." In *Research in Transportation Economics*. Vol. 1, ed. T. E. Keeler. Greenwich, Conn.: JAI Press 1983, pp. 27–74.

Small, Kenneth A., and Clifford Winston. "Welfare Effects of Marginal-Cost Taxation of Motor Freight Transportation: A Study of Infrastructure Pricing." In *Studies in State and Local Public Finance*, ed. Harvey S. Rosen. Chicago: University of Chicago Press, 1986, pp. 113–28.

Smeeding, Timothy M. "Alternative Methods for Evaluating Selected In-Kind Transfer Benefits and Measuring Their Effect on Poverty." Technical Paper 50. Washington, D.C.: U.S. Bureau of the Census, U.S. Government Printing Office, 1982.

Smith, Adam. *The Wealth of Nations*. London: J. M. Dent and Sons, 1977 (1776).

Smith, V. Kerry, ed. *Environmental Policy under Reagan's Executive Order: The Role of Benefit-Cost Analysis*. Chapel Hill: University of North Carolina Press, Urban and Regional Policy and Development Studies, 1984.

Smith, Vernon L. "Microeconomic Systems as an Experimental Science." *American Economic Review* 72, no. 5 (December 1982), pp. 923–55.

Special Committee on Aging, U.S. Senate. *Medicare and the Health Costs of Older Americans: The Extent and Effects of Cost Sharing*. Washington, D.C.: U.S. Government Printing Office, 1984.

Stafford, Frank P. "Income-Maintenance Policy and Work Effort: Learning from Experiments and Labor-Market Studies." In *Social Experimentation*, ed. Jerry A. Hausman and David A. Wise. Chicago: University of Chicago Press, 1985.

Starr, Paul, "Health Care for the Poor: The Past 20 Years." In *Fighting Poverty: What Works and What Doesn't*, ed. Sheldon H. Danziger and Daniel H. Weinberg. Cambridge, Mass.: Harvard University Press, pp. 106–32.

Stern, Nicholas H. "On the Specification of Models of Optimum Income Taxation." *Journal of Public Economics* 6, nos. 1, 2 (July–August 1976), pp. 123–62.

Steuerle, Eugene, and Michael Hartzmark. "Individual Income Taxation, 1974–79." *National Tax Journal* 34 (June 1981), pp. 145–66.

Stevenson, Richard W. "Competition for Contracts Trims Costs for Pentagon." *New York Times*, March 31, 1988, pp. A1, D2.

Stigler, George J. "Director's Law of Public Income Distribution." *Journal of Law and Economics* 13 (April 1970), pp. 1–10.

Stigler, George J. "Free-Riders and Collective Action." *Bell Journal of Economics* 5 (1974), pp. 359–65.

Stiglitz, Joseph E. "Taxation, Corporate Financial Policy, and the Cost of Capital." *Journal of Public Economics* 2 (1973), pp. 1–34.

Stiglitz, Joseph E. "Notes on Estate Taxes, Redistribution, and the Concept of Balanced Growth Path Incidence." *Journal of Political Economy* 86 (1978), pp. S137–50.

Stockfisch, J. A. "Value-Added Taxes and the Size of Government: Some Evidence." *National Tax Journal* 38, no. 4 (December 1985), pp. 547–52.

Stockman, David A. "The Triumph of Politics—Why the Reagan Revolution Failed." *Newsweek,* April 21, 1986, pp. 40–59.

Stone, Lawrence. *The Family, Sex, and Marriage in England, 1500–1800.* New York: Harper & Row, 1977.

Stuckart, Wilhelm, and Hans Globke. "Civil Rights and the Natural Inequality of Man." In *Nazi Culture,* ed. George L. Morse. New York: Universal Library, 1968.

Suits, Daniel B., and Ronald C. Fisher. "A Balanced Budget Constitutional Amendment: Economic Complexities and Uncertainties." *National Tax Journal,* 38, no. 4 (December 1985), pp. 467–78.

Sunley, Emil M., Jr. "Summary of the Conference Discussion." In *Comprehensive Income Taxation,* ed. Joseph A. Pechman. Washington, D.C.: Brookings Institution, 1977.

Tait, Alan A. *Value-Added Tax—International Practice and Problems.* Washington, D.C.: International Monetary Fund, 1988.

Tanzi, Vito. "Inflationary Expectations, Economic Activity, Taxes, and Interest Rates." *American Economic Review* 70 (March 1980), pp. 12–21.

Tax Foundation. *Tax Features* 28, no. 8 (November–December 1984), p. 1.

Tax Policy Guide. Washington, D.C.: Citizens for Tax Justice, June 1982.

Thurow, Lester C. "The Income Distribution as a Pure Public Good." *Quarterly Journal of Economics,* May 1971, pp. 327–36.

Tideman, T. Nicolaus, and Gordon Tullock. "A New and Superior Process for Making Social Choices." *Journal of Political Economy* 84 (December 1976), pp. 1145–60.

Tiebout, Charles. "A Pure Theory of Local Expenditures." *Journal of Political Economy* 64 (1956), pp. 416–24.

Tobin, James. "Liquidity Preference as Attitude toward Risk." *Review of Economic Studies* 25 (February 1958), pp. 65–86.

Tobin, James. "On Limiting the Domain of Inequality." *Journal of Law and Economics* 13 (1970), pp. 263–77.

Tresch, Richard W. *Public Finance: A Normative Theory.* Plano, Texas: Business Publications, 1981.

Tucker, Robert C., ed. *The Marx-Engels Reader.* 2d ed. New York: W. W. Norton, 1978.

Tucker, William. *America in the Age of Environmentalism.* New York: Doubleday Publishing, 1982.

Tufte, Edward R. *Political Control of the Economy.* Princeton, N.J.: Princeton University Press, 1978.

Tyles, Gus. "Caught in the Doldrums." *The New Leader,* June 13, 1988, p. 10.

U.S. Bureau of the Census. *Historical Statistics of the United States, Colonial Times to 1970.* Washington, D.C.: U.S. Government Printing Office, 1975.

U.S. Bureau of the Census. *Statistical Abstract of the United States: 1986.* 106th ed. Washington, D.C.: U.S. Government Printing Office, 1985.

U.S. Bureau of the Census. *Current Population Reports. Household Wealth and Asset Ownership: 1984,* Series P-70, No. 7, Washington, D.C.: U.S. Government Printing Office, 1986.

U.S. Bureau of the Census. *Current Population Reports. Money Income and Poverty Status of Families and Persons in the United States: 1989,* Series P-60, No. 168. Washington, D.C.: U.S. Government Printing Office, 1990.

U.S. Bureau of the Census. *Statistical Abstract of the United States: 1990.* 110th ed. Washington, D.C.: U.S. Government Printing Office, 1990.

U.S. Congress. Senate Subcommittee on Water Resources. *Corps of Engineers and Soil Conservation Service Projects.* 93rd Congress, 1973.

U.S. Department of Commerce, Bureau of the Census. *Governmental Finances in 1989–90.* GF84, No. 5, Washington, D.C.: U.S. Government Printing Office, 1990.

U.S. Department of Health and Human Services. *Social Security Bulletin* 52, no. 1 (January 1989).

U.S. Department of Labor. *Comparison of State Unemployment Insurance Laws.* Washington, D.C.: U.S. Government Printing Office, 1985, revised September 1990.

U.S. Department of the Treasury. *Tax Reform for Fairness, Simplicity and Economic Growth.* Washington, D.C., November 1984.

U.S. General Accounting Office. *Report by the U.S.G.A.O., The Job Training Partnership Act: An Analysis of Support Cost Limits and Participant Characteristics.* GAO/HRD 86–16, November 6, 1985.

U.S. General Accounting Office. *Profiles of Major Components of the Tax Gap.* Washington, D.C., April 1990.

Venti, S. F., and D. A. Wise. "IRAs and Saving." In *The Effects of Taxation on Income Accumulation,* ed. Martin Feldstein. Chicago: University of Chicago Press, 1987, pp. 7–48.

Viscusi, W. Kip. *Risk by Choice.* Cambridge, Mass.: Harvard University Press, 1983.

Wanniski, Jude. *The Way the World Works.* New York: Simon & Schuster, 1978.

"Weaning Congress from the Pork Barrel." *New York Times,* March 23, 1986, p. E5.

Weicher, John C. "Urban Housing Policy." In *Current Issues in Economics,* ed. Peter

Mieszkowski and Mahlon R. Straszheim. Baltimore: Johns Hopkins University Press, 1979, pp. 469–508.

Weicher, John C. *Housing— Federal Policies and Programs.* Washington, D.C.: American Enterprise Institute, 1980.

Weidenbaum, Murray L. "Reducing the Hidden Cost of Big Government." *Tax Review* 39, no. 7 (July 1978), pp. 31–34.

Weitzman, Martin L. "Efficient Incentive Contracts." *Quarterly Journal of Economics* 114, no. 4 (June 1980), pp. 719–30.

White, Lawrence J. "Effluent Charges as a Faster Means of Achieving Pollution Abatement." *Public Policy* 24, no. 1 (Winter 1976), pp. 111–25.

White, Michelle J. "Fiscal Zoning in Fragmented Metropolitan Areas." In *Fiscal Zoning and Land Use Controls,* ed. Edwin S. Mills and Wallace E. Oates. Lexington, Mass.: D.C. Heath, 1975, pp. 31–100.

White, Michelle J. "Property Taxes and Firm Location: Evidence from Proposition 13." In *Studies in State and Local Public Finance,* ed. Harvey S. Rosen. Chicago: University of Chicago Press, 1986, pp. 83–112.

Wiehl, Lis. "Private Justice for a Fee: Profits and Problems." *New York Times,* February 17, 1989, p. 85.

Wilkins, J. G. "The Role of Tax Policy in Meeting the Competitive Challenge." Washington, D.C.: Coopers & Lybrand, 1990, Mimeo.

Will, George F. "Power to the President." *Newsweek,* October 12, 1981, p. 120.

Will, George F. "The Soul of Conservatism." *Newsweek,* November 11, 1985a.

Will, George F. "You Ain't Seen Nothing Yet!" *Newsweek,* December 23, 1985b, p. 84.

Will, George F. "Gramm-Rudman's Mindless Music." *Newsweek,* February 17, 1986, p. 80.

Willig, Robert. "Consumer's Surplus without Apology." *American Economic Review,* September 1976, pp. 589–97.

The Windfall Profits Tax: A Comparative Analysis of Two Bills. Congressional Budget Office, Staff Working Paper. Washington, D.C., 1979.

Yarrow, George. "Privatization in Theory and Practice." *Economic Policy: A European Forum* 1, no. 2 (April 1986), pp. 324–77.

Yellen, Janet L. "Symposium on the Budget Deficit." *Journal of Economic Perspectives,* Spring 1989, pp. 17–22.

Yitzhaki, Shlomo. "A Note on Optimal Taxation and Administrative Costs." *American Economic Review* 69, no. 3 (June 1979), pp. 475–80.

"Your Stake in the Fight over Social Security." *Consumer Reports,* September 1981, pp. 503–10.

Author Index

Subject Index

Government surpluses and deficits, 1939–1990
(1986 dollars)*

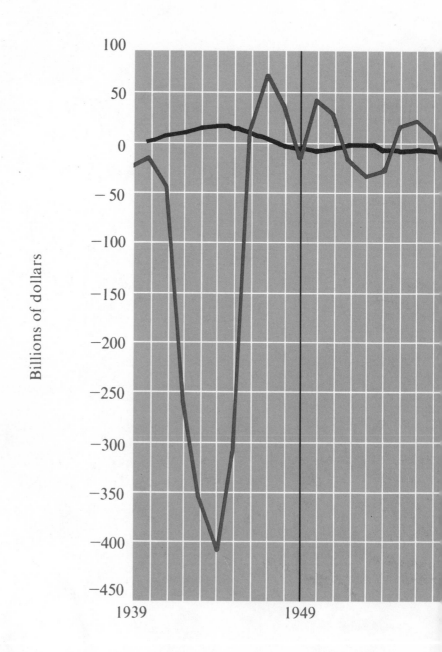

*Positive numbers are surpluses; negative numbers are deficits
Source: *Economic Report of the President 1991*, pp. 290, 37